C000020057

Canada

Managing editor: Liz Coghill
English translation: Cedilla Translations, Vanessa Dowell, Jane Moseley
Editorial: Maria Morgan, Clare Thomson, Timothy Wright, Stephen Guise, Julie Pickard

Additional research and assistance: Michael Hutchinson, Sofi Mogensen, Kate Williams, Michael Summers, Eileen Townsend-Jones, Trista Selous
Index: Dorothy Frame

Series director: Philippe Gloaguen
Series creators: Philippe Gloaguen, Michel Duval
Chief editor: Pierre Josse
Assistant chief editor: Benoît Lucchini
Coordination director: Florence Charmetant

Editorial team: Yves Couprie, Olivier Page, Véronique de Chardon, Amanda Keravel, Isabelle Al Subaihi, Anne-Caroline Dumas, Carole Bordes, Bénédicte Bazaille, André Poncelet, Jérôme de Gubernatis, Marie Burin des Roziers and Thierry Brouard.

Our guides provide independent advice. The authors and compilers do not accept any remuneration for the inclusion of addresses in this guide. Please note that we cannot accept any responsibility for any loss, injury or inconvenience sustained by anyone as a result of any information or advice contained in this guide.

Feedback
We have done our best to ensure the accuracy of the information contained in this guide. However, addresses, phone numbers, opening times etc. do invariably change from time to time, so if you find a discrepancy please do let us know and help us update the guides. As prices may change so may other circumstances – a restaurant may change hands or the standard of service at a hotel may deteriorate since our researchers made their visit. Again, we do our best to ensure information is accurate, but if you notice any discrepancy, please let us know. You can contact us at: hachetteuk@orionbooks.co.uk or write to us at Cassell & Co, address below.

Price guide
Because of rapid inflation in many countries, it is impossible to give an accurate indication of prices in hotels and restaurants. Prices can change enormously from one year to the next. As a result we have adopted a system of categories for the prices in the guides: 'Budget', 'Moderate', 'Chic' and 'Très Chic' (in the guides to France), otherwise 'Expensive' and 'Splash Out' in the others.

First published in the United Kingdom in 2002 by Cassell & Co
© English Translation Cassell & Co 2002
© Hachette Livre (Hachette Tourisme) 2001
© Cartography Hachette Tourisme

Distributed in the United States of America by Sterling Publishing Co., Inc. 387 Park Avenue South, New York, NY 10016-8810.

A CIP catalogue for this book is available from the British Library.

ISBN 1 84202 031 5

Typeset at The Spartan Press Ltd, Lymington, Hants.
Printed and bound by Aubin, France. E-mail: sales@aubin-imprimeur.fr

Cover design by Emmanuel Le Vallois (Hachette Livre) and Paul Cooper.
Cover photo © Telegraph Colour Library/Peter Gridley. Back cover photo © Superstock.

Cassell & Co, Wellington House, 125 Strand, London WC2R 0BB

routard

Canada

**The ultimate
food, drink and
accommodation guide**

HACHETTE

Contents

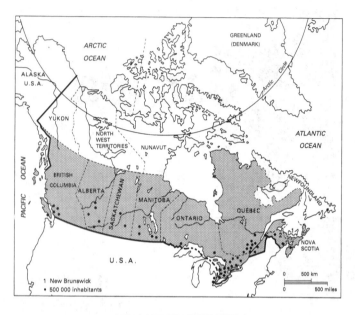

AREAS COVERED IN THE GUIDE

GETTING THERE 13

GENERAL INFORMATION 24

BACKGROUND 57

ONTARIO 88

MANITOBA 158

SASKATCHEWAN 170

ALBERTA 172

NOVA SCOTIA 575

Map List

Just Exactly Who or What is a Routard?

You are. Yes, you! The fact that you are reading this book means that you are a Routard. You are probably still none the wiser, so to explain we will take you back to the origin of the guides. Routard was the brainchild of a Frenchman named Philippe Gloaguen, who compiled the first guide some 25 years ago with his friend Michel Duval. They simply could not find the kind of guide book they wanted and so the solution was clear – they would just have to write it themselves. When it came to naming the guide, Philippe came up with the term Routard, which at the time did not exist as a bona fide word – at least, not in conventional dictionary terms. Today, if you look the word up in a French-English dictionary you will find that it means 'traveller' or 'globetrotter' – so there you have it, that's what you are!

From this humble beginning has grown a vast collection of some 100 titles to destinations all over the world. Routard is now the bestselling guide book series in France. The guides have been translated into five different languages, so keep an eye out for fellow Routard readers on your travels.

What exactly do the guides do?
The short answer is that they provide all the information you need to enable you to have a successful holiday or trip. Routards' great strength however, lies in their listings. The guides provide comprehensive listings for accommodation, eating and drinking – ranging from campsites and youth hostels through to four-star hotels – and from bars, clubs and greasy spoons to tearooms, cafés and restaurants. Each entry is accompanied by a detailed and frank appraisal of the address, rather like a friend coming back from holiday who is recommending all the good places to go (or even the places to avoid!). The guides aim to help you find the best addresses and the best value for money within your price range, while giving you invaluable insider advice at the same time.

Anything else?
Routard also provides oceans of practical advice on how to get along in the country or city you are visiting plus an insight into the character and customs of the people. How do you negotiate your way around the transport system? Will you offend if you bare your knees in the temple? And so on. In addition, you will find plenty of sightseeing information, backed up by historical and cultural detail, interesting facts and figures, addresses and opening times. The humanitarian aspect is also of great importance, with the guides commenting freely and often pithily, and most titles contain a section on human rights.

Routard are truly useful guides that are convivial, irreverent, down-to-earth and honest. We very much hope you enjoy them and that they will serve you well during your stay.

Happy travelling.

Symbols Used in the Guide

Please note that not all the symbols below appear in every guide.

- ■ Useful addresses
- ⓗ Tourist office
- ✉ Post office
- ☎ Telephone
- 🚂 Railway station
- 🚌 Bus station
- 🚖 Shared taxi
- ⓣ Tram
- ⛴ River transport
- ⛴ Sea transport
- ✈ Airport
- ⬥ Where to stay

- ✕ Where to eat
- ⱦ Where to go for a drink
- ♪ Where to listen to music
- ⸙ Where to go for an ice-cream
- ★ To see
- 🛍 Shopping
- ● 'Other'
- ⓟ Parking
- ⚔ Castle
- ∴ Ruins

- ⚓ Diving site
- ⛉ Shelter
- ⛺ Campsite
- ▲ Peak
- ● Site
- ○ Town
- ✕ Hill
- ⚲ Abbey, chapel
- ⛊ Lookout
- ⛱ Beach
- ⛯ Lighthouse

Getting There

By Air

FROM BRITAIN

Air Canada and **British Airways** fly directly to Canada. Airlines flying to Canada with stops en route include **Air France**, **American Airlines**, **KLM**, **Northwest** and **United Airlines**.

Up to five direct Air Canada flights leave London Heathrow every day for Toronto, Pearson International Airport. Air Canada fly twice a day directly to Vancouver and Calgary, and once a day directly to Halifax, Montreal, Ottawa and Edmonton. One Air Canada flight a day travels directly to Toronto from Glasgow and Manchester. British Airways fly daily non-stop from Heathrow to Toronto, Montreal and Vancouver, and daily from Birmingham to Toronto, via New York. Air France fly four times daily, from Heathrow, to both Montreal and Toronto. Air France fly to all other destinations in Canada, via Paris and Montreal. American Airlines fly daily, from Gatwick, to Toronto, Montreal, Ottawa and Halifax, usually via New York, Chicago or Dallas. KLM fly, from Heathrow and regional airports, to major Canadian cities, via Amsterdam.

Journey time on direct flights from London is 8 hours to Toronto and 9 hours to Vancouver, with increases for time spent in stopovers.

Midweek advance return fares to Toronto from London start at around £250, but can exceed £700. The average flight to Toronto costs about £550. Fares to Montreal and Hamilton are priced at similar levels. Midweek advance returns to Vancouver, Calgary, Edmonton or Winnipeg start at about £450 and can exceed £800. Most schedule airlines offer 'open jaw' tickets, which enable you to fly into one city and out of another, for only slightly more than the standard return fare. Fares to Canada are highest between June and August, with a second peak for the winter ski season from November to January. Early booking will reduce your fare, whenever the date of departure. Advance booking of at least 21 days is required for APEX (advance purchase excursion) fares. APEX fares usually limit your stay to more than one week and less than one month.

Charter flights, on airlines such as **Air 3000** and **Air Transat**, can be the most economical way of visiting Canada. Charter flights, sold by high-street travel agents, usually leave or arrive at inconvenient times, have limited availability in high season and are generally unsuitable for travellers intending to stay in Canada for longer than two or three weeks.

London to Canada is a popular route and there's every chance of bargain fares, even in summer. The travel pages of the weekend broadsheet newspapers, teletext, websites such as www.cheapflights.com, www.expedia.com and www.lastminute.com advertise good package and air ticket bargains. If cheap flights are booked up, check flights to New York, which can sell for as low as £170. Canada is a straightforward bus or train journey from New York. For more on travel from the United States, *see* 'Getting There by Train' and 'Getting There by Bus'.

Ensure that any airline or travel agent is ABTA endorsed. Contact the **Air Travel Advisory Bureau** for information on airlines and prices.

● **Air Canada**: 7–8 Conduit Street, London W1R 9TG. ☎ (0990) 247226. Website: www.aircanada.com

● **Air France**: 10 Warwick Street, First Floor, London W1R 5RA. ☎ (0845) 084 5111. Website: www.airfrance.com

● **American Airlines**: 45–46 Piccadilly, London W1J 0DS. ☎ (0845) 778 9789. Website: www.aa.com

● **British Airways**: Waterside, PO Box 365, Harmondsworth UB7 OGB. ☎ (0845) 773 3377. Website: www.britishairways.com

● **KLM Royal Dutch Airlines**: Endeavour House, Stansted Airport CM24 1RS. ☎ (0870) 575 0900. Website: www.klm.com

● **Northwest Airlines**: Northwest House, Tinsley Lane, Crawley RH10 2TP. ☎ (01293) 561000. Website: www.nwa.com

● **United Airlines**: 7–8 Conduit Street, London W1R 9TG. ☎ (0845) 844 4777. Website: www.ual.com

● **The Air Travel Advisory Bureau**: Columbus House, 28 Charles Square, London N1 6HT. ☎ (020) 7635 5000. Website: www.atab.co.uk

TRAVEL AGENTS

■ **Airline Network**: (discount flights by phone only) ☎ (0870) 241 0019.

■ **Bridge the World**: (discount flights and packages) 47 Chalk Farm Road, London NW1 8AJ. ☎ (0870) 444 7474. Website: www.bridgetheworld.com

■ **Flightbookers**: (discount flights and packages) 177–178 Tottenham Court Road, London W1P 0LX. ☎ (0870) 010 7000. Website: www.ebookers.com

■ **STA Travel**: (students and those under 26) 86 Old Brompton Road, London SW7 3LQ. ☎ (020) 7851 4132. Website: www.statravel.co.uk

■ **Thomas Cook**: (flights and packages, branches nationwide). ☎ (0990) 666 222. Website: www.thomascook.com

■ **Trailfinders**: (discounts and specialist itineraries) 194 Kensington High Street, London W8 7RG. ☎ (020) 7938 3939. Website: www.trailfinders.com

■ **USIT Campus Travel**: (students and those under 26) 52 Grosvenor Gardens, London SW1 0AG. ☎ (0870) 240 1010. Website: www.usitcampus.co.uk

SPECIALIST TRAVEL AGENTS

■ **AmeriCan Adventures and Roadrunner International**: (adventure tours) 64 Mount Pleasant Avenue, Tunbridge Wells TN1 1QY. ☎ (01892) 512700. Website: www.americanadventures.co.uk

■ **American Travel**: (fly-drive, packages, itineraries) 598 Green Lanes, Palmers Green, London N13 5RY. ☎ (020) 8886 8880. Website: www. americantravel.com

■ **Footloose Adventure Travel**: (trekking tours) 105 Leeds Road, Ilkley LS29 8EG. ☎ (01943) 604030. Website: www.footlooseadventures.co.uk

■ **Go Fishing Canada / Windows on the Wild**: (nature and wilderness holidays) 2 Oxford House, 24 Oxford Road, London WC1 4DH. ☎ (020) 8742 1556. Website: www.go-fishing-worldwide.com

■ **Leisurail**: (rail holidays in Canada and rail passes) 17 Coningsby Road, Peterborough PE3 8SB. ☎ 01733 335599. Website: www.leisurail.co.uk

■ **North America Travel Service**: (fly-drive, packages, itineraries) 48 Deansgate, Manchester M3 2FE. ☎ (0161) 839 8844. Website: www. americatravelservice.com

■ **Trek America**: (group adventure travel) 4 Waterperry Court, Middleton Road, Banbury OX1 4QB. ☎ (01295) 256777. Website: www.trekamerica. co.uk

FROM IRELAND

British Airways fly daily from Dublin to Toronto, Montreal and Vancouver, via London Heathrow. British Airways will quote through fares from Belfast to Toronto, via London. **Air France** fly up to four times daily from Dublin to Montreal, via Paris and twice daily from Dublin to Toronto, via Paris. **Delta Airlines** fly daily from Dublin to Toronto, via New York.

Flight times to Montreal and Toronto from Dublin start at 11 hours, and increase in proportion to time spent in stopovers.

Prices for a standard return from Dublin to Toronto start at around IR£650 in low season and can exceed IR£2000 from July to August and November to January. Fares from Belfast are more expensive.

❶ **Air France**: Dublin Airport, Dublin. ☎ (01) 605 0383. Website: www. airfrance.com

❶ **British Airways**: 13 St Stephen's Green, Dublin 1. ☎ 1-800-626-747. For enquiries from Northern Ireland ☎ (0345) 222 111. Website: www.british airways.com

❶ **Delta Airlines**: 3 Dawson Street, First Floor, Dublin 2. ☎ (01) 407 3165. Website: www.delta.com

TRAVEL AGENTS

■ **American Express Travel**: 116 Grafton Street, Dublin 2. ☎ (01) 677 2874.

■ **Budget Travel**: 134 Lower Baggot Street, Dublin 2. ☎ (01) 661 3122.

■ **Budget Travel Shops**: 63 Main Street, Finglas 11, Dublin. ☎ (01) 834 0637.

GETTING THERE

■ **Thomas Cook**: 11 Donegall Place, Belfast BT1 6ET. ☎ (01232) 554 455. 118 Grafton Street, Dublin. ☎ (01) 677 1721. Website: www.thomascook. com

■ **Trailfinders**: 4–5 Dawson Street, Dublin 2. ☎ (01) 677 7888. Website: www.trailfinders.com

■ **Usit NOW**: 19–21 Aston Quay, O'Donnell Bridge, Dublin. ☎ (01) 602 1700. 13B Fountain Centre, College Street, Belfast BT61 6ET. ☎ (01232) 324 4073. Website: www.usitnow.ie

SPECIALIST TRAVEL AGENTS

■ **American Holidays**: (packages, ski, fly-drive, itineraries) 38–39 Pearse Street, Dublin 2. ☎ (01) 679 8800. Website: www.american-holidays.com

■ **Exodus**: (adventure travel) Colette Pearson Travel, 64 South William Street, Dublin 2. ☎ (01) 677 1029. Email: cptravel@indigo.ie. Website: www.exodus.co.uk

Most travel agents in Britain can also arrange travel to Canada. For more details, *see* 'Specialist Travel Agents in Britain'.

FROM THE UNITED STATES

There are hundreds of daily flights between the United States and Canada. **Air Canada** sends round-the-clock planes from cities across the United States to all destinations in Canada. Other airlines flying direct to Canada include **American Airlines**, **British Airways**, **Continental Airlines**, **Delta Airlines**, **Northwest Airlines**, **TWA, United Airlines** and **US Air**. Charter flights, sold by travel agents, are worth considering if you're planning a short trip and you don't mind antisocial flight times.

Toronto, Vancouver and Montreal are the busiest air destinations. Edmonton, Halifax and Winnipeg are also popular.

As a guide, flights from New York to Toronto start at around US$200. Prices are higher from the west coast, with fares from Los Angeles to Toronto beginning at approximately US$300. Fares increase by about US$25 to US$75 for a flight from either destination to Montreal. 'Open jaw' tickets, which enable you to fly into one city and out of another, cost only slightly more than the standard return fare. Seasonal variations apply, with high prices in summer and around the winter holiday, but the further in advance you book, the cheaper the fare, whenever you plan to depart. The cheapest APEX (advance purchase excursion) fares must be booked at least 21 days in advance. APEX tickets usually require a stay of at least seven days and no longer than one month.

Airlines are competing for your business on routes across North America, and a little research usually brings up low-price fares. 'Price wars' between airlines can lower fares to rock-bottom prices. Consult your travel agent and keep an eye on the websites of the airlines themselves, as these are often where the deals are posted first.

Travel sections of newspapers, such as the *LA Times*, *San Francisco Chronicle*, *New York Times* and *Chicago Tribune* carry advertisements for flight and package bargains. It's worth investigating internet travel sites such as www.lowestfare.com, www.priceline.com, www.previewtravel.com, www.travelocity.com, www.expedia.com. Travel clubs, which offer discounts on travel services for an annual fee, can be worthwhile if you need additional services, such as car hire.

Always ensure that any travel agent is endorsed by ASTA or is a member of USTOA.

✪ **Air Canada**: Satellite Airline Terminal, 125 Park Avenue, New York, New York 10017. ☎ 1-888-247-2262. Website: www.aircanada.com

✪ **American Airlines**: 4200 Amon Carter, PD 2400, Fort Worth, Texas. ☎ 1-800-433-7300. Website: www.aa.com

✪ **Continental Airlines**: 2929 Alan Parkway, PO Box 4607, Houston, Texas. ☎ 1-800-525-0280. Website: www.continental.com

✪ **Delta Airlines**: PO Box 20980, Atlanta, Georgia 30320. ☎ 1-800-221-1212. Website: www.delta.com

✪ **Northwest Airlines**: 100 East 42nd Street, Second Floor, New York, New York 10017. ☎ 1-800-447-4747. Website: www.nwa.com

✪ **TWA**: 650 Anton Boulevard, Suite F, Costa Mesa, California 91364. ☎ 1-800-982-4141. Website: www.twa.com

✪ **United Airlines**: ☎ 1-800-241-6522. Website: www.ual.com.

✪ **US Air**: 10 Eyck Plaza, 40 North Pearl Street, Albany, New York 12207. ☎ 1-800-428-432. Website: www.usairways.com

TRAVEL AGENTS

■ **Air Courier Association**: 191 University Boulevard, Suite 300, Denver, Colorado 80206. ☎ (303) 278 8810 or 1-800-282-1202. Website: www.aircourier.org

■ **Last Minute Travel Club**: (standby deals) 132 Brookline Avenue, Boston, Massachusetts 02215. ☎ 1-800-LAST MIN.

■ **STA Travel**: (students and those under 26. Branches nationwide) 48 East 11th Street, New York, New York 10003. ☎ 1-800-781-4040. Website: www.statravel.com

■ **USIT (Council Travel) USA**: (students and those under 26. Over 60 branches nationwide) 931 Westwood Boulevard, Westwood, Los Angeles, California 90024. ☎ 1-800-226-8624. Website: www.counciltravel.com

SPECIALIST TRAVEL AGENTS

■ **AmeriCan Adventures and Roadrunner**: (adventure tours) PO Box 1155, Gardena, California 90249. ☎ 1-800-873-5872. Website: www.americanadventures.com

■ **Backroads**: (cycling and general activity holidays) 801 Cedar Street, Berkeley, California 94710. ☎ 1-800-462-2848. Website: www.backroads. com

■ **Odyssey Adventures**: (canoeing and activity holidays) Box 76, Ashland, Missouri 65010. ☎ 1-800-677-7099. Website: www.odyssey-adventures. com

■ **Suntrek**: (adventure holidays) Sun Plaza, 77 West Third Street, Santa Rosa, California 95401. ☎ (707) 523 1800. Website: www.suntrek.com

■ **The World Outside**: (wilderness holidays) 2840 Wilderness Place, Suite F, Boulder, Colorado 80301. ☎ (303) 413 0938. Website: www.theworld outside.com

■ **Trek America**: (group adventure travel) PO Box 189, Rockaway, New Jersey 07866. ☎ 1-800-221-0596. Website: www.trekamerica.com

FROM AUSTRALIA AND NEW ZEALAND

All flights from Australia or New Zealand to Canada involve at least one stop, usually in Honolulu or Los Angeles. Vancouver is the main entry point, although many flights route through Los Angeles to destinations in Canada.

Air Canada fly three times daily from Sydney to Vancouver, via Honolulu and Los Angeles, and fly from Vancouver to all domestic destinations in Canada.

Qantas fly up to eight times a day from Sydney and Melbourne to Toronto, via Los Angeles, and sometimes an additional stop. Up to four daily Qantas flights depart Sydney and Melbourne for Vancouver, via Los Angeles. Qantas also fly three times daily from Auckland to Vancouver only, via Los Angeles.

Other airlines that fly from Sydney and Auckland to Canada include **JAL Japan Airlines**, via Japan, and **KLM**, via Los Angeles. **Cathay Pacific** fly twice daily from Sydney to Toronto, via Hong Kong, **Delta Airlines** fly regularly to Toronto, via New York, and **United Airlines** fly to various Canadian destinations from Sydney, via Los Angeles.

Journey time to Toronto from Sydney starts at 20 hours 30 minutes, for a flight with one stopover, and increases according to time spent in additional stopovers. Journey time from Sydney to Vancouver starts at 18 hours 30 minutes. The shortest flight time, including two stopovers, from Auckland to Toronto is 29 hours.

The cheapest fares are to Vancouver. Low-season return fares can be as cheap as AUD$1700, with advance booking, but usually start at around AUD$2500. Return flights in high season start at around AUD$3000. For flights to destinations other than Vancouver, you should expect to pay at least AUD$500, or NZ$600, in addition to the basic fare. Fares are highest for departures in summer and during the winter holiday. Early booking will reduce the price of your ticket, whenever your date of departure.

➍ **Air Canada**: Comaltech House, Level One, Sydney 2000. ☎ (02) 286-8900. 18 Shortland Street, Sixth Floor, Auckland 1. ☎ (09) 379-3371. Website: www.aircanada.com

✪ British Airways: Chifley Square, 70 Hunter Street, Sydney 2000. ☎ (02) 9258-3300. Auckland International Airport, Auckland. ☎ (09) 356-8690. Website: www.britishairways.com

✪ Cathay Pacific: 3/F International Terminal, Sydney International Airport, Mascot, Sydney 2020. ☎ 13 26 27. Arthur Andersen Tower, 11th Floor, 205–209 Queen Street, PO Box 1313, Auckland 1. ☎ (09) 379-0861. Website: www.cathaypacific.com

✪ Delta Airlines: 189 Kent Street, Level Nine, PO Box N117, Sydney 2000. ☎ (02) 9251-3211. 18 Shortland Street, Sixth Floor, Auckland 1. ☎ (09) 379-3370. Website: www.delta.com

✪ JAL Japan Airlines: Darling Park, Level 14, 201 Sussex Street, Sydney 2000. ☎ (02) 9272-1111. Westpac Tower, 12th Floor, 120 Albert Street, Auckland 1. ☎ (09) 379-9906. Website: www.jal.com

✪ KLM / Alitalia: 115 Pitt Street, Level 13, Sydney 2000. ☎ (02) 9922-1555. Salvation Army Building, Second Floor, 369 Queen Street, Auckland 1. ☎ (09) 309-1782. Website: www.klm.com

✪ Qantas: Qantas Centre, 203 Coward Street, Mascot, Sydney 2020. ☎ 13 12 11 or (02) 9691-3636. 191 Queen Street, Auckland 1. ☎ (09) 357-8900 or 0800-808-967. Website: www.qantas.com

✪ United Airlines: 10 Barrack Street, Level Five, Sydney 2000. ☎ (02) 9292 4111. 1 Queen Street, 17th Floor, Auckland Central, Private Bag 92137. Auckland 1. ☎ (0800) 508 648. Website: www.ual.com

TRAVEL AGENTS

■ **Flight Centres**: 33 Berry Street, Level 13, North Sydney 2060. ☎ (02) 924-2422. 205 Queen Street, Auckland 1. ☎ (09) 309-6171. ☎ 1-1300-131-600 for nearest branch.

■ **STA Travel**: 855 George Street, Sydney 2000. ☎ (02) 9212-1255 (72 branches). 90 Cashel Street, Christchurch. ☎ (03) 379-9098 (13 branches). For nearest branch ☎ 13 17 76. Website: www.statravel.com.au

■ **Thomas Cook**: 175 Pitt Street, Sydney 2000 ☎ 1-300-728-748 (branches nationwide) 96 Anzac Avenue, Auckland. ☎ 0800-500-600 (branches nationwide). Websites: www.thomascook.com.au; www.thomas cook.com.nz

■ **Trailfinders**: 91 Elizabeth Street, Brisbane, Queensland 4000. ☎ (07) 3229-0887. Website: www.trailfinders.com/australia

SPECIALIST TRAVEL AGENTS

■ **Adventure World**: 73 Walker Street, North Sydney 2000. ☎ (02) 9956-7766. Website: www.adventureworld.com

■ **Peregrine Adventures**: 38 York Street, Fifth Floor, Sydney 2000. ☎ (02) 9290-2770. Website: www.peregrine.net.au

■ **Top Deck**: 123 Clarence Street, Level Two, Sydney 2000. ☎ 1-300-656-566. Email: topdeck@deckers.com.au

FROM SOUTH AFRICA

Air Canada fly from Johannesburg to Toronto, via Frankfurt and Paris, twice daily in summer and once daily in winter. **Air France** fly once daily throughout the year to Toronto, via Paris. **British Airways** fly twice a day from Johannesburg to Toronto, via London.

Flight time from Johannesburg to Toronto begins at 25 hours for flights with the shortest stopovers.

Fares for a standard return from Johannesburg to Toronto start at around R6000, but can increase to over R20000. Prices increase for departures in summer, winter and at weekends. The cheapest tickets on international flights from South Africa book up quickly. The further in advance you book, the more chance you have of getting the cheapest fares.

➊ **Air Canada**: Sandton Terrace, 137C 11th Street, Parkmore, Benmore 2010. ☎ (011) 884-7788. Website: www.aircanada.com

➊ **Air France**: Oxford Manor, First Floor, Oxford Road, Ilovo 2196. ☎ (0860) 340 340. Website: www.airfrance.com

➊ **British Airways**: Grovesnor Court, 195 Grosvenor Corner, Rosebank, Johannesburg 2196. ☎ (0860) 011 747 or (011) 441-8600. Website: www.britishairways.com

TRAVEL AGENTS IN SOUTH AFRICA

■ **STA Travel**: Leslie Social Sciences Building, Level Three, University of Cape Town, Rondebosch 7700, Cape Town. ☎ (021) 685-1808. Website: www.statravel.co.za

■ **USIT Adventures**: Rondebosch Shopping Centre, Rondebosch Main Road, Rondebosch, Cape Town. ☎ (021) 685-2226. Website: www.usit campus.co.uk

By Train

FROM THE UNITED STATES

Amtrak trains are a scenic and comfortable way to travel to Canada, but journey times are slightly longer than by bus.

There are four main train routes from the United States to Canada. The **Maple Leaf** runs 11 times daily from New York to Toronto, via Buffalo and Niagara Falls. The journey takes 12 hours and costs from US$65 in low season for a one-way ticket. The **Adirondack** runs daily from New York to Montreal, via Alberta and Platsburg, taking 10 hours and costing from US$60 for a one-way ticket. The **International** travels daily between Chicago and Toronto in just over 11 hours and costs from US$100 for a one-way ticket. There is a daily train between Seattle and Vancouver, costing around US$25 for a one-way trip. Ticket prices increase by around US$30 for travel during summer and some public holidays.

Amtrak services connect with trains run by **VIA Rail Canada**, the Canadian national railway company.

Amtrak: 60 Massachusetts Avenue North East, Washington, DC 20002. ☎ 1-800-872-7245 or (215) 824 1600. Website: www.amtrak.com

VIA Rail Canada: PO Box 8116, Station A, Montreal H3C 3N3. ☎ 1-888-842-7245. Website: www.viarail.ca

By Sea

FROM THE UNITED STATES

The **Victoria Clipper** carries foot passengers between Seattle and Victoria, Vancouver Island, in British Columbia. The ferry sails three times daily from mid-May to mid-September and once daily in autumn and early spring. Prices start at around US$60 for a one-way ticket and US$100 for a return, with increases for departures during holiday periods. **Washington State Ferries** carry cars and passengers from Anacortes, Washington State, to Sidney, Vancouver Island. Ferries sail twice daily in summer and once daily in winter. Adult one-way tickets cost around $11 and vehicle and driver fares begin at US$30. Prices increase by around $10 in summer. The **Scotia Prince** departs Portland, Maine, daily at 9pm, between May and October, for Yarmouth, Nova Scotia. Journey time is 11 hours. Adult one-way tickets begin at around US$60 in low season and one-way vehicle and driver fares begin at US$85. Prices increase by around US$30 in July and August. Cabins are available at additional cost. The **Cat Ferry** sails from Bar Harbour, Maine, to Yarmouth, Nova Scotia, daily from May to October. Journey time is 4 hours. An adult one-way ticket begins at approximately US$45 in low season. The one-way fare for vehicle and driver begins at US$85. Fares increase by $10 in July and August.

Reservations are usually recommended and are necessary if you are taking a vehicle.

Cat Ferry: 121 Eden Street, Bar Harbour, Maine 04609 ☎ 1-888-249-7245. Website: www.catferry.com

Scotia Prince: Portland International Ferry Terminal, 468 Commercial Street, Portland, Maine. ☎ 1-800-845-4073. Website: www.scotiaprince. com

Victoria Clipper: 2701 Alaskan Way, Pier 69, Seattle, Washington 98121. ☎ 1-800-888-2535. Website: www.victoriaclipper.com

Washington State Ferries: 2911 Second Avenue, Seattle, Washington 98121. ☎ 1-888-808-7977. Website: www.wsdot.wa.gov

By Car

FROM THE UNITED STATES

Travelling by car is the best way to get off the beaten track in Canada.

The major Canadian cities, Winnipeg and Calgary in the middle, Vancouver in the west, and Montreal and Toronto in the east, are all within an hour's drive of the border. The United States Interstate Highway System leads directly into Canada at the following main points: I–95 from Maine to New Brunswick; I–91 and I–89 from Vermont to Quebec; 1–87 from New York to Quebec; I–81 and a fork off I–90 from New York to Ontario; I–94, I–96 and I–75 from Michigan to Ontario; I–29 from North Dakota to Manitoba; I–15 from Montana to Alberta; and I-5 from Washington State to British Columbia. Most of these connections link to the Trans-Canada Highway within a couple of miles.

Crossing the border can be a hassle, with long queues during summer and at weekends. Popular crossing points include Niagara Falls (both sides of the border), Windsor (Ontario), Buffalo (New York State), Rouses Point (New York State), Fort Erie (Ontario) and Detroit (Michigan).

Visitors carrying United States or United Kingdom passports may bring their car into Canada for up to six months. Driving rules differ across the provinces, but all require you to wear seatbelts (and use infant seats). Speed limits outside cities vary, but are usually about 50–60 mph (90–100 kph). Road signs in Quebec are in French only.

Those without a car might be able to drive to Canada with **Driveaway** by delivering a car. You pay a deposit of about US$300 and have a certain time period in which to deliver the car.

■ **Driveaway**: 2500 East Hallandale Beach Boulevard, Suite 205A, Hallandale, Florida 3309. ☎ (954) 456 2277. Website: www.driveaway.com

By Bus

FROM THE UNITED STATES

Greyhound buses link United States cities with destinations in Canada.

Eight daily buses leave New York for Montreal. The journey lasts 8 hours and costs around US$80 for an adult one-way ticket. Five daily buses also leave Boston for Montreal, a journey taking just over 8 hours and the adult one-way fare costs around US$75. There are regular buses between Chicago and Toronto (15 hours, approximately US$80 one way). Eight daily buses leave for the 3-hour journey from Buffalo, New York, to Canada. Single one-way fares start at around US$35. The cheapest bus journey, from Seattle to Vancouver (4 hours), costs from US$25 one-way.

Return fares are usually double the single fare, less 20 per cent. Some concessions are available.

Greyhound Ameripasses are not valid in Canada, but you can travel to Canada with your last destination on the Ameripass. Greyhound offers a Canada Travel Pass, which includes unlimited travel for 7 (US$250), 15 (US$385), 30 (US$450) or 60 days (US$580), with concessions available. Passes are not normally valid for travel during major holiday periods such as Thanksgiving, Christmas and New Year.

Greyhound: PO Box 660689, MS 4490, Dallas, Texas 75266. ☎ 1-800-229-9424. Website: www.greyhound.com

GETTING THERE

General Information

The spirit of the Great North still breathes in Canada: images of forests reaching to the horizon, huskies pulling sleds, gleaming lakes, igloos, leaping salmon, spouting whales and wild bears are deeply embedded in the country's mythology. Glowing maples, hunters' hats with racoon tails, lumberjacks and hydroplanes are all part of this somewhat clichéd image of the country that, while true, is only a small part of the mystery of the immense Canadian landscape.

Canada has long been popular with holidaymakers, attracted to its immense and arresting wilderness. Humans have struggled to survive it, but whether First Nations or white settler, they have always admired it. The land's sheer vastness commands a respect that has long dissipated from Western Europe. From the moment you set foot in Canada, it's inescapable.

Canada is a wondrous place in all seasons, but it's increasingly a winter destination, when the snow affords excellent skiing and the country turns white for as far as the eye can see. In autumn, when the maple leaves turn, the hills are incandescent with colour. In the springtime thaws the skies are soft blue and the change of season is marked by music and street festivals. In summer the beaches are full as people flock to the lakes and oceans where, if you're lucky, you might get to see some whales.

Canada is a good deal more than wildlife and scenery. The Canadian people are generally warm and welcoming, the towns and cities have been built with care, there are many important festivals and the cultural life is rich and varied.

ACCOMMODATION

BOOKING

Book well in advance. The Rockies and Vancouver Island are popular destinations, particularly with American and Japanese tourists, but hotels are few and far between. So if you plan to stay in Banff (or anywhere else in the Rockies), or if you want to visit the Pacific Rim National Park or Vancouver, it's really worth booking early to avoid disappointment. Otherwise, you could arrive to find the only available room is over 100 kilometres (60 miles) away. These places are favourite spots for cruises, and if there's a convention in town you could find that all the decent hotels are full. September is still a busy month even though the holidays are over.

CAMPSITES

Campsites in Canada are among the best organized in the world, but a large number of them close after Labour Day, at the beginning of September. The sites are clean, very spacious and well equipped with electricity, showers, washing machines and picnic tables for meals. Many sites have designated places for campfires and wood can be bought when you register. Most campsites are also either equipped with washer-dryers, areas under cover or special rooms for drying washing in wet weather. In the National Parks, campsites are run on the same lines. You can get comprehensive lists of campsites and maps from Canadian tourist offices. A book giving details of all the provinces is available from the Montréal tourist office.

Prices are reasonable and vary according to the location and the facilities on offer. You pay for the pitch itself, and each site is designed for a particular use (tents, trailers etc.) and number of people. This means they are never overcrowded, but it's advisable to book in summer. On some very remote sites, just put your payment in an envelope and post it in a special box; every so often a ranger will collect it.

If camping in May and June come well prepared because it can still be very cold. Non-campers can also enjoy sleeping in the great outdoors: many sites rent cabins, some with private washing facilities, and generally equipped with crockery and cooking facilities and a barbecue outside.

Insects are a real problem so bring some repellent; Muskoil is a miracle product that will protect you from gnats, flies and mosquitoes.

YOUTH HOSTELS

As a rule, Canadian youth hostels are excellent. They are welcoming and hassle-free and often cheaper than campsites – in fact you can often camp in the grounds of a youth hostel. They will be able to give you masses of information about the surrounding region, which is as good as going to a local tourist office. Unfortunately, many hostels have had to shut down in recent years, but you will find an up-to-date list of hostels at the local tourist offices. To use a hostel, you must be a current Youth Hostel Association (YHA) member. Membership cards can be bought locally for $25 plus taxes. Alternatively, you can buy a stamp for each night you spend in a hostel, $4 plus taxes per night; after six nights you will be given a card. This applies only in the English-speaking provinces. In Québec, although they are called 'youth hostels', the hostels are not part of the international hostelling network, so some of them don't expect you to be a member.

Joining in Britain

For information about joining before you arrive, contact the **Youth Hostel Association (YHA)** for membership details and other information. An international YHA card costs £12 for adults for a year and is valid worldwide. The **International Youth Hostel Federation (IYHF)** will issue the card. They also produce guidebooks to hostels overseas and run an international booking network from the same number.

■ **YHA**: Trevelyan House, Matlock, Derbyshire DE4 3YH. ☎ (0870) 870 8808. Fax: (01727) 844126. Email: customerservices@yha.org.uk. Website: www.yha.org.uk

■ **IYHF**: First Floor, Fountain House, Parkway, Welwyn Garden City, Herts AL1 6JH. ☎ (01707) 324170. Email: iyhf@iyhf.org. Website: www.iyhf.org

■ International booking site: www.hostelbooking.com

■ Irish website: www.irelandyha.org

■ Scottish website: www.syha.org.uk

HOTELS AND MOTELS

Hotels in Canada are comfortable and functional although they don't always have atmosphere or charm; the older ones can be delightful. Main railway stations often have telephones that connect you directly to a variety of hotels listed on a board with a description of services. Some hotels will even pay for the taxi from the station.

Motels can be very practical. Even small towns are likely to have at least one motel, often on the outskirts of town. The only drawback for independent travellers is the cost – for a single person, a motel room can be quite costly but for a group of three or more they are very reasonable. Prices can work out even cheaper than youth hostels, and are often lower during the winter season, from September. However, room rates in hotels can be negotiated. Hoteliers often have offers and it's always worth asking if discounts are available for cash payment.

It's worth knowing that dogs are not usually accepted in hotels, gîtes or restaurants.

■ **Alberta Hotel Association**: Suite 401, 5241 Calgary Trail South, Edmonton AB TRH 5G8. ☎ (403) 436-6112 or ☎ 1-800-661-8888 (toll-free). Fax: (403) 436-5404. The association publishes a free guide entitled *Accommodation* that lists all types of lodging, including ranches.

STUDENT RESIDENCES

Lodging in university residences is not always a great idea, as campuses are usually well away from town and prices are not really good value. On the other hand, there are usually communal cooking facilities, the rooms are comfortable and they often have their own bathroom.

BED & BREAKFASTS

If you want to spend a little more on accommodation, opt for a B&B (known as '*Couette et Café*' – literally 'quilt and coffee' in Québec) rather than a hotel. Throughout the country there are networks of friendly associations to find you a room with cheery families where the welcome is as generous as the breakfast included in the price. This option will be much better value than a hotel room at the same price. Obviously you must remember that you are staying in someone's home and, while you cannot expect hotel-style services, contact with your hosts will be much more personal. Make your bookings at the local tourist office. If the places suggested in here are full up, they will have a longer list you can consult. Two indispensable guides are the *British Columbia and Alberta Bed & Breakfast Guide* (published by Gordon Soules) and *The Canadian Bed & Breakfast Guide* (Penguin Books).

In Québec you will come across the words *Gîtes du Passant*. This is not a general phrase meaning B&B but a reputable badge of recognition given by **Agricotours**, which assesses these establishments on a regular basis. Places displaying this badge will have met an exacting set of selection criteria that include cleanliness, comfort, security and quality of the welcome. You can be sure that all the addresses with a *Gîte du Passant* logo offer accommodation of a good quality. However, prices will not necessarily be any higher than anywhere else, making this an attractive option.

A number of tourist offices stock copies of a book produced by the Association, which lists all its establishments and gives their exact location on a map.

Another association in the same mould is **Gîtes Classifiés**, covering Québec and New Brunswick; addresses are classified by a system of hearts. A map of their establishments is readily available. The price quoted for a night in a gîte is a price for two people, but remember that most accommodation in gîtes is subject to a 15 per cent tax. The exception to this is in establishments where there is a limited number of rooms.

- **Agricotours**: 4545 avenue Pierre-de-Coubertin, CP 1000. Succursale M, Montréal, Québec H1V 3R2. ☎ (514) 252-3138. Fax: (514) 252-3173. Website: www.giteetaubergedupassant.com

- **Gîtes Classifiés**: (gîte listings) 808 Bellevue Ouest, route 132, Les Méchins, Québec G0J 1T0. ☎ and fax: (418) 729-3483. Email: aggite@gites-classifies.qc.ca. Website: www.gites-classifies.qc.ca. You can email them to receive a free map of their gîte listings. The website has photographs of the gîtes.

- **Québec Hôtellerie Champêtre**: (resorts and country inns) Bureau 114, 445 rue St Antoine Ouest, Montréal, Québec HSZ 1J1. ☎ (514) 861-1024.

RANCHES

If you have always dreamed of being a cowboy in the Wild West, now's your chance. More and more ranches in Alberta and British Columbia are opening up to visitors so you can sample ranch life for yourself. Ranches are immense and most are in the arid interior plateau of British Columbia, in the wide plains of Alberta or in the Rocky Mountain foothills. They are usually very close to lakes or rivers so, as well as horse-riding, you can also go trekking, mountain climbing, canoeing, white-water rafting, fishing or swimming. Some ranches are open all year round.

Accommodation can be in dormitories, individual log cabins or in the ranch house. For a really cheap deal, you can also camp. There's a choice of B&B or full board, and some all-inclusive deals include horse riding (with lessons for beginners) and other sporting activities. Children are always welcome.

There are roughly a dozen guest ranches in British Columbia and close to 20 in Alberta. All are inspected and licensed yearly by the provinces' tourist offices, which then publish a list of approved ranches. You can book directly with the ranch, but you will need to book very early to avoid disappointment because Canadian families often book ranch holidays a long time in advance.

There are three main types of ranch:

Working Ranches

These offer an authentic western experience. They raise cattle or horses and the cowboys are the genuine article. To supplement their income the ranch-owner will take in 8 to 30 visitors. You can help with work such as herding the cattle or feeding and tending the other livestock. Working ranches are not all that cheap but offer a folksy, friendly stay.

Guest Ranches

The main activity of **guest ranches** is tourism, even though some still raise cattle or horses. The cowboys are mainly there to take you riding and ensure you have a good time. These ranches tend to be larger (accommodating up to 100 people), better equipped and more comfortable than working ranches.

Ranch Resorts

These are super-luxurious and are more like leisure complexes, with swimming pools and tennis courts. Meals are generous and the speciality is often barbecues, cooked and served in the open air.

■ **British Columbia Guest Ranchers' Association**: Box 3301, Kamloops, BC V2C 6B9. Website: www.bcguestranches.com (For information on British Columbia and ranch reservations)

LODGES, LOG CABINS AND RESORTS

If you want to stay out in the Canadian wilds, there are yet more choices. Some lodges are exclusively for hunters or fishermen, but they are always havens of peace and tranquillity. The air is always remarkably pure and peace is guaranteed. You will often find them near national or provincial parks, situated on the banks of great, fast-moving rivers or crystal-clear lakes. Lodges usually offer accommodation in chalets or log cabins (usually just a few), with numerous sports facilities and activities. You'll find some addresses in the *Accommodation* guide (*see above*) and can obtain others through the Canadian tourist offices, which sometimes produce a guide to lodges only. These guides are also available from the provincial tourist offices.

HOUSE AND APARTMENT SWAPS

■ **Intervac**: 230 boulevard Voltaire, 75011 Paris, France. ☎ + 33-(0)1-43-70-21-22. Fax: +33-(0)1-43-70-73-35. Website: www.intervac.org. This international organization arranges house or apartment swaps with Canadians. The company charges reasonable rates to advertise your home (with a photograph) in four or five catalogues of your choice. It's then up to you to choose your accommodation, via the intermediary. It's a practical, pleasant and frequently economical option.

■ **Vacances Amitiés internationales:** 2242 Cartier, Montréal, Québec. Fax: (514) 525-0115. This organization will send you the address of a person or family who will either take in a guest as part of the family in exchange for a return visit under the same conditions or will swap either their main or second home. Either write to VAI or send them a fax to obtain an application questionnaire, which gives full details of the terms and conditions. There's a fixed charge of approximately $85.

BUDGET

To give you some help in planning your budget, here is a guide to the sort of prices you can expect in Canada, giving average prices in four categories. These are by no means comprehensive, nor an exact reflection of what you will find and are for guidance only. Note that all dollar prices in the guides refer to Canadian dollars, unless otherwise specified.

ACCOMMODATION

Prices listed are based on the average cost and are given without allowing for local taxes, which most establishments will add on. As with most other places, prices can be subject to change. Occasionally, for example, some hotels, motels or B&Bs increase their prices at the height of the tourist season (for example, in summer or at Christmas). During these periods, prices will be outside the range quoted.

Budget: from $15 to $50 per person per night for two sharing a double room in some of the cheaper B&Bs. You'll pay less than $20 per person or per tent in a campsite. Youth hostels are usually the best bet in this category.

Moderate: $50–80 per night for two sharing a double room. Most B&Bs and motels fall into this price bracket.

Expensive: $80–120 per night for two.

Splash out: more than $120 per night for two.

EATING OUT

These price guides do not include taxes (add around 15 per cent) or service (10–15 per cent), see 'Taxes' and 'Tipping'. In western Canada you will rarely find set menus with an all-inclusive price. You are more likely to have a choice of starters, main courses and desserts. A main course could be a simple snack or a main dish with vegetables, and it usually comes with a salad as well. When it comes to tipping, it's interesting to know that waiters have to pay tax on their tips, which are considered to be part of their salary. Many Europeans are unused to leaving tips of more than five per cent so restaurateurs now add the tip to the bill to make sure that the staff get what they deserve (10 per cent or more).

It's impossible to list all the dishes that a restaurant or café offers in the guide, or even to quote all the prices, so those given can be seen as 'average' for the establishment's fixed-price menu.

Budget: less than $13 for a main course.

Moderate: $13–20 for a main course.

Expensive: $20–25 for a main course.

Splash out: more than $25 for a main course.

CLIMATE

Canada stretches from the Atlantic to the Pacific; the Northwest Territories are inside the Arctic Circle, Vancouver on the Pacific coast is at almost the same latitude as Paris, and Ottawa is farther south still, almost level with Milan. Given this vast land mass, it's impossible to generalize about climate. However, you can get good leaflets from the tourist offices (*see* 'Tourist Offices'), which include information about the average temperatures in their respective areas, with advice about clothing for different seasons.

GENERAL GUIDELINES

The climate is warmer in the southern part of any province, near the border with the United States, and this is where the majority of the population has settled. **January** and **February** are very, very cold, although the days can be superbly sunny. This is the time of year for skiing, going out on snowshoes or on a skidoo. It's also the time of year for a strong wind known as the *barbier*, or 'barber', which is guaranteed to turn any moustache into a mass of stalactites. In **March** and **April** the weather is changeable but getting warmer. When the thaw begins, the city streets are full of slush, although the weather is by then often very pleasant and sunny, and you're likely to find a few terrace cafés opening whenever they can. Generally, in this southern strip of the country the days are warm from **May** to **September**, but the nights are cool. Don't go over the top clothes-wise though – there's no need for cold weather gear during this period. **June** is hot. **July** and **August** are very hot and mainly dry. **October** is cool to cold. **November** is cold and the frosts begin. **December**, like January and February, is very cold.

If you intend to go **whale watching** at any time of year, remember that it will be very cold out on the water, even in summer, so take sweaters, thick socks and a scarf. It's worth noting that the Canadians have mastered temperature control; **air-conditioning** works exceedingly well and operates everywhere. In fact, it works so well you may even need a sweater if you go into a shopping mall or a restaurant. In winter, it's just the opposite and homes and public places are often overheated. The answer is to wear layers of clothing.

REGIONAL GUIDELINES

Western Canada

In western Canada the climate varies enormously and there are three distinct climatic areas. The Pacific coast benefits from a warm and wet microclimate. It rains a good deal in winter but the summers are very pleasant. Vancouver is rarely swelteringly hot. The interior of British Columbia, around Kamloops and the Okanagan valley, on the other hand, is virtually a desert, and the weather can be so oppressive that you'll long for a cool swim in the lakes. The third region is the Rocky Mountains, which has an alpine climate, with bitterly cold winters but pleasant, dry summers. Alberta is one of the sunniest provinces.

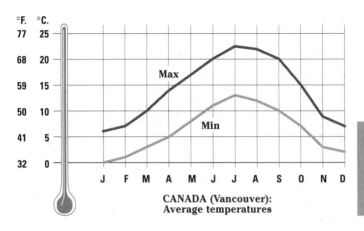

CANADA (Vancouver):
Average temperatures

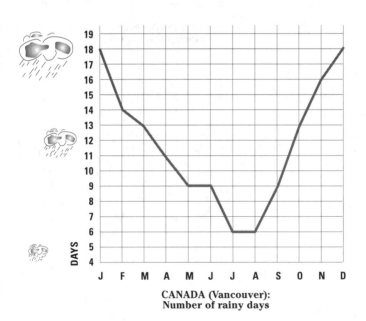

CANADA (Vancouver):
Number of rainy days

In southern Ontario, around the Niagara Falls region, the weather is mild enough for vineyards. In the winter, a celebrated ice wine is produced locally; it's a delicious beverage made from the juice of frozen grapes. If you visit Canada in winter or early spring, don't miss out on the uniquely spectacular Niagara Falls, which are partly frozen at this time of year.

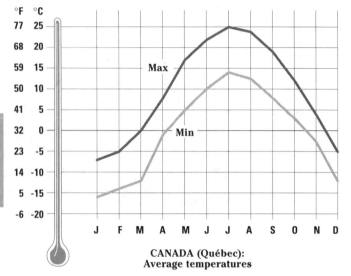

CANADA (Québec):
Average temperatures

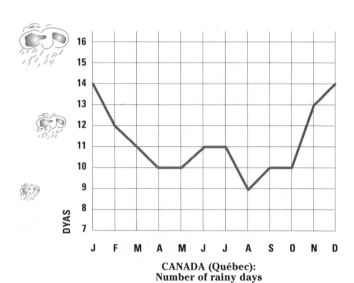

CANADA (Québec):
Number of rainy days

Québec

Winter in Québec

In order to really understand the Québécois you need to get the measure of
how winter is lodged in the collective memory. Their ancestors experienced
life through many a freezing winter without the benefits of any of today's

facilities. Despite this, the people of Québec will often tell you that they dream of being wealthy enough to be able to spend winter in sunny Florida in order to escape the long, dark months where, even in the heart of Montréal, the icy trees look like brilliant crystal chandeliers. In the old days, the whole town would turn out to line the banks of the St Lawrence river to wait for the spectacle of the ice breaking up. These days, however, almost a million of them leave the country during this period, and head south either for a few weeks' break or for the whole winter. In fact, 300,000 Québécois own a second or third home somewhere warmer.

Nowadays, in a world where central heating, electric blankets and thermal insulation are the norm, the Québec winter is still a challenge, but one that the people have got the knack of dealing with.

Indian summers

The arrival of autumn is punctuated by a phenomenon that truly belongs to the North American continent – the Indian summer. Soon after the first chill of autumn (just before mid-October usually) comes a week – sometimes more, sometimes less – when temperatures soar and there's a final flash of summer before the first snows arrive. This short heat explosion seems to put the Québécois into a sort of collective euphoria and is the magic moment to visit. The leaves stop falling temporarily and nature provides a show of autumn colour that is unique to the New World – a sight celebrated in music by a famous immigrant, Antonín Dvořák. Immediately after the week of sunshine the snow will start to fall day after day.

A word on the meaning of the name 'Indian' summer – the Native Americans, or 'Indians' in the early days used to take advantage of this brief period of warm weather to establish their camps deep in the woods and re-establish their reservations.

COMMUNICATIONS

POST

Any item sent to a general delivery or *poste restante* must be collected by the addressee in person within two weeks of arrival, otherwise it is returned to the sender. If you need mail sent to you and are not sure when you can collect it, you would be safer having it sent c/o American Express agencies who keep it longer. In the major cities of Québec, you'll find that the post offices are often not very central, although there will be small post offices within convenience stores and even in dry cleaners, as well as in pharmacy chains such as *Pharmaprix* or the *Jean Coutu* stores.

TELEPHONE

Making a Call

Local calls

For local calls you do not need to use the area code (e.g. 514 for Montréal).

Regional calls

Making long-distance calls is a little more complicated. First of all, you have to use the area code for all calls between towns, and this applies even if the area codes are the same (for example, for a call to Berthierville from Montréal use the code 450). The cost of the call will vary according to the distance, and it won't be cheap either way.

Regional Dialling Codes

Barrie (Ontario)	705	Québec	418
Calgary	403	Regina	306
Chatham	519	Saskatoon	306
Edmonton	403	Sault Ste-Marie	705
Halifax	902	Stratford	519
Montréal	514	Toronto	416
Niagara Falls	416	Vancouver	604
Ottawa	613	Victoria	250
Peterborough	705	Winnipeg	204

International calls

To call Canada from Britain, dial 00 + 1 + three-digit area code + the number.

International dialling codes from Canada:

– To Great Britain:	+44
– To Ireland:	+353
– To the USA:	+1
– To Australia:	+61
– To New Zealand:	+64
– To South Africa:	+27

Toll-free numbers (1-800-xxx-xxxx or 1-877-xxx-xxxx) are free from within Canada and the USA, but standard international rates apply if you call these numbers from overseas.

Cost of Calls

Public telephones

Local calls from a phone kiosk cost 25 cents per call. You should ideally buy a phonecard (*see below*), but be aware that there are still some phone kiosks that are not equipped to take phonecards so you will need change. Rates vary according to the time of day so make the most of your card by calling outside peak hours. Note that there are no **public telephones** in post offices as the two services are separate in North America.

Some public telephones, particularly in airports, train stations and major hotels in cities, take credit cards, but charges can be astronomical, so save for emergency calls only. The same is true of calls made from your hotel room – the rates will be extortionate, so use sparingly.

Phonecards

Phonecards make calling abroad much simpler as most phone companies don't accept credit cards. There is a wide choice of pre-paid phonecards to choose from, so ask in local newsagents for details.

– **Making a call**: Dial the toll-free prefix (e.g. 1-800), followed by the number on your card. Every time you make a call, the amount remaining on your card will be displayed.

You can buy a **Bell Telephone** 'Hello Phone Pass' in units of $10, 20, 50 or 100 from numerous outlets, including tourist offices, shops, metro stations and automatic dispensers at airports. They come in five languages, including English and French, and you can call anywhere in the world from any telephone kiosk in Canada or the United States. In Québec, the pre-paid phonecards are issued by **La puce de Bell** and cost $5, 10 or 20. These cards are sold mainly at telephone company offices, Bell shops, main **Via Rail** railway stations, as well as in some tourist information offices and occasionally in youth hostels.

– **United States residents** should use dial-around services that allow you to bill your home phone or credit card. Toll-free access numbers in Canada include AT&T (☎ 5-5288), MCI (☎ 1-800-888-8000), and Sprint (☎ 1-800-366-2555).

– **United Kingdom residents** can obtain a BT Chargecard, which will charge all calls you make overseas to your home phone bill.

– Another option is the **AT&T Calling Card**. Available free to American Express, MasterCard and Visa cardholders, you can use this to call more than 200 countries from the USA and Canada. It can also be used in the 72 countries that offer the 'AT&T World Connect' service. Calls are charged direct to your credit card. The AT&T Calling Card also gives you access to the company's international services: Language Line (interpreters), Message Service, information, freephone numbers, multifax and telephone conferencing. Available through AT&T in the UK ☎ 0800 890011. Delivery usually takes about three weeks so leave plenty of time before you intend to travel.

Emergency Long-distance Calls

In an emergency, the best option for non-United States residents is to make a **reverse-charge (collect)** call. Dial a Canadian operator, such as AT&T (☎ 1-800-445-5667), MCI (☎ 1-800-444-2162), or Sprint (☎ 1-800-800-0008) and ask to be put through to a BT operator or an operator for your phone company in Australia, New Zealand or South Africa. This will incur an international operator fee.

GENERAL INFORMATION

CONVERSION TABLES

Men's sizes

Shirts

UK	USA	EUROPE
14	14	36
14½	14½	37
15	15	38
15½	15½	39
16	16	41
16½	16½	42
17	17	43
17½	17½	44
18	18	46

Suits

UK	USA	EUROPE
36	36	46
38	38	48
40	40	50
42	42	52
44	44	54
46	46	56

Shoes

UK	USA	EUROPE
8	9	42
9	10	43
10	11	44
11	12	46
12	13	47

Women's sizes

Shirts/dresses

UK	USA	EUROPE
8	6	36
10	8	38
12	10	40
14	12	42
16	14	44
18	16	46
20	18	48

Sweaters

UK	USA	EUROPE
8	6	44
10	8	46
12	10	48
14	12	50
16	14	52
18	16	54
20	18	56

Shoes

UK	USA	EUROPE
3	5	36
4	6	37
5	7	38
6	8	39
7	9	40
8	10	42

Temperature

- To convert °C to °F, multiply by 1.8 and add 32.
- To convert °F to °C, subtract 32 and multiply by 5/9 (0.55). 0°C=32°F

US weights and measures

1 centimetre	0.39 inches	1 inch	2.54 centimetres
1 metre	3.28 feet	1 foot	0.30 metres
1 metre	1.09 yards	1 yard	0.91 metres
1 kilometre	0.62 miles	1 mile	1.61 kilometres
1 hectare	2.47 acres	1 acre	0.40 hectares
1 litre	1.76 pints	1 pint	0.57 litres
1 litre	0.26 gallons	1 gallon	3.79 litres
1 gram	0.035 ounces	1 ounce	28.35 grams
1 kilogram	2.2 pounds	1 pound	0.45 kilograms

DISABLED ACCESS

Disabled facilities are usually very good in Canada. However, B&Bs are usually in older buildings that are more difficult to adapt and often cannot be suitably converted, so it's wise to check first. Motels and hotels tend to be better equipped.

ELECTRICITY

The current in Canada is 110 volts AC. Plugs are of the North American type (two flat pins) so you'll need an international adaptor.

EMBASSIES AND CONSULATES

CANADIAN EMBASSIES OVERSEAS

United Kingdom: Canadian High Commission, 38 Grosvenor Street, London W1K 4AA. ☎ (0906) 861 6644 (premium rates apply). Fax: (020) 7258 6506. Website: www.canada.org.uk

Ireland: Canadian Embassy, 65 St Stephen's Green, Dublin 2. ☎ (01) 478 1988. Fax: (01) 478 1285

United States: Canadian Embassy, 501 Pennsylvania Avenue North West, Washington DC 20001. ☎ (202) 682-1740 Fax: (202) 682-7726. Website: www.canadianembassy.org

Australia: Canadian High Commission, Commonwealth Avenue, Canberra ACT 2600. ☎ (02) 6720-4000. Fax: (02) 6273-3285. Website: www.canada.org.au

New Zealand: Canadian High Commission, 61 Molesworth Street, Third Floor, Thorndon, Wellington. ☎ (04) 473-9577. Fax: (04) 471-2082. Website: www.dfait-maeci.gc.ca/newzealand

South Africa: Canadian High Commission, 1103 Arcadia Street, Corner Arcadia and Hilda Streets, Hatfield 0028, Pretoria. ☎ (012) 422-3053. Fax: (012) 422-3054

OVERSEAS EMBASSIES IN CANADA

United Kingdom: British High Commission, 80 Elgin Street, Ottawa, Ontario K1P 5K7. ☎ (613) 237-2008. Fax: (613) 237-6357. Website: www.britain-in-canada.org

Ireland: Embassy of Ireland, 130 Albert Street, Ottawa, Ontario K1P 5G4. ☎ (613) 233-6281. Fax: (613) 233-6281.

United States: United States Embassy, 490 Sussex Drive, Ottawa, Ontario K1N 1G8. ☎ (613) 238-5335. Fax: (613) 688-3082. Website: www.usembassycanada.gov

Australia: Australian High Commission, Suite 710, Seventh Floor, 50 O'Connor Street, Ottawa, Ontario K1P 6L2. ☎ (613) 236-0841. Fax: (613) 236-4376. Website: www.ahc-ottawa.org

New Zealand: New Zealand High Commission, Suite 727, Metropolitan House, 99 Bank Street, Ottawa, Ontario K1P 6G3. ☎ (613) 238-5991. Fax: (613) 238-5707. Website: www.nzhcottawa.org

South Africa: South African High Commission, 15 Sussex Drive, Ottawa, Ontario K1M 1M8. ☎ (613) 744-0330. Fax: (613) 744-1639.

EMERGENCIES

For all emergencies (police, fire brigade and ambulance) call ☎ 911.

ENTRY FORMALITIES

UNITED STATES CITIZENS

Visitors from the United States do not need a passport if they are entering from the United States, but do need proof of identity. A driver's licence is usually sufficient for crossing the land border, but, if you don't take your passport, you should carry a certificate of birth, citizenship or naturalization. Non-United States citizens resident in the country should carry their green card and United States citizens arriving from a country other than the United States should carry their passport.

CITIZENS OF OTHER COUNTRIES

Those travelling to Canada from any country other than the United States must have a passport with at least six months validity to enter Canada. Customs formalities are less strict than those on entry to the United States, but you may be requested to show a return ticket or proof of sufficient funds to finance your stay. A credit card, or around $400 per week, should be sufficient.

Citizens of the European Union, Australia and New Zealand do not need a visa to enter Canada, unless they plan to work in the country. You are usually given a 90-day visa on arrival. If you require a six-month visa, contact your local Canadian consulate well before departure.

Citizens of South Africa must obtain a visa from the Canadian High Commission before departure. Single-entry visitor visas are valid for six months and multiple-entry visas can be used over a two-year period, as long as no single stay exceeds six months. Extensions must be applied for at a Canadian Immigration Centre one month before the current visa expires.

Remember that if you plan to visit the United States, even for a very short period, you will need a visa. However, citizens of some countries (such as Great Britain) are eligible for the visa waiver scheme. If you do not need a visa to enter the United States and you cross the land border, you will be charged a US$6 entry fee. You will be expected to have an onward or return ticket out of the United States in your possession.

For more information on visas for work in Canada, *see* 'Working in Canada'.

HEALTH AND INSURANCE

Canada is a typical First World country with respect to health, and the health service is excellent. It is very expensive however, particularly for foreigners, and all visitors to Canada should arrange comprehensive health insurance cover before they leave. For treatment in Canada, you will usually have to pay up-front – often in cash – and claim back expenses later, so you should take out a travel insurance policy that will cover immediate expenses and any emergency repatriation costs.

No vaccinations are required for travel in the country, but you should check that your tetanus jabs are up to date, particularly if you plan to do any walking or trekking. If you take prescription medications, bring all your supplies with you. You should also pack a copy of your prescription to avoid problems at customs. It's worthwhile packing a basic first-aid kit, especially if you plan to drive in Canada or get off the beaten track.

INSECT REPELLENTS

Canada is a land of lakes and forests, so expect an onslaught of mosquitoes and other biting insects during spring. These insects are not disease-carriers, but it's still advisable to take the necessary precautions, as they can make your stay extremely uncomfortable. A number of sprays, creams and lotions sold in retail outlets and even in pharmacies offer little or no protection against mosquitoes. However, there is a solution called **Bayrepel** that offers long protection, doesn't smell too awful and is easy to apply. It can even be used on children as young as two years. Brand names include Autan Family (for children and for delicate skins) and Autan Active (for use during outdoor activities and in tropical climates). Other recognized and recommended treatments include **Insect Ecran Peau**, which contains 50 per cent DEET (or diethyltomide). This one should not be used on children under three years. Another is **Cinq sur Cinq Tropic**, containing an ingredient called 35/35. This one works in much the same way but is safe to use on young children.

Whatever you use, treat all exposed parts of the body at intervals of not more than four hours.

LANGUAGE

English and French are the two official languages of Canada, as stipulated in the Official Languages Act of September 1969, and both languages have equal status – at least in theory. Former Prime Minister Pierre Elliott Trudeau, was a formidable supporter of bilingualism and was determined to keep French-speaking Québec within the Canadian Federation. He was deeply

GENERAL INFORMATION

committed to making the country genuinely bilingual, but his dream was only partially realized.

The extent of bilingualism is largely limited to the administration of the federal government. Signs at airports or customs, in national parks and post offices are in both languages and the translations can appear somewhat quaint. Canadian English has diverged from British English, and Canadian French has diverged from French as spoken in France, so the translations may well go back to more historic usage.

You should be able to manage pretty well with English everywhere in Canada but the population in Ottawa (Ontario), the capital, is largely bilingual. Ontario has an estimated 1 million inhabitants who have French as their only language. There is also a French-speaking community of around 12,000 in Manitoba province – descendants of the French-Canadian pioneers of the 19th century – who live in the district of St Boniface in Winnipeg. Canadian accents vary from region to region – whether in English, French or French-Canadian English – although not nearly as much as in Britain.

In Québec, French has been the only official language since 1977. A number of expressions in Canadian French are different from the French spoken in France, and these even vary from one part of Québec to another, and it is often the case that words and phrases that people have never heard of or used in Montréal or Québec can be readily heard in Charlevoix or on the Gaspé Peninsula. For English-speakers here are two pieces of useful information. First, don't be surprised to hear everyone using the '*tu*' form, even the policemen. The second is that meals are confusingly not called what you would expect, as '*déjeuner*' means 'breakfast', '*dîner*' means lunch and '*souper*' means supper.

In parts of the west Japanese is an unofficial 'third' language. Before the slump in the Tiger economies, there was massive Japanese investment in tourist resorts, mainly in the Rockies and especially in the hotels of the famous Canadian Pacific chain. At the Banff Springs Hotel or the Château Lac Louise, everything is written in Japanese characters and the luxury boutiques are often Japanese-owned.

DIALECTS

Across the territory of modern Canada there are some 50 different native languages or dialects, belonging to 10 major linguistic groups: Algonquian, Iroquoian, Siouan, Athapaskan, Kootenayan, Salishan, Wakashan, Tsimshian, Haida and Tlingit. However, their distribution and use are extremely complex and enough to confuse even the most meticulous student of linguistics. For example, the Wakashan family of the Pacific coast brings together the Haisla, Heiltsuk, Kwakiutl, Nuuchalnulth, Nootka and Nitinat languages, while Athapaskan from around the Rocky Mountains includes the following languages: Beaver, Porter, Chilcotin, Tcippewayan, Flan-de-chien, Han, Hare, Kaska, Kutchin, Sarsi, Sakani, Slave, Tagish, Tahitan and Tutchoni.

MONEY

The Canadian dollar ($) has a much more favourable exchange rate than its American neighbour. It is divided into 100 cents and all prices in this guide refer to Canadian dollars, unless otherwise indicated. The exchange rate hovers around $2.20 to £1, but check the latest rate before you leave. This makes prices very reasonable, although you are likely to spend more in the eastern provinces than in the west. When exchanging money, try to do it in towns rather than at the airport, as the exchange rates are better.

It's as well to know that Canada is not the cheapest place in which to travel independently, especially when it comes to lodging and food, both of which cost more than they do in the US. In addition, most parks and museums charge an admission fee, so you need to go prepared.

Banks

In the west banks are open Monday–Friday 10am–5pm. Some also open on Saturdays. Cash machines where you can withdraw money with a credit or debit card are found everywhere. In Québec, banks are open Monday–Friday 10am–3pm; most stay open until 8pm on Thursday and Friday, when the shops stay open late.

Traveller's Cheques

It's best to buy them in Canadian dollars (rather than US$), as most shops will accept them. When you change traveller's cheques, you will usually be charged a commission of about $2.50.

Credit/Debit Cards

Using your debit card is an easy way to withdraw money from most cash dispensing machines (ATMs). They will take most cards, but be aware that you pay a fee for each withdrawal whatever the total value, so if you withdraw cash every day you could end up paying a lot for the privilege. You can use a MasterCard to draw cash at the Banque de Montréal. Both are accepted in shops, hotels and restaurants, but they don't take debit cards in supermarkets. In some regions you can pay for your stay in a youth hostel with a Visa card.

If your card is lost or stolen, cancel it as soon as possible by calling the card provider in your own country; make sure you have the 24-hour contact number with you. British holders of American Express, Barclaycard and Visa cards can phone the UK from Canada for assistance:

American Express (24-hour)   ☎ 44 (0)1273 696933
Barclaycard (24-hour)   ☎ 44 (0)1604 234234
Visa (24-hour)   ☎ 44 (0)1383 621166

Money Transfer

If you need cash urgently, for whatever reason, Western Union Money Transfer can arrange speedy transfers. Make your way to the nearest office or call them (freephone): ☎ 1-800-325-6000.

French Words for Money

In Québec, people often use the word *piastre* (pronounced 'piass') instead of dollar, and either '*sous*' or '*cennes*' for cents. In Québécois shops you might be asked if you want to pay '*comptant*' which means 'in cash'.

PARKS AND NATURE

The protection of the environment is taken very seriously in Canada and there are more than 30 national parks, as well as numerous provincial parks, that are managed by the governments of each province. The main purpose of the parks is to protect the indigenous flora and fauna while ensuring that visitors can enjoy the wealth of nature.

The quality of services in each park is a testament to their success. The 'welcome centres' are staffed by nature experts who can provide information and advice about walks or rambles to suit all abilities and itineraries. The staff are passionate about what they do and will enthusiastically answer any questions you have – so ask away. The parks have splendid campsites (equipped with showers and washing machines), picnic areas and so on.

Canadians are all careful to respect nature, and visitors are requested to do the same when in the parks: do not smoke, do not pick any flowers or plants, take away your rubbish and dispose of it only in proper bins outside the park. Under no circumstances allow yourself to be bewitched by the bear cubs or peaceful wild lambs; feeding wild animals is strictly forbidden as the park authorities do not want them to become dependent on humans.

The sign for the national parks is a picture of a beaver. National parks are open all year round, but services are reduced out of season, usually from Labour Day (first Monday in September). You will need a permit to enter a park, which you can buy at the rangers' reception area as you arrive. Free maps and brochures are available.

THE QUÉBEC FORESTS

The forests of Québec make up 20 per cent of Canada's total forested area, which consists of four different zones of vegetation from south to north: a mixture of broad-leaved trees (firs and yellow birches), sub-Arctic trees (spruces, pines and silver birches), taiga (conifers) and tundra. The timber industry, which employs 200,000 people either directly or indirectly, exports 28 per cent of its output, and this represents about 20 per cent of Canada's total exports. More than 50 types of tree are grown, with none under threat except the elm, which has suffered badly throughout North America. A decline in the number of maples has become noticeable but no cause has yet been identified.

The government of Québec itself manages 90 per cent of its forestry manpower. Since a law passed in 1986, felling has been strictly controlled, and no trees are felled around lakes and along riverbanks.

PUBLIC HOLIDAYS

National Holidays

– New Year's Day (1 January)

– Good Friday

– Easter Monday

– Victoria Day (the Monday before 25 May)

– Canada Day (1 July)

– Labour Day (first Monday in September)

– Thanksgiving (second Monday in October)

– Remembrance Day (11 November)

– Christmas Day and Boxing Day (25 and 26 December)

> **TIP** Although it's a holiday, most museums and many other attractions are open to the public on **Labour Day**, but hours may be limited and some might be closed. Check on opening times and possible restricted travel services with the tourist offices. It's also the last weekend before children return to school, and traffic into the cities could be quite congested. Make sure you book hotels or B&Bs for this weekend well in advance to avoid disappointment.

Provincial Holidays

Alberta – Alberta Family Day (third Monday in February)

Newfoundland – Celebrated on nearest Monday: St Patrick's Day (March 17); St George's Day (April 23); Discovery Day (June 24); Memorial Day (July 1); Orangemen's Day (July 12); Regatta Day/Civic Holiday (fixed by municipal council orders)

Nova Scotia – Natal Day (first Monday of August, except in Halifax where it varies from year to year, usually August or July)

Ontario, **Nova Scotia**, **New Brunswick**, **Manitoba**, **British Columbia**, **Saskatchewan**, **Alberta** and **Northwest Territories** – Civic Holiday (first Monday in August)

Québec – Fête de Dollard-des-Ormeaux – festival commemorating a French officer killed by the Iroquois (third Monday in May); Fête de la Reine (third Monday in May); National Day (June 24)

Prince Edward Island – Natal Day (by proclamation, usually on first Monday of August)

Yukon – Discovery Day (third Monday in August)

SHOPPING

– The famous **Hudson's Bay Company blanket** made of 100 per cent wool is on sale in the Bay chain of shops, which is the descendant of the great colonial trading company. Their design of green, red, yellow and black stripes on a natural background has never changed. You can also find '*canadiennes*' which are warm, fur-lined jackets.

– **Roots**, a Canadian chain of stores, can be found throughout the country. Their goods are a little expensive but ruggedly made; look out for leather bags, hiking boots, jeans and checked shirts.

– If you want to taste the local tipple, **Crown Royal** is a special Canadian whisky.

– All **sports clothes and accessories** are good value, from cycling helmets to golf clubs and fishing equipment.

– **Native Indian crafts**: these artefacts are very attractive but costly. You can also find a variety of cheap 'ethnic' trinkets. Where possible, try to buy this kind of thing on the reserve rather than in the shops. Not only does the money then go straight back to the producer but it's bound to cost less as you won't pay any local taxes! Look out for such items as peace-pipes, moccasins, small figures and native jewellery. You will find the most famous Amerindian artists in the West. Bill Reid's imposing sculptures are exhibited in the Anthropological Museum in Vancouver. The museum shop sells very beautiful reproductions. Other lesser-known artists make beautiful pieces which make splendid presents: finely carved pipes, unusual silver jewellery and wooden figures.

– **Inuit art**: a significant number of shops and galleries keep a large stock of Inuit figures and carvings in soapstone. If you buy an original work by an Inuit artist, it should have a special sticker of an igloo on it, the official Canadian Government sign certifying the piece is authentic.

– **Snowshoes**: good either as a souvenir or a gift. These are the speciality of the First Nation people, especially the Hurons.

– *Catalognes en guenilles*: these are brightly coloured covers made using narrow strips of old material (*guenilles* means 'rags'). The best place to buy these is on the Gaspé Peninsula between Forillon and Percé.

– If you're after a western look, you can buy **cowboy boots and hats** in Alberta, as well as wide leather belts and boot-lace ties. If you're really into it, buy yourself a collection of country-music CDs – the choice is huge.

– **Maple syrup** (*le sirop d'érable*): this Canadian national delight has finally become affordable once more. In Québec the main areas of production are Beauce, which considers itself to be the world capital of maple products, and les Bois-Francs. Almost every farm has maple syrup for sale and you will also find it in the markets of Montréal as well as in some food shops. Even if you don't manage to taste it where it is made, it's available tinned or bottled. Buy the best quality (the clearer the better) and don't be fobbed off with the watery imitations made from sweet corn that you find in some restaurants.

– **Blueberry wine** (*le vin de bleuet*): this fantastic Québécois aperitif is fairly cheap and goes by the name of du Bleuet or Minaki. Production is centred around the Lac Saint-Jean, especially at Mistassini, where there is a 'blueberry festival' every year in July. Cousin to the European bilberry, the blueberry produces a wine that is best drunk chilled. Try also a drink called '*ricaneux*', a wine made with raspberries and strawberries, or '*caribou*', which is a blend of spirits and red wine. In Québec, this is a popular beverage for keeping warm during the winter carnival and is drunk from a hip flask.

– **Good deals**: all **CDs** are much cheaper, as are clothes, particularly jeans. **Electronic equipment** such as fax machines, computers, mobile phones and cameras are worth a look, although you need to be sure about the voltage and buy a transformer to use your equipment back home. And to make things even cheaper, you can get the tax back (*see* 'Taxes'). Look for the sales or discount promotions that are advertised in newspapers. The department stores often sell them at incredibly knocked-down prices.

GENERAL
INFORMATION

SMOKING

Nicotine-dependants should note that the majority of B&Bs and lodges are non-smoking. If you can't do without a late-night fix, double-check for particular 'late-night' policies when you book. Rules can be pretty strict, not least because so many houses are built out of wood. What's more, the law forbids smoking in commercial or public buildings such as shops, as well as on all domestic flights on Canadian airlines. Airports, trains and buses are also smoke-free zones. Restaurants usually have separate sections for smoking and non-smoking guests. However, in more and more cases, particularly in Toronto and Vancouver, smoking is very often simply forbidden. Smokers, you have been warned.

TAXES

Beware of hidden costs for services (restaurants etc.) or products as two different taxes will be added. Province Sales Tax (**PST**, called **TVQ** in Québec) can be 7–8 per cent depending on the province, although in Alberta a sales tax of 5 per cent is added only to hotel room charges. On top of that is Goods and Services Tax (**GST**, called **TPS** in Québec) of 7 per cent, adding around 15 per cent to the price displayed.

CLAIMING BACK THE SALES TAX

The politicians wanted to be sure they weren't killing the goose that laid the golden egg – tourism is a source of significant revenue – so, if you are not resident in Canada, you can claim back the PST. It's not exactly straightforward, but you can get a leaflet and application form from the tourist office or from customs at the airport.

Basically, PST is reimbursed on the cost of temporary lodging (hotels and B&Bs, but not campsites unless you have pre-booked and paid from abroad), and on most consumer products that you are likely to take home.

You can't claim back the tax on meals, alcohol, tobacco, car hire, petrol, food or second-hand goods of value, such as antiques. However, on a three-week trip you might pay a significant amount of tax that you could claim back so it's worth looking into.

If you want to make a claim, you'll need to send all your bills and receipts, so don't forget to keep them. Be sure to ask the hotel or B&B staff to write down the amount of PST clearly and also the number of nights you have stayed. In order to qualify for reimbursement each receipt must total a minimum of $50 (before tax), so it's best to buy things at the same time when shopping, and the total sum of goods purchased must be at least $200 (before tax).You will have to complete the form in the PST brochure (available from tourist offices or airport customs), and send it with the original bills. The cheque (in Canadian dollars) may take a few weeks to arrive and you might be charged a fee to pay it into your bank.

If you want to avoid the hassle, you can arrange to be reimbursed in the tax-free shops you'll find at international airports, but some specify a minimum of $500 before they will reimburse you. You will need to produce two separate proofs of identity, one showing your home address and the other with a photograph. You will also need your plane ticket, as recent legislation has ruled that if you are travelling by car you will be reimbursed by post. Furthermore, you must be able to show the goods themselves.

Reimbursements are not normally made through bureaux on purchases of electronic goods or valuable items. For these, you will need to make a postal application.

In Montréal, you can get your reimbursement at the Maple Leaf Bureau (☎ (514) 847-0982; fax: (514) 847-1019) on the 4th level of the Eaton Centre, although there is a 15 per cent service charge on every transaction.

TIME

There are six time zones across Canada. When it's 5pm in Britain, it's noon in Québec and Ontario (Greenwich Mean Time –5), 1pm in New Brunswick and Nova Scotia, 11am in Manitoba, 10am in Alberta, Saskatchewan and the Northwest Territories, and 9am in the Yukon and British Columbia. And, just to keep you on your toes, 1.30pm in Newfoundland and Labrador.

TIPPING

Tips are not included on restaurant bills, but it's customary to leave about 15 per cent of the price, excluding tax. If you are paying by credit card, there is a space left for you to fill in the tip. A word of caution: the amount on the credit card slip will be the bill including tax, so make sure you calculate the tip on the pre-tax price that's shown on the menu. So, if the bill comes to $100, expect to pay an extra 15 per cent tax plus 15 per cent for the tip (about 30 per cent in total), making $130. Remember that the serving staff rely on their tips to live and waiters are in fact obliged to declare their tips as part of their wages, for tax purposes.

Remember when settling a restaurant bill with a credit card that you need to complete the 'service' box yourself. If you don't, you're asking for trouble as you run the risk of the restaurant completing it for you. Finding out when you get home that your meal cost a fortune won't make a good end to the holiday.

With regard to taxis, you are expected to give between 10 and 15 per cent of the metered fare as a tip. If you don't, you can expect to be told in no uncertain terms what the driver thinks of you.

TOURIST OFFICES

Tourist offices are very easy to find and are indicated by a sign with a large question mark on it. They are usually excellent. You will get a warm welcome from competent, courteous staff who will happily provide general information and hand out maps, town plans, accommodation lists and so on. They will also answer any questions, and also offer suggestions on where to go and what to see. In addition each region produces its own useful mini Tourist Guide. These are clear and extremely well produced, with lots of detail. Better still, they are up to date, as new editions appear every year. Bear in mind, though, that the advertisements in the guides are paid for.

TOURIST OFFICES IN CANADA

Canadian Tourism Commission: Eighth Floor West, 235 Queen Street, Ottawa, Ontario K1A OH6. ☎ (613) 946-1000. Website: www.canadatourism.com

Tourisme Québec: PO Box 979, Montréal, Québec H3C 2W3. ☎ 1-800-363-7777 or (514) 873 2015. Website: www.bonjourquebec.com

Provincial Tourism Commissions

Travel Ontario: Level One, Eaton Centre, 220 Yonge Street, PO Box 104 Toronto, Ontario M5B 2H1. ☎ 1-800-ONTARIO. Website: www.ontariotravel.net

Travel Alberta: Suite 500, 999 Eighth Street South West, Calgary, Alberta T2R 1J5. ☎ 1-800-661-8888 or (780) 427-4321. Website: www.travelalberta.com

Tourism British Columbia: Parliament Buildings, Victoria, British Columbia V8V 1X4. ☎ 1-800-HELLO-BC. Website: www.hellobc.com

Travel Manitoba: Department CU8, 155 Carleton Street, Seventh Floor, Winnipeg, Manitoba R3C 3H8. ☎ 1-800-665-0040. Website: www.travelmanitoba.com

Tourism New Brunswick: Department 243, PO Box 12345, Campbelton, New Brunswick E3N 2EB. ☎ 1-800-561-0123. Website: tourismnbcanada.com

Nova Scotia Tourism: PO Box 519, Halifax, Nova Scotia B3J 2M7. ☎ 1-800-565-0000 or (902) 425-5181. Website: www.exploregove.ns.ca

GENERAL INFORMATION

Prince Edward Island Tourism: Visitor Services, PO Box 940, Charlottetown, Prince Edward Island C1A 7M5. ☎ 1-888-PEI-PLAY or (902) 629-2400.

Tourism Saskatchewan: 1922 Park Street, Regina, Saskatchewan S4P 3V7. ☎ 1-877-237-2273. Website: www.sasktourism.com

City Tourist Information

Tourism Toronto: Queen's Quay Terminal, Suite 590, 207 Queen's Quay West, Toronto, Ontario M5J 1A7. ☎ (416) 203-2600. Email: toronto @torcvb.com. Website: www.torontotourism.com

Tourisme du Grand Montréal: Bureau 600, 1555 rue Peel, Montréal, Québec H3A 1X6. ☎ (514) 844-5400. Website: www.tourisme-montreal.org

Calgary Convention and Visitor Bureau: Suite 200, 238 11th Avenue South East, Calgary, Alberta T2G OX8. ☎ 1-800-661-1678 or (403) 263 8510. Website: www.tourismcalgary.com

Tourism Victoria: 812 Wharf Street, Victoria, British Columbia V8W 1T3. ☎ 1-800-663-3883 or (250) 953-2033. Email: info@tourismvictoria.com. Website: www.tourismvictoria.com

Tourism Vancouver Island: Old City Square, Suite 203, 335 Wesley Street, Nanaimo, British Columbia V9R 2T5. ☎ (250) 754-3000. Website: www.islandsbc.ca

TOURIST INFORMATION OUTSIDE CANADA

Britain

There is no walk-in tourist office in Britain, but you can obtain brochures and information from Visit Canada, or the Canada Centre in London.

■ **Visit Canada**: PO Box 5396, Northampton NN1 2FA. ☎ 0906 871 5000 (premium rate). Email: visitcanada@dialpipex.com

■ At the **Canada Centre**, Trafalgar Square, London SW1Y 5BJ, there is a dedicated phone from which you can dial **Visit Canada** for free.

■ **Québec Tourist Information**: c/o Bridge Marketing Ltd, PO Box 1939, Maidenhead SL6 1AJ. ☎ 0990 561 705.

Other Countries

United States: c/o Canadian Embassy, 501 Pennsylvania Avenue North West, Washington DC 20001. ☎ (202) 682-1740

Australia: c/o Canadian High Commission, Commonwealth Avenue, Canberra ACT 2600. ☎ (02) 9954-3377. Website: www.canada.trav.net

New Zealand: c/o Canadian High Commission, 61 Molesworth Street, Third Floor, Thorndon, Wellington. ☎ (04) 473-9577. Website: www.canada.co.nz

South Africa: c/o Canadian High Commission, 1103 Arcadia Street, Corner Arcadia and Hilda Streets, Hatfield 0028, Pretoria. ☎ (012) 422-3053. Fax: (012) 422-3054.

Representatives of Québec Overseas

United Kingdom: Délégation du Québec, 59 Pall Mall, London SW1Y 5JH. ☎ (020) 7766 5900. Email: qc.londres@mri.gouv.qc.ca

TRANSPORT

AIR TRAVEL

Air Canada offers very few attractive deals on domestic flights if you book in the country. But if you buy your return ticket in Europe, Australia and New Zealand or elsewhere, the airlines offer add-on flights at 30 per cent discount. **Canadian Airlines** has a wide-ranging network of flights out of Toronto.

BUSES AND COACHES

This is the most practical way of getting around and buses and coaches are often faster than the train. The buses are often older than those used in the US, but there are good, frequent connections to most towns and cities. You can cover very long distances in Canada and down to the United States as long as you are prepared to put up with a degree of discomfort, especially when travelling overnight. All vehicles have toilets, and some have TVs. The terminals are often quite basic; some have private washroom cubicles (25 cents) but none have showers apart from Winnipeg.

It's a good idea to plan to arrive at the bus station 45 minutes before your departure time.

Bus Companies

Eastern Canada (Ontario and Québec) is served by the **Voyageur/Orléans Express** network, which offers numerous daily connections between the cities and towns in the two provinces. The west of the country is served by **Greyhound** and its affiliates (*see* 'Useful Addresses' in the destinations). There is also a Greyhound office in Montréal: ☎ (514) 842-2281. Be aware that while their quoted prices are always accurate, they occasionally deviate from the advertised schedules. Check out www.greyhound.ca for more details.

Bus Stations

Montréal	☎ (514) 842-2281
Ottawa	☎ (613) 238-5900
Québec	☎ (418) 525-3000
Toronto	☎ (416) 393-7911
Vancouver	☎ (604) 661-0325

GENERAL INFORMATION

Excursion Fares and Discounts

On buses, as on trains, the thing to ask for is an 'excursion fare', which will often be 30–40 per cent cheaper.

– For discounts while still in Great Britain, contact **The Independent Traveller**: Devonshire House, Devonshire Lane, Loughborough LE11 3DF. ☎ (01509) 618800. Fax: (01509) 610585. Or ask your travel agent or tour operator for details. In Canada, call one of the bus stations for information (*see above*).

– **Greyhound** offers an all-inclusive package covering 7–60 days. The trips include New York and, for a little extra, Québec and the eastern provinces. There is also a deal combining overnight stays in youth hostels for 15 or 30 days. Again, check www.greyhound.ca before you leave for more information.

– **Voyageur/Orléans Express** offer **Tour Pass** tickets, which are valid for 7, 14 or 18 days consecutively (only in the summertime). These tickets can be used throughout both provinces on buses operated by any bus company in the network. Useful if you're planning on staying around for a period of time but less useful if your visit is a short one as you hardly have enough time to recoup your investment.

– Other bus companies also offer regional connections and most of them give a discount to students.

TRAINS

The trains operated by the Canadian national railway company, **VIA Rail**, are slower and more expensive than bus services, but they offer by far the most scenic and comfortable way to travel across Canada. For routes and train times, pick up the National Timetable at any VIA Rail station.

A low-season cabin fare on the sleeper train from Montréal to Toronto would cost from $90 one way, including tax. Other sample low-season fares are Ottawa to Montréal at around $50 one way and Niagara Falls to Toronto at around $100 one way.

The most expensive times to travel are during public holidays and the summer season, particularly in July and August. Ticket prices are highest for travel on Fridays and Sundays all year round. Prices do drop considerably with advance booking and Via Rail sometimes introduces cheap or companion fare deals in the low season. Buying your ticket at least five days in advance always reduces the fare, whenever you plan to depart. Senior citizens, students and children are eligible for concessionary fares, which vary according to the date of travel.

To book tickets in Canada, call at any train station, use the freephone number below, or access the website. To book in the United Kingdom, contact **Leisurail**.

The Canrail Pass

The **Canrail Pass**, available to citizens of Canada and overseas visitors, is a great way to save money if you're planning lots of long-distance travel. The pass allows you 12 days of standard-class travel within a 30-day period. The

Distances between the major Canadian towns (in kilometres)

	CALGARY	CHICOUTIMI	EDMONTON	GASPÉ	HALIFAX	JASPER	MONCTON	MONTRÉAL	OTTAWA	QUÉBEC	REGINA	SAINT JOHN'S	TORONTO	VANCOUVER	VICTORIA	WHITEHORSE	WINNIPEG
WINNIPEG	1 336	2 884	1 357	3 359	3 656	1 725	3 431	2 408	2 218	2 678	571	5 010	2 099	2 232	2 337	3 524	
WHITEHORSE	2 385	6 326	2 086	6 801	7 099	2 247	6 874	5 850	5 660	6 120	2 871	8 452	5 528	2 697	2 802		3 524
VICTORIA	1 162	5 382	1 349	5 856	6 154	980	5 929	4 905	5 126	5 176	1 926	7 775	4 596	105		2 802	2 337
VANCOUVER	1 057	5 277	1 244	5 752	6 050	875	5 824	4 801	4 611	5 071	1 822	7 403	4 492		105	2 697	2 232
TORONTO	3 434	1 015	3 455	1 490	1 788	3 824	1 536	539	399	809	2 670	3 141		4 492	4 596	5 528	2 099
SAINT JOHN'S	6 334	2 338	6 367	2 248	1 503	6 735	1 579	2 602	2 792	2 363	5 581		3 141	7 403	7 775	8 452	5 010
REGINA	764	3 455	785	3 930	4 228	1 154	4 002	2 979	2 789	3 249		5 581	2 670	1 822	1 926	2 871	571
QUÉBEC	4 014	206	4 035	703	982	4 403	784	270	460		3 249	2 363	809	5 071	5 176	6 210	2 678
OTTAWA	3 553	666	3 547	1 141	1 439	3 943	1 213	190		460	2 789	2 792	399	4 611	5 126	5 660	2 218
MONTRÉAL	3 743	476	3 764	951	1 249	4 133	1 024		190	270	2 979	2 602	539	4 801	4 905	5 850	2 408
MONCTON	4 756	760	4 788	669	275	5 156		1 024	1 213	784	4 002	1 579	1 536	5 824	5 929	6 874	3 431
JASPER	415	4 609	369	5 084	5 382		5 156	4 133	3 943	4 403	1 154	6 735	3 824	875	980	2 247	1 725
HALIFAX	4 973	977	5 013	945		5 382	275	1 249	1 439	982	4 228	1 503	1 788	6 050	6 154	7 099	3 656
GASPÉ	4 694	679	4 715		945	5 084	669	951	1 141	703	3 930	2 248	1 490	5 752	5 856	6 801	3 359
EDMONTON	299	3 294		4 715	5 013	369	4 788	3 764	3 547	4 035	785	6 367	3 455	1 244	1 349	2 086	1 357
CHICOUTIMI	4 220		3 294	679	977	4 609	760	476	666	206	3 455	2 338	1 015	5 277	5 382	6 326	2 884
CALGARY		4 220	299	4 694	4 973	415	4 756	3 743	3 553	4 014	764	6 334	3 434	1 057	1 162	2 385	1 336

pass costs from $500 in the low season for adults, and from $450 for students, seniors and those under 24. Between June and mid-October, the price of the pass increases to around $650 for adults and $580 for concessions. You can purchase up to three extra days of travel and also pay supplements if you wish to take sleepers on overnight services.

You can buy the Canrail pass at any VIA Rail office, from Canadian travel agents or from Leisurail in the United Kingdom.

📧 **VIA Rail Canada**: PO Box 8116, Station A, Montréal, Québec H3C 3N3. ☎ 1-888-842-7245. Website: www.viarail.ca

📧 **Leisurail**: 17 Coningsby Road, Peterborough PE3 8SB. ☎ 01733 335599. Website: www.leisurail.co.uk

The Rocky Mountaineer

If you have a bit of money to spend, then take a ride on the 'Rocky Mountaineer' train that runs east from Vancouver to Kamloops in British Columbia then on to the national parks of Jasper and Banff. You can go as far as Calgary in Alberta. And of course, you could also do the trip in reverse, ending up in Vancouver. The journey takes two days because the train only travels in the daytime – the price includes a night in a hotel in Kamloops. The views are spectacular: the snowy Rocky Mountains, the canyons of the Fraser and Thomson rivers, glaciers, vast wilderness parks and breathtaking views. And if you really want to treat yourself, there's a super-luxurious carriage. The Dome Coach has two decks and you get panoramic views from the glass-enclosed upper floor. There are only 74 seats and the dining room accommodates only 36 people. If you have the chance, this is the journey of a lifetime. The 'Rocky Mountaineer' runs from May to October.

DRIVING

British driving licences are accepted in Canada, as are Irish, New Zealand and Australian licences. An International Driving Permit is not a legal requirement in Canada, but the Canadian Automobile Association (CAA) recommends it for all foreign tourists.

– The **speed limit** is 50kph (30mph) in town and 100kph (60mph) on highways. Note that traffic lights are positioned on the far side of the intersection, so be careful not to end up stopping at a red light in the middle of the junction.

– **Please note**: When a school bus stops to pick up or drop off children, a 'STOP sign' with flashing lights swings out on the driver's side of the bus. Cars travelling in both directions must stop until the flashing sign is withdrawn. Do not move off before this happens, even if there are no children. This is the law, and if you don't obey it, you could face a hefty fine.

– **Car parking**: car parks are expensive, particularly in the big cities, so set aside a chunk of your budget to cover the costs. For on-street parking, in signposted areas you must not park between 7–9am and 4–6pm or sometimes 3.30–6.30pm. Always check the time limits on the signs as your car will be impounded very quickly if you infringe them. It is very expensive to get your car back, and you will be charged even if your car is in the process of being hooked to the tow truck. Note that you are not allowed to park in front of a fire hydrant, even if there is no sign telling you so.

CAR HIRE

The big car-hire companies, such as Hertz or Avis, are not necessarily the most expensive and their vehicles are always in excellent condition. It's always worth phoning to check on special offers, and shop around for the best deal. If your route takes you along the Canada–US border, it's worth hiring your car in the US, where prices tend to be lower.

– You must be at least 21 or 25 years of age (depending on the company) to hire a car in Canada, so it's essential to check when booking. Most companies ask for payment by credit card, although it's not compulsory. Avis and Hertz, in particular, will accept cash or retain your air tickets as a guarantee.

In winter, particularly in Québec, always ask for a vehicle fitted with snow tyres (*les pneus-neige*), as all-weather tyres are not effective in the Canadian winter. Since you are likely to be covering considerable distances, it's best to take the unlimited mileage option. You will probably find yourself with a car with automatic gear-shift – don't panic, you'll get used to it in no time.

– Note that if you buy a fly-drive package from a tour operator or travel agent in Britain for a stay in the western provinces, check whether there are any charges if you leave your car in a different town from where you picked it up.

– **Hertz** offers a wide range of vehicles and has agencies in most cities and larger towns as well as at the principal airports. There's a 24-hour relay service if you break down. You'll get a better rate if you book from Britain, by calling the national reservations line: ☎ (0870) 599 6699.

– **Auto Escape**: ☎ (0800) 920940 (freephone in Britain). Email: info@ autoescape.com. Website: www.autoescape.com. This is a new concept in car hire. The company buys large blocks of hire-car time from other agencies at huge discounts that they can then pass on to their customers. Their services are free because they operate on commission from the hire companies. Essentially Auto Escape acts as a central reservation office. You don't pay any penalties if you change your contract after your initial booking and you receive a full refund should you cancel. You enjoy unlimited mileage in most countries and the company constantly checks what others are doing to ensure the best prices. It's advisable to book before you leave home to get their best rate and to be sure that your car will be in the right place for collection on your arrival.

MOTOR HOMES

Hiring a motor home (campervan or recreational vehicle) can be a good option for families or groups. Many tour operators or travel agents sell packages with motor-home travel or can arrange hire. There are many options, including travel from A to B or pre-planned circuits returning to the starting point; some deals also include unlimited travel. An international driving licence is usually required. This is a very popular option, so it's advisable to book early.

For further information in Québec, contact: **Société d'Assurance auto-mobile du Québec** in Montréal: ☎ (514) 873-7620.

HITCHHIKING

While hitching on the highways is tolerated in Québec, it is prohibited in the English-speaking provinces, so you will find lots of hitchhikers on the edge of villages and small towns. Truck stops are good places to pick up rides and drivers won't mind if you ask them where they're going. **Allô-Stop** is a system that puts hitchhikers in touch with truck drivers – you just pay a subscription to join the network, which operates in many towns. There are Allô-Stop offices in Montréal, Ottawa, Toronto, Sherbrooke, Québec, Rimouski, Jonquière and Chicoutimi, but note that there are none beyond Rimouski. In Montréal, the office is at 4317 rue Saint-Denis. ☎ 985-3032.

In summer there's a lot of competition for rides on the Trans-Canada Highway. It will take a good week to hitch from Montréal to Vancouver, but there are lots of good youth hostels along the route. Take the bus to get to the outskirts of the city or town and to get on the right road.

In Québec, as well as knowing that it's legal to hitchhike on highways, you have a good chance of getting a ride anywhere connected with the forestry and logging industries. This is especially true in the north of Québec.

Hitchhiking is called *faire du pouce* in Québec.

WORKING IN CANADA

Canadian citizens are first in line for job opportunities and it's not easy to get a work permit. Unless you have a Canadian parent or your adult children have a Canadian passport, your only chance is to find a Canadian employer prepared to sponsor your application and to write to your local Canadian consulate or embassy on your behalf.

Australians and New Zealanders between the ages of 18 and 30 are eligible for one-year working-holiday visas to Canada. There are only a limited amount of such visas, so you should contact your High Commission as early as possible and at least three months before you plan to depart. You are unrestricted as to the job that you take but most travellers work in restaurants, bars and resorts, or as seasonal pickers on farms.

United Kingdom and Irish students should investigate the **Bunac (British Universities North America Club) Work Canada Programme.** Bunac arranges for gap year school leavers or students under 29 to work in Canada for up to 12 months at jobs of their choice. Bunac organizes your flights and visas and gives advice on job hunting. Students and recent graduates from Ireland or the United Kingdom can also work in Canada for up to 12 months on visas arranged by **Council Exchanges**. You must usually be under 30 years old and take a job that is relevant in some way to your full-time career. Contact **Council Exchanges** or **Usit NOW** in Ireland (see 'Travel Agents in Ireland') for more details. South African students can work in Canada at any job of their choice for up to six months on a visa scheme arranged by **SASTS Working Adventures**.

All of these programmes are oversubscribed and competition for places is fierce so you should contact the organizers as soon as you start to consider working in Canada.

Useful Addresses

■ **Council on International Educational Exchange-Programme Work and Travel Canada**: 52 Poland Street, London W1V 4JQ. ☎ (020) 7478 2000. Website: www.councilexchanges.org. The council helps students, undergraduates or new postgrads (within 12 months of graduating) find work in Canada. However, it is not an employment agency. It can also arrange visas and work permits, and offers support once you get to Canada. An internship can last between 2 and 12 months. There is no restriction on the type of job you do to qualify for their assistance; it really depends on what interests you, so get in touch with them for more information.

■ **The British Universities North America Club (BUNAC)**: 16 Bowling Green Lane, London EC1R OQH. ☎ (020) 7251 0215. Website: www. bunac.co.uk. To qualify for support, students must be in full-time education or wish to fill a gap year. Students can stay for up to 12 months. BUNAC publishes job listings, helps arrange work before you leave and also sorts out the necessary work permits with the Canadian High Commission. You do not have to have a job to go to, nor are you restricted to taking a particular job; the scheme means that students are entitled to take any temporary or casual work to finance their stay in Canada. However, you must provide proof of minimum funds and a return ticket. The programmes run all year round.

Work permits: these usually take 2–4 weeks from receipt of your application. For further information either call BUNAC or contact the Canadian High Commission. If your application is urgent, you can call in person to the Visa section of the Canadian High Commission, 38 Grosvenor Street, London W1K 4AA.

■ **The Student General Working Holiday Programme** is run by the Canadian High Commission. To qualify for a work permit you must have a written job offer indicating the job title, wage, working hours and duration of employment. For further information, write to the Canadian High Commission Immigration Section, London W1X 0AA, UK. Write SGWHP in the top left-hand corner of the envelope and enclose a large, stamped, self-addressed envelope. ☎ (020) 7258 6350 (fax-back).

■ **Travel Cuts**: Regent Street, London W1. ☎ (020) 7255 2191. Run by the Canadian Federation of Students, this outfit can give you information about the **Student Work Abroad Programme**.

■ **Work via the Internet**: if you are interested in following an internship related to your course of studies, you will find help on the net. Try the **Association of Universities and Canadian Colleges**: website:

www.aucc.ca or the **Association of Canadian Community Colleges**: website: www.accc.ca.

■ **SASTS Working Adventures**: 11 Bree Street, Cape Town 8001. ☎ (021) 418-3794. Website: www.sasts.org.za

Background

To the outsider or first-time visitor, this vast country has a somewhat ill-defined identity. The Hollywood image of the Wild West evoking a landscape of canyons and prairies populated by cowboys and Indians has tainted the imagination and is not the real Canada. These clichés of the Canadian west have been further embedded in many minds through the stories of American novelist Jack London (1876–1916), author of *The Call of the Wild* and *White Fang*. While such images have contributed to the fabric of Canadian life, things are rather different now. And certainly, while many a dream journey will be made to Niagara Falls, there is much more to this immense land, which has been settled by Europeans for over three centuries.

VITAL STATISTICS

Area: 9,970,160 square kilometres (3,849,674 square miles)

Population: 29.6 million

Capital: Ottawa (Ontario)

Official languages: English and French

Currency: Canadian dollar (about $2.20 to £1)

Political system: Parliamentary democracy

Head of government: Jean Chrétien (Prime Minister since 1993)

HISTORY

Canada was established officially as a nation in 1867 and its identity has evolved through successive waves of immigrants. The fur trappers, harvesting skins for the great fur-trading companies, gradually penetrated inland and those pioneers who arrived later were keen to settle the new land that was full of promise and far from the Old Europe they were glad to leave behind. From the beginning, Canada was a multicultural rather than an integrationist nation, and is rightly proud of its success. Toronto, for example, sees itself as the most cosmopolitan city on the planet, where everyone lives in harmony and there are no ghettos.

But Canada has fought to build its own identity, and the fight continues to this day, as demonstrated by the October 1995 referendum on independence in Québec. The 'No' votes won by a slim margin but caused the Canadian federalists great concern. In the Québec provincial elections held in November 1998, Lucien Bouchard's Parti Québécois won, but only narrowly. Consequently, the Liberal Party and the Parti Québécois have had to work closely together. Bouchard has been determined not to risk the possibility of losing another referendum (should one be called), so the project has been put on hold for the time being. However, the issue of independence for Québec is a major preoccupation for both Québécois and English-speaking Canadians, and there are almost daily opinion polls. As a result, the public has become weary of the subject and polls now show that no one even wants another referendum, let alone independence.

ANCIENT HISTORY

The current academic view is that the Native American Indians, the Amerindians (known as First Nations), were originally Asiatic peoples who travelled from Northern Asia to Alaska. The first wave of tribal movements dates back some 40,000 years. They were hunter-gatherers who followed the migrating herds over what is now the Bering Strait in search of food. Over time, as the tribal groups dispersed throughout the territories of the Americas, each created original, identifiable civilizations which were often remarkably brilliant. There were still nomadic tribes in the Canadian territories when the first European settlers landed, while other tribes had settled and become farmers. Prior to European colonization, the tribes had belief systems incorporating animist deities, and ancestral culture was handed down principally through oral tradition. Equally, there was a fundamental respect for the abiding balance between humans and nature that surrounded and nourished the people. Ownership of land was anathema, and everyone had a right to its use.

The First Settlers

Early European exploration began along the eastern seaboard of Canada. Vikings from Iceland and Greenland travelled to Labrador and the island of Newfoundland, and there are traces of early habitation on the north shore of the Gulf of St Lawrence. Some ethnologists believe that there were also Viking settlements along the Atlantic coast as far south as Virginia. A Norse village, l'Anse aux Meadows in Newfoundland, is thought to have been occupied by AD 1000. There may well have been some interbreeding with the native tribes, although it is thought that this was discouraged so that the newcomers would not be lost by assimilation into the aboriginal peoples.

OFFICIAL DISCOVERY

The Italian navigator John Cabot (around 1450–98) made the first 'official discovery' of Canada in 1497, followed by a number of other 'discoverers'. Giovanni da Verrazano (1485–1528) recorded a short visit in 1524, but the only commemoration of his passage is a bridge in New York named after him. The French explorer Jacques Cartier (1491–1557) made three voyages to Canada, and in 1534 he claimed the country in the name of François I of France. When he sailed up the Gulf of St Lawrence, Cartier believed he had discovered the route to China. He sailed up the river to where the village of Hochelaga now stands, and named the hill Mont Réal (Mount Royal) in honour of his king. A little farther on he was stopped by rapids, to which he gave the name Lachine (from the French la Chine, meaning 'China'), believing that China lay just a little farther upriver. The oriental look of the indigenous peoples led him to believe that the East was not far away. He rather unimaginatively named the river itself after St Lawrence, whose name was celebrated on that day. Cartier made his last trip to Canada in

1541. The origins of the name Québec are disputed, but some say it comes from an Algonquin Indian word meaning 'contraction', since the river narrows at Québec City.

IN THE DAYS WHEN AMERICA SPOKE FRENCH

The powerful French minister Cardinal Richelieu adopted the policy followed by the British in their American colonies and founded the Compagnie des Cent-Associés (Company of the Hundred Associates) in Canada. From 1629 to 1644 this company had the monopoly over trade throughout the St Lawrence valley and imported its products to France tax-free. In exchange the French agreed to bring 300 new colonizers (Catholics only) to New France annually and to provide three priests for each settlement. Canada soon became the favourite target of the French missionaries – who themselves became the favourite target of the First Nations. However, commercially speaking, colonization did not bear the expected fruit. The company went bankrupt and, more than 30 years after its foundation, there were a mere 2,000 French living in the vastness of North America. This failure was due largely to the severe climate and to the fact that, unlike the British (mostly Quakers or Puritans who had few friends at home), the French Catholics did not suffer persecution in France and were in fact the only religious group allowed to emigrate. These people had no reason to leave home apart from the hope of becoming rich, which was not a very likely outcome. Also, the French authorities themselves were not particularly encouraging. Finance minister Colbert, for example, said that, 'It would not be prudent to depopulate the kingdom of France in order to populate Canada.' In 1663 King Louis XIV dissolved the company and New France became a royal province, run, like the French provinces, by a governor and a senior official known as the *intendant*.

BACKGROUND

THE BRITISH REACTION

The French were not the only nation to take an interest in the New World. Their old adversaries the British were also keen to get a foothold on the new continent. Two years after the arrival of Samuel de Champlain, who founded Québec City in 1608, the English navigator Henry Hudson (around 1565–1611) was convinced he had discovered the famous passage to the Orient. He sailed into a vast bay, and upon realizing he was alone, named it Hudson Bay. However a life of adventure has its price, and in 1611 it cost him dear. When his crew mutinied, unceremoniously dumping him in a canoe in the icy Arctic waters, Hudson lost his life to the bay that had taken his name.

The French and the British Battle It Out

Despite the fact that the Europeans had failed to find China and its fabulous treasures, they decided to stay in Canada. The rivalry between the British and the French for dominance over the territory began with Hudson's discovery. The Hudson's Bay Trading Company was established in 1670 and, while the English sought to control trade in the vast bay, French expansion was to the west and north. A small and courageous group worked desperately in very difficult and snowy conditions to establish the French colony known as New France. Although the French settlements along the banks of the St Lawrence were small, they were a cause of great concern to the British, as were the other Canadian territories conquered by France. The British controlled the eastern coast of the United States, but they were cut off on the inland side. The French had opened a route from the St Lawrence to the Gulf of Mexico, but the British were more far-sighted than the King of France when it came to understanding its potential.

Acadia, on the Atlantic coast, was a hotspot between the two European powers. The First Nations allied themselves with one side or the other, determined not to be robbed of their land. The British sided with the Iroquois Indians, while the French courted the Hurons, which led to ferocious, bloody battles. To prevent any French takeover of the North American continent, the British attacked from the north. In 1690 Sir William Phips sailed from Boston and conquered Acadia, which was renamed Nova Scotia. He then led his fleet of small vessels (including a few fishing boats) up the St Lawrence to demand the surrender of Québec City. The governor, Louis de Buade, Count of Frontenac, refused and Phips attacked; but he lost the battle. Despite this defeat and the fact that France had an enormous geographical advantage, the French decline was swift. The 70,000 French Canadians were powerless against the 1.5 million British who had settled in the south. Meanwhile King Louis XIV was deeply embroiled in his struggle for domination in Europe and his people showed little interest in emigrating.

THE FUR TRADE

Even though there was no fabulous oriental gold or jewels to be had in Canada, there were vast fortunes to be made from the trade in furs and pelts. The lure of wealth drove the adventurers to penetrate westwards across the country, and this migration continued over the next few centuries.

This flurry of fortune-seeking revolved around the beaver, whose pelt was used to make felt for hats. Tricorns and top hats were fashionable among the gentry of the time and were also worn by imperial soldiers. Hats made from beaver-felt were fashionable until silk hats replaced them in the 19th century. The beaver was already rare by the mid-16th century in the Old World because it had been hunted with such determination.

The trappers and fur traders soon discovered there were vast populations of the rodent with the golden pelt in North America; and that they could buy the skins for derisory prices. European merchants fought desperately to control this lucrative trade, and battles also took place between the First Nations. Those in the interior of the country hunted and trapped the beavers, and supplied the skins to middlemen who sold them on at trading posts. Their common ambition was to get rich quick. However, a group of young Frenchmen decided that the best way to go about this was to cut out the middleman and deal directly with the native Indians in their remote villages. These explorers and traders were nicknamed 'coureurs des bois' and lived wild in the woods. These men were strongly disapproved of by the authorities, who wanted to control the fur trade from Montréal and keep the settlers in the colonies to develop agriculture and increase the population. The men were outlawed and, whenever their furs fell into the hands of the authorities, they were confiscated and the traders were fined. The administrators found it impossible to cope with their independent ways and disapproved of their relationships with the Indians and their mixed-race children.

Étienne Brûlé: More Than a Trapper

Some of these *coureurs des bois* provided a great service to the colony. A 17-year-old Frenchman named Étienne Brûlé arrived in the town of Québec, which had just been founded in 1608 by Samuel de Champlain. Brûlé was then exchanged for a young Indian whom Champlain took back to France. Brûlé lived with the Hurons, learned their language, and also the secrets of the forest, the geography and the peoples of the interior. His knowledge later served Champlain well when he was hired as an interpreter. But Brûlé had an explorer's spirit and became one of the great discoverers of Ontario. He was the first European to reach Georgian Bay and the banks of the Great Lakes. He set up camp at the location of modern Toronto, on the shores of Lake Ontario. History does not relate why he was slaughtered and devoured by the Hurons when he was 41 years old, however one theory is that he was a little too interested in a particular young woman. Other rumours and legends claim that he betrayed his Huron brothers by trying to make a new commercial deal between the French and other tribes.

THE HUDSON'S BAY COMPANY

Two other French *coureurs des bois* played a pivotal role in the history of Canada to the benefit of the English. In 1659, Médard Chouart des Groseilliers and Pierre-Esprit Radisson, his young brother-in-law, embarked on a long trading journey which took them first to the Great Lakes then north to Hudson Bay, where they found many beavers with fur of remarkable quality. The two men bought large numbers of pelts from the Cree Indians, which they brought back, surviving repeated skirmishes with the Iroquois. Their success was in vain: their trade was illegal and most of their skins were confiscated by the Governor of New France.

Worse still, their plan to open a trading post in the Hudson Bay area was frowned upon by the French, who blocked the idea of westward expansion. Their policy was first of all to find new immigrants to settle their lands. Since the French wouldn't support them, des Groseilliers and Radisson turned to the English, who at that time were not at war with France. King Charles II was enthusiastic about their project and, in 1670, signed a Royal Charter creating the 'Company of Merchant Adventurers of the Hudson's Bay'. This not only gave the governor a monopoly over all trade, but also the right to colonize Rupert's Land – named after Prince Rupert, the king's cousin – one of the richest sources of animal skins in the world. This charter was signed with no regard for the indigenous peoples of the lands. By refusing to sanction the creation of the Hudson's Bay Company, the French gave away not only control over trade but also all rights to the vast land – five times the size of France. The territory encompassed most of northern Ontario and northern Québec, all of Manitoba, most of Saskatchewan, the southern half of Alberta and a large part of the Northwest Territories.

BACKGROUND

For the next 200 years, until 1867, when Rupert's Land was incorporated into the Dominion of Canada, the simple fur-trading enterprise evolved into a trading and exploration company that reached to the west coast of Canada, south to Oregon in the USA, north to the Arctic and east to Ungava Bay. The company had agents in Chile, Hawaii, California and Siberia. In addition, it was a land development company with vast holdings in the prairie provinces, and a merchandizing and natural resources development company. It is Canada's oldest corporation and one of its largest retailers today.

RIVALRY BETWEEN '*VOYAGEURS*'

After the establishment of the Hudson's Bay Company, the French tried to thwart it and, during its first decades in business, French and British warships battled for control of its trading posts. The rivalry was finally settled in the company's favour by the Treaty of Utrecht in 1713. This provided the British with an opportunity to make the French acknowledge their failure in North America. France formally ceded Hudson Bay, Newfoundland and Nova Scotia and in 1755 the British expelled the French Acadians from Nova Scotia, an event known as *le Grand Dérangement* (the Great Disturbance). Many were deported, while others fled to Louisiana or returned to France. This event was a factor in the Seven Years War, which the British won thanks to their naval supremacy. Each side had its First Nation allies, the Iroquois fighting with the British and the Hurons with the French.

Then, in 1759, the British routed the French army at the Battle of the Heights of Abraham, when the fortress of Québec fell, and the remaining French forces capitulated at Montréal a year later. Under the Treaty of Paris in 1759, all French-Canadian territories (except the islands of Saint-Pierre and Miquelon) were ceded to the British Crown. After 150 years of occupation, the inhospitable territory of New France was abandoned. The army burned its flags and returned to France, followed by almost all the colony's merchants and other important people. Only the poorest of the French were left behind, most of them prisoners of the British.

But there was no flood of British emigrants keen to colonize the wintry lands of Québec, and the new governor, James Murray, was sympathetic to the French inhabitants, whose courage he greatly admired. The Québec Act of 1774 gave the Catholic clergy back their privileges and tithes, even though the official Church was now the Church of England. Murray also gave French speakers seats on the governing council.

Despite the British conquest, the French continued to play an important role in exploring the land, becoming '*voyageurs*' for the fur companies. Unlike their ancestors the '*coureurs des bois*', these *voyageurs* were engaged in a fully legal and recognized capacity in the fur trade. Powerful rivals had emerged to challenge the supremacy of the Hudson's Bay Company, of which the most formidable was the North West Company, comprising primarily Scottish-Canadian traders from Montréal, pushing north and west in defiance of the charter. The North West Company employed a good 30 First Nations interpreters and 1,200 *voyageurs*, many of whom were French-Canadian. The number of trading posts multiplied and rivalry between the companies to control hunting rights negotiated with the First Nations was intense.

The *voyageurs* were brave mercenaries who would carry vast quantities of furs or trading goods in birch-bark canoes on long and perilous expeditions. Their staple diet consisted of *pemmican*, an Indian food of dried bison or moose meat. Trade with the First Nations was based on the value of a beaver, which represented six large knives or a pound (454 grams) of necklace beads or 4 pounds (1.8 kilograms) of lead shot. A braided uniform was valued at six beavers and a gun at four beavers.

LINGUISTIC ECHOES

The ambivalent attitude of the Québécois towards English-speaking Canada, reflected in their intermittent desire for independence, has its roots in this period. The fact that they had been abandoned by both their own middle class and their home country left the 70,000 French Canadians feeling like orphans. All things considered, the British were 'no worse', particularly in the early days of their common history, when France had just given up its Canadian territories. Popular Québécois expressions often have precise 'emotional' roots, for example the phrase '*c'est pas pire*' ('it's no worse') is used both literally and as an expression of great approval.

This ambivalence manifested itself in 1775, when the American rebels invaded Québec, thinking its inhabitants would rally to their cause of independence. In fact the French Canadians sided with the British. The American revolution marked Canada very deeply. Thousands of 'Americano-British' refugees crossed the border in order to remain loyal to the British crown, and King George III paid more than £4 million to the United States in compensation for their loss. Since then this game of cat-and-mouse between French- and English-speakers has had cultural repercussions for both communities.

One of the most obvious examples is *joual*, the dialect of Québec. In its 330 years of independent evolution the French of Canada has taken on a life of its own and adapted to the needs of the modern world. Along the way it has absorbed and digested quite a few English influences, in both grammar and vocabulary. For example, the English word 'chum' has been turned into '*tchumme*', while the noun 'job' has evolved a verbal form (*je jobe*) and variants such as '*jobine*' and '*jobette*' are used to describe menial types of work.

CONQUEST BY SEA AND RIVER

Meanwhile the country was still being exploited for its fur trade. In the second half of the 18th century, Spanish vessels from Mexico sailed up the British Columbian coast and Russian traders led many expeditions down the western coast in search of sealskins for sale to China. Having taken part in the conquest of Québec (1759) as a British Naval officer, Captain James Cook returned to Canada in 1778, this time to the Pacific coast. He initiated trade with the Nootka Indians, buying some beautiful otter skins from them, which he then sold on to the Chinese.

The Constitutional Act of 1791 split the colony into Lower Canada, with a largely French-speaking population with its own independent government and laws, and Upper Canada, which was organized and governed on the British model. In 1792, George Vancouver, who gave his name to the city, followed the path of his friend Cook and sailed up the northwest coast of North America. His task was to draw the first map of the coast.

THE BIRTH OF CANADA

With the onset of the Anglo-American war the Americans again tried to incorporate Canada into the United States. Fighting was particularly fierce on the border near Niagara Falls, with the French, Indians and British combining forces against the Americans. However, the American 'invasion' failed and Canada's definitive border with the United States was agreed in a treaty of 1814, signed in the Belgian town of Ghent. In addition, after years of intense rivalry, the two great trading companies (Hudson's Bay Company and the North West Company) finally merged in 1821 under the name of the Hudson's Bay Company.

Independence for Lower Canada (Québec)

The first attempt to gain independence for Lower Canada (Québec) was led by Louis-Joseph Papineau, who wanted to establish a French-speaking republic on the banks of the St Lawrence. In Upper Canada the same year, William Lyon Mackenzie led a rebellion against the British. His idea was to found a second republic, modelled on that of the United States. The British, faced with trouble from both sides, sent in Lord Durham, who was known as 'Radical Jack', to sort things out. He did not like the Québécois, describing them as 'a people without history and without literature', who represented a threat to English-speaking Canada. He advocated reunifying the two Canadian provinces so that the English-speakers would dominate the French. This plan was implemented in 1840, when a single government was established for Canada's 1 million inhabitants.

This union proved unworkable, failing to produce any greater political stability between the two communities. There were similar numbers of French- and English-speakers, making the country ungovernable. The word 'union' implies one capital for the whole territory; however the choice of Québec City would have given the French-speakers the advantage, while Toronto would have been more favourable to the English-speakers. Eventually Queen Victoria was asked for her opinion. She studied the map and chose a very small place called Bytown, on the Ottawa river at the border between Upper and Lower Canada. Bytown was duly selected as the capital and renamed Ottawa.

The 'Dominion of Canada' is Formed

With the outbreak of the American Civil War in 1861, the British-American settlers were apprehensive that the victorious armies would surge into their lands to annex them to the United States. George Brown, John A. Macdonald and George-Étienne Cartier formed a coalition in 1864 to seek federal union of all the colonies. This they achieved with the British North America Act, passed in London in 1867, making Canada a British Dominion and joining Québec, Ontario, Nova Scotia and New Brunswick. On 1 July 1867 Canada duly became the 'Dominion of Canada' and the anniversary of this date is officially celebrated as Canada's national day.

To protect itself further from potential incursions from its American neighbour, the new government undertook long, tortuous negotiations with the Hudson's Bay Company to purchase Rupert's Land, paying £1.5 million for the territory and, in 1869, concluded the biggest property deal in the country's history.

By this time immigration from Scotland and Ireland had swelled the population of Upper Canada, so that it was larger than that of French-speaking Canada. The federation was eventually born out of economic necessity, as the country needed an east-west rail link across all its territories, and the necessary funds had to be raised. The federation was not an instant success; in fact Newfoundland did not join until 1949.

Canada became independent in 1931, but remains a member of the British Commonwealth. The red-and-white Canadian flag, with its maple leaf design, was finally chosen in 1965, when it replaced the Union Jack.

THE MÉTIS REVOLT (RED RIVER REBELLION)

The new Canadian government misjudged the potential seriousness of the situation concerning the Métis – the mixed-race sons of French traders and Indians, who lived along the Red River, a significant trading area of the Hudson's Bay Company, now part of Manitoba. They were the first to penetrate deep into the unknown country alongside French colonists. At the time of the purchase of Rupert's Land there were several thousand Métis who lived off the crops they grew and the bison they hunted.

Without negotiation, the Canadian government shamelessly despatched surveyors to parcel up their land for the benefit of future generations of English-speakers in Ontario. In 1869, resistance was organized under the leadership of Louis Riel, a fulminating 25-year-old. His efforts ensured that Manitoba became a province of Canada, with specific rights protecting the Métis peoples and the French-speakers. Riel was accused of murdering an Ontarian who opposed the Rebellion and he fled to the United States. In 1884, he returned to Canada to support his compatriots, this time in Saskatchewan where many Métis had fled after the earlier revolt. They lost this battle and, following a historic trial, Riel was hanged in 1885 to great outcry in Québec. Until quite recently Louis Riel was thought of as a traitor by some English-speaking Canadians, but his actions have been reassessed and he has finally been granted his rightful place in Canada's history.

THE CANADIAN RAILWAY

These incidents, however tragic, were quickly forgotten, and Canada set about becoming a great country without regard for the Métis and the indigenous peoples. Once the border with the United States was drawn along the 49th parallel, Canada's first prime minister, John A. MacDonald, threw down the challenge of laying a railway across vast areas of wilderness with fewer than 3 million inhabitants. His proud ambition was to link Canada from coast to coast and, based on MacDonald's commitment that the railway would reach the Pacific coast, British Columbia agreed to join the Canadian Confederation in 1871.

Once the Rocky Mountains were traversed, the 4,600 kilometres (2,900 miles) of steel road finally reached the Pacific in 1885. To achieve this enormous task, the Canadian Pacific Company received huge subsidies and lands previously belonging to the Hudson's Bay Company. In return, Canadian Pacific was required to find new immigrants to settle along the route.

Thousands of Chinese from San Francisco were brought in to work on the railway, only to be paid a pittance and treated miserably despite their tireless labour. They were forbidden to marry in Canada and were forced to leave the country after their work was over.

Other settlers were more warmly welcomed, especially Americans who knew how to cultivate arid lands and, of course, the British. Other Europeans were also encouraged to settle, especially if they were farmers. Among them were numerous German, Czech, Hungarian and Ukrainian settlers, whose descendants can be found in the great cities of the west. The initial immigrants were lured to the West by the promise of owning their land after 10 years, providing they cultivated it to produce crops. Between the end of the 19th century and World War I, over 2 million pioneers emigrated to Canada. The Canadian Pacific Railway, or 'Iron Horse' as it was known colloquially, was the key to the development and colonization of the Prairies, and many towns and villages sprang up in its wake.

THE GOLD RUSH

As the fur trade began to collapse, another magnet attracted a new wave of adventurers to western Canada – gold. British Columbia was rich in gold, and two fruitful seams were found: in the great Fraser River (in 1858) and farther north in the Caribou Mountains (in 1862). Thousands of prospectors flocked from California, where there wasn't a nugget to be found, and the gold-bearing seams were quickly exhausted. Then rumours began to circulate about another El Dorado – the Klondike.

The Klondike river flows through the Yukon, a virtually unexplored and unexploited region of Canada bordering on Alaska, which the United States had recently purchased from Russia. This was to be the most frenetic gold rush in history. The thousands of Americans who took to the road to dig and pan for gold were a fanatical bunch and there was often trouble. The Royal Canadian Mounted Police, the famous Mounties in their scarlet tunics, were called in to establish the peace and to keep some kind of order during the invasion of the Yukon. One notable visitor of the time was the novelist Jack London, who recorded much of the period in his stories.

Fortunes were created overnight and settlements ballooned, particularly Dawson City, then the capital of the region. But by the beginning of the 20th century the seams were exhausted and the population had dwindled.

THE INFLUENCE OF THE UNITED STATES

The Big Neighbour Next Door continued to eye up the young Canada, hoping to absorb even only some part of it, though without success. However, the economic histories of the two countries are inextricably bound together. While each community is distinctive, the American influence is considerable nonetheless. The fast-food-eating, Coke-drinking American way of life is everywhere to be seen. In the 1920s the attractions of the American Dream were such that the French community feared a takeover and teenagers were forbidden to go to the cinema.

NEW CHALLENGES

Constitutional disputes around the question of Québec largely influenced the federal election results of October 1993. Though the Liberal leader Jean Chrétien, the prime minister of Canada and a Québécois, has a substantial majority in the House of Commons in Ottawa, he has to take account of two new 'regionalist' groups. The Reform Party, an ultra-conservative, populist party widely considered to be Francophobic, is militant in its determination to suppress bilingualism in the Federal Institutions. Meanwhile in Québec itself, the Parti Québécois is the official opposition and it still pursues the separatist cause of an independent Québec. (*See* 'The Québec Question'.)

BACKGROUND

THE FIRST NATIONS

After centuries of cohabitation, relations between the Canadians and the indigenous peoples are highly charged with misapprehensions and ignorance, and are often burdened with prejudice and mutual resentment. Even the terms used to identify the parties are problematic. In the early decades of the 20th century, the most common word used, particularly in history books, was 'savages', when discussing the 'redskins' or 'Indians'. The native people were so called by the first navigators who believed that they had found the route to the Indies. Today, the word 'indigenous' is more commonly used, or 'First Nations' – a term that also encompasses the Inuit, who are not native American Indians.

The Settlers and Ensuing Problems

The arrival of French and English immigrants in what was to become New France (and later the Dominion of Canada) caused a profound upheaval in the ordered life of the First Nations' peoples. However, it's important to put this into perspective. Canada has always been very sparsely populated, and today 29 million people inhabit a territory 20 times the size of France, which has around twice the population. As the colonizers occupied land for settlements and farming and plundered the natural resources, it was inevitable that conflicts would erupt and it is true that the indigenous peoples were treated brutally by the settlers. There is no question that tribal groups were deported, relocated, dispossessed and persecuted as the white settlers encroached and overran their historical lands. Equally, new illnesses

Iroquois group :		Attikameks	**Inuits**
■ Hurons-Wendat	◁ Cree	
▣ Mohawks	▽ Malécites	
Algonquin group :	◩ Micmacs	
△ Abénaquis	◩ Montagnais	
▲ Algonquins	◪ Naskapis	

200 km
200 miles

Ivujivik
Salluit
Kangiqsujuaq
Akulivik
Quaqtaq
Puvirnituq
Kangirsuk
Taqpangajuk
Aupaluk
LABRADOR
Inukjuak
Tasiujaq
Kangiqsualujjuaq
SEA
Hudson
Bay
Kuujjuaq
Umiujaq
Kawawachikamach
Kuujjuarapik
Matimekosh
Whapmagoostui
Chisasibi
Wemindji
Eastmain
Nemiscau
Pakuashipi
Waskaganish
Uashat and
Maliotenam
Mingan
La Romaine
Mistissini
Waswanipi
Ouié-Bougoumou
Natashquan
ONTARIO
Betsiamites
Pikogan
Obedjiwan
Mashteuiatsh
Les Escoumins
Gaspé
Témiscamingue
Lac Simon
Weymontachie
Gesgapegiag
Grand Lac
Winneway
Victoria
Manouane
Whitworth and Cacouna
Hunter's Point
Lac Rapide
Restigouche
Wendake
NEW
Kebaowek
Maniwaki
Wôlinak
BRUNSWICK
Kânesatake
Odanak
Akwesasne
Kahnawake
NOVA
SCOTIA
ATLANTIC
U.S.A.
OCEAN
NEWFOUNDLAND

FIRST NATION COMMUNITIES IN QUÉBEC

brought by the Europeans decimated the local people. In the whole of North America it is estimated that, between 1520 and 1700, a terrifying 90 per cent of the indigenous populations were wiped out by disease.

Direct confrontations between the colonists and the First Nations in Canada took place mainly in the fertile lands where control of the territory was at stake, such as on the St Lawrence plains and around the shores of the Great Lakes. However, away from the lakes and sea coasts, contact was rarer and largely confined to trade.

Raising Awareness and Guilt

Canadians know that wrongs were done and there is a sense of historic guilt. However, many arguments point out how well the indigenous peoples have benefited from enormous privileges – often tax benefits. The First Nations, on the other hand, strive to maintain their difference and their culture (which is often attacked by modern life). They still feel exploited and make claims to repossess their ancestral territories, to which they believe they still have rights. Their claims are as legitimate as those of the separatists in Québec, and the government constantly reviews the issues.

The last decades of the 20th century have seen fundamental social changes that have been as rapid as they have been radical. For example, 50 years ago the Inuit and a large majority of native Indians lived a nomadic life. Now they have lost their roots and there is a distinct social and economic divide between them and the modern life of the majority of Canadians.

Worrying Statistics

'Registered Indians' number around 533,000 (according to 1993 figures) and are distributed throughout Canada, constituting about 1.9 per cent of the total population. The majority (around 60 per cent) live in the western provinces of Manitoba, Saskatchewan, Alberta and British Columbia, with 25 per cent of the population in Ontario. It should be remembered that there were around half a million indigenous people in the country when white settlers arrived, demonstrating zero growth in the native population over the last four centuries. Today, more than half the First Nations are under 25 years old, and it is estimated that the number of registered Indians has reached 623,000, representing some 2.1 per cent of the population. The increase is partly explained by a law passed in 1985, when 85,000 were granted registration rights for the first time.

'Indian Law'

Under the Canadian Constitution, the federal government has the right to promulgate laws affecting 'The Indians and the Lands Reserved for the Indians'. The first 'Indian Law' was passed in 1876 and has been amended numerous times since. Prior to 1960, 'registered Indians' (those who qualified for registration under the law) who lived on reservations did not have the right to vote in federal elections. It was not until 1969 that the indigenous Indians obtained the right to vote in provincial elections. In 1985, their rights were incorporated into the Canadian Charter of Rights and Liberties.

Prior to that, the Indians, as they were called, could have their status of 'registered Indian' withdrawn. This particularly affected Indian women, as any who married non-Indian men immediately lost their 'Indian' status. This was called 'emancipation', and the process took away their rights as Indians but extended to them equal rights with all other Canadians. It was a convoluted, dehumanizing experience that requires some time to understand.

Even though advances have been made, the federal government has acknowledged that the Indian laws 'continue to impede their social, economic and political development' and that 'it cannot satisfy the contemporary aspirations of the Indians'. The community self-government negotiation process was established by the federal government in 1986 and designed to respond to proposals from Indian and Inuit communities which sought to establish self-government arrangements beyond the current limits of the Indian Act. This led the leaders of the First Nations and the Ministry of Justice and Indian and Northern Affairs to work together to effect changes in government and administrative powers.

The First Nation Question Today

The issues remain complex and require careful thought to resolve. After the native peoples were accorded full rights as citizens they were first held at arms' length and treated in some ways as colonial subjects of 'Her Majesty'. When territorial issues were addressed, a Chiefs' Council, which had political status, was called and proposals to confer rights by treaty were discussed. The system of reservations has meant the peoples are segregated, with limits imposed on their rights to the use of their ancestral hunting grounds.

Today, much is being done to rehabilitate the image of the First Nations in all parts of the country. Gradually, due respect is being paid to the native peoples: their culture is now displayed in exhibitions, as well as being introduced into mainstream culture, and they are given their proper place in the history books. All their demands may not be met or understood by the majority of the population, but the most important step, that of recognition, has been made.

In 1912 Québec officially recognised that its 'savage inhabitants' also had territorial rights, which could then be traded for financial compensation, as is still the case today. This process allowed the conquerors 'legally' to dispossess the occupied peoples of their wealth before they even realized what was happening. A parallel social system was established for them, giving the members of the First Nations specific rights which can only be seen as a clumsy attempt to make amends for past mistakes.

The Gulf of Oka crisis

While most Canadians tend to be ignorant of the entire 'Indian question', this is not true in Québec, where even those who were not particularly interested in the issue heard it continually discussed during the summer of 1990. It all started with a project to turn an Amerindian pine forest into a golf course. The Mohawk warriors of the Kahnesatake Reserve south of the Island of Montréal were fiercely opposed to the idea and, concentrating all their resentment on this new territorial violation, went into battle. They seized and vandalized houses belonging to white people and blocked off the Mercier bridge. Their refusal to negotiate meant that the terrified inhabitants had to drive miles out of their way to get to their workplaces in Montréal and a policeman was killed during the first attack. All the old resentments and lack of understanding flared up on both sides during that blazing hot summer, but more importantly the affair acted as a catalyst. Now everyone has the feeling that something must change so that both sides can live together.

In Québec, and elsewhere in Canada, confrontation now seems to have been replaced by negotiation, however there is certainly still a lot of tension.

The thorny question of fishing and hunting rights is often in the headlines, as is the issue of territorial claims. However both the federal and provincial governments prefer talking to fighting.

Constitutional Rights

The First Nations now enjoy all the rights and advantages of other Canadians. A 'registered Indian' has the right to live on a reservation – there are 2,300 in Canada and about 60 per cent of the native population lives on them – and the right not to pay tax on income earned on the reserve. There are also some provincial tax exemption benefits. Various other benefits include free health care and subsidized housing and tertiary education.

Political and social organization

With compulsory schooling and access to the country's wealth came the regime of equal rights and the modern administrative system. The native villages elect political representatives and govern themselves. For example, each native village in Québec is run by a group council, consisting of a chief (who may be a woman, as is now the case in the Huron village near Québec City) and elected councillors. As well as governing their communities the group councils monitor the implementation of various government programmes and are now increasingly taking over responsibility for education and local economic and cultural development. The chief speaks for the village when dealing with the outside world. Native Canadians stand as candidates in provincial and federal elections, and some are elected. Today native demands are generally taken to the courts, where they are defended by lawyers who are members of the native communities. The old treaties are being reviewed and new concessions traded for services and money. The native lobby has become a major force and has made important gains.

But all these legal and political battles, some won, some lost, will never be more than the revenge of defeated peoples beating their conquerors at their own game. Their cultural losses are irreversible; some suffer from delinquency, alcoholism and all the other social problems linked to the breakdown of identity and the difficulty of finding their place in a world which is no longer that of their ancestors. No compensation can ever make up for these things. They can only try to prevent their culture draining away and demand recognition for their ancestral rights, while remaining caught up in an irreversible process of adjustment to the white, industrialized and resolutely modern society.

THE INUIT

The Inuit (meaning 'men', plural of *Innu* in the Inuktitut language) used to be known as Eskimos. They are the native peoples of northern Canada, living above the 60th parallel and in the north of Québec and Labrador. The Indian Law does not apply to them, and the Ministry of Indian and Northern Affairs does not keep a census record although it is thought that there are some 40,000 Inuit in northern Canada, about a quarter of their total world population.

The Inuit have an entirely distinct culture from the Indians of Canada. They appeared in northeastern Canada around 4,500 years ago, which is very recent compared to the tens of thousands of years of the American Indians. Until the second half of the 20th century the Inuit of northern Québec had encountered few white men – just the occasional Basque fisherman or English or American whaler. A few brigades of the Canadian army went on reconnaissance missions in northern Canada; some anthropologists and a few explorers also passed through, while some Christian missionaries stayed to do their work. The cultural shock did not occur until the establishment of various military bases, and government education and health services were brought into Inuit territories in the 1950s.

The Inuit are still mainly nomadic, moving their settlements according to the season and living from hunting and fishing. In summer their dwellings are made from skins and, in winter, they build igloos. Everything they require for subsistence is patiently sought out in the harsh environment but the Canadian climate does little to help them – farming is impossible, so famines are frequent and mortality is high. Only the strongest survive. However none of this prevents the Inuit from being a deeply joyous and generous people.

Unwanted Consequences of Modern Life

While material goods have eased aspects of Inuit life, there have been some disastrous consequences. The Inuit have a particular genetic make-up that has been conditioned by their traditional way of life. They have an exceedingly efficient metabolism and can survive on very little food. The government gave them houses to live in which has led to a more sedentary lifestyle, and now the Inuit are too warm, they eat too much and are not sufficiently active. Consequently, even though their expectations have been raised to a certain degree, their health has deteriorated considerably. Their culture is based on migration and a close relationship with nature, but this has been seriously eroded by a combination of TV, evangelization and the early years of the education system.

Renewal of Culture

Under the Convention of James Bay and North Québec that was signed in 1975, the Inuit began to take control of their own destiny. Financial grants made it possible for the Inuit to identify their own needs and manage developments themselves. These included purchasing modern fishing boats, setting up a radio station and newspaper, starting a regional airline, Air Inuit, and even purchasing another air company which served the Northwest Territories. Air travel is vital in an area lacking roads.

Inuit culture is recovering lost ground. The young people are asking their elders to teach ancestral wisdom. They write their own history books and dictionaries. Traditional objects and artefacts which had been taken south are being brought home, and traditional carvings of bone, ivory, caribou antlers or soapstone are being rediscovered. In some areas, such as Cape Dorset, the sale of traditional carvings is a major source of income for the local economy, and they command significant prices in specialist galleries in Montréal or New York.

But pride and dynamism are the driving forces behind the renewal of this land of the walrus, the narwhal and the polar bear. On 1 April 1999, Nunavut ('our land' in Inuktitut) officially became Inuit territory, with its own government in the capital, Iqaluit. Nunavut is part of Northwest Territories, covering some 350,000 square kilometres (910,000 square miles), which has been claimed by the Inuit since 1976. The first task has been to set up an administration run entirely by the Inuit. The prospects for this new territory are bleak; unemployment is high and few are well educated. Equally, revenue is very low. But the Canadian government greatly supports this development in self-government and believes that it will stimulate the region's economy. These administrative and political advances have now enabled them to take over responsibility for their own educational system, which uses the Inuit language, and to control the development and exploitation of all the territory of Québec above the 55th parallel, amounting to a third of the entire province. However, another land claim – that of the Inuit of Labrador – still has to be addressed.

THE AMERINDIANS

The territory of Québec is almost five times the size of Britain and is home to around 63,000 recognized members of native groups. This is about 1 per cent of the province's entire population. In ethnological terms, these native groups include ten nations that fall into two broad categories: the Amerindians and the Inuit.

There are more Amerindians than Inuit, making up around 90 per cent of all the native inhabitants of Québec. The nations in this category are divided into two main cultural and linguistic groups. The *Algonquins* are traditionally nomadic peoples living in the forests, including the true Algonquins, the Abenakis, the Attikameks, the Cree, the Malecites, the Micmacs, the Montagnais and the Naskapis. The *Iroquois* on the other hand farm the fertile lands of the St Lawrence valley and, in Québec, include the Mohawks and the Hurons (other Iroquois groups are present in Ontario and in some American states along the Canadian border).

The Algonquin Nations

The Abenakis (*Wabanaki*, 'Land of the Dawn')
These former hunter-gatherers, whose homelands lay in the northeastern United States, joined forces with the French colonials against the British and are thought to have taught the Europeans how to make maple syrup. When they were driven north, they settled on the southern banks of the St Lawrence, opposite Trois-Rivières. There are about 1,600 Wabanakis in Québec.

The Algonquins (*Nishnabi*, 'Real Men')
Around 4,000 Algonquins, probably originally from the Atlantic coast, now live in nine communities in the Outaouais and Abitibi-Temiscamingue regions. Before the arrival of the Europeans they survived by hunting and gathering, but took advantage of the fur trade, in particular by taxing the Hurons who used the Ottawa river as a route to the trading posts of New France. They still move to their hunting grounds in winter and the Algonquin

language, used in the broadcasts of the community radio station, is very much alive.

The Attikameks

Described as 'peaceful' by the first French missionaries, the Attikameks were decimated in the 17th century, as much by European diseases as by wars with the Iroquois over issues to do with the fur trade. Threatened with total disappearance, the survivors took refuge with their friendly Cree and Montagnais neighbours. This has enabled them to survive to the present day with a mixed culture. During the 20th century things were made more difficult for them by the exploitation of the forests and the construction of hydro-electric dams. Today they number about 4,000, living in three communities in Haute Mauricie.

The Cree

There are about 10,500 Cree living in nine villages deep in the northern forests. They have been living by hunting and gathering in the James Bay area for 4,000 years. The Cree also traded furs with the whites, but kept far enough away from European settlements to reduce the effects of colonization, at least until the second half of the 20th century. When state education programmes were introduced and, more importantly, large hydro-electric dams were built in the 1970s, flooding hundreds of square miles of land, the Cree reacted swiftly. Today their political organization is a model of efficiency and has brought them the recognition of their ancestral land rights, financial compensation for the loss of use of the flooded lands, the right to govern their own people and territory as well as the exclusive right to continue their ancestral way of life over 150,000 square kilometres (60,000 square miles) of forest and lakes, where they still live by hunting and fishing. The Cree Grand Council has close links with its Inuit neighbours and has learned how to play the political game. It often embarrasses the Québécois government through large-scale actions designed for maximum media exposure and publicity. Most of the Cree population speak the Cree language.

The Malecites

The Malecites are more numerous in New Brunswick, with only 270 in Québec. They are scattered among the white population and have only a tiny amount of land on which they can exercise their ancestral rights. Today they all speak French.

The Micmacs (*Mig'mawag*, 'People of the Dawn')

There are 15,000 Micmacs living in Canada's maritime east, including 3,850 people living in three villages in the Gaspésie Provincial Park. They are a seafaring people who also do some basic farming. They became allies of the French, becoming involved in a battle against the British in Chaleur Bay in 1760. A French ship, *Le Marquis de Malauze*, which was sunk in this battle, was recently raised by the inhabitants of the Restigouche Reservation and is now a tourist attraction.

The Montagnais (Innuat)

The 12,000-strong Montagnais nation of Québec also has members in Newfoundland's Coast of Labrador. According to their oral history they saw, and sometimes made contact with, white fishermen who arrived in boats long before the time of Cabot and Cartier. The Montagnais were involved in the fur trade with the whites and, as hunter-gatherers, divided their time between summer camps for food collection and winter camps where they set their traps. This migration, which dates from time immemorial, is now being revived. In each of their villages, shared with the Attikameks, the Montagnais have a radio station broadcasting in their language and a newspaper. There is even a Montagnais rock band, 'Kashtin', which recently made it onto the radio play-lists.

The Naskapis (from the Montagnais *Unaskahpiwaki*, 'People from the Place Where it Disappears')
The only Naskapi village in Canada is near Shefferville in Nouveau-Québec. Its 488 residents have exclusive hunting and fishing rights over 4,000 square kilometres (1,500 square miles). They are highly skilled caribou hunters and have long lived off the products of this activity, including meat, clothing and tools. Recently the Naskapis discovered a major source of revenue in the form of adventure tourism and expedition guiding in the north (dog-sleighs, snow-mobiles, long hunting trips etc.).

The Iroquois Nations

The Hurons (*Wendat*, 'Inhabitants of the Peninsula')
This is one of the most urbanized of Québec's Amerindian nations. Approximately 950 Huron-Wendats live in a single community in the suburbs of Québec City and more than 1,500 others are intermixed with the whites. However, this small population does not reflect the importance of the historical role played by their ancestors.

Originally from southeastern Ontario, where they formed the Huronia confederation of four nations who practised settled agriculture (18,000 inhabitants in 1640, living in around 20 fortified villages), the Huron-Wendats sided with the French and were for a long time their most important partners in the fur trade. This meant that the decline in French power and fortunes put an end to Huron prosperity at a time when the population was also being decimated by wars with the Iroquois and by raging epidemics. The nation owes its survival in Québec to 300 Huron-Wendat converts to Christianity, who had fled there in 1649, living under the protection of the Jesuits.

The Huron-Wendat have largely interbred with the white population and now speak French, having lost their own language. They make their living from a flourishing industry producing craft objects, which are highly prized by the many tourists who visit the reservation. They have skilfully used Canadian law to obtain recognition of their rights over a much greater area than they currently occupy, basing their negotiations on a treaty signed by the first British governor, James Murray, in 1760.

The Mohawks (*Kanienkehaka*, 'People of Flint')
After the Huron-Wendats, the Mohawks are the most urbanized of Québec's native peoples. This is because their ancestral lands were in the St Lawrence plain, where most of the European colonizers also settled. Almost all Québec's 12,000 Mohawks now live in three villages on the outskirts of Montréal.

By the time the whites arrived in Canada the Mohawks had already acquired a reputation for independence and dynamism which they have kept to this day. They have also long had a sophisticated political organization and are famous for the architecture of their 'long houses'. Skilled farmers and clever traders, they formerly held commercial and military sway over a territory stretching from Québec to Chicago. They were by turns friends and enemies to the French and also profited from the British and Dutch demand for fur. Because of their rather lukewarm collaboration with New France the Mohawks have been dogged by a notoriety as the 'bad guys', which is promoted by simplistic history books describing the 'horrors' for which they have been condemned without a fair trial, such as massacring colonizers and torturing missionaries.

Now that the spread of modern Montréal has rendered traditional forms of agriculture impossible, the Mohawk communities have turned almost exclusively to an economy based on small-scale trade. As a result anyone driving through a Mohawk village would find it hard to tell it apart from the surrounding suburbs. The 'Gulf of Oka crisis' was played out in the Mohawk area of the Montréal suburbs in the summer of 1990 (*see* 'The First Nations').

THE QUÉBEC QUESTION

THE ISSUE OF QUÉBEC

We do not propose to discuss the issues fully here, rather our aim is simply to provide you with a few historical pointers so that you have a basic grasp of a very complex situation. It is a problem that will be brought to your attention over and over again throughout your stay, by the people you meet, through cultural events and in many other aspects of life in Québec.

The history of Québec cannot be separated from that of Canada as a whole. Historically speaking the French Canadians should have been more or less entirely assimilated into the English-speaking nation; however this is not what happened, for a number of reasons. Firstly, in 1763 there were too few English-speakers to impose their language and laws on the French. Then, in 1774, London gave the French Canadians a degree of independence to stop them forming an alliance with the American rebels who were demanding independence from the British crown. They were allowed to live 'as French'. Later came the 'revenge of the cradles', when Québec's birth-rate was much higher than those of the other Canadian provinces – between 1760 and 1850 its population doubled every 25 years. Another factor was the primarily rural nature of Québec society, which did not encourage assimilation. Lastly, the demands of the French Canadians were often supported by liberal English-speakers in Upper Canada.

In 1867 the British North-America Act finally established the legal right of the Québécois to use their language, organize their own education system and control their own administration. This relative autonomy was made possible by the federal system with its four provinces. However, ultimate control over trade and industry remained in the hands of the English-speakers. Between 1867 and 1960 Québec continued to assert its identity and gain new rights.

In the later years of this period the province was deeply marked by what became known as *duplessisme*. Between 1936 and 1960 Maurice Duplessis, leader of the Union Nationale party and a man whose motto could have been 'Work, Family, Country', governed Québec with paternalistic authority. During this time the province was unified around the traditional values he represented, and its development came to an almost total halt as a result.

Yet *duplessisme* had the positive effect of preserving Québec once again from the Anglo-Saxon lifestyles and ways of thinking that were taking over in many other places. It was also at this time that the province adopted its own distinctive blue-and-white flag with a fleur-de-lys design.

'LONG LIVE FREE QUÉBEC!'

Since 1960 Québec society has undergone a profound transformation. Major energy projects, industrialization and the movement of ideas have brought it onto the international stage.

In 1967 preparations for the Expo '67 exhibition in Montréal provided the backdrop to Canada's centenary celebrations and Québec was quick to seize this opportunity to distinguish itself from the other provinces and make its mark on the international scene. In the late-1960s, a time of global turmoil, the Québécois separatists argued their cause in the provincial election, while other militants went much further, launching terrorist attacks. It was in this climate of unrest that General de Gaulle (temporarily forgetting that, during World War II, Québec had supported the Vichy regime which ruled France in collaboration with the Nazis) astounded the world with the words, 'Long live free Québec!' This respected and respectable figure of international politics was apparently giving public support to what some regarded as a terrorist cause promoted by young trouble-makers. Many commentators have tried to explain what De Gaulle meant by this call. With hindsight the most plausible explanation is probably that he was seizing an opportunity to sow a little panic among the British and Americans. He had always been something of a maverick and he was still smarting over the Yalta conference at the end of World War II, at which Churchill, Roosevelt and Stalin agreed to divide control of Germany and the Eastern bloc countries between them, to the exclusion of France. Despite sending shockwaves round the world, De Gaulle's exclamation was never followed up by any kind of material help from France to bring the Québécois nearer to independence.

A year later the separatist Parti Québécois (PQ) was founded by René Lévesque, a Liberal Party dissident and influential television journalist. In 1970 they won 24 per cent of the vote and a few seats. It was at this time that impatient young Québécois with little faith in their institutions created the FLQ (Québec Liberation Front) and turned to terrorist methods.

TRUDEAU AND THE FLQ

Meanwhile, Pierre Elliott Trudeau, a refined, bilingual lawyer from Montréal and the Liberal Party leader, had become the youngest ever Prime Minister of Canada in 1968, at the age of 49. He had previously been a very progressive Minister of Justice, reforming the laws on homosexuality, divorce, contraception and abortion. Trudeau was exactly the kind of French Canadian the English-speaking Canadians could like, but his reforms made him particularly unpopular in Québec, where the grip of the Catholic Church was still extremely strong. Although Trudeau showed some sympathy for Québec's requests for linguistic equality, he was fiercely opposed to any notion of independence. The FLQ stepped up its terrorist action, abducting James Cross, the British trade commissioner, and assassinating the Québécois Labour Minister, Pierre Laporte, in October 1970 (these events are known as the 'October Crisis'). The FLQ was banned, after which Trudeau invoked the 'war measures law' and sent 10,000 men into Québec to make hundreds of arrests. The shockwaves caused by the FLQ were to have important consequences.

Québécois singer and songwriter Félix Leclerc wrote a beautiful song called *L'Alouette en colère* ('The Angry Lark'), in which a father describes how and, more importantly, why 'his son' became a murderer. This song had a major impact, particularly among the older inhabitants of Québec, who had turned against any idea of independence following the terrorist attacks. Another consequence of the general climate of unrest was that many English-speakers left Québec for Toronto, which began, as a result, to outstrip Montréal both in size and in financial and cultural importance.

ESTABLISHING QUÉBEC'S IDENTITY

The Parti Québécois won the provincial election of 1976 with 41 per cent of the vote. This gave René Lévesque confidence and encouraged him to hold the 1980 referendum on 'Associative Sovereignty'. He was looking for a political mandate to negotiate Québec's total control over its own destiny, as a sovereign state linked to Canada in a kind of common market. Despite the support of popular figures like singer-songwriters Félix Leclerc, Gilles Vigneault and Robert Charlebois, the proposal was endorsed by only 41 per cent of voters and was therefore rejected. Those who came out against it included the business and commercial communities, most of the English-speaking minority (20 per cent of the population of Québec), people frightened by the prospect of change they regarded as too rapid and, of course, all those who preferred to stay within the federation. By contrast most young and working-class people voted 'yes'. Some assumed this negative result would be confirmed by defeat for the PQ in the next provincial election. However, in fact the result was quite the opposite, with more votes and seats for the PQ than in the preceding parliament.

The lesson of this action-packed political soap-opera is that, while the majority of Québécois were not ready for radical change at that time, they were keen to assert their own distinctive character. It is significant that some Montréal neighbourhoods with large numbers of Greek and Italian immigrants abandoned the provincial Liberal Party in favour of the PQ, and that two successful PQ candidates were English-speakers. To some extent the election result also reflected the desire among the Québécois to express their dissatisfaction with the Americanization of Canada as much as to assert their own identity.

Despite the 1977 'Law 101', which made French the only official language of Québec, the province asserted its individuality once again in 1982, refusing to ratify an amendment to the constitution which would have permanently established Canada's political identity by freeing it of the obligation to have changes to its constitution approved by the British govenment. This amendment also included a Charter of Rights and Freedoms, similar to the French Declaration of the Rights of Man.

At the federal level, having been in power for almost 15 years (with one brief interruption), in September 1984 Trudeau's Liberal Party was replaced by the Conservative Party, and Brian Mulroney took over as Prime Minister. Meanwhile in Québec the Parti Québécois lost the December 1985 election to the Liberal Party and Robert Bourassa became Prime Minister. A few years later the PQ also lost René Lévesque, one of its founder members, who died on 1 November 1987.

René Lévesque was a colourful figure on the political scene, who will always be remembered as the man who first asserted Québec's right to be different, and who won the respect of his opponents as well as his friends. Brian Mulroney, the Conservative Prime Minister, promised Québec that he would enable it to sign up to the Canadian constitution with 'enthusiasm and dignity'. In April 1987 he proved himself as good as his word, signing the Meech Lake Accord with the ten provincial prime ministers. This agreement set out seven amendments to the 1982 constitution, including recognition of Québec as a 'distinct society'. To become legally binding it had to be approved by all 11 Canadian parliaments before June 1990; however, in the meantime three of the prime ministers who had signed the Accord were replaced by successors who took a different view.

It should be said that there are more than a million French-speaking Canadians living in other provinces, particularly in Ontario and New Brunswick, who are still threatened with assimilation into the English-speaking world. This danger would clearly be heightened by any change in the status of Québec since, as the only French-speaking province, it upholds the status of the French language at federal level.

NEW CHALLENGES

In 1994 Jacques Parizeau's pro-independence Parti Québécois won the provincial legislative election. In the following year it lost the referendum on sovereignty, though by a small margin: 49.6 per cent voted 'yes' compared to 50.4 per cent voting 'no'. Parizeau resigned and was replaced by Lucien Bouchard (the former head of the Québécois bloc in Ottawa) as leader of both the pro-independence PQ and the provincial government.

In the much anticipated federal elections of 2 June 1997, which saw a comparative victory for the Liberal Party, 60 per cent of Québec's population voted for other parties. The Québécois bloc lost its status as the Canadian official opposition to the Reform Party, whose origins lay in western Canada.

In the last provincial elections of November 1998, Lucien Bouchard's PQ was returned to power, but only just, and the Liberal Party and the PQ are now neck-and-neck. Lucien Bouchard has said he does not want to lose another referendum, and has put the project on hold for the present time. Could a referendum like that of 1985 still represent a first step towards independence? Both the Québécois and the English-speaking Canadians are obsessed with this question and there is not a day that passes without the media chewing it over yet again. The result of all this exposure is that the general public are becoming very weary of the whole thing and all the polls suggest that the Québécois just do not want any more referendums.

QUÉBÉCOIS 'DISTINCTIVENESS'

The French of Canada avoided the social disintegration suffered by some immigrant populations because many of them emigrated in groups of more than one family, or as whole villages. They turned to each other for support in a dangerous environment and soon became a far more homogeneous social group than the French of France, where provinces differed greatly from each other. This social cohesion saw the emergence of a new mentality in Québec. On this point it is interesting to mention the importance of the rows of houses they live in, *le rang*, a form of organization specific to Québécois society, and used as an address in the countryside. When the Québécois settled, they always built their houses close together in a line along a river or road. This turned every farm into a long strip of land, enabling villagers to get help from their immediate neighbours quickly. Settlement in rows increased the sense of solidarity and unity within villages, in contrast to the American West, where settlement tended to be more isolated and individualistic. In Québec the classic three-pronged power structure of French villages, consisting of the lord, the priest and local officials, was reduced to the priest alone. The parishes also acted as the civil administration, organizing schooling and dealing with social issues.

Another factor was that French Canadians were far more likely than their English-speaking counterparts to establish amicable, neighbourly relations with the indigenous tribes. Although there was little in the way of real cultural exchange, the Native Americans communicated their independence, freedom and love of nature to the Québécois. By the time the Treaty of Paris ceded Canada to Britain, the French Canadians had by and large already acquired their distinctive characteristics and social organization, and it was this that enabled them to survive and to keep their own identity for two centuries.

The 'French of France' formed the elite made up of merchants and members of the administration. They stayed in their towns and were the first to depart in 1763, leaving only the villages with their all-powerful priests. Those remaining were bound together by religion and managed to retain their cultural heritage, language and customs. This goes some way to explaining the egalitarian attitudes and sociable nature of the Québécois.

POLITICS

Canada is a constitutional monarchy under Queen Elizabeth II, who nominally has considerable power. In practice, the powers of the Crown are exercised in the Queen's name by the Governor General, now always a Canadian, whom she appoints on the advice of the prime minister of Canada. The legislature consists of the Queen, a nominated Senate and the House of Commons, which is elected by universal suffrage. General elections for the House of Commons must be held at least once every five years.

The federal parliament, which is responsible for federal policies and foreign affairs, is elected by the Canadian people. There are also provincial parliaments responsible for all matters affecting the province. Each province has a great deal of autonomy in terms of education, housing and natural resources. Historically, two main political parties have dominated the federal government. One is the Liberal Party, which has its roots in the pre-Confederation reform parties that fought for the establishment of a parliamentary responsible government in the 1840s. The other is the Progressive Conservative Party, which traces its origins to a coalition of moderate conservatives and moderate reformers in the province of Canada in 1854. The present name was adopted in 1942. The New Democratic Party plays a minor role and is a more recent political force, created in 1961 out of the major trade-union federation, the Canadian Labour Congress, and the Co-operative Commonwealth Federation.

Prior to 1993, the two main parties dominated the federal government, but the general election of that year caused such ructions that no one was prepared for the upheaval. The Progressive Conservative Party was wiped out, winning only two seats in parliament. This left fruitful ground for two new 'regionalist' parties to develop. The Reform Party, based mainly in the west is populist and ultra-conservative, while the Parti Québécois gained many new followers in its call for an independent Québec and became the official opposition. In the 1997 federal elections the Liberal Party won a second term under Prime Minister Jean Chrétien, with the Reform Party this time elected as the official opposition.

HUMAN RIGHTS

Canada has one of the world's better records on human rights. In contrast to most countries, human rights have been a live issue in Canada in recent years, and a new Charter of Rights and Freedoms was enacted in 1982 as part of a new constitution. The federal states of Canada have, for the most part, accepted the constraints this imposed, and the courts have made good use of it in the protection of a wide variety of rights.

The most pressing human rights issue in recent Canadian history has been that of aboriginal or First Nation rights. However, even here the government's reputation has been reasonably good, certainly when compared with similar situations elsewhere including the United States and Australia. The 1982 constitution recognized ancestral land rights, and as a result various forms of reparation have been awarded. Probably the best example is the Nunavut land agreement, which granted effective autonomy to the Inuit in the Eastern Arctic, covering almost two million square kilometres (772,000 square miles).

In addition, a Royal Commission reported on the situation of aboriginal peoples in 1996, and made a number of wide-ranging recommendations aimed at improving the lives of the minority population. However, here the government has moved rather slowly, and there is concern over the speed with which the report is being implemented. There are numerous issues concerning the First Nation inhabitants of Canada that have to be addressed, ranging from allegations of police brutality, to concerns about their generally poor economic status. It is clear that there is widespread discrimination against them across much of Canadian society. While government legislation is a blunt instrument for creating social change, in the light of the Royal Commission report, there are some important changes required.

In Canada women suffer from various, familiar, forms of discrimination; in the workplace, in politics and in society generally. As with the First Nation rights, the government has made some efforts to address this problem. The Employment Equity Act entered force in 1996, establishing a compliance regime that requires federal departments to ensure that women, persons belonging to aboriginal and visible minorities and disabled persons constitute a fair proportion of their workforce. Compared with other nations, this is quite a strong piece of legislation. However, it will probably do little to address the more striking problems of inequality in Canada. In particular, aboriginal women until recently lost their aboriginal status if they married outside their people. While this has been reversed, the new law applies only to the woman and her children; further descendants can still be denied membership of their community. There has also been considerable concern over the very high levels of poverty among single mothers in Canada.

Recently, in common with much of the Western world, Canada has seen the arrival of numerous asylum seekers. A number of organizations have expressed concern over the long periods for which they are often detained while their applications are being examined. There have also been recent allegations that Canada has endangered asylum seekers by returning them to hostile states.

– For more information visit the Amnesty International websites: www. amnesty.ca and www.amnesty.org.uk.

FOOD AND DRINK

Don't expect to find a standard North American style of cooking in Canada. Cuisine in the English-speaking parts of the country may be more Americanized than in French-speaking Québec, where traditions of French gastronomy are very much alive, but elsewhere the range and freshness may surprise you. You're unlikely to be overwhelmed by the culinary inventiveness on the menus in smaller towns and villages or roadside diners, but you can find chunky, satisfying club sandwiches, plate-sized pizzas, and assorted fruit tarts.

As elsewhere in the world, there's a growing interest in healthy eating, and a greater variety available in many restaurants. In Toronto and Vancouver and, to a lesser extent, in Calgary and Edmonton there are many excellent restaurants where creative chefs try to challenge the status quo. But prices can be high.

– Alberta is cowboy land, so you'll never be disappointed if you order **steak** – it should be tender, tasty and very reasonably priced. But beware of waiters brandishing huge pepper mills that they will grind over your T-bone before you can blink.

– British Columbia is **salmon** country – fresh, cold-smoked or hot-smoked, it is superb. **Seafood**, harvested from the Pacific, is splendid and sparklingly fresh; the flavours are sensational whether simply grilled, barbecued or steamed, or served with a variety of sauces. It's all delicious and very cheap.

– You'll find a proliferation of **exotic restaurants** in the bigger towns and cities, certainly in Toronto and Vancouver, and the choice is ever widening. Although Toronto once had a reputation for being pretty severe or strait-laced and provincial, it's now a cosmopolitan city with a profusion of Chinese, Italian, Greek, Jewish and Portuguese restaurants, cafés and food markets (among many others).

– Restaurants generally tend to be more functional than imaginative, although themed restaurants or bars are all the rage. Whatever the theme – cowboy, circus, ice hockey – a restaurant can draw a faithful crowd of regulars who make for a lively atmosphere and a permanent party mood. Wherever you decide to eat, you'll find a friendly, easy-going welcome.

Useful Tips

– Remember that taxes are not usually included in listed prices on menus. If in doubt, always ask before you order (*see* 'Taxes' *and* 'Tipping').

– In most (if not all) restaurants, you'll be brought a tumbler of water, often filled with ice. You'll also be brought a basket of rolls, often hot, and individual portions of butter.

– If you're on the move, there are plenty of food shops in the cities and there will always be at least one in a small town that opens long hours and even on Sunday and public holidays (such as the Seven/Eleven chain). These late-night stores are more expensive than supermarkets. You'll find huge shopping malls on the outskirts of towns and cities containing a wide selection of shops. They often have extended opening hours (8am–11pm) and offer an immense choice of goods. Credit cards are generally accepted.

– Organic foods are available everywhere in the country, and you'll also readily find specialized food shops and markets. There are also exclusively organic restaurants, although prices can be high.

DRINKS

– The **legal drinking age** is set by the individual provincial governments. It's 18 in Québec, Manitoba and Alberta and 19 everywhere else.

– **Beer** is reasonably priced and Canadians consume vast quantities in winter and summer. It's unquestionably the national drink. Even though there is a growing fashion in the west, and particularly in Vancouver, for non-alcoholic bars (often non-smoking too), a cool Molson, Labatt's or Canadian will be full of flavour and very refreshing. 'Dry' beers that are sweeter and without an after-taste are fashionable, as are cold-filtered 'ice' beers. Beers from local **micro-breweries** are also popular across the whole country. If you're in Vancouver, try the Granville Pale Ale.

– Canadian **wines** are remarkably good and much more affordable than imported bottles. Ontario and British Columbia have excellent vineyards producing quality wines that you'll find in all good supermarkets. Sadly, they are not often available in restaurants because of the limited quantities produced. You'll find the local whites are better than the reds.

– **Tea** is served black, with milk or lemon provided, and in summer refreshing iced tea is often available.

– Most good restaurants and cafés serve excellent **coffee**, so you can indulge your espresso and cappuccino habit. British Columbia and Ontario in particular have many chain coffee shops, with which you may already be familiar. Refills of filter coffee in restaurants are free.

MUSIC

From the singing games of the native Inuit communities in the northern part of the country, to the songs and melodies of the French and Celtic settlers on the east coast, Canada has a surprising diversity of traditional music to offer the unsuspecting listener. It also boasts a long list of popular singer-songwriters, among them Leonard Cohen, Joni Mitchell, and folk singer Stan Rogers, as well as more contemporary artists who have made their mark on the international music scene, including Celine Dion, k.d. lang and The Cowboy Junkies.

The music of the native Inuit people is based around the drum and the percussive abilities of the human voice, including a special style of singing that produces sounds from deep in the throat. This technique is used in the singing games which form an integral part of Inuit culture. Performed by women, they are used as a social and educational tool, bonding female members of the community and stimulating children to learn new activities. The songs can sound strange to the Western ear, particularly in the game known as *Katajjaq* which is centred around the complex rhythmic interaction of a mixture of grunting, breathing, animal-like noises and high-pitched vocal sounds that often makes it difficult to distinguish individual voices.

Today, the Inuit are no longer isolated from modern technological innovations, but while the arrival of European settlers in the 19th century and the advent of radio and television in the 20th century have had a considerable influence on their music (e.g. the introduction of traditional European instruments and the popularity of country music), the younger generations continue to embrace their traditional culture. This has resulted in some interesting fusions of Inuit music with modern rock and pop styles.

On Indian reservations across the northern reaches of Canada, the indigenous Amerindian population also maintain a rich musical heritage. Like the functional music of the Inuits, drums and voices are at the heart of native Amerindian powwow music. During the traditional ceremony of the powwow, they provide a powerful accompaniment to the spectacular displays of tribal dancing. External influences have resulted in some surprising musical developments among native Amerindians, notably the development of fiddle playing among the Cree population of northern Québec. The folk singer Buffy Sainte-Marie (born on a Cree reservation) and musician Robbie Robertson (part Mohawk, raised on the Six Nations reservation) have both made names for themselves working with a mix of musical styles including powwow music, country, folk, blues and electronic music.

Aside from its native communities, Canada is also home to the descendants of European migrants who came to start a new life abroad. These included workmen who helped build the Canadian Pacific Railway, sailors who worked on the whaling ships, fur trappers employed by large fur-trading companies and farmers who came to work the land. Their rich and varied musical legacy can be heard throughout Canada, most notably on the east coast. The arrival of French settlers in the 17th century, for example, had an enormous social and cultural impact on the natives. Many of the French fur traders took wives from the local tribes and their progeny, the mixed-race descendants of French traders and native Indians, became known as the Métis. This cultural integration led to the gradual adoption of European instruments among native communities (such as the fiddle and the accordion), and the absorption of French songs into the local musical repertoire. Later generations of musicians, such as well-known singers Gilles Vigneault and Félix Leclerc, did much to popularize these hybrid forms, writing their own patriotic Canadian songs in the style of French chansons.

This synthesis of European and native Canadian styles provided a spring-board for the folk revival of the 1970s led by La Bottine Souriante, an extraordinary band whose energy and commitment to the music of Québec has won them many followers and awards over the years. Originally formed in 1976 with five band members, the group has evolved over the past 25 years to include a total of nine musicians. Playing a heady mix of traditional Québécois tunes with Scottish and French folk music as well as salsa, jazz and cajun influences, they are currently one of Canada's top musical exports. Their unique sound and style is reflected in their eclectic choice of instruments including fiddle, guitar, button accordion, mandolin, acoustic and electric bass, piano, saxophone, trumpet, trombone, bass trombone, drums, harmonica, jew's harp and spoons. The complex foot percussion (a traditional feature of French-Canadian music known as *accords de pieds*) of multi-instrumentalist Michel Bordeleau and the charismatic singing of the only original band member, singer Yves Lambert, complete the distinctive sound of 'The Smiling Boot'. With 10 albums and over half a million copies sold worldwide, La Bottine Souriante continue to be a major force in the dissemination of Québécois folk music, regularly playing at folk festivals around the world.

Other notable performers to have come out of the folk music revival in Québec include Montréal sisters Kate and Anna McGarrigle who sing in both English and French, the talented duo of Québécois singer and instrumental-ist Bertrand Gosselin and American folk singer Jim Corcoran, and the guitar, accordion and violin trio of Le Rêve du Diable, who have been entertaining audiences in various guises since 1974.

While French settlers made their mark on the music of Québec, the arrival of English, Irish and Scots migrants in the 19th century helped shape the music of the east coast, notably in Nova Scotia. On Cape Breton Island, several generations of the Rankin and Barra MacNeil families have ensured the future of Scottish traditional music on the island, particularly fiddle playing, inspiring young musicians such as Natalie MacMaster and Ashley MacIsaac. The former is both an accomplished fiddler (like her uncle the legendary Buddy MacMaster) and a step-dancer, often combining the two activities on stage to tremendous effect. Meanwhile, fiddler Ashley MacIsaac has made an unforgettable impact on the traditional music scene, pushing the boundaries of improvisation to the limit with his fast and furious brand of Cape Breton jigs and reels. In New Brunswick and on Prince Edward Island, the fusion of Scottish and Irish fiddle music with French songs brought over by the first settlers in North America has given rise to Acadian music (a reference to the former French colony of Acadia now called Nova Scotia). The young and talented group known as Barachois (from Prince Edward Island) have played a major part in the promotion of Acadian music, playing a lively mix of traditional melodies on fiddle, guitar, trumpet, piano and bass with foot-tapping accompaniment.

Wherever you go in Canada, you'll find different communities from around the world sharing their musical traditions. From the gospel music of Nova Scotia's Afro-Canadian population to the musical traditions of Manitoba's Ukrainian community, you'll soon discover that there seems to be no end to the musical possibilities of such a cosmopolitan population. The social history of the country has played a vital part in the dissemination and integration of these musical styles among its inhabitants and coupled with the revival of interest in traditional music, sparked by the 'world music' craze of the 1980s and 1990s, the future of Canadian music looks brighter than ever.

SUGGESTED READING

The Penguin History of Canada (Kenneth McNaught, 1988). This is a comprehensive, readable digest of Canadian history.

The Collected Works of Billy the Kid (Michael Ondaatje, 1970). This account of the factual and fictional life of the notorious outlaw won Ondaatje his first Governor General's Award in 1970, and was adapted for stage and produced at Stratford, Toronto and New York. His novel *In the Skin of a Lion* (1987) is set in Toronto in the 1930s.

Federalism and the French Canadians (Pierre Elliott Trudeau, 1968). Canadian prime minister in 1968–79 and 1980–84, Trudeau became a sharp critic of contemporary Québec nationalism and argued for a Canadian federalism in which English and French Canada would find a new equality.

Red Fox (Antony Hyde, 1986). Robert Thorne, a journalist and specialist on Russia, arrives in the small port of Halifax on Canada's eastern seaboard to investigate the sudden disappearance of a wealthy fur importer. His enquiries take him further than he had expected, and lead him back to the early rumblings of the Russian Revolution.

The Call of the Wild (Jack London, 1903). London's famous novel set in late 19th-century Alaska is the story of a dog sold to Klondike gold prospectors. When his owners die, he is inexplicably drawn to the forests by the call of the wild. He abandons the world of man and joins the wolves, his wild brothers, in the mountains.

The Passionate Trilogy (Peter C. Newman). This recounts the history of the hugely powerful British Hudson's Bay Company of Canada's pioneering days. The last volume includes portraits of the personalities and explorers.

Kiss of the Fur Queen (Tomson Highway, 1998). Highway is one of the most creatively successful of Canada's native authors. This novel follows the lives of two brothers who leave an idyllic childhood when they go to a religious boarding school. The story is of their struggle to adapt on their own terms to a European-based culture and their resistance to forced assimilation.

The Edible Woman (Margaret Atwood, 1969).This was a great success for Canada's most famous novelist and poet, author of five collections of short fiction, 14 volumes of poetry and nine novels. Her themes are contemporary ones of Canadian identity, feminism and ecology. Her writing is steely, her style energetic. *The Edible Woman* is set in Toronto and unwinds a wickedly funny tale of a woman and her relationships. *Circle Game* (1966) won the Governor General's Award, *The Handmaid's Tale* (1986) was shortlisted for the Booker Prize and *The Blind Assassin* bettered that by winning the Booker in 2000.

The Deptford and Cornish Trilogies (Robertson Davies, 1970–75). The patriarch of Canadian literature in English was a man of the theatre, a critic and a journalist. Born in Ontario, he died in 1995. Davies wrote two bestselling trilogies in which he juxtaposed the supernatural and astrology.

Stranger Music: Selected Poems and Songs (Leonard Cohen, 1993). The archetypal troubadour of the 1960s, Leonard Cohen has had a prolific and fruitful career as a writer, and this is a major volume of his works. In 1994, his 60th birthday was marked by the compilation album *Take This Waltz: A Celebration of Leonard Cohen*. His work has been widely translated, and he is especially popular in France, Germany, Scandinavia and the Netherlands.

BACKGROUND

Ontario

Refer to the first colour plate section for a general map of Ontario and West Canada, and maps of Toronto, Ottawa and Vancouver.

In Ontario you will find . . . big modern cities, vast open spaces, friendly towns and villages rich in history, museums and jazz bars, and kind, smiling Canadians wherever you go.

It covers a huge area, bordered by the Great Lakes in the south and Hudson Bay to the north. It is Canada's most economically productive province, in terms of both industry and agriculture and has a variable and pleasant climate (which even permits grapes to grow in the Niagara region), largely thanks to the influence of the Great Lakes on weather patterns.

Most people live in the towns and cities along and a bit north of the Great Lakes (such as Toronto and Ottawa).

Mention Ontario and many people will think of the Niagara Falls. However, there is much more to Ontario than this famous waterfall, and the visitor will find much of interest in the smaller towns and cities around Toronto. The province is dotted with thousands of lakes, criss-crossed by numerous rivers and waterways (easy to explore by canoe), and farther north is the Canadian Shield, a great expanse of rocky outcrop: in Ontario you don't have to go far to find rampant, unspoiled wilderness. To make the most of your trip to the province try to combine visits to towns and cities with more adventurous expeditions such as walking trails or canoeing adventures, particularly through Algonquin Park. This is the best possible way to get an idea of the vastness of the country and to understand the difficulties the pioneers must have met when it was virgin territory.

Smokers should be aware that theirs is not a popular habit in Ontario. Smoking areas are few and far between in restaurants in Toronto and are generally so unappealing that they are more effective than a nicotine patch.

TORONTO   DIALLING CODE: 416

For maps of Toronto, see the first colour plate section.

Once a small industrial city, Toronto has changed radically and developed into a more cosmopolitan metropolis (with all its faults and qualities), competing with Montréal on both economic and cultural fronts. Indeed, Toronto aims to be recognized as the most cosmopolitan city in the world. The city sprawls into endless industrial suburbs, dissected by long arterial roads. One of the key areas to explore during your visit is Downtown, which is the best place to stay. Here you'll find numerous ethnic communities with their own rhythms of life and cuisine, which add to the colourful and vibrant cultural dynamic of the city as a whole. The streets are clean, the locals are usually friendly and it's all relatively stress-free. Despite the profusion of skyscrapers built in the Downtown area since the 1960s, you never get the feeling that the city is overcrowded. Many of these skyscrapers are connected to each other and to subway stations by great expanses of underground walkways, making it entirely possible to live in Toronto without ever having to go outside.

Among the Downtown communities you'll find **Chinatown**, which is always lively, and **Queen Street West** and **Kensington Market**, where you'll find alternative lifestyles of all kinds. **Cabbagetown** has undergone a make-over and is home to young city workers. Along **College Street** is an Italian area that's quite trendy, and there are others along **St Clair Avenue West** (a bit out of the Downtown area). The Greek quarter on Danforth Avenue is known as 'the Danforth'.

If on the face of it this city appears a little cold, under the surface you'll discover streets festooned with flowers, little parks, warm and welcoming districts with a wide range of ethnic groups, and fabulous little restaurants. There are lots of really nice (often cheap) bars where the music is as good as the beer. Although there is so much going on, it may take a while to get to know the 'hidden' Toronto.

The cultural life of the city comes into focus twice a year, with the Jazz Festival in June and the International Film Festival in September.

GETTING THERE

❶ **The airport** is 32 kilometres (20 miles) northwest of the town centre.

– **Information**: ☎ 247-7678 between 8am and 10pm. Information available in several languages.

– **From the airport to Downtown by car**: take Highway 427 south, then QE east. It should take about 25 minutes.

A word of advice to prevent you from having an accident at your first crossroads: the three-coloured traffic lights are on the **other side** of the intersection.

– **Airport Express bus to Downtown**: departures every 20 minutes from 6.25am to 12.45am, stopping at most of the major Downtown hotels with the final stop at the bus terminal. The journey takes about 40 minutes, and students enjoy a 10 per cent discount.

– **Taxis with Airport Services**: ☎ (416) 255-2211.

ORIENTATION

Toronto is a sprawling city and the interesting places can be quite far from each other. But the Downtown area extends to **Front Street** in the south, **Bloor Street** in the north, **Jarvis Street** in the east and **Bathurst Street** in the west. In the very centre, **Yonge Street**, which goes north–south, is useful for getting your bearings. It's the dividing line in town, from where all the parallel roads are called either East or West. Yonge Street is claimed to be the longest road in the world.

GETTING AROUND

Even though distances may be great, having a car in Toronto is often a drawback as visitors are frequently obliged to park in private, pay car-parks – which can be convenient but expensive. You would need strong legs, though, to walk everywhere, so your other option is the TTC (the Toronto

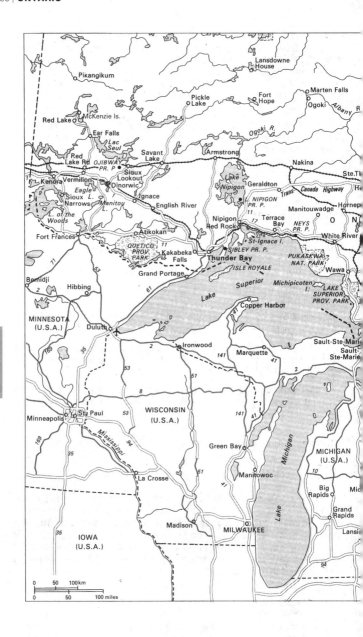

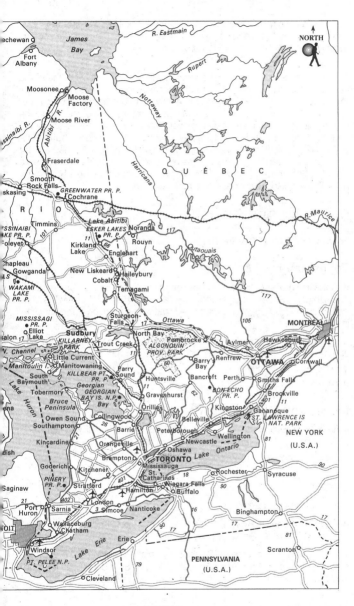

ONTARIO

Transit Commission). Take the subway: the Bloor–Danforth line runs east and west, and the Yonge–University line runs north and south looping around Union Station, which is clean, quick and easy to use and open from about 6am to 12.30am.

The bus service (same hours of operation as the subway) covers the whole city (with several night buses) and a streetcar service (24 hours a day) covers the whole of Downtown. The drivers are always happy to help you find your way. You can buy tokens in the subway stations that can be used on all the city transport services. When you pay your fare, ask for a transfer or get one from the steel box just inside the subway (there should be a red button that you push). You can then transfer onto the next leg of your journey without paying again, even if it involves a different mode of transport. This will save you a lot of money. If you get stuck, just ask a member of the TTC staff for help. There's also a 'day-pass' that easily pays for itself.

USEFUL ADDRESSES

For maps of Toronto, see the first colour plate section.

Tourist Information

◩ **Ontario Tourist Information Center** (map II, C3, **1**): Eaton Centre, Level 1, 220 Yonge Street. Open Monday–Friday 10am–9pm. Saturday 9.30am–7pm. Sunday noon–5pm. Well-informed staff will help you organize your stay in the province.

■ **Information by telephone**: ☎ 1-800-668-2746 (toll-free). The number can be dialled from anywhere in Canada (except Toronto). A tourism expert will answer your questions.

■ **Website**: www.toronto.com.

Money and Exchanging Money

■ **American Express**: if your money is lost or stolen call ☎ 1-800-221-7282. Office: 101 McNabb Street, Markham. ☎ (905) 4746-8000.

■ **Visa**: ☎ 1-800-732-1322 (toll-free).

Health

■ **Emergencies**: ☎ 911.

■ **Toronto General Hospital**: 200 Elizabeth Street. Accident and emergency: ☎ 340-4800. Subway: Queen's Park.

■ **24-hour pharmacy** (map II, C3, **8**): Shoppers' Drug Mart, 700 Bay Street, on the corner of Gerrard Street. ☎ 979-2424. Call Shoppers' Drug Mart toll-free ☎ 1-800-363-1020 for information on the nearest pharmacy.

Transport

🚆 **Union Station** (main station; map II, C3-4): 65 Front Street, between Bay Street and York Street. Via Rail: ☎ 366-8411. Website: www.viarail.ca. Numerous daily departures for Montréal and Ottawa.

🚌 **Bus station** (map II, C2): on the corner of Bay Street and Dundas Street. Information and reservations: ☎ 1-800-661-8747 (toll-free). Buses to many towns and cities, one-way or round-trip tickets available for all routes.

■ **Car hire**: there are several small car-hire companies. The larger ones include National Car Rental Canada: ☎ 922-2000 and Hertz: ☎ 620-9620.

■ **Bicycle hire** (map II, C4, **3**): McBride, on the corner of York and Queens Quay West. ☎ 763-5651. Open from May to October. Main shop: 2799 Dundas Street West (a distance from the city centre).

All-night Services

■ **Dominion**: opposite 360 Bloor Street West. The supermarket is open 24 hours a day.

■ **Shoppers' Drug Mart**: 700 Bay Street. Also open 24 hours.

Entertainment

■ **T.O. TIX**: Buy half-price theatre or concert tickets for the same evening from the kiosk at Eaton Centre, Level 2, Dundas Mall Corridor. Open Tuesday to Friday noon–7.30pm. Saturday noon–7pm. Sunday noon–6pm.

■ **International Press Centre** (map II, B1, **5**): 124 Yorkville Avenue. Subway: Bay. *Now* and *Eye* are free listings magazines giving details of all the current shows and cultural attractions around town. Pick them up in many restaurants or from steel boxes on Downtown street corners.

■ **Internet cafés and venues**: **@Cyber Space** (map II, A1, **7**), 561 Bloor Street West. **Cyberland Café** (map II, C2, **9**), 257 Yonge Street. **Hostelling International Toronto**, 76 Church Street. **Global Village Backpackers**, 460 King Street West.

■ **Swimming pools**: All public pools are free. Ask for details at the tourist office or telephone the Pool Hotline: ☎ 392-7838.

WHERE TO STAY

For maps of Toronto, see the first colour plate section.

Finding accommodation in Toronto is difficult and can be expensive. There is no camping near to Downtown; the universities offer rooms but they are not cheap. This leaves the central Youth Hostel. If you have more funds, opt for B&Bs rather than hotels. For the same price, you will be closer to the centre, breakfast is included in the price and you will meet nice people. It's vital to book ahead.

Campsites

⚓ **Indian Line Tourist Campground**: 7625 Finch Avenue, Brampton. ☎ (905) 678-1233 or ☎ 1-800-304-9728 (toll-free). Fax: (905) 678-1305. Email: www.iline@trca.on.ac. This is a large campsite on the outskirts of the city, with sheltered sites. Facilities are not spotless, but it's about the closest you'll get to Toronto (it's still a long way though, and not very easy to get to and from Downtown without a car).

⊠ Budget (around $20)

⛺ **Hostelling International Toronto** (map II, C3, **20**): 76 Church Street. ☎ 971-4440 or toll-free (outside Toronto): ☎ 1-800-668-4487. Fax: 971-4088. Open 24 hours a day. It's advisable to book to secure a bed. The reception room is divided into small relaxation areas equipped with guidebooks and other reading matter. There's a huge kitchen, a laundry, a TV room and an Internet café (costing $1 for 10 minutes online). The atmosphere is young and friendly. The youth hostel organizes a few two-day excursions (various prices and destinations).

⛺ **The Rosa Tourist House** (map I, A4, **21**): 1584 King Street West, Sunnyside. ☎ 536-8225. Prices are reduced for stays of more than a week, and there's also a car-park. It's 20 minutes from Downtown, and the streetcar stop – either the No. 501 (Queen car) or the No. 504 (King car) – is very close to the hostel. The clientele is mainly European.

⛺ **Leslieville Home Hostel** (map I, D3, **22**): 185 Leslie Street. ☎ 461-7258. Fax: 469-9938. From Queen Street, take the streetcar east to Leslie Street. It's around 10 minutes' drive from Downtown and has dormitories and single or double rooms. If you want more independence, the landlady rents out double rooms or apartments in another house that's a little farther away but much quieter.

⛺ **Global Village Backpackers** (map II, B3, **23**): 460 King Street West. ☎ 703-8540 or 1-888-844-7875 (toll-free). Fax: 703-3887. Website: www.globalbackpackers.com. Located in the heart of Toronto, 5 minutes' walk from the SkyDome and the CN Tower. You may be forgiven for thinking you've entered a nightclub due to the rock music, psychedelic bar and trendy,

but relaxed atmosphere. You'll find a kitchen, TV room, cybernet café, piano, billiard table and even a pub. Highly recommended.

⛺ **The Planet Traveler's Hostel**: 175 Augusta Avenue, behind Kensington Market. ☎ 599-6789. Website: www.theplanettraveler.com. Take the Dundas streetcar and get off one stop west of Spadina Avenue. The cost is $20 per person per night in spacious six-bed dorms. This brand new youth hostel, housed in a renovated Victorian building, is very clean and equipped with a kitchen and TV room. Anthony will give you a warm welcome and is always helpful. A generous breakfast is included, consisting of muffins, fruit and endless drinks. Word is spreading – you'll be wise to book ahead to avoid disappointment.

University Accommodation

Around $25 per person per night, and rooms can be rented by the night, the week or the month.

⛺ **Neill Wycik College Hotel** (map II, C2, **24**): 96 Gerrard Street East, between Jarvis and Church Streets. Subway: College. ☎ 977-2320 or 1-800-268-4358. Fax: 977-2809. Email: wycik@inforamp.net. Good location, and offers discounts for students, over-50s and members of the Youth Hostelling Association. The large students' residence is open from mid-May till the end of August and has 185 functional and not entirely spotless rooms. Sheets, towels and soap are supplied. There are shared facilities, one kitchen for every 10 rooms and a cafeteria for breakfast. You can even enjoy a sauna and roof terrace with barbecue. There's no curfew. An additional folding bed in a room costs very little and two children under 17 years of age can share a room with their parents at no extra cost.

♠ **Tartu College** (map II, B1, **25**): 310 Bloor Street West. ☎ 925-9405. Fax: 925-2295. Email: info@ tartucollege.com. Subways: Spadina or St George. Half price after the second night's stay. Open to tourists from 1 May till the end of August. The office is open from 9am to 4pm. This is a functional, but rather gloomy students' residence which has shared facilities (including bathrooms), and one kitchen for every six rooms. It's quite central and there's no curfew.

♠ **University of Toronto** (map II, B1, **26**): Summer residence accommodation at Sir Daniel Wilson Residence, 73 St George Street. ☎ 978-2532. Fax: 946-5386. Website: www.toronto.ca/ucres. Open from May till the end of August only and a minimum stay of one week is required. A single room costs $100 per week. There are over 200 single and double rooms (the latter are harder to come by), some overlooking the park. The rooms are spartan, furnished in polished wood and the facilities are spotless. The kitchen is rather minimalist, with a fridge and a microwave. Curfew at 11pm. This picturesque spot is reminiscent of the film *Dead Poets Society*.

♠ **YWCA** (map I, C2, **27**): 80 Woodlawn Avenue East. Subway: Summerhill. ☎ 923-8454. Fax: 923-1950. Open all year round, 24 hours a day. Dormitories or individual rooms for female guests only. Breakfast is included.

Bed & Breakfast Associations

There are five B&B associations. They all offer very similar prices, and prices vary according to the class of the house and its proximity to the centre of town.

■ **Metropolitan Bed & Breakfast Registry of Toronto**: ☎ 964-2566. Fax: 960-9526.

■ **Toronto Bed & Breakfast**: ☎ 588-8800. Fax: 927-9526 (evenings and weekends).

■ **Downtown Toronto Association of Bed & Breakfast Guesthouses**: PO Box 190, Station B, Toronto. ☎ 368-1420. Fax: 368-1653. Offers expensive but very central accommodation.

■ **Bed & Breakfast Homes of Toronto**: ☎ 363-6362.

■ **Abodes of Choice Bed & Breakfast Association of Toronto**, PO Box 46093, College Park Post Office, Toronto M5B 248. ☎ 694-6491. Fax: 537-7629.

☆☆ Moderate ($60–80)

♠ **Les Amis** (map II, C2, **36**): 31 Granby Street. ☎ 591-0635. Fax: 591-8546. Subway: College. Email: les-amis@bbtoronto.com. Double rooms cost from $75 to $90, with shared facilities. It is well named ('Les Amis' means friends), with a warm welcome and peaceful atmosphere. The owners are vegetarians and serve delicious breakfasts.

♠ **Havinn** (map I, B2-3, **38**): 118 Spadina Road (near Casa Loma). Subway: Dupont. ☎ 922-5220. E-mail: havinn@echo-on.net. Double rooms for $60 per night ($350 per week). They have four modest rooms with TV and shared facilities plus use of the kitchen.

♠ **Grayona Tourist Home** (map I, A4, **28**): 1546 King Street West. ☎ 535-5443. Take the No. 504 streetcar and get off at the stop before Roncesvalles. The streetcar stop is outside the door. It's about 20 minutes from Downtown. The house is simple, clean and pleasant, and run by a friendly, chatty Australian woman who loves to meet people from around the world. There are six rooms, a small studio with a corner kitchen and private bathroom. Opt for the quieter rooms at the back. Some have a view of the lake. Impeccably clean facilities and reasonable prices, but no breakfast. Non-smoking.

⚑ **Global Guest House** (map II, A-B1, **29**): 9 Spadina Road (near Bloor Street). ☎ 923-4004. Fax: 923-1208. Subway: Spadina. There are frescoes and painted murals in the corridor and the rooms (the owner is an artist). The 10 rooms (some with air-conditioning) are somewhat old-fashioned, and the red bath is a must-see. No breakfast but there's a kitchen available for guests to use. Also TV and car-parking.

⚑ **Vanderkooy** (map I, C2, **32**): 53 Walker Avenue. ☎ 925-8765. Subway: Summerhill. Situated in a quiet and leafy street that opens onto Yonge Street, north of Bloor Street, this is a lovely house with a terrace and garden. The rooms are very comfortable, it's all impeccably clean and there's also air-conditioning. The welcome is friendly.

☆☆☆ Expensive ($80–120)

⚑ **Beverly Place** (map II, B2, **30**): 235 Beverly Street, off College Street. ☎ 977-0077. This is a very classy house situated in a residential street which is rather poorly sign-posted. It has five pretty rooms, all of them spotless. The elegant interior includes paintings, period furniture, thick carpets or polished parquet flooring. There are five larger rooms with similar decor in another house across the street. Breakfast is included and can be enjoyed in the garden. You can smoke in the kitchen or outside but not in the bedrooms. It's a lovely spot.

⚑ **La Terrasse** (map I, B2, **31**): 52 Austin Terrace. ☎ 535-1493. Fax: 535-9616. Email: terracehouse bandb@sympatico.ca. Subway: St Clair West. Austin Terrace is a pretty little road off Bathurst Street, just north of Davenport Road, and very close to Casa Loma. This early 20th-

century house is run by Suzanne Charbonneau and her husband who are French-speaking Canadians originally from Québec. It's a lovely spot, surrounded by greenery and one of the rooms has a private sitting room with a view of the garden, from which you can watch the racoons. You'll get a tasty and generous breakfast. The house is air-conditioned and for non-smokers only.

⚑ **Annex House** (map I, B2-3, **33**): 147 Madison Avenue. ☎ and fax: 920-3922. Subway: Dupont. Well located on a pretty, quiet and leafy street, this splendid early 20th-century house has four huge double rooms that are well maintained and very comfortable. It's a little more expensive than the other B&Bs listed but it's still reasonable. No hotel could offer the same level of comfort or charm for these prices. It's a good spot, ideal for those looking for a certain degree of comfort. Free private parking.

⚑ **Executive Motor Hotel** (map II, A3-4, **39**): 621 King Street West. ☎ 504-7441. Fax: 504-4722. Well located, near the SkyDome, Ontario Place and Harbourfront, this classic American-style motel represents good value for money in the city centre.

☆☆☆☆ Splash Out (over $150)

⚑ **Royal York** (map II, C3, **34**): 100 Front Street West, opposite Union Station. ☎ 368-2511. Fax: 368-2884. Thick carpets, glistening copper, stunning crystal lights, a hushed atmosphere and impeccable service – you can enjoy all these if your budget stretches this far. An airport bus stops at the door every 30 minutes (from 5.30am to 11pm).

⚑ **The Strathcona Hotel** (map II, C3, **35**): 60 York Street. ☎ 363-3321. Fax: 363-4679. This classic hotel is slightly old-fashioned in a way that might appeal to the more

romantically minded and mature traveller.

WHERE TO EAT

For maps of Toronto, see the first colour plate section.

Toronto is a young city with a lively restaurant scene. You'll find a wide range of ethnic cuisines to choose from, brought to the city by its many immigrants who have re-created the various culinary specialities of their home countries.

Chinatown

☆ Budget (less than $10)

You'll find many cheap eateries worth a try near the intersection of Spadina Avenue and Dundas Street West.

✕ **Tung Hing Bakery** (map II, B2, **40**): 428 Dundas Street West. Excellent Chinese cakes and other delicacies to take away.

✕ **Saigon Lai Restaurant** (map II, B2, **41**): 434 Dundas Street West. ☎ 592-9155. Open 10am–10pm (Saturday until 11pm). In the heart of Chinatown, this restaurant's menu price includes tea and soya salad. The dining room is gently air-conditioned and you'll find Chinese families seated at round tables enjoying tasty cuisine from Saigon. If you're hungry but hard up, fill up on the soup.

✕ **Saigon Palace Restaurant** (map II, B2, **42**): 454 Spadina Avenue, next to El Mocambo (near College Street). ☎ 968-1623. Open 9am–10pm (Saturday to 11pm). The atmosphere is canteen-like, and it's very popular with the Chinese locals. A huge variety of exotic fruit juices and vegetables are on offer, so it's ideal if you're after a healthy snack.

Kensington Market Area

☆☆ Moderate ($10–20)

Baldwin Street offers a huge range of restaurants, some better than others.

✕ **Dessert Sensation Café** (map II, B2, **43**): 26 Baldwin Street. ☎ 348-0731. Open daily 11.30am–midnight. A good choice of really substantial cakes. Very nice terrace and the atmosphere is peaceful.

✕ **John's Italian Café** (map II, B2, **44**): 27 Baldwin Street. Open noon–11pm. Classic, relaxed Italian café with a terrace that catches the sun in the afternoon. There's a limited but enticing menu of pizzas, soups and pasta. After a stroll through Kensington Market (at the other end of Baldwin Street), it's an ideal spot to relax and write postcards home.

✕ **Margarita's** (map II, B2, **45**): 14 Baldwin Street. ☎ 977-5525. The food is good value but drinks are expensive at this fun Mexican restaurant with ponchos and sombreros hanging on the walls. Attractive terrace on the first floor. The food is pleasantly spicy. It's best to phone ahead as opening hours can be unreliable.

TORONTO

Queen Street West

⌨ Moderate (around $15)

✗ **Tortilla Flats** (map II, B3, **46**): 429 Queen Street West; east of Spadina Avenue. ☎ 593-9870. Open 11am–2am (Sunday to midnight). This Tex-Mex restaurant and bar with pleasant patio serves delicious fajitas that are a must – go on Tuesday evening when they're half price. Try also the reasonably priced and rather decadent desserts. A good choice.

Near Front Street

⌨ Moderate (around $15)

✗ **The Old Spaghetti Factory** (map II, C3, **48**): 54 The Esplanade, near Scott Street. Open Monday–Thursday 1–10pm. Friday and Saturday 11.30am–midnight. You'll find a variety of inedible objects throughout the restaurant: sewing-machine tables, wooden horses, Western-style chairs, large multicoloured bay windows and streetcars, all contributing to the rather baroque style of this Italian restaurant. There are a number of spaghetti dishes to choose from, unpretentious and reasonably priced; there's also a children's menu.

✗ **Shopsy** (map II, C3, **55**): 33 Yonge Street, on the corner of Front Street. Open 6.30am–9pm (but times can vary depending on the day). This deli was established in 1922, making it one of the oldest in town. It seats over 250 people and is decorated like an old-style railway station brasserie, with wooden benches and celebrity photos on the walls. The food isn't sophisticated (hamburgers, steak and chips, cooked deli meats and salads) but you can eat well and the portions are big.

✗ **Le Papillon** (map II, C3, **56**): 16 Church Street, near Scott Street.

✗ **The Rivoli** (map II, B3, **54**): 332 Queen Street West. ☎ 596-1908. Open 11am–2am. This designer restaurant/bar serves original dishes inspired by Asian and Italian cuisine, together with local hamburgers and a large selection of wines for a trendy clientele. Lots of young people. There's a performance space in the back that hosts original exhibitions of work by local artists every month. It's best to visit in the evening or simply enjoy a drink on the terrace.

☎ 363-3773. Open Monday to Saturday 11.30am–10pm. Specialities from Québec, served in a sophisticated interior. The service is professional with a dash of spontaneity and natural charm – as it often is in Québec. The food is good but you won't be able to fill up on the starter as you can in other places. It makes a welcome change from the traditional cuisine of Ontario.

✗ **Restaurant Marché Mövenpick** (map II, C3, **57**): 42 Yonge Street, in BCE Place. ☎ 366-8986. Open daily 7.30am–2am. Serves a selection of dishes, savoury and sweet, from $4. This rather unusual restaurant, with its attractive interior and seating for 500 people, is the flagship of the Mövenpick chain. As the name suggests, it's rather like a village market, offering a colourful selection of appetizing dishes, including pizzas and pastries, plus a wine counter. Wander around, selecting your meal from the vast selections, but keep your eye on the final bill. Best to book ahead.

✗ **Café Bar Masquerade** (map II, C3, **58**): 42 Yonge Street, opposite Marché Mövenpick. ☎ 363-8971. Open Monday to Saturday 7.30am–

10pm. This is a very modern restaurant and bar with brightly coloured furniture and an Italian carnival-like atmosphere. Antipasti, pasta and pizza on the menu. Good spot for a coffee (great espresso).

Bloor Street West

☆ Budget (around $10)

✕ **Country Style** (map II, A1, **49**): 450 Bloor Street West. ☎ 537-1745. Open daily 11am–10pm. Also does take-aways. An excellent Hungarian restaurant in a narrow, rather sombre dining room where you can savour the best of Hungary's specialities. Come here for the quality of the cooking, not the decor. This is one of the places the Hungarians of Toronto gather to enjoy excellent goulash or beef with paprikash onions.

✕ **Swiss Chalet** (map II, B1, **53**): 234 Bloor Street West. ☎ 972-6831. Open 11am–10 or 11pm. This is one of a chain of restaurants specializing in a variety of chicken dishes. The rooms are airy and rather alpine in style. Good value for money in the business district.

✕ **Madison Avenue Pub** (map II, A-B1, **59**): 14 Madison Avenue. ☎ 927-1722. Open 11am–2am. Enjoy 'Happy Hour' for certain dishes from 3pm to 6pm. This English pub with its classic exterior is a veritable labyrinth, housed in two adjoining houses with numerous rooms and terraces on different levels. The bar holds as many as 500 customers at a time. Locals come here for a pint after work and they squeeze together round big wooden tables on the patio, even in winter when the terraces are kept warm by huge suspended gas heaters. There are competitive games of billiards and darts. You can even stay the night (from $90) if you don't think you'll make it home.

Yorkville District

☆☆☆ Expensive (around $20)

✕ **Pilot Tavern** (map II, C1, **47**): 22 Cumberland Street. Open until 1am. In 1987, an aviation enthusiasts' club took over this legendary bar. The large, dark room downstairs exhibits some of the brave exploits of the war pilots. The 'Flight Deck' (a roof terrace) is of little interest. Enjoy salads, hamburgers and club sandwiches. No desserts, but you can always pop into **Dinah's Cupboard** at No. 50 for a delicious cake.

✕ **Hemingway's** (map II, B1, **50**): 142 Cumberland Street. Open until 2am. The food is very acceptable in this rather typically up-market spot in Yorkville. There are comfortable sofas in which businessmen enjoy their shorts on the rocks, but the atmosphere is better on the roof terrace, where things are a bit more relaxed.

Near Yonge and Wellesley Streets

✕ **Spiral** (map II, C1, **61**): 582 Church Street. Open from 11.30am. Located in the gay district, this is a fashionable spot, popular with the local yuppies. Decorated with pastel blue and green walls, wooden floors and furniture, it's a pleasant place with a lovely terrace for warm days. Tasty dishes include chicken spring rolls and mango salad.

✕ **Coach House** (map II, C1, **62**): 574 Yonge Street. Open every day.

This is a large American-style bar with revolving footstools and a 1970s metal fridge. The service can be a bit slow, but you can always enjoy a beer while you wait (or watch TV like the regulars). You'll feel as if you've stepped onto an old American movie set.

Near the Skydome

☆ Budget (around $15)

✕ **The Second City** (map II, B3, **51**): 56 Blue Jays Way. ☎ 863-1111. This theatre-restaurant is one of the best places in Toronto to appreciate Canadian humour. Eat your fill at **Leoni's** (same entrance) where they serve Italian dishes in a vast dining room.

✕ **Ed's Restaurant** (map II, B-C3, **52**): 270 King Street West. Several gigantic restaurants are housed in two whole street blocks. They close at 10pm (11pm on Sunday). Superb kitsch decor. You'll find a variety of cuisine on offer – Italian, Chinese, seafood and excellent meat dishes. The owner is making a fortune with his restaurants and he has plastered the facade of the place with reviews that proclaim his success. He's also written a book entitled *How to Succeed in 121 Lessons*.

✕ **Le St Tropez** (map II, B3, **60**): 315 King St West. Open 11.30am–11pm. The food is French with a difference and served in a dining room or on the terrace. You'll spot a few French touches, including a bottle of Cointreau and a picture of a 2CV car. The coffee is good.

✕ **ACME Grill** (map II, B3, **63**): 86 John Street. ☎ 340-9700. This large brick building over a car-park has a long room split in two, brick walls and Western chairs. The first part is a bar and the second a restaurant serving hamburgers, club sandwiches and other similar dishes. Country music will be playing in the background and you can watch the baseball on the TV screens, only minutes from the real thing.

WHERE TO HAVE A DRINK

For maps of Toronto, see the first colour plate section.

Kensington Area

❢ **Amadeus Bar** (map II, A-B2, **70**): on the corner of Augusta Street and Denison Square. Open 10am–2am. There's a terrace which is a pleasant place to have a drink and chat with friends. It seems to be from another time, but it's friendly nonetheless. Portuguese specialities and seafood.

Yorkville

❢ **Lettieri** (map II, B1, **71**): 96 Cumberland Street, on the corner of Bellair Street. This is a pleasant café with a terrace where Toronto's in-crowd come to hang out and be noticed.

Queen Street West and King Street West

❢ **Bovine Sex Club** (map II, A3, **72**): 542 Queen Street West, east of Bathurst Street. Open 10pm–3am. Despite the name, this is not a seedy club but a really friendly bar with a punk-rock atmosphere, easily identifiable by the bicycles, prams and kitchen utensils hanging from the wall above the door. The interior is quite something – see for yourself. Concerts are held here from time to time.

♥ Amsterdam Brewing Company (map II, B3, **80**): 600 King Street West. Open daily 11.30am–2am. This big bar has a wooden counter at least 20 metres (66 feet) long, and you drink downstairs under the copper vats used to brew the beer. Choose from the house beers or many others, either on draught or in bottles. You can also have a snack. It's a bit pricey.

Other Friendly Bars

♥ Chick 'n' Deli (map I, C1, **81**): 744 Mount Pleasant Road. A typical bar that might feature in an American soap opera, with bottles of beer lined up behind the bar and soft lights. It's often packed as rock bands play every night. Relaxed and unpretentious atmosphere.

♥ Future Bakery Café (map II, A1, **83**): 483 Bloor Street West. Open daily 7am–1am. Serving mostly Polish food, it also makes its own bread. It feels like a university cafeteria, or an old bistro, crammed with intellectuals, artists and students, who all come for a drink, to revise for exams or to leaf quietly through the daily papers. It's relatively inexpensive. There's a bulletin board with information about concerts and various cultural activities.

NIGHTLIFE

For maps of Toronto, see the first colour plate section.

The music scene in Toronto reaches a climax during the Jazz Festival at the end of June, when the nightclubs host excellent bands from around the world – and don't charge a fortune to let the public in. Wander around Queen Street West and dive in and out of the clubs to enjoy as much variety as you can. It's a great way of meeting all sorts of unexpected people.

♥ The Bamboo (map II, B3, **73**): 312 Queen Street West. ☎ 593-5771. Open Monday to Saturday 11.30am–3am. Entrance is controlled, and sports shoes are forbidden at night. Sometimes the concerts spill out onto the pavement. It has a pleasant patio, and at the end of the long room there's a small stage where progressive or reggae bands play. The decor is a blend of modern and bamboo, with an atmosphere of the islands. It's also a restaurant serving Malaysian, Thai and tropical vegetarian dishes.

♥ HorseShoe Tavern (map II, B3, **74**): 370 Queen Street West. ☎ 598-4753. There's a bar in the front room and a band plays in the back room (modest entry charge). You can hear the music from the front room, so if you're hard up just have a drink and listen in. If the band doesn't appeal to you, just stay at the bar or play a game of pool. The bands tend to be of the country and western type.

♥ The Bohemian Café (map I, B2, **75**): 128 Pears Street; near Avenue Road and Davenport Road. ☎ 944-3550. Bar open Monday to Friday 4pm–1am. It's best to come here on Thursday nights when you can listen to good jazz bands while sitting comfortably in worn-out sofas.

♥ Lee's Palace (map II, A1, **76**): 529 Bloor Street West. Open noon–1am. A really nice bar on two levels, with a painted facade of bright, wild colours. Gigs every night on the

TORONTO

ground floor, and a disco on the first floor that's often packed. Small admission charge at the weekend.

❢ **The Olde Brunswick House** (map II, A1, **77**): 481 Bloor Street West. Open noon–1am. Has gigs most nights and the bands are usually pretty good. It has a reputation for being a riot, and has very sturdy tables and benches, just in case people get a bit too exuberant. It's best to come in a group and on foot, because you may drink more than you planned. The cover charge varies depending on the band.

❢ **The Government** (map II, C4, **78**): 132 Queen's Quay East. Closed Tuesday and Wednesday. One of the most famous clubs in Toronto. There are professional dancers, sometimes locked in cages, sometimes flying above the gigantic dance floor on swings. You'll find loads of pool tables, cheap drinks and, not surprisingly, a fairly young clientele.

❢ **Big Bop** (map II, A3, **79**): 651 Queen Street West, on the corner of Bathurst Street. Open Wednesday, Friday and Saturday night only. This nightclub, spread over two floors, is not very original but the music's good. Every Wednesday is hard-rock night. Watch yourself around here, as it can get a bit rough late at night.

WHAT TO SEE

For maps of Toronto, see the first colour plate section.

Museums

★ **Royal Ontario Museum** (map II, B1, **100**): 100 Queen's Park Crescent. ☎ 586-8000. Subway: Museum. Open daily 10am–6pm (Sunday from 11am and Tuesday until 8pm). Entrance charge $15 (weekdays), $20 (weekends). Free entry on Friday from 4.30pm to 9.30pm. Student reductions. The ROM is one of the most prestigious museums in Canada and North America. There are 30 different sections, so you're bound to find something of particular interest.

– **The Chinese collection** is one of the most significant in the world. In just a few hours it covers several thousand years of Chinese art, from archaeological finds to recent exhibits from the Manchu dynasty. Of particular interest is the gallery of tombs from the Ming dynasty, which includes an imposing mortuary collection with a number of doors, protective figures and huge stone camels lining the entrance. Don't miss the three 13th-century mural paintings in the **Bishop White gallery** depicting Buddhist and Taoist divinities. Also on exhibit are some superb Buddhist sculptures in wood from the 12th and 16th centuries. Still in the Chinese collection is a gallery of funeral furniture that gives an arresting glimpse into the importance attached to the dead. Take a look at the realism of the figures that accompany the dead.

– The **Natural history** galleries have a remarkable display of 13 genuine dinosaur skeletons displayed in a reproduction of their natural habitat.

– In the **Gallery of Discoveries** small groups of visitors can explore the nature of different objects using the sense of touch, and vision, amplified by a microscope.

– Other galleries worth visiting are those showing archaeological remains from the first civilizations of the Mediterranean basin (Egyptian, Greek, Etruscan, Roman), and a gallery of Islamic art.

– Finally there are the galleries of the **Canadian Nation** where you can discover the history, culture and various achievements of the diverse peoples of Canada.

★ **Art Gallery of Ontario** (map II, B2-3, **101**): 317 Dundas Street West. ☎ 979-6648. Subway: St Patrick. Open in summer Tuesday–Friday noon–9pm. Saturday–Sunday 10am–5.30pm. Entrance charges vary according to the exhibitions.

The exhibition space of the gallery has doubled to incorporate **The Grange**, the oldest brick house in Toronto. The gallery has an extraordinary collection of original plaster works by the English sculptor Henry Moore (1898–1986), highlighted by the natural lighting designed especially for his work. The **Canadian Collection** shows paintings by the famous 1920s Group of Seven, an influential group of painters who threw out the precepts of Canadian painting and drew from various elements of European Impressionism. Another highlight is the superb collection of European paintings, including Flemish masters (Rembrandt, Van Dyck, Frans Hals), painters from the French school (Poussin, Boucher), the Italian school (Canaletto, Bordone) and the English school (Hogarth, Raeburn, Reynolds). Also included are painters from the late 19th and early 20th centuries (Derain, Delaunay, Picasso, Chagall, Dufy, Van Gogh, Renoir, Monet, Pissarro, Cézanne etc.). One department displays a surprising collection of sculpture with works by Rodin, Degas, and a head by Picasso. The gallery also regularly shows contemporary art by both Canadian and international artists.

★ **Ontario Science Centre** (map I, D1, **102**): 770 Don Mills Road at Eglinton Avenue East. ☎ 696-3147. Open daily 10am–6pm. Entrance charge $8. A considerable distance from the centre but worth the trip. Take the Yonge Street subway to Eglinton (north from Downtown), then the Eglinton East bus to Don Mills Road. By car, take the Don Valley Parkway (you can get onto it at Front Street, near the lake) and follow the signs for Don Mills Road North (it will take between 20 and 30 minutes). Imagine a super-temple dedicated to inventions where you can participate in all sorts of fun and informative experiments. The workshop presentations are eye-opening and instructive. Very cool. Avoid going at the weekend.

★ **Bata Shoe Museum** (map II, B1, **103**): 327 Bloor Street West. ☎ 979-7799. Subway: St George. Open Tuesday 10am–8pm. Wednesday–Saturday 10am–5pm. Sunday noon-5pm. Entrance charge $6. A small interactive and informative museum, displaying a selection of unique footwear, such as Sir Elton John's platform boots.

Sporting Attractions

★ **Baseball at the Skydome** (map II, B4, **113**): Seats start at $7. Canadian families love watching baseball and the Toronto team, The Blue Jays, are local heroes. A huge screen transmits the match and statistics throughout the game. With cheerleaders, mascots and lotteries it's a great atmosphere.

★ **Skydome Tour Experience** (map II, B4, **113**): 1 Blue Jay Way, at the foot of the CN Tower. ☎ 341-2770. This huge white dome is famous for its retractable four-part roof. Daily tours every hour until 5pm (except on match days) last around 90 minutes and cost $10.50. You'll notice how high up the hair-dryers are and how tall the doorways have to be to accommodate the players. It's like a town in itself, with bars, restaurants, a Hard Rock Café and even a hotel with rooms overlooking the pitch. It was in one of these rooms that a couple indulged in a spot of off-pitch activity, much to the amusement of the stadium and the local press.

★ **Air Canada Centre** (map II, C4, **112**): 20 Bay Street, just a few minutes' walk from the CN Tower. ☎ 214-2255. Open daily 10am–3pm. This is home to Toronto's other sporting heroes – the Maple Leaf ice hockey team. The atmosphere is electric in the stadium in the winter. In summer the basketball team, the Raptors, take over. Ticket prices depend on individual matches. You can take a 1-hour, behind-the-scenes tour of the stadium and visit the small museum for $9.

★ **Hockey Hall of Fame** (map II, C3, **114**): in the BCE building on the corner of Yonge and Front Streets. ☎ 360-7735. Open daily in summer 9.30am–6pm (10am–6pm on Sunday and 10am–5pm out of season). Entrance charge $12. The venue includes a museum, shops and games area dedicated to Canada's national sport of ice hockey, its heroes and history. There's no shortage of cups, ice hockey sticks, video shows and other paraphernalia. It's very popular with Canadians – and particularly with Canadian children.

Other Venues

★ **Casa Loma** (map I, B2, **111**): 1 Austin Terrace. ☎ 923-1171. Subway: Dupont, then a 5-minute walk up the hill (north). Open daily 9.30am–4pm. Entrance charge $9 plus parking. The chateau was built between 1911 and 1914 by Sir Henri Pellat, a very wealthy, eccentric businessman. The 98 rooms in the building have sophisticated interiors, but sadly the furniture isn't original, the latter having been sold at less than 10 per cent of its value when the owner went bankrupt. The tour lasts between 1.5 and 2 hours.

★ **Spadina House** (map I, B2, **115**): 285 Spadina Road. ☎ 392-6910. Subway: Dupont. Open daily April to September noon–5pm. Entrance charge $5. Located near Casa Loma, this is a typical early 20th-century bourgeois building and everything has been carefully restored. Four generations of the Austin family lived here until fairly recently. The guided tour is appropriately British in flavour.

★ **Toronto City Hall** (map II, C3, **105**): Nathan Phillips Square. Subway: Dundas or Queen. As you wander around the district, you can't fail to notice the ultra-modern lines of this building. It actually comprises three buildings: two towers shaped like quarter circles form an arc around a lower building that looks like a giant flying saucer.

★ **Old City Hall** (map II, C3, **104**): This is an impressive old building that looks out of character in the newly built district. But it's worth a look, as is The Bay, the largest and oldest example of this Canadian chain of department stores.

★ **CN (Canadian National) Tower** (map II, B4, **106**): The entrance is on Front Street West at John Street. Open 9am–11pm. Friday and Saturday 8am–11pm. Entrance charge $22 (reductions for children and seniors). It's hard to miss the rocket-shaped (and controversial) concrete tower. The building has the highest self-stabilizing structures in the world. The high-speed lift takes you up 447 metres (1,466 feet), and the aerial reaches 533 metres (1,748 feet). Before you pay for your ticket, check that the visibility is good. On a clear day, you'll have a brilliant view of the city, the lake and even across it into the United States. At the top, 350 metres (1,148 feet) above the ground, there's a nightclub and a revolving restaurant. A glass floor has been installed, but some visitors are too frightened to walk on it. Unsurprisingly, this is a busy place with long queues at the weekend, so try to visit on a weekday morning.

★ **Black Creek Pioneer Village**: 1000 Murray Ross. Near York University campus. ☎ 736-1733. Take the subway north to Downsview, then the No. 106 bus and get off on the west side of the campus. Entrance charge $8. The reconstruction of a pioneers' village has about 40 houses dating from the middle of the 19th century, with a farm, a mill, the smithy and so on. The whole thing is brought to life by people wearing period costume.

Attractions

★ **Ontario Place** (map I, B4, **107**): 955 Lake Shore Boulevard West. Open from mid-May to mid-September 10.30am–midnight. Entrance charge. Kids are king in this large, well-laid-out park with lots of attractions and numerous activities in big, open, green spaces. For grown-ups there are restaurants but, above all, open-air concerts every evening (included in the price), sometimes featuring international performers but the prices remain the same. Arrive fairly early for concerts to secure a good seat and bring a picnic and a blanket. The performers play on a circular, revolving stage.

★ **Toronto Islands** (map II, C4, **108**): take the ferry from the terminal at the foot of Bay Street behind the Westin Harbour Castle Hotel. Frequent departures until 11.30pm. Crossings cost $5. Call for departure times: ☎ 392-8194. There's a great view of Downtown from the ferry, not to be confused with Toronto Tours, which offers crossings via the islands at $20. You'll find a lovely park where you can chill out on the grass and watch the baseball games. Unfortunately, Lake Ontario is quite polluted, but despite this it's a very popular spot at the weekend when the weather is hot, so you'll have to like crowds. Or you could rent a bike and try to escape them on some of the lovely cycle paths around the islands.

★ **High Park** (map I, A3, **109**), Subway: High Park. This pleasant place is the largest developed park in Toronto, where for two weeks during the summer you can see plays performed (*see* 'Culture' *below*). There's a small zoo in the middle of the park, and several swimming pools and playgrounds for the children.

★ **Metro Toronto Zoo**: 361A Old Finch Avenue (40 kilometres/25 miles from the centre), on Highway 401, Meadowvale exit, Scarborough. ☎ 392-5900. Entrance charge $12 (reductions possible). Open in summer Monday to Friday 9am–7.30pm (Saturday and Sunday to 6.30pm). As it's one of the biggest zoological parks in the world, the Metro is well equipped both for visitors and for the animals.

★ **Fort York** (map II, A4, **110**): Open in high season 10am–5pm, in low season 10am–4pm. Entrance charge $5. This is the birthplace of Toronto and the site of confrontation between the English and the Americans, which led to the fort's destruction in 1813. In reprisal, the English marched to Washington and burned the American political office, which was painted white to hide traces of the fire and became known as The White House. Fort York was rebuilt and escaped the building contractors in 1934. It's on a lovely site tucked in between the railway, the Gardner Expressway and the surrounding city. Once over the threshold, you can begin to imagine what life was like in the past when it was a working fort.

Walks and Excursions

★ **Kensington Market**: in the square bordered by Augusta and Spadina avenues and Nassau and College streets. Open Monday to Saturday 8am–7pm. Here you'll find brightly painted food shops, second-hand clothes shops, charming little cafés and the space and time to stop to chat a while. Kensington is one of the most welcoming parts of Toronto.

The first residents here were English immigrants, at the beginning of the 20th century. When they moved on, the area became home to the many Central European Jewish immigrants. It was this wave of immigrants who gave the district its truly popular identity. Small shops flourished and the market today is still as colourful as it used to be. The 1950s saw an influx of new minorities, such as the Hungarians and Italians, who created a little bit of 'back home' in the street life of the district.

During this period, various influential and seemingly well-intentioned real estate magnates tried to find a host of good reasons to pull the district down and rebuild. In 1982, a campaign was launched to stop live chickens and ducks from being sold in the market. Since then, Portuguese immigrants arrived and added another international dimension to the area, which is now truly multicultural – even a few worn out punks are still hanging around.

★ **Chinatown**: follows along Dundas Street, from Spadina Avenue to University Avenue, and then south on Spadina Avenue towards Queen Street, and north up to College Street. Chinatown can be said to have been founded in 1878, when Sam Ching opened his laundry on Adelaide Street West. The area then grew gradually until swelled by a wave of Hong Kong Chinese immigrants in the early 1960s. Toronto's Chinese community has now grown to 200,000, making it the third biggest in North America after San Francisco and Vancouver. The area has also become a favourite meeting place for the city's non-Chinese residents, and stands as proof of successful social integration. There are five Chinese daily newspapers.

This is the only part of town that's really lively on Sunday, when Chinese families come to do their shopping, have a meal or visit friends in the suburbs. On Dundas Street you can still see a few of the 19th-century buildings that have been covered with illuminated red-and-yellow signs in Chinese characters. Further up are air-conditioned shopping centres where you can shelter from the freezing winters.

★ **Queen Street West**: this is where a lot of the young people of Toronto gather. It's a bit like SoHo in New York, and has many huge warehouses that were taken over by artists in the 1970s and turned into studios. Since then,

TORONTO

shops selling clothes and gadgets, together with ultra-trendy restaurants, have moved in to make the most of the changes taking place in the area. These have also boosted the original population of mainly Ukrainians, Poles and Jewish communities from many countries. The area has also become popular with new-wave youth, and attracts a whole crowd of Toronto's interesting 20–30-somethings. The area is worth exploring on Saturday afternoon and, of course, at night as it's full of really good bars (see 'Where to Have a Drink').

★ **Cabbagetown**: Nothing much happens here, but it's a lovely, green and popular residential area. It's reminiscent of parts of San Francisco: little cottages painted in different colours and planted with flowers, tall, narrow houses, charming Victorian buildings and so on. In the 1960s, the area was very run down and there were many plans to demolish and rebuild it. Instead, it was renovated and gentrified to become a very chic place to live. Professional and business people have flooded into the area between Jarvis and Parliament streets on one side and Gerrard Street East and King Street East on the other. Cabbagetown is located farther north and east of these streets.

Walk east along Wellesley Street East (past Parliament Street), to Sackville Street, Amelia Street and Metcalfe Street, all of which are lined with beautiful gardens and bushes. The early 20th-century houses create an old-world ambience.

★ **Yorkville**: In this small area the old houses have been renovated and turned into art galleries, chic boutiques and luxury restaurants and there are also a few really trendy bars. It's very popular with young professionals and the smart set.

★ **St Lawrence Market**: 103 Front Street, at the corner of Jarvis Street. Open Tuesday to Saturday 8am–6pm (5pm on Saturday). An old brick building houses this big covered market.

★ **The Danforth**: If you take a drive (or the subway) east of the centre to Danforth Avenue, between Broadview Avenue and Pape Avenue, you'll find the Greek area of Toronto. The main street's a bit too wide to create a community atmosphere, and the street signs translated into Greek don't really do the trick, but there are some good Greek restaurants. Sunland Fruit Market is also reputed to be the best for fresh fruit and vegetables.

★ **Corso Italia**: around St Clair Avenue West, between Lansdowne Avenue and Dufferin Street. On Saturdays, this small Italian district comes alive with families shopping, visiting and chatting in cafés.

★ **Sailing on Lake Ontario**: To enjoy a different view of Toronto, a trip on the lake is really pleasant in summer. Canadians do a lot of boating and you'll find numerous marinas along the shore. There are no particular dangers but it's worth being cautious with so many other boats around. **Sailing School Club**: 275 Queens Quay West, near the CN Tower and the SkyDome. ☎ 203-3000. Fax: 203-8000. From Union Station, take the LRT to Harbour-front and get off at Rees Street. You can rent a sailing dinghy for a day or half-day, and also motorboats (cash deposit or credit card). Sailing lessons are available in summer for adults and children at $50 an hour (with reductions for over 3 hours). The young staff at the centre are very friendly and will provide you with a map of the port. The equipment is in good order.

CULTURAL LIFE

For maps of Toronto, see the first colour plate section.

■ **The Royal Alexandra Theater** (map II, C3, **6**): 260 King Street West ☎ 872-1212 or **Roy Thompson Hall** at 60 Simcoe Street ☎ 593-4828 are worth a visit. Alternatively, watch productions by the **Toronto Free Theater**, which are even more appealing since they are free and in the open air. They are held during a fortnight in summer in High Park (on Bloor Street, at the corner of Parkside Drive). Subway: High Park. For programme information: ☎ 368-3110.

– If you are passionate about classical music catch the **Toronto Symphony Orchestra** at Roy Thompson Hall. ☎ 593-4828.

FESTIVALS AND EVENTS

– **Du Maurier Downtown Jazz Festival**: end of June. Information: ☎ 363-8717. You can hear a number of well-known and top-quality bands performing in the bars along Queen Street West. There's a great atmosphere and the entrance charges are not expensive.

– **Caribana Carnival**: from mid-July to the beginning of August. This is the carnival of the Afro-Canadians and attracts people from all the surrounding areas. It's a festival of fabulous costumes and brilliant colours, of dancing and music. The high point of the carnival is the parade that takes place on the last day of the festivities. Ask about the route at the tourist office. It goes on all afternoon. After the parade there's a big celebration on the Toronto islands for the next two days.

– **International Film Festival**: the second week in September, give or take a day. More than 250 films from around the world are showcased here. Call the tourist office for information (*see* 'Useful Addresses').

– For the huge number of other festivals and events, read the free magazines *Now* and *Eye* that you'll find everywhere around town.

SHOPPING

🔒 **Honest Ed's** (map II, A1, **90**): 581 Bloor Street West, on the corner of Bathurst Street. Subway: Bathurst. This is probably the cheapest shop in Toronto, selling clothes and many useful and useless things. The facade, with its glaring neon signs, would give a Las Vegas casino a run for its money. The motto reads: 'Don't just stand here, buy something.'

🔒 **The World's Biggest Book-store** (map II, C2, **91**): 20 Edward Street, close to Yonge and Dundas Streets. The name says it all really . . .

🔒 **Eaton Centre** (map II, C2, **93**): Yonge Street, between Queen and Dundas streets. Open Monday to Friday 10am–9pm. Saturday 9.30am–6pm. Sunday noon–5pm. This gigantic shopping centre is

one of the biggest in the world and sells just about everything.
≞ The Bay (map II, C3, **92**): 176 Yonge Street (on the corner of Queen Street West). Open Monday to Friday 10am–9pm. Saturday 8am–7pm. Sunday noon–6pm. A branch of the popular Canadian department store. You can not only shop here, but also have a drink or something to eat in either the restaurant, the bar or the café.

LEAVING TORONTO

By Plane

There are two ways of getting to the airport:

– Take the express bus that leaves every 30 minutes from the larger Downtown hotels. The journey takes 40 minutes. You can also get airport buses from some subway stations (check with the tourist office).

– Take the subway to Lawrence West, then the No. 58 bus to the airport (the cheaper alternative, remember to ask for transfers).

By Car

– **For Hamilton** and **Niagara Falls**: Take Highway 2 (Lakeshore Boulevard) or the Gardiner Expressway, and then the Queen Elizabeth Way (QEW). Continue on to Niagara Falls or take Highway 55 towards Niagara-on-the-Lake. From there, take the Niagara Parkway that leads to Niagara Falls – much more appealing than the highway.

– **For Montréal**: Drive north on Yonge Street to Highway 401 and go east. Alternatively, take the Don Valley Parkway from Downtown: go east on Dundas Street or follow Lakeshore Boulevard East to the DVP, and then go north to Highway 401 eastbound.

By Bus

Bus station (map II, C2), Bay and Dundas Streets. ☎ 393-7911. Frequent departures all day for Ottawa, Montréal and Niagara Falls. There's also a regular Greyhound bus that goes as far as North Bay (north of Toronto).

From Toronto to Niagara Falls

The strip of land between Lake Ontario and Lake Erie is mainly planted with orchards and vineyards. Take time to stop, as there are daily wine-tastings and Ontario wines have improved greatly over the years. After Toronto and its industrial suburbs, it's great to breathe in the fresh air. This region is often referred to as Ontario's fruit belt. It has its own micro-climate, thanks to the two great lakes.

It's probably more interesting to tour Niagara-on-the-Lake before taking the superb Niagara Parkway along the Niagara River to Niagara Falls. On the right of the road throughout the summer you'll find numerous farms selling excellent and inexpensive cherries and strawberries. Don't think twice about stopping to buy some.

HAMILTON

This industrial town is about halfway between Toronto and Niagara, 50 kilometres (30 miles) west of Toronto on Highway 2 and 60 kilometres (37 miles) east of Niagara along Route 8 North. There's not much to see, but if you need to stop here, at least visit Castle Dundurn on York Boulevard. Open daily 10am–4pm from 15 June to 1 September and noon–4pm from 2 September to 14 June. Castle Dundurn was the first 'Tuscan-style' villa built in North America, and it's in what was the heart of the area of the ruling classes of Eastern Canada in the 19th century. It was built in 1835 by Sir Allan Napier MacNab, Prime Minister of the United Province of Canada (Ontario, plus today's Québec). Its 35 rooms are admirably furnished and show the life of a rich Victorian gentleman. There's a wonderful view of Lake Ontario from the splendid estate.

NIAGARA-ON-THE-LAKE

Everything is very pretty though expensive in this village of charming 19th-century homes, which have been attractively restored and now mostly transformed into B&Bs. There's a rather English feel about the place with its huge green parks and beautiful location. It's a really pleasant and tranquil spot, a perfect contrast to the frenetic tourism of Niagara Falls.

NIAGARA

USEFUL ADDRESS

🄱 **Chamber of Commerce** (tourist information; map A-B1): on the corner of King Street and Prideaux Street, on the main street. ☎ 468-4263. Open Monday to Friday 9am–5pm in summer. Saturday to Sunday 10am–5pm. Staff can arrange hotel or B&B reservations.

WHERE TO STAY

Staying in the village is very expensive and there is no real reason to stay anyway, unless you're on your honeymoon. In any case, book ahead as it's very touristy here.

☆☆ Moderate ($55–85)

🛏 **Mrs Dietlinde Witt** (map A1, **3**): 341 Dorchester Street. ☎ 468-3989. Three rooms with double beds in this B&B run by a lovely and friendly elderly couple. It's like staying with your grandparents.

Even the birds have their own B&B.

🛏 **Jerri's Bunny Hutch** (map A1, **6**): 305 Centre Street. ☎ 468-3377. The house is decorated with numerous handmade cloth rabbits. You'll receive a warm welcome. Recommended.

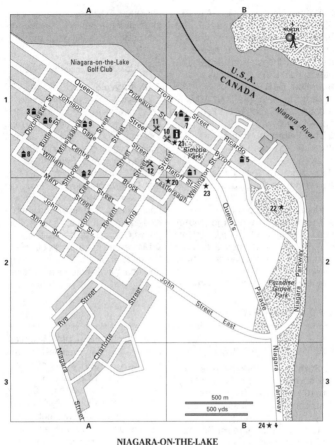

NIAGARA-ON-THE-LAKE

NIAGARA

■ **Useful Address**

🄷 Chamber of Commerce – Tourist Information

🛏 **Where to Stay**

1 Moffat Inn
2 Avalon B&B
3 Mrs Dietlinde Witt
4 The Leighton House
5 The Royal Anchorage Motel
6 Jerri's Bunny Hutch
7 The Old Bank House
8 Almar House
9 Hickoryvale

✕ **Where to Eat**

10 Stagecoach Family Restaurant and Ice Cream Parlour
11 Old Town Ice Cream Shoppe and Restaurant
12 Angel Inn

★ **What to See**

20 Niagara Historical Museum
21 Niagara Apothecary
22 Fort George
23 Shaw Festival Theatre
24 Inniskillin Wines

⌂ **Almar House** (map A1, **8**): 339 Mary Street. ☎ 468-2409. The owner, Marie-Jane, offers guests a charming reading room and bunnies, as in the previous entry. The atmosphere is very peaceful.

⌂ **Avalon B&B** (map A2, **2**): 189 William Street. ☎ 468-2091. This is a comfortable spot with three adequate bedrooms.

⌂ **The Leighton House** (map B1, **4**): 16 Front Street. ☎ 468-3789. A lovely house near the lake which dates from 1820 and has lots of period furniture, floral rugs, paintings and knick-knacks. Breakfast is included. Charming owners.

⌂ **The Royal Anchorage Motel** (map B1, **5**): 186 Ricardo Street. ☎ 468-2141. This is more expensive than a B&B in the summer months. It overlooks the Marina and is not very central. Recently renovated, it

has about 20 en suite rooms and a large dining room with terrace. It's particularly pleasant in summer.

☆☆☆ Expensive ($90–150)

⌂ **Hickoryvale** (map A1, **9**): 276 Mississauga Street. ☎ 468-3015. There are several comfortable and attractive rooms (some overlooking the park), together with a kitchen, sitting room and swimming pool.

⌂ **The Old Bank House** (map B1, **7**): 10 Front Street. ☎ 468-7136. Eight very beautiful rooms in an old bank. Ask for rooms with a view over Lake Ontario. It's very expensive but also quite luxurious, and a very generous breakfast is included.

⌂ **Moffat Inn** (map B2, **1**): 60 Picton Street. ☎ 468-4116. This is a central and charming place, located opposite the park.

WHERE TO EAT

☆☆ Moderate (around $10)

✕ **Stagecoach Family Restaurant and Ice Cream Parlour** (map A1, **10**): 45 Queen Street. A cheap American-style restaurant, open daily 7am–9pm.

✕ **Old Town Ice Cream Shoppe and Restaurant** (map A1, **11**): 61–63 Queen Street. Open 7.30am–

9pm in summer (7pm in winter). Enjoy a decent breakfast in this typically Canadian venue offering a wide selection of ice-cream.

✕ **Angel Inn** (map A1, **12**): 224 Regent Street. Open daily 11.30am–1.30pm. This Irish-style pub has a sombre dining room with a fireplace and small windows with indoor shutters; the food is European.

WHAT TO SEE AND DO

★ **Niagara Historical Museum** (map A–B2, **20**): corner of Castlereagh and Davy streets. Open May to October 10am–5pm and November to April 1pm–5pm. Entrance charge $3 (reductions possible). This was the first museum to be built in the town, in 1907. It houses various collections from the beginning of the 20th century, including military uniforms, crockery, furniture and utensils from daily life. Enjoy a short and nostalgic tour through your grandparents' generation.

★ **Niagara Apothecary** (map B1, **21**): 5 Queen Street, on the corner of King Street. Open mid-May to September noon-6pm. Free entry. This restored pharmacy, dating from 1866, was still operating up to 1964. Ceramic jars, wooden caskets and coloured-glass bottles greet you along with the scent of camphor and polished wood. Note the sculpted wood ceiling with magnificent rose motifs.

★ **Fort George** (map B2, **22**): 26 Queen Street. Open April to October 10am–5pm. Entrance charge $6 (reduced rates possible). Completed in 1802, the fort was built to replace Fort Niagara, which passed into the hands of the Americans and was destroyed in 1813. Guided tours and military manoeuvres by students in uniform bring the 19th century back to life.

★ **Shaw Festival Theatre** (map B2, **23**): 10 Queens Parade. This theatre festival takes place every year from March to November, featuring the works of George Bernard Shaw and several of his contemporaries. Information and tickets: kiosk on corner of Wellington and Picton Streets. ☎ 468-2172.

In the Area

★ **Wineries**: several wineries arrange guided tours. These two are the most interesting and also offer tastings. They're open until 5pm.

– **Inniskillin Wines** (map B3, off **24**): go through Niagara-on-the-Lake and follow the Niagara Parkway for a few kilometres. Look for the sign. ☎ 468-2187. Guided tour at 2.30pm in summer.

– **Hillebrand Winery**: Highway 55, not far from Niagara-on-the-Lake, at exit 38A. ☎ 468-7123. Guided tours at 11am, 1pm, 3pm and 5pm.

– Keep your eyes open for the numerous **fruit markets** all along the Niagara Parkway as you head for Niagara Falls.

NIAGARA FALLS   DIALLING CODE: 905

If you're expecting to find a wild and protected spot, you'll be disappointed – the falls are just outside the town centre, itself a mass of illuminated signs directing visitors to all sorts of different activities. Niagara Falls is like a miniature Las Vegas. Once over the initial surprise, go and see the huge and magnificent falls that make the journey worthwhile. To enjoy the site fully, visit early in the morning, before the crowds of tourists, to appreciate the genuine majesty of the place. According to an old Iroquois legend, the falls were pacified only by the sacrifice of Indian virgins to Niagara, the 'Great Thunder of the Water'.

How Niagara Falls Became So Popular

Joseph Bonaparte, the brother of the Emperor Napoleon, is partly responsible for the fashion of honeymooning at the Falls. Intrigued by the account the French writer and diplomat the Vicomte de Chateaubriand had given of them, in 1803 he decided to make a journey with his young wife, all the way from Louisiana by horse-drawn coach. On his return he gave such a glowing report to the important and influential people of Louisiana that they all followed suit. In the inter-war years of the 20th century, the craze among honeymooners took off as car-ownership increased. Later, when actress Marilyn Monroe (1926–62) went to shoot the film *Niagara* (directed by Henry Hathaway in 1952), the publicity claimed '*Niagara,* the film where two wonders of the world share star billing'. Today there are dozens of attractions, all equally tacky, designed to persuade to visitors that they're having a really good time. (There's even an Elvis Presley Museum.) At night the Falls are illuminated with all the colours of the rainbow.

A Few Statistics

In the summer over 6,810,000 litres (1.5 million gallons) of water cascade over the 54-metre (177-feet) high Falls every second. In the 1950s the limestone was eroding at the rate of 1 metre (3 feet) a year, but since then the water supply to the hydroelectric generators has slowed this down to 30 centimetres (12 inches) a year. The horseshoe of the Falls is 675 metres (2,214 feet) wide. Their spectacular quality comes from their massive power – as much as 5 million horsepower – and the surreal foaming that the waters produce.

Challenging the Falls

In 1859, Jean-François Gravelet, the French acrobat known as Blondin, was the first to challenge the Falls when he walked a tightrope across the river from the American to the Canadian banks, carrying his impresario on his shoulders. In 1901, Annie Taylor, a primary schoolteacher from Michigan, was the first person to go over the Falls successfully in a barrel (she couldn't even swim). However, in 1950 these sort of madcap ventures were banned.

USEFUL ADDRESSES

🛈 Tourist information (map A4): Table Rock House, in front of the Canadian Falls. ☎ 1-800-56FALLS (toll-free). Website: www.niagarafalls tourism.com

■ **Greater Niagara General Hospital** (map A3, **1**): Accident and Emergencies: 5400 Main Street. ☎ 358-0171.

■ **Useful Addresses**

🛈 Tourist Information
1 Greater Niagara General Hospital

🛏 Where to Stay

10 Niagara Youth Hostel
11 Niagara Glen View
12 Happyness Inn
13 Empire Motel
14 Chestnut Inn
15 Glenn Mhor Guesthouse
16 Butterfly Manor
17 Fairway Motel

✕ Where to Eat

31 La Fiesta

★ What to See and Do

40 Table Rock House and Journey Behind the Falls
41 Great Gorge Adventure
42 Maid of the Mist
43 Skylon Tower
44 Helicopter tours
45 Spanish Aero Car
46 Butterfly Conservatory

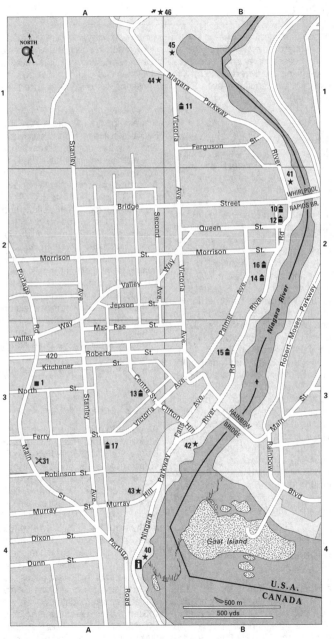

NORTH

A ★ 46

45 ★

44 ★ Niagara Parkway

🏛 11 Victoria

Ferguson St.

River

41 ★ WHIRLPOOL

Bridge Street RAPIDS BR.

10 🏛 St. Rd

Queen St. 12 🏛

Morrison Morrison St.

16 🏛 Ave.

Valley 14 🏛

St.

Way Victoria Ave. Palmer Niagara River Robert Moses Parkway

Jepson St.

Mac Rae St. Ave.

Roberts St. 15 🏛

420 Kitchener St. Ave. RAINBOW St.

■ 1 North St. 13 🏛 Centre St. BRIDGE Main

Victoria Clifton Hill River Ave.

Stanley St. Falls

Ferry St. 🏛 17

✕ 31 Robinson St. 42 ★

Ave. St.

Murray St. Murray 43 ★ Hill

Dixon St. Niagara Parkway Goat Island

Main St. Portage Dunn St. 40 ★ ℹ

Rainbow Blvd

500 m
500 yds

U.S.A.
CANADA

NIAGARA

A B

NIAGARA FALLS

WHERE TO STAY

Although it's well worth a visit, within 3 hours you'll have seen all you need and written home about it, so there's no real reason to spend the night here. In any case, motel prices double in peak season. However, the town is undergoing rapid development with new places opening and closing with extraordinary regularity; even the Falls museum has become a hotel and restaurant.

☆ Budget

⌂ **Niagara Youth Hostel** (map B2, **10**): 4549 Cataract Avenue. ☎ 357-0770. Near the Niagara River, about 3 kilometres (2 miles) from the Falls, and close to the train station. Head towards the river along the road with the train station and Greyhound bus station. It's an attractive building about 100 metres on the right, set back slightly. There are 170 beds, with a dorm bed costing $18 per night and a double room $20 ($25 for non-members). Breakfast is $3.50. You can surf the net for $1 for 10 minutes. Equipped kitchens and bike hire. In summer it's advisable to book by phone, but you must get there before 6pm. Free parking.

⌂ **Niagara Glen View campsite** (map B1, **11**): 3950 Victoria Avenue, near River Road. ☎ 358-8689. It costs about $40 for a pitch in summer at this site, about 3 kilometres (2 miles) from the Falls. There's a shuttle bus every 20 minutes from 10am to 10pm. This is a huge site with spacious, shady sites and a family atmosphere. Facilities include a grocer's shop and small pool. It can be noisy because of the helicopter landing pad nearby.

☆☆ Moderate ($60–90, depending on season and location)

⌂ **Happyness Inn** (map B2, **12**): 4181 Queen Street. ☎ 354-1688. Fax: 354-0041. This renovated motel is in a tranquil spot on the edge of the Niagara River, 2 kilo-

metres (about a mile) from the Falls. Facilities include a fridge, microwave and TV in the room and breakfast is free after two nights' stay. The welcome is friendly.

⌂ **Empire Motel** (map A3, **13**): 5046 Centre Street. ☎ 357-2550. Central, with restaurants, shops and attractions, but can be noisy.

⌂ **Fairway Motel** (map A3, **17**): 5958 Buchanan Avenue. ☎ 357-3005. Fax: 357-3659. Has a swimming pool, and offers the best value for money given its location and the local fluctuation in prices.

– There are several other motels on Lundy's Lane, served by the Falls shuttle bus that runs from 8am to 11pm. Alternatively, take the No. 3 bus in the summer. The farther you stay from the Falls, the lower the price.

☆☆☆ Expensive (over $90)

As you approach from the Niagara Parkway, along River Road and before you reach the Falls, you'll come across a number places to stay with 'Tourist Home' boards hanging outside. Here are a few good places (it's advisable to book):

⌂ **Chestnut Inn** (map B2, **14**): 4983 River Road. ☎ 374-7623. A modern house which looks a bit Victorian, with very well-maintained rooms, two of which have direct access to the roof terrace. Some of the rooms can also accommodate children.

⌂ **Glen Mhor Guesthouse** (map B3, **15**): 5381 River Road. ☎ 354-2600. Five tasteful rooms, and a superb patio where you can enjoy breakfast, including freshly baked bread. Private parking.

⚓ **Butterfly Manor** (map B2, **16**): 4917 River Road. ☎ and fax: 358-8988. Lovely rooms with splendid bathrooms. Real luxury but with prices to match.

In the Area

⚓ **Crystal Beach Motel**: 122 Ridgeway Rd. ☎ 894-1750. Fax: 894-3691. Rooms start at $67, and facilities include air-conditioning, TV, microwave and fridge. Also has a swimming pool.

WHERE TO EAT

This is a tricky question, as all that's on offer is Burger King, Pizza Hut and Planet Hollywood, plus other variations such as Wendy, Swiss Chalet and Red Lobster. However, there is one alternative:

✕ **La Fiesta** (map A3, **31**): 6072 Main Street, north of Robinson Street. Open Monday to Friday 11am–8pm. Saturday to Sunday 11am–9pm. The walls are decorated with fishing nets and starfish. The food is simple but good and includes delicious homemade cakes. Fish and chips cost $4–15 and takeaways are available. Private parking.

WHAT TO SEE AND DO

The Falls are much more beautiful on the Canadian side, from where you get an impressive horseshoe-shaped vista. In comparison, all you see from the American side is a tiny trickle. There is, however, a lovely walk in the park on the US side. If you come by bus from Buffalo (United States), don't forget your passport.

★ **Table Rock House** (map A4, **40**): In the centre of the balcony that looks over the Falls, apart from the superb view of the Falls, take a look at the interesting array of people who have travelled from around the world to see the spectacle. You can also change money here.

★ **Journey behind the Falls** (map A4, **40**): The ticket office is in Table Rock House, open 9am–10pm. Pay $6.50 and then don a canary-yellow waterproof jacket before taking the lift to the entrance of the mysterious underground tunnels. There are three narrow views of the Falls, two of them from underneath and the other a little farther away. It's an amazing feeling to realize you are behind the waterfalls, but all you actually see is a curtain of water.

★ **Skylon Tower** (map A4, **43**): Enjoy a spectacular view of the Falls from the top of the tower, and pay $8.50 for the pleasure.

★ **Maid of the Mist** (map B3, **42**): The boat operates from 9am to 8pm and costs $10.65. This exciting and good-value trip is the best way of getting inside the Falls (well, almost). Dressed in blue waterproofs, you'll be transported amid the mists.

★ **Great Gorge Adventure** (map B2, **41**): A good way of spending extra time and money is to take this walk along the Niagara River for $5.25.

★ **Helicopter trips** (map A1, **44**): Enjoy spectacular flights over the Falls for $85.

NIAGARA

– **Spanish Aero Car** (map B1, **45**): Open 9am–6pm (weather permitting). $5.50 ($2.75 for children). You'll find yourself in a metal cockpit above the natural pool downstream from the Falls.

– Pop music fans may like to visit the large **Rainbow Bridge** that crosses the river, as sung about by Jimi Hendrix. But even pedestrians have to pay the toll into Canada.

– **Butterfly Conservatory** (map, off A1, **46**): 2665 Niagara Parkway, in the Niagara Parks Botanical Garden. Open 9am–8pm (9pm in high season). Entrance charge $8 (reductions possible). Enjoy the exotic atmosphere of this large greenhouse, surrounded by fluttering butterflies. You can even attend their hatchings in the nursery.

IN THE AREA

★ **Fort Erie**: Open 10am–6pm mid-May to October. Set in a superb park near the mouth of the Niagara River on Lake Erie, with a lovely view across to Buffalo in the United States. The old fortress, destroyed by the Americans in 1814, still looks imposing. Its museum exhibits historic English and American military uniforms. There are guided tours, and shows and firing practice by students take place throughout the day.

★ **Welland Canal**: Situated about 15 kilometres (9 miles) from Niagara Falls, the canal has a series of locks of impressive proportions, through which enormous tankers navigate up the narrow channel from Lake Ontario to Lake Erie. The best view is from the Observation Deck high above lock No. 3.

★ **Crystal Beach**: If you continue beyond Fort Erie you'll reach this popular holiday resort with a large, clean beach, but you have to pay for the pleasure. Besides the charming lakeside holiday homes belonging to Americans and Torontonians, there isn't much to see but you can stay in one of the nearby motels if you fancy spending the night.

Kitchener and Waterloo

This is an area of real countryside, full of orchards and dotted with lots of elegant little Victorian towns. The region is noted for the Mennonite communities established by descendants of some of the first German immigrants. You'll find them in the villages of **St Jacobs** or **Elmira**: take Highway 86 north from Waterloo (10 kilometres/6 miles) where, every April, they hold the Maple Syrup Festival. Members of this Protestant sect still live as they did at the beginning of the 19th century – without electricity or cars, travelling only in horse-drawn traps. The men wear broad-brimmed black hats, while the women wear tight bonnets covering their hair. However, these outwardly austere, frugal peasant farmers are often very rich landowners. They are also the only pork butchers in Ontario, making sausages of all kinds.

ST JACOBS

DIALLING CODE: 519

A pretty little riverside village in the heart of the Mennonite region, St-Jacobs has lots to offer visitors, and is very good for shopping, in particular at the Farmers' Market (*see below*).

USEFUL ADDRESS

🛈 Tourist information: 33 King St. Open Monday–Saturday 11am–5pm. Sunday 1.30–5pm.

WHAT TO SEE AND DO

★ **Museum**: 33 King St. In the same place as the tourist information office is this exhibition of the history and lifestyle of the Mennonites.

★ **Arts and Crafts shops**: You'll find a variety in the town centre.

★ **St Jacobs' Farmers' Market**: Located between Waterloo and St Jacobs. Open Thursday and Saturday 7am–3.30pm (also Tuesday in summer, 8am–3pm). As many as 350 local farmers (Mennonites and others) come here to display and sell their farm produce and crafts in huge wooden barns. The market is one of the most extraordinary in eastern Canada – a festival of colours and smells, such as spices and maple.

– **The Quilt Festival**: Held every year during the second two weeks in May, this is a wonderful exhibition of patchworks and quilts.

ELORA

DIALLING CODE: 519

Situated about 20 kilometres (13 miles) north of Waterloo, Elora is a small town that has managed to retain the charm of its old stonework. Take a stroll before enjoying a picnic in the Grand River Park, where the water flows into the base of a canyon.

🛈 Tourist information: 128 Geddes St. ☎ 846-9841. Open daily 10am–6pm (in winter 8.30am–4.30pm). The office is just down the road from the public library.

WHAT TO SEE

★ **Town centre**: The windmill, now converted into an inn, the narrow streets and 19th-century houses are worth a look.

★ **Grand River Park**: 400 Clyde Road. ☎ 621-2761. Fax: 621-4844. Website: www.grandriver.on.ca. Open April to October. Entrance charge $3.50. As in most Canadian parks, this is geared towards camping, and a pitch costs $10. You can enjoy various activities in the gorges around the falls. It's a popular spot for family picnics at the weekend and also a meeting place for clubs.

ONTARIO

★ **Elora Festival**: Held from mid-July to mid-August, there's something for every taste and budget ($10–40), from jazz and classical music to pop concerts and dance. Contact the Elora Festival Office, 33 Henderson St. ☎ 846-0331. Fax: 846-5947. Website: www.elora.org

★ **West Montrose**: south of Elora. This is the last remaining covered bridge of its kind in Ontario, built in 1880 and still in operation. It crosses the Grand River and is 60 metres (197 feet) in length.

STRATFORD   DIALLING CODE: 519

This large market town is full of charm, and follows the rhythm of the Theatre Festival that attracts more and more people every year. Many Toronto dwellers come for the weekend to see one or two stage productions and to enjoy walking in the many parks along the river. The Shakespeare Festival produces an average of 13 plays in 6 months. The programme is of both modern and classical plays. On Monday evenings the plays are replaced by classical music and jazz concerts.

USEFUL ADDRESSES

Tourist information: 30 York Street, near the river. ☎ 273-3352 or 1-800-561-SWAN (toll-free). Open in summer Tuesday to Saturday 9am–8pm. Sunday and Monday 9am–5pm. A notice-board displays photographs of houses offering tourist accommodation in town, with prices. You can also check out the menus of the local restaurants in this helpful and informative office.

Bus terminal: 101 Shakespeare Street, at the train station. ☎ 1-800-265-6037 (toll-free) or 271-7870.
■ **Police**: ☎ 271-4141.
■ **Hospital**: ☎ 272-8210.
■ **Bicycle hire**: Maiden Inn Store, 123 Church Street. ☎ 271-7129. Best to book ahead.

WHERE TO STAY

Stratford Trailer Park: 20 Glastonbury Drive. ☎ 271-5832. This central and clean site has over 200 pitches, costing $12–16 per night.
Brunswick House: 109 Brunswick Street. ☎ 271-4546. In a well-known spot near the Avon Theatre is this lovely house dating back to 1857, prettily decorated and run by charming people. There's a large room that can accommodate four. Breakfast is available.

Burnside Guest-Home: 139 William Street. ☎ 271-7076. Pleasant little house with four comfortable and clean rooms (student reductions of $25). Pretty garden on the riverbank. Good breakfast of muffins and homemade jams. Non-smokers only.
Rosecourt Motel: 599 Erie Street (across from Jarvis Street). ☎ 271-6005. Out of town, and closed between November and April. The friendly owner is of Hawaiian origin. Breakfast is available.

WHERE TO EAT

☆☆ Moderate (under $10)

✗ **York Street Kitchen**: 41 York Street, opposite the tourist office. Open 8am–8pm. Sandwiches and tasty salads are served, including large take-away sandwiches with a choice of fillings. Alternatively you can eat in the small pastel-coloured dining room.

✗ **Ellam's**: 115 Ontario Street. Open 7am–11pm. Substantial breakfasts are on offer at this pleasant but kitsch and brightly lit spot.

✗ **Elizabethan Restaurant**: 95 Ontario Street. Open Monday to Saturday 9am–7pm. You'll get a warm welcome here. There are four dining rooms with small tables covered with red checked tablecloths. It's a bit dingy and shabby, but the meals are generous and cheap.

– You'll find other nice restaurants and bars in **Ontario Street** and there are a number of fairly smart and pretty pricey restaurants clustered around the little square in the centre of town.

WHERE TO HAVE A DRINK

❢ **Down The Street**: 30 Ontario Street. ☎ 273-5886. Open Monday to Saturday 11am–midnight. This is a trendy spot, so booking's advisable. Try to get the table at the back for attractive river views.

WHAT TO SEE AND DO

★ **The Gallery Stratford**: 54 Romeo Street, just outside the centre. Open 9am–6pm (noon–7pm on Monday in July and August); in winter 10am–5pm. Entrance charge $8. This is a small gallery showing interesting temporary exhibitions of sculpture, ceramics and design.

– **Stratford Shakespeare Festival**: After a faltering start in 1953, the Festival gradually became established with famous theatre companies and developed a real following. In addition to Shakespeare's plays, it also includes works by Molière, Wilde, Chekhov and others.

Performances take place most days between May and November (except on Monday) at 2pm and 8pm in one of three theatres: **The Festival**, **The Avon** and **The Tom Patterson**. Tickets cost $20–75. The cheapest (rush) seats are on sale from 9am only on the day of the performance, at the Festival Theatre box office. There are no rush seats for the Tom Patterson. Note that some seats at the Avon Theatre have restricted views of the stage. Make sure to ask about the special performances for students.

The Festival Theatre is near the river and Queen's Park; the Avon Theatre is on George Street, not far from City Hall; and the Tom Patterson Theatre is near the river between Waterloo and Nile Streets.

Information: ☎ (416) 363-4471 (Toronto); 1-800-567-1600 (Stratford). Details are available from the Festival Theatre or the tourist office. To book in writing: Stratford Festival Box Office, P.O. Box 520, Stratford, Ontario, Canada N5A 6V2. Website: www.stratford-festival.on.ca. In Toronto, you can buy tickets from the Roy Thomson Hall at 60 Simcoe Street.

ONTARIO

– **Festival City Days**: Ask for a list of the festivities at the tourist office. A programme of events starts in May.

GRAND BEND
DIALLING CODE: 519

Many Canadians spend their holidays at this small resort on the shore of Lake Huron, with lovely beaches and relatively unpolluted water. The sunset reflected in the lake is superb. Night owls can stay in the village and enjoy the pleasant, trendy atmosphere.

USEFUL ADDRESSES

❸ Tourist office: corner of Highway Street and Main Street, on the left, set back a little from the road. ☎ 238-2001. Open 10am–7pm in summer only.

■ **Police**: ☎ 238-2345.
■ **Medical centre**: ☎ 238-2362.

WHERE TO STAY AND EAT

– There are a number of smart hotels across from the beach on the right as you arrive, along the main road. If you're here midweek, don't hesitate to ask for a big discount and haggle.

– All the restaurants are expensive and not very good, so stock up at the grocery stores and picnic on the beach.

â Pinary Provincial Park: entrance on Highway 21, a few kilometres from Grand Bend. ☎ 243-2220. Reservations: ☎ 243-3099. Open 8am–10pm. Several areas of the park have been laid out as campsites, where pitches cost around $30. Dune Campground is the most popular and therefore the busiest. Burley Campground is quieter and more pleasant, but a little farther away. Both are near the beach.
â Fountainblue Motel: 30 Highway 21N, between Oak Street and Main Street. ☎ 238-2339. Rooms cost $80. The carpets are worn and the interior is rather tired, but it does have a swimming pool.

WHAT TO DO

★ **Pinary Provincial Park**: a few kilometres from Grand Bend. ☎ 243-2220. Open daily 8am–10pm. Entrance charge $8 per vehicle. Those in search of peace and quiet should try this park which offers a range of walks through a wonderful pine forest perched on high sandy dunes.

However, one drawback is poison ivy, which is essential to the local ecosystem and grows almost everywhere in the park. The rangers will help you to identify it. Animals and birds love it but if humans have even the slightest physical contact with the plant it causes skin irritation and serious itching. It's rather like a nettle sting but much worse. If you do get stung, wash with soap and water and try not to scratch.

– **Pinary Antique Flea Market**: held every Sunday between April and October 8.30am–5pm. You'll find this on the left-hand side of the road along Highway 21 between Grand Bend and the park.

– **Swimming**: Pinary park has nearly 10 kilometres (6 miles) of beaches. Since most people head to the same few spots, there are many others where you can enjoy the sun and lake, relatively undisturbed.

– **Canoeing**: You can hire boats from the centre of the park for an enjoyable trip along the river, but it gets very busy at the weekend. **Bicycles** are also available for $6 per hour.

– **Walking trails**: The park rangers distribute maps at the entrance detailing 10 walks. The Wilderness Trail (3 kilometres/2 miles) takes you through the dunes, past some lovely views of the lake and ends on a very beautiful beach with fine sand.

Grand Bend to Owen Sound

Highway 21 takes you from Grand Bend to Owen Sound along the shores of Lake Huron, via a succession of small provincial parks, golf courses, campsites, small airports and peaceful market towns. Many inhabitants of Toronto spend their weekends in this relatively isolated lakeside spot. The local villages are not particularly lively, but they do have a pleasant holiday feel.

USEFUL ADDRESSES

🚻 **Owen Sound Visitor's Information Centre**: 1155 First Avenue West, in the former station building on the edge of the Sydenham River. ☎ 371-9833. Fax: 371-8628. Open Monday to Friday between May and September 8.30am–5pm. Saturday and Sunday noon–4pm.

🚌 **Bus terminal**: corner of 3rd and 10th streets, Owen Sound. ☎ 376-5375. Three daily departures to Toronto Monday to Saturday, and two departures on Sunday. The journey takes 3 hours 30 minutes.

WHERE TO STAY AND EAT

🛏 **The Bluffs Motel**: 5 kilometres (3 miles) before Goderich on Highway 21. ☎ 524-9199. Rooms start at $50 at this unpretentious and friendly motel run by Bill and Dorothy.

🛏 **Colborne** and **Huron campsites**: Point Farms Provincial Park. Information and reservations: ☎ 524-7124.

In Owen Sound

🛏 **Diamond Motor Inn**: 713 Ninth Avenue East, at Highway 6 and 10. ☎ (519) 371-2011. Fax: 371-9460. There are 22 well-maintained rooms with kitchenette from $89. The owner will advise you enthusiastically on which local sights to visit.

🍴 **Channing Restaurant**: 1002 Second Avenue. ☎ (519) 376-0718. Open 11am or noon to between 9 and 11.30pm depending on the day. Generous portions of tasty Canadian and Chinese specialities to suit all palates from around $6.

ONTARIO

WHAT TO SEE

★ **Goderich**: This is a very typical small, conservative town. With parallel streets, tidy lawns and flowerbeds in front of lovely homes sporting national flags, there's a slightly smug feel about it. The town's main streets radiate from the courthouse, and there's a sense of social order about the place. Stop by the lakeside at dusk to watch the sunset over the water.

– A little to the north of Goderich is **Point Farms Provincial Park**, which is less attractive than Pinary Park, but has two lovely campsites at the water's edge (*see* 'Where to Stay').

★ **Owen Sound**: This is a small town on the road to the Bruce Peninsula.

★ **Ingils Falls**: Scenic Route, on 2nd Avenue East. Of course nothing compares with Niagara Falls, but this is a pretty little corner where nature is still unspoiled and you can forget that there's a town nearby. Enjoy the lovely view over the forest and Harrison Park.

THE BRUCE–TOBERMORY PENINSULA

DIALLING CODE: 519

The Bruce Peninsula, 80 kilometres (50 miles) in length, is effectively the Niagara escarpment and separates Georgia Bay from the main basin of Lake Huron.

GETTING THERE

– From Owen Sound, take Highway 6 north towards Tobermory.

– For a more scenic route, follow the shoreline of Owen Sound to Tobermory and enjoy a lovely view of Georgia Bay. The waters are blue and transparent but very cold. There are lots of small country roads lined with fields, pine trees and farms.

USEFUL ADDRESSES

🛈 Visitor's Centre: Tobermory Chamber of Commerce, Highway 6 (as you enter town). ☎ 596-2452. Open 9am–9pm in summer.
🛈 National Park Visitor's Centre: in the port. ☎ 596-2233. Open 9am–9pm in summer only. Information about the peninsula's two national parks – Bruce Peninsula Park and National Marine Park.
■ **Clinic**: ☎ 596-2305.
■ **Police**: ☎ 1-800-310-1122 or 596-2426.

■ **Canoe hire**: Cedar Grove Cottages, near Cameron Lake. ☎ 596-2267 or Tobermory Adventure, 112 Bay South. ☎ 596-2289.
■ **Bicycle hire**: Lands End Park Campground. ☎ 596-2523 or Tobermory Adventure, 112 Bay South. ☎ 596-2289.
■ **Bank**: Royal Bank, 7371 Highway 6, on the left just before town, virtually opposite the Esso station.

ONTARIO

WHERE TO STAY

🛏 **Tobermory Village Campground**: 3 kilometres (2 miles) south of Tobermory, on Highway 6. ☎ 596-2689. Well-run campsite with swimming pool.

🛏 **Cyprus Lake Campground**: Bruce Peninsula Park, 10 kilometres (6 miles) south of Tobermory. Open May–September. Bookings taken Monday to Friday 8am–4pm. ☎ 596-2263. Fax: 596-2433. Camp out in the wilds at the water's edge.

There are really lovely walks, canoe trips or bike rides, but watch out for the mosquitoes.

🛏 **Peacock Villa Motel**: From Highway 6, take the small road on the left by the port (it's signposted). ☎ 596-2242. A good location with double rooms at $63 and chalets from $73. Choose between a classic, motel-style room and a picturesque wooden chalet in the trees. Barbecues are available for the use of guests.

WHERE TO EAT

✗ **Lion's Head Restaurant**: 8 Helen Street, Lion's Head. Open Monday to Saturday 11am–11pm. Sunday noon–8pm. Dishes cost between $6 and $14 in this English pub with a covered terrace, serving traditional American food.

✗ **Shipwreck Lee's**: on the left as you head down to the port. ☎ 596-2177. Open May to September.

Dishes cost $6–17. Masks from all over the world decorate the walls and the menu is designed like a newspaper, with information, games and puzzles. The waiters will give you a free spray of mosquito repellent during your meal.

✗ **Crowsnest**: opposite Shipwreck Lee's, above. A selection of reasonably priced breakfast specials.

WHAT TO SEE AND DO

★ **Singing Sands**: Dorcas Bay Road, 5 kilometres (3 miles) south of Tobermory, on the shore of Lake Huron. The beach has a border of pine trees and you can swim in warm water about 1 metre deep for over 2 kilometres (1 mile). Canadians come here for family picnics on summer evenings.

★ **Bruce Peninsula Park**: 10 kilometres (6 miles) south of Tobermory, on Highway 6. Entrance charge $6 per car. Information: ☎ 596-2233. Lots of marked walking trails crisscross the park, including a selection that take about an hour and depart from Lake Cyprus.

– **The Bruce Trail** stretches for about 800 kilometres (500 miles) along the Niagara escarpment from Queenston to Tobermory and reveals some really impressive countryside. For further information, contact the Bruce Trail Association in Hamilton. ☎ 1-800-665-4453 (toll-free) or ☎ (905) 529-6821.

– **The Georgian Bay** trail leads to the edge of the escarpment and offers fantastic panoramas, steep cliffs, caves, white pebble beaches and crystal-clear waters. On reaching Halfway Rock you should be able to make out Flowerport and Bears Rump Islands in the distance before passing through a natural arch and a cave, both carved out of the porous dolomite rock by the waves.

★ **Fathom Five National Marine Park**: This group of five islands includes the famous Flowerpot Island, whose limpid waters, wrecks and rocky depths

ONTARIO

make it one of the best places for freshwater diving in Canada. Both experienced divers and beginners congregate here. Wrecks are visible from the boats sailing to Flowerpot Island. Information is available from the Divers' Registration Centre in the port: ☎ 596-2503

– The islands: Several ferry companies, all based in the harbour, organize similar trips around the islands for around $10 per person. There are frequent departures every day in summer, from 9am. The views, rocks and light-houses are all unusually striking. If you have an entire day to spare, spend the morning on an island and enjoy a picnic. But bring provisions as you can't buy water or food on the islands.

MANITOULIN ISLAND   DIALLING CODE: 705

The largest island surrounded by fresh water in the world, this strip of land – bathed by the chilly waters of Lake Huron and Georgia Bay – is 100 kilometres (60 miles) long and 40 kilometres (25 miles) wide. It's a quiet spot hardly spoiled by tourists. As there's no public transport you'll need a car or a bike. One thing is for sure: you come here to make the most of nature rather than to party. However, the island does liven up during the first weekend of August when the annual powwows (traditional tribal festivals) take place, as a third of its inhabitants are originally from First Nation tribes.

GETTING THERE

⚓ **Chi-Cheemaun Schedule**: the ferry from Tobermory harbour to South Baymouth on Manitoulin Island also takes cars. Information at the ferry terminal in Tobermory: ☎ (519) 596-2510 or the terminal at South Baymouth: ☎ (705) 859-3161. Departures leave Tobermory at 7am, 11.20am, 3.40pm and 8pm in the summer. Go to Manitoulin Island just for the day (the last ferry leaves South Baymouth at 10pm).

USEFUL ADDRESSES

🛈 **Tourist information**: two offices to choose from:
– Arrival by road: **Manitoulin Information Centre**, Little Current (on the right after the bridge). Open end-April to end-October. ☎ 368-3021. Fax: 368-3802. The centre will make ferry reservations for you.
– Arrival by ferry: South Baymouth ferry terminal. Open 8am–8pm.
■ **Sue's taxi**: ☎ 368-3293.

WHERE TO STAY

🛏 **Providence Bay Park Campsite**: Providence Bay. ☎ 377-4650. Open daily 9am–9pm. It's fairly central, across the road from the beach, and is used mainly by families and overseas visitors.

🛏 **Bridgeway Motel**: Little Current, Highway 6 North on the road to Espanola. ☎ 368-2242. Simple, practical rooms at reasonable prices.

WHAT TO SEE

★ The fine sandy beach at **Providence Bay** is fabulous.

★ There's a fantastic viewpoint at **Cup & Saucer**, on Highway 540 between West Bay and Little Current. The walking trail takes about 1 hour and offers truly magnificent panoramic views of the forest and the lakes.

★ **Indian Reservations**: West Bay and Wikwemikong. These have nothing special to see outside the tribal festival events, but there are some shops selling native crafts.

BLUE MOUNTAIN DISTRICT   DIALLING CODE: 705

From Thornbury to Collingwood

The small village of Thornbury is known for its skiing, but if you descend too fast you may end up in the lake.

Craigleith is a small and peaceful town at the foot of the Blue Mountains that's gradually becoming *the* place to ski. It also marks the highest point in the Niagara escarpment.

USEFUL ADDRESSES

目 Tourist Information Centre: 601 First Street, Collingwood, at the junction with Highway 26. ☎ 445-7722 or 445-0748. It can arrange hotel bookings.

■ Ski and bicycle hire: There are several shops below the Blue Mountain Auberge and the ski lifts in Craigleith.

WHERE TO STAY

🛏 Blue Mountain Auberge: Craigleith, near the ski lifts and Blue Mountain Inn complex (don't confuse the two). ☎ 445-1497. There are 83 beds in this charming mountain chalet, costing from $70 per night (half price for youth hostel members). Phone ahead for availability. Facilities include kitchens, a sauna, large sitting room with cosy open fire. There are walking trails nearby and you can hire mountain bikes in the summer, opposite the inn at the foot of the hill.

WHAT TO SEE AND DO

★ **Scenic Caves**: Scenic Caves Road, just before Collingwood. Open mid-May to mid-October (weather permitting). ☎ 446-0256. Entrance charge $8 (reductions possible). Here you can look at the fossils and stunning panoramas, and follow a trail to the summit of the mountain (about 1 hour 30 minutes) for superb views over Nottawasaga Bay.

– **Skiing**: Available from mid-December to mid-March in Craigleith and Thornbury.

– **Hiking** and **mountain biking** (*see* Blue Mountain Auberge for bike rental).

ONTARIO

WASAGA BEACH   DIALLING CODE: 705

The long beaches of Nottawasaga Bay are becoming increasingly popular and touristy. There's no feeling of wilderness here, but the beaches here are still fabulous. At 14 kilometres (about 9 miles), Wasaga Beach is claimed to be the world's longest stretch of freshwater beach.

USEFUL ADDRESS

⊟ Visitor Information: Beach areas 1 and 2, near the amusement park. ☎ 429-1120. Open 10am–5pm in summer only.

WHERE TO STAY

– The town is full of motels, properties and rooms for rent by the day, week or month on the waterfront and on Highway 92. They are generally expensive and of variable quality.

– There's no municipal campsite and the private campsite costs from $30 per night. They tend to be very busy and pack you in like sardines.

⚐ Jell-E-Bean Park Camping Ground: No. 121 on Highway 26, just before the junction with Highway 92. ☎ 429-5418. A family campsite with small swimming pool, just 2 minutes' walk from the beach.

⚐ Cedar Grove Park: opposite the Jell-E-Bean Park, with the same prices. ☎ 429-2134. Good facilities, plus moorings, bicycles and canoes for hire.

WHAT TO SEE AND DO

★ **Nancy Island Historic Site**: Mosley Street, in the centre opposite the tourist office. ☎ 429-2728. The museum is free but you pay to park. Nancy Island is composed of alluvial soil that gathered around the wreck of the British ship the *Nancy* that sank in the Nottawasaga River while seeking cover from American attacks.

– **Water World**: Beach area 1. There's a giant water slide and a variety of swimming pools.

PENETANGUISHENE   DIALLING CODE: 705

'The place of rolling white sands' in the local tribal language is a very well-protected small port in the very heart of Huron country. The Hurons were a partially settled tribe and sworn enemies of the Iroquois. The town is also known by the shorter name 'Penetang'. Leaving the little port there's a superb trip through the Thirty Thousand Islands. Worth visiting are the very interesting naval and military establishments.

USEFUL ADDRESSES

🅑 **Tourist office**: in the port. ☎ 549-2232. Open daily in summer 9am–5pm.

🚌 **Bus terminal**: PMCL, Robert Street (on the corner of Main Street).

To Toronto: three departures daily from 10 Robert Street, in front of the church. For information on fares and timetables: ☎ 549-3388. Website: www.midlandtours.com

WHERE TO STAY

☆ Budget

⚓ **Awenda Provincial Park Campground**: at the tip of the peninsula, a few kilometres out of town. ☎ 549-2231. Open 8am–8pm. A simple campground in total harmony with nature, charging from $20 per night. It's a really lovely place not far from the lake (but some distance from the beach), with lots of walking trails.

☆☆ Moderate ($50–80)

⚓ **Chesham Grove Bed & Breakfast**: 72 Church Street. ☎ 549-3740. The cheapest B&B in Penetang is near the town centre and offers clean and quiet rooms with excellent breakfast.

⚓ **Chez Vous Chez Nous Couette et Café** ('quilt and coffee' B&B): 160 Lafontaine Road West, Lafontaine (3 kilometres/2 miles from Penetanguishene). ☎ 533-2237. Housed in a large white building amid the fields in this village where some 60 per cent of the inhabitants speak French. Georgette will charm you with her hospitality and culinary expertise. The brightly coloured rooms have been decorated with care and it's an ideal spot for large families. Her husband will gladly recount the tale of the 'wolf of Lafontaine'.

⚓ **1 Jury Drive Bed & Breakfast**: 1 Jury Drive. ☎ 549-6851. Website: www.jurydrbb.huronia.com. Near the theatre and Harbour Discovery. It's number one on the street and on the list of B&Bs in the area. Everything is perfect, except perhaps for the lack of bike hire.

WHERE TO EAT

☆☆ Moderate (around $10)

✖ **Chez France, Naturellement**: 63 Main Street. Enjoy pizzas and salads at $4–8. This is the canteen attached to the Centre d'Activités Françaises where you can enjoy a meal while watching what is going on in the radio studio. This is just the spot to practise your French.

✖ **Memories Road House**: 32 Main Street. Open daily until 9pm. Decent food at a venue that owes its name to the antiques displayed in the dining room.

✖ **The Dock Lunch**: in the port. Open 8am–9pm (later on Friday and Saturday). American snackbar where you can almost dip your toes in the water. Perfect for filling a hole after a trip around Thirty Thousand Islands. A hamburger comes with every conceivable condiment, including onions, olives, sweetcorn, ketchup and sauces in every shade and flavour you've ever heard of (and some you haven't).

ONTARIO

WHAT TO SEE AND DO

★ **Discovery Harbour**: end of Jury Drive, 3 kilometres (2 miles) from town. Follow signs for King's Wharf Theatre from town. Open 10am–5pm (last admission 4.15pm). Entrance charge (student reduction). This early 19th-century arsenal has been converted into a museum enlivened by students in period costume. Consisting of 15 buildings, it used to be part of the fort which was the English headquarters during the war against the Americans in 1812. Each building presents a different aspect of life in the arsenal – warehouses, living quarters, the dockyard and even a theatre. Children can also take an active part by learning how to tie knots or helping to repair a boat. There are also lovely views of the surrounding countryside and seascape from here.

★ **Cedar Point and Christian Island**: In the extreme south of the peninsula is a tiny port where a ferry crosses to Christian Island – a reservation belonging to the Ojibwe tribe. There are several departures Monday to Friday 7am–5pm and Saturday and Sunday 7am–7pm. A return trip with car costs $40, and $8 for foot passengers. The Hurons took refuge on this very poor island, as did the Jesuit missionaries after the massacre of Fort Sainte-Marie in 1649. When they started out to cross the frozen lake, the ice broke, sounding the death knell for the Huron Nation. The reservation holds no particular attractions but it gives an insight into the plight of one of the First Nations in Canada. The visit is instructive, but don't take any photos. You can also camp here.

– **Boat trip**: You can take a lovely cruise through the Thirty Thousand Islands on the steamer *Georgian Queen*. ☎ 549-7795. It departs at 2pm from the left of the tourist office between June and September, takes 3 hours and costs $15. You can eat on board and enjoy the wild countryside and jagged coastline, bathed in light.

Adventure Sailing Plus: Sailing enthusiasts can enjoy different activities from around $39. ☎ 549-1032.

– **Beaches**: As you follow the southwest coast of the peninsula from Penetang, you'll come across a multitude of wide, sandy beaches and small rocky creeks, including Balm Beach, Rowntree Beach, Tiny Beach and Lafontaine Beach. The routes leading to the beaches traverse wooded countryside lined with tiny villages such as **Lafontaine**, with its charming red-roofed church.

MIDLAND   DIALLING CODE: 705

Midland is a very popular holiday resort (although don't expect Mediterranean-style nightlife) with a significant place in Huron history. This is where the French Jesuits distinguished themselves in their determination to convert the Huron Indians, and there's still a substantial community of French-speakers and Huron Indians in the area. It's a multi-faceted place but, despite its pretty houses, only of limited interest.

A BRIEF HISTORY

The word 'Huron' comes from the French 'hure'. Whenever the French sailors saw a Huron they would shriek: 'Quelles hures!' ('Look at the boar's heads!'), because of the native's startling crested haircut that reminded the sailors of the neck hair of a boar or pig. The Hurons' actual name was the *Ouendat*. There were 30,000 of them at the time the French Jesuit Jean de Brébeuf first described them. They were farmers living in settlements, but quickly turned to trading furs with the French who brought them flour, tobacco, corn and other provisions and goods. The Iroquois, the Hurons' enemies and thus enemies of the French, launched numerous attacks that gradually decimated the poorly armed tribe.

This was the situation the first missionaries (reformed Franciscan monks) and then the Jesuits came to know during the years from 1615 to 1650. They brought the Good Word with them, but in fact they contributed to the moral and physical annihilation of the Hurons, sowing discord among families and deepening the hatred of the Iroquois.

USEFUL ADDRESSES

🛈 **Tourist Information**: Midland Chamber of Commerce, 208 King Street. ☎ 526-7884. Fax: 526-1744. Open Monday to Friday 8am–6pm in summer. Saturday and Sunday 10am–6pm. Closed Saturday and Sunday in winter.
✉ **Post Office**: 525 Dominion Avenue.

■ **Police**: 250 Second Street. ☎ 526-2201.
🚌 **Bus terminal**: PMCL, 475 Bay Street. ☎ 526-0161. For Toronto: three daily departures (7.10am, 11.45am and 5pm).
■ **Car hire**: Budget Rent-a-Car, 725 Vinden Street. ☎ 526-4300.
■ **Hospital**: 1112 St Andrews Drive. ☎ 526-3751.

WHERE TO STAY

☆ Budget (from $15)

There are very large campsites, and you can also rent cottages by the week in high season. A complete list of accommodation is available from the tourist office.
♨ **Bayfort Camp**: end of Ogden's Beach Road, behind the memorial to Canadian martyrs. ☎ 526-8704. On the shore of Lake Huron is this very well-equipped campsite, but the washing facilities are a bit old. Pitches are $18 per night. It has a small beach.
♨ **Smith's Trailer Park & Camp**: King Street, near Little Lake. ☎ 526-4339. Centrally located and open throughout the year (some people even spend all year here), this costs from $17 per night. Pitch your tent among the mobile homes and enjoy a swim in the lake. The supermarket and facilities are in need of updating.

☆☆ Moderate (around $50)

♨ **Shamrock Motel**: 955 Yonge Street (west of Midland). ☎ 526-7851. Double rooms cost $60 and are equipped with TV, fridge, microwave and air-conditioning. Modest establishment outside the centre with a view over Little Lake Park.

ONTARIO

☆☆☆ Expensive ($85–100)

⌂ **Little Lake**: 669 Yonge Street. ☎ 526-2750. Fax: 526-9005. Well located by the lake, close to the museum. Some rooms have en-suite bathrooms and others share facilities at $70 per night. The yellow room is the most expensive, and boasts a magnificent view of the park, a separate entrance, plus two private sitting areas (inside and on the terrace) and a dressing room. The owners are friendly and the house is tastefully decorated.

⌂ **Mark & Margie's B&B**: 670 Hugel Avenue. ☎ 526-4441. Slightly less expensive than Little Lake, but more classic, this is a romantic spot where you'll get a warm welcome.

WHERE TO EAT

☆☆ Moderate (around $15)

✕ **Scully's**: opposite the harbour. Open daily 11am–11pm. ☎ 526-2125. Dishes cost $7–17 at this large bar and restaurant, with original all-wood decor, pool table, baseball on video and beer to quench your thirst. Enjoy a selection of good-value fish dishes. There's a pleasant terrace with a view of the marina.

✕ **Whalen's Wharf**: 238 Midland Avenue, on the corner of Dominion Avenue. ☎ 627-5427. Pastel interior decorated in a naive marine theme, with framed shells, miniatures in bottles and fake fish. The food (costing $5–20) is traditional at lunch but more elaborate and expensive in the evening.

✕ **Freda's Restaurant**: 342 King Street. ☎ 526-4851. Open Monday to Friday 11am–2pm and from 5pm. This dolls' house has been converted into a very British restaurant with embroidered tablecloths and floral crockery. It's a lovely spot serving an English version of nouvelle cuisine. There's a larger selection of dishes in the evening, but the prices are higher too.

✕ **Sha-na-na's**: 519 Hugel Avenue. ☎ 526-2266. Dishes cost $6–12. This is the place where adults refuse to grow up. It's got a rather 1960s feel to it, with its mini jukebox, celebrity photos, old petrol pumps and American music. The food is American-style too, of course, and after the kitchen closes at 10pm, the bar continues.

WHAT TO SEE AND DO

★ **Huronia Museum**: Little Lake Park, King Street. Open 9am–5pm (6pm in July and August). Entrance charge $6 (reductions possible), valid for the museum and nearby village (*see below*). The building consists of two large rooms, the first of which contains a pile of dusty objects that look as if they belong on a second-hand stall. In fact, they are items brought by the pioneers and include clothes, toys, furniture, utensils and jewellery (categorized thematically). The second room houses an exhibition of Indian artefacts from daily life.

★ **Huron Indian Village**: near the Huronia Museum. ☎ 526-2844. Ask for the handy map on your way into this well-constructed exhibit. A high wooden palisade surrounds the rebuilt Huron village where you can see communal 'long houses' covered with bark where several Indian families lived. A tour round the village gives a good insight into the natives' way of life before white men put an end to it. There's a place where pots were made, the medicine man's room, food store and sauna (no longer in use), and in a tepee, animal skins are drying out.

★ **Ste-Marie among the Hurons**: ☎ 526-7838. 5 kilometres (3 miles) east of Midland on the north side of Highway 12. Open daily end-May–October 10am–7pm (last admission 4.15). Entrance charge $10.

The village is an exact reconstruction of (and in the same location as) the first Jesuit mission in Ontario, built in 1639 and burned down 10 years later. Very knowledgeable guides in period costume will first show you an excellent slide show lasting about 20 minutes, which plunges you back into the 17th century. It recounts the destruction of the Huron tribe by foreign diseases and the failure of the Jesuits, weakened by famine and attacks by the Iroquois. You'll learn of their flight first to Christian Island and then to the Ste-Marie II mission and how, following winter and famine, they made their way to Orleans Island and then to Québec.

At its height this mission included a number of lay members and craftsmen who had come to transform it into a real village that would welcome the baptized Hurons. The Hurons saw it as an example of 17th-century French culture, and it was a sanctuary for the missionaries. Visitors are entertained by students playing the roles of missionaries, blacksmiths, Hurons and farmers. You don't need too much imagination to appreciate the cultural shock that the Indians must have experienced with the arrival of the white man. In the church you can see the tombs of Jean de Brébeuf and Gabriel Lalemant, who were horrifyingly martyred by the Iroquois. If you have any questions for the guides, don't hesitate to ask – there's no chance of catching them out. This live reconstruction is so successful you'll wish you were in costume and could take part.

★ **Sanctuary of the Canadian Martyrs**: located in an enormous park south of Highway 12, opposite the Ste-Marie Mission, east of Midland. Open daily May to September 7.30am–9pm. Here you'll find the church that was built in 1926 in honour of the martyrs. The architecture is not particularly interesting and, indeed, there's not all that much else to see here. However, Pope John Paul II came here to pray in September 1984. You can also follow the Stations of the Cross.

– **Wye Marsh Wildlife Centre**: next to the Ste-Marie Mission. Open daily in summer 10am–6pm. ☎ 526-7809. Entrance charge $5. The centre offers wilderness walking trails during which you'll come across the trillium, a rare and small white flower with three petals which is the emblem of the Province of Ontario. Book ahead for guided canoe tours or snowshoe trails in winter.

– **Boat trips through the Thirty Thousand Islands**: departures from the port daily in summer at 10.45am and 1.45pm (and late afternoon during certain periods). ☎ 549-3388. The trip lasts 2 hours 30 minutes and tickets cost $15 (reductions possible). If you have more time, leave from Parry Island to the west of Parry Sound. This is Canada as you have always imagined it: colourful wooden houses on tidy, forested islands with boathouses and the occasional seaplane of the very rich inhabitants. Enjoy a stroll dreaming of a peaceful life in the natural environment. It's paradise.

ONTARIO

THE MUSKOKA LAKES

There's no alternative route from Nottawasaga Bay to Algonquin Park. This superb region is considered by many Ontarians to be a real paradise, and it includes Lake Muskoka, Lake Rousseau and Lake Joseph. The circuit round Lake Muskoka can be done in 3 hours leaving either Gravenhurst or Bracebridge. Many activities take place on Lake Muskoka and you can enjoy a historic crossing on the oldest steamer still in operation in Ontario. On Lake Gull concerts are held on floating barges during the summer. There are many viewpoints that make the area a condensed digest of everything that's typical in Ontario.

★ **Orillia**: This small and peaceful town to the north of Lake Simcoe is rapidly expanding, with the construction of several hotels following the opening of the huge Casino Rama. It's owned by the local Ogibway Indians, and big international stars come to perform there. Less famous and more modest personalities in traditional Scottish dress entertain the crowds during the Orillia Scottish Festival, held annually in July.

★ **Gravenhurst**: This is the gateway to the Muskoka region, and a town that is developing slowly while managing to retain its peaceful and serene air. Keep an eye out for the beautiful Victorian homes.

★ **Bracebridge**: Make sure to have a look at the waterfalls, right in the heart of town.

★ **Huntsville**: Pop in quickly on your way to beautiful Algonquin Park, the focus of the town's tourism.

USEFUL ADDRESSES

🅑 **Bracebridge tourist office**: corner of Ecclestone Drive and Ontario Street, above the waterfalls. ☎ 645-5231.

🅑 **Port Carling tourist office**: past the bridge, on the right of the main street. ☎ 765-5336. Open 10am–4pm in summer only. Some local information is available.

Boat Hire

The best way to explore the lakes and discover the beautiful countryside is at the wheel of a motorboat. It's not that expensive and is really worthwhile. You'll need a driving licence to hire a boat. Note that, as well as the deposit and tax (15 per cent), you should also budget for petrol.

■ **Beaumaris Marina**: Highway 118 West. Take the Beaumaris Road exit (halfway between Bracebridge and Port Carling). ☎ 764-1171. Motorboat or canoe hire, minimum of 4 hours.

■ **Ryans' Sea-Doo Rentals**: ☎ 1-888-766-8690 (toll-free). Boat and jet-ski hire by the day.

WHERE TO HAVE A DRINK

♪ The Boat House: in the Carling Cove Inn, Port Carling. Next to the bridge and the service station, you can enjoy a drink and superb views of Lake Rousseau.

ALGONQUIN PARK   DIALLING CODE: 705/613

Only a few hours from Toronto is this immense national park covering 7,700 square kilometres (480 square miles) – almost as large as Wales. It's an area of wild and abundant nature, dotted with thousands of lakes. Cars are banned in the park itself, but you can drive across the southern part of the park on Highway 60, which is the only way in by car from the south. This road exists to facilitate access for nature-lovers wanting to walk the trails or canoe along some of the 1,600 kilometres (1,000 miles) of navigable rivers and streams. There are 29 access points to the park, but the busiest entrance is still the one off Highway 60. You'll need a permit for camping or canoeing. Prices are $10 per car per day and $40 per car for more than four days. However, it's free to drive across Highway 60 (and thus the park), providing you don't stop along the way.

This is where the real Canada begins – the Canada of tall trees, clear lakes with water clean enough to drink, evenings in front of an open fire trying to identify the whispers and cries in the night, and waking up by the edge of a misty lake. This encounter with the wildneress and the feeling of isolation will be one of the strongest feelings you will encounter on your visit. A voyage of discovery on the lakes by canoe is the ideal way to get to know the real Canada, so make the most of the opportunity here.

USEFUL ADDRESSES

Drivers are at an advantage, since the bus only stops at Huntsville, some way from the park entrance. It takes an hour to cross the park by car.

🅗 Park Information Centres: At the east and west gates of the park, on Highway 60. Open daily in summer 8am–9pm (10pm on Friday). In winter 9am–4pm. ☎ 633-5572. You'll find all the leaflets and information you need on the park at these excellent centres. They can also provide a weather forecast for 3–5 days ahead.

■ **Park emergencies**: ☎ 633-5583.
■ **Police**: ☎ 1-888-310-1122.
■ **Hospital**: Huntsville ☎ (705) 789-2311; Barry's Bay ☎ (613) 756-3044.
■ **Anti-poison centre**: ☎ 1-800-267-1373.
■ **Park information on radio**: 102.7 FM.

WHERE TO STAY

There are several hotels in the park, but they're all extremely expensive. It's better to find accommodation in the small towns at the entrances to the park, such as Dwight or Huntsville near the west gate and Whitney near the east gate.

🛏 **The Curv Inn**: 5 kilometres (3 miles) from the west gate. ☎ 635-1892. Accommodation costs $30–50, or you can pitch your tent for $10. This motel is closest to the park and, oddly enough, is the cheapest. Five quite big country rooms (sometimes cleanliness leaves something to be desired). Above the souvenir shop/restaurant/foyer and filling station are five more rooms with shared bathroom. These are cheaper than the rooms in the motel, a bit noisy but decent enough. You can also hire canoes from here.

Campsites

There are eight campsites along Highway 60, each on the shore of one of the lakes. Campsite reservations: ☎ 1-888-668-7275. A pitch costs from $20 per night. You can stay at the same site for a maximum of 23 consecutive days. The sites are clean, as respecting nature is a concept that has long been accepted by the Canadians; Europeans could learn much from them.

Pick up a free information sheet on Algonquin Provincial Park describing all the facilities and detailing maps of the walking trails. If you're not a walker and would like to camp instead, choose a campsite where motor boats are not permitted, or even one with no showers. It's the only way to avoid the weekend crowds.

🛏 A couple of recommendations are the **Canisbay** campsite (25 kilometres/15 miles from the west gate) or the one at **Pog Lake** (about 37 kilometres/23 miles from the west gate). Both are quite isolated and less crowded than the others.

WHERE TO EAT

It's advisable to buy all your foodstuffs before entering the park, where the few shops are on the expensive side.

BEARS

Even though their fur is soft, bears are not sweet. Relax, you're very unlikely to meet one, but for cohabitation to work well you must avoid leaving food or rubbish behind: leave all foodstuffs in the boot of your car. Never try to approach a bear should you see one, and never feed them. The park rangers can offer helpful advice.

WALKING AND BACKPACKING TRAILS

There are 16 trails, 8–11 kilometres (5–7 miles) in length, starting from Highway 60. Well marked with blue, yellow and brown signposts, the trails have individual themes such as wildlife, park ecology etc., detailed in English or French in a small guidebook available at the beginning of the walk. Use it on the walk and return it at the end or buy it for a modest sum.

Among the best trails are:

– **Lookout** (almost 2 kilometres/1 mile): For those pressed for time or feeling a bit lazy, with superb views of the park halfway along the route.

– **Booth's Rock** (about 5 kilometres/3 miles): Discover the various types of landscape in the park.

– **Mizzy Lake** (11 kilometres/7 miles): This leads past a series of ponds and small lakes and is a good trail for observing animals.

– **Whiskey Rapids Trail** (about 2 kilometres/1 mile): This walk follows the river and the rapids.

Long-distance Trails

Pick up a topographical map at the information centre and inform the guides of your choice of route and intended campsite. There are three possible routes, each with camping spots marked with a small red triangle on the map. At these spots you will find a simple clearing with an area set aside for lighting a fire. Do not light a fire other than at a designated fireplace. Dig a hole for a toilet and refill it when you leave. Two routes start from Highway 60, and the number of campers is restricted.

– **Western Uplands**: three circuits 32, 55 and 88 kilometres (20, 34 and 55 miles) in length. Allow 3–7 days to complete the trip. These are the most varied trails; note the spots marked for lighting fires. Buy your permits at the park's west gate.

– **Highland Backpacking Trail**: two circuits of 19 and 35 kilometres (12 and 22 miles). Allow 2–3 days, and buy your permits at the Cache Lake Information Centre on Highway 60. These circuits are less demanding than the Western Uplands trails.

– **Eastern Pines**: two circuits of 5.5 and 15.5 kilometres (3.5 and 9 miles) at the eastern side of the park. Permits available at the east gate.

Things to Remember

– a lightweight tent and a good-quality sleeping bag

– good walking boots that lace up and cover the ankles

– two pairs of socks, one thin and another thicker pair

– a swimming costume

– a rainproof and windproof jacket or a raincape or poncho that you can use to protect your backpack on your back or in the canoe

– a pair of light trousers and a light, long-sleeved shirt to protect you from the sun

– a small first-aid kit

– a torch, some string, a knife, waterproof matches, a can opener, a compass, a waterproof watch, some newspaper for kindling (the wood isn't always dry)

ONTARIO

– some food: dried fruit, dehydrated soups, chocolate snack bars

– a mess-tin with two sets of cutlery

– water-purifying tablets (the water in the lakes is drinkable, but use these to be on the safe side)

– a map

– insect repellent (so you avoid being totally disfigured – black flies are a pest in Algonquin Park)

CANOEING ROUTES

The best way to have a real adventure – to feel the pioneering spirit, to follow the Indian way and penetrate deep in the wild forests, to fish and grill your catch on an open fire, to really take off without wearing out your walking boots – is to go by canoe. Algonquin Park is like a starry night where each star is a lake. Trails have been marked out between the lakes. The canoeing routes comprise all the navigable waterways and portaging between them, which means that you can carry your canoe on your back to get to the next stretch of navigable water. Even the uninitiated can go on short expeditions lasting a few days. Don't forget that the canoe is completely different from the kayak, which requires real technical competence and long training to use. Also, if it rains (and this is quite possible), you balance the canoe upside down between two rocks to make an excellent shelter.

Canoeing in Algonquin Park is relatively safe because there are no rapids, just calm lakes and peaceful waterways. As you journey through the wild, majestic nature, the only real danger depends on yourself and whether you have prepared properly for your trip. The best way to do this is to discuss the various possible routes with the rangers at the Park Information Centre and work out the ones with shorter portage distances so you don't get disheartened. Every day in July and August the rangers offer programmes to familiarize visitors with the wilderness which include canoeing lessons and lots of information about preparing for your trip. Canoe hire is not expensive, especially by the week. Telephone for information (*see* 'Useful Adresses').

– On summer weekends the most accessible lakes are very busy. If you want peace and quiet avoid **Canoe Lake** at the weekend. As a rule, if you choose a lake you have to portage into at the beginning of your trip, it's likely to be a less busy lake. The farther north you go the more you'll be on your own. It's also true for the lakes that don't have a departure point from Highway 60. On the map, access to the park is shown by a red diamond. In the west is Entrance 3 to **Magnetawan Lake** or, right in the north, **Cedar Lake**. This is an excellent route with complete isolation guaranteed.

– During the week take **Smoke Lake**, off Highway 60, and go down as far as **Ragged Lake** – not much portage and not too many people.

Organizing Your Trip

– If you have a Canadian friend who owns a canoe and who knows the region, all you have to do is paddle and have a good look around at the beautiful surroundings.

– If you haven't got the equipment you can hire a canoe on the spot (but it's more expensive, *see* 'Specialized Shops' *below*) or in Toronto or Ottawa. Prepare your route with the help of a ranger and start by buying a copy of the indispensable *Algonquin Provincial Park Canoe Routes.* It shows all the campsites, as well as all the possible routes with portage distances. Ask the ranger as many questions as you like. Read all the explanations and advice that appear on the back of the map with great care and go to one of the regular slide shows at the Log Lake Outdoor Theatre (in July and August).

A badly organized trip can turn into a nightmare. On the other hand, a little care over the preparation will really pay off. Don't forget that there are no telephones in the bush and a small problem can turn into a major crisis. To prepare for your main trip, it's worth camping for a day or two by the side of Highway 60 planning how much and what food to take, which route, how long will it take etc.

– If you're a complete novice at canoeing, but have a lot of money to spare, you can visit one of the hire shops or route outfitters. They can put together a very well-organized package to suit the amount of time you want to stay and your itinerary: canoe, sleeping bag, food in watertight containers etc. They can even supply a guide, although you won't really need one.

Specialized Shops

The price and quality of service are similar in all three shops:

■ **Algonquin Outfitters**: Highway 60. About 8 kilometres (5 miles) outside the west gate, on the left (signposted). ☎ 635-2243. They're open all year round and have a variety of things for hire. They also give good advice. All-inclusive hire prices for two people for a 3-day trip are around $100–120 per person (half price if you bring your own camping equipment and food). At the end of your trip you can return your canoe to one of their two shops in the park: Brent Store, on Cedar Lake (in the north) or Opeongo Store.

■ **Portage Store**: 14 kilometres (9 miles) into the park from the west gate, on the left of Highway 60. ☎ 633-5622.

■ **Opeongo Store**: in the east of the park, near Lake Opeongo. ☎ (613) 637-2075. Open 8am–8pm in July and August.

WHAT TO SEE BY ROAD

★ **Algonquin Visitor's Centre**: Highway 60, 43 kilometres (27 miles) from the west gate. Open 9am–9pm in summer. Facilities include a cafeteria, bookshop and the small, free **Algonquin Park Museum**, which describes the fauna of the park (bears, elks, deer etc). Oddly enough, Highway 60 offers the best chance of seeing elks. In May and June they enjoy the pools of water along the roadside, which still taste of the salt used to clear the roads. It's best to avoid driving through the parks at night, the elk can get pretty aggressive during the rutting season. Headlights attract them and they will charge towards the car. You won't see them until the very last moment, just before you hit them, and this can result in quite a crash.

★ **Logging Museum**: at the entrance to the park. Open 10am–6pm. This enjoyable outdoor exhibition is set in the natural environment over a distance of just over 1 kilometre, and displays the different tools and materials used by loggers in the 19th century, including paddle-boats, carts and locomotives. There's also a good slide show. In 1861, 112 companies were cutting trees in Algonquin Park – demand was so high that almost total chaos reigned which inevitably destroyed that aspect of the forest. There were no holds barred and even young trees were cut down to satisfy the demand. The experts anticipated the continuing exploitation of the forest for the next 700 years and, 70 years on, people were wondering what happened to the forest. In 1893, they decided to create a park, to control logging and to avoid a further catastrophe. If the museum is closed, take a small guide from the dispenser at the beginning of the path and follow the route on you own.

★ **Algonquin Gallery**: 20 kilometres (about 12 miles) along Highway 60. Open June–October 10am–6pm. Entrance charge (student reductions possible). Temporary exhibitions are held every summer.

ACID RAIN

Sulphur dioxide and nitrogen dioxide are the two main enemies of the Canadian lakes. They're belched into the atmosphere mainly by factories in the industrial belts. The emissions then turn into sulphate and nitrate particles which, combined with water, fall as weak solutions of sulphuric and nitric acid. The prevailing winds blow them great distances before they fall as rain on the northern land and lakes. This results in the pH of the lakes falling below 4.6 – fish, frogs and other creatures need a pH value of above 5 to survive and reproduce. In Ontario a 1984 research project into 4,000 lakes showed that 4 per cent of them had such high levels of acidity that they could no longer support aquatic life; a programme was then developed to counteract the damage caused.

Algonquin Park to Ottawa

There's one piece of advice for this route: just follow the Ottawa River. As you leave the park, take Route 60 East, then Route 62 East as far as Pembroke and follow the riverbank all the way to Ottawa.

After you leave Algonquin Park, enjoy a pit stop in **Barry's Bay**, where things have been developing at a less brutal pace.

WHERE TO STAY AND EAT

⌂ ✕ **The Ash Grove Inn**: Highway 62 South, opposite Lake Kamaniskeg. ☎ 1-888-756-7672 (toll-free). Rooms cost $50 and meals from $7 to $14. Have a hamburger on the terrace while remembering your adventures and experiences in Algonquin Park.

⌂ **Victoria House B&B**: on the main street approaching on Highway 21. ☎ (613) 646-7638. Double rooms cost $45–75. There are a few pleasant rooms with old-fashioned interiors, one of which houses a Chinese emperor's bed that is over 150 years old.

WHERE TO GO RAFTING

– In **Forester's Falls**, at the junction of Highways 21 and 48, fans of whitewater rafting will find themselves in paradise. Enjoy dramatic and spectacular rapids as you descend the Ottawa and Madawaska rivers. A day's rafting (including a meal) on a Saturday in summer will set you back around $100. There are three operating companies whose prices vary according to the season, day and number of people. Package deals including two days' rafting and shelter are possible. It gets very busy at weekends. Access to the different sites is well marked as you approach Forester's Falls.

■ **Wilderness Tours**: ☎ (613) 646-2291 or 1-800-267-9166 (toll-free). The staff are very enthusiastic.

■ **RiverRun**: ☎ (613) 646-2501 or 1-800-267-8504.

OTTAWA — DIALLING CODE: 613

For maps of Ottawa, see the first colour plate section.

Ottawa is the most uniformly bilingual city in English-speaking Canada, so you'll be able to get around in English or French. Ottawa was chosen as the capital of Canada by Queen Victoria in 1857, more because of its strategic position between the two language areas than for its real political importance. Formerly known as Bytown, it was renamed Ottawa, meaning 'river trade' in the Algonquin language. So you will find an interesting mismatch between the seriousness of the skyscrapers and parliament buildings and the very provincial ease of the wide avenues lined with parks. At the weekend, boats sail up the Ottawa River and the Rideau Canal which goes through the city. In the evenings, young people look for their entertainment in the renovated area around Byward Market. Placid Ottawa also has some superb museums, which are another good reason to make a stop.

USEFUL ADDRESSES

🛈 **Infocentre** (map B2): 90 Wellington Street, on the corner of Metcalfe Street opposite the parliament buildings. ☎ 1-800-465-1867 (toll-free) or ☎ 239-5000. Open daily 8.30am–9pm in summer.

■ **American Express Travel Service** (map B2, **2**): 220 Laurier Avenue. ☎ 563-0231 or ☎ 1-800-668-2639 (toll-free). Open Monday to Saturday 8.30am–5.30pm. Currency exchange facilities.

■ **United States Embassy** (map B2, **5**): Sussex Drive, opposite Clarence Street. ☎ 238-5335.

■ **Emergency services**: ☎ 911.

■ **General hospital**: 501 Smyth Road. ☎ 737-7777.

■ **Police** (map C3, **6**): 474 Elgin St. ☎ 236-1222.

■ **Internet** (map C2, **11**): Cybercafé Agora, 135 Besserer Street.

OTTAWA

Transport

🚆 **Train station** (map, off A2 and D2): Tremblay Road. **Via Rail**: ☎ 244-8289. Several departures a day to Toronto (via Kingston), Montréal and Québec.

🚌 **Bus station** (Voyageur Colonial and Greyhound; map C3, **7**): 265 Catherine Street. ☎ 238-5900. Many departures to Toronto and also the USA. Departures for Montréal every hour except at 11am and 3pm.

➕ **Airport**: ☎ 998-3151.

■ **Air Canada** (map B2, **10**): 275 Slater Street. ☎ 247-5000. ☎ 1-800-268-7240 (toll-free).

■ **Rent-a-Bicycle**: 1 Rideau St, behind Château Laurier. ☎ 241-4140.

WHERE TO STAY

For maps of Ottawa, see the first colour plate section.

⊡ Budget (under $20)

🛏 **Breton** campsite (map A3, **20**): corner of Booth and Fleet streets, 5 minutes from the parliament buildings. ☎ 236-1251. Open mid-June to early September. For tents only, it's well equipped and fairly cheap, but noisy and the washing facilities are not always up to standard. Cars are left at the entrance.

🛏 **Ottawa International Inn** (map C2, **21**): 75 Nicholas Street, on the corner of Daly Avenue. ☎ 235-2595. Take bus No. 95 from the station or No. 4 North from the bus terminal. This is in the old town prison, where you'll get a friendly welcome from the 'inmates'. There's a curfew at 2am in winter. Guests sleep four, six or eight per cell, and the rooms have no windows. There are also three double rooms. Facilities include kitchen, wash house and message board. It's more or less clean.

🛏 **Ottawa Backpackers Inn** (map C1, **25**): 203 York Street. ☎ 241-3402. Website: www.ottawahostel.com. This is a classic red-brick building with 30 beds for those on a tight budget. You'll be greeted by a pile of shoes and a multilingual sign asking you to remove and add yours to the collection. It has a pleasant atmosphere, but it's not spotless.

⊡⊡ Moderate (less than $65)

🛏 **University of Ottawa** (map, C2, **22**): 100 University Street. Reception is in the Stanton building. ☎ 564-5400. Open May to end-June for visitors. On offer are 1,200 very clean, top-quality rooms at reasonable prices for students. For others prices vary.

🛏 **YMCA and YWCA** (map C3, **23**): 180 Argyle Street, on the corner of O'Connor Street near the bus station. ☎ 237-1320. Open all year. Large, pretty dismal student residence with 75 beds for travellers. The swimming pool and health club are good quality and free. One to try if you're stuck.

🛏 **Lyon Guesthouse** (map B3, **31**): 479 Slater Street. ☎ 236-3904. Not far from the centre, this is a small house with not much charm in need of a clean.

🛏 **A Voyageur's Guesthouse** (map B3, **32**): 95 Arlington Avenue, behind the bus terminal. ☎ 238-6445. Open 24 hours so worth a try if you arrive at night, but otherwise don't bother.

⊡⊡⊡ Expensive ($70–85)

🛏 **Australis** (map D2, **24**): 35 Marlborough Avenue. ☎ 235-8461. A peaceful house with a few large rooms, run by Carol Waters, a friendly Australian. It's only 15 minutes from the centre, in the residential district among the embassies. Generous breakfast included. Free car-parking.

♠ **Le Gîte** (map C3, **27**): 54 Park Avenue. ☎ 230-9131. A beautiful renovated house in a quiet district, run by Anne-Marie, a charming, bilingual and welcoming woman originally from Brittany.

♠ **Auberge du Marché** (map C1, **28**): 87 Guigues Avenue. ☎ 241-6610. Very close to the centre is this pretty, typically Canadian house from the early 20th century with three single rooms in very good taste. Quiet and relaxing place.

⊞ Splash Out ($85–100)

♠ **Ottawa House** (map D1, **26**): 264 Stewart Street. ☎ 789-4433. Fax: 789-6440. Connie McElman de-scribes her house as a jewel of Victorian architecture, with its embroidered sheets, old-fashioned bathtubs and generous breakfast. It's a matter of honour that her guests are satisfied. Ask for a room with balcony overlooking the garden.

♠ **The King Edward Inn** (map C2, **29**): 525 King Edward Avenue. ☎ 565-6700. As soon as you cross the threshold of this pretty house, you'll be enchanted by the sitting room. It's a very pleasant setting, where the hosts will give you a warm welcome. There are a few clean and comfortable rooms, and the food is excellent.

♠ **Haydon House** (map, C2, **30**): 18 The Driveway, on the corner of Queen Elizabeth Promenade and Somerset Street. ☎ 230-2697. This impressive building has a sophisticated interior and three large rooms.

WHERE TO EAT

For maps of Ottawa, see the first colour plate section.

Byward Market District

This is the oldest, liveliest district (especially around Clarence Street) and houses more than 250 restaurants, bars, snack bars and cafés.

⊞ Budget

✕ **Bagel-Bagel** (map C1, **40**): 92 Clarence Street. A dull decor, but the place is very popular with young people and opens very late at the weekend. Features bagels of all kinds, including an excellent one with smoked meat. A pleasant meeting place.

✕ **Zack's** (map C2, **41**): 16 Byward Market, near Clarence Street. An American 1950s diner type of place with jukebox, comfortable benches and delicious milkshakes.

✕ **Memories** (map B2, **46**): 7 Clarence Street. ☎ 241-1882. Open daily 11am–11pm. Good menu of appetizing cakes. Try warm apple pie with ice-cream and have some perfectly creamy hot chocolate.

✕ **Mamma Grazzis** (map C2, **47**): 25 George Street (in the Courtyard). ☎ 241-8656. Open daily 11am–10pm. This Italian restaurant on two floors also has a big sunny terrace. Pasta and pizzas are the specialities: the pasta Gambari is delicious. You'll find a really friendly atmosphere here.

⊞ Expensive

✕ **The Fish Market** (map C2, **42**): 54 York Street next to Byward Market and William Street. ☎ 241-3474. Open until 10pm. Very attractive decor and the atmosphere is quite smart. Cajun cooking with a variety of excellent fish dishes. Try the sautéed shrimps with curry.

✗ **Nagina Indian Cuisine** (map C2, **50**): 217 Rideau Street. ☎ 562-0060. Open daily until 11pm. Tasty Indian food, plus Indian music, decor and staff are all part of the pleasant atmosphere.

✗ **Mangia** (map C1, **51**): 121 Clarence Street. ☎ 562-4725. Open daily 11.30am–11pm. This corner restaurant has a dark interior decorated with posters, filtered lighting and a sophisticated menu.

✗ **The Crêperie** (map C2, **52**): 47 York Street. ☎ 241-8805. Open until 11.30pm every evening. Enjoy sweet and savoury pancakes while sipping a glass of American-style cider in this elegant spot with hushed atmosphere.

Somerset Village

On Somerset Street, between O'Connor and Bank streets, is an interesting district with several restaurants serving Italian and American specialities. The atmosphere is friendly and the prices attractive.

☆☆ Moderate ($10–20)

✗ **Full House** (map C3, **44**): 337 Somerset Street. ☎ 238-6734. Open daily 5–11.30pm. Dishes cost around $16 and there's a full menu available at $21. The Piano Parlour is on the first floor, intimate, select and well worth a visit.

✗ **Olé! Tapas** (map B3, **53**): 352 Somerset Street. Open Monday to Thursday 4–11pm. Friday and Saturday 5pm–2am. Happy hour for tapas daily 4–6pm. Enjoy live music on Thursday and Flamenco concerts on Friday and Saturday evenings. The young Hispanic community meets here, but there's no Spanish beer.

Farther Out

Ottawa's Chinatown centres on Somerset Street, between Bay and Preston Streets and in Little Italy, along Preston Street, you'll find numerous Italian restaurants.

☆☆ Moderate ($10–20)

✗ **The Ritz** (map C3, **43**): 274 Elgin Street. ☎ 235-7027. Open Monday to Friday to 10pm (11pm Saturday and Sunday). Closed Saturday and Sunday lunchtime. The dining room is long and narrow in this intimate, friendly place serving refined Italian cooking.

✗ **Druxy's** (map B2, **45**): 100 Metcalfe Street, on the corner of Slater Street. There's also one on Laurier Street, on the corner of O'Connor Street. Open Monday–Friday 6am–6.30pm. Saturday 7.30am–3.30pm. Sunday 9.30am–3pm. Part of a res-

taurant chain specializing in salads and smoked meat.

✗ **The Mekong Restaurant** (map B3, **48**): 637 Somerset Street. Open daily 11am–midnight. Right in the middle of Chinatown, serving good Vietnamese cooking. Unfussy decor, smiling, efficient staff and large portions make this a good-value and popular choice.

✗ **Il Piccolino** (map, off A3, **49**): 449 Preston Street, slightly out of the centre of town. ☎ 236-8158. Open Monday to Friday 11.30am–2.30pm and 5–10pm. Saturday 5–10pm. This intimate little Italian restaurant with a charming welcome serves excellent

OTTAWA

pizzas. There's a ravishing patio smothered with Virginia creeper.

✕ **Newport Restaurant** (map, off A3, **57**): 334 Richmond Road.

☎ 722-9070. This small restaurant is like a corner shop and serves classic cuisine. Elvis Presley fans will love the memorabilia.

WHERE TO HAVE A DRINK

For maps of Ottawa, see the first colour plate section.

Byward Market

❣ **Rainbow Bistro** (map C1, **61**): Murray Street, at the corner of Parent Avenue. Entrance charge. On the first floor, this bistro has good bands playing blues or jazz every evening.

❣ **The Collection and Mercury Lounge** (map C2, **65**): 56 Byward. Open daily from 4pm. These two trendy bars are popular with the young and fashionable set, sipping colourful cocktails.

Towards Bank Street

❣ **Royal Oak** (map B3, **62**): 318 Bank Street. Open daily 11am–1am. Pleasant, good-value pub serving snacks and a good selection of draught beers in a young and friendly atmosphere. Another branch is at 161 Laurier Avenue East, on the corner of King Edward.

❣ **The Celtic Cross Pub & Restaurant** (map B3, **63**): 265 Bank Street. ☎ 237-9493. Open 11am–2pm. Good beer and Celtic music (Thursday, Friday, Saturday) in a guaranteed Irish atmosphere.

NIGHTLIFE

The minimum age for entrance to a nightclub is 19 in Ontario and 18 in Québec, so it may be wise to take proof of your date of birth (identity card or passport) to avoid potential trouble on the door.

❣ **Atomic** (map C2, **66**): 137 Besseser Street. Open Thursday to Sunday from 10pm. This is the only nightclub in town that closes at 3am on Friday and 7am on Saturday. Free entry Thursday and Sunday. It's on two dimly lit floors with really hip house and

underground music. Special evenings with international DJs at the helm.

❣ **Reactors** (map C2, **68**): 18 York Street. Open Thursday to Saturday 10pm–2am. Young, easy-going crowd, cheap beer, pool tables and terrace.

WHAT TO SEE

For maps of Ottawa, see the first colour plate section.

★ **Parliament Hill** (map B2, **80**): Open in summer Monday to Friday 9am–8pm. Saturday and Sunday 9am–5pm. A huge, U-shaped building in neo-Gothic style surrounded by wide lawns, this is the strategic centre of town where everyone gathers for the festivities on 1 July. You can take a free guided tour of the Centre Building and the East Building, leaving every 30 minutes from the Info tent to the right of the Parliament Building. This informative place will help you understand more clearly the workings of Canada's political and democratic system (House of Commons, Senate etc.) and allows you to attend debates during parliamentary sessions.

– **Centre Building**: A fire in 1916 destroyed everything except for the superb library resembling the nave of a Gothic cathedral. It's considered lucky to touch the doors to the library as, prior to the fire, an employee had locked these very doors, thereby saving the works inside from the flames. The rest was rebuilt in neo-Gothic style, topped by copper roofs. There are finely worked wooden panels in white pine with hundreds of carved rosettes. The edifice is built of fossilized limestone from Manitoba. With highly competent guides and English and French commentary, this makes an interesting visit. It's best to take the tour in the evening when there are fewer people and the view over the city from the top of the tower is much more beautiful. Buy your ticket early in the morning.

★ **The Rideau Canal locks** (map B2, **81**): Wellington street, next to the Château Laurier Hotel. Exhibition open 8.30am–4.30pm in high season. This series of locks connecting the Rideau Canal to the Ottawa River are still worked by hand. The canal was dug by the first soldiers in the area, but was never used. In summer pleasure boats ply the canal and in winter, when it's frozen, many people (quite possibly even important civil servants) skate to work. The Rideau Canal, along with several other sites (Rideau Centre, Rideau Street, Rideau Falls and the Rideau River) owe their name to the fact that, on discovering the falls in Ottawa, Samuel Champlin declared that they looked like a *rideau* ('curtain' in French).

★ **The Bytown Museum** (map B2, **82**): on the left by the locks. Open Monday to Saturday 10am–5pm. Sunday 1–5pm. Built in 1827, this former British military depot now houses an exhibition about the construction of the canal. Worth a look only if you have time.

★ **National Aviation Museum** (map B1, off **83**): Rockcliffe Airport, near St Laurent Boulevard. ☎ 993-2010. Open daily 9am–5pm (late closing on Thursday). Entrance charge $6. More than 100 aircraft recount the history of flight in Canada.

★ **Château Laurier Hotel** (map C2, **84**): 1 Rideau Street, above the falls. You can't fail to notice the attractively medieval architecture of this luxury hotel, the only building with a French influence in Ottawa.

★ **Byward Market** (map C2): This is the liveliest district of Ottawa at night, with restaurants and cafés spread out along Byward, Clarence, Parent, York, George and William streets. A restoration programme has preserved all the old buildings. It's a really pleasant market during the day, selling seasonal fruit in summer at unbeatable prices. It's also the meeting place of Ottawa Motorcycle Club, who proudly display their gleaming machines to passers-by.

★ **Canadian Museum of Civilization** (map B1, **85**): 100 Laurier Street, Hull, opposite Parliament Hill. ☎ (819) 776-7000. Open daily in summer 9am–6pm (Thursday to 9pm). Entrance charge $8 (reductions possible; free on Sunday 9am–noon).

The architecture of this superb building is an allegory for the Canadian countryside, created by natural erosion by the glaciers, the winds and the waters. An immense glass gallery contains life-size reconstructions of different Amerindian habitats complete with majestic totem poles and canoes. The upper level recounts the settlement and everyday life of the different peoples who came to Canada. There are many very realistic slide shows, under a dome some 17 metres (56 feet) high, which reconstruct events such as the arrival of the Vikings and whale-hunting. Other exhibits include a whole 18th-century street from New France, a mixed-race encampment on the Prairies, a street in Ontario, a naval dockyard and a 19th-century saw mill. There are also numerous displays of folk art; it's really quite exceptional and you should allow 3 hours to see it all.

★ **Canadian Museum of Nature** (map C3, **86**): 240 McLeod Street. ☎ 566-4700. Entrance charge $5 (student reductions possible). Open throughout the week in summer 9.30am–5pm (8pm on Thursday).

The ground floor has sections about 'Life through the Ages' and 'The Earth'. These vast, complex subjects are approached using really attractive methods of explanation that are very interesting but never annoying. The sections on 'The Mammals of Canada' and 'The Birds of Canada' have some hyper-realistic dioramas where you can see herds of bison crossing snow-covered land, or colonies of sea birds on the cliffs of the Atlantic coast. Don't miss the collection of dinosaur skeletons, some of which exist nowhere else in the world. Another must-see is the fascinating (and permanent) display of live insects and rodents. This is a really enjoyable museum.

★ **National Gallery** (map B1, **87**): 380 Sussex Drive. ☎ 990-1985. Open daily in summer 10am–6pm (8pm on Friday). In winter 10am–5pm. Entry charge $10 for temporary exhibitions, otherwise free. A superb museum that makes wonderful use of space and light, whose glass dome in geometric shapes shows the daring and modernity of Mashe Safdi's concept (he's half Canadian, half Israeli). Inside you can see the oratory of Rideau chapel (29.7 metres/97 feet long and 7.6 metres/25 feet high), which was condemned to be destroyed and only saved *in extremis*. It was taken apart piece by piece, restored and then reassembled. Take a look at the ceiling rose in carved wood. The ancient sculptures and their modern environment are in remarkable harmony. Also worth a look is the collection of early Canadian art, including the famous Group of Seven, founded in 1920 shortly after the death of the leader of New Painting in Canada, Tom Thomson, many of whose works are exhibited. Note also the wonderful view of Parliament Hill from the second floor. And don't miss the exhibition of Inuit art, but you'll have to flex your muscles to open the huge doors.

★ **War Museum** (map B1, **88**): 330 Sussex Drive. ☎ 776-8600. Open 9.30am–5pm (8pm on Thursday). Entrance charge $4 (free on Sunday 9.30am–noon). This is an excellent small museum, whatever your thoughts on war. It's on three floors that lead chronologically through the various roles played by the Canadian army in all international conflicts of the last 200 years. The final exhibit focuses on the Canadian Blue Berets. It's full of photographs, paintings and models of all kinds. The museum is destined for new, larger premises in 2004 next to the National Aviation Museum in Rockliffe (*see below*).

★ **Royal Canadian Mint** (map B1, **89**): 320 Sussex Drive, next to the War Museum. ☎ 993-8990. Open daily 9am–5pm. Guided tours by appointment, phone to book. Tours every 15 minutes from 8.30am lasting 45 minutes. Entrance charge $2 ($1 Saturday and Sunday). Employees finish work at 3pm, so try to visit in the morning to watch them at work. Collectors' coins and medals are minted here, and Canadian currency is minted in Winnipeg. You'll get an interesting explanation, although sometimes it can get a bit too technical. Sadly, no free samples are given out at the end of the visit.

★ **National Museum of Science and Technology** (map, off B1, **94**): 1867 Saint Laurent Boulevard. ☎ 991-3044. Open daily. Push, pull, hold, press . . . take an active part in the discovery of the laws of physics. It's a sort of Palace of Discovery that's been dusted down. You'll also find a collection of old cars.

WHAT TO DO

Boat Trips on the Ottawa River

★ **Amphibus** (map B2, **90**): corner of Spark and Elgin Streets. ☎ 852-1132 or 524-2789. Operates daily 9am–5pm (9pm in July). Departures are every 2 hours and the trips lasts 90 minutes. This is a great concept and a unique experience – a red bus/boat piloted by a uniformed captain. The first part of the trip is on land, past the main buildings in Ottawa. You then glide onto the river to enjoy the last part of the adventure.

★ **The Ottawa Riverboat Company** (map B2, **92**): leaves from below the lock gates. ☎ 562-4888. Open May to mid-October. Tours start at 10am, 11.30am, 1pm, 3pm, 5pm and 7pm.

★ **Paul's Boat Lines** (map B2, **93**): ☎ 235-8409. Tours at 11am, 2pm, 4pm and 7.30pm, lasting 1 hour 30 minutes. Student rates possible. The 7.30 trip offers the chance to see Parliament Hill beautifully lit. There are also excursions on the Rideau Canal with frequent departures from the Conference Centre, lasting 1 hour 15 minutes.

City Tours

★ **Capital Double Decker and Trolley Tours** (map B2, **91**): corner of Sparks and Metcalfe streets. ☎ 749-3666. The tour is accompanied by a bilingual commentary, and you can take your time, since the day ticket allows you to hop on and off whenever you like. There's a free shuttle bus to and from your hotel (☎ 749-3666), and coupons for the museums. The company also offers a steam-train trip between Hull and Wakefield, lasting 5 hours with one departure daily.

★ **Car tours**: If you want to explore the elegant districts of Ottawa, drive past the Parliament Buildings and turn onto Sussex Drive. You'll pass the National Gallery with its proud, geometric glass towers. Continue on, past the Department of External Affairs (supposed to be reminiscent of a sphinx), then the Town Hall built on an island, and finally you'll come to the various embassies. Keep going and you'll reach the residential area of Rockcliffe, with its green, wooded hills. Many of the influential civil servants live out here in large mansions; the Prime Minster's residence is also here. You'll find many styles of house: English cottages, Californian houses, little castles and big palaces.

– Bicycle tours: There are lots of cycle paths in and around Ottawa. Get yourself a free *Tourist Cycle Guide* from the tourist office, which is really helpful. As well as these paths, on Sunday mornings in summer the routes along the Ottawa River and Rockcliffe are also closed to cars. Everyone is out on their bikes or roller-blades.

– If you're feeling lazy, another less tiring way of exploring the town is to go for a ride in a **pousse-pousse** while strong students push you through Ottawa for just a few dollars. You can find them pretty well everywhere around the market, mostly on the corner of George Street and William Street. Prices are about the same as for a taxi.

FESTIVALS AND ATTRACTIONS

– In spring Ottawa shows off its superb gardens, with a floral spectacle whose stars are unquestionably the millions of tulips. These are a gift to Canada every year from the people of Holland because the country allowed the Dutch queen to give birth in a room that was declared to be Dutch territory – the Dutch royal family took refuge in Ottawa during World War II. It's the biggest festival of tulips in the world.

– **Son et lumière**: at La Croisée des Vents (the 'crossroads of the winds') in front of the Parliament Building. This excellent spectacle is held in French and English on summer evenings and lasts 30 minutes. Find out more at the tourist office. This is a great way to learn about the history of the country as you relax on the lawns. And what's more, it's free.

– Changing of the Guard: You can enjoy this event between 9.30am and 10am every morning in summer (in good weather). It's actually more like a parade, leading from Cartier Place to Parliament Hill.

– Franco-Ontario festival: This takes place at the end of June.

– 1 July: This is the date of many festivities in the city, including an air show, musical groups, dozens of boats brightening up the river, and a stunning firework display at night. Thousands of families gather on Parliament Hill, and there's an easy-going, friendly atmosphere.

– Jazz Festival: Held in the second two weeks in July, this is not as big as Montréal's festival, but lots of good groups play in the streets of Ottawa. Information: ☎ 241-2633.

– Snow Ball: This takes place during the first three weekends in February, and includes several activities such as canoe races and ice-sculpture competitions.

SHOPPING

🔒 **Rideau Centre** (map C2): This is the only shopping centre located in downtown Ottawa, but out of town there is also the larger St Laurent centre.

🔒 **Byward Market** (map C2): Here you'll find superb fruit and vegetables at excellent prices in a pleasant atmosphere.

IN THE AREA

★ **Gatineau Park**: Drive northwest for 20 minutes from downtown Ottawa across the Ottawa River and you get to a magnificent park of dense forests and wild lakes that's pretty amazing given how close it is to the city. It's a really lovely place to take a break in the middle of your trip, but not at the weekend. There are also three budget campsites: Lake Philippe is the biggest and the busiest; Lake Taylor is wilder but you're not allowed to swim; and the one at Fish Lake is only accessible by boat (which you can hire on site). It's a super place that's really peaceful, and there's a lifeguard on the beach. Get yourself a free map of the park and just explore. For more information about the park and the campsites: ☎ (819) 827-2020. Fax: (819) 827-3337.

– There are over 125 kilometres (78 miles) of walking trails, 90 kilometres (56 miles) of mountain-bike routes and 200 kilometres (125 miles) of cross-country skiing trails in the winter.

– There are also about five public beaches in the park, and the three biggest lakes (Meech, Philippe and Fish) have guarded beaches (entry charge). Bike and canoe hire is available at Lake Philippe, and the path around Lake Pink has lots of signs explaining the lake's ecology.

★ **Omega Park**: You'll find this at Montebello, roughly halfway between Ottawa (80 kilometres/50 miles) and Montréal (110 kilometres/69 miles), on Route 323 north. ☎ (819) 423-5487 or 5023. Fax: (819) 423-5427. Open all year 10am–dusk. The park covers 800 hectares (about 2,000 acres) of superb countryside. Drive round or go on foot in search of bison, wapitis (North American elk), moose, black bears, ibex and wild boar, plus birds of prey in summer.

HULL   DIALLING CODE: 819

For maps of Ottawa and Hull, see the first colour plate section.

While in Ottawa, don't hesitate to cross the river to Hull on the Québec side. Start your visit with a walk in **Gatineau Park** (*see above* 'In the Area') and then relax in one of the newly fashionable lounge-style bars in the lovely **Place Aubry** (*see* 'Where to Eat and Have a Drink').

USEFUL ADDRESS

🚹 **Tourist office** (map A1, **12**): 103 rue Laurier, at the foot of Alexandra Bridge. Tel 237-9493 or 1-800-265-7822 (toll-free). Open Monday to Friday 8.30am–8pm. Saturday and Sunday 9am–6pm. The office has extensive local information and will greet you warmly.

WHERE TO STAY

☆☆ **Moderate ($50–60)**

🏠 **Au Gîte du Parc** (map A1, **35**): 258 rue Rédempteur. ☎ 819-777-7981. Fax: 819-771-1621.

Unpretentious establishment with somewhat old-fashioned decor, but you're sure of a warm welcome from Jacqueline and Marcel.

⚓ **Couette et Croissant** (map A1, **36**): 330 rue Champlin. ☎ 819-771-2200. The owner makes muffins in advance ready for guests. There are two pretty rooms and a small sitting room in this sweet place.

WHERE TO EAT AND HAVE A DRINK

✕ **Restaurant Barbe** (map A1–2, **55**): 122 rue Eddy. Dishes cost around $10. Before the factories closed, this was where the workers would come for breakfast before work. It then became a bar for customers leaving the nightclub. It's been refurbished and is now a small restaurant serving Canadian specialities, including the famous meat pie.

✕ **Le Tartuffe** (map A1, **56**): 133 rue Notre-Dame, at the junction with Papineau Street. ☎ 819-776-6424. Closed Sunday and Monday. The dining room in this tall building near the Canadian Museum of Civilization is small, intimate and sophisticated. The French-style food is quite good and dishes cost around $12 for lunch ($24 for dinner).

❢ **Place Aubry** (map A2, **64**): 179 Promenade du Portage. Named after a former mayor of Hull, this charming pedestrianized square is where the trendy young people meet and enjoy a drink in the **Bop Bar** or the **Bistrot**.

❢ **Aux 4 Jeudis**: 44 rue Laval, next to Place Aubry. This is a favourite comfort zone for students from the UQAH (University of Québec in Hull).

ALONG THE ST LAWRENCE RIVER

The parks along the St Lawrence, the area between Cornwall and Ganonoque, are beautiful. **Morrisburg**, 139 kilometres (87 miles) north of Kingston on Highway 401, was one of the first regions of Canada to be colonized, and the construction of the St Lawrence shipping route led to a rise in the water level here.

WHERE TO STAY

You'll find several campsites in the area. For information contact the St Lawrence Parks Commission in Morrisburg: ☎ 543-3704. Fax: 543-2847. Website: www.parks.on.ca. You can also pick up a brochure from the Kingston tourist office or from the kiosk at the car-park in Upper Canadian Village. The administrative office is a few kilometres east of Gananoque, at the edge of the Thousand Islands Parkway.

⚓ **Héron Bleu**: 11583 Lakeshore Drive, 10 minutes from Upper Canadian Village off Highway 2. ☎ 652-2601. Fax: 652-1112. Website: www.bbcanada.com. Rooms cost $50 at this attractive building with relaxed atmosphere, opposite the St Lawrence River. Hosts Paul and Pierrette have three simple but spotless rooms for non-smokers only. You can relax in the sitting room downstairs. Pierrette is an inventive cook who makes her own muffins and jams for breakfast.

WHAT TO SEE

★ **Upper Canada Village**: 11 kilometres (7 miles) east of Morrisburg on Highway 2. Open daily mid-May to mid-October 9.30am–5pm. Entrance charge $15 (student reductions possible). This is a collection of 19th-century buildings saved from the rising water, dismantled and then rebuilt on the new riverbank. A village has been reconstructed with a mill, forge, church, school and sawmill, and costumed actors play the roles of villagers. It's touristy but well done and best visited during the week. Tourist information is available in the car-park.

★ **Prescott**: This attractive provincial market town has a certain charm about it.

★ **Fort Wellington**: at the entrance to town. Open in summer daily 10am–5pm. This well-preserved fort was built by the English in the 19th century to defend the St Lawrence against attack by the Americans. Enjoy the costumed guides and wonderful reconstructions.

★ **Battle of the Windmill**: just before you get to Fort Wellington, on Highway 2, is this attractive site with accounts of the battle available in English and French.

GANANOQUE
DIALLING CODE: 613

The entrance to this elongated town is not particularly welcoming, but once you get past the main street – with its motels, restaurants, department stores and shops of all kinds – you'll discover the real Gananoque. It's the best departure point for the Thousand Islands.

USEFUL ADDRESS

Tourist office: 2 King St (between the town hall and the bridge) ☎ 382-3250 or ☎ 1-888-855-4555 (toll-free). Open daily in summer 8am–8pm. In winter 9am–5pm.

WHERE TO STAY

There are several campsites on Thousand Islands Parkway and, if you can afford it, stay on the islands. The owner of the Amaryllis House-boat will collect you by boat. ☎ 659-3513.

🛏 **The Landon Bay Centre**: 302 Thousand Islands Parkway. ☎ 382-2719. Open mid-May to October. A pitch costs from $16 at this shaded campsite with pool.

🛏 **Leanhaven Farms**: 3940 Highway 2, 8 kilometres (5 miles) from Gananoque. ☎ 382-2698. Double rooms cost $60 (reductions after several nights). This family farm in the countryside has several rooms, one accommodating a large family. If you don't fancy the outdoors, you can always watch TV. This is a perfect location if you're catching the morning boat from Gananoque to the Thousand Islands.

🛏 **Tea & Crumpets**: 260 King Street East. ☎ 382-2683. Double rooms cost $65–125. The Butterfly

Room has a private jacuzzi in this fine B&B. A very English and pleas-ant breakfast is served on lovely porcelain.

WHERE TO EAT

✗ **Maple Leaf**: 65 King Street East. Open daily until 10pm (later in summer). Run by an expat Czech couple who serve delicious food, including generous salads and Eastern European specialities. Save some room for the tasty desserts such as the delightful Apfelstrudel.

✗ **Titania**: 740 King St West (as you leave town). Open daily 7am–9pm (8pm on Sunday). Two light and airy rooms in which you can eat speedy and well-priced fare.

WHAT TO DO

– **Thousand Island boat trip**: To qualify as an island there must be at least 0.5 square metres (6 square feet) of land and one tree. This means that some houses are larger than the islands on which they stand. Many of the islands were sold by the First Nations to the government, which then sold them on (one by one) for one or two dollars. Nowadays, American senators and senior civil servants own second homes on the islands.

– **Gananoque Boat Line**: Tickets are sold in the port. ☎ 382-2144. Duration 1 or 3 hours, with departures every hour. The 3-hour tour stops at an American island to view **Boldt Castle**, a wonderful unfinished home built by the owner of the Waldorf Astoria Hotel in New York. You may be asked to show your passport when you land on the island.

– **Thousand Island Air**: 101A South Street, on the waterfront. ☎ 382-7111. Open daily 9am–8pm. At least two passengers are needed for the flight in a seaplane (otherwise single passengers pay double). Several flights per day. Viewing the landscape and the river from 460 metres (1,500 feet) up is absolutely magnificent and worth breaking the bank for. You get a real appreciation of the number of islands in the crystal waters. It's obviously more expensive and noisy than the boat, but a real privilege and delight.

KINGSTON   DIALLING CODE: 613

A quiet resort on the St Lawrence estuary south of the Rideau Canal, Kingston attracts lots of pleasure boats. The town expanded greatly between 1841 and 1844, having been designed as the capital of United Canada before Queen Victoria chose Ottawa. The City Hall, across from the port, was intended to be the Canadian Parliament. You'll find a good number of wealthy 19th-century residences in Kingston, which give it a rare historic feel, and you can feel the influence of its Scottish roots. You'll find many smart, relaxed holidaymakers as it's a pleasant stop on the route between Montréal and Toronto. Note, however, that it's hard to find accommodation in September.

ONTARIO

USEFUL ADDRESSES

🗊 Visitor's and Convention Bureau: 209 Ontario Street, opposite City Hall, in the port. ☎ 548-4415 or 1-888-855-4555. Fax: 548-4549. Open daily 9am–8pm in summer (9am–5pm in winter).

■ **Post office**: 120 Clarence Street. ☎ 545-8560.

■ **American Express**: Dailey Travel Agency, 842 Gardiner Road. ☎ 384-3933 or 1-800-881-3812 (toll-free. Open 9am–5.30pm (Saturday to 4pm).

🚌 **Bus station**: 175 Counter Street. ☎ 547-4916. Information from the Visitor's Bureau. Seven daily departures to Toronto and Montréal, each taking about 2 hours 30 minutes. Four daily departures to Ottawa, taking 2 hours.

🚂 **Train station**: Take the Woodbine Park Bus on Brock Street, behind City Hall, to the station. **Via Rail**: ☎ 544-5600. Several departures daily to Toronto, Ottawa and Montréal.

■ **General Hospital**: 76 Stuart Street. ☎ 548-3232.

■ **Bicycle hire**: Ahoy Rentals, 23 Ontario Street. ☎ 539-3202.

WHERE TO STAY

☒ Budget (under $20–30)

🛏 **Lake Ontario Park**: 4 kilometres (2.5 miles) west of town, towards the psychiatric hospital. ☎ 542-6574. Fax: 542-5699. Open May to September, it's a clean and well-equipped campsite. Four buses daily, leaving from the centre of Kingston.

🛏 **Hi-Lo Hichory Campground**: Wolfe Island, across from Kingston. Take the free (car) ferry from the port for the 20-minute journey. When you reach the island, take Highway 96 East for about 12 kilometres (7 miles) and you'll find wonderful isolated spots and natural beaches.

🛏 **Queen's University**: Queen's Crescent Street, on the corner of Albert Street ☎ 545-2531. Open May to August only. Go to Victoria Hall, where you'll find simple but clean and spacious student rooms with a buffet breakfast included in the price.

☒☒ Moderate ($20–70)

🛏 **Alexander Henry**: 55 Ontario Street (near the Marine Museum). ☎ 542-2261. Fax: 542-0043. Open May to September. This is an original and attractive option for adventurous travellers – sleeping on board a decommissioned ice-breaker. Officers' cabins are larger and more expensive, but the price includes breakfast.

🛏 **Louise House**: 329 Johnson St. ☎ 385-2033. Open May to September (houses university students at other times). Centrally located, with large, functional rooms and comfortable facilities. You'll receive a warm welcome.

🛏 **Glen Lawrence B&B**: Highway 2 East, P.O. Box 1325. 6 kilometres (4 miles) east of Kingston, opposite Glen Lawrence Farm. ☎ 548-4293. You'll get a warm welcome from linguists Marion and Hans Westenberg. Their superb and tastefully decorated house is deep in the woods only 2 minutes from the St Lawrence River. Come here for silence and rest. Breakfast is extra.

🛏 **Wellington Street**: 60 Wellington Street. ☎ 544-9919. This isn't a charming inn, but it has the advantage of being near the centre.

☆☆☆☆ Splash Out ($110–250)

⚓ **The Hotel Belvedere**: 141 King Street East. ☎ 548-1565. Very beautiful, classic residence that's superbly decorated. If you have the money, ask for room 202. The huge bed and stylish furniture gives a sense of authenticity to the place. Breakfast included, served on the terrace in summer.

WHERE TO EAT

☆☆ Moderate (under $15)

✕ **The Pilot House of Kingston**: 265 King Street East. This corner restaurant owes its name to the sailors who used to shelter here. The café has retained a friendly and warm atmosphere and its decor is typical of taverns of the period. Enjoy specialities such as meat pie.

✕ **Stoney's**: Ontario Street, not far from the tourist office. Open Monday to Friday 10am–10pm. Saturday and Sunday 10am–11pm. Bare stone walls, and very popular at lunchtime, serving a large choice of cheap salads, pizzas and American specialities in large portions. There's a bar in the evening.

✕ **Hoppin' Eddy's**: 393 Princess Street. A large, very lively restaurant with several rooms, a terrace and New Orleans-style food and interior. Enjoy a 10 per cent discount if you've visited Fort Henry.

🍴 **White Mountain**: 176 Ontario Street, opposite Stoney's. Open daily 10am–11.30pm. You can't miss this ice-cream parlour as there's always a crowd outside. Excellent homemade ice-creams, and even the cornets are made before your very eyes.

☆☆☆ Expensive (around $20 for dinner, slightly less for lunch)

✕ **Le Caveau**: 354 King Street East. Wine bar and restaurant with lovely, intimate rooms on three levels in a narrow building. Cuisine is innovative, served in a rather French atmosphere.

✕ **Mino's Restaurant**: 250 Ontario Street, to the right of City Hall, next to the car-park. ☎ 548-4654. Tasty and generous portions of Greek food are served in a pleasant neo-Greek atmosphere. Always busy.

✕ **Chez Piggy**: 68 Princess Street. ☎ 549-7673. Next to No. 72 is a cul-de-sac with a small courtyard. The restaurant is on the right, housed in a 19th-century building with a lovely terrace. It has the best reputation in town, serving good wines.

WHERE TO HAVE A DRINK

🍸 **Toucan Bar**: Princess Street. Open Monday to Friday till 1am. Saturday and Sunday until 2am. This English pub in the same courtyard as Chez Piggy (*see above*) actually specializes in Irish beers. You'll find the inevitable darts games and sometimes live rock bands. Food also served.

🍸 **Margaritaville**: 25 Ontario Street, opposite Mino's Restaurant. Open daily 11am–midnight. With the first rays of spring sun the restaurant, bar and terrace come to life. Barrels for tables, nachos with a drink, a little music and there you go. Spicy Mexican food.

ONTARIO

♪ The Kingston Brewing Co: corner of Clarence Street and Ontario Street. Open daily until 1am. Another more or less English pub, but this one brews its own beer, and it's very good too. Very well known locally as the 'Brew Pub'. Pleasant patio.

ENTERTAINMENT

– **AJ's Hangar**: 393 Princess Street. Look for the small unobtrusive entrance next to Hoppin' Eddy's restaurant. Open daily. AJ's Hangar is decorated in 1960s style, with aeroplanes suspended from the ceiling. Great atmosphere, rock 'n' roll and beer. Lots of people each night to hear the touring bands or have a blast on Tuesday retro nights or Thursday and Saturday disco nights. Entrance charge for themed evenings.

– **Stages**: 390 Princess Street, opposite AJ's Hangar. Closed Tuesday and Sunday. Entrance charge. The most fashionable nightclub at the moment draws a young crowd.

– **Cocamo**: 172 Ontario Street. Open daily until 2am (3am on Saturday). Free entry to women on Thursday. This is the hot spot in the resort, where Kingston's golden youth come to break out to the dance tunes. It's a bit pretentious – amazing for Canada! For those little gaps at the end of an evening there's a pizza stand at the entrance. The nightclub is also a restaurant during the day.

– **Grand Theatre**: 218 Princess Street. ☎ 530-2050. Kingston's community performing arts centre, comprising two performance spaces. The Regina Rosen Auditorium puts on music, theatre and dance by local and touring groups; the Baby Grand Studio features more avant-garde drama.

– **Domino Theatre**: 370 King Street West. ☎ 546-5460. Opposite Ellerbeck Street. A focus point for amateur theatre in Kingston, with performances almost every evening in summer.

WHAT TO SEE

★ **Fort Henry**: east of Kingston on Highway 2, 30 minutes' walk from the centre (signposted). ☎ 542-7388. Open 10am–5pm. Entrance charge $10. Guided tours available. A programme detailing parade times is available from the tourist office. The Fort was built in 1832 to protect the entrance to the Rideau Canal at a time when relations between the British and the Americans weren't particularly harmonious.

It now houses an interesting collection of uniforms and arms, and you can visit the officers' quarters as they were in 1867. Some World War II prisoners were incarcerated here but escaped through the latrines. The uniformed parades, processions and demonstrations of military discipline of the period are authentic, informative and entertaining. Children can even have a go at marching and saluting in time with the professionals. This is one of the best living museums of its kind in Ontario.

★ **Murney Tower**: corner of King and Barnes streets, on the shores of Lake Ontario. Open mid-May to mid-September 10am–5pm (6pm in July and August). This small museum is linked to Fort Henry and housed in one of the large, squat Martello towers built to defend the town.

★ **Bellevue House**: 35 Centre Street. ☎ 545-8666. Open 10am–5pm. Entrance charge inexpensive (student discounts). This house of Tuscan influence was the home of a rich businessman who lost his fortune. Sir John A. MacDonald – then a rather insignificant lawyer – lived in it from 1848 to 1849 before he became Canada's first Prime Minister in 1867. The house shows what bourgeois life was like in the 19th century, and there's a short documentary film you can watch.

★ **Marine Museum of the Great Lakes**: 55 Ontario Street. ☎ 542-2261. Open daily 10am–5pm. Entrance charge includes the ice-breaker (and B&B) *Alexander Henry* (*see* 'Where to Stay') as well as the Pump House at 23 Ontario Street, where you'll see navigational instruments, several lovely models, and various bits of flotsam. There's also an exhibition of photographs relating to naval boat-building on the Great Lakes, which centred on Hamilton in the 19th century.

LEAVING KINGSTON

Hitchhikers beware: there are six large prisons in the vicinity of Kingston, so try to avoid the escaped convict look!

Drivers with time on their hands are advised to take Route 33 via Picton rather than the highway, as it passes fields of apple trees, small ports and the green landscape.

A vast plain stretches from Ontario to the Rockies, so immense that it's hard to imagine. This huge expanse of flat land that sits under deep-blue skies in summer, swept by the wind, divided into plots and traversed by the Trans-Canada Highway, appears to be uninhabited. In fact, the region is 1,300 kilometres (812 miles) wide with a population of 4.5 million, clustered mainly around the towns of Winnipeg (Manitoba), Regina (Saskatchewan), Calgary and Edmonton (Alberta).

Manitoba

WINNIPEG
DIALLING CODE: 204

Winnipeg is a big, apparently soulless town that seems to stretch to infinity, just like the immense prairies that surround it. The lively areas are very spread out, so you'll need a car, as the districts stretch towards never-ending suburbs with wide streets. You'll wonder where the inhabitants have gone because there's so much space. In fact, the city was built in this spot because it was ideal for the grain business, and Winnipeg is essentially a huge cereal warehouse. All that was missing in the early days was a railway to turn this crossroads of the Great Prairies into a real city. Luckily, Ukrainian, Russian, Mennonite, Italian, Polish and Chinese immigrants were drawn here to settle and breathe some life into the Prairies.

One of the few attractions in a one or two day stay in Winnipeg is the French-speaking quarter of St Boniface and a visit to the excellent Manitoba Man and Nature Museum. Nature-lovers can make their way north to the shores of Lake Winnipeg, where the fishermen bring in some extraordinary catches.

A GLIMPSE OF THE PAST

Initially an old fur-trading post, Winnipeg developed mainly on the right bank of the Red River, site of the present-day St Boniface district. This is where the Métis community developed – born of intermarriages between the original white settlers (fur-company administrators and workers) and the Indian women, generally from the Cree tribe. It was here that the Métis rebellion against the Canadian government was fomented, led by their chief, Louis Riel. For more on this *see* 'The Métis Revolt' *in* 'Background'.

GETTING THERE

❶ **Winnipeg International Airport**: about 10 kilometres (6 miles) north-west of the city centre. ☎ 744-0031. Take the orange or yellow shuttle bus into town.
■ **Air Canada**: ☎ 943-9361.
🚇 **Train station** (map D3): Main Street.

■ **Via Rail**: Reservations: ☎ 1-800-561-8630 (toll-free)
🚌 **Greyhound** (map B3): corner of Portage Avenue and Colony Memorial Boulevard. ☎ 783-8840.
■ **Grey Goose Bus Lines**: 301 Burnell Street. ☎ 786-8891.

USEFUL ADDRESSES

❶ **Visitor's Information Centre** (map C3): Legislative Building, corner of Broadway and Osborne Street. ☎ 945-3777 ext. 36 or 1-800-665-0040 (toll-free). Open 8am–9pm in summer.

❶ **Information Bureau** (map C3): Convention Centre, 232–375 York Avenue. ☎ 943-1970.
✉ **Post office** (map C2): 266 Graham Avenue. ☎ 983-5481. Open 8.30am–5.30pm.

WINNIPEG

■ **Police**: ☎ 986-6222.
■ **Health Science Centre (hospital)**: 820 Sherbrook Street. Emergencies: ☎ 787-3167.

■ **The Canadian Park Service**: 457 Main Street. ☎ 983-2290. Open Monday to Friday 8.30am–5pm. Information centre for campsites, provincial parks and fishing and hunting licences.

WHERE TO STAY

A really pleasant way to visit Manitoba is to stay on different farms through **Manitoba Farm Vacations**. Contact: Felix Kuehn, 525 Kylemore Avenue, Winnipeg, Manitoba R3L 1B5. ☎ 475-6624. The rates are not giveaway prices for lodging in the country, but are decent enough.

🛏 **Ivey House International Hostel**: 210 Maryland Street. ☎ 772-3022. Closed 9am–4pm. About 15 minutes' walk from town is this clean, welcoming little house with 40 beds in a variety of rooms. Use of kitchen, fridge and small sitting room. Really nice and not expensive. Bike hire available.

🛏 **University of Manitoba**: Pembina Highway. ☎ 474-9942. The Pembina Bus from downtown to the University stops 2 minutes away from the residence reception in Pembina Hall. If you arrive after 5pm, ask the night porter to open the door. There are 30 student rooms at fairly cheap rates, but it's closed to tourists from September. There's a cafeteria and restaurant in

the University Centre Building. This isn't a very practical place to stay, as it's quite far from town.

🛏 **Saint James Hotel**: 1719 Portage Avenue. ☎ 888-2341. Clean and not very expensive. Take the Red-Express bus on Portage Avenue.

🛏 **Guesthouse International**: 168 Maryland Street. ☎ 772-1272. Cheap and you'll get a friendly welcome. There's a dining room and kitchen. There's a maximum of three beds per room, a bathroom on every floor, and showers and washroom in the basement.

🛏 **Gîte de la Cathédrale** (map F3): 581 rue Langevin. ☎ 233-7792. This B&B in the St Boniface district has four rooms with communal bathroom and offers a very friendly welcome.

WHERE TO EAT

☆ Budget

✕ **Redtop**: 219 Saint Mary's Road. The best hamburgers in town at real basement prices.

✕ **Kelekis**: 1100 Main Street. The best hot dogs around. The walls are covered with signed photographs of celebrities and other visitors, giving a pictorial biography of Mr Kelekis, the owner. The place has a very good reputation in Winnipeg.

– In the **Fourche district** (see 'What to See') a variety of kiosks offer really excellent Chinese, Sri

Lankan, Ukrainian, Italian or Jamaican meals at unbeatable prices.

☆☆ Moderate

✕ **Alycia's**: 559 Cathedral Avenue. ☎ 582-8789. Families come from afar to eat in this excellent Ukrainian, family-run restaurant, serving great soups, sauerkraut and delicious *piroshki* (filled savoury pastries). However, the kitsch decor includes portraits and photos of the Pope. Next door, the **Daly Store** does take-aways.

THE PRAIRIES

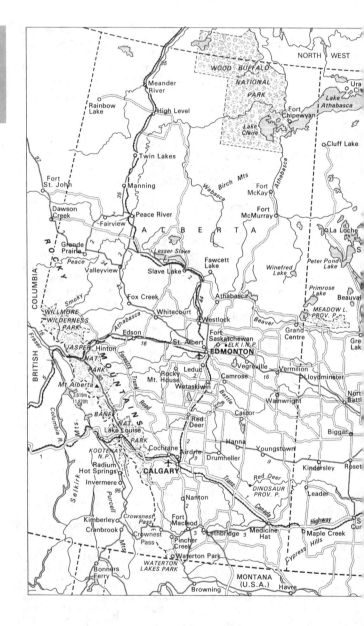

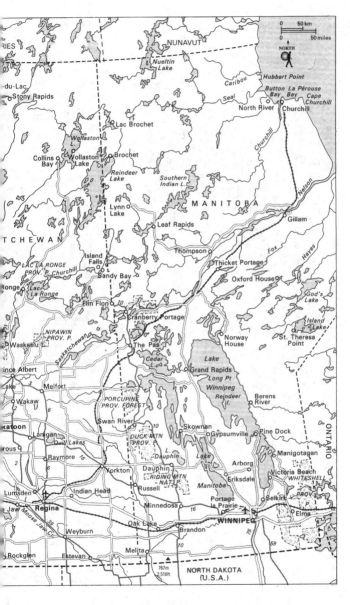

THE PRAIRIES

WINNIPEG

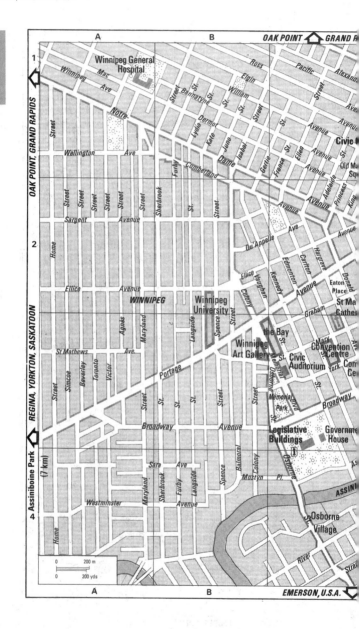

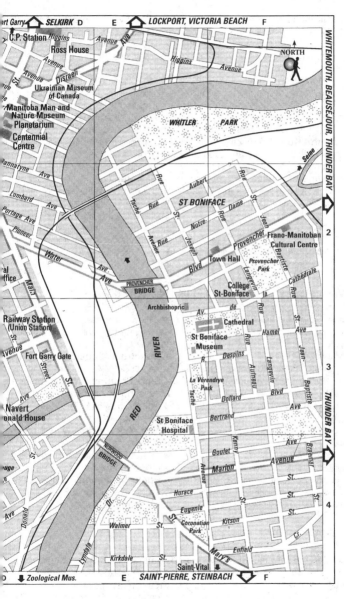

WINNIPEG

✕ **Chopin**: 84 Albert Street. ☎ 943-0727. This is a good downtown café serving excellent Polish soups and a number of other well-prepared dishes.

✕ **Impression Café**: 102 Sherbrook Street. Very popular café with a European feel where you can read a newspaper or play chess. It has good cakes and also a few Russian dishes.

✕ **Kum Koon**: 257 King Street. ☎ 943-4655. A pretty animated atmosphere in this Chinese restaurant.

✕ **Emperor Palace**: 277 Ruppert Avenue, Chinatown. Another pretty good Chinese restaurant.

☆☆☆ Expensive

✕ **Acropolis**: 172 Sherbrook Street. Good Greek restaurant, serving souvlaki, gyros (doner kebabs) and taramasalata.

✕ **D'8 Schtove**: 1842 Pembina Highway, near the university. ☎ 275-2294. Mennonite dishes cooked by a Vietnamese chef, including highly recommended puddings.

✕ **Picasso's**: 615 Sargent Avenue. Seafood specialities in a pretty smart place. If you're not careful, the bill could be quite substantial; best to opt for the salads or appetizers.

✕ **Yamato**: 667 Stratford Street, on the corner of Pembina Highway. ☎ 452-1166. A Japanese restaurant where you take off your shoes at the door. It's expensive but the side dishes will satisfy your hunger without putting you in financial trouble.

WHERE TO HAVE A DRINK, NIGHTLIFE

🍸 ✕ **Café Jardin-Terrasse Daniel Lavoie** (map F2): 340 Boulevard Provencher, in the Franco-Manitoban Cultural Centre in St Boniface. French-Canadian cuisine – savoury tarts, soups gratinée, pasta, pumpkin pie – at lunchtime only. On Tuesday there are jazz gigs. Check their programme for occasional groups on other evenings.

– **Rorie Street Marble Club**: 65 Rorie Street. ☎ 943-4222. A big, very American disco with a 'Top 50' group every evening. Pretty convivial, and the only place with a bit of life in town. There's a dress code so you might not get in wearing jeans and trainers.

– **Spectrum Cabaret**: 176 Fort Street. ☎ 943-6487. For rock fans.

– **Club Soda** and **Night Moves**: Windsor Park Inn, 1034 Elizabeth Road. ☎ 253-2641. These are the most fashionable clubs in town.

– **Yuk Yuk's Komedy Kabaret**: 108 Osborne Street, second floor. ☎ 475-9857. It's in the lively Osborne Village district.

– **Rumor's Comedy Club**: 2025 Corydon Avenue. ☎ 488-4520. Comedy shows from 9pm.

WHAT TO SEE

★ **Manitoba Museum of Man and Nature** (map D1): 190 Ruppert Avenue. ☎ 943-3139. Open daily 10am–6pm. This excellent museum is the cultural must in town, and there's not really much point in stopping in Winnipeg if you don't visit it. You'll learn a great deal about the way Canada developed. Different sections recount the history of the country through very realistic slide shows: the climate, flora and fauna are clearly explained. The section devoted to the Algonquin Indians is particularly good. In fact, you'll find yourself in the middle of a village – a lively reconstruction of a road in

Winnipeg from the beginning of the 20th century. Also worth a look is an impressive replica of the *Nonsuch*, the first boat that traded furs in the 17th century.

★ **St Boniface Museum** (map E3): Taché Avenue, near Boulevard Provencher. ☎ 237-4500. Open 9am–9pm (5pm on Saturday). The museum is in the old convent of the 'Grey Sisters' – four nuns who travelled 59 days by canoe from Montréal to Winnipeg. This is the oldest building in Winnipeg. In addition to a few relics belonging to the nuns, the museum's upper floor also has a number of everyday utensils that show the life of the fairly wealthy in the mid-19th century. In the chapel, be sure to look at the Virgin made of papier mâché.

The museum also has a room dedicated to Jean-Baptiste Lagimodière, a local figure renowned for having carried a very urgent message from Winnipeg to Montréal, in the middle of the dreadful winter of 1815–16.

Before she became a nun, the founder of the convent was married to an alcoholic and bootlegger. The prevailing joke was that her husband was always '*gris*' (meaning grey, and French slang for drunk). The nun must have had a sense of humour because she apparently chose this colour for the order's habits.

★ **St Boniface Cathedral** (map E–F3): Avenue de la Cathédrale. The cathedral burned down in 1968, and a ghastly church rebuilt just behind it. The only parts of the original cathedral now remaining are the superb neo-Romanesque facade, a few pillars and the statue of St Boniface.

Opposite the cathedral is a small **cemetery** where you'll find the tombs of many Winnipeg personalities, including those who came to Winnipeg in 1818 to provide a religious presence for the French and Métis population.

★ **Winnipeg Art Gallery** (map B–C3): 300 Memorial Boulevard, on the corner of St Mary Avenue. ☎ 775-7297. Open Tuesday, Friday and Saturday 11am–5pm. Wednesday and Thursday 11am–9pm. Closed Monday and public holidays. Free every Wednesday. It was built in 1970 of fossilized stone from Manitoba and houses, among other things, a superb collection of Inuit sculptures (in the mezzanine). The Inuit pieces are fascinating for the respect they command. The materials are never finely worked, resulting in a kind of crudeness that creates a softness in the sculpted faces. The groups of people are often still attached to the stone, as if to keep them warm. You'll also notice that the figures are always engaged in some activity, but that their backs are hunched over and stiff to reflect the harshness of Inuit life. The Floor Gallery exhibits Flemish and German wooden pieces from the 16th century. The gallery also hosts temporary exhibitions of contemporary art.

★ **Ukrainian Museum of Canada** (map D1): 1175 Main Street. ☎ 582 7345. Closed Monday. The museum shows the vitality of Ukrainian culture in the region, and includes a collection of richly embroidered pioneer costumes from the 19th century.

★ **Osborne Village** (map C4): There's a small section of Osborne Street, between River and Stradbrook avenues, where you'll find a few bars and restaurants. It's hardly Greenwich Village, but it's one of the liveliest parts of town and where the local young people get together.

★ **Exchange District** (map D1–2): Along Main Street, just north of Portage Avenue, you'll find some of Winnipeg's oldest buildings, built at the beginning of the 20th century. This is where fortunes were made in a day, with the Hudson's Bay Company being the trailblazer of the fur trade. The grain industry also flourished here during a time of continuous expansion between 1880 and 1920. This area is still the heart Canada's cereal industry.

★ **Main Street** (map D1): This huge thoroughfare, running north–south through the city, is so wide at the junction with Portage and Main that the Mall outside Buckingham Palace in London looks as narrow as a train track in comparison. Back in the mid-19th century the ox-drawn carts cut up the town's muddy roads so much that they often had to move to different ruts, thus making the roads wider and wider. Main Street and Portage Avenue, which were the main routes for the fur traders, were particularly badly damaged. Nowadays people say that the roads are 'as wide as seven Red River carts'.

While on Main Street, don't miss the Ukrainian Orthodox Cathedral with its black-and-gold domes.

★ **The Forks**: at the confluence of the Assiniboine River and Red River, behind the Via Rail station. An attractive area, the Forks has become the liveliest area in Winnipeg – the result of a redevelopment project that encompassed one of the most important historical sites of both Winnpeg and Manitoba. It's now essentially a leisure area, with beautifully arranged walks along the riverbanks (panels give interesting explanations of the history and culture). There's also a group of buildings and old warehouses that have been converted into attractive shops, restaurants, cafés, ice-cream parlours and grocery stores stocking products from all the ethnic groups in Manitoba; they all sell snacks to eat in or take away. You can also rent bikes here by the hour or by the day.

WHAT TO DO

– **Grand Beach**: about 130 kilometres (80 miles) north of Winnipeg, on Highway 59. If you're in Winnipeg for a few days and the pressing Prairie heat is taking its toll, go and have a swim at this beautiful beach, frequented at the weekend by Winnipeg's inhabitants. There's a well-organized campsite in Grand Beach Provincial Park. ☎ 754-2212.

– **Fishing**: The Winnipeg tourist office has lots of information about the amazing fishing here, and the best places to visit north of town (*see* 'Useful Addresses').

– The **Legislative Assembly of Manitoba** sits from March or April to June or July, and members of the public and visitors are welcome to attend. Passes for the public gallery must be obtained from the security office in the main front lobby. The most exciting debates usually occur in the Question Periods, which are also regularly televised.

– **Shows**: In the summer on the Rainbow Stage, in Kildonan Park on North Main Street, you can see shows such as *My Fair Lady, The King and I* or *Annie*.

– **Folklorama**: This is a multicultural festival, held in tents in different parts of the city, where each ethnic community offers dances, song and cuisine from their country of origin. It takes place every year, during the first two weeks in August, and is touristy and quite expensive. Information: ☎ 944-9793.

– **Winnipeg Folk Festival**: Bird's Hill Provincial Park, 20 kilometres (12 miles) north of the city. ☎ 231-0096. This 3-day annual open-air event, held at the beginning of July, is much more interesting than Folklorama, and is the biggest and most famous festival in the country. It's a celebration of 'World Music', bringing together 100 or so international musicians playing many different styles of music. A cosmopolitan audience travels from all over the continent to attend what's certainly one of Canada's musical traditions.

IN THE AREA

★ **Lower Fort Garry**: 32 kilometres north of Winnipeg along Main Street north, which becomes Highway 9. ☎ 983-6341. Open daily 10am–6pm. Modest entrance charge. The fort was built between 1831 and 1848 for the fur trade and was the economic centre of the Red River colony. It was once the home of Governor George Simpson and, later, Governor Colville. English envoys signed contracts for three or five years to work here, and they didn't employ Indians, who were more likely to be trappers. At the time, the fort was the westernmost limit of Rupert's Land.

You can visit several well-preserved buildings, one of which has been completely refurbished. Costumed staff play the roles of former residents, and you can also visit the blacksmith's shop where the kids can help to make nails.

One of the most interesting areas is the fur loft, where hundreds of furs were stored. A beaver pelt had both long and short hair, and a rubbing technique was used to make the longer hair (which was too hard) fall out, leaving the short hair. When trading began, the Indians were amazed that the traders were more interested in used (already worn) furs than newer ones. To turn beaver skins into felt (for hats) they were soaked in a mixture of mercury and lead. This process gave off very toxic fumes that drove the hat-makers mad, without anyone understanding why. This is the origin of the expression 'as mad as a hatter' used by Lewis Caroll in *Alice's Adventures in Wonderland* (1865) for the character the Mad Hatter. Top hats were all the rage in England in the 1800s, and this fascination for felt was one of the reasons for Winnipeg's prosperity and the disappearance of the beaver.

★ **Mennonite Village Museum**: just north of Steinbach about 60 kilometres (37 miles) from Winnipeg; take Highway 1 east, then Highway 12 south. Open in summer Monday to Saturday 9am–8pm. Sunday noon–8pm. Entrance charge. Here you'll find reconstructions of houses from various villages built by Mennonites who emigrated from Holland and Germany between 1874 and 1880. The site includes a printer's workshop, stores, a school, church and a lovely windmill. A small museum near the entrance displays typical period costumes and a map showing the great migrations of Mennonites fleeing from successive persecutions.

The sect comes from the Anabaptists (similar to the Amish in the United States), and was founded by Menno Simonsz, a 16th-century Dutch reformer. Their creed is based on the Bible and their own conscience. However, in contrast to the Amish, the Mennonites have always been open to technological progress and are well integrated into modern life. To see for yourself, take a trip to Steinbach, an exclusively Mennonite community, where only the most conservative women are recognizable from their little navy-blue hats pinned to the back of their hair, and their rather long skirts.

✗ The village **restaurant** serves good-quality, typical Mennonite dishes. Particularly recommended are the rhubarb cake and the *pluma moos*, a cooked, dried fruit salad.

CHURCHILL
DIALLING CODE: 204

A place only for the brave and the poetic, Churchill is a small village of 1,300 inhabitants lost somewhere near the end of the world – actually on the shore of Hudson Bay. It's a beautiful way of discovering the Canadian north, and the last Cree village before Inuit country.

The journey in by train is so long and slow that you'll have lots of time to meet your co-travellers, and look at the countryside (the ever-thinning forest gives way to pine forest and peat bogs, and finally tundra). And there are lots of wild animals to look out for, including elk, foxes and various others, depending on the season. You'll also stop in mining towns such as The Pas and Thompson along the way.

This journey to the north is a very strange one, and you'll see many unique things in this unquestionably remarkable place. As late as mid-July, Hudson Bay is still covered with icebergs forming a great barrier that closes off the horizon. It's breathtaking.

GETTING THERE

There's no road, so you have to go by plane or, preferably, by **train**. There are three trains a week from Winnipeg. The trip covers 3,200 kilometres (nearly 2,000 miles), takes three days each way and is not expensive, given the distance and experience. Give yourself at least a week for this trip: the return journey will take you five days and six nights, with three days in Churchill.

If you buy your ticket in Winnipeg at least seven days in advance, you'll get a 40 per cent discount.

Plane services are operated by Calm Air ☎ (204) 778-6471, a subsidiary of Air Canada. Flights leave Winnipeg airport throughout the week and take about three hours.

WHAT TO SEE

★ **The tundra**: This is a frozen desert in the winter, with not a tree to be seen; everything is flat, and it stretches off to the horizon.

★ **The Inuit**: Churchill is still a native, indigenous village and the hospital and social services (among others) are located here, which brings many Inuit into town. Look for signs written in the Inuit language. There's also a good native museum.

★ **Tribal Village**: You'll have to go to Eskimo Point, 300 kilometres (186 miles) north of Churchill by plane or on foot. The latter is not really recommended, since you may never come back.

★ **Polar bears**: Bears live all around Churchill and from the beginning of October they wait for Hudson Bay to freeze over so that they can fish for seals. Therefore, the best time to see them is from mid-October to mid-November, and it's difficult to find accommodation in Churchill at this time. Beware: polar bears are dangerous and afraid of nothing – they kill someone once every two or three years.

★ **Aurora borealis** (the northern lights). Churchill is the ideal spot to view this spectacular natural phenomenon, especially in December and January. The colours are incredibly bright and very beautiful.

★ **The Cereal Terminal**: ☎ 675-8863. Guided tours organized by Parks Canada. Quite amazing, these 70-metre (230-feet) high grain silos are what the railway was built for.

■ **Northern Expeditions**: ☎ 675-2793. The company organizes various (fairly expensive) excursions from Churchill to watch bears or photograph white whales. They also offer daily expeditions across the tundra for the more adventurous visitors (and those who don't feel the cold).

Saskatchewan

Saskatchewan is Canada's wheat field, where the crops stretch to the horizon in all directions. The province covers 651,900 square kilometres (over 250,000 square miles), and has a population of 1,050,000. As well as grain farming, the region also has flourishing industries producing potash, oil and natural gas.

It's a province of rivers, forests and lakes, including some of the most beautiful watercourses in Canada. Among them are the Saskatchewan River (an Indian name meaning 'river flowing sweetly') and the powerful Churchill River that pounds its way through the Precambrian rocks, forging spectacular landscapes that dwarf the canoeists paddling by.

All along the roads in the province you'll come across dozens of small towns and villages with grain silos visible from far away. And wherever you go you'll find ranches or farms where you can stay.

Many people living in Saskatchewan are direct descendants of European immigrants from Russia or Scandinavia who arrived in Canada at the end of the 19th and the beginning of the 20th centuries. You'll find them hospitable and friendly, and they've kept their folklore and customs alive.

REGINA
DIALLING CODE: 306

Regina is the capital of Saskatchewan and its main commercial city. It's in the middle of the vast prairies where the wheat grows abundantly, about 160 kilometres (100 miles) north of the US border. The city was named in honour of Queen Victoria, but was previously known as Pile o' Bones, being a site where the Indians and the Métis used to hunt bison.

In 1882, Regina was chosen as the northwest headquarters of the Royal Canadian Mounted Police, and later, in 1883, became the capital of the North West Territories. The city is populated by a wide range of ethnic groups, with a large minority of German origin.

USEFUL ADDRESSES

Convention and Visitor's Bureau: Center of the Arts, 200 Lakeshore Drive. ☎ 789-5099.
Regina Tourism Center: Cornwall Center, 2100 Saskatchewan Drive. ☎ 787-2300. In the city centre.

Saskatchewan Tourism: 2103 11th Avenue. ☎ 565-2300. Toll-free: ☎ 1-800-667-5822. A source of very good leaflets.
– The daily paper, *The Leader-Post*, gives all the information about the cultural life of the town.

WHERE TO STAY

YMCA (Family YMCA of Regina): 2400 13th Avenue. ☎ 757-9622. Fax: 525-5508.

YWCA (YWCA Big Sisters of Regina): 1940 McIntyre Street. ☎ 525-2141. Fax: 525-2171. Email: regina ywca@ywca.regina.sk.ca

⌂ Youth Hostel: 2310 McIntyre Street. ☎ 791-8165. Set in a renovated historical monument, it's the most beautiful youth hostel in Canada. It's clean, newly renovated and well situated, but closes at 10pm.

– There are also numerous bed & breakfast places in town.

WHERE TO EAT

✖ **Butler's Quarters**: 2171 Lorne Street. ☎ 781-6945. Not far from the youth hostel, this budget place has a pleasant atmosphere and good food and drinks, including Irish whiskey. A notable patron is Ernest Hemingway's grandson, who lives in Regina and drops by once in a while.

WHAT TO SEE AND DO

★ **The Wascana Center**: Dominating the city is this huge park of 800 hectares (nearly 2,000 acres), on the banks of the artificial Lake Wascana. This is where you'll find the city's main government buildings, including:

– **The Legislative Assembly**: This is a cruciform building of Manitoba stone, with finishing materials imported from various countries. Inside, the arches and the ceiling ornamentation draw your eyes up to the tower and 56-metre (184-feet) high dome. The view from the top of the dome is well worth the effort of getting up there.

The building also houses the **Saskatchewan Gallery**, which contains an important collection of paintings of Prairie Indians depicting the heroic era of colonization.

– **Saskatchewan Museum of Natural History**: Here you'll find a remarkable collection of wild animals, birds, reptiles and fossils. The gallery on Manitoba takes the life of the Prairie Indians as its theme.

– The **University of Regina** is housed in futuristic buildings designed by Minoru Yamasaki, the architect of the Wascana Center.

– **Norman Mackenzie Art Gallery**: Located on the university campus, the gallery houses a permanent collection of Chinese, Egyptian and Mesopotamian artefacts, plus European paintings from the 15th to the 19th century. It also features regular exhibitions of works by contemporary Canadian artists.

– **The Trial of Louis Riel**: Each year, from the end of June to August, this play is performed at Saskatchewan House, on Dewdney Avenue, west of Alexandra Street. Riel led the Métis rebellion against the central government which had refused to recognize the territorial claims of the Métis. The play gives a fascinating insight into the origins and history of Canada. For more on this see 'The Métis Revolt' in 'Background'.

SASKATCHEWAN

Alberta

Alberta is the land of cowboys and Prairie Indians, Mounties and oil barons. Not far from the big, modern cities of Edmonton (the capital) and Calgary (the centre of Canada's oil industry), Albertans raise cattle on vast ranches. The abundance of nature is unrestrained in Alberta. The sky seems huge, the land rolls on and on and the lakes are turquoise, even when it rains, because of the powdered rock particles washed down by the melting glaciers in June.

Travelling west you reach the foothills that rise into the Rocky Mountains (the natural frontier with British Columbia) – a vast and awesome mountain range which astonished the first explorers. You'll find the most beautiful of Canada's national parks, Banff and Jasper, each a fabulous wilderness of narrow canyons, clear lakes and thick forests. The Alberta landscape has remained much as it was when the first Europeans arrived.

CALGARY   DIALLING CODE: 403

As the home of the biggest rodeo in Canada, Calgary was already famous for its Stampede, but has become better known since it hosted the Winter Olympics in 1988. However, unless you're around during the Stampede, it's not absolutely essential to stop here.

The history of the city perfectly sums up its present atmosphere. It has known three successive booms. First, the Royal Canadian Mounted Police (Mounties) was set up here in 1875, in a fort right in the middle of the Prairies. Colonel Brisebois, the commander of the fort, simply gave the place his own name. Having ruled the isolated fort like a dictator he was decommissioned and the new police commander renamed the place 'Calgary' – which means 'clear water' in Scots Gaelic.

The second boom came with the arrival of the railway in 1883, which brought hundreds of new immigrants on their way west to the hypothetical promised land. When oil was struck in 1914 Calgary went from small village to town, and subsequently developed into a city which has continued to make considerable progress. Today several hundred oil companies (86 per cent of the producers in the country) have their offices in multi-storey office blocks which have sprung up.

So why should you stop here? Simply for the annual Stampede when, for 10 days in July, it's complete madness. Everyone, from bar staff to business-men (and even prostitutes), dresses up in cowboy gear of jeans, stetson and boots. There's a fantastic atmosphere in the bars and the streets as people drink their way through the festivities.

After the madness of the Stampede, a relaxing break in the mountains is just the solution – Calgary is the perfect departure point for a marvellous journey across the legendary Rocky Mountain passes.

GETTING THERE

– If you're travelling across Canada by train, note that Via Rail no longer goes to Calgary. The nearest station is Edmonton, from where you'll have to take the bus south.

GETTING AROUND

Note that **hitchhiking** is prohibited in the province generally, but the ban is strictly enforced in Calgary and hitching can lead to a hefty fine.

From the Airport

– **By bus**: Shuttle every 30 minutes from 6.30am to 11.30pm to the big hotels in town. ☎ 531-3909.

– **By car**: Follow signs towards the city centre. As you leave the airport, turn onto Barlow Trail and follow it to its end, just by Bow River. Turn west to reach downtown on 4th Avenue SE, about 15 minutes' drive.

Orientation

It's easy to get your bearings once you've sussed out the system. The city is divided into four quadrants: northeast, southeast, southwest and northwest. The Bow River and Memorial Drive divide the north from the south and Centre Street divides east from west. Avenues run east and west, streets run north and south, with the numbering beginning at the demarcation lines. So, 7th Avenue SW is simply the 7th avenue south of Bow River, and located to the west of Centre Street.

To locate specific houses or buildings, first look at the last two digits of the address and then look at the first one or two, which will tell you the nearest street or avenue. So, 456 3rd Avenue is not far from 4th street, and 2345 13th Street, is near 23rd Avenue. However, you'll still need to know which quadrant you're looking in. The system lacks charm but you'll soon find out how practical it is.

Transport

Public transport in Calgary can be unreliable, so having a car is practically essential.

🚃 **The C-Train**: A sort of tram or light-rail train that runs from 6am to 2am along two lines making the shape of a 'Y'. The train going south (passing Stampede Park) is called 'Anderson'; the one going northwest is called 'Brentwood' and the one going northeast is 'Whitehorn'. There are shuttle connections to the city centre terminal and the Greyhound terminal. It's quick and practical and costs the same as the bus (it's free along the 7th Avenue section).

🚌 **Bus**: Buses run from 6am to midnight and many routes connect with the C-Train stations.

CALGARY

USEFUL ADDRESSES

❶ Tourist information at the airport: open until 10pm.

❶ Tourist information (map B3): Calgary Tower, at the foot of the mushroom, 131 9th Avenue SW. ☎ 263-8510 ext. 397 (Visitors' Information Centre). Website: www.tourismcalgary.com. Open 8am–8pm mid-May to beginning of September, and 8am–5pm the rest of the year. Very friendly, helpful staff. Pick up the *Calgary Attractions* brochure, which gives discounts on various activities in town.

✉ Post office (map B3): 207 9th Avenue SW. ☎ 974-2078.

■ United States Consulate (map B2, **1**): 1000 615 Macleod Trail SE. ☎ 266-8962.

■ Calgary General Hospital (map C2, **2**): Bow Valley Centre, 841 Centre Avenue. ☎ 291-8505.

■ Emergency services: 911 (national number).

🚌 Greyhound bus (map A2): 850 16th Street SW. (Bow Trail at the corner of 9th Avenue SW). ☎ 265-9111 or 1-800-667-8747.

■ Car hire: Rent-a-Wreck, 113 42nd Avenue SW. ☎ 287-9703. Budget (map B2, **4**): corner of 1st Street SE and 6th Avenue SE. ☎ 226-0000.

■ Mobile home hire: Three companies rent out mobile homes:
Canadream Hire (2508 24th Avenue NE. ☎ 291-1000); **Go West** (5515 Crowchild Trail SW, in the 'ATCO' park. ☎ 240-1814);
Motorhome Vacations Rentals (3640 26th Avenue NE. ☎ 291-9450).

WHERE TO STAY

Accommodation is not very practical in Calgary as in the downtown area you'll only find hotel chains that are expensive and impersonal. The B&Bs are much more pleasant but they're usually farther out of town. If you're here for the Stampede, make sure you book well in advance as accommodation is hard to find around that time. That's unless, of course, you've already booked a place on a ranch (see 'Accommodation' in 'General Information').

☆ Budget

🛏 Calgary West KOA Campground: Highway 1 towards Banff, about 1 kilometre on the left after Olympic Park. ☎ 288-0411. A private campsite from the KOA chain with all facilities: shower, electricity, washrooms etc., but a little more expensive than usual.

🛏 Calgary International Youth Hostel (map C2, **10**): 520 7th Avenue SE, just east of City Hall. ☎ 269-8239. Fax: 266-6227. Website: Chostel@hostellingIntl.ca. Not far from downtown is this hostel in a two-floor, long wooden house, in a wasteland of car-parks. You must

arrive between 6.30pm and midnight, and curfew is at 2am. There are 114 beds in dormitories sleeping six to eight, with a few family rooms in low season. Also a big, bright kitchen with fridge, plus laundry facilities. Breakfast, lunch and dinner are very simple and very cheap. This hostel is the best value for money in town. The free C-Train is nearby. There's also a daily bus service to the youth hostels as far away as Jasper in the Rockies.

🛏 YWCA (map C2, **11**): 320 5th Avenue SE. ☎ 232-1599. A 15-minute walk from Stampede Park where the rodeos are held, and two blocks from the City Hall and the closest C-Train station. It's very clean and has 40 single or double rooms (with or without bathroom) for women and children only. There's also a cafeteria, washroom, TV room and gym.

⌂ **University of Calgary** (map off A1, **17**): 2500 University Drive NW. ☎ 220-3210 (September to April); 220-3203 (May to August). Fax: 220-6760. Bookings in writing to: University Housing Office, Room 18, Dining Centre, University of Calgary, 2500 University Drive NW, Calgary, Alberta T2N 1N4. Just outside town; take bus No. 9 to opposite Kanasaskis Hall. Some of the buildings were erected for the Olympic Games, and a somewhat minimalist double room will cost around $20 per person, or $40 for a fully equipped apartment.

⌂ **Southern Alberta Institute of Technology** (SAIT; map A1, **12**): 1301 16th Avenue NW. The women's residence is at Owasina Hall. ☎ 284-8012. Fax: 284-8435. From mid-May to mid-August you can stay in small apartments like university residences, with kitchen and some private bathrooms. There's also a washroom and TV room. Phone ahead as there are plans for this type of accommodation to be made unavailable for people just passing through.

CALGARY

■ **Useful Addresses**

  🛈 Tourist information
  ✉ Post office
  🚌 Greyhound bus
  1 United States Consulate
  2 Calgary General Hospital
  4 Budget car hire

⌂ **Where to Stay**

  10 Calgary International Youth Hostel
  11 YWCA
  12 Southern Alberta Institute of Technology (SAIT)
  13 A Good Knight B&B
  14 Tumble Inn
  15 Lions Park B&B
  16 Inglewood B&B
  17 University of Calgary
  19 Elbow River Inn

✖ **Where to Eat**

  30 Pied Pickle
  31 Earl's
  32 Singapore Sam's
  33 Divino
  34 Unicorn
  35 Silver Dragon
  36 Cannery Row
  37 River Café
  38 Señor Frogs
  39 Sukiyaki House
  40 La Caille on the Bow

♟ **Where to Have a Drink**

  34 Unicom
  38 Señor Frogs
  50 The Rose and Crown
  60 The King's Horses
  61 Concorde
  64 The Drink
  65 King Edward Hotel
  66 Dusty's
  67 The Ranchman

★ **What to See and Do**

  70 Stampede Park
  71 Glenbow Museum
  72 Grain Academy
  73 Calgary Tower
  74 Devonian Gardens
  75 Fort Calgary
  76 The Deane House
  77 The Energeum
  78 Heritage Park
  79 Zoo

CALGARY

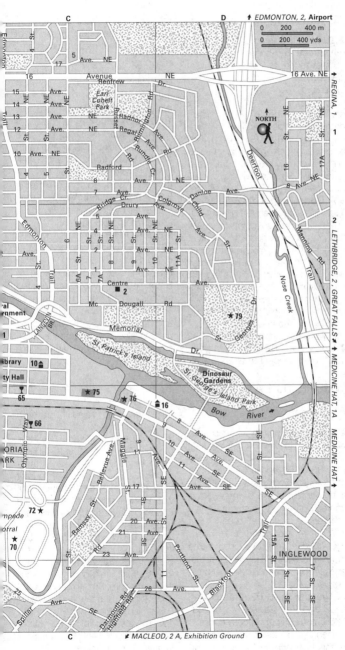

☆☆ Moderate

⚑ **Tumble Inn** (map B3, **14**): 1507 6th Street SW, between 15th and 16th avenues. ☎ 228-6167. A very well-located B&B that's not too expensive, especially if you stay several nights. There are three very comfortable rooms with shared bathroom in this beautiful Victorian-style house built in 1912. It's owned by a young, easy-going couple who will give you a warm welcome. Arrive between 5.30 and 7pm or by arrangement if you phone in advance.

⚑ **A Good Knight B&B** (map A1, **13**): 1728 7th Avenue NW. ☎ 270-7628. It's worth going this far out to this cosy little place in a very quiet residential area. You'll find three prettily decorated, spotless rooms with private bathroom. The biggest room is much more expensive although the facilities are not significantly better. Note that children, the wearing of shoes and smoking are not allowed upstairs.

⚑ **Lions Park B&B** (map A1, **15**): 1331 15th Street NW. ☎ 282-2728.

Fax: 289-3485. You'll receive a very warm welcome and the choice of three very well-maintained rooms with handbasin and shared bathroom. You might find the decor a little kitsch, but the prices are reasonable.

⚑ **Inglewood B&B** (map C–D3, **16**): 1006 8th Avenue SE. ☎ 262-6570. Open all year. Not far from the centre, in a quiet residential area 15 minutes' walk from Calgary Tower. Take 9th Avenue past Fort Calgary, then turn left. This non-smoking B&B in an elegant Victorian-style house has three comfortable rooms, a veranda and big garden.

⚑ **Elbow River Inn** (map B3, **19**): 1919 MacLeod Trail SE. ☎ 269-6771. Fax: 237-5181. The Elbow River Inn is a good alternative to B&Bs: near the lively areas, not too expensive and very close to a C-Train station. It also has a casino and free car-park. However, the hotel is also near Stampede Park, so bookings are often made up to a year in advance.

WHERE TO EAT

☆ Budget

✕ **Singapore Sam's** (map B3, **32**): 524 11th Avenue SW. ☎ 234-8088. Fax: 237-5748. Open daily until 3pm. $6–9 per dish. In spite of the grimacing dragons and traditional lanterns, this is more like a canteen than a restaurant. It's self-service, with set menus that include a Mongolian grill where you choose your own ingredients (noodles, vegetables, various meats) and a chef cooks it for you on a hotplate.

✕ **Unicorn** (map B2, **34**): 8th Avenue and 2nd Street SW. ☎ 233-2666. You can get various snacks at reasonable prices in the basement of this Irish pub, including fish and

chips, assorted salads and even some Mexican food.

✕ **Pied Pickle** (map B2, **30**): 522 6th Avenue SW. ☎ 234-0050. Open Monday to Saturday 11am–midnight. This bar-cum-restaurant is typically American–Canadian, but with a few touches of Italian in the cooking. Nothing really great, but good-quality, inexpensive food.

✕ **Silver Dragon** (map B2, **35**): 106 3rd Avenue SE, on the corner of Centre Street. ☎ 264-5326. Fax: 262-1575. Open Monday–Thursday 10.30am–1pm. Friday and Saturday 10am–2pm. Sunday and holidays 9.30am–10.30pm. Dishes cost $7–15. There's a quiet family atmosphere and you'll get perfect service in this Chinese restaurant in Calgary's very small Chinatown. The huge upstairs dining room has a sober, elegant decor, and with over 200 dishes on the menu, you're bound to find something you like.

☆☆ Moderate

✕ **Earl's** (map B2, **31**): Banker's Hall, 315 8th Avenue SW (Stephen Avenue Mall). ☎ 265-3275. Fax: 233-7554. Open Monday to Thursday 11am–midnight. Friday and Saturday 11am–1am. Sunday 11am–10pm. Part of a chain of restaurants found in all the big towns and cities of western Canada. The decor is very colourful and the atmosphere lively. Their slogan is 'Eat a little, eat a lot, fun to share!' On the menu you'll find everything very American in style. Next door is a bar catering to a young crowd where the floor is strewn with peanuts.

✕ **Divino** (map B2, **33**): 817 1st Street SW. ☎ 263-5869. Open until midnight. Closed Sunday. The decor here is fairly restrained, with a certain elegance and a hint of high-tech. You'll find an exhibition of modern pictures on the walls in this very European atmosphere – a bit classical, a touch intellectual and definitely warm. The delicious cooking is dominated by Italian and Californian influences: lots of inventive pasta dishes and salads. Specials are listed on the blackboard.

✕ **Cannery Row** (map B3, **36**): 317 10th Avenue SW. ☎ 269-8889. Fax: 269-1447. Open daily (except lunch at the weekend). Expect to pay between $16 and $23 per dish in this huge dining room overwhelmed by a vast bar. There's also a café area near the street and a small terrace in summer. The varied dishes include good light lunches and a wide selection of wines from around the world. Upstairs, a similar but smarter restaur-

ant called **McQueen** has jazz playing in the background.

✕ **Sukiyaki House** (map B3, **39**): 517 10th Avenue SW. ☎ 263-3003. Fax: 269-4082. $10–15 per dish. A Japanese restaurant to its very fingertips, with waitresses in traditional costume, screens, prints and traditional music. You can even have lunch or dinner on a tatami (straw mat), set away from the other tables (but booking is advisable for this).

✕ **Señor Frogs** (map B2, **38**): 739 2nd Avenue SW, on the corner of 7th Street. ☎ 264-5100. A big Mexican restaurant on several different levels in a beautiful yellow house with warm and colourful decor. Lots of good-quality food is on offer, but some people come here purely for a spot of salsa dancing to Latin music every evening (live or DJ). Great atmosphere.

☆☆☆ Expensive

✕ **River Café** (map B2, **37**): Prince's Island Park. ☎ 261-7670. Fax: 261-8795. From $16 a dish. Come for a meal after a walk in the park. You'll find very nice decor, complete with fishing theme, and excellent local food cooked on a wood fire, plus a good wine list. Brunch served at the weekend.

✕ **La Caille on the Bow** (map B2, **40**): 7th Street and 1st Avenue SW, next to Señor Frogs. ☎ 262-5554. Fax: 237-6108. Dishes cost from $16 in this attractive ochre and green house near Bow River, with a lovely view over the park. This large restaurant consists of a number of self-contained rooms and small sitting rooms over two floors. The bar comes alive at the weekend with concerts, and there's also a welcoming terrace on the edge of the park. It's a place that's both romantic (there's a fireplace in each room) and relaxed. The cuisine isn't brilliant but it's of good quality and it's a successful venue. It's very well known in Calgary, so it's wise to book ahead.

WHERE TO HAVE A DRINK

Nearly all the hotel bars have rock, jazz or blues bands in the evening during the Stampede – they're nearly all the same. If you like crowds and noise you'll have every chance to find what you want. The bars are usually open until 2 or 2.30am. Just leave your car behind (drink-drive laws are very strict in Canada) and go from bar to bar, wherever takes your fancy.

♥ Unicorn (map B2, **34**): 8th Avenue SW and 2nd Street. ☎ 233-2666. A basement bar with wood-and-brick decor and a big, oblong counter. Come here for your first drink, and have a Guinness after shaking off the dust from crossing the prairie. You can listen to excellent rock music, and at the weekend it's a boisterous Irish-style pub. There's a pool table and darts, and also a restaurant next door.

♥ The Rose and Crown (map B3, **50**): 1503 4th Street SW, on the corner of 15th Avenue. ☎ 244-7757. Another friendly Irish pub, with a warm atmosphere, regular happy hours and a very good brunch menu from noon to 3pm.

♥ The King's Horses (map B3, **60**): Near the corner of 11th Avenue and 5th Street, this is just the pub for a place for the over 20-somethings. Old barrels hang from the ceiling and there's a corner salon with ample armchairs, booths and a billiard table, plus darts and live music. By the end of the week it's so full that you can't move for people. On Sunday happy hours are noon–6pm on billiards and 6–10pm on drinks. There's a doorway through to the similar **Fox & Firkin** bar next door.

♥ Señor Frogs (map B2, **38**): *See* 'Where to Eat'.

♥ The Drink (map B3, **64**): 355 10th Avenue SW. ☎ 264-0202. A vast bar and restaurant on two levels in a sort of Roman style – columns with capitals in imitation marble.

There's billiards and a dance floor, and people of all ages gather here all week.

♥ King Edward Hotel (map C3, **65**): 438 9th Avenue SE, along a bit from the Calgary Tower. ☎ 262-1680. This likeable old hotel is Calgary's temple of the blues, holding memorable concerts on the ground floor (modest entry charge). There are three sets from 9.30pm, and often a jam session on Sunday. The regulars are blues-lovers and it also attracts buskers and backpackers. It's very smoky and the tables are too small to hold all the beers, but it all adds to the atmosphere. Photos of the famous and glamorous who have performed here adorn the walls.

♥ Concorde (map B3, **61**): 510 17th Avenue SW. ☎ 228-4757. Open for lunch and again in the evening until 2am. If you want a change from the pub atmosphere, this really popular, smart bar with a resolutely modern decor is where the golden youth of Calgary hang out. Snacks are served, and there are concerts from time to time.

♥ The Ranchman (map B4 off, **67**): 9615 MacLeod Trail South, 12 kilometres (7 miles) south of town. Open until 2am. You'll need a car to reach the best place for country music in Calgary, where stetson and cowboy boots are just about essential. There's a dance floor and billiards, plus bands on some nights.

♥ **Dusty's** (map C3, **66**): corner of 11th Avenue SE and Olympic Way. ☎ 263-5345. The decor of this country music venue is in light wood, much like a saloon. On one side is billiards and a corner bar propped up by cowboys, on the other a stage and scuffed-up dance floor, with tables solid enough to take the weight of the festivities. The atmosphere buzzes, especially during the Stampede which is held close by.

WHAT TO SEE

★ **The Stampede** (Stampede Park; map C3, **70**): This is what you've come for. It takes place over 10 days from the beginning of July. Each year tens of thousands of Canadians and Americans come to participate in this festival of horse and rider. The activities take over the streets, particularly along 8th Avenue, where there's a fabulous parade of cowboys, First Nations, Mounties and majorettes on opening day. And throughout the festivities you'll find entertainment of all kinds, from musical groups to native Indian dancers, on every street corner.

The rodeo itself takes place at Stampede Park. Before you actually arrive at the stadium entrance there's a huge funfair which will help put you in the mood.

Three types of competition are held in the stadium, usually at 1.30–5pm and from 7.30pm. In the afternoon it's **rodeo** time: with one arm high in the air the rider straddles a bucking mount for at least 8 seconds. The horses aren't wild – they're aggravated by slightly tightening a thong that squeezes their genitals so that they quickly revert to a wild state. After the competition the thong is loosened, and the horse quietens down.

The second competition is **calf-roping** (always in the afternoon) where a cowboy has to lasso a calf, leap from his horse, bring the calf to the ground and tie three of its feet together in less than 10 seconds.

The third competition is the **chuck-wagon race** (in the evening), which is like a cavalcade of pioneers' rickety wagons. Teams have to load a wagon (pulled by four horses) with various utensils, go round a course in the ring then race at full speed round the track.

It's a good idea to book tickets in advance, but there are always some on sale on competitions days. Note that advance tickets to the rodeo include entrance to the whole event, so won't have to pay again to see more than one competition.

– **Information**: Calgary Exhibition and Stampede, P.O. Box 1060, Station M, Calgary, Alberta T2P 2L8. ☎ 269-9822, 261-0101 or 1-800-661-1260 (toll-free). Website: www.calgary-stampede.com

★ **Glenbow Museum** (map B2–3, **71**): 130 9th Avenue SE. ☎ 268-4100 and 268-4208. Open daily 9am–5pm (9pm Thursday and Friday). This excellent museum specializes in contemporary works of art, but also contains a rich collection of native Indian and Inuit artefacts and other diverse exhibitions.

Among the items representing native cultures are superb Inuit arts and crafts, kayaks covered in caribou skins, and fishing utensils. The collection of artefacts from the Prairie Indians includes finely worked clothes and beautiful

CALGARY

embroidered horse blankets. There's also a section covering medicine men, with small totem poles and other items, and also a section on trappers and the fur trade.

The galleries dedicated to the conquerors of Canada display domestic objects, old agricultural machines and colonial furniture, plus material about the discovery of oil. In 'Heritage from the Homeland', you'll see items that the immigrants brought from their home countries that contributed to Canada's development. There are also displays from the 1920s contrasting the boom years and the Depression.

In the section 'Indians of the American West', rare documents show the development of the treaties with Canada's native tribes and how their lands were gradually seized. This gives a rare insight into the natives' plight, as proof that the decline of the First Nations coincided with the arrival of the whites is rarely publicized, and native exhibits are usually limited to a parade of costumes. But here you can even read a begging letter that an old, blind and destitute Indian showed to passers-by. Next to it is the history of the rebellion of Louis Riel.

On the 2nd floor you'll find a fine display of Asian art, including a rare walking Buddha from Sukothai (15th century), protective Tibetan statues from Lhasa and Hindu sculptures. You'll also see examples of 19th- and 20th-century Canadian works by artists such as Emily Carr, Riopelle, and McLeod. The museum also houses a collection of arms and uniforms, and a mineralogy gallery.

★ **Heritage Park** (map, off A4, **78**): 1900 Heritage Drive SW. ☎ 259-1900. Fax: 252-3528. Open mid-May to August daily 9am–5pm. From September to mid-October Saturday, Sunday and occasionally during the week (check in advance). From downtown, take the MacLeod Trail for a few kilometres then turn right onto Heritage Drive. The park is a little farther on, on the left (about 20 minutes' drive). It was funded by sponsorship from a number of industrialists and individual donations.

Bring a picnic, as you'll easily spend a few interesting hours here. This vast park boasts a dozen or so shops and houses dating from the early 20th century, and a very realistic-looking village has been tastefully reconstructed close to the lake. It's a real pleasure to wander round the streets among the staff (all in period costume) or to take the authentic steam train that links the various points of interest in the park.

There's a saloon, a train station, a school, a blacksmith's forge, a workshop where trains were repaired, the railway turntable and an excellent pastry shop (where breakfast is served free from 9 to 10am if you show your entrance ticket). Some summer programmes even invite children to relive the period on the village farms.

Also on display is the big wheel from a Chicago funfair dating from the early 20th century. Another attraction is a trip on the lake aboard the SS *Moyie*. Or you can follow signposted walking trails to learn more about three important periods in Calgary's history: the fur trade in 1860, the colonization of the prairie in 1880 and small-town life in the West in 1910.

★ **The Zoo** (map D2, **79**): Take the C-Train to the Zoo Station. ☎ 232-9300. Open daily 9am (closing times vary). Calgary's zoo is the pride of the city. The section about the Rockies is particularly interesting, as is the park containing life-size prehistoric animals.

★ **Grain Academy** (map C3, **72**): in Stampede Park. ☎ 263-4594. Open April to September, Monday to Friday 10am–4pm. Saturday noon–4pm. Free entry. This small museum about agriculture in Alberta is run by a farmers' cooperative that's proud to talk about its business. Exhibits include photographs, audiovisual displays, tools and models.

★ **Calgary Tower** (map B3, **73**): corner of Centre Street and 9th Avenue South (you can't miss it). ☎ 266-7171. Open 7am–11pm (8am–10pm off-season). The tower is 190 metres (623 feet) high and was constructed in 1967 by the unique method of pouring the cement for 24 hours non-stop. You'd be hard-pushed to say it was an aesthetic success, but it's much better from the top, which you can reach by lift in 62 seconds. One side looks out over the vast expanse of prairie, while on the other you can pick out the expanse of the Rocky Mountains. There is a bar and restaurant at the top, but watch out as prices are sky-high.

★ **Devonian Gardens** (map B2, **74**): While in the shopping area between 2nd and 3rd Streets SW, pop into the 4th floor of Toronto Dominion Square, where this glasshouse with hanging garden covers more than 1 hectare (2.5 acres).

★ **Fort Calgary** (map C3, **75**): Interpretative Centre, 750 9th Avenue SE. ☎ 290-1875. Fax: 265-6534. Open daily 9am–5pm May to mid-October. Nothing remains of the Mounties' former barracks except this big, green open space where a few students in period costume re-enact scenes of life in the fort. However, there are some artefacts, tools and uniforms, and an audiovisual show.

★ **The Deane House** (map C3, **76**): opposite Fort Calgary. ☎ 269-7747. Open daily 11am–2pm. Guided tours by arrangement. Built in 1906, this is one of the oldest houses in Calgary. Formerly the residence of Fort Calgary's commander, it's now a restaurant and tea-room. On Friday evening, at around 6pm, it hosts *Mystery from History*, an interactive dinner show that must be booked in advance. Behind the house is the oldest building in Calgary – a small hunting lodge built in 1876 by the local representative of the Hudson's Bay Company.

★ **The Energeum** (Energy Resources Building; map B2, **77**): 640 5th Avenue SW. ☎ 297-4293. Open Monday to Friday 10.30am–4.30pm (also Saturday during holidays and May to August). Kids interested in how things work will love this place. They can learn about geology and power in Alberta, and about all its resources (oil, natural gas, coal, hydro-electric power). There are even some simple interactive machines.

★ **Aerospace Museum of Calgary**: 4629 McCall Way NE. ☎ 250-3752. Fax: 250-8399. Open daily 10am–5pm. This is one of the most important aviation museums in North America. Among its exhibits are the famous Sopwith Triplane (invaluable in World War I), the Hawker Hurricane (distinguished in the Battle of Britain), the Beech D18S, the Mosquito, the mighty Lancaster and many other civil and military aircraft.

FESTIVALS

– **Caribbean Festival**: This usually takes place during the second week in June on Olympic Square and Prince's Island.

– **Jazz Festival**: Jazz bands perform all over town during the last week of June.

– **Canada Day**: On 1 July this national holiday is marked by various attractions on Prince's Island, including concerts, workshops for the kids and lots of games. Don't forget your Canadian flag.

– **Free concerts** are held on Saturday in the summer (during the day) in Riley Park and Heritage Park.

SHOPPING

– All along 8th Avenue SW are **cowboy** shops where you'll find a good selection of belts, boots, stetsons, shirts and lassos – everything in fact you need for the *Little House on the Prairie* look.

🔒 **Riley & MacCormick**: 209 8th Avenue SW (☎ 1-800-661-1585). This is the place where real cowboys go for the best North American brands: Boulet boots, Wrangler jeans (choose them long so they cover your boots well), Rockmount Ranchwear shirts with insets and wide cuffs, Montana belt buckles, Watson gloves and stetson hats. There are sales all year long, but particularly after the Stampede.

🔒 **Grand Saddlery and Western Wear**: 108 8th Avenue SE. ☎ 269-3293.

🔒 **Hudson's Bay Company**: 1st Street and Stephen Avenue (8th Avenue SW). This outlet of the famous chain that opened on 2 May 1670 is set in beautiful arcades.

🔒 **Eau Claire Market**: corner of 2nd Avenue and 2nd Street SW. ☎ 264-6460. This is one of the few decent markets in town, where you'll find a great variety, including stalls selling fresh fruit and vegetables and even local wines.

IN THE AREA

★ **Tyrrell Museum of Palaeontology**: 6 kilometres (4 miles) northwest of Drumheller and 138 kilometres (86 miles) from Calgary. About 90 minutes' drive northeast on Highway 9. ☎ (403) 823-7707. Website: www.tyrell museum.com. Open daily mid-May to early September 10am–5pm. This area is called the Badlands and it's a remarkable setting for one of the most impressive museums of palaeontology in the world. It's named after Joseph Burr Tyrrell, who discovered the first dinosaur remains in 1884. You'll see interesting models of prehistoric animals in their natural habitat, earth's evolution, the appearance of various lifeforms and, of course, the arrival of the dinosaurs. One of the many highlights is the complete reconstruction of a Tyrannosaurus Rex. In a particularly informative and successful approach, children can also amuse themselves and learn at the same time on the computers provided. Allow 2 hours for your visit.

★ **Dinosaur Park**: near the small town of Brooks, in a desert of rocks and sand 2 hours east of Calgary. ☎ (403) 378-4342. One of the richest fossil sites on the planet (and designated a UNESCO World Heritage Site), this marvellous attraction is an actual dinosaur cemetery. Phone in advance, as opening times can be erratic.

★ **Head Smashed-In Buffalo Jump**: 66 kilometres (41 miles) west of Lethbridge and 160 kilometres (99 miles) south of Calgary. From the intersection of Highway 2 with Route 785 take Route 785 west for 16 kilometres (10 miles). Open 9am–7pm from Victoria Day (third Monday in May) to Labour Day (first Monday in September), and 9am–5pm the rest of the year. Free entrance. ☎ (403) 553-2731. When you arrive in this superb place, designated a UNESCO World Heritage Site in 1981, you'll find a very beautiful museum and centre for interpretation, built on seven terraced levels and remarkably integrated into the cliff. This was the largest site where bison were massacred in the whole of North America. For nearly 6,000 years the Prairie Indians herded the animals to the edge of the cliff. Carried away by their speed and their terror, the enormous creatures smashed on top of each other some tens of metres below, where other hunters were waiting to finish them off with spears or tomahawks. The collection of bison bones is truly amazing, and films, displays, models and maps give an excellent introduction to life on the Prairies. There's a 2-kilometre (1-mile) walk along attractive, easy paths that run from the foot of the cliffs up to the top, with stunning views over the green plain below.

★ **Fort MacLeod**: 20 kilometres (12 miles) east of Head Smashed-In Buffalo Jump on Highway 2, and 165 kilometres (102 miles) south of Calgary. Information: Fort Museum, P.O. Box 776, Fort McLeod AB T0L 0Z0. ☎ (403) 553-4703. Open May to October 9am–5pm (7pm in July and August). Entrance charge. The fort was built on an island in 1874 and was the first North West Royal Mounted Police outpost in the west. Rebuilt in 1957 and turned into a museum, it tells of the life of the horsemen, the Indians and the pioneers from this region. In July and August the Mounties perform a musical parade four times a day.

★ **Hammerhead Tours**: 4714 14th Street NW, Calgary. ☎ 547-1566. They organize guided tours for small groups in the south of Alberta, visiting remarkable historic sites, particularly those following the path of the dinosaurs ('Dinosaur Adventure' includes a visit to the Tyrrell Museum), and Head Smashed-In Buffalo Jump.

LEAVING CALGARY

– If you want to go **north**, towards Banff and the Rockies, it's best to go by car as it would be a pity if you couldn't stop where you wanted.

– There is no regular **train** from Calgary to **Banff** and **Vancouver**. The only line across western Canada goes through Winnipeg, Edmonton, Jasper and Vancouver. Only the Rocky Mountains Train, specially adapted for tourists from May to October, links Calgary and Vancouver, but it's quite pricey. For information: ☎ 1-800-665-7245.

– If you are going **east**, it's best by plane across the vast prairies.

By Bus

🚌 **Greyhound bus**: 850 16th Street SW. ☎ 265-9111 or 1-800-661-8747 (from outside Calgary).

– **For Vancouver**: five departures daily.

– **For Winnipeg**, **Toronto** and **Montréal**: five departures daily, including three that go as far Montréal. The journey takes several days.

By bus: to Banff, six departures daily.

The Rocky Mountains

Crossing the Rocky Mountains is the highlight of any trip to Canada. From Banff to Jasper, you embark on a journey of over 400 kilometres (250 miles), along a beautiful highway with unforgettable views and a constantly changing panorama. Take Highway 1, and then Highway 93 north, through the Banff and Jasper National Parks on the eastern side of the mountains, in Alberta. Yoho and Kootenay National Parks are on the west side of the Rockies, in British Columbia. To get to them you need to leave the main road. The parks form a single rocky chain, administratively divided into four regions totalling 20,155 square kilometres (7,780 square miles).

But don't hesitate to leave the security of the road and explore some of the natural marvels on foot. You should allow several days if you want to enjoy the route's pleasures to the full, see the wildlife, go rafting and walk the national parks' tourist trails. There's something for everyone, from healthy walks lasting a few hours to hikes lasting several days.

The best time for a trip to the Rockies is at the end of May and the beginning of June: not only will you find hardly anyone else there, but the weather is usually good and the motels and B&Bs are cheaper. There are also numerous reasonably priced campsites and youth hostels all along the route. Don't forget, though, that the lakes won't have melted completely yet and the pathways are only open from June. There are so many wonderful walks that it would be a shame if the weather forced you to rush through without the chance to get off the well-trodden paths.

A LITTLE PREHISTORY

Some 57 million years ago the Rocky Mountains were forced out of the ground by the pressure of the earth's crust and the oceans. As they rose they pulled masses of rock with them which were forced upwards and then broken into sheer peaks, forming a barrier more than 4,000 kilometres (2,480 miles) long, from the north of the Yukon territories south to the Mexican border.

The Rockies bear a close resemblance to the Alps, with their sloping peaks, well-defined strata of rocks, deep, wooded valleys, eternal snows and glaciers creeping down the mountains. Vast pine forests grow very densely in the humidity, and you'll see lakes large and small with wild shorelines and

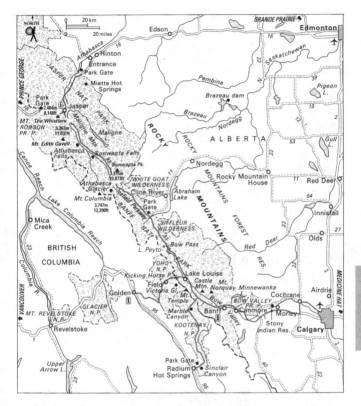

THE ROCKY MOUNTAINS

sometimes more tranquil surroundings that resemble a postcard, where the intensity of the colours is beyond imagination. Here your sensitivity to colours and shapes is constantly on the alert, and the vistas are as different as they are amazing.

Since they were created the Rockies have undergone at least four glacial periods, the last of which was about 10,000 years ago. This has allowed the glaciers to stay young and they've gouged out huge U-shaped valleys as they have thawed. Five great river systems drain from the valleys and wash down the debris from the erosions. The Rocky Mountains of the national parks are unspoiled. Apart from the villages you come across, humans have never exploited this region, so please respect this beautiful area.

A BIT OF ADVICE

– As in all the parks, campsites are limited. The rangers are there to give you a hand and to help you find places depending on your itinerary. Don't hesitate to ask them for advice, as they'll certainly communicate their love of the mountains.

– Remember that you are in bear country, so pick up a brochure about what to do if you see a bear, and read it carefully. There's advice in it that is evidently not always taken, since tourists are attacked each year. For example, do not keep any food in your tent, as the bears' well-developed sense of smell will sniff it out. Also, don't try to take photographs of the cubs as their mother might not take too kindly to it.

– Respect the environment – the rubbish bins are there for a reason, so don't leave a trail of litter in your wake.

– Be careful when you're on the highway as it's quite common to see herds of deer and even a few elk wandering about. Do not stop and feed them as this would mean they would eventually get used to humans, making their presence on the road ultimately very dangerous.

– Pack some warm clothing for the cool evenings.

– Watch out for mosquitoes and horse flies.

From Calgary to Banff

This journey of 129 kilometres (80 miles) starts by picking up Highway 1, at the end of 16th Avenue NW in Calgary, which crosses the Rockies. About 12 kilometres (7 miles) along on the left you can see the Olympic ski jump. As you leave the wide plateaux of the prairies you enter the foothills with their big cattle ranches. About 20 kilometres (12 miles) farther on the landscape changes again as you enter pine forests and steep valleys. When you get to Canmore, on the left, you'll see the Three Sisters, a mountain with three peaks.

CANMORE
DIALLING CODE: 403

The small town of Canmore isn't exactly a happening place, but it's a good base for hiking and exploring in the Rockies and has some advantages over nearby Banff. Accommodation is easier to find and prices are the same or lower than in Banff. You'll also find adequate shops and restaurants along Main Street (8th Street).

WHERE TO STAY

≜ **Cougar Canyon B&B**: 3 Canyon Road. ☎ and fax: 678-6636. ☎ 1-800-289-9731 (toll-free). Email: gailusaf @telusmapet.net. Two rooms with bathroom at $95 a night in this beautiful blue house with pleasant decor in a quiet part of town. Very friendly, homely and with super breakfast.

≜ **A Room with a View B&B**: 711 Larch Plane. ☎ and fax: 678-6624. Email: bestbnb@telusmapet. net. About $130 a night. Your host, Jean-Daniel, is a French ex-pat who knows the area like the back of his hand. There's a choice between a pleasant room in light wood or a more expensive mini-apartment downstairs (bedroom, TV room, kitchenette). Jacuzzi and sauna available in both cases.

⛟ A Touch Oh'Brass B&B: 510 Larch Plane. ☎ and fax: 678-4220. Email: mgfbrass@telusmapet.net. Two rooms with kitsch decor at prices the same as elsewhere, plus a jacuzzi.

WHERE TO EAT

✕ **Famous**: 629 8th Street, on the corner of 6th Avenue. ☎ 678-9351. Open daily except Monday in low season. As is often the case in western Canada, the Chinese restaurant is often the answer for eating well and cheaply. This one's not at all bad even though the setting isn't great.

✕ **The Sherwood House**: on the corner of Main Street and 8th Avenue. ☎ 678-5211. A log cabin with a terrace where you can sit in good weather. The inside is sober but in good taste, a family atmosphere. Traditional, good-quality cooking with a few touches of extravagance.

✕ **Sinclair's**: 637 Main Street. ☎ 678-5370. The decor is a bit dated but it's one of the few restaurants in town offering more than the usual burger-salad-pasta formula. Reasonable prices at lunchtime, more expensive in the evening.

BANFF	**DIALLING CODE: 403**

Banff is 56 kilometres (35 miles) from Lake Louise, 120 kilometres (74 miles) from Calgary and 228 kilometres (141 miles) from Jasper. It's the nearest mountain resort to Calgary, and a very popular and smart place. The main activity in town is centred along the main street, Banff Avenue, which is always very lively.

Banff was first developed at the beginning of the 20th century following the discovery of its sulphurous waters, which inspired the creation of the first national park in Canada. The Banff Springs Hotel, built at that time, quickly became the meeting place for the influential people of the region. There is also a renowned arts centre, the Banff Centre, which attracts writers, artists and performers from around the world.

All around you'll find short walks and great hikes that start at the edge of town. It is not uncommon to see deer walking calmly down the streets in the early morning, happily munching the green hedges around the houses or causing mini traffic jams. Sometimes you'll even find elk, which are much more aggressive.

If you want to drive around in the park, you must buy a day pass. If you're likely to be here for more than seven days, an annual pass is worthwhile. It's expensive, but you'll understand why when you see the quality of the organization and service in the national parks. You can camp out in the wilderness, but you'll need to do a bit of planning and get a licence from the park rangers. It's a form of registration, and you'll need to ask in advance because the number of permits issued each day is limited. And watch out for the bears!

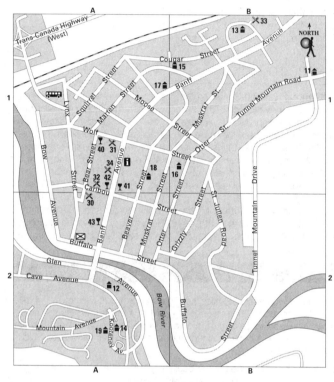

BANFF

■ **Useful Addresses**

🅸 Park information and tourist office

✉ Post office

🚌 Greyhound bus

🛏 **Where to Stay**

11 Banff International Hostel
12 Y Mountain Lodge
13 Spruce Grove Motel
14 Cascade Court B&B
15 A Good Night's Rest Chalet B&B
16 Rocky Mountain B&B
17 Red Carpet Inn

18 Beaver Street Cabins
19 Eleanor's House B&B

✕ **Where to Eat**

30 Magpie and Stump
31 Earl's
32 Coyote's Deli and Grill
33 Bumper's The Beef House
34 The Grizzli House

🍸 **Where to Have a Drink**

40 Saint James' Gate
41 Rose and Crown
42 Wild Bill's
43 Barbary Coast

GETTING AROUND

Banff Transit Service: For $1 a day you can have unlimited use of the town's somewhat kitsch buses. There are two routes: from the beginning of Banff Avenue (Trailer–RV park) to Banff Springs Hotel and from Tunnel Mountain Hotel to Banff Avenue.

USEFUL ADDRESSES

Park information and tourist office (map A1): 224 Banff Avenue, next to the church. ☎ 762-1550. From 21 June to 6 September open 8am–8pm. From 1–20 June and 7–26 September 8am–6pm. In winter 9am–5pm. On one side is the tourist office for the town of Banff; on the other, friendly rangers from the national parks will give you information and advice. There are also many brochures packed with information, including the excellent *Don't Waste Your Time in the Canadian Rockies,* which is a selection of views and tips. For example, avoid walking in the high forests where you can't see the country or landscape, as it's a lot of effort for not very much. If you want to explore on foot, buy a detailed map. There's also a very informative slide show. Pick up your information leaflets in Banff because the selection is better than at Lake Louise. The weather forecasts also seem more reliable than those at Lake Louise. You can also get up-to-date information about hotels from the very practical and affable staff. Finally, every evening in high season a ranger holds filmshows, gives talks (such as on the fauna and flora) or chairs discussions.

Bus terminal (map A1): Gopher Street. ☎ 762-2286. Five buses a day for Calgary. Also five a day for Calgary airport in summer, fewer in winter. Check for times.

Greyhound bus: ☎ 762-1092.

Transport in Banff: the Banff Explore Transit Service does a circuit of the hotels and campsites from 8am to 9pm June to September.

Police: ☎ 762-2226.

Mineral Springs Hospital (map A1): at the corner of Bow Avenue and Wolf Street. ☎ 762-2222.

Park keeper: ☎ 762-4506 (emergencies, 24 hours a day). Non-urgent calls: ☎ 762-1470.

Bank of Montréal: 107 Banff Avenue. ☎ 762-2275. Open 10am–4pm (6pm on Friday).

Post office (map A2): corner of Buffalo Street and Bear Street (☎ 762-2586); also Cascade Plaza, 317 Banff Avenue (☎ 762-2245).

Bicycle hire: Bactrax, 225 Bear Street. ☎ 762-8177. Open 8am–8pm. The least expensive in Banff, with discounts for Youth Hostel members with card

Performance: 208 Bear Street. ☎ 762-8222. Fax: 762-8411. You can hire bicycles, mountain bikes, tents, camping, hiking, and climbing equipment.

WHERE TO STAY

☆ Budget

Tunnel Mountain Village Campsite: 9 kilometres (6 miles) northeast of Banff. Take Tunnel Mountain Road all the way to the end. A large, very well-equipped campsite with showers, but it gets packed.

Banff International Hostel (map B1, **11**): Tunnel Mountain Road. ☎ 762-4122. Quite far out. Registration from 3pm to midnight, but if you arrive after midnight the watchman will let you in. This is a well-equipped, modern hostel with a lovely sitting room with fireplace, and another room with a piano. There are 154 beds in dormitories for four to six people, as well as family rooms, plus a kitchen, small cafeteria and washing machines. A really nice place full of friendly people. You can sign up for a day's rafting in the mountains nearby at attractive prices, and also for other activities, excursions and hikes.

Y Mountain Lodge (map A2, **12**): 102 Spray Avenue. ☎ 762-3560. Fax: 760-3202. A modern building, on the left after the bridge coming from Banff. Very clean with a range of accommodation, including small dormitories, family rooms and double rooms, plus a large, pleasant sitting room. You'll find the cheapest en suite room in town. If you have a bunk bed, you must sleep in a sleeping bag. Low prices in high season (15 May to 30 October). Booking advisable. The cafeteria is open 7am–1pm. There are no cooking facilities and no curfew. A lot of the young people who work in town during the tourist season stay here.

Spruce Grove Motel (map B1, **13**): 545 Banff Avenue. ☎ 762-2112. Fax: 760-5043. The cheapest motel in town is clean, has pleasant rooms and you'll get a nice welcome. Booking is essential in high season.

☆☆ Moderate

Because the area is very touristy, it's best to book rooms in B&Bs well in advance. You can get a list from the tourist office, but here are a few suggestions:

Cascade Court B&B (map A2, **14**): 2 Cascade Court. ☎ 762-2956. Fax: 762-5653. This very lovely house, with an interior that could be out of a glossy magazine, has spacious rooms, and a billiard table. You'll get an excellent welcome and a filling breakfast.

A Good Night's Rest Chalet B&B (map B1, **15**): 437 Marten Street. ☎ 762-2984. Fax: 762-8883. Choose from three rooms with communal bathroom or a mini-apartment with bathroom, fridge and TV. A very friendly welcome and prices are among the cheapest in town.

Rocky Mountain B&B (map B1, **16**): 223 Otter Street (on the corner of Wolf). ☎ 762-4811. Open May to November. This is a big, attractively decorated house with 11 rooms, with or without bathroom, at reasonable prices. There's also a more expensive suite on the third floor which can sleep up to six. Reductions in low season.

☆☆☆ Expensive

Red Carpet Inn (map A1, **17**): 425 Banff Avenue. ☎ 762-4184. Fax: 762-4894. An old 'inn' that's been turned into a hotel. The rooms are spotless and have one to three double beds in each. These can be very good value for large groups; otherwise, they're a bit expensive.

Beaver Street Cabins (map A1, **18**): 220 Beaver Street. ☎ 762-5077. Fax: 762-5071. Open all year to families (but very young children are not accepted) or small groups. You can rent pleasant and comfortable small chalets (sleeping up to four) at very reasonable prices, for a minimum of one week.

Eleanor's House B&B (map A2, **19**): 125 Kootenay Avenue. ☎ 760-2457. Fax: 762-3852. Open May to October and in the skiing season (rental by the week only during the

COLOUR MAPS

SECTION 1

The colour maps in this section refer
to the first half of the guide and refer
to the following chapters: Ontario and
British Columbia

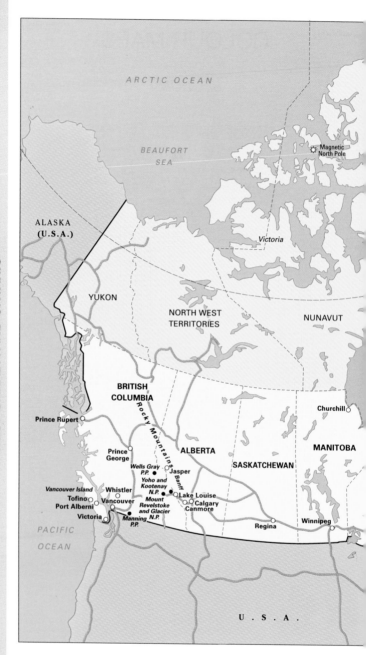

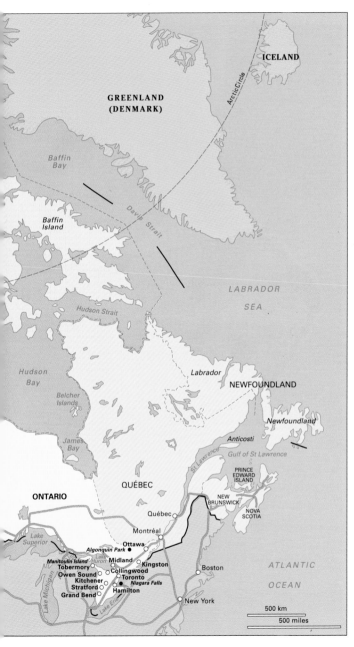

ICELAND

GREENLAND
(DENMARK)

Baffin
Bay

Arctic Circle

Baffin
Island

Davis Strait

LABRADOR
SEA

Hudson Strait

Hudson
Bay

Labrador

NEWFOUNDLAND

Belcher
Islands

Newfoundland

James
Bay

Anticosti

Gulf of St Lawrence

St Lawrence

QUÉBEC

PRINCE
EDWARD
ISLAND

ONTARIO

Québec

NEW
BRUNSWICK

NOVA
SCOTIA

Montréal

Lake
Superior

Ottawa
Algonquin Park

ATLANTIC

Lake
Huron

Midland
Kingston

Manitoulin Island
Tobermory
Owen Sound
Kitchener
Stratford
Grand Bend

Collingwood
Toronto
Hamilton

Niagara Falls

Boston

OCEAN

Lake
Michigan

New York

Lake Erie

500 km

500 miles

WEST CANADA AND ONTARIO

VANCOUVER (MAP I)

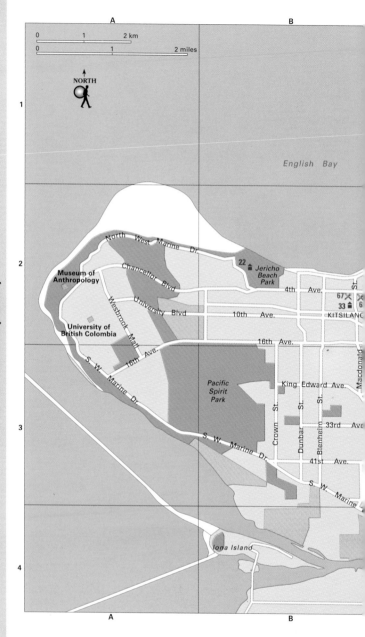

0   1   2 km
0   1   2 miles

NORTH

1

English Bay

North West Marine Dr.

2

Chancellor Blvd

Museum of Anthropology

Westbrook Mall

University Blvd

10th   Ave.

University of British Colombia

16th   Ave.

S. W.   Marine   Dr.

16th   Ave.

22 ⌂ *Jericho Beach Park*

4th   Ave.

67 ✕
33 ⌂   ✕ 6
KITSILANO

Macdonald

Pacific Spirit Park

King Edward Ave.

Crown St.

Dunbar St.

Blenheim St.

33rd   Ave

3

S. W.   Marine   Dr.

41st   Ave.

S. W.   Marine

4

Iona Island

A   B

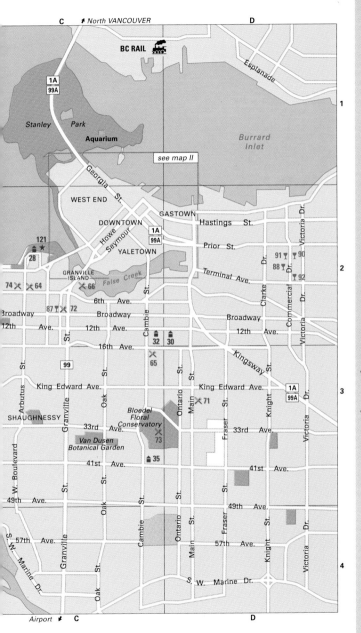

VANCOUVER (MAP I)

VANCOUVER (MAP II)

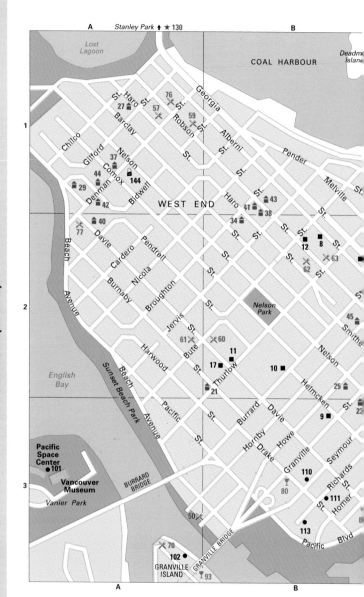

Stanley Park ↑ ★ 130

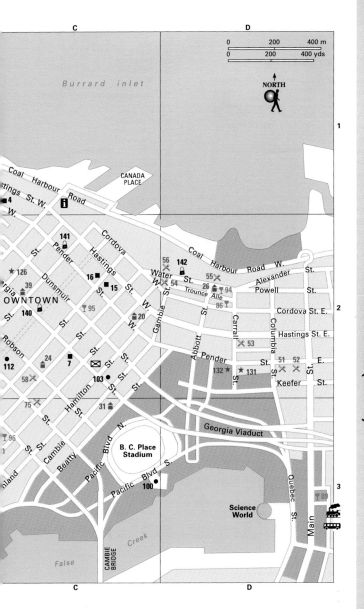

VANCOUVER (MAP II)

VANCOUVER – KEY TO MAP I

■ **Useful Addresses**

🚈 Train station (BC Rail)

🏠 **Where to Stay**

22 Hostelling International Vancouver, Jericho Beach
28 Kitsilano Point B&B
30 Douglas Guesthouse B&B
32 The Manor
33 The Penny Farthing Inn
35 Beautiful B&B

✕ **Where to Eat**

64 Sophie's
65 Sala Thai
66 Isadora's
67 Nyala
69 Naam
71 Accord
72 Tama Sushi
73 Seasons in the Park
74 Bishops

🍸 Where to Have a Drink, Nightlife

87 Carnegie's
88 Bukowski's
90 Joe's Café
91 The Quena
92 Waazubee Café

★ **What to See**

121 Maritime Museum

VANCOUVER – KEY TO MAP II

■ **Useful Addresses**

🄸 Tourism Vancouver Convention and Visitor's Bureau
✉ Post office
🚌 Greyhound bus terminal
🚈 Train station (Via Rail)
4 United States Consulate
6 Canadian Airlines
7 Budget
8 Tilden
9 Lo-Cost
10 St Paul Hospital
11 Shoppers Drug Mart
12 London Drug
13 American Express
15 International Travel Maps
16 Lingo Cyberbistro
17 Internet Coffee
18 The Byte Place

🏠 **Where to Stay**

20 Vincent's New Backpackers Hostel
21 Vancouver Hostel
23 Global Village Backpackers
24 The Kingston Hotel
25 Royal Hotel
26 The Dominion Hotel
27 Buchan Hotel
29 Sylvia Hotel
31 YWCA Hotel-Residence
34 The West End House
37 Shato Inn
38 Barclay
39 Georgia
40 Best Western Sands
41 Robsonstrasse Hotel
42 English Bay Apartment Hotel
43 Tropicana Motor Inn
44 Oceanside Apartment Hotel
45 Wedgewood Hotel

✕ **Where to Eat**

50 C Restaurant
51 Kam Gok Yuen
52 New Capital Smorgasbord
53 The Only Fish and Oyster Café
54 Water Street Café
55 The Old Spaghetti Factory
56 Umberto Al Porto
57 Poncho's Mexican Restaurant
58 Café S'il Vous Plaît
59 Capers
60 Doll and Penny's
61 Hamburger Mary's
62 Cactus Club Café
63 Joe Fortes
70 Bridges Bistro
75 Subeez
77 Liliget Feast House

🍸 Where to Have a Drink

80 The Yale
81 Automotive Billiards Club
82 Soho Café and Billiards
83 Bar None
84 Yale Town Brewing Company
86 Hungry Eye
89 The Ivanhoe Pub
93 Arts Club Lounge
94 The Town Pump
95 Railway Club
96 Starfish Room

🍸 Nightlife

100 Yuk Yuk's
101 Theater Sports
102 Arts Club Theater
103 Queen Elizabeth Theater
110 Luv-a-fair
111 The Grace Land
112 The Commodore
113 Mars Bar
114 Richard's on Richards

★ **What to See**

125 Vancouver Art Gallery
126 The Canadian Craft Museum
131 Sun Yat Sen Park and Garden
132 Building Sam Kee

🛍 **Shopping**

140 Pacific Center
141 Inuit Art and Sculpture
142 Hill's Indian Crafts
144 Lush

TORONTO – KEY TO MAP I

⌂ Where to Stay

21 The Rosa Tourist House
22 Leslieville Home Hostel
27 YWCA
28 Grayona Tourist Home
31 La Terrasse
32 Vanderkooy
33 Annex House
38 Havinn

♆ Where to Have a Drink

75 Le Bohemian Café
81 Chick'n'Deli

★ What to See

102 Ontario Science Center
107 Ontario Place
109 High Park
111 Casa Loma
115 Spadina House

TORONTO – KEY TO MAP II

■ Useful Addresses

🏢 Ontario Tourist Information Center
🚉 Union Station
🚌 Greyhound
3 Location de vélos
5 Maison de la Presse Internationale
6 Royal Alexander Theater
7 Cyber Space
8 24-hour pharmacy
9 Cyberland Café

⌂ Where to Stay

20 Hostelling International Toronto
23 Global Village Backpackers
24 Neill Wycik College Hotel
25 Tartu College
26 University of Toronto
29 Global Guest House
30 Beverly Place
34 Royal York
35 The Strathcona Hotel
36 Les Amis
39 Executive Motor Hotel

✕ Where to Eat

40 Tung Hing Bakery
41 Saigon Lai Restaurant
42 Saigon Palace Restaurant
43 Dessert Sensation Café
44 John's Italian Café
45 Margarita's
46 Tortilla Flats
47 Pilot Tavern
48 The Old Spaghetti Factory
49 Country Style
50 Hemingway's
51 The Second City
52 Ed's Restaurant
53 Swiss Chalet
54 The Rivoli
55 Le Papillon
57 Restaurant Marché Mövenpick
58 Café Bar Masquerade
59 Madison Avenue Pub
60 Le St Tropez
61 Spiral
62 Coach House
63 ACME Grill

♆ Where to Have a Drink

70 Amadeus Bar
71 Lettieri
72 Bovine Sex Club
73 The Bamboo
74 HorseShoe Tavern
76 Lee's Palace
77 The Olde Brunswick House
78 The Government
79 Big Bop
80 Amsterdam Brewing Company
83 Future Bakery Café

★ What to See

100 Royal Ontario Museum
101 Art Gallery of Ontario
103 Bata Shoe Museum
104 Old City Hall
105 Toronto City Hall
106 CN Tower
108 Embarkation for ferry to Toronto Islands
110 Fort York
112 Air Canada Center
113 Skydome Tour Experience
114 Hockey Hall of Fame

🛍 Shopping

90 Honest Ed's
91 The World's Biggest Bookstore
92 The Bay
93 Eaton Center

TORONTO – KEY TO MAPS I AND II

TORONTO (MAP I)

NORTH

A

B

Lawrence West

Caledonia

Dufferin Ave.

Lawrence

Glengrove Ave.

Glengrove

Allen

Marlee

Hillmount Ave.

Glencairn

Stayner Ave.

Castlefield Ave.

Roselawn

Keele St.

Eglinton Ave.

Kane

Caledonia

Mc Roberts

Rogers Rd

Rogers

Old Weston Rd.

St Clair

Davenport

Dundas St.

Dupont

High Park

Bloor

Keele

High Park ★ 109

High Park Blvd

Garden Ave.

Gardiner

Lake Ontario

0   1   2 km

0   1   2 miles

Bathurst

Glenmount Ave.

Glencairn

Glencairn

Briar

Hill

Roselawn

Chaplin

Glenholme

Winnett

Eglinton West

Ava

Dedarvdegar Park

Arlington

Northcliffe

St Clair

Davenport

Road

Oakwood

Dovercourt

Dupont

Hallam

Lansdowne

Dufferin

Dundas West

Emerson Ave.

Lansdowne

Brock

Dufferin

College

High Park's Dr

Roncesvalles

Soraluren Ave.

Lansdowne Ave.

Queen

Dunn Ave.

King St.

21

28

Dundas

College St.

Lansdowne

Dufferin

Bloor

Ossington

Dovercourt

Crawford

Ossington Rd.

Christie

Davenport

Dupont

Barton Ave.

Bathurst

Harbord

Palmerston

Grace

College

Crawford

Dundas

Queen

Adelaide St. W.

King

Strachan Ave.

Lake Shore Blvd

Expressway

107 ★

Eglinton Park

W. Eglinto

Oriole Pkwy

Old Orest Cres.

Spadina Rd

Hilti Rd

Burton Rd

Kilbarry

Lonsdale Rd

Heath St. W.

St Clair West Ave.

Spadina Rd

31 Road ★ 111 ★ 115

Dupont 75

38 33

Bernard Ave.

Lowther

Bathurst St. Spadina

St George

Spadina

Dundas

Queen

Adelaide St

Front

Bathurst

Christie

Toronto City Centre Airport

see map II

TORONTO (MAP I)

TORONTO (MAP II)

TORONTO (MAP II)

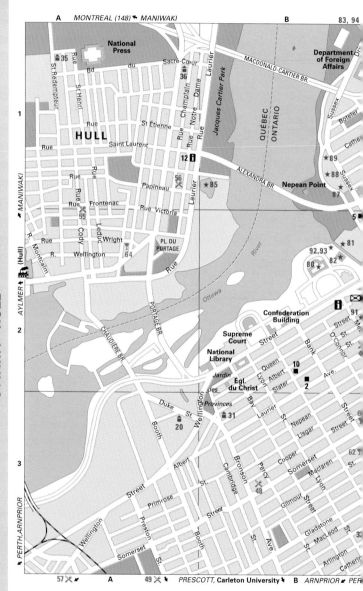

OTTAWA – HULL

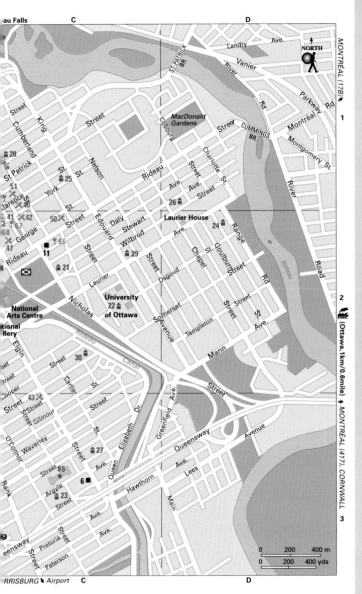

OTTAWA – HULL

KEY TO MAP OTTAWA – HULL

■ Useful Addresses

- **⊞** Infocentre
- **⊠** Post office
- **🚆** Train stations
- **🚌** National bus station
- **2** American Express Travel Service
- **5** United States Embassy
- **6** Police
- **🚌 7** Bus/Greyhound station
- **10** Air Canada
- **11** Cybercafé Agora
- **⊞ 12** Tourist Information, Hull

⌂ Where to Stay

- **20** Breton campsite
- **21** Ottawa International Inn
- **22** University of Ottawa
- **23** YMCA and YWCA
- **24** Australis
- **25** Ottawa Backpackers Inn
- **26** Ottawa House
- **27** Le Gîte
- **28** Auberge du Marché
- **29** The King Edward Inn
- **30** Haydon House
- **31** Lyon Guesthouse
- **32** A Voyageur's Guesthouse
- **35** Au Gîte du Parc
- **36** Couette et Croissant

✕ Where to Eat

- **40** Bagel-Bagel
- **41** Zack's
- **42** The Fish Market
- **43** The Ritz
- **44** Full House
- **45** Druxy's
- **46** Memories
- **47** Mamma Grazzis
- **48** The Mekong Restaurant
- **49** Il Picolino
- **50** Nagina Indian Cuisine
- **51** Mangia
- **52** The Creperie
- **53** Olé! Tapas
- **55** Restaurant Barbe
- **56** Le Tartuffe
- **57** Newport Restaurant

🍸 Where to Have a Drink, Nightlife

- **61** Rainbow Bistro
- **62** Royal Oak
- **63** The Celtic Cross Pub & Restaurant
- **64** Place Aubry
- **66** Atomic
- **67** The Collection and Mercury Lounge
- **68** Reactors

★ What to See

- **80** Parliament Hill
- **81** Rideau Canal locks
- **82** Bytown Museum
- **83** National Aviation Museum
- **84** Château Laurier Hotel
- **85** Canadian Museum of Civilization
- **86** Canadian Museum of Nature
- **87** National Gallery
- **88** War Museum
- **89** Royal Canadian Mint
- **94** National Museum of Science and Technology

★ What to Do

- **90** Amphibus
- **91** Double Decker & Trolley Tours
- **92** The Ottawa Riverboat Company
- **93** Paul's Boat Lines

latter). The best B&B in Banff offers four themed room – the 'Turret' (magnificent view of the Rockies), the 'Artist's View' (for romantics), the 'Homestead' (full of souvenirs from the owner's childhood) and the 'Ranger's Cabin' (this has twin beds, while the other three have doubles). With a big sitting room for guests and a nice fireplace, this is real luxury and good value. Very pleasant hosts.

WHERE TO EAT

The places below are mainly restaurants, but don't forget that you can also have a snack in most bars (*see* 'Where to Have a Drink').

☆–☆☆ Budget to Moderate

✕ **Magpie and Stump** (map A1–2, **30**): 203 Caribou Street, on the corner of Bear Street. ☎ 762-4067. Open noon–2am. Without doubt the best Mexican restaurant in town, with warm decor, totally in wood, and a family atmosphere. It's also a very popular bar with the local youth, and bands play on some evenings. The lunch menu offers nachos, French fries and combination platter. Dinner includes classic Mexican dishes (excellent guacamole, ceviche, burritos and enchiladas) and grilled meat Canadian-style (for the less adventurous as it says on the menu). This is serious cooking, distinctive and generously served. If you're in a group it's a good idea not to all order the same thing, as the starters are generous enough to share.

✕ **Earl's** (map A1, **31**): 299 Banff Avenue, on the corner of Wolf Street. ☎ 762-4414. Fax: 762-4735. Another in the chain, with locally inspired decor showing photographs and pictures of the Old Continent; and a big warthog presides in the middle of the room. Traditional dishes, mainly burgers, not very imaginative but of good quality.

✕ **Coyote's Deli and Grill** (map A1, **32**): 206 Caribou Street. ☎ 762-3963. Open daily 7.30am–11pm. Budget cuisine with Mexican and Mediterranean flavours, often well balanced and attractively presented. The blue corn bread is excellent.

✕ **Bumper's The Beef House** (map B1, **33**): 603 Banff Avenue, on the corner of Marmot Crescent. ☎ 762-2622 or 762-4001. As you might have guessed, the local speciality is good beef from the prairies. The cook cuts the meat to the thickness of your choice: from the 'Ladies' size to 'Mountain Man' size ('so thick you won't believe your eyes' as the menu explains). The cooked meat is so tender that you could cut it with your finger. Included in the price is a self-service salad bar, where you can eat as much as you like. Pretty, chalet-style setting.

☆☆☆ Expensive

✕ **The Grizzli House** (map A1, **34**): 207 Banff Avenue. ☎ 762-4055. The decor is very Indian trapper and, sitting between a totem pole and stuffed animal heads, you can try a variety of tasty but costly dishes, from alligator to caribou. The two specialities of the house are 'hot rocks' and fondues where, if a woman drops a chunk of meat into the oil, she owes a kiss to the man with her. But if the man does it, he must buy a round for the whole table. The impressive wine list has over 100 to choose from.

WHERE TO HAVE A DRINK

Most of the bars in Banff are also restaurants: you can have a meal while those sharing your table can be downing a beer or two. Sometimes the bar area is so busy that it overwhelms the restaurant.

Ⴘ Saint James' Gate (map A1, **40**): 207 Wolf Street. ☎ 762-9355. A really great Irish pub with a vast central bar where the stout flows freely. There are 33 beers on draught and 50 single malts. It's undoubtedly one of the nicest places in town, which is why it's so full. Live music from time to time.

Ⴘ Rose and Crown (map A1, **41**): 202 Banff Avenue, first floor. ☎ 762-2121. One of the busiest bars in town, mainly attracting young people and the atmosphere is really friendly. There's billiards, and live music from time to time. The restaurant side is decent but over-priced.

Ⴘ Wild Bill's (map A1, **42**): 201 Banff Avenue, first floor. ☎ 762-0333. Fax: 762-0399. Meals served until 11pm. Bar and music until 1.30am. Has various bars that look like saloons, all with a friendly atmosphere, plus an attractive menu offering soup, salads, pizzas, barbecues, Tex-Mex, burgers, pasta and steak.

Ⴘ Barbary Coast (map A2, **43**): 119 Banff Avenue, first floor. ☎ 762-7673. Same style as Wild Bill's but a bit less smart – bar pillars, tatty billiard tables and floor strewn with peanuts. The restaurant next door has a particularly local decor and a very relaxed atmosphere. Again there's a California-style menu with a bit of everything.

SHOPPING

The speciality in Banff is without doubt chocolate, and it's hard to resist all the shops on Banff Avenue selling homemade delights. But there's also a whole lot more than chocolate in Banff.

⌂ The Fudgery: 215 Banff Avenue. ☎ 762-3003. Follow your nose to find this very inviting shop producing fudge. It opens onto the road and has an overwhelming selection to choose from.

⌂ Chocolaterie Bernard Callebaut: 127 Banff Avenue. ☎ 762-4106. Altogether a higher class of establishment with very finely made goodies for the aristocrats of chocolate. Bernard won the top prize in the International Festival of Chocolate in Roanne, France.

⌂ Welch: 126 Banff Avenue. ☎ 762-3737. At this large sweet shop both children and adults succumb to temptation when faced with the incredible choice of confection in all shapes and sizes.

⌂ Art Inuit: Sedna Art Gallery, 205A Wolf Street. ☎ 760-8676. Fax: 760-8675. Yvonne Macey exhibits pieces by the grand masters at all prices and is delighted to explain to you the Inuit art that is so unjustly ignored in Europe. You'll see lovely examples of pictures, sculptures and totems that give an insight into Canadian art and its variety. Yvonne also has a shop in Samson Mall in Lake Louise.

⌂ Sportswear: You just have to walk along Banff Avenue to realize that it's a bit like a ski resort such as Chamonix, and the prices are correspondingly high. It's best to compare prices and stick to buying in summer during the sales. Unless, of course, what you want isn't available back home. One recommendation among the multitude of shops is **Relaxed n'Rugged**, 124 Banff Avenue (☎ 762-0450). Here you'll find the best brands at the best prices, and sometimes flash sales with 25 per cent discount on some items.

🔒 **Banff Indian Trading Post**: Banff Avenue on the corner of Birch and Cave, near the Banff Spring Hotel. ☎ 762-2456. If you're determined to take some Indian crafts home, this is the place for **native clothing** and **souvenirs**. Don't be reluctant to bargain a bit, because the items are not cheap.

WHAT TO SEE

★ **Cave and Basin**: 311 Cave Avenue, a little outside town. ☎ 762-1557. Open daily 9am–6pm May to September. Guided tours available. The thermal springs here have been commercially exploited since the railway was built in 1883. In 1885, a dispute between several of their 'discoverers' over the ownership of the springs led the government to declare Banff to be the property of all Canadians. This eventually led to the creation of the first national park. A swimming pool has been built, retaining the walls of the earlier buildings. The water temperature varies between 29°C and 32°C (84–90°F) but, sadly, you can't swim there any more. You can, however, visit the small grotto from where the spring of sulphur waters flows, caused by rain and snow falling on the other side of Sulphur Mountain. The water seeps through the earth's crust (for more than 2 kilometres (1 mile)) where it is heated up; it also absorbs mineral salts that are released when the waters reach the surface again. The waters gained a reputation among the first tourists in the 19th century as a cure for gout, dyspepsia, depression and even gunshot wounds.

★ **Upper Hot Springs**: Mountain Avenue. ☎ 762-1515 or 1-800-767-1611 (toll-free). Open daily 9am–11pm mid-June to mid-September. In low season 10am–10pm. Entrance charge about $3. This stunning setting offers much the same sort of thing as the Cave and Basin but it's more modern and, therefore, less appealing. The water here is hot (40°C/104°F), and you can at least have a Turkish bath (spa) and massage.

★ **Sulphur Mountain Gondola**: Mountain Avenue (go up Spray Avenue towards Banff Springs Hotel and turn right). Signposted. ☎ 762-2523. Fax: 762-7493. Open 7.30am–9pm end-June to early September. Enjoy the 8-minute cable-car ride to the top of Mount Sulphur (2,270 metres/7,446 feet). It's expensive but the expansive views of the Rockies and Bow River, the colour of slightly milky emerald, are grandiose. A narrow path leads to the old meteorological station.

★ **Luxton Museum**: Go over the bridge at the end of Banff Avenue and turn right. ☎ 762-2388. Open 9am–9pm in summer. A fort protected by a big wooden palisade houses the most interesting museum in town. It recounts the life of the Plains Indians from the north, through displays of their environment and their clothing. The faces aren't brilliantly done, but the settings accurately reflect their lives, and offer a better understanding of these nomadic Indians and how they moved camp to follow the migration of the bison.

★ **Park Museum**: At the bottom of Banff Avenue, on the right near the riverbank. ☎ 762-1558. Open in high season 10am–6pm (10am–5pm other times). Guided tours at 11am and 3pm. Located on the edge of a small park, the museum is housed in a huge, wooden pagoda-style building, furbished in a historical manner. It's full of stuffed birds and animals, a selection of the fauna you'll find in the Rockies. The museum also includes a rich collection of birds, particularly owls. There are often musical performances under a shelter in the park.

★ **Bow Falls**: Cross Banff Avenue, turn left after the little bridge and follow the arrows to reach this picturesque little waterfall. It's best to go early in the morning before the busloads of tourists arrive. The falls are part of a lovely walk along the river, but beware of mosquitoes.

★ **Whyte Museum of the Canadian Rockies**: 111 Bear Street. ☎ 762-2291. Open summer daily 10am–5pm. *The* place for fans of mountain climbing and related sports gives an overview of man and the mountains since the beginning of time. You'll see wonderful landscapes, souvenirs, historic photos, ancient mountain-climbing equipment and items belonging to famous guides or local personalities of the past.

★ **Natural History Museum**: 112 Banff Avenue. ☎ 762-4747. Open 11am–8pm in summer. No entry charge for the Clock Tower. This is a small museum that explains the formation of the Rockies. There's an audiovisual show and geological exhibits of minerals, plus models, slides, stones of all sorts and fossils (including four dinosaur skulls).

★ **Mount Norquay**: 5 kilometres (3 miles) from town; go under the Trans-Canada Highway and follow the road up to the end. ☎ 762-4421. This mountain overlooks Banff and the lakes around it, and offers great skiing in winter and wonderful views from the summit in summer. Guided walks of 3–5 hours are a good opportunity to learn about the local flora and fauna.

WHAT TO DO

– **Cycling**: Most hire shops are on Bear Street. Compare prices and don't stint on the quality of the equipment, particularly not if you have grand plans. A few recommendations include:

■ **Mountain Magic Equipment**: 224 Bear Street (☎ 762-2591). Excellent value for money, with very friendly and competent staff who really know the area and can offer advice on the most suitable routes. You might find, however, that the equipment you want is not available in high season.

■ **The Ski Stop**: This has two shops, one near the entrance at the Banff Springs Hotel (☎ 762-5333) and the other at 203 Bear Street in town (☎ 760-1650).

■ **Bactrax**: 225 Bear Street. ☎ 762-8177.

A few routes to consider:

– **From Cave and Basin to Sundance Canyon**: The circuit takes about 1 hour along the river and through the forest. No cars are allowed after Cave and Basin.

– **Lake Minnewanka Trail**: A 3-hour ride that takes you to Lake Minnewanka north of town. Take drinking water with you, there's also a small grocer's at the lake.

– **Vermilion Lakes**: This circuit around the three small lakes takes about 1 hour and is fine on foot or by bike. It starts from Mount Norquay Drive, just before the Trans-Canada Highway. Don't forget your binoculars so you can watch beavers, wild geese, eagles, muskrats, egrets etc.

– **Fenland**: This starts at the beginning of the Vermilion Lakes walk. The path is about 2 kilometres (1 mile) long and takes you from the marsh into the forest, with the chance to see a few beavers and waterbirds along the way.

– **Fairy Chimneys routes**: These offer lovely views over Bow Valley and Mount Rundle.

– **Spray River and Goat Creek**: This excellent but demanding circuit is best done as a round trip, but you'll need to be fit as it's equally difficult in either direction. The views are also quite different. Allow at least 6 hours to cover 19 kilometres (about 11 miles) each way. If you leave early in the morning, you might be lucky enough to come across herds of deer in the mists.

– **Rafting**: For fairly relaxed paddling, try a 1- to 2-hour trip with **Rocky Mountain Raft Tours**: ☎ 762-3632. If you fancy something a little more adventurous, **Adventures Unlimited/Hydra** (209 Bear Street. ☎ 762-4554) offer half- or full-day options on the Kicking Horse River.

– **Canoeing**: **Bow River Canoe Rentals** at the end of Wolf Street in Banff (☎ 762-3632) rent canoes by the hour or by the day for trips on Bow River and Vermilion Lakes. Note that there are no rental facilities at Vermilion Lakes itself

– **Horse riding**: You can book 1-, 2- or 3-hour rides with **Holiday on Horseback** at the Trail Rider Store, 132 Banff Avenue. ☎ 762-4551.

– **Fishing**: Fishing licences are available at the tourist office in Banff (*see* Useful Addresses). For river or lake fishing equipment and advice try **Fishing Unlimited**: ☎ 762-4936.

BANFF NATIONAL PARK

★ A few kilometres inside the park gate you'll see an exit for lovely **Lake Minnewanka** (5 kilometres/3 miles) at the foot of the mountains. It's ideal for boating or canoeing in the summer. Follow the rock dyke up as far as Two Jack Lake and Johnson Lake. It's best to go early in the morning, and you can get some superb photos on the rocky dam. On the river to the left of Lake Minnewanka there's a path to Stewart Canyon, Aylmer Pass and Devil's Gap.

★ Along the route of the lake you'll see an old mining shaft just before the site of **Bankhead South**, a town that was once more important than Banff. The coal mine opened in 1903 and employed 300 miners underground and 150 on the surface. Warehouses, workshops, houses, schools and shops developed around the area, but problems of viability and strikes for better wages and working conditions led to the mine's closure in 1922. Everything was dismantled quickly, leaving only a few vestiges. However, there's a short trail with explanatory signs that bring this chapter of working history to life. It's an interesting walk and the valley is beautiful early in the morning.

– Many campsites have been set up throughout the park, including:

⛺ **Two Jack Main Campground**: 13 kilometres northwest of Banff, near the lake on the right-hand side of the road. Open from mid-May to first Monday in September, this has toilets but no showers.

⛺ **Two Jack Lake Side**: Open mid-May to September. Arrive before 11pm. A smaller site on the lake's shore, with showers.

WALKING TRAILS AROUND BANFF

Guidebooks, Brochures and Information

For walks of a day or more it's essential to buy a detailed map of the region. In addition to those listed below, you can also pick up numerous other guides and maps at the Park Information Office shop.

– There are more than 1,300 kilometres (806 miles) of marked trails to follow, some of which can be done in a day, while others take several days. For short walks (lasting up to one day) the indispensable *Walks and Easy Hikes in the Canadian Rockies,* by Graeme Pole, gives details of a selection of the 95 best trails.

If you're after something more ambitious, *The Canadian Rockies Trail Guide* (by Brain Patton and Bart Robinson) is excellent and details over 250 walks taking a day or more. The guide includes maps, accurate descriptions, duration, landmarks and photographs, and is available in any local bookshop.

– Also essential reading is the brochure called *Walks and Excursions in Banff and Its Environs* is, available free from the Park Information Office. Read it carefully, as everything you'll need to know is explained in great detail – options, general advice, examples of day-long walks etc.

– Also get the *Visitors Guide to the Hinterland* which is stuffed full of useful information.

– The gazette *Banff National Park – Visitors' Guide* contains a diary of the organized walks led by rangers.

A Few Superb Walks

Here's just small selection of walks. Ask the park rangers for precise itineraries, and don't forget that in most years not all the lakes are completely thawed before the end of June.

– **Bourgeau Lake**: This round trip will take less than a day and is not too difficult. Bourgeau is a wild lake surrounded by scree and pine trees, where you're likely to see a few mountain goats.

– **Rock Bound Lake**: Although fairly demanding, this can be done in a day and the view is worth the effort – superb, sub-alpine landscapes reflected in the green waters of the lake.

– **Twin Lakes**: There are two possible routes into the quiet, restful lakes, taking up to about 3 hours 30 minutes. The view of the peaks is also impressive.

– **Elk Lake**: You can complete this walk in a day with no major difficulties, but you can also spend the night here. The lake is in the middle of an amphitheatre of mountains, with varied, open views.

– **Mystic Lake**: This classic route for hikers takes 6–8 hours and includes delightful streams, sub-alpine landscapes and dense forests. There are numerous campsites along the way. You can also extend the walk by going as far as Johnston Canyon.

– **Fish Lakes**: Allow about 6 hours, and there's a long climb following the pass. From the lakes you'll see open, unrestricted landscapes, and Upper Fish Lake is the starting point for other very pleasant walks. You might want to stay here for some time.

Local Fauna

It's an unfortunate statistic that around 60 large mammals are killed on Banff's roads every year, and quite a number of car drivers are also injured. So drive carefully, noting the lower speed limits in places (and travel even more slowly at dawn or dusk). Here are the most common animals in the park:

– **Wapiti** (North American elk): You sometimes see these along the side of secondary roads. You'll recognize them easily since 'wapiti' means 'white rump'. The elk has antlers, and its neck and legs are darker than its coat. It's best to keep your distance (at least 30 metres) in the spring, when the females defend their young with determination (watch out for their pointed hooves), and in September and October when the males can be particularly aggressive if you make them nervous by getting too close. It's also best to photograph them from a distance during these periods (if you must). It's estimated that there are no more than 3,200 wapitis.

– **Moose**: This is easily recognizable by its wide, flat antlers, great size and lack of white rump. The moose is a very solitary animal that's seldom seen, except in marshy areas like Lake Waterfowl and Bow Mountain. It's very aggressive in the spring and autumn for the same reasons as the wapitis. Estimates put their number here at only 50 to 80.

– **Mule deer**: Smaller and more common, with a straight white tail, white rump and long ears, it sometimes risks coming into towns.

– **White-tailed deer**: Its tail is actually brown on top and white underneath and moves characteristically fast, like a white flag being waved. The deer number somewhere between 250 and 350.

– **Conan**: This is sometimes confused with the caribou, but it's more modestly built and has a very strong body odour. It's now virtually extinct, although it was the animal that the Prairie Indians respected the most.

– **Mountain sheep**: Seen at the roadsides, often in small groups, they have short, pale-brown hair, a white rump and tiny tail. It's unwise to feed them because it makes them dependent. There are between 2,000 and 2,600 in the area.

– **Mountain goats**: These are also called *lemenaheze* (their name in the Cree language). They look very striking – a long, white coat and small head with two small horns as hard and sharp as steel daggers. You'll rarely see them from the road, and they number around 800–900.

– **Grizzly bear**: Bigger than the black bear, with a flatter, more concave face, its fur is usually cinnamon coloured but sometimes it looks almost black. Amazingly, a grizzly cub weighs a mere 300–500 grams (11–18 ounces) at birth – just a tiny scrap. There are between 80 and 100 of them in the park.

– **Black bear**: This has a narrower head than the grizzly and a black coat. However, identification can be difficult because the fur on the head can be brown, cinnamon or even white. There are about 50 to 60 black bears in the park.

To see the bears, pick up the brochure *You Are in Bear Country*, which is full of useful advice, then ask the rangers where they're usually found.

– **Other animals**: There are around 200 **coyotes** in the park, which are often hit by cars around Banff. **Caribou** only number about 25 and cougars around 10 to 15. The **bison** is the only species not threatened with extinction here, but don't get out of the car, as they weigh 600 kilograms (1,320 pounds) and have a huge, hairy head that will push you back in no time! Finally, there are about six packs of **wolves** (about 50 to 60 in all), which attract a lot of attention from the park authorities.

From Banff to Lake Louise

After leaving Banff and picking up the Trans-Canada Highway, take the Bow Valley Parkway (1A) a few kilometres farther on, which will take you to Lake Louise by a route that is initially much more picturesque than the Trans-Canada. This 64-kilometre (40-mile) route is actually superb in places, and offers every chance of coming across some wapitis. Among the several lovely stretches are:

★ **Johnston Canyon**: On the left, after about 25 kilometres (16 miles), is the Johnston Canyon campsite. ☎ 762-1581. Open June to September 7am–midnight (you can call early or late). A little farther along, on the right, you'll find a coffee shop as well as the start of a lovely trail that follows the sinuous course of **Johnston River** for several kilometres. Follow the paved path under the pines for 1 kilometre until you reach a really charming waterfall that has gouged out a round basin in the rocks below. Almost another 6 kilometres (4 miles) farther on you get to the **Inkpots**, a series of springs that run into splendid ponds. It's a pleasant hike, and you'll find a clear, illustrated map for sale at the campsite.

★ **Castle Mountain**: If you take the route on the right, you'll see Castle Mountain appearing in the middle, as if in a fairy story. It's a huge mass of rock in the shape of a pyramid that reaches up to the sky, and it blends in like a sculpture. The route seems to take you right into the rocky castle where your Prince (or Princess) Charming undoubtedly awaits.

WHERE TO STAY AND EAT

☆–☆☆ Budget to Moderate

♠ **Castle Mountain Youth Hostel**: ☎ 762-2367. When just about opposite Castle Mountain, turn left for Castle Mountain Village (small grocery store and bungalows for rent) then left again for the hostel in the woods. (You're at the junction where Highway 93 leads south to Kootenay National Park in British Columbia.) You can book in from 8 to 10am and from 5 to 10pm, although it's open all the time. The refurbished hostel is clean and has 36 beds in all. There's also a pleasant sitting room and equipped kitchen.

♠ **Whiskey Jack Youth Hostel**: Open mid-June to mid-September. If you take the road for Yoho Park, this place at the foot of the fantastic Takakkaw Falls is highly recommended. It accommodates 27 people in three dormitories and takes bookings from Calgary or Banff.

☆☆–☆☆☆ Moderate to Expensive

♠ **Johnston Canyon Resort**: as you enter Johnston Canyon, on the 1A. ☎ 762-2971. Open mid-May to mid-October. Pleasant, small wooden chalets without kitchenettes start at $95–143 for four.

There are also more luxurious (and more expensive) chalets with equipped kitchen for four. You'll get a warm welcome. A cafeteria is near the bottom.

♠ **Castle Mountain Village**: 32 kilometres (20 miles) from Banff and 29 kilometres (18 miles) from Lake Louise. ☎ 762-3868. Fax: 762-8629. Open all year. About 20 lovely and very well-equipped chalets spread through the trees along the 1A. You'll get a friendly welcome from the proprietor who regularly wins awards for running her chalets so well. Also summer cottages for two or four, pine, cedar log chalets for four and a deluxe (with jacuzzi) for six people. This is the best value for money in the area. You can buy groceries and petrol in the village.

♠ **Baker Creek Chalets**: before Lake Louise Village. ☎ 522-3761. Fax: 522-2270. Comfortable chalets with kitchenette, but pretty expensive, at $150 per night (but good value for families or groups). The surroundings are charming.

✕ **Baker Creek Bistro**: ☎ 522-2182. This small restaurant with a pleasant terrace sells budget snacks and salads at lunchtime, and more substantial dishes in the evening.

FROM BANFF TO JASPER

LAKE LOUISE

DIALLING CODE: 403

First you come to the tiny village of Lake Louise, with just a service station and a shopping mall. Another 4 kilometres (2.5 miles) along the road, you then reach one of the jewels of the Rockies – Lake Louise itself, with its famous Château Lake Louise (a deluxe hotel, though you might not guess it from the dull architectural frontage). The lake's emerald waters and its location at the foot of a sweep of mountains – with an amphitheatre of ice at the centre and flanked by steep, rocky peaks smothered with pines – have long made it an essential stop for busloads of tourists. For that reason it's best avoided at weekends. In 1980 the picture-postcard lake was designated a World Heritage Site by UNESCO – a sure indication of its beauty.

USEFUL ADDRESSES

🛈 **Lake Louise Visitors' Centre**: near Samson Mall. ☎ 522-3833. Open 8am–6pm, with seasonal variations. The weather forecasts displayed can sometimes be unreliable, so it's best just to wait and see.

■ **Lake Louise Park Administration**: ☎ 522-3763.

■ **Watchman's office**: ☎ 522-3866 (24 hours).

🚌 **Buses**: at Samson Mall. Going east, six departures from 3am. Going west, four departures between 10am and 1.35am. There's a direct bus to Jasper at 4.15pm; another in the morning stops at the Athabasca Glacier but is more expensive (a round trip).

■ **Police**: ☎ 522-3811.

■ **Lake Louise Medical Clinic**: ☎ 522-2184.

WHERE TO STAY

Lake Louise only exists because of tourism and has no permanent residents. Therefore, you won't find any B&Bs, but there are hotels and also cabins to rent. In either case, you'll have to break the bank, especially in high season. This is why you'll find more tourists than backpackers roaming about.

☆–☆☆ Budget to Moderate

🛖 **Lake Louise Campsite**: Cross the village, take the road towards Lake Louise and immediately fork left onto Sentinel Fairview Road. The campsite is on the right and is open all year. It's quite big and very busy. There's a shelter with a stove and tables in case of rain.

🛖 **The Canadian Alpine Centre and International Hostel**: Lake Louise Village. ☎ 522-2200. Fax: 522-2253. This hotel complex for mountaineers and young people is the only place with accommodation at acceptable prices. Lovely wooden buildings have rooms for four to six people and 14 double rooms, some with private bathroom. It's advisable to book at least six months in advance for high season. Bookings must be made by credit card or the reservation is cancelled at 6pm. There's also a library, games room, sauna etc.

☆☆☆ Expensive

🛖 **Paradise Lodge and Bungalows**: Lake Louise Drive. ☎ 522-3595. Fax: 522-3987. Pretty little chalets in the forest for two or four people, with or without corner kitchenette. Prices starting at around $143, but are virtually the same for all chalets.

🛖 **Lake Louise Inn**: Lake Louise Village. ☎ 522-3791 or 1-800-661-9237 (toll-free). Fax: 522-2018. Double rooms start at $90 in high season and $60 in low season. The reasonably priced restaurants serve excellent seafood chowder and New York steak.

FROM BANFF TO JASPER

☆☆☆☆ Splash Out

⚓ **Post Hotel**: Lake Louise Village. ☎ 522-3989. Fax: 522-3966. This is the place for real occasions such as weddings. You'll find the same quality as at the Château Lake Louise but with a great deal more charm. Every evening staff put a weather forecast in your room for the following day. Some evenings storytellers come to recount the history of the Canadian Rockies, or visiting guides give talks on respecting the environment. There's a drawing room/library with a big open fire. This is a must, but only affordable out of season or if you take one of the smallest rooms with a view over the back rather than over the river.

WHERE TO EAT

☆–☆☆ Budget to Moderate

✗ **Bill Peyto Café**: in the International Hostel (see 'Where to Stay'). Open daily 7am–9pm. The setting is pleasant, and you'll find a menu on the blackboard with not a bad choice (including a good breakfast). It has a young, convivial atmosphere, and you give the staff a hand by helping to clear your own table – but you're not expected to do the washing up.

✗ **Mountain Restaurant**: 200 Village Road, next to the Esso service station. Unpretentious food for breakfast, lunch and dinner at reasonable prices for the area, plus quick, smiling service. It may not be the Himalayas, but you'll be satisfied. The lovely shirts and embroidered jeans worn by the waiting staff are on sale in the boutique as you leave the restaurant.

✗ **Deer Lodge**: Lake Louise Drive. ☎ 522-3747. A great setting in dark wood. At lunchtime you can find good-quality light dishes and, above all, a little peace and quiet. Watch out for soaring prices in the evening.

✗ **Timberwolf**: in the Lake Louise Inn (see 'Where to Stay'). This is the more affordable and the less pretentious of the hotel's two restaurants. The huge pizzas are excellent, and there are TV screens for sports fans.

✗ **Lake Louise Station**: at the end of Sentinel Road. ☎ 522-2600. In the old train station, very well renovated. The setting is great, sort of 1920s, with soft lights. It's a pity that the cooking is not always up to the same standard; nonetheless, you'll still find something good to eat.

☆☆☆–☆☆☆☆ Expensive to Splash Out

The Restaurants of Château Lake Louise: on the shores of Lake Louise:

✗ **Poppy Room**: A restaurant with a vaguely Tyrolean decor and a view over the lake. Varied menu with hints of Italian and Austrian, plus a fun menu for the kids.

✗ **Walliser Stube**: This is open only in the evening and has a pretty decent wine bar and German-inspired cuisine.

✗ **Tom Wilson**: On the seventh floor overlooking the lake, this also opens for dinner only, but with good Italian dishes at higher prices.

– The Château's other restaurants are luxurious, but very expensive given the quality of the food.

✗ **Post Hotel Restaurant**: This is without a doubt the best restaurant in Lake Louise, but at serious prices – it's difficult to escape without paying less than $70 per person.

FROM BANFF TO JASPER

WHAT TO SEE

★ **Northern Art Impression Gallery**: Samson Mall. ☎ 522-2038. You'll receive an excellent introduction to Inuit art in this small gallery, where some superb works by famous artists are also on sale.

★ **Lake Moraine**: about 13 kilometres (8 miles) along the highway from the junction with Lake Louise. The road is often very congested in summer. This is much wilder than Lake Louise, surrounded by lots of severe-looking rocky structures called 'the Valley of the Ten Peaks'. The spectacle of these immense cliffs, with austere colours softened by a green cloak at their bases, just before they disappear into the dazzling blue waters of the lake, is an unforgettable sight. On the left of the lake there's a field of scree that holds back the watercourse, creating the lake. On the left, just before you get to the lake, you'll see the Tower of Babel, an enormous, lonely monolith reaching skywards.

– Three **hiking** trails start from the Lake Moraine car-park, and they are among the most beautiful in the region. The **Lake Moraine Rockpile trail**, a round trip of 1.4 kilometres, takes about 30 minutes. The path along **Lake Moraine**, to the end of the lake, also takes 30 minutes. Finally, there's the very attractive path (2 hours round trip) deep in the woods that ends at the superb **Consolation Lake**. It's inaccessible to cars and therefore pretty quiet. At the end of the lake is a wonderful glacier. The return trip involves a steep descent.

WHAT TO DO

– **Prepared paths**: There are many trails through the undergrowth beneath the spruce trees, detailed in the booklet *Walks and Excursions Around Lake Louise and the Environs*. These include really lovely walks at **Paradise Valley** (18 kilometres/11 miles round trip), **Sentinel Pass** (12 kilometres/7 miles) and **Lake Moraine** (*see* 'What to See'). If you have a little time, take the path on the left from Château Lake Louise to **Lake Mirror** and **Lake Agnes**. It will take about 45 minutes to reach Lake Mirror and another 15 minutes to get to Lake Agnes, where there's a tea-house (open from mid-June). Depending on the season, you can get up to the **Beehive**, from where there is a dazzling view of the lake. Some 7 kilometres (4 miles) west of the junction between Highway 1A and Lake Louise Drive, at the summit of Vermilion Pass (1,651 metres/5,415 feet), you'll find the trail marking the **Great Divide**. It runs between the Kootenay and Banff national parks and between the hydrographic basins of the Pacific and the Atlantic Ocean (the point where waters flow west to the Pacific or east to the Atlantic). It's also the spot where a huge forest fire laid waste the Vermilion Pass in 1968. The **Epilobe interpretative trail** (a circuit of 800 metres) takes you through the burned lands to witness how the forest has begun to regenerate

– **Cycling**: You can hire mountain bikes from **Wilson Mountain Sports** on the square in Samson Mall (at the corner of Lake Louise Drive and Village Road). ☎ 522-3636. You'll find helpful and experienced staff, and impeccable service and equipment. Prices are about $30 a day.

– **Horse riding**: **Brewster Lake Louise Stables** take bookings through Guest Service at Château Lake Louise or you can call ☎ 522-3511, ext. 1210 or 1142. They offer a range of rides, from an hour, half day or a whole day, and even three days for experienced riders (with a night camping out, cooking over a wood fire etc.). Trails usually go to Lake Agnes or the Plain of Six Glaciers. Another choice is **Timberline Tours** (☎ 522-3743), with similar rides that are a little less expensive. However, they charge by the half-hour. Rides leave from behind Deer Lodge.

– **Rafting**: Prices for equipment hire are very similar from one company to another, in accordance with strict regulations to guarantee absolute safety. Check with the tourist offices or rafting companies for further information. Equipment includes a full wetsuit, helmet and life jacket. You can do a half-day trip, in which case it's best to go in the afternoon when the water is warmer.

Two rafting companies stand out from the crowd: **Wild Water Adventures** (☎ 522-2211) and **Wet 'n' Wild Adventures** (☎ (250) 344-6546). Trips leave from Banff, stopping at Lake Louise to pick up more people before heading towards Golden in British Columbia. If your itinerary takes you to Banff first and then to Lake Louise, wait until you get to Lake Louise before you start your whitewater rafting descent (this way you'll avoid an unnecessary round trip from Banff to Lake Louise).

– **Canoeing** and **boating**: There are hire facilities at Lake Louise and Lake Moraine, but it's fairly expensive.

– **Mount Whitehorn cable car**: 3 kilometres (2 miles) from Lake Louise. ☎ 522-3555. Open 8am–9pm (8pm in winter). Several footpaths start from the top of the run, where there's also a restaurant.

The Icefields Parkway

This superb drive from Lake Louise to Jasper along Highway 93 takes you 236 kilometres (146 miles) through a region of great splendour, with lakes, glaciers, sharp peaks and forests.

If you're on foot and you don't want to hitchhike (although this works really well), ask about the daily bus service linking all the youth hostels between Calgary and Jasper from mid-May until the end of November. All bus times are subject to change.

USEFUL ADDRESS

🛈 **Icefield Information Centre**: Athabasca Glacier (see 'What to See'). You'll find this in a huge new complex complete with hotel, souvenir shops and two restaurants – the one on the left only caters for individuals and is quite expensive; the other one only accepts groups.

WHERE TO STAY

All the youth hostels located along the route (and there are lots of them) are usually open every day, and definitely from mid-May to mid-October. Most are open all year but are closed on some days in low season. Note that

FROM BANFF TO JASPER

opening times may vary. For information about the hostels and for bookings, contact Banff International Hostel: ☎ (403) 762-4122. For hostels from Beauty Creek onwards contact Whistler Mountain Hostel, near Jasper: ☎ (780) 852-3215.

– The hostels are listed in order of distance along Highway 93 from Lake Louise, and the measurement given is an aid to their location.

⚑ **Mosquito Creek Hostel**: 24 kilometres (15 miles). Closed Monday and Tuesday in low season, except at Christmas. The hostel and campsite are close to each other. The hostel has 38 places in four chalets, including two family rooms. There's also a kitchen, sitting room and sauna.

⚑ **Water Fowl Lake Campsite**: 57 kilometres (35 miles). A path from the campsite leads to two beautiful lakes in about 90 minutes.

⚑ **The Crossing**: 80 kilometres (50 miles), at the junction of Highway 93 and Highway 11. ☎ 761-7000. Fax: 761-7006. This small motel has decent rooms for two (but that can squeeze in four) at fair prices, especially out of season. For a lunchtime snack, try the small pub behind the motel, where you can make your own burger quite cheaply. The dining room in the main building isn't great for dinner, but there's not much else in the area.

⚑ **Rampart Creek Hostel**: 88 kilometres (55 miles), just off the road on the right, in a clearing at the foot of the mountain. Closed Wednesday and Thursday in low season. This has 30 places, and is next to a campsite.

⚑ **Hilda Creek Hostel**: 118 kilometres (73 miles), on the left. Open daily mid-May to mid-October. Thursday to Saturday end-January to mid-May. Closed mid-October to end-January, except over Christmas. This very simple building has room for 21 people, modest facilities and a sauna. Surrounded by pines and quite far from the road, it's the

departure point for the Parker Ridge Trail.

⚑ **Wilcox Creek Campground** and **Columbia Icefield Campground**: 124 and 125 kilometres (about 77 miles). Two small campsites on the right-hand side of the road; the Columbia is better equipped, but only as far as the tents go.

⚑ **Hotel Columbia Icefield Chalet**: overlooking Athabasca Glacier (see 'What to See'). ☎ (780) 852-6550. Fax: (780) 852-6568. Open May to mid-October. This large complex has 32 lovely, very comfortable rooms, several with a mezzanine. Some large rooms can accommodate up to six people. Prices are based on two people sharing, and in high season it's quite expensive unless there are lots of you sharing. Prices are very affordable in May and October. Non-smoking.

⚑ **Beauty Creek Hostel**: 144 kilometres (89 miles), on the left of the valley, squeezed in between the road and a wide river. Open daily all year (but only for groups from October to end-April). It's a good departure point for walkers.

⚑ **Jonas Creek Campground**: 153 kilometres (95 miles). A small campsite on the right-hand side of the road.

⚑ **Athabasca Falls Hostel**: 198 kilometres (123 miles), on the right-hand side, just after the emergency telephone. Open 5–11pm. Closed Tuesday in low season (except at Christmas). Not far from the falls (unsurprisingly), with 40 places.

⚑ **Mount Edith Cavell Hostel**: Mount Edith Cavell Road; take Highway 93A from Athabasca Falls or south from Jasper, then a little climb up the deeply forested road. The hostel is a little off the route but the surroundings here are really superb. From mid-October to mid-June it's open only to groups and, even then, only if the road conditions allow access. There is accommodation for 32 people. The kitchen is in a separate building that's heated by two beautiful stoves. You'll find lovely walks nearby, and also places for experienced climbers.

WHAT TO SEE

The following attractions are also listed by distance along Highway 93 from Lake Louise.

★ **Lake Hector**: 16 kilometres (10 miles). From here you'll get a superb view of the lake's emerald waters surrounded by pine trees with a lick of snow that comes down from the mountain peaks. Note that the next service station is about 250 kilometres (155 miles) away – still another 150 kilometres (93 miles) from Jasper.

★ At 34 kilometres (21 miles), on the left, there's a lovely view of **Bow Lake** and, just before it, of **Crowfoot Glacier** at the foot of the amphitheatre.

★ **Lake Peyto**: 46 kilometres (29 miles). At this point there's a magnificent panoramic view of what has to be the greenest of the lakes in the Rockies. To avoid the crowds in high season at the lake path, continue for another 2 kilometres (1 mile) and you'll find an alternative path that takes you to the lake in about 20 minutes.

★ **Athabasca Glacier**: 127 kilometres (79 miles). On the left-hand side of the road, the glacier stretches out a tongue of ice 7 kilometres (4 miles) long, 1 kilometre wide and 400 metres (1,312 feet) thick. To get to the glacier on foot, park at the information centre and climb the last few hundred metres. The glacier is obviously very slippery and you should not walk on it unless accompanied by a guide. Superb walks lasting 3–5 hours depart daily at 11am. Trips onto the glacier in a big-wheeled vehicle to take photos are also available.

Like the Saskatchewan and Columbia glaciers, Athabasca came from the vast Columbia Icefield – an impressive icecap covering more than 300 square kilometres (116 square miles) with a maximum thickness of 900 metres (2,952 feet). The Athabasca Glacier has receded 1.5 kilometres since 1878, while the Columbia Glacier on the other side of the mountain range has advanced 1 kilometre since about 1990. Some 20 million years ago, the cooling of the earth's crust brought about the creation of glaciers in the northern mountainous regions. These glacial advances were interrupted by warmer interglacial periods. The current interglacial period began some 10,000 years ago.

★ **Stutfield Glacier**: 135 kilometres (84 miles). Visible far away on the left as you descend the valley is this glacier where the landscape is already less rugged and the valley is opening out.

★ **Sunwapta Falls**: 175 kilometres (109 miles). Turn left, to the car-park 500 metres farther on, and you'll find a really pleasant path through the undergrowth that leads to the falls.

FROM BANFF TO JASPER

★ **Athabasca Falls**: 199 kilometres (123 miles); turn left after a few hundred metres. The waters of the Athabasca plunge with such great force into a narrow canyon that the energy of these falls is amazing. The water slowly gouges an ever-wider course over time, digging out larger and larger pools and hollowing out ever-deeper cavities. The concrete handrails somehow destroy some of the charm.

WHAT TO DO

– **Hiking in Jasper National Park**: A permit to use the park is compulsory for excursions of more than one day, and buying a permit means you can avoid the crowds and that the park will be protected. You must obtain it at least 24 hours in advance, either from the Icefield Information Centre at Athabasca Glacier or from the information centre in Jasper (*see* 'Useful Addresses'). You have to apply in person, which gives you the opportunity of discussing your plans with the rangers and finding out about the weather forecast and the state of the paths. To be sure you'll get a permit, you can make a provisional booking by telephone: ☎ (780) 852-6177.

JASPER
DIALLING CODE: 780

A small bathing resort set in the expansive Jasper National Park, surrounded by impressive rocky peaks, Jasper is less smart than Banff – it has fewer appealing shops, more ordinary people and more affordable restaurants. Jasper comprises three parallel roads, including the main street (Connaught Drive), flanked by the railway and shops and restaurants. Along Patricia Street you'll find old wooden houses with brightly coloured roofs and charming little gardens with white picket fences. There are also a few churches and a number of historic buildings, including the firemen's barracks, the tourist office and the post office (in mountain stone).

Jasper is also the major rendezvous for mountain-bikers who organize pretty unbelievable endurance tests through the mountains. This is also an excellent departure point for walks to the superb lakes in the area. You can also hire kayaks or go rafting.

USEFUL ADDRESSES

🛈 **Tourist information**: 500 Connaught Drive, in the middle of the small park in the town centre. ☎ 852-6162 (emergencies, 24 hours) and 852-6176. Open 8am–7pm May to mid-June. 9am–5pm September to mid-October. You can get information and advice about walks in the park; ask for the brochure *One-day Excursions in Jasper National Park*, which details several circuits. For information about the area's wild animals check out the weekly *Bear Report* or the *Wildlife Observation Book*, a daily log of all appearances of the various animals.

■ **Parks Canada**: ☎ 852-6161. This very useful emergency number can put you in touch with the service you need if you have a problem. It can also provide information on road conditions.

🚂 🚌 **Station and bus terminal**: 314 Connaught Drive.

✉ **Post office**: Patricia Street, behind the information centre.

■ **Medical emergencies**: 518 Robson Street. ☎ 852-3344. The doctors' surgery is at 507 Turret Street. ☎ 852-4885.

■ **Police**: ☎ 852-4848.

■ **Weather forecast**: ☎ 852-3185.

■ **Car hire**: **National Tilden** is in the train station. ☎ 852-1117. Fax: 852-4303. **Hertz** is also at the station. ☎ 852-3888. The **Budget** office is in the Shell station on Connaught Drive, not far from the train station. ☎ 852-3222.

■ **Jasper Taxi**: ☎ 852-3146.

■ **Bike hire**: **Free Wheel Cycle**, 618 Patricia Street, in the centre. ☎ 852-3898. Bikes are also available from **On-line Sport & Tackle**, almost opposite at 600 Patricia Street. ☎ 852-3630. Not expensive.

WHERE TO STAY

All the hotels in Jasper are pretty expensive, so opt for the youth hostels or private rooms. A chalet can be quite reasonable for a group of four or more. There are also several modest retirement homes housing B&Bs.

☆ Budget

⌂ **Whistler Mountain Hostel**: Whistler Road, 7 kilometres (4 miles) south of Jasper, at the foot of Whistler Mountain. ☎ 852-3215. Open 5–11pm. Situated in a wild area is this really pleasant house with accommodation for 80 people. There's a big dormitory on the ground floor, three family rooms, a pleasant sitting room and a kitchen with lots of burners. Everyone helps to clean up, sweeping, taking out the bins etc. It's a pity curfew is so early (11pm) and that the hostel is more expensive than the others in the park. But it does offer cheap mountain-bike hire.

⌂ **Maligne Canyon Hostel**: 11 kilometres (7 miles) east of Jasper on Maligne Canyon Road (there's a turning on the right about 4 kilometres (2.5 miles) beyond the village. Open all year, but closed Wednesday from October to end-April. Bookings for summer are made through the Whistler Mountain Hostel (*see above*). About $10 with a Youth Hostel membership card. This small chalet, near the Maligne River and at the foot of the sheer cliffs of the canyon, has 24 places, with a kitchen and camp fire. It's more modern, but less expensive, than Whistler Mountain Hostel. You'll find it spartan but comfortable, with complete immersion in the wild guaranteed.

⌂ **Whistler Campsite**: take Whistler Road, on the left 3 kilometres (2 miles) before Jasper. Open early May to mid-October. This is one of the biggest and best-equipped campsites in the park, along with the Wapiti and Wabasso sites. The **Wapiti** site, 4 kilometres (2.5 miles) from Jasper, is open mid-June to mid-September. **Wabasso** campsite is 16 kilometres (10 miles) from Jasper and is open from May to September.

Private Lodgings

Several agencies arrange stays in private homes, and it's wise to go through them for accommodation at weekends and during the holidays. Be sure to book in advance.

Most of the guest rooms are on Connaught Drive and Patricia Street, indicated by the sign 'Approved Accommodation'. If you don't find anything on either of these streets, try Geikie Street where there are probably a few places that aren't too expensive.

■ **Jasper Travel Agency**: in the train station. ☎ 852-4400. Fax: 852-3030. Email: jtravel@telusmapet. net.

■ **Jasper Adventure Centre**: 608 Connaught Drive, in the cinema. ☎ 852-5595. Fax: 852-3127. Email: tours@telusmapet.net. This agency takes bookings not just for rooms, but also for all activities in Jasper.

♦ **Mrs McLay**: 719 Patricia Street. ☎ 852-4543. Open all year. This is one of the cheapest – a white house with a small studio with kitchenette. The hostess is very punctilious and prefers guests who are looking for peace and quiet.

♦ **Mrs S. de Silvestri**: 729 Patricia Street. ☎ 852-3615. You'll get a warm welcome here and the offer of a small studio for up to five people, with kitchen, living room, bath and shower.

♦ **Lena and Pat Hollenbeck**: 716 Connaught Drive. ☎ 852-4567. Email: hollen@incenter.net. They have one double and one twin room, plus one room with two double beds. The rooms with double beds are less expensive. As much coffee or tea as you like. Not expensive.

♦ **Gloria Kongsrud**: 712 Connaught Drive. ☎ 852-3763. Modern house with pleasant rooms.

♦ **Bill and Gloria Unrau B&B**: 204 Colin Crescent. ☎ 852-4345. Decent, quiet basement rooms (bathroom outside) at very modest prices. Also a small garden. No breakfast, and the welcome is so-so.

☆☆–☆☆☆ Chalets (moderate to expensive)

Chalets are more appealing than traditional motels and hotels, but you'll need to book well in advance. They're usually open from the end of April to Thanksgiving (second Monday in October).

♦ **Alpine Village**: Highway 93 (Icefields Parkway), a few kilometres before Jasper (coming from Banff). ☎ 852-3285. A mini village of delightful log-cabin-type chalets hidden in the trees, surrounded by flowers and only a few paces from the Athabasca River. Each cabin has charming interior decor, a huge stone fireplace and a lawn with sunny terrace. Average prices are $80–160 for four depending on the quality and facilities.

♦ **Becker's Chalets**: Highway 93, 5 kilometres (3 miles) from Jasper. ☎ 852-3779. Fax: 852-7202. More lovely cabins that are charming and comfortable.

♦ **Jasper House Bungalows**: ☎ 852-4535. Fax: 852-5335. Same style as Becker's Chalets.

♦ **Bonhomme Bungalows**: 100 Bonhomme Street, three blocks from Connaught Drive. ☎ 852-3209. Fax: 852-3099. Open mid-April to October. A pleasant collection of cabins right in the centre of town, but in a quiet neighbourhood. You'll get a friendly welcome. Facilities include sauna, jacuzzi, barbecue and mountain-bike hire. Prices are $80–100 for two and just over $120 for four (with kitchenette and open fire).

WHERE TO EAT

☆ Budget

✗ **Jasper Pizza Place**: Connaught Drive, after the tourist office. ☎ 852-3225. Open daily until 1am. Tacos, hamburgers and pizzas for

about $12. It's where many of the young people gather. Roof terrace with mountain views.

✗ **A & W**: 624 Connaught Drive, opposite the steam train. ☎ 852-

4930. Open 7am–10pm in summer, until 9pm in winter. This is the cheapest place in Jasper – a fast-food outlet in the train station serving hamburgers, steaks, etc.

✕ **Cantonese Restaurant**: Connaught Drive. ☎ 852-3559. Fax: 852-3047. Open daily 11am–11pm. Clean, pleasant place with set menus of soup, main course and rice for around $12.50.

☆☆ Moderate

✕ **Kim Chi House**: 407 Patricia Street. ☎ 852-5022. But for the big sign saying 'Korean Restaurant' outside a small house that looks like all the others, you wouldn't know this restaurant was here. It has a family atmosphere, where diners feel like house guests. Good Korean specialities such as pan-fried dumplings at very reasonable prices.

✕ **Earl's**: 600 Patricia Street. ☎ 852-2393. Another in the chain, similar to the branches in Banff and Calgary. It's packed in high season.

✕ **L. and W. Family Restaurant**: corner of Patricia Street and Hazel Street. ☎ 852-4114. Open until 1am in summer and 10pm in winter. The Californian-style decor is a bit garish, but it's spacious, and lots of green plants, rosy hues and white

wood give it a freshness. Generous portions of Italian and Greek cuisine – fish, scallops, pasta, BBQ chicken and spare-ribs, Alberta prime rib, T-bone grilled over a charcoal fire and good salads. Good value for money.

✕ **Something Else**: 621 Patricia Street. ☎ 852-3850. Open until midnight. The setting is overwhelmingly plastic but the atmosphere is warm and quite lively. The particularly eclectic cuisine includes souvlaki, pizzas, pasta, Cajun dishes, seafood, BBQ ribs and, for lunch, burgers and sandwiches.

✕ **Papa George's**: 404 Connaught Drive. ☎ 852-3351. Fax: (780) 852-5472. Open from breakfast to dinner. Closed mid-October to mid-December. On offer are a few basic salads and burgers, but mostly lots of cooked meat and fish dishes (very good fillet of halibut), all served with a degree of style.

✕ ❏ **Bear's Paw Bakery**: Cedar Avenue, near Connaught Drive. ☎ 852-3233. Highly recommended is this bakery that sells bread of all sorts, and particularly excellent Viennese pastries and cakes to take out or to eat in with a cup of tea or coffee. It's perfect for breakfast.

WHERE TO HAVE A DRINK

❢ **Atha-B Pub**: corner of Miette Avenue and Patricia Street, next to the Athabasca Hotel. In addition to being a bar, this is the only place in town with live bands in the evening.

WHAT TO SEE

★ **Den Wildlife Museum**: Connaught Drive and Miette Avenue, in the basement of Whistlers Inn. ☎ 852-3361. Open daily 9am–10pm. Entrance charge expensive. All the animals native to the region can be seen in their natural habitat at this small, but must-see, museum.

★ **Jasper Yellowhead Museum**: 400 Pyramid Lake Road (opposite the swimming pool). ☎ 852-3013. Open in summer 10am–9pm. 10am–5pm the rest of the year. This little museum details the history of Jasper and the region, the pioneer fur trappers and the arrival of the railway. Numerous exhibits and old photographs illustrate the explanatory panels, and there are also films on the local fauna. A small room is set aside for children to learn about nature in the form of a game.

IN THE AREA

★ **Patricia and Pyramid lakes**: 10 minutes northeast of Jasper. These are easily accessible by bike, and it's ideal to continue as far as Pyramid Lake where you can hire canoes to explore tranquil, wooded surroundings. Pretty (but quite expensive) log cabins overlook the lake at Pyramid Lake Resort. ☎ 852-4900. Open all year.

★ **The Whistler (Jasper Tramway)**: take Whistler Road about 3 kilometres (2 miles) south of Jasper and continue right to the end (another 3 kilometres). ☎ (403) 852-3093. Fax: (403) 852-5779. Open mid-April to mid-October. Departures 8am–10pm in high season. Last departure at 4pm in low season. It's a bit expensive. Enjoy breathtaking views of the valley, the neighbouring mountains, the shimmering rivers and the peaceful lakes on a magnificent cable-car ride up Mount Whistler (2,469 metres/8,098 feet). Alternatively, there's a challenging, really steep hike up 1,200 metres (3,936 feet) of uneven ground over 7 kilometres (4 miles). A path then leads to the summit of the peak, 200 metres (124 feet) higher, where you'll see a grandiose panoramic view. The mountain owes its name to the whistles of the woodchucks that you can sometimes see below the higher cable car.

★ **Lake Edith and Lake Annette**: 5 kilometres (3 miles) out of town, on the road to Jasper Park Lodge. Here you'll find two really adorable lakes that are very seldom visited. It's a pretty civilized spot, with toilets, car-park and picnic area, but no restaurant or souvenir shop. The landscape around Lake Edith is softer and superbly lit at sunset. The shores are so sandy that you might even believe you were on a beach. The water is not as cold as elsewhere and can reach 20°C (68°F) in July – ideal for a swim.

★ **Maligne Canyon**: 11.5 kilometres (7 miles) from Jasper; 3 kilometres (2 miles) north of town turn right, over a little bridge. There's a car-park and an interpretative trail. The Maligne Valley extends for 65 kilometres (40 miles) between the mountains. The six bridges that cross the canyon are the most important stages of the route. There's a superb 23-metre (75-foot) waterfall where the waters snake along a narrow canyon with pleasant, very informative trails about the valley. The layers of rock are clearly visible in the canyon, and you might even see some of the small birds that nest in the tiny holes in the rock face.

★ **Medicine Lake**: 15.5 kilometres (10 miles) beyond Maligne Canyon (*see above*). Sometimes this lake is nearly dry; its waters come from Lake Maligne, via an underground river, and filter up through the softer layers of rock. It's not a really beautiful lake, but the mountains on the left (the Queen Elizabeth Range) have clearly defined vertical stratifications – proof of the phenomenal upheaval of the earth's crust that formed them.

★ **Lake Maligne**: about 33 kilometres (20 miles) beyond Medicine Lake (*see above*). It's marvellous here, and you might even catch a glimpse of some mountain goats. When the light is soft and the sky is slightly cloudy, the spectacle is breathtaking. On one side the rounded hills rise gently from the lake shores, at the end are snowy peaks and in the middle the waters of the lake stretch 22 kilometres (14 miles) into the distance. The narrowness of the lake gives it an intimate feeling. Right at the end is Spirit Island, the most famous image of the lake. To see it at its most splendid come early in the morning and hire a boat from the old boatyard (open 8am–6pm), where a pioneer guide in the 1930s built rowing boats. Fishing is also permitted.

The lake is best avoided on Wednesday, when organized coach parties arrive. Further information is available in Maligne. There's a large cafeteria (open 9am–7pm end-June to 10 September, until 6pm at other times).

– Boat trips: Maligne Tours, 626 Connaught Drive. ☎ 852-3770. Open mid-May to mid-October daily 10am–5pm. Departures every hour in high season, and about every 2 hours out of season. It's rather expensive, though. You can also hire canoes.

★ Miette Hot Springs: 61 kilometres (38 miles) northeast of Jasper on Highway 16 towards Edmonton; turn right at Pocahontas and go past Punchbowl Falls. ☎ 866-3939. Open 8am–10.30pm end-June to early September. 10.30am–9pm mid-May to end-June and in September. The spa comprises two very hot swimming pools – the 'cool' one is 40°C (104°F), compared to a water temperature of 54°C (129°F) when it emerges from the rocks. There's also a cold pool and a picnic area.

★ Mount Edith Cavell: 30 kilometres (19 miles) south of Jasper on Highways 93 and 93A. This is a real attraction in the region, but the very narrow and winding ascent is impassable for wide vehicles such as motorhomes, caravans and buses.

★ Historic Ukrainian Village: outside Elk Island National Park, east of Edmonton. ☎ (403) 662-3640. A little farther afield is this interesting site where you can gain an insight into the everyday life of Ukrainian immigrants who arrived between 1891 and 1925, as represented by young actors. The village includes a domed church, station, police station, mechanic's workshop, general store, hardware store and blacksmith's shop, all in Ukrainian architecture. You can also sample the authentic cuisine. Set aside about 2–3 hours.

WHAT TO DO

– The park rangers organize daily **themed excursions**, which are all detailed (with times) in *Profil*, a free newspaper. These are an excellent introduction to the flora and fauna of the region.

– **Kayaking**: Amateurs will find the Maligne River is one of the best spots in the Rockies, but pretty scary. Kayak hire is available in Jasper.

– **Rafting**: The rivers in Jasper are great for rafting, and the Athabasca River is ideal for beginners. Experienced rafters (or those with nerves of steel) should head for the Maligne River – it's unmissable and will give you a huge buzz. Trips are not cheap but certainly worth it for the experience of a lifetime.

A few operators include **Jasper Raft Tour** in the bus station at the Brewster agency. The company offers trips down the Athabasca River for beginners and softies. **White Water Rafting** has lots of outlets in town. ☎ 852-7238. It has superbly organized trips on the Athabasca, the Sunwapta and the Maligne rivers in a really nice atmosphere. For great programmes on the Athabasca, Sunwapta and Kakwa rivers try **Maligne Rafting Adventure**, at 626 Connaught Drive (☎ 852-3370; fax: 852-3390) and 627 Patricia Street (☎ 852-5208).

– **Mountain biking**: Enthusiasts will be in seventh heaven riding circuits on well-marked walking paths. Information is available from the tourist office. You can also get the latest from people returning from rides, as a few always hang around with their bikes near the tourist office in the small park. For bike hire *see* 'Useful Addresses'.

– **Horse riding**: Pyramid Stables, in the direction of Pyramid Lake. ☎ 852-3562. The stables are about 3.5 kilometres (2 miles) above Pyramid Lake Road and offer rides lasting 1–3 hours, with ponies for the kids. It's best to book in advance.

– **Mountain hiking**: There are plenty of opportunities for hikes of several days into the mountains. Pick up the *Guide to the Wilderness for Visitors – Jasper National Park* at the tourist office. Don't forget that you must buy a park permit for camping in the wild: $6 per night up to a maximum of $30 per trip, or an annual permit for $42.

A two-day circuit of **Saturday Night Lake** will undoubtedly get you hooked, and it's a fairly easy path. Of all the possible three-day routes, the one along the **Tonquin Valley** takes in marvellous wild landscapes. The **Skyline** is also highly recommended.

LEAVING JASPER

By Bus

🚌 **Greyhound** and **Brewster**: 314 Connaught Drive. ☎ 852-3332. Fax: 852-3211. The two operators are in the same office in the station. Time-tables are often subject to change.

– **For Banff**: The express bus leaves at 1.30pm. There are three other departures throughout the day but the buses stop everywhere.

– **For Edmonton**: Two departures early in the morning (around 6am), one at 1.45pm and another at 7.30pm.

– **For Vancouver**: One departure at noon, and two night departures (1am and 4am).

– **For Kamloops**: One bus in the morning and one in the afternoon.

By Train

Canadian trains are what you might call simple but functional, and it's a real pleasure to find a little taste of the retro.

🚆 **Station**: 314 Connaught Drive. Reservations: ☎ 1-800-561-8630 (toll-free). Information in Jasper: ☎ 852-4102.

– **For Vancouver**: Services on Monday and Saturday at 4.25pm. The Jasper–Vancouver journey crosses the Rockies and really exceptional landscapes. it takes 4 hours 30 minutes.

– **For Edmonton** and **Winnipeg**: Services on Monday, Wednesday and Saturday at 2.05pm. Journey time around 5 hours to Edmonton and about 15 to Winnipeg.

– **For Prince Rupert**: Wednesday, Friday and Sunday at 12.45pm. You stay overnight in Prince George and arrive in Prince Rupert the following evening.

British Columbia

In the province of British Columbia you'll find the most varied and grandiose landscapes and the most splendid forests in the whole of Canada. The west coast, broken up by inlets and thousands of small islands, is formed by immense snow-capped mountains that fall precipitously into the ocean. The abundant rainfall and generally wet climate encourages the growth of luxurious tropical vegetation. The warm summers and the appeal of the sea attract increasingly more tourists, particularly to Vancouver – a superb modern city that has the deepest respect for the natural environment.

Over the next few years the population of British Columbia is expected to rise by 40 per cent, accompanied by a matching increase in traffic. But measures are already being taken to improve the infrastructure of the province, including road improvement schemes, the modernization of the ferry fleet and increased sailings.

The Rockies and the Yoho and Kootenay national parks are significant attractions. British Columbia is a place of infinite space, with lakes and an impressive array of superb hiking trails flanked by rocky peaks. In short, it's one of the most pleasurable of the Canadian provinces to visit.

VANCOUVER   DIALLING CODE: 604

For maps of Vancouver, see the first colour plate section.

This is Canada's California – a city of wide avenues, vast, well-tended (but somehow still wild) parks, lively nightlife and people who take life as it comes. Although surrounded by mountains and ocean, Vancouver is a city on a human scale that can dispel the usual stresses of a big city. This is helped by the climate which ensures it's neither too cold in the winter (rarely below 0°C/ 32°F) nor too hot in summer.

It's often compared to San Francisco, as both cities are easy-going, pleasant places to live, and smoking is forbidden in all commercial establishments where children might be present. And then Vancouver also has a vibrant and cultural life that's always on the move. It's essentially a place not to be missed, and most of its attractions are Downtown, on the peninsula to the northwest.

Just a few kilometres across the sea from the modern city is Vancouver Island – a chunk of land both preserved by and protected from humans that complements the city. Discovered by Captain James Cook (1728–79) in 1778, George Vancouver subsequently took possession of it in 1792 in the name of the British Crown.

GETTING THERE

By Plane

✪ **Vancouver International Airport**: about 15 kilometres (9 miles) from town, a drive of about 25 minutes. ☎ 276-6101. The shuttle bus from the Greyhound bus terminal (150 Dunsmuir) costs $10 and leaves from Platform 20 every 30 minutes from 6.12am to 10.10pm, and takes 40 minutes.

The Airport Express bus also runs every 30 minutes to most of the big hotels. ☎ 273-9023.

– For groups of three or more travelling together, it's much better to take a taxi for $20–30.

By Train

🚆 **BC Rail** (map I, C–D1): 1311 West 1st Street, North Vancouver. ☎ 984-5246 and 631-3500. Fax: 984-5005. Website: www.bcrail.com/bcrpass.

🚆 **Via Rail** (map II, D3): 1150 Station Street. ☎ 669-3050 or 1-800-561-8630 (toll-free). Website: www.viarail.ca

🚆 **Amtrak**: ☎ 1-800-USA. Email: amtrak-p@ix.netcom.com. One train daily from Seattle in the United States.

By Bus

🚌 **Greyhound Bus Terminal** (map II, D3): 1150 Station Street. ☎ 482-8747 or 1-800-231-2222 (toll-free).

GETTING AROUND

– **By car**: Driving is best for visiting districts outside Downtown (walking is fine in the centre). Drivers should note that the authorities here are very strict on illegal parking, and that cars will be impounded immediately. However, the retrieval fee isn't that high. If your car is towed away, it will be taken to 1410 Granville Street by **Unitow**: ☎ 606-1250.

– **By bus**: The bus system is fast and very efficient. Information: **BC Transit**. ☎ 521-0400. Ticket prices cover three zones ($1.50, $2.25 and $3), with discounts for students. Make sure you have the right change. There's also a very attractively priced **Daypass** that's also valid on the **Skytrain** and **Seabus**. You can also buy a **monthly pass** or a book of tickets. Buses for most of the main routes leave from **Granville Street**.

– **Seabus**: from Water Front Station. This ferry between Vancouver and North Vancouver operates daily every 15–30 minutes, with the crossing taking about 12 minutes. You'll see a very beautiful view of the city. Prices and ticketing are the same as for the buses.

– **Skytrain**: This is a magnetically propelled overhead subway or light-rail system (only 4 of the 17 stations are underground). The single line, 24.5 kilometres (15 miles) in length, links Vancouver with the eastern suburbs of Burnaby, New Westminster and Surrey.

– **Cycling**: Bikes are also excellent for touring Vancouver, and mountain bikes are probably best to tackle the hills around the city. One enjoyable journey is the **Vancouver Seaside Route**, a splendid 15-kilometre (9-mile) tour from Stanley Park to Spanish Banks, via False Creek. Useful numbers include **Bicycle Hotline**, ☎ 871-6070 (information service on the town), and **Parks and Recreation Board**, ☎ 681-1141.

VANCOUVER

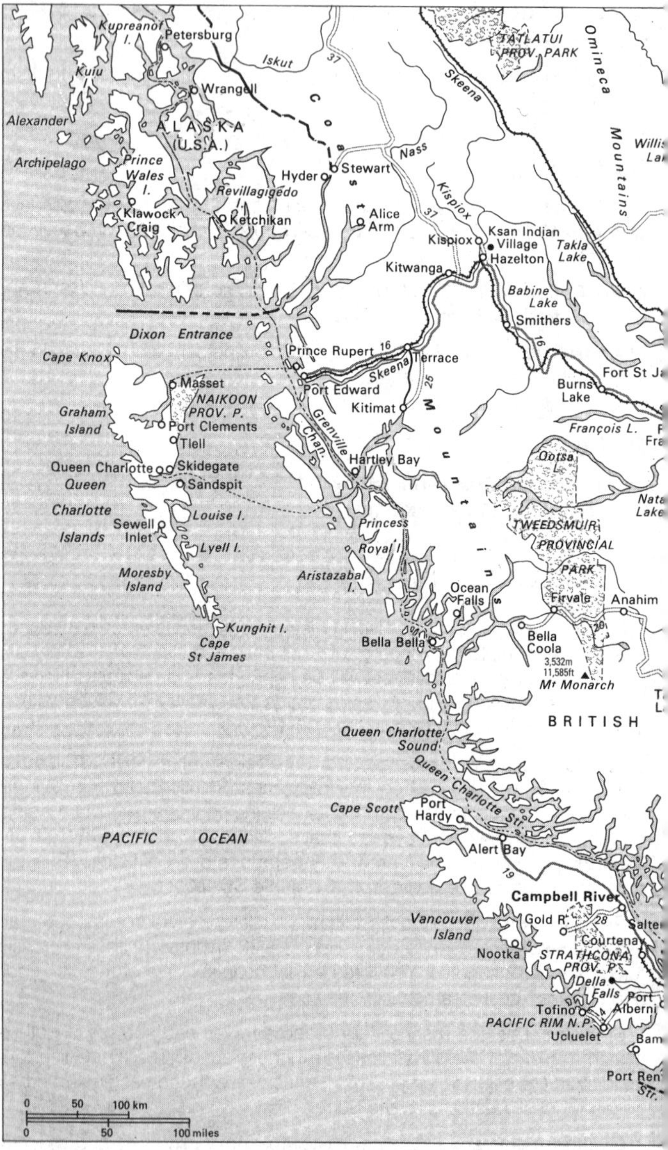

BRITISH COLUMBIA

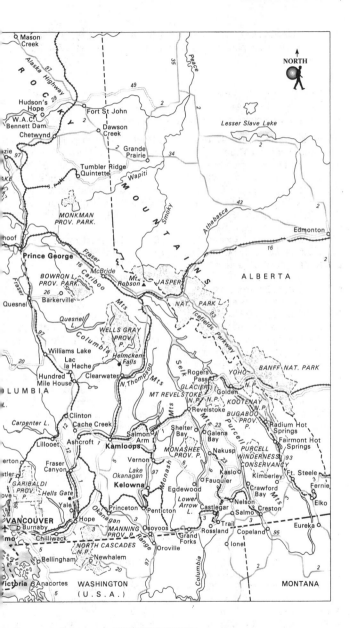

BRITISH COLUMBIA

– **Boats**: Although fairly exorbitant to rent, these are great fun to get around in. There's a hire company around Cardero and Georgia, just before Stanley Park. ☎ 682-6257.

USEFUL ADDRESSES

For maps of Vancouver, see the first colour plate section.

🖪 Tourism Vancouver Convention and Visitor's Bureau (map II, C1): Water Front Center, Plaza Level, 200 Burrard Street. ☎ 683-2000 or 1-800-663-6000 (toll-free). Fax: 682-6839. Open daily 8am–6pm in season. Rest of the year 8.30am–5pm (9am Saturday). Closed Sunday. This excellent new tourist office with brilliant staff has plenty of brochures and information.

🖪 Tourist Info Center: airport arrivals hall, just before the exit. ☎ 303-3601. Fax: 271-0924. Website: www.tourism-vancouver.org. Efficient, friendly staff will offer advice, find you a hotel to suit your budget and preferred location and will give you a voucher after confirming your reservation by telephone. There's also an **information kiosk** on the corner of Georgia and Granville streets.

Transport

🚌 Greyhound bus terminal (map II, D3): 1150 Station Street, at Main Street and Terminal. ☎ 482-8747 (24-hour) or 1-800-231-2222 (toll-free). Fax: 683-0144. Website: www.greyhound.ca. Departures to destinations throughout Canada and the United States.

🚌 BC Transit: 108 Surrey Avenue, New Westminster. ☎ 521-0400 (intercity information, 6am–11.30pm). Website: www.bctransit.com

🚆 Train station (**Via Rail**; map II, D3): 1150 Station Street, at Main Street and Terminal. Reservations: ☎ 1-800-561-8630 (toll-free).

✉ Post office (map II, C2): 349 West Georgia Street. ☎ 662-5722. Open Monday–Friday 8am–5.30pm.

■ **United States Consulate** (map II, C1, **4**): 1095 West Pender Street. ☎ 685-4311. Open Monday to Friday 8am–4.30pm. Closed public holidays.

■ **St Paul Hospital** (map II, B2, **10**): 1081 Burrard Street, Downtown. ☎ 682-2344/2157.

■ **Emergencies**: ☎ 911.

■ **Pharmacies**: **Shoppers Drug Mart** (map II, B2, **11**), 1125 Davie Street, on the corner of Thurlow Street. ☎ 685-2424. Also at 1650 David Street. Open Monday to Saturday 9am–11pm. Sunday and school holidays 10am–10pm.

– **London Drug** (map II, B2, **12**): 1187 Robson Street. ☎ 669-7374. Open daily until 10pm.

■ **American Express** (map II, C2, **13**): 666 Burrard Street. ☎ 669-2813.

■ **Train station** (**BC Rail**; 1311 West First Street, North Vancouver. ☎ 984-5503. Fax: 984-5565. Website: www.bcrail.com/bcrpass

■ **Air Canada**: 1088 West Georgia Street. ☎ 688-5515.

■ **Air France**: ☎ 1-800-361-7257 (toll-free).

■ **Canadian Airlines** (map II, B2, **6**): 1030 West Georgia Street. ☎ 279-6611.

■ **Thrifty**: Century Plaza Hotel, 1015 Burrard Street. ☎ 606-1695. Car hire, also at 1400 Robson Street (☎ 681-4869) and at 4071 3rd

Street, Richmond, near the airport (☎ 276-1840).

■ **Budget** (map II, C2, **7**): 501 West Georgia Street at Richards Street. ☎ 668-7068. Also at 99 West Pender Street. ☎ 683-5666. Open Monday to Saturday 7.30am–6pm. Sunday 8.30am–6pm.

■ **Tilden** (map II, B2, **8**): 1140 Alberni Street (near Thurlow Street). ☎ 685-6111. Also at 1128 West Georgia Street.

■ **Rent-a-Wreck**: 1083 Hornby Street. ☎ 688-0001.

■ **Lo-Cost** (map II, B3, **9**): 1105 Granville Street. ☎ 689-9664. 1835

Marine Drive. ☎ 986-1266. Canada Place, 'Cruise Ship Level'. ☎ 682-7333. Another rental agency at this address offers excellent weekend rates (three days).

■ **Taxis**: Vancouver Taxi: ☎ 871-1111. Yellow Cab: ☎ 681-1111.

– **Bike hire**: Most hire companies are concentrated near the coner of Robson and Denman streets. Prices are fairly similar but double-check the rates as they may differ from those advertised. Also check the condition of the equipment.

The Media

■ **International Travel Maps** (map II, C2, **15**): 552 Seymour Street. ☎ 687-3320. Fax: 687-5925. Open Monday to Saturday 9am–6.30pm. Sunday noon–5pm. Guides, road maps and topographic maps of the whole world, and a particularly huge choice on Canada and the USA.

■ The main daily newspapers in English for local and regional news are the *Vancouver Sun* and *The Province*. A monthly, *Vancouver* ($3.50) and two free sheets, *Georgia Straight* and *Where Vancouver*, offer a wealth of listings, information about shops and how and where to meet people. You'll find them in most cafés.

Websites

● **www.tourism-vancouver.org**: The website of the Vancouver tourist office has very little general information about the city, but does have very complete listings for accommodation, restaurants, bars etc.

● **www.culturenet.ca/vca**: A diary of cultural events and general information about artistic events in Vancouver.

Internet Access

As this is part of North American life, there are terminals everywhere, in different settings and at different prices. Here are a few places around the downtown area, but you'll have no problem finding others.

■ **Lingo Cyberbistro** (map II, C2, **16**): 547 Seymour Street, opposite A&B Sound. ☎ 331-9345. Website: www.ilsc-vancouver.com/lingo/. Open Monday to Friday 8am–8pm. Saturday 8am–4am. Sunday 8am–7pm. $4.50 for 30 minutes, $8 per hour to surf the web. Good sand-

wiches and a few Tex-Mex dishes also available.

■ **Student Center**: 616 Seymour Street. ☎ 488-1441. Open daily 10.30am–7.30pm. This place is fairly new and you can use the Internet for short stretches – a good place to scan photos to send back home. $2 for less than 20 minutes, $6 per hour. You can also buy phone cards here.

■ **Internet Coffee** (map II, B2, **17**): 1104 Davie Street. ☎ 682-6668. Email: internetcoffee98@yahoo.fr. Open daily 9am–3am (Saturday to 4am). As well as the Internet services, Italian-style coffee and fresh fruit juice are on offer.

■ **The Byte Place** (map I, A1, **18**): 1636 Robson Street, below Tama Sushi (*see* 'Where to Eat'). ☎ 683-2688. Email: byteplace@ yahoo.com. Open daily 10am– midnight (2am Friday and Saturday). The decor is 1970s in style but the technology is more cutting-edge and includes Internet access, photocopiers and fax machines – everything you need to keep in touch. There's also a bar.

WHERE TO STAY

For maps of Vancouver, see the first colour plate section.

Booking Agencies: There's no shortage of booking agencies, some of which are listed below. However, do remember that B&B accommodation is not a cheap option. A good Bed & Breakfast guide, listing all the licensed places, is available from tourist offices and at the establishments themselves. Website: www.wcbbia.com.

■ **A Home Away From Home**: 1441 Howard Avenue, Burnaby, BC. ☎ 294-1760. Fax: 294-0799.

■ **Canada West Accommodations**: ☎ 929-1424 or 1-800-561-3223 (toll-free). Fax: 929-6692. Covers B&Bs in Vancouver, Victoria and Whistler.

■ **Old English Bed & Breakfast Registry**: 1226 Silverwood Crescent, North Vancouver. ☎ 986-5069. Fax: 986-8810.

■ **AAA Bed & Breakfast Registry**: ☎ 875-8888 or 1-800-463-9933 (toll-free).

■ **Vancouver B&B Registry**: ☎ 298-8815. Fax: 298-5917.

☆ Budget

There are only a few campsites in Vancouver and they're not central. The following listings include a few suggestions for committed campers.

⚑ **Capilano RV Park** (map 1, C1): 295 Tomahawk Avenue, North Vancouver. ☎ 987-4722. Fax: 987-2015. The nearest campsite to town, just cross the Lion's Gate Bridge and you're in Stanley Park, 10 minutes from Downtown by bus. It costs $25 for two plus car and tent. Facilities include a washroom, swimming pool and jacuzzi. The only drawback is that it's quite noisy because of the traffic.

⚑ **Richmond RV Park and Campground**: 6200 River Road, Richmond. ☎ 270-7878 or 1-800-755-4905 (toll-free). Fax: 244-9713. Open April to October. The is the closest campsite to town, only about 10 kilometres (6 miles) south, on Lulu Island. The bus to Downtown is just a 5-minute walk away. Pitches cost around $15 for two.

⚑ **Dogwood Campgrounds of BC**: 15151 112th Avenue, Surrey. ☎ 583-5585. Fax: 583-4725. Around 30 kilometres (18 miles) southeast, not far from Highway 1 (the Trans-Canada).

⚑ **Peace Arch RV Park**: 14601 40th Avenue, Surrey. ☎ 594-7009. Around 40 kilometres (24 miles) southeast of Vancouver, not far from Highway 99. It's comfortable, has a heated swimming pool and the sites are in a nice wooded area.

There's a bus from the campsite to the Skytrain.

♠ **Vincent's New Backpackers Hostel** (ex-Vincent's Guesthouse; map II, C2, **20**): 347 West Pender Street. ☎ 688-0112. Prices range from $10 a night in a dorm for four or six, to $25 for a single room and $30 for a double. It's good for one night or if you're on a really tight budget, but it's not always spotless. Very much a backpackers' atmosphere, but no curfew. Kitchen and TV room.

♠ **Vancouver Hostel** (map II, B2, **21**): 1114 Burnaby Street, on the corner of Thurlow Street. ☎ 684-4565 or 1-888-203-4302 (toll-free). Fax: 684-4540. Email: van-downtown@hihostels.bc.ca. Centrally located in a pretty quiet district, not far from Nelson Park. Single rooms are around $20 a night for members ($24 for non-members) and doubles are $55 (or $64). Private or shared rooms (maximum four people). Reception is open round the clock. The location, welcome and services at this new hostel make it a good place to stay, even for families. It has a garden, lounges, equipped kitchens, dining room, laundrette, bookshop, games room and bicycle hire. Disabled access, and non-smokers only.

♠ **Hostelling International Vancouver, Jericho Beach** (map I, B2, **22**): 1515 Discovery Street. ☎ 224-3208 or 1-888-203-4303 (toll-free). Fax: 224-4852. Email: van-jericho@hihostels.bc.ca. Open 24 hours. You'll find this in Jericho Park, 5 minutes from Jericho and Locarno beaches, south of town. Bus No. 4 from Granville Street heading towards UBC stops a 5-minute walk from the hostel – a big white building with blue windows. There are two floors of rather spartan, single-sex dormitories divided into sections of four beds ($17 per person for Youth Hostel members and $21.50 for non-members), plus four individual rooms at about $50. Clean washing facilities, cafeteria, laundrette and kitchenette, plus a billiard table and tennis next door. Note the no-smoking policy.

♠ **Global Village Backpackers** (map II, B2–3, **23**): 1018 Granville Street, opposite the Royal Hotel. ☎ 682-8226 or 1-888-844-7875 (toll-free). Fax: 682-8240. Website: www.globalbackpackers.com. You can't miss it, look for the bright colours. The price is $18 a night, plus a few individual rooms at $56. Ideally situated near the bars and Gastown, not far from the crazy life on Robson Street. Very cool atmosphere, you don't stay on your own for long, you're immersed as soon as you enter the door.

♠ **YWCA Hotel/Residence** (map II, C3, **31**): 733 Beatty Street. ☎ 895-5830 or 1-800-663-1424 (toll-free). Fax: 681-2550. Website: www.ywcavan.org. This is a real hotel in a new building that's modern and very central, near the renovated district of Yaletown. It has 155 rooms for one to five people, at $48–63 for singles, $60–96 for doubles and around $90 for triples (about $80 in low season). Disabled access. Private or shared bathrooms, and TV in some rooms. There are several kitchens, laundrette, TV room and air-conditioning. The atmosphere and welcome are a bit frosty. Free use of the sports and health centre about 15 minutes' walk away. Best to book.

☆☆ Moderate

♠ **The Kingston Hotel** (map II, C2, **24**): 757 Richards Street, at Robson and Richards streets. ☎ 684-9024 or 1-888-713-3304 (toll-free). Fax: 684-9917. Website: www.vancouver-bc.com/kingstonhotel. Singles $45–75, doubles $55–85, with communal showers and toilets on each floor. Also sauna, laundry facilities and parking. Only a few blocks from the stadium and the shops on Robson Street is this practical B&B for covering the whole city centre. A very clean, unpretentious, family hotel at unbeatable value for money.

â **Royal Hotel** (map II, B2, **25**): 1025 Granville Street. ☎ 685-5335 or 1-877-685-5337 (toll-free). Fax: 685-5351. Email: frontdesk@atthe royal.com. Rooms cost $69–89 at this completely refurbished hotel with a yellow-and-black front. It feels almost too new, but its central location and reasonable prices will attract lots of people. Pretty quiet despite the pub below.

â **The Dominion Hotel** (map II, D2, **26**): 210 Abbott Street, on the corner of Water Street, Gastown. ☎ 681-6666. Fax: 681-5855. Website: www.dominionhotel.bc.ca/ gastown. Doubles without bathroom cost from $96 in season ($115–128 with bathroom), including breakfast. Worlds away from the antiseptic chain hotel, this hotel has a historical flavour and charm. The hotel has been open since 1899 and is in one of the oldest buildings in Gastown. The rooms differ and feel a little shabby, the decor is minimal and the walls are brick, with all the charm and disadvantages that implies. Those overlooking Water Street can be noisy, and loud bands that sometimes play at the Lamplighter's Pub on the ground floor of the hotel will also seriously disturb your sleep. Breakfast is served in the coffee shop next door until 11am. Friendly welcome.

â **Buchan Hotel** (map II, A1, **27**): 1906 Haro Street, parallel to Robson Street. ☎ 685-5354 or 1-800-668-6654 (toll-free). Fax: 685-5367. Website: www.3bc.sympatico.ca/ buchan. This is a small three-storey hotel, built in the 1940s in a quiet

residential area only two blocks from Stanley Park. Surrounded by trees, it has a very pleasant setting. You'll find very well-maintained rooms (with or without bathroom) with open fireplaces, plus a friendly welcome. Attractive prices by the week. Non-smoking, and booking advised.

â **Kitsilano Point B&B** (map I, C2, **28**): 1936 McNicoll Avenue, very close to Burrard Street. ☎ 738-9576. In a good location not far from Kitsilano beach and Vanier Park is this traditional, early 20th-century house offering pleasant rooms for around $75. Hosts Jennifer and Larry are really nice. It's essential to book either in writing or by phone.

☆☆ – ☆☆☆ Moderate to Expensive

â **Sylvia Hotel** (map II, A1, **29**): 1154 Gilford Street. ☎ 681-9321. Fax: 682-3551. Rooms cost $65–115 (including kitchenette if required) and lovely suites are available at $125–175. Parking is $5 per night. This is on the shore of English Bay, with its lovely beach, and also very close to Stanley Park. The area has many lovely lawns and this hotel, with its majestic, ivy-covered facade, is easy to find. In 1912, the hotel was considered to be the most beautiful building in the West End and, until 1950, it was also the highest. It's now surrounded by many smart but identical chain hotels. It offers remarkable value and charm for the money, with functional and spacious rooms – eight have a view directly over the bay (the most expensive) and many of the others offer at least a glimpse. Booking is essential.

â **Douglas Guest House B&B** (map I, D2, **30**): 456 West 13th Avenue, at the corner of Cambie Street. ☎ 872-3060 or 1-888-872-3060 (toll-free). Fax: 873-1147. Website: www.dougwin.com.

Pleasant, light rooms from $95 to $110. No smoking. An Edwardian house that's not very discreet (the exterior is in shades of orange) but which has all the necessary facilities. You'll get superb cooking with breakfast served on the terrace. If it's full, try the blue-and-white Cambie Lodge next door, which is owned by the same proprietor.

♠ **The Manor** (map I, C2, **32**): 345 West 13th Avenue. ☎ 876-8494. Fax: 876-5763. This Edwardian house in a leafy residential district has elegant internal wood panelling. There are 10 pleasant rooms ranging from $85 to $170, some of which are in the basement (not much light, but very clean). On the top floor there's a superb and very bright family suite with kitchen, balcony and a view of Downtown. Private parking. Booking strongly recommended.

♠ **The Penny Farthing Inn** (map I, B2, **33**): 2855 West 6th Avenue, near MacDonald. ☎ 739-9002. Fax: 739-9004. Website: www.penny farthinginn.com. This charming B&B in a pleasant district has three rooms at $110, one suite at $165, and a garden overflowing with flowers. Smokers, children under 12 and anyone allergic to cats (there are three), should stay away. The Edwardian house dates from 1912 and has an attractive raised veranda. The house is adorably decorated, with lots of lace and English furniture, and the rooms are given English names such as Abigail, Lucinda, Sophie and Bettina (a luxury suite with open fire, TV, stereo and veranda). You'll get a substantial breakfast and booking is highly recommended.

♠ **The West End House** (map II, B2, **34**): 1362 Haro Street. ☎ 681-2889. Fax: 688-8812. Just a block from lively Robson Street and 600 metres from Stanley Park. Prices start from $120 a night at this comfortable and attractive early 20th-century house with Victorian charm, brass beds and period furniture, and a pleasant terrace. For non-smokers only, and a minimum stay of two days. Booking is essential.

♠ **Beautiful B&B** (map I, C3, **35**): 428 West 40th Avenue, at the corner of Cambie Street. ☎ 327-1102. Fax: 327-2299. Website: www.beautifulbandb.bc.ca. This is well located in the heart of a residential area between Downtown (5 minutes' drive) and Vancouver airport (12 minutes). Alternatively, the centre is 15 minutes away on the Cambie Street bus. A single room is $100, a double $110 and a suite is $200 in this superb colonial mansion with impeccable rooms and rustic furniture. You'll get a lovely welcome from the owner, Corinne.

♠ **Shato Inn** (map II, A1, **37**): 1825 Comox Street. ☎ 681-8920. Around $110 for a double. There are a few rooms in this wooden house in a quiet street, a short walk from English Bay. It's perfect for families, and there's free parking in the basement. Friendly welcome.

♠ **Barclay** (map II, B1–2, **38**): 1348 Robson Street. ☎ 688-8850. Fax: 688-2534. Website: www.barclay hotel.com. Well located between the business district and the restaurants on Denman Street. Single rooms for $75–95, doubles $95–125. The building's entrance and attractive facade might lead you to imagine that the rooms would have more character, but in fact they're rather functional. But the hotel is on a human scale, and altogether a good place to stay.

☆☆☆ – ☆☆☆☆ Expensive to Splash Out

♠ **Georgia** (map II, C2, **39**): 801 West Georgia Street. ☎ 682-5566 or 1-800-663-1111 (toll-free). Fax: 642-5579. Website: www.hotelgeorgia.

VANCOUVER

bc.ca This vast hotel has a retro charm, but the rooms are like motel rooms. You'll pay around $279 for a single and $400 for a double.

⚓ **Best Western Sands** (map II, A2, **40**): 1755 Davie Street. ☎ 682-1831 or 1-800-661-7887 (toll-free). Fax: 682-3546. Rooms cost around $180 during the week and $200 at the weekend; half the rooms are non-smoking. A classic, functional, American-style motel very well located only 100 metres from English Bay and not far from Stanley Park. The fifth-floor rooms have a small balcony with splendid view of the ocean, and only cost a fraction more.

⚓ **Wedgewood Hotel** (map II, B2, **45**): 845 Hornby Street. ☎ 689-7777 or 1-800-663-0666 (toll-free). Fax: 608-5348. Website: www.wedgewoodhotel.com. Double rooms cost from $200 and suites range from $440 to $640 in this luxury hotel, full of English charm, pastel pink shades and floral wallpaper, situated right in the heart of town. It has a restaurant and bar and afternoon tea is served in the Bacchus Lounge.

Apartments

Rental by the day is a good-value option for four sharing a big apartment with fully equipped kitchen, which will help save on restaurant bills.

⚓ **Robsonstrasse Hotel** (map II, B1, **41**): 1394 Robson Street. ☎ 687-1674 or 1-888-667-8877 (toll-free). Fax: 685-7808. Website: www.vancouver-bc.com/Robson strasseHotel. At the edge of the pleasant Robson Street area with boutiques, low-rise houses, lively streets etc. These very clean, large apartments with bathrooms and kitchens, and big bay windows cost around $139 a night. Just opposite, the **Riviera** is a large, new apartment building in vivid green that also has comfortable apartments, but they're more expensive ($169).

⚓ **English Bay Apartment Hotel** (map II, A1, **42**): 1150 Denman Street, on the corner of Pendrell Street. ☎ 685-2231. Fax: 685-2291. Run by a smiling Chinese man, this is only 2 minutes from English Bay beach in a district that's always buzzing, and three blocks from Stanley Park. Clean, spacious rooms with bathroom and kitchen for $90 a night.

⚓ **Tropicana Motor Inn** (map II, B1, **43**): 1361 Robson Street. ☎ 687-6631. Fax: 687-5724. Email: 693687@ican.net. You'll pay around $139 per night (less in low season). The same set-up and area as the previous two, and it has a swimming pool and sauna, plus free parking.

⚓ **Oceanside Apartment Hotel** (map II, A1, **44**): 1847 Pendrell Street. ☎ 682-5641. Fax: 687-2340. Large, bright apartments (kitchen/dining room plus sitting room) for $150 a night ($100 out of season), and there's free parking. You'll get a so-so welcome. It's very well located, near English Bay and Stanley Park, even though it might be time to rename it . . . don't bother craning your neck for a glimpse of the ocean, it's now blocked by the private residences of Ocean Towers.

WHERE TO EAT

For maps of Vancouver, see the first colour plate section.

You'll eat very well in Vancouver, as the cuisine matches the city's ethnic mix. The budget places really are cheap, and you can even treat yourself in a smarter place without breaking the bank. The eateries listed are divided into two geographically distinct areas: Downtown and south of Downtown – the other side of Granville and Cambie bridges (a gastronomically appealing district). The areas can be covered quickly by car.

Chinatown

Chinatown suffers from being close to Hastings Street, one of the few streets you should avoid in Vancouver (quite a number of smaller restaurants have given up). You can still eat quite cheaply in the many noodle restaurants, but the district closes down more or less around 8pm and it's best not to hang around much longer. Anyway, it's livelier and more interesting during the day.

✖ **Kam Gok Yuen** (map II, D2, **51**): 142 East Pender Street. ☎ 683-3822. Open until midnight (12.45am on Saturday). Allow about $6 per dish in one of the few Chinese restaurants that stays open late in the evening. It's very gloomy inside, with neon lights and waitresses in yellow uniforms. The portions are huge and cheap, and BBQ is a speciality.

✖ **New Capital Smorgasbord** (map II, D2, **52**): 158 East Pender Street. ☎ 681-1828. Open until 11pm. Closed Wednesday. This basement restaurant is clean and a good place if you're famished. Order the smorgasbord (buffet) and for less than $8 you can help yourself as often as you like. The selection includes salad bar, soups, fish, chicken, pork, beef curry, noodles and various vegetables. Good service.

Gastown

✖ **The Only Fish and Oyster Café** (map II, D2, **53**): 20 East Hastings Street. ☎ 681-6546. Open Monday to Saturday 11.30am–8.30pm. Sunday noon–7pm. Less than $10 for a meal. Asian restaurant. You don't come for the decor (yellow Formica and tiled floor) or the atmosphere, but for the cheap seafood. This is not grand cuisine; in fact it's fairly basic, but it's an experience you should try if you want to dine in a Vancouver institution.

✖ **The Old Spaghetti Factory** (map II, D2, **55**): 53 Water Street, between Abbott and Carrall streets. ☎ 684-1288. Open 11.30am–10pm (11pm on Saturday). With dishes for $10–15, this is a classic in Canada and the United States. Warm atmosphere, the waitresses are delightful, the food won't disappoint and the bill is fair. It's always full, but you won't wait for very long. (*See also*

'Where to Eat' in Toronto for another one.)

✖ **Water Street Café** (map II, D2, **54**): 300 Water Street (on the corner of Cambie, opposite the steam clock). ☎ 689-2832. Housed inside the old Hotel Regina, one of few buildings that survived the fire of 1886, serving fairly predictable but well-cooked main courses for $6–12. Specialities include seafood salad, tomato salad with croutons and goat's cheese. Huge bay windows look out onto the steam clock and make the dining room very bright, and there's a welcoming little terrace with spaces even on sunny days.

✖ **Umberto Al Porto** (map II, D2, **56**): 321 Water Street. ☎ 669-3732. Fax: 669-9723. Website: www.umberto.com. Open daily 11.30am–10pm, Friday and Saturday until 11pm. Closed at lunchtime on Saturday and Sunday. Yuppies come here for finely prepared Italian dishes and a wide choice of American, French and local wines. Main courses cost $12–13 at lunchtime ($10 for a plate of pasta) and only slightly more in the evening. You can eat in the warm Tuscan dining room downstairs, or enjoy views over North Vancouver and its snow-capped peaks and over the bay from upstairs. You'll get a warm welcome here.

The West End

☆ Budget

✕ **Benny's Bagels** (map II, A1–2, **78**): 1780 Davie Street, ☎ 685-7600. Open daily 7am–11pm. Various set breakfasts or lunch for less than $5, with sandwiches at $3–5 and $3 for six take-away bagels. This is part of a chain (there are other outlets on the university campus, 102 University Boulevard), but the 15 different bagel varieties are baked on the premises. Enjoy them as you relax on the terrace overlooking English Bay, absorbing the rhythm of West End life.

✕ **Bread Garden** (map II, A1, **68**): 1040 Denman Street. ☎ 685-2996. Fax: 685-5703. Branches also in Robson Street, at Bute Street and in Kitsilano. Open daily 6am–midnight (2am Saturday and Sunday). Sandwiches cost around $5, and they also serve fruit juices, cappuccino, desserts and fresh biscuits. This is a chain of sandwich cafés that the Canadians do so well, and offers fresh produce, a warm wooden interior and a lovely heated terrace. Perfect for a quick break before exploring Stanley Park.

✕ **Great Wall Mongolian BBQ** (map II, A1, **76**): 717 Denman Street. ☎ 688-2121. Open daily. This is a pleasant self-service restaurant featuring fresh pasta, bowls of soup

✕ **C Restaurant** (map II, A–B3, **50**): 1600 Howe Street. ☎ 681-1164. Fax: 605-8263. The entrance is quite easy to miss (be careful not to, because you'll find yourself on Granville Bridge), but don't fret too much. Everyone in Vancouver knows this contemporary, award-winning fish restaurant. Prices are high (about $25 without wine) but the cooking is excellent. An attractive selection of wines, and a pleasant terrace.

and rice bread at reasonable prices. At lunchtime you'll pay $5.95 for a bowl of salad or $7.95 for the 'all you can eat' option (11.30am–3pm). The buffet selection of meats, vegetables and tasty sauces is prepared before your eyes.

✕ **Poncho's Mexican Restaurant** (map II, A1, **57**): 827 Denman Street. ☎ 683-7286. Open Tuesday to Sunday 5–11pm. You'll get a really nice welcome and, good, filling Mexican food, with specialities costing around $12.50. A simple but warm setting (with big sombreros for lampshades) and the house margarita will relax you right away.

✕ **Café S'il Vous Plaît** (map II, C2, **58**): 500 Robson Street, on the corner of Richards Street. ☎ 688-7216. Open Monday to Friday 9am–10pm. Saturday 9am–midnight. A quiet, unpretentious little snack bar, completely out of place since the Yaletown area was redeveloped. It has really decent food at under $10 for both counter and table service.

✕ **Capers** (map II, A1, **59**): 1675 Robson Street. Open daily 8am–10pm. You'll spot it from far away – it's a green colour that fits in with the philosophy of the place. There's a heated, sheltered terrace with big wooden chairs, or you can eat inside at the high tables. It's also a little supermarket selling natural and organic produce. The appetizing displays of fruit and vegetables are wonderful, and the watering system keeps them permanently cool. Sandwiches for around $6, very good salads and all kinds of bread are on offer. It's an ideal place to put together a picnic, and also worth coming back for souvenirs. On the first Wednesday of the month, 5 per cent of the takings are given to charity. It's politically correct in every way.

✕ **Doll and Penny's** (map II, B2, **60**): 1167 Davie Street. ☎ 685-3417. Open until 2 or 3am at the weekend, and it's more common to go towards the end of the evening. To give you some idea, on Friday there's a drag-queen show on the little stage at the end of the room, and reservations are essential. The place has a theatrical decor, a bit like a nightclub, with all manner of local bits and pieces on the walls to admire as you sink into one of the sofas. It's a place with atmosphere where people come to make new friends. But it's also a restaurant where you can eat for less than $10, but the food is not that important at such a late hour. Indeed, there's hardly enough light to see what's on your plate, but it's likely to be good, well-garnished burgers.

✕ **Hamburger Mary's** (map II, A2, **61**): 1202, on the corner of Bute and Davie streets. ☎ 687-1293. Open 24 hours. It has a blatantly American 1950s diner decor and is famous for its breakfasts that range from simple pancakes at $8 to more substantial selections, including the West Coast (eggs and smoked salmon) at $8.50. The Bute Street Express (egg, bacon, sausage, fried potatoes and toast) deserves a mention at only $4.29. You can also have dinner; try the burgers for around $10 and sip a margarita out on the small terrace.

☆☆ Moderate

✕ **Liliget Feast House** (map II, A2, **77**): 1724 Davie Street, close to Denman Street. ☎ 681-7044. Open 5–10pm. It's hardly visible from the road – a sign points to the small staircase leading to the basement restaurant. Soup costs around $5, with main courses at $10 (more for seafood dishes). Traditional American Indian cuisine, from Pacific salmon to various game (guinea fowl to caribou) dishes. The main courses with the most outlandish names are the best: potlatch platter (grilled salmon, oysters, mussels and smoked *oolican*). Just give in.

✕ **Café de Paris** (map II, A1, **76**): 751 Denman Street. ☎ 687-1418. Open Monday–Friday 11.30–2pm, 5.30–10pm. Also for brunch on Sunday. For 20 years this restaurant has attracted everyone with a taste for good cuisine typical of a French bistro. Dishes include Toulouse cassoulet and Provençal bouillabaisse, adapted French cooking (smoked bison on celeriac with a remoulade sauce), cheese platters and a sweet trolley. Main courses cost $15–20, starters around $6, plus special prices in the basement.

✕ **Cactus Club Café** (map II, B2, **62**): 1136 Robson Street. ☎ 687-3278. Fax: 681-3274. Obviously the formula works, as there are nine Cactus Clubs in Canada serving good, burger-style food. There's a young atmosphere, with TVs everywhere tuned to different sports or music channels, but it's pretty good fun. You'll get a dynamic welcome and it's lively and noisy all day.

☆☆☆ Expensive

✕ **Joe Forte's** (map II, B2, **63**): 777 Thurlow Street, on the corner of Robson Street. ☎ 669-1940 or 1-877-669-JOES (toll-free). Fax: 669-

4426. Email: joefortes@intouch.bc.ca. Open Monday to Thursday noon–11pm. Friday and Saturday noon–midnight. Sunday noon–10pm. Joe Seraphin Fortes was one of the greatest local figures: first a sailor then a barman, he spent his retirement teaching thousands of children how to swim and how to be lifesavers. In 1923, at his burial, there was the longest funeral cortège in the history of Vancouver. This restaurant is an immense, high-ceilinged room that's noisy and full of life. It has a reputation as one of the best singles bars in town. The U-shaped bar is always packed, as is the terrace. Amazing selection of Scotch whiskies and beers on draught, and it's also well known for its fish and oysters, including special pan-fried Cajun oysters, Joe's lite clam chowder, fish trio (mako shark, local halibut, sockeye salmon). Book or be prepared to join the long queue.

Yaletown

✖ **Subeez** (map II, C3, **75**): 891 Homer Street, on the corner of Homer and Smith. ☎ 687-6143. The gigantic concrete pillars and the aluminium conduits are light years away from what might be described as a warm setting, but this old shed with high ceilings and big windows is truly welcoming. You might think the music is deafening but the young, techno crowd can't get enough of it. It's one of the new vogue places in Yaletown, and fine for a quick, light lunch and good seafood salads (cob salad $10.95; hot seafood salad $12.95). More substantial dishes include lasagne, plus vegetarian dishes such as pesto, jambalaya and curries. The choice of wines and draught beers is listed on huge blackboards. On the restaurant side, you're given a menu at the entrance and you choose at your table. The menu highlights the slow service as a feature of the place to head off any complaints.

South of Downtown

☆–☆☆ Budget to Moderate

✖ **Sophie's** (Cosmic Café; map I, C2, **64**): 2095 West 4th Avenue; north of Broadway, on the corner of Arbutus Street. ☎ 732-6810. Open daily 8am–9.30pm. A fun setting, with a fantasy decor (kids' cars, hats, posters, etc.) that's particularly kitsch and colourful. Families and young locals squeeze onto the leatherette benches and create a vibrant, lively atmosphere. Dishes of the day are chalked on the blackboard at around $6–7 for eggs with all the sauces, burgers and club sandwiches. A few Cajun and Québec-inspired specialities include po'-boy Louisiana, oyster burger, Santa Fé chicken and Cajun shrimp.

✖ **Sala Thai** (map I, C3, **65**): 3364 Cambie Street. ☎ 875-6999. Open Monday to Friday 11.30am–2.30pm and every evening until 10pm. Note the grey-and-pink Corinthian columns. Main courses cost around $8 and you'll get excellent Thai cooking in generous portions. Dishes include three types of *tom yam* (a deliciously spicy soup), various salads, beef in oyster sauce, pork with garlic, *Sala Thai ruam mitr* (shrimp, clams, cuttlefish and fish), noodles and rice.

✖ **Isadora's** (map I, C2, **66**): 1540 Old Bridge Street, Granville Island, just by the Granville Street bridge. ☎ 681-3748. Fax: 681-4538. Open Monday to Friday 11.30am–5.30pm, dinner 5.30–9pm (except

Monday). Saturday and Sunday 9am–2.30pm, 3–5.30pm. This is a restaurant/cooperative supported by 1,500 shareholders, and all the profits are reinvested in community projects. The shareholders receive dividends in the form of an annual feast. There's space in the dining room and mezzanine for many diners. It's one of the most family-friendly restaurants in town, with a warm, animated atmosphere and lots of things for the kids (outdoor playground outside, small tables and chairs, etc.). Very good food at extremely reasonable prices: for lunch try *babaghannouj* (aubergine dip), seafood chowder, burgers, salads, fish stew. Dinner includes baked snapper, wild Chinook salad and vegetarian lasagne, and delicious desserts such as carrot cake and apple crumble.

✕ **Nyala** (map I, B2, **67**): 2930 West 4th Avenue, on the corner of Bayswater. ☎ 731-7899. Website: www.nyala.com. Open daily 5–11pm (to 2am Thursday to Saturday). You just can't miss this flashy restaurant painted in brilliant African colours, offering an attractive and tasty introduction to Ethiopian cooking. There are salads for around $5, main courses for $12–15 and, on Wednesday and Sunday, there's a vegetarian 'all you can eat' option at $10.95. Some of the typical, highly flavoured dishes include *yedoro watt* (chicken marinated in lemon, garlic and ginger), *yedoro kay watt* (lamb with red pepper sauce), *yasa watt* (fresh fish with Berber sauce), *kitfo* (Ethiopian steak tartare), kid with Berber sauce, etc.

✕ **Naam** (map I, B2, **69**): 2724 West 4th Avenue, on the corner of Stephens. ☎ 738-7151. Open daily 24 hours. This lovely, friendly restaurant is where older people, students, greens and local workers all rub shoulders happily in the mostly wooden decor, full of spicy fragrances and folk music. There's a terrace festooned with greenery and a few tables in the sun. It serves a good selection of exceptionally tasty vegetarian dishes: naam burgers, pasta, stir-fry, dragon bowl, and also delicious cakes with chocolate or pecan nuts. Sometimes there's music in the evening from 7 to 10pm.

✕ **Bridges Bistro** (map II, A3, **70**): 1696 Durenleau Street, Granville Island. ☎ 687-4400. Open 11am–11pm. On the ground floor of this smart restaurant there's a sort of brasserie serving local-style burgers, seafood, sandwiches and various salads at around $15 per dish. But it has also one of the most beguiling terraces in Vancouver, overlooking the pleasure-boat harbour and Burrard Bridge, with the cry of the wheeling seagulls in the background. Yuppies throng here after work, and it's a really lovely place for a drink in the evening.

✕ **Accord** (map I, D3, **71**): 4298 Main Street, near 27th Avenue, and Queen Elizabeth Park. ☎ 876-6110 and 876-3963. Open 5pm–3am. This is quite a way from the centre and is therefore only of interest if you have a car or an interest in Chinese food and adventure off the beaten track. Unpretentious (not a Chinese lantern or a dragon in sight), it's popular with Asian families who come to enjoy generous servings of authentic cuisine. The atmosphere is festive. Choose a small dish, rather than medium or large, when selecting soup, noodles or other dishes. There's a large menu with lots of tasty seafood dishes, sizzling hotpots and *tappans*.

☆☆ – ☆☆☆ Moderate to Expensive

✕ **Tama Sushi** (map I, C2, **72**): 1595 West Broadway. ☎ 738-0119. Open Monday–Friday

11.30am–2pm (a little longer in summer) and in the evening until 10.15pm (10.45pm Friday and Saturday). Go around The Byte Place Internet café on the right and up the steps. Ignore the soulless building and its banal concrete surroundings – the setting of this little sushi paradise is in complete contrast to the interior. Here it's all space and light, simple but fresh decor that's contemporary and warm at the same time. You could say it has a discreet elegance. You'll get a nice welcome and a smile of near familiarity. You can leave your shoes at the entrance and kneel in one of the lovely cubicles for your meal. Alternatively, there are normal tables or a long counter from where you can watch the sushi and sashimi being prepared from marvellously fresh fish. There's an excellent choice of sushi, sashimi combo, chicken teriyaki, chicken and scallops, steak and tempura, and a seafood boat for two. Main courses cost around $7 and a 'Tama Box' or 'Bento Box' costs under $10 (including miso soup, rice salad and sushi or tempura) – entirely reasonable bearing in mind the quality of the produce.

✗ **Seasons in the Park** (map I, C3, **73**): 33rd Avenue and Cambie Street, in Queen Elizabeth Park, next to Bloedel Floral Conservatory. ☎ 874-8008 or 1-800-632-9422 (toll-free). Fax: 874-7101. Email: info@settingsun.com. This is where presidents Bill Clinton and Boris Yeltsin dined during the 1993 Vancouver Summit. They enjoyed crab with spinach ravioli, with a scattering of parmesan and a marvellous view over Vancouver, with the gardens in the foreground and the mountains in the distance. Lunch costs around $12–15, and dinner almost double that.

☆☆☆☆ Splash Out

✗ **Bishops** (map I, C2, **74**): 2183 West 4th Avenue. ☎ 738-2025. Fax: 738-4222. Open Monday to Saturday 5–10pm (9pm on Sunday). A meal will cost at least $25 in this very elegant setting with Indian paintings and sculpture and enormous bunches of fresh flowers. The atmosphere and clientele are really smart and the welcome formal. Here you'll taste New British Columbia Cuisine. It's inventive, full of inspiration with subtle combinations of flavours and wonderfully complementary vegetables. Try the light scallops with fresh, baby vegetables, delicately flavoured steamed clams or mussels, salmon fillet poached in yoghurt, vegetarian curry with basmati rice, chargrilled fillet of beef (with sun-dried cherries and cognac), grilled skewer of sea scallops, etc. The wines are expensive.

WHERE TO HAVE A DRINK

For maps of Vancouver, see the first colour plate section.

Vancouver is known for its dynamic musical life. The folk festival may draw the crowds, but the rock and blues scene is certainly the most vibrant in Canada. Lots of high-quality bands have belted out their stuff on the hot, narrow stages of the sweltering clubs and pubs, and still do. Open a door to one of these furnaces and Vancouver nights are full-on rock! And if these nocturnal break-outs aren't enough for you and you want to make your home shake with the Vancouver sound, drop into the excellent record shops in Seymour Street, between Dunsmuir and Pender, or tune into C-Fox (99.3 FM) and CITR (101.9 FM), the university radio station. You'll have to pay a cover charge to get into most clubs, but it's not ruinous. There are several café/restaurants with sometimes odd decor along Commercial Drive, between William Street and 1st Avenue.

Here's a small selection of clubs, pubs, bars and other venues to suit all tastes.

♟ The Yale (map II, B3, **80**): 1300 Granville Street, on the corner of Drake, just after Granville Bridge (from the island). Open Monday to Friday 11.30am–1.30am. Saturday 1.30pm–1.30am. Sunday 2pm–midnight. This hotel bar is the city's most famous place for blues and R&B, a rite of passage for musicians. It's got an excellent atmosphere at the end of the week, and good beers on draught.

♟ Automotive Billiards Club (map II, C3, **81**): 1095 Homer Street. ☎ 682-0040. Immense, with about 20 billiard tables, but you can only drink fruit juice at the tables (there's a designated place elsewhere in the club to drink beer). It's where the local youth gather, and has good music (acid-jazz).

♟ Soho Café and Billiards (map II, B3, **82**): 1144 Homer Street. ☎ 688-1180. Open Monday to Friday from 11am until late. Saturday and Sunday from noon. Set in a historic warehouse building with bare brick walls and a lovely view of False Creek. You drink at tables (but not while playing billiards).

♟ Bar None (map II, B3, **83**): 1122 Hamilton Street. ☎ 689-7000. Entrance charge $5. Smart dress required, but they're quite tolerant. You'll find big rooms, bar and billiards, and a lively, 30-something clientele who opt out of the modish 'in' places for the reassuring strains of funk. Good music, it's a hot spot with soft lights; sort of classy.

♟ Yale Town Brewing Company (map II, C3, **84**): 1110 Hamilton and 1111 Mainland. ☎ 688-0039. Open until 1am. The bar is jammed with a young, stylish crowd. They brew six types of beer on the premises, from a light ale to a more bitter and nourishing dark beer. There's also a restaurant serving pizzas, pasta, grilled fish and meat.

♟ Hungry Eye (map II, D2, **86**): 23 West Cordova Street. ☎ 688-5331. An excellent list of gigs, and a young, slightly off-beat crowd.

♟ Carnegie's (map I, C2, **87**): 1619 West Broadway. ☎ 733-4141. A very Californian-style American bar, with a mainly yuppie clientele. Good jazz concerts nearly every evening (except Sunday), and there's also a restaurant.

♟ The Ivanhoe Pub (map II, D3, **89**): Main and National, opposite the railway station. An enormous pub with an elbow-shaped bar in the middle. The clientele varies according to the time of day, but the afternoon attracts all sorts, including a few outsiders – well-known regulars, old people from the area, local workers and yuppies, and a few punks with shocking pink mohicans – all here for the cheapest beer in the district.

♟ Joe's Café (map I, D2, **90**): on the corner of Commercial Drive and William Street. Open until 1am. It's in a working-class area quite far from town, run by a former Portuguese matador who hung up his cape after injury. Cool, with a buzz to it. In summer the drinkers spill onto the pavement to enjoy Joe's very good espresso in the sun, and also some extremely tasty deli sandwiches. There are several billiard tables, payable by the hour.

♟ The Quena (map I, D2, **91**): 1111 Commercial Drive. ☎ 251-6626. Open 11am–11pm (8pm on Monday). This really nice coffee shop is popular with the communities from El Salvador and Nicaragua, students, ecologists and left-wing militants. On offer are (vegetarian) South American dishes or sandwiches and good cappuccino. There's a billboard with local small ads. On some evenings there are musical shows, poetry readings etc.

☉ Waazubee cafe (map I, D2, **92**): 1622 Commercial Drive, between 1st Avenue and Graveley. ☎ 253-5299. Open daily until about 1am.

☉ Bukowski's (map I, D2, **88**): 1447 Commercial Drive. The Beat Generation writer would no doubt have found this place too clean for his taste, but it draws quite a crowd with its DJs and non-stop music. A few scribbles and photos of the poet and novelist are on the tables, plus a great terrace.

☉ The Town Pump (map II, D2, **94**): 66 Water Street, near Abott Street. ☎ 683-6695. Open every evening. Cover charge. This has wood and brick decor, several rooms with intimate corners, exhibitions of pictures and photographs and a dance floor. The bands play rock 'n' roll, and it's usually excellent. Come early at the end of the week, otherwise you'll have to queue.

☉ Railway Club (map II, C2, **95**): 579 Dunsmuir Street, on the corner of Seymour and Dunsmuir streets. ☎ 681-1625. This comprises a big room on the first floor, where small bands play every evening. The crowd is sort of new wave and well behaved.

☉ Starfish Room (map II, C3, **96**): 1055 Homer Street. Open every evening. One of the favourite places for Vancouver's rock fans it puts on good gigs.

☉ Arts Club Lounge (map II, A3, **93**): 1585 Johnston Street, Granville Island. Hot, smoky, American-style billiard room that gets pretty lively during certain gigs, and attracts young people from the neighbourhood. There's a really pleasant little terrace that's virtually in the water. In June some acts from the Jazz Maurier Festival play here.

Nightlife

– **Yuk Yuk's** (map II, C3, **100**): 750 Pacific Boulevard South. ☎ 687-5233. Open Wednesday to Sunday. This comedy theatre is the only one of its kind in Vancouver, so it's best to book. Generally three separate comics perform every evening.

– **Theatre Sports** (map II, A3, **101**): Pacific Space Center, 1100 Chestnut Street. ☎ 738-7827. This generally features an excellent show (and often improvisations), from Wednesday to Sunday at 8pm, and at 10pm on Friday and Saturday.

– **Arts Club Theater** (map II, A3, **102**): 1585 Johnston Street, Granville Island. ☎ 687-1644. Its social themes make this a Vancouver institution, with two auditoriums and a nice bar where you can extend the evening.

– **Queen Elizabeth Theater** (map II, C2, **103**): corner of Hamilton Street and West Georgia Street. ☎ 665-3050. Built by two Montréal architects, these three auditoriums opened in 1959 as precursors to the Lincoln Center in New York and the Place des Arts in Montreal.

– **Luv-a-fair** (map II, B3, **110**): 1275 Seymour Street, near Drake Street. ☎ 685-3288. You'll have to show your passport at the door. *The* best club as far as the young in town are concerned, where stylish punks and new-wave kids get together for a beer. There's a small mezzanine with pinball machines. You can hear a variety of music, including hip-hop, industrial, jazz, grunge, house, etc.

– **The Grace Land** (map II, B3, **111**): 1250 Richards Street. ☎ 688-2648. This cutting-edge place boasts very large rooms with high-tech decor in shades of grey. The place does its best to appear cold but the crowd is warm, and there's a good ethnic mix of people. There are dancers on stage at the weekend, and the music's new wave and 1980s rock, plus reggae on Wednesday and sometimes hip-hop. They're not too fussy on the door.

– **The Commodore** (map II, C2, **112**): 870 Granville Street Mall. ☎ 681-7838. Right in the middle of the mall is this huge, recently refur-

bished nightclub where the big groups on tour gig. On Tuesday in the summer they have a *Saturday Night Fever*-style disco night, and a lot of African music too. It's just amazing, and you'll spend at least an hour queueing.

– **Mars Bar** (map II, B3, **113**): south of Richards Street. Modern setting for a really hot techno dance club, and the crowd is 20–30-something.

– **Richard's on Richards** (map II, C3, **114**): 1036 Richards Street, not far from Helmcken Street. ☎ 687-6794. Also known as 'Dick on Dick', this has a rather meat-market-cum-yuppie atmosphere. Dress smartly and smile at the highly selective bouncers. Good bands from time to time.

WHAT TO SEE

For maps of Vancouver, see the first colour plate section.

★ **Museum of Anthropology** (map I, A2): 6393 NW Marine Drive, in the centre of the university (signposted). ☎ 822-5087. Website: www.moa.ubc.ca. Open 10am–5pm (until 9pm on Tuesday from September to June). Closed Monday from September to mid-May. This unmissable museum is a superb example of modern architecture, inspired by the dwellings of the First Nations people, with intelligent thought given to light and space. The museum offers a high-quality glimpse of the seven cultural and linguistic groups that live along the northwest Pacific coast through sculpture, tools and other exhibits.

– However, the main feature of the museum is the collection of Indian **totem poles**. Each one is illuminated by a shaft of light from the sky, which highlights the grandeur of these huge woodcarvings. The exhibition area also has displays of other strange and beautiful wooden objects. The room opens onto a huge bay window through which you can see other totem poles in a small clearing. These were usually erected in front of Indian lodges. The totem pole was the symbol of family pride, or was raised in honour of someone who had died. The forms are frequently taken from nature and their very complex symbolism can be read on many levels and is open to different interpretations. Some of the designs are obvious, while others are clear only to the artist or his family. You will often find a frog, beaver, wolf, bear, or eagle in these sculpted forms. Some of the totems also have long protruding beaks that break up the vertical rhythm of the work.

– On the right, in the **Great Hall**, you will see vessels used for a feast: huge, hollow dishes with little wheels hooked to each other. At each end are two carved snakes' heads, with spoons in their mouths. The dishes contained sugar, which was given as a gift during potlatches (ceremonial feasts) at the beginning of the 20th century. During the ceremonies, for celebrating marriages or paying homage to the dead, by their very presence the guests were the guarantors of the continuity of tradition. Other objects on display here include storage chests, canoes, wall panels and family tombs.

– **Gallery of Art**: This contains a collection of the very best of First Nations' culture – remarkably worked and engraved pieces in gold, silver, ivory, horn, wood and bone, all aesthetically extremely fine. There are also domestic objects, spoons, combs, 'soul-captors' in bone, hair ornaments, crockery and various figures.

– **Research Collections**: Here you'll find a wide range of Indian art, but the presentation is somewhat crammed, and only specialists would know their way about. There are lots of masks and a rich selection of objects from the Arctic such as games, baskets and fishing tools. You can also see sculptures by the great Indian artist Bill Reid, in particular *Legend of the Raven* and the *First Humans* in yellow cedar.

– **Gallery of Other Cultures**: Here, too, is a fascinating presentation of Indonesian, Chinese, Melanesian, Australian Aboriginal and other cultures. Among the extensive collections are some superb pieces of Chinese jade porcelain, Korean masks, etc. Not to be missed, to the left in the entrance hall, is the ceramic gallery that includes a German polychrome pot from 1560, bottles from Ukrainian Anabaptists and Italian majolica.

★ **Maritime Museum** (map I, C2, **121**): 1905 Ogden Avenue, near Vanier Park. ☎ 257-8300. Open 10am–5pm (last admission 4pm). Closed Monday from November to the beginning of May. The Saint Roch room is also closed on Monday from 9 September to 18 May. Not far from the Planetarium, this is a small museum full of some very lovely maritime models. You'll see a reconstruction of the helmsman's cabin from a sloop of war, lovely etchings, engravings and uniforms. Every 20 minutes you can visit the restored *Saint Roch*, the first vessel to cross the waters of the Arctic from Halifax to Vancouver, in 1944. There is an interesting guided tour you can take. Also have a look at the remarkable temporary exhibitions. In a creek 200 metres farther on there's a small Heritage Harbour with a junk and two steamers (the *Ivanhoe* and the *Master*).

★ **University of British Columbia** (map I, A2): between SW Marine Drive and Westbrook Mall, next to the Museum of Anthropology. Bus No. 4 or No. 10 south from Granville Street Mall. Free tours of the campus are available from 8.30am to 4.30pm. Reservations: ☎ 822-3131. The third university of Canada also has a 763-hectare (1,885-acre) park, a Japanese garden, a nautical centre and a geology museum.

★ **Vancouver Museum** (map II, A3): 1100 Chestnut Street, west of Burrard Bridge in Vanier Park. ☎ 736-4431. Bus No. 22. Open daily 9am–5pm (9pm Thursday and Friday). Closed Monday out of season. Entrance charge $15 (under-19s $10, under-fives free). The organization of the museum has undergone some changes, but there are always temporary exhibitions on the history of Vancouver and the surrounding area, and other interesting ones on the numerous immigrant communities in Vancouver.

★ **Pacific Space Center** (map II, A3): 1100 Chestnut Street (same address as Vancouver Museum). ☎ 738-7827. Open Tuesday to Sunday 10am–5pm (daily in July and August). Entrance charge $12 (reductions for children). Shows at 3, 7.30 and 9pm. Extra shows at noon, 1pm and 2pm on Saturday and Sunday and during the holidays. There's nothing exceptional about this planetarium compared to any other, but it's fascinating for first-timers.

★ **Vancouver Art Gallery** (map II, C2, **125**): 750 Hornby Street, on the corner of Robson Street, in the old Court House. ☎ 662-4700. Open 10am–5pm (from noon on Sunday). Free entrance on Thursday 5–9pm. The gallery essentially shows temporary exhibitions of paintings and sculpture. The only permanent exhibition is the biggest collection of work by Emily Carr in Canada, and this is worth seeing. Emily Carr (1871–1945) set about painting totem poles and Indian landscapes as she *felt* them. The Indians nicknamed her 'The one who lives'. The painting of *The Crying Totem* perfectly depicts the sensation she had, going beyond the Indian sculpture through painting. What emerges is a strong impression that sometimes causes uneasiness. Indeed, some forest landscapes, which seem cold at first, gradually become clear. You can find textures created by the depth of the greens and feel you are being drawn into the picture. There are also some works by contemporaries of Emily Carr, such as Georgia O'Keeffe and Irène Hoffar Reid. There's another gallery of Canadian landscapes, and also one of still lifes.

★ **The Canadian Craft Museum** (map II, C2, **126**): 639 Hornby Street, at the junction with Georgia; the entrance is on Cathedral Place. ☎ 687-8266. Fax: 684-7174. Open Monday to Wednesday, Friday and Saturday 10am–5pm. Thursday 10am–9pm. Sunday and public holidays noon–5pm. This museum is very beautiful and you can enjoy the best in Canadian crafts in temporary, themed exhibitions. Current exhibitions are posted outside.

★ **Bloedel Floral Conservatory** (map I, C3): Queen Elizabeth Park, 33rd Avenue and Cambie Street. ☎ 872-5513. Bus No. 15 on Burrard. Open Monday to Friday 9am–8pm (5pm in winter). Saturday and Sunday 10am–9pm. Set in a green park of 53 hectares (130 acres) is this living museum of vegetation, with superb flowers and scents. Beautiful tropical plants flourish under a dome. Especially fascinating are the strange, mottled birds. From the terrace at the front there's a magnificent panoramic view of the city. Make the most of it and go for a walk in the splendid Sunken Garden.

★ **Van Dusen Botanical Garden** (map I, C3): 37th Street and Oak Street. ☎ 266-7194. Bus No. 17 from the town centre. Open 10am–sunset. Free guided tour every Sunday at 2pm. Entrance charge $5.50 (student and family reductions). The extensive garden, each part of which represents a different part of the world, has perfumed flowers (fuchsias, roses etc.) and painstakingly maintained lawns. It's a wonderful place to go for a walk, either with an organized tour or on your own, aided by a brief explanatory leaflet given free at the entrance.

★ **Stanley Park** (map I, C1). ☎ 261-5100. Take bus No. 19 on West Pender Street, between Homer and Cambie streets. This is a fantastic place, in the heart of Vancouver, situated on the eastern point of the peninsula overlooking the ocean. It's a vast park, covering as big an area as Downtown, that gives the city its charm and perhaps its Californian character. You'll find lots of open green space, swimming pools, statues, cycle trails, pony rides, mini-golf, observation points over the ocean – and all just 10 minutes from the heart of town. There are also huge Douglas fir trees, drowned in luxuriant vegetation because of the wet climate.

A great way to explore the park is to hire a bike – spend an afternoon riding around the park then return in the evening by the path along English Bay that follows the road from Stanley Park right into the centre of town. There's lots to see and the sunsets over the bay are brilliant. While you're here, you could also visit the aquarium (see below).

Near Brockton Point there are some very beautiful Indian totem poles, and a lot of tourists come to have their photograph taken. When you get near the access to Lion's Gate Bridge, there's a breathtaking view of the bay from Prospect Point. There is talk about replacing the old bridge, because of increasing vehicle traffic. But for many, the loss of one of Vancouver's most famous landmarks would be very sad, as it's such an important image of the city.

Towards Third Beach you'll see some giant pine trees and the lovely sandy beach. The cycle trail from east to west follows Beaver Lake with its huge trees. In summer, from Victoria Day to Labour Day, the beaches are supervised from 11.30am to 9pm. For information ☎ 738-8535.

★ **The Aquarium** (map I, C1): ☎ 682-1118. Open daily 9.30am–8pm 1 July to 6 September, 10am–5.30pm the rest of the year. Take bus No. 19 west on Pender Street. At the weekend, from April to October, there is a connection with bus No. 52 on the Stanley Park Loop. The entrance charge is not cheap, but the income goes to the local Cousteau officers. This is one of the best-conceived aquariums, and the most interesting, in North America. There are displays of fish from every ocean, housed in wide aquariums, most of which are genuine works of art. There are a few sharks and some gigantic fish from South America.

But the most interesting section is the one dedicated to the whale, and there's a killer whale show. Killer or grampus whales (*Orcinusorca*) are so named because they attack other whales and not humans. There are also a few beluga (white) whales that live in large groups (gams) that travel a long way up the St Lawrence River. Their heads are peculiar and their wide smile makes them look somewhat friendly.

In the basement there's an excellent exhibition on other marine mammals.

★ **Robson Square** (map II, C2): around Hornby Street and Robson Street. Right in the heart of the city is this wide esplanade on several levels, embellished by fountains, terraces, walks and restaurants, that's a meeting place for officer workers at lunchtime. There's not much to do here but the surrounding area is worth a visit for its architecture. The old apartment buildings have been retained, without being overwhelmed by more modern buildings. In fact, the architectural styles blend in harmoniously, leaving open spaces where the sun can get in. Take a look at the new Court House, topped by a vast glass structure that leans at an angle of 45° and reflects the light. It's astonishing in its daring and lack of ostentation. Farther on, note the austere columns of the old Court House. All around the big green space, banks with modern lines and hotels from the beginning of the 20th century stand side by side. That said, there's not much life around here in the afternoon or the evening, when it's best to make tracks for Davie and Denman streets (*see below*).

★ **Denman and Davie streets**: At the end of Robson Street near the ocean, Denman Street and Davie Street form one of the liveliest parts of town, day and night. It's an area that has a distinctively European look and feel, with smart boutiques, cafés with terraces and restaurants from every corner of the world. The area is hilly, recalling San Francisco in many ways, and the atmosphere is very easy-going. Every evening in the summer young people come cruising around here in their cars. At the end of Denman Street, before you turn onto Davie Street, you get to **English Bay Beach**. The most popular beach in Vancouver, it has a holiday atmosphere with lots of green spaces, cyclists and ice-cream sellers. In the evening couples come to watch the sun setting on the ships and boats anchored in the bay.

★ **Gastown** (map II, D2): Centred along Water Street, this is the oldest part of town, but over the last few years its warehouses and old buildings have been renovated and refurbished in a more contemporary style. Smart little shops, restaurants and businesses of every kind have meant that a few of the charming 19th-century brick houses have been saved, along with some lovely grey-stone buildings ornamented by friezes, all of which were due to be torn down. In spite of this, the area hasn't entirely escaped a sort of overblown false smartness. But it's still worth a visit, if only to take a look at the **steam clock** on Water Street, at the corner of Cambie Street. In Maple Tree Square you will also see the **statue of Gassy Jack**, the person who gave the district its name. His real name was John Deighton, and he opened a saloon in 1867 for the loggers who worked in the area. He soon acquired a great reputation with them and became known as Gassy Jack. More recently, people went so far as to erect this statue of the alcoholic to regenerate and relaunch the area (perhaps a little artificially).

It's best to avoid some of the streets between Gastown and Chinatown where vagrants and drug addicts congregate, as they're not entirely safe.

★ **Chinatown** (map II, D2): East Pender Street, between Carrall Street and Gore Avenue. Bus No. 22 north from Burrard or No. 19 or No. 22 east on Pender Street. A lot less attractive but much more authentic than Gastown, Chinatown doesn't need an excuse to exist – its past and present are enough. This is the second largest Chinese community in North America, after San Francisco. There are two TV channels, three radio stations and as many newspapers in Cantonese.

The Chinese started to arrive during the gold rush. But later, in the 1880s, they arrived by the hundreds and endured hard labour on the railway to help their families back home. However, the majority of them settled here, retaining their customs and, above all, their community spirit. Despite constant social and economic persecution (punitive raids, slave wages, etc) the venerable community thrived. After World War II the area was further invigorated by a new wave of immigrants. More recent arrivals from Taiwan, China and, above all, from Hong Kong have created a base in Vancouver with lucrative property and financial enterprises.

As you stroll the streets of Chinatown during the day you'll come across amazing herbalist shops, small restaurants, religious artefacts and much more. However, take care at night, particularly around Main Street and Hastings Street, an area which has a bad reputation by day and night.

– **Sun Yat Sen Park and Garden** (map II, D2, **131**): 50 East Pender Street and 578 Carrall Street. ☎ 689-7133. Open 10am–4.30pm. Entrance charge to garden, but you can see the main parts of the garden from the park. This is a lovely oasis in the centre of town, with a lake covered in water lilies and home to paddling turtles. A faithful reconstruction of a Ming Dynasty garden, it was one of the first to be built on this scale outside China, and is made from imported materials. If you're walking in this lovely spot, be sure to try the cup of jasmine tea that you are graciously given free just before the exit. There's also a kiosk in the middle of the park. On Friday in summer you can hear concerts of Chinese music.

– **The Sam Kee Building** (map II, D2, **132**): Carrall and Pender streets. This is not so much spectacular as revelatory of something of the spirit of North America. In 1913, when the road was widened and part of the building destroyed to make way, the owner continued with his business, despite the circumstances. On the narrow strip of land that was left, he constructed a new building 1.8 metres (6 feet) wide and 33 metres (108 feet) long, with shops on the ground floor and offices above. Since then, this has appeared in *The Guinness Book of Records* as the narrowest commercial building in the world.

– On Sunday morning, go to **Queen Elizabeth Park** to watch hundreds of Chinese practising martial arts. It's really impressive, especially the sight of numerous children wielding sabres and kendo staffs.

★ **Granville Street** (map II, B3): By day this is the banking district and department store area (Eaton Centre, on the corner of Georgia Street). But by night Granville Street is home to a motley crowd of vagrants and prostitutes. There are also many cinemas along here, so it's busy at the weekend and on half-price Tuesday nights. Most of the bus services go along this street.

★ **Granville Island** (map II, A3): This renovated old industrial sector is located directly under the Granville Bridge. The BC transit No. 50 bus (False Creek) stops at the edge of the island; the Granville Island No. 51 goes from Granville Street as far as the Public Market. You can also take the crossing from the bottom of Hornby Street, and there's also a link from the Maritime Museum by the Granville Island Ferry. However, it's much better to go on foot or by bike. The information centre is open 9am–6pm. ☎ 666-5784.

You'll find many attractions and restaurants among the repair shops and merchants selling boats and spare parts, including:

– The **Public Market**, which is open daily 9am–6pm. Built in 1917 as a cable factory, the original building burned down in the 1950s. It's now a very colourful market selling fresh fruit and excellent seafood.

– **Kids Only**: Open 10am–6pm (9pm on Friday). As the name suggests, this shop is just for the kids, but keep an eye on how much you spend.

– **Granville Island Brewing Company**: 1441 Cartwright Street. ☎ 687-2631. Open Monday to Thursday 9am–7pm. Friday and Saturday 9am–9pm. Guided tours at noon, 2 and 4pm. Be sure to drop in while you're in the area.

– Cultural life is far from missing, with two good theatres on the island. And, to enjoy a well-earned rest, there's a choice of two superb terraces: the **Bridges** and the **Backstage Lounge**.

WHAT TO DO

Ocean Swimming

– **Jericho Beach**: 5 minutes' walk from the Hostelling International Vancouver, on the eastern point of Jericho Park (*see* 'Where to Stay'). This is not a very crowded beach, and you can hire dinghies and windsurfers.

– **Kitsilano Beach**: Known as Kits Beach, this popular and busy spot is the Côte d'Azur of Vancouver.

– **Wreck Beach**: To reach this nudist beach take the path to the right of the Museum of Anthropology on the UBC campus (*see* 'What to See'). Then take the left fork once you've gone round the totem poles, and join up with the path that goes through the undergrowth.

FESTIVALS AND EVENTS

– **Polar Bear Swim**: A number of enthusiastic and possibly crazy people 'enjoy' a swim off English Bay Beach on 1 January.

– **Chinese New Year**: In mid-February two weeks of festivals take place in Chinatown, mostly around Sun Yat Sen Park, including parades, concerts and fortune tellers.

– **Bard on the Beach Shakespeare Festival**: June to September. Plays are performed in tents on English Bay Beach, and it's good as long as the weather holds. Programmes are available from the tourist office or from newspaper kiosks.

– **Summer Francophone Festival of Vancouver**: Mid-June. This does not automatically mean that performances are in French, and there is a surprising number of shows on the programme, both with African influences and from Québec folklore.

– **Du Maurier Jazz Festival**: End-June to early July. The city's jazz venues host some of the great names on the international scene. Don't miss it.

– **Vancouver Folk Music Festival**: On Jericho Beach, near the University of British Columbia. In July Canadian and American folk groups perform at this event that's similar to the Winnipeg Folk Festival but not as big (*see* 'What to Do' *in* 'Winnipeg').

– **Symphony of Fire**: End-July to early August. The whole town looks towards the ocean to enjoy the international fireworks competition over English Bay Beach that draws enormous crowds.

– **Vancouver International Film Festival**: End-September to early October. Website: www.viff.or. With around 300 films from 50 countries, this festival is getting a name for itself.

– For sports events and more: ☎ 661-7373 (24 hours). Another useful number is Vancouver's Free Arts Hot Line (☎ 684-ARTS) for information about music, dance, theatre and cinema.

SHOPPING

For maps of Vancouver, see the first colour plate section.

If you ask a local where to go shopping they'll send you straight to Robson Street, where prices are scarcely less affordable than in Europe. You'll find all the latest names and brands, including DNKY, Gap, Guess, Banana Republic and Bebe. If you're in any doubt about the hottest fashions, just check out what the Japanese girls are wearing. Pop into the 'techno' shops for a spot of retail therapy to the sound of the DJ's latest mixes.

🔒 **Pacific Center** (map II, C2, **140**): 700 West Georgia Street. A commercial gallery connecting the Vancouver Centre shopping mall to the Eaton and Bay department stores. You'll find mostly clothes here, but it's of no particular interest as far as choice or price are concerned.

🔒 **Inuit Art and Sculpture** (map II, C2, **141**): Marion Scott Ltd, 481 Howe Street (on the corner of Pender). You'll find a good selection of works by various artists, including some key figures such as George Tatanic and Olivoo Tunnillic. You could try haggling.

🔒 **Spirit Wrestler Gallery**: 8 Water Street. ☎ 669-8813. On sale here are sculptures, masks, drawings and paintings, including works by some masters such as Judas Oollooha.

🔒 **Inuit Gallery** (map II, D2): 345 Water Street. ☎ 688-7323. This features a particularly lovely collection of masks and sculptures, but you must really haggle here.

🔒 **Maple Delights, Gourmet Bistro & Shoppe** (map II, C2): ☎ 682-6175. Fax: 682-6245. Open Monday to Friday 6.30am–11pm. Saturday and Sunday 1–11pm. Everyone knows about maple syrup, but try a taste of the chocolate, jam and even the salad dressing. Take some souvenirs home in attractive bottles or stylish wooden gift boxes.

🔒 **Hill's Indian Crafts** (map II, D2, **142**): 165 Water Street, Gastown. ☎ 685-1828. On offer here are lovely woollens knitted by the Cowichan Indians from the east coast of Vancouver Island.

🔒 **Lush** (map II, A1, **144**): 1118 Denman Street. Open daily 10am–11pm. Hot from London, this shop has become a real hit in Canada. Even the singer Madonna is a big fan of the soaps and creams in every conceivable flavour, perfume and texture, sold by weight as in a deli.

🔒 **Taj Mahal Trading Center** (map II, D2): 44 Water Street. ☎ 685-1934. This is a small, unpretentious shop, apparently no different from many others on Water Street, but here you can get T-shirts and sweatshirts printed with the design of your choice at pretty unbeatable prices. Save time, money and energy shopping here.

– **CDs**: Customers benefit from price wars between **A&B Sound** of 556 Seymour Street (plus two other branches in Hastings Street and Marine Drive), ☎ 687-5837, and **Virgin Megastore** at 788 Burrard Street, ☎ 669-2289.

IN THE AREA

★ **Capilano Suspension Bridge**: 3735 Capilano Road. ☎ 985-7474. Open May–October 8.30am–8pm. November–April 9am–5pm. Entrance charge $9.95 (reductions for children and students, under-sixes free). By car, take Georgia Street through Stanley Park, then across Lion's Gate Bridge as far as Marine Drive. Turn right and then left onto Capilano Road, and it's a few kilometres farther on the left. By bus, take the No. 246 Highland West on Georgia Street to Ridge Wood and Capilano, and then walk from there.

The 137-metre (450-foot) bridge across a deep gorge is exciting and frightening at the same time as you're swung by the vibrations and swaying of the bridge. However, it doesn't necessarily merit a special trip, and you may find it a little disappointing. Alternatively, it might be better to go to **Lynn Canyon**, from where the view of the suspension bridge is undoubtedly less impressive, but it's free and less crowded.

★ **Grouse Mountain**: Continue along Capilano Road past the suspension bridge and take the cable car to the top of Grouse Mountain. By bus, take No. 236 (Grouse Mountain) from the Seabus terminal in North Vancouver (summer only) or the No. 246 Highland West on Georgia Street and transfer at Edgemont Village for the No. 232. ☎ 984-0661. The cable car runs every 15 minutes from 9am to10pm all year round. At the summit you can enjoy magnificent views over Vancouver.

★ Still going north, **Mount Seymour Provincial Park** has some lovely walking trails.

★ **Horseshoe Bay**: Take Marine Drive west from North Vancouver and follow the coast road through wild undergrowth. When the forest canopy is less dense, you'll come across some picturesque creeks and a few mansions with superb views over the bay. Horseshoe Bay is a small harbour surrounded by green mountains and lots of tiny islands. From here you can get the ferry to Nanaimo on Vancouver Island, (*see* 'Leaving Vancouver' *below*) or some of the smaller islands just off the mainland.

★ **Squamish**: 67 kilometres (42 miles) north of Vancouver, before Garibaldi Park. Squamish is well known to mountaineers of all levels as the site of **Stawamus Chief**, the second biggest granite monolith in the world. Loggers also come here in August for the World Championships of Loggers' Sports. But it's the white-headed eagles that attract most people to Squamish. These eagles come to feed on the salmon from the end of November to mid-February. The peak is in January when a festival is held and the number of eagles is recorded. Visitors come to take photos, go on expeditions, see exhibitions etc. The most famous observation point is in Brackendale, a residential area between Tenderfoot Creek and downtown Squamish.

★ **Whistler** and **Garibaldi Park**: After you leave Horseshoe Bay there's a very lovely route up to Whistler. On the way, you can stop at the British Columbia Museum: ☎ 688-8735 and 896-2233. This mining museum is open between 15 May and 15 October if you fancy a go at prospecting.

★ Just after this you can visit the impressive **Shannon Falls,** and then **Brandywine Falls,** so named by two railway workers who threw two bottles of brandy and wine over them. You'll find lots of well-equipped campsites here, including the one at Porteau Cove that's popular with divers – the diving around here is renowned.

★ **The Sunshine Coast**: This excursion by car and ferry covers a wild and very little-used route, with lots of campsites along the way. For this trip you'll need some time and to enjoy travelling by boat. And you'll also enjoy going to places that others overlook. A map of the area is essential.

Take the ferry from Horseshoe Bay to Langdale, then drive from Langdale to Earl's Cove and take another ferry to Saltery Bay. From there, drive as far as Powell River then take the ferry to Comox on Vancouver Island for the drive down the coast to Nanaimo. You can then cross back on the ferry to Horseshoe Bay or continue towards Victoria. From Victoria, you can then push on to Vancouver or Seattle in Washington State (USA).

LEAVING VANCOUVER

By Car

Three main routes leave Vancouver. Highway 99 will take you north to Whistler in under 2 hours; the same highway southbound connects with Interstate 5 for Seattle. Finally, the Trans-Canada Highway 1 is the route to the national parks and the rest of Canada.

– **Auto Drive-away**: 1080A Marine Drive, North Vancouver. ☎ 985-0936.

By Plane

Vancouver Airport is privately run, and there is an 'airport improvement charge' of $15 when you check in.

By Train

🚆 **BC Rail** (colour map I, C–D1): 1311 West 1st Street, North Vancouver. ☎ 984-5246 and 631-3500. Fax: 984-5005. Website: www.bcrail.com/bcrpass. Services only to other British Columbia destinations.

– **For Prince George**: Three departures a week with BC Rail at 7.30am.

– Via Rail has connections across Canada, going through **Kamloops, Jasper, Edmonton, Saskatoon, Winnipeg,** and across **Ontario.** Departures Tuesday and Friday. The trip east takes three days.

– **For Seattle**: Daily trains with Amtrak.

By Bus

🚌 **Greyhound Bus Terminal** (colour map II, D3): 1150 Station Street. ☎ 482-8747 or 1-800-231-2222 (toll-free).

– **For Seattle**: Five departures daily.

– **For Calgary**: Six departures daily, from 7am to 1am, both direct or with connections.

– **For Toronto**: Four departures daily. Some buses continue to Montréal. With a ticket valid for 30 days you can break and resume your journey wherever you like along the route.

– **For Jasper**: Three departures daily, between 7am and 6pm.

– **For White Horse**: One departure at 8am daily (except Saturday).

🚌 **Pacific Coach Lines**: Pacific Central Station, 1150 Station Street. ☎ 662-7575.

– **For Vancouver Island**: Some bus and coach services include ferry crossings from Tsawwassen or Horseshoe Bay (*see below*).The journey from the city centre to the centre of Victoria, including the ferry crossing from Tsawwassen, takes about 3 hours 15 minutes. There are several departures a day. It's a lovely crossing through the islands.

– Tip: smart travellers use local transport. Take bus No. 601 from the corner of Granville Avenue and Broadway (9th Avenue) to the terminus at Ladner Exchange. Then take No. 680 (No. 404 from 15 April to second Monday in October) to the boarding point in Tsawwassen and buy a walk-on ticket for the ferry. Alternatively, take bus No. 99 south on Granville and transfer to the No. 17 going to the ferries.

By Ferry

⚓ There are two departure points for ferries to **Victoria** and **Nanaimo** on **Vancouver Island**. The main port is in **Tsawwassen**, about 30 minutes by car south of Downtown Vancouver, which serves both Victoria and Nanaimo. The other is in **Horseshoe Bay**, about 20 kilometres (12 miles) north of town, with ferries to Nanaimo (the crossing takes from 90 minutes to 2 hours) and some of smaller islands up the Sunshine Coast (*see* 'In the Area' *above*).

– If you're on foot, short of time or don't want to go to Victoria (which would be a pity), it's better to take the ferry from Tsawwassen.

■ **BC Ferries**: ☎ (604) 444-2890 or 1-800-724-5223 (toll-free). Fax: 381-5452. Website: www.bcferries.bc.ca. If you have a vehicle, it's best to book.

– **From Tsawwassen**: Departures are every hour from 7am to 10pm. When you get to Vancouver Island, take bus No. 70 into Victoria to save some time and money. By car, at busy times, you can wait for an hour at the ferry terminal. It's best to take the first ferry, leaving at 7am. Boarding starts between 6.30 and 6.45am, and you pay on board (Visa and MasterCard accepted).

– **From Horseshoe Bay**: Take bus No. 250 or No. 257 on Georgia, or No. 99 North that goes via Granville Street. The ferries leave for Nanaimo from 7am to 10pm, with about 15 services a day in the summer.

WHISTLER

Vancouver's major ski resort has also become a Mecca for mountain-bikers and golfers in the summer. If you don't have time to tour British Columbia, this smart and fairly relaxed resort gives you a sort of pocket version of the ocean and the mountains. And the route from Vancouver to Whistler is absolutely breathtaking. Whistler is very busy in all seasons and, like any other ski resort, is relatively expensive. But don't forget that low season here means the summer.

Whistler developed with the increase in tourism, and although the area is not that big, it's quite spread out. From Vancouver, you first reach Whistler Creekside and Lake Alta before finding the centre of the resort, Whistler Village and Village North. Farther up, Blackcomb Mountain completes the resort. Be careful about the distances and check your route before you get off the highway.

USEFUL ADDRESSES

🏢 **Chamber of Commerce**: Right in the centre of Whistler Village. ☎ 932-5528. Bookings: ☎ 1-800-944-7853 (toll-free).

🚌 **Maverick Coach Lines**: ☎ 932-5031. In Vancouver: ☎ 255-1171. For services to downtown Vancouver. Booking advisable.

🚈 **BC Rail**: North Vancouver station. ☎ 932-2134.

■ **Bicycle hire**: Several outlets include Carleton Lodge, Day Lodge, Château Whistler, Glacier Lodge, etc. (see also 'What to Do').

■ **Taxi**: ☎ 932-3333.

■ **Whistler Internet Café**: Town Plaza, in North Village near the Val d'Isère Restaurant. ☎ 905-2980. Internet access, drinks and cakes.

WHERE TO STAY

🛏 **Hostelling International Whistler**: 5678 Alta Lake Road. ☎ 932-5492. Fax: 932-4687. Email: whistler@hihostels.bc.ca This is a bit difficult to find, but it's in one of the most beautiful settings in Whistler. Before you reach Whistler, follow the signs to Les Deux Gros restaurant and follow the lake for a few kilometres. Four return buses daily from Whistler Village. The clientele tends to be young, and there are significant reductions for children. Prices are $18.50 a night for Youth Hostel members ($23 for non-members). The wooden cabin is just on the lakeshore with the mountains behind. There's a big sitting room with open fire, comfy sofas, billiards,

piano and also a sauna. Canoes, mountain bikes and snowmobiles are available on loan or hire.

🛏 **The Shoestring Lodge**: 7124 Nancy Greene Drive; continue on Highway 99 a little past Whistler Village. ☎ 932-3338 or 1-877-551-4954 (toll-free). Fax: 932-8347. Website: www.shoestringlodge.com. Next to the Boot Pub, dormitories for four cost $16 in summer (up to $25 in high season), and doubles are $50 ($80 in winter). It's very clean and each dorm has its own bathroom. The rooms are not very appealing, but it's hard to find anything cheaper in Whistler. You'll find a friendly atmosphere here and there's a shuttle bus service to the ski runs.

♨ **Blackcomb Lodge**: 4220 Gateway Drive, on the main square. ☎ 932-4155 or 1-800-667-2855 (toll-free). Fax: 932-6826. Website: www.blackcomblodge.com. Prices start at a hefty $145 for a double room in this centrally located spot.

♨ **Chateau Whistler Resort**: 4599 Château Boulevard, in Blackcomb. ☎ 938-8000 or 1-800-268-9411 (toll-free). Fax: 938-2070. Website: www.sunnygolf.com/chatrst.ht. You'll pay around $189 a night at this hotel, one of Whistler's finest, situated at the foot of the ski runs.

WHERE TO EAT

✕ **Old Spaghetti Factory**: 4154 Village Green, in Crystal Lodge, Whistler Village. ☎ 938-1081. Open noon–10pm. A main course will cost around $15 in this restaurant belonging to the well-known Canadian chain. You'll get no surprises, but it's good value for money.

✕ **La Bocca**: 4232 Village Stroll, on the main square in Whistler Village. ☎ 932-2112. Run by the same owner as the Brasserie des Artistes next door, this has a warm, colourful decor with a nice atmosphere, and the wine list is longer than the menu. Pasta for $16, Fondue Savoyarde or Chinese (with vegetables) for $20.

✕ **Val d'Isère**: in Village North, the other side of Village Gate Boulevard from Whistler. ☎ 932-4666. Fax: 932-2186. Main courses from $8 to $18, and around $30 for a full meal. Game and trout are specialities prepared by a French ex-pat, Roland Pfaff.

✕ **Les Deux Gros**: right near the Highway, before Whistler by Lake Alta. ☎ 932-4611. Fax: 932-2744. Open in the evening. As you might guess from the name, this a French restaurant and there's even a flag and a place to play boules. You can eat well here for around $25 per person.

WHERE TO HAVE A DRINK, NIGHTLIFE

Whistler doesn't sleep much at night and a day's skiing is often finished off in one of the many bars and clubs dotted around the village. Check in the bars to see if you can get free entry to the clubs or evening gigs.

♫ For your first drink in town try **La Brasserie des Artistes** at 4232 Village Stroll (☎ 932-3569) or the **Amsterdam Pub** next door.
♫ **Boot Pub**: 7124 Nancy Greene Way. ☎ 932-3338. Just north of the

village as you head along Highway 99, this is best known for its blues concerts.
♫ **Maxx Fish**: On the main square in Whistler is this venue for hip-hop, concerts, DJs, blues and funk.

SHOPPING

🔒 **Cow's Whistler**: 102-4295 Blackcomb Way, Whistler Village. There's a bovine theme here, with cows everywhere – as alarm clocks, on aprons, helmets, socks and posters. You can also buy ice-creams, made with real milk, naturally.

WHAT TO DO

The three resorts of Whistler Village, Blackcomb and Whistler's South Side together make up the biggest ski area in Canada, but there are plenty of other sports on the agenda:

– **Rafting**: Various options are on offer depending on age and experience, from a few hours to a whole day. Enjoy a picnic and some birdwatching, particularly the eagles. Operators include **C3 Rafting** (☎ 938-1821), **Wedge Rafting** (☎ 932-7171) and **Whistler River Adventures** (☎ 932-3552).

– **Canoeing/kayaking**: For a relaxed experience the magnificent setting of Lake Alta is lovely for canoeing, with absolutely no danger. If you're prepared to get wet, go a bit farther up and run the rapids on Green Lake. **Whistler Sailing and Watersports Centre** offers canoe and kayak hire, and guided tours. ☎ 932-7245.

– **Mountain Bikes**: These are the most widely used means of transport on Whistler in the summer. You'll find lots of prepared trails, with guides available at the Chamber of Commerce and in the hire shops (*see* 'Useful Addresses'). Other outlets include **Glacier Shop** (☎ 938-7744), **Wild Willie's** (☎ 938-8036) and **Whistler Mountain Bike Park and Learning Centre** (☎ 932-3434).

– **Walking**: You'll find superb trails to follow around Whistler that are not as hard going as you might think. But beware of the bears, though. In winter some come into the village, so you have every chance of meeting one. **Whistler Summer Adventures** (☎ 932-8484) offer guided walks lasting 2–4 hours. Take the Last Lake Loops, one of many marked trails that goes to the lake, picnic sites and to places that have been prepared for swimming.

Vancouver Island

An island of contrasts, 34,000 square kilometres (13,124 square miles) in area, this shelters the southern coasts of British Columbia. The island is barely inhabited outside the southern part, where you'll find Victoria – the pretty, very British capital, with its numerous meticulously maintained gardens. This is also the island where the seriously rich of Vancouver have their second homes.

A few kilometres to the north, the island rapidly becomes an immense wilderness that, for the most part, has remained undeveloped. The dense vegetation and gigantic trees, the lack of a road network, and the wild animals that live there contribute to making the island one of the last unspoiled bastions of nature. The farthest and most inaccessible places are a few tiny villages that will delight travellers in search of the authentic, as well as experienced fishermen and hikers.

The island was owned by the Hudson's Bay Company when Fort Victoria was founded in 1843. It then became a colony of the Crown in 1848 before being attached to British Columbia in 1866. Two years later, Victoria became its capital and, in addition to splendid gardens where the great and good took their walks, a bunch of public buildings also flourished.

VICTORIA

British Columbia's capital has a population of 75,467 and is the main town on the island. The people of Victoria have adopted a very English style of life, with flower gardens, Victorian houses, brick storehouses and various warehouses in good architectural style. Here the road network is not the standard chessboard grid because originally it had to link the farms. Victoria's British character and temperate climate have attracted many retired people, rich Americans and tourists. But don't be misled, partakers of afternoon tea are few and far between and the proximity of the university stops the town from going to sleep when the sun sets. For the last decade more and more of the warehouses and storehouses have been turned into warm bars and restaurants which fill up in the evening. Victoria is charming and very lively and is a good starting point for a tour of the island, as well as a welcome stopping place for weary travellers.

USEFUL ADDRESSES

■ **Travel InfoCentre** (map II, A2): 812 Wharf Street; above the port, almost opposite the Empress Hotel. ☎ 953-2033 or 1-800-663-3883 (toll-free bookings). Fax: 382-6539. Website: www.tourismvictoria.com. Open daily 8.30am–5.30pm in season. As in Vancouver, you'll receive perfect service, and virtually exhaustive documentation about the island and the town of Victoria.

■ **Tourism Association of Vancouver Island** (map II, A2): Bastion Square, Suite 302-45. ☎ 382-3551. Fax: 382-3523. For more specific information on the whole island (trails, etc.), with extensive documentation.

■ **Provincial Park Office**: ☎ 387-4550. For information on the island's provincial parks.

✉ **Post office**: The main post office is at 714 Yates Street, which can be reached on the No. 5 bus. Most mail services, however, are provided by the city's pharmacies – which also sell videos.

■ **Royal Jubilee Hospital** (map I, off D2): 1900 Fort Street. ☎ 370-8000. Emergencies: ☎ 370-8212.

■ **Cyber Station** (map II, B2, **6**): 1113 Blanshard Street. ☎ 386-4687. Website: www.cyber.bc.ca. Open Monday to Friday 8.30am–10pm. Saturday 10am–10pm. Sunday 10am–5pm. Internet access, printers and scanners are available for around $5.50 for 30 minutes (or $1 for 5 minutes if you're really fast).

■ **Left luggage**: at the bus station on Belleville Street, opposite the Crystal Court Motel.

GETTING THERE

By bus/ferry: *see* 'Leaving Vancouver'.

By plane: Victoria International Airport: in Sydney, 38 kilometres (24 miles) north of Victoria. There's an Airporter Service bus: ☎ 386-2526.

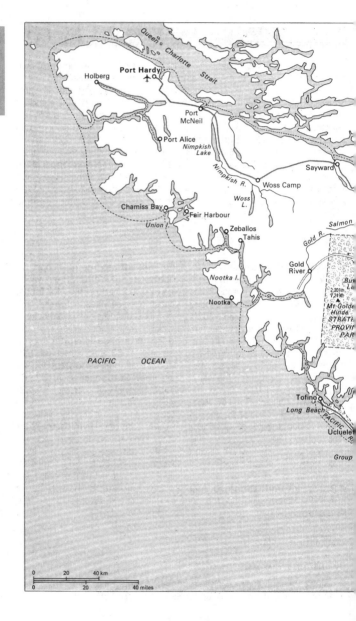

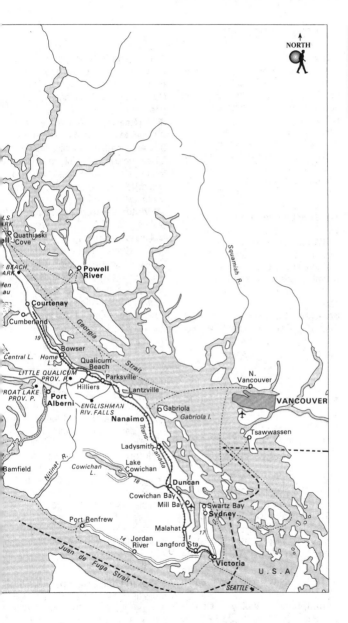

NORTH

Quathiaski Cove

BEACH PARK

Powell River

Courtenay

Cumberland

19

Bowser

Home L.

Qualicum Beach

Central L.

LITTLE QUALICUM PROV. P.

Hilliers

Parksville

Lantzville

ROAT LAKE PROV. P.

Port Alberni

ENGLISHMAN RIV. FALLS

Nanaimo

Gabriola

Gabriola I.

Squamish R.

Georgia

Strait

Trans Canada

N. Vancouver

VANCOUVER

Tsawwassen

Ladysmith

Nitinat R.

Cowichan

Cowichan L.

Lake Cowichan

Bamfield

18

Duncan

Cowichan Bay

Mill Bay

Swartz Bay

Sydney

Port Renfrew

Malahat

Jordan River

Langford Sta.

14

1

17

Victoria

U.S.A

Juan de Fuga Strait

SEATTLE

VANCOUVER ISLAND

GETTING AROUND

■ **Bike hire**
– **Harbours Rentals**: 811 Wharf Street, next to the Travel InfoCentre. ☎ 995-1661. Open daily. Bike and scooter rental at reasonable prices.

■ **Car hire**
– **Budget Rent-a-Car** (map II, A3, **7**): 757 Douglas Street. ☎ 953-5300.
– **Avis Rent-a-Car**, 843 Douglas Street. ☎ 386-8468.
– **Rent-a-Wreck** (map I, B1, **8**): 2634 Douglas Street. ☎ 384-5343. A little more expensive.

🚌 **Gray Line Victoria** (map II, A3, **9**): 700 Douglas Street. ☎ 388-5248. Fax: 388-9461. Tours in Victoria and the surrounding area.

🚌 **BC Transit**: ☎ 382-6161. Very useful buses around town. Make sure to pick up the excellent brochure.

🚌 **Island Coachlines** (map II, A3, **10**): 700 Douglas Street. ☎ 385-4411. Regular buses to Nanaimo, Parkville, Port Alberni and Tofino, plus a service from Nanaimo to Courtenay and Port Hardy. Left luggage.

🚆 **Via Rail** (map II, A1): 450 Pandora Avenue. ☎ 383-4324 or 1-800-561-8630 (toll-free). Air-conditioned autorail on the line from Victoria to Courtenay, via Chemainus, Nanaimo, Parksville and other very scenic spots, with regular stops.

⛴ **Victoria Harbour Ferry**: in the port. ☎ 708-0201. This serves several stops, including the Empress Hotel, Ocean Point Resort and Coast Harbourside Hotel, with daily departures every 15 minutes. For a change, take a *kabukis cab* or a carriage, the little taxi-boats do hops along Victoria Harbour for the price of a bus ticket ($2.50).

WHERE TO STAY

Campsites

🛏 **Fort Victoria RV Park**: 340 Island Highway. ☎ 479-8112. Fax: 479-5806. Website: www.fortvicrv. com. Take Douglas Street north (which becomes Highway 1), turn left onto Helmaken, then right when you get to Highway 1A. Bus Nos. 14 or 15. The site has decent facilities, but it's a long way out.

🛏 **Thetis Lake Campground**: 1-1938 West Park Lane, not far from Highway 1. ☎ 478-3845. Fax: 478-6151. Open all year. This campsite is shady, has 100 pitches, showers and a laundrette. Hiking paths and a lake close by.

🛏 **Humpback Valley Campground**: 2960 Irwin Road RR6, 20 kilometres (12.5 miles) along Highway 1 towards Nanaimo. When you reach the Shell station after 16 kilometres (10 miles), turn left onto Sooke Lake Road. ☎ 478-6960. Open 15 May to 15 September. The site's in a pleasant forest landscape and has good facilities, plus kayak hire.

🛏 **Victoria East**: Saanichton, 20 kilometres (12.5 miles) from Victoria on Highway 17 and 11 kilometres (7 miles) from Swartz Bay. Turn at Mount Newton X, then go as far as Waddling Dog Inn. ☎ 652-3232. Comfortable and shady, with access to the beach.

☆ Budget

🛏 **Ocean Island Backpackers Inn** (map II, B1–2, **21**): 791 Pandora Avenue. ☎ 385-1788 or 1-888-888-4180 (toll-free). Website: www. oceanisland.com. Very central, just a few blocks from Market Square, and inexpensive at $16 per night, with doubles under $40. Clientele tends to be surfers and body-piercing types. Reception open 24 hours, and has parking.

Youth Hostel (map II, A2, **20**): 516 Yates Street. ☎ 385-4511. Fax: 385-3232. Email: victoria@hi hostels.bc.ca. Open all year. Closes at 9.30pm; be punctual, or you'll sleep outside. This really nice place right in the centre of town has 120 places in two big dormitories, plus a few rooms. A dormitory bed for a night is $16 for members ($20 non-members), and $36 ($40) for a double room. It's in one of the town's oldest warehouses (built in 1882) and has been attractively re-novated, with a small sitting room, kitchen. Emergency items such as razors and toothbrushes on sale.

Selkirk Guesthouse (map I, off A1, **36**): 934 Selkirk Avenue. ☎ 389-1213 or 1-800-974-6638 (toll-free). Fax: 389-1313. It seems a long way out, but in fact it's easy to get here. From the centre of town, drive across Johnson bridge, turn right into Tyee Road, go straight down Skinner, then Craigflower, turn right into Arcadia and you get to Selkirk.

Otherwise, take bus No. 14 Craig-flower from Douglas and Yates to the Tillicum stop. It's only 10 minutes by bus, 30 minutes on foot and about the same by canoe. There are charming rooms for couples and families with bathroom and kitchenette for $40–60, and two 10-bed dormitories at $18–20 a night. You'll get a really laid-back reception. The garden's a real paradise for the kids, with barbecue, jaccuzzi and tram-poline. You can even hop into a canoe for a trip to the shops. This is one of the nicest places in Canada, so phone in advance as it gets full very quickly, and it's really hard to leave.

YMCA and **YWCA** (map II, B2, **22**): 800 Courtney Street, on the corner of Quadra Street. ☎ 386-7511. You'll pay around $20 for a dorm bed and $55 for one of the six private rooms. It's modern and clean, and better than a hotel (but not as good as the youth hostel). If you arrive late the bell is to the left of the entrance, quite high up. There's a café and laundry facilities, plus access to the swimming pool and gym nearby.

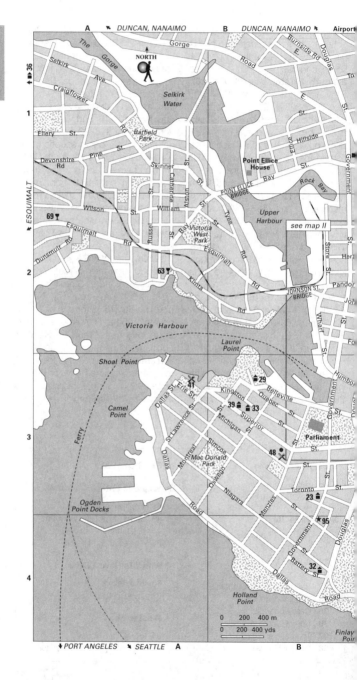

VICTORIA

☆☆ – ☆☆☆ Moderate to Expensive

🛏 **Dominion Hotel** (map II, B2, **26**): 759 Yates Street. ☎ 384-4136. Fax: 382-6416 or 1-800-663-6101 (toll-free). In this renovated old building in town you'll find charm and comfort at reasonable prices, starting at $90 for a double. The pastel-coloured rooms are bright, spacious and pleasant. Hunter's is a good bar-restaurant on the ground floor.

🛏 **The James Bay Inn** (map I, B3, **23**): 270 Government Street. ☎ 384-7151 or 1-800-836-2649 (toll-free). Fax: 385-2311. Email: info @jamesbayinn.bc.ca. Very well located, not far from the centre and three blocks from Beacon Hill Park, in the heart of a residential area. Doubles cost $104–117, depending on the view. The refurbished hotel has an attractive facade, welcoming interior and bay windows that illuminate the spacious rooms. Good value for money.

🛏 **Crystal Court Motel** (map II, A3, **24**): 701 Belleville Street, on the corner of Douglas Street. ☎ 384-

---

- ■ **Useful Addresses**

    - 🛈 Travel InfoCentre
    - 🛈 Tourism Association of Vancouver Island
    - 🚂 Train Station (Via Rail)
    - 6 Cyberstation
    - 7 Budget Rent-a-car
    - 9 Gray Line Victoria
    - 10 Island Coachlines
    - 110 Black Ball Transports or M.V. Coho
    - 111 Victoria Express Passenger Ferry
    - 112 Victoria Clipper

- 🛏 **Where to Stay**

    - 20 Youth Hostel
    - 21 Ocean Island Backpackers Inn
    - 22 YMCA and YWCA
    - 24 Crystal Court Motel
    - 25 Helm's Inn
    - 26 Dominion Hotel
    - 28 Royal Scot Inn
    - 34 Taj Mahal Agra House

- ✕ **Where to Eat**

    - 40 John's Place
    - 42 Day and Night
    - 44 Pagliacci's
    - 45 Don Mee
    - 46 Café Mexico
    - 47 Kwong Tung Seafood Restaurant
    - 49 Chandlers

    - 50 The Keg
    - 51 Milestone's
    - 53 Pescatore's
    - 92 Camille's
    - 94 The Empress

- 🍷 **Where to Have a Drink, Nightlife**

    - 26 Hunter's Steakhouse and Lounge
    - 61 The Sticky Wicket
    - 62 Swan's
    - 64 Millennium
    - 65 Legends
    - 66 House of Blues
    - 67 The Jet Lounge
    - 70 Hugo's

- ★ **What to See**

    - 90 Royal British Columbia Museum
    - 91 Thunderbird Park, Helmcken House
    - 92 Maritime Museum of British Columbia
    - 93 Parliament Building
    - 94 Empress Hotel
    - 97 Market Square

- 🛍 **Shopping**

    - 81 Rogers'
    - 100 Christmas
    - 101 Victoria Eaton Center

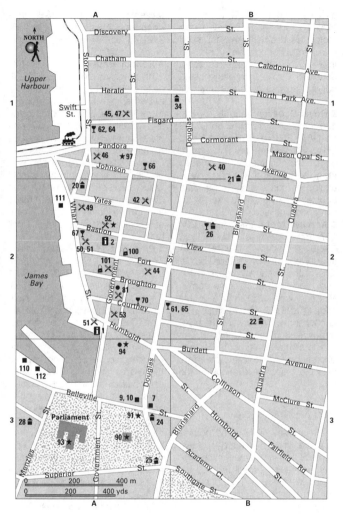

VICTORIA (MAP II)

0551. Fax: 384-5125. Website: www.victoriabc.com/accom/crystal. Doubles cost $80 ($60 out of season), and slightly more for three or four people at this little blue-and-white motel right in the centre, with functional rooms that are very clean.

♚ **Helm's Inn** (map II, A3, **25**): 600 Douglas Street, on the corner of Superior at the foot of Beacon Hill Park, a few blocks from the port. ☎ 385-5767 or 1-800-66-4356 (toll-free). Fax: 385-2221. Website: www.helmsinn.com. In the same block as the Royal British Columbia Museum and the Crystal Court Motel, this is a very pleasant motel with bright, comfortable rooms and free parking. Allow $99–109 for a double ($10 more with kitchen), and out of season prices are very attractive.

â **Royal Scot Inn** (map II, A3, **28**): 425 Québec Street. ☎ 388-5463 or 1-800-663-7515 (toll-free). Fax: 388-5452. Website: www.royalscot. com. This motel is 50 metres from the port and has huge, well-equipped rooms at $99–159 for a double. Also has a sauna, swimming pool and jacuzzi.

â **Admiral Motel** (map I, B3, **29**): 257 Belleville Street. ☎ and fax: 388-6267; 1-888-8ADMIRAL (toll-free). Website: www.admiral.bc.ca. One of the cheapest motels in the port, particularly out of season in May and June, at $125 for a double and up to $169 mid-summer. The anchor above the door and the blue-and-white frontage set the tone. The rooms all have bathroom, TV, telephone, fridge and coffee machine, plus big balconies overlooking the bay.

Bed & Breakfast

There are several hundred houses available in and around Victoria. Some B&Bs are no more expensive than modestly priced motels. It's impossible to check them all out, so contact the tourist office or any of the services listed below:

■ **Best Canadian B&B Network**: 1064 Balfour Avenue. ☎ 738-7207. Fax: 732-4998.

■ **Canada West Reservation Service**: ☎ 990-6730 or 1-800-561-3223 (toll-free). Fax: 990-5876. Website: www.b-b.com

■ **Vacations West**: 185–911 Yates Street. ☎ 383-1863. Fax: 383-0144. Website: www.vacations west.ca

■ **Western Canada B&B Innkeepers Association**: ☎ 255-9191. Fax: 642-7538. Website: www.wcbbia.com

â **Renouf House** (map I, D2, **38**): 2010 Stanley Avenue. ☎ 595-4774. Fax: 598-1515. Email: renouf@ islandnet.com. From the centre of town, take Pandora Avenue to the fork with Begbie Street, then turn left onto Stanley Avenue; or take bus No. 22 to Fernwood and Gladstone. Doubles cost $45–70 a night, with or without bathroom in this simple white house, dating from 1912. Run by a very nice young couple, it offers a warm welcome and the charm of a B&B for the price of a small hotel.

â **Piermont Place B&B** (formerly **Trudy's**; map I, D3, **31**): 810 Piermont Place. ☎ 592-5703 or 1-800-487-8397 (toll-free). Fax: 592-5703. Email: piermont@ampsc.com. Near Government House and Craigdarroch Castle, this is a bit far out unless you have a car. Otherwise, the owner will pick you up from the bus station or ferry and take you into town in the morning. This modern and comfortable B&B is in a superb residential area, and peace is guaranteed. You'll get a lovely welcome, and a pleasant breakfast served at the bay window. Four rooms with or without bathroom cost $90–110 (reductions for children under 12), and some sleep four people. Credit cards are accepted, and booking is advisable.

â **The Laird's** (**Campus View House**; map I, off D1, **37**): 1840 Midgard Avenue, off Shelbourne Street, below McKenzie. ☎ 477-3069 or 1-800-597-9119 (toll-free). Located 10 minutes' drive east of town, in a residential area one block from the university, is this modern residence in the middle of a garden. You'll get a courteous welcome, and the emphasis is on the peace of the neighbourhood and of the house, which is great if that's what you're looking for. You can arrange a free ride from town. There are three rooms (two with private bathroom) at $75 for a double, and you'll get a pleasant breakfast in the sun-room. Non-smokers only. Credit cards accepted.

⌂ **Battery Street Guesthouse** (map I, B4, **32**): 670 Battery Street. ☎ 385-4632. Only a block from the ocean and Beacon Hill Park, this house dates from 1898. It has a long balcony, six decent double rooms and a little garden with a few pear treas. No smoking.

⌂ **Andersen House** (map I, B3, **33**): 301 Kingston Street, on the corner of Pendray. ☎ 388-4565. Fax: 388-4563. Email: andersen@islandnet. com. Very close to Victoria Harbour and the Parliament building, this is a Victorian house that has retained all its old charm. It has a colourful facade, high-ceilinged veranda, stucco decoration, old fireplaces and lovely furniture in four comfortable rooms. Prices are between $100 and $150 in high season, but it's really superb. One room has a huge balcony, another has a double jacuzzi. One of the larger rooms has a kitchenette and a corner sitting room, and each room has a CD player. The decoration is very personalized, particularly the ceramics, which were made by the owner. There are several small terraces. You can also sleep on the boat moored nearby in the harbour. You'll get a pleasant welcome, and a good breakfast.

⌂ **Taj Mahal Agra House** (map II, B1, **34**): 679 Herald Street. ☎ 380-1099 and 383-4662. Fax: 380-1099. Located in an elegant road on the edge of Chinatown, not far from the centre on foot. This is a fun and well-run B&B that's more like a small hotel, with a stylized version of Mongolian architecture. Except for the two with pleasant Indian decor –

cosy furnishings, green plants, etc. – that are a bit more expensive, most of the rooms lack any particular charm. The facilities are good, though, and credit cards are accepted. Non-smokers only.

⌂ **Ryan's B&B** (map I, B3, **39**): 224 Superior Street. ☎ 389-0012. Fax: 389-2857. Website: www.bc1. com/users/ryans. The exterior of this superb house, built in 1892, is flowery and colourful. The interior has been restored with a great deal of taste and a hint of eccentricity that adds to its charm. You leave your shoes at the door, the better to appreciate the 10-centimetre (4-inch) thick carpets! The rooms are expensive at $135–175 per night, but personalized, spacious and pleasant. And you'll get a very nice welcome.

☆☆☆☆ Splash Out

⌂ **Dashwood Manor** (map I, C4, **35**): 1 Cook Street. ☎ 385-5517 or 1-800-667-5517. Fax: 383-1760. Website: www.dashwoodmanor. com. This very substantial mock-Tudor residence on the edge of Beacon Hill Park, only 10 metres from the ocean, has 14 suites. Prices range from about $75 out of season to about $165 in the summer, depending on the suite. There's a very old English atmosphere created by beautiful period furnishing, refined decor and lovely ornaments, aided by rooms named 'Buckingham' or 'Windsor'. There are some spectacular views over the ocean and also some great views of the mountains. Suites have open fireplace, jacuzzi and kitchen, and the fridge is replenished daily so that you can make your own breakfast. Credit cards accepted.

⌂ **Oak Bay Beach Hotel** (map I off D4, **27**): 1175 Beach Drive (along the coast towards Oak Bay Village). ☎ 598-4556 or 1-800-668-758 (toll-free). Fax: 598-6180. Email: reser vations@oakbaybeachhotel.bc.ca. A superb mock-Tudor building over-looking the sea offering rooms from $185 to $265 in season ($114–155 off-peak), plus sumptuous suites from $300. The terraced garden leading down to the beach is a little paradise. The British touch is evi-dent from floor to the ceiling – quaint wooden beams, pastel shades, flowery wallpaper, as warm a setting as the welcome. You could imagine you were an English Lord . . .

WHERE TO EAT

☆ Budget

✕ **John's Place** (map II, B1, **40**): 723 Pandora Avenue. ☎ 389-0711. Open Monday to Thursday 7am–10pm. Friday and Saturday 7am–11pm. Sunday 7am–3pm, 5–10pm. Breakfast menus cost from $6, brunch on Sunday about $7. A pleasant American-style decor, with light wood and leatherette seats, and old photographs on the walls. It has a young and student clientele. Good, budget food, with a few specialities such as eggs Valentine (with asparagus and salmon) or popular flapjacks for breakfast. For something a bit more exotic try the Egyptian or Indonesian chicken and Chanlong's honey garlic ribs (sau-téed with garlic and onions). For dessert there are four varieties of cheesecake.

✕ **Paradiso di Stelle**: 10 Bastion Square, opposite the Tourism Asso-ciation of Vancouver Island. ☎ 920-7266. An Italian café that's very popular for its real ice-cream, pas-tries and sandwiches. You can also get really strong coffee and possibly the best iced-tea in town.

✕ **Barb's Place** (map I, A3, **41**): Fisherman's Wharf, 310 Erie Street, at the end of Ontario. If you don't have a car, you can take the Victoria Harbour Ferry. ☎ 384-6515. Open daily May to October 10am–sunset, weather permitting. Breakfast ($3) is served until 11am. After that you can get fresh fish and chips wrapped in newspaper for about $6. You can also dine on halibut, oysters, sea-food chowder, fish burgers or salads outside at big tables that people lounge around on in fine weather, or even on the wharf. Make the most of it and have a look at the interest-ing houseboats a bit farther on. It's a very popular place at weekends, a romantic spot for travellers on a budget.

✕ **Day and Night** (map II, A2, **42**): 622 Yates Street, not far from the youth hostel. Open daily 24 hours. Serves 'Pasta express' for $4.50 and a full breakfast menu for less than $4. The special is always ad-vertised in the window. This place attracts a local crowd, including insomniacs and a few ladies of the night. It's the cheapest eaterie in town but the atmosphere's not great.

✕ **The Blethering Place** (map I, off D4, **82**): 2250 Oak Bay Avenue, at the entrance to Oak Bay Village. ☎ 598-1413 or 1-888-598-1413 (toll free). If you're after some British spirit in Victoria, just go to the un-doubtedly English Oak Bay Village, only 10 minutes from town. 'Village' is a bit of a misnomer (don't go looking for the church or the village green), but Oak Bay prides itself in perpetuating traditions like after-noon tea. In the charming Blethering Place you'll find flowers adorning everything, from the tables, table-cloths, walls and carpet, to the wait-resses' aprons. You can have a substantial breakfast, or tea with scones and a large selection of homemade cakes; the cream tea costs less than $5. There are also (Celtic) music concerts in the evening.

☆☆ Moderate

✕ **Milestone's** (map II, A2, **51**): 812 Wharf Street, below the Travel InfoCentre, opposite the port. ☎ 381-2244. Open Monday to Friday from 11am. Saturday and Sunday from 9am. Allow about $10 per head for a meal in this decent chain restaurant much appreciated for its terrace at the water's edge. International cuisine with a few dishes of Mediterranean influence (pitta with red peppers and hummus) and others with a Chinese or local flavour.

✕ **Med Grill** (map II, B2): 1010 Yates Street. ☎ 888-0597. One of the last places in Victoria that's smart and not really expensive, with starters at $6 and main courses around $15. An old carpet shop has been converted into a lovely high-ceilinged room with a warm, carefully decorated interior. The huge bar offers a view of the whole kitchen. Meat and fish is prepared with taste and originality; ask for the 'fish feature' of the day. You'll get efficient, friendly service, and there's a lovely terrace for good weather.

✕ **Pagliacci's** (map II, A2, **44**): 1011 Broad Street, near Fort Street, a small street between Government and Douglas streets. ☎ 386-1662. Open 11.30am–midnight for meals and then live music. Sunday brunch 11am–1pm. You'll find youthful, colourful decor, including a mural of New York and photos hanging from the cornice round the room, all so dimly lit by candles that you can hardly see what's on your plate. However, the number of customers here suggests it's quality cuisine. You can choose from dishes with fun names such as the Mae West (veal with white wine and lemon), the

Hot Transvestite (sautéed chicken with artichokes) or prawns al Capone. Affordable prices at lunchtime and still acceptable in the evening. A really good place with a lively, noisy atmosphere. Very busy and often full in the summer, so it's best to book for the evening.

✕ **Don Mee** (map II, A1, **45**): 538 Fisgard, between Store and Government streets. ☎ 383-1032. Open daily. Main courses cost $12–16, seafood dishes around $15 and set menus $14. This first-floor Chinese restaurant has a good reputation, particularly for the *dim sum* on Sunday (11am–2pm). Take a number at the entrance, the wait won't be long. While you're waiting have a look at the little carts that are pushed around the tables. Arrive early because lots of the delicacies, such as the delicately perfumed clams, sell out quickly. À la carte includes grilled or steamed crab with the preparation of your choice, Don Mee's assorted cold platter, etc. Lots of Chinese families here is a good sign.

✕ **Café Mexico** (map II, A1, **46**): 1425 Store Street, on the first floor of Market Square. ☎ 386-5454. Open for lunch and dinner. This offers good Mexican cooking at really modest prices (chilli $6, *quesadillas* $5–8) plus interesting desserts. The inviting decor is very green, with quiet little corners, and there's a pleasant little terrace on Market Square where you can have a cocktail. Take-away also available.

✕ **Kwong Tung Seafood Restaurant** (map II, A1, **47**): 548 Fisgard Street. ☎ 381-1223. Open for lunch and dinner daily. The setting is pretty dreary and the Szechuan cooking a little expensive for à la carte, but the set menus are good value at around $10. It serves *dim sum* even in the evening, which is a cheap solution for groups.

✖ **James Bay Tea-Room and Restaurant** (map I, B3, **48**): 332 Menzies Street, on the corner of Superior Street just behind the Parliament Building. ☎ 382-8282. Open daily 7am–9pm (8am on Sunday). This small white house with flowers and a pointed roof is cosy yet kitsch, with lace curtains at the window. Here you can have tea among portraits of the British royal family and Sir Winston Churchill in a deliciously British atmosphere, with breakfast served until 11.30am and afternoon tea from 1pm to 4.30pm. You'll get traditional English dishes, including steak and kidney pie, Welsh rarebit, roast beef and Yorkshire pudding and Cornish pasty, and good desserts such as homemade sherry trifle and cheesecakes. There are also nightly dinner specials with soup, or salad and fresh vegetables.

✖ **The Cheesecake Café** (map II, A2): 910 Government Street, next to the Eaton Center. ☎ 382-2253. This is the temple of cheesecake, with drinks and cakes for under $5. You'll learn to love cheesecake at this place (if you weren't already a fan), as there are no fewer than 16 different types, fresh daily. Alternatively, there are excellent salads (spinach, potato and shrimp). They also do take-away.

☆☆–☆☆☆ Moderate to Expensive

✖ **The Keg** (map II, A2, **50**): 500 Fort Street. ☎ 479-1651. Open Sunday–Thursday 4.30–10pm. Friday and Saturday 4.30–11pm. Relaxed restaurant for those who swear only by steaks weighing more than 200 grams (7 ounces). Generous portions for $17–$22. The music is sometimes invasive, but the first floor is less noisy, with nooks and crannies everywhere. You'll get efficient service, excellent cocktails

and house wine at reasonable prices.

✖ **Chandlers** (map II, A2, **49**): 1250 Wharf Street, on the corner of Yates Street. ☎ 385-3474 and 386-3232. Open for lunch and dinner until 11pm. Housed in an old brick warehouse that was the 19th-century headquarters of the Yukon Gold Rush Trade, this is one of the stops on tourist bus routes, despite the prices. The cooking, mainly fish and seafood, holds its own and there's a good choice of salmon dishes and first-rate grilled halibut. The special of the day is always generously served. At noon there's a set lunch, snacks and seafood express. Main courses cost $14–20 in the evening, when it's more expensive and smarter.

✖ **Camille's** (map II, A2, **92**): 45 Bastion Square, opposite the Maritime Museum. ☎ 381-3433. Open from 5.30pm. This basement restaurant is one of the trendy places in Victoria, serving west-coast cuisine that's very delicate, plus a wide selection of regional wines. Main courses cost $16–20. Booking advisable.

✖ **Pescatore's** (map II, A2, **53**): 614 Humboldt Street, near the junction with Government Street. ☎ 385-4512. Open from 4.30pm, reservations strongly advised. Main courses start from $20, as this is one of the most popular fish and seafood restaurants in town. It has very colourful pseudo-colonial decor (wood panels, ceiling fans, parquet floor). You can also dine in the bar. A very convivial atmosphere. Specialities include Indian curried shrimps, seafood salad, salmon fritters, halibut and oysters. Booking advisable.

✖ a **The Empress** (map II, A3, **94**): 721 Government Street. ☎ 384-8111 or 1-800-268-9411 (toll-free). Extremely chic, with all the charm of the early 20th century, you can take afternoon tea here in the recently refurbished Tea Lobby or the elegant Palm Court. But you won't find many backpackers fighting their way in – not because of the smart dress code, but because of the $40 price!

WHERE TO HAVE A DRINK, NIGHTLIFE

New bars are opening up all the time in Victoria's old, dilapidated storehouses and warehouses, whose high ceilings and atmosphere are perfect for the job. However, Victoria is not really lively enough to sustain this increase in venues. Some bars have happy hours on starters and drinks on weekdays; just follow the crowds of students to find them. You'll also find nightclubs inside pubs or in hotels, often with a small cover charge of about $5. Drinks are usually moderately priced. You need to arrive early to get a seat and avoid the long queues. Clubs often close fairly early (between 1 and 2am). Although smoking is banned in public places, some bars don't seem to take much notice of this because it's the smoker who pays the fine.

The Sticky Wicket (map II, A–B2, **61**): 919 Douglas Street. Lots of rooms and bars all over the place, with a rich decor of carved mahogany and engraved mirrors, plus a games room with darts, pool, etc. Right at the back is a small, lively dance floor. This connects with Cuckoo's Nest and the quirky, atmospheric Big Bad John's, also in the Strathcona Hotel.

Swan's (map II, A1, **62**): 506 Pandora Street, on the corner of Store Street. ☎ 361-3310 or 1-800-668-7926 (toll-free). This is a good example of a converted storehouse, built in 1913, with red-brick walls that give it a certain class. There are a few young people, but it's mainly aimed at 40-somethings. In summer there's a pleasant, flowery patio exclusively for the restaurant's clientele. You can eat lunch, dinner and brunch on Sunday until 2pm. Good halibut and chips. The bar has beers and local wines.

Spinnakers (map I, A2, **63**): 308 Catherine Street. ☎ 386-2739. This pub overlooks the ocean and the American coast in the distance. It's particularly lively, popular as much for the breakfast as for the wide choice of beers on draught.

The Jet Lounge (map II, A2, **67**): Wharf Street. $5 Entrance charge $5. A very popular nightclub with different music every night. Candles and old junk sofas create a style that has its imitators in Victoria. Get there early at the weekend.

Hugo's (map II, A2, **70**): 625 Courtney Street, under the Magnolia Hotel. As the evening progresses the lights are dimmed and the music level rises. Bands on some evenings. This is rather smart and fashionable, and you sip house cocktails on elevated benches facing each other. There's a direct line to a taxi company so you can get home at the end of the evening.

Hunter's Steakhouse and Lounge (map II, B2, **26**): Dominion Hotel, 759 Yates Street. ☎ 384-7494. Near the cinemas, this is where the young locals come before or after a film. Youthful atmosphere, and a nice place to start the evening. If you're feeling a little hungry, try their decent grills and tapas.

Millennium (map II, A1, **64**): 1605 Store Street, next to Swan's (*see above*). ☎ 383-2340. Pretty youthful club, clean and lively, especially at the weekend.

❢ **Legends** (map II, A–B2, **65**): 919 Douglas Street. ☎ 383-7137. A vast venue with a crazy atmosphere at the weekend. The DJ orbits in a capsule in the middle of the room. Stark fluorescent and neon lights, TV sets that crackle, pool tables, table football. The crowd is friendly, young and noisy.

❢ **House of Blues** (map II, A1, **66**): 603 Pandora Avenue. ☎ 386-1717.

Middle-class youngsters form an orderly queue to get in here on a Saturday night.

❢ **Esquimalt Inn** (map I, A2, **69**): 856 Esquimalt Road. ☎ 382-7161. A typical country and western venue. Groups play from 9pm, and there are free line dancing lessons some evenings. Reasonably priced drinks and lots of opportunities to make friends.

WHAT TO SEE

★ **Royal British Columbia Museum** (map II, A3, **90**): 675 Belleville Street, on the corner of Douglas Street. ☎ 387-3014. Open July to September 9.30am–7pm. Rest of the year 10am–5.30pm. Closed Christmas Day and New Year's Day. This well-funded museum has exhibits in giant dioramas and informative and lively commentary, with audio recordings and explanatory panels. Some of these are absolutely marvellous (particularly the reconstructed farm). You can also learn of the succession of hardships endured by the First Nations people.

First floor: Here you'll find the natural history collections – local flora and fauna shown in a natural environment. The impressive displays are extremely informative, and almost life-size dioramas of the coastline and its forest include giant trees such as Douglas firs and Western red cedars. There are even some mammoths.

Second floor: The first section is dedicated to tribal culture, including crafts, fishing techniques, weaving, rituals, cosmogony, Haida Indian carvings (this is a major centre for shamanism), a model of a Shedan village, magnificent Kwakiutl ceremonial costumes, traditional totems and masks. There's also an exhibition of carved and engraved objects in argilite, a carbon mineral from which the Haidas created a unique art form. You'll also learn about the arrival and impact of the whites, and about various treaties, promises and native Indian grievances that were never addressed.

The other part of the floor has a remarkable reconstruction of a small village from the Canadian west (1870–1920) featuring an amazingly realistic soundtrack. There are high-quality dioramas and objects on display, plus reconstructions of the logging industry, a fish cannery, a gold mine with watermill, and an impressive farm. There's also a section on science, explorers and other adventurers, and colonization – including a visit by George Vancouver aboard the *Discovery*.

★ **Thunderbird Park** (map II, A3, **91**): Outside the Royal British Columbia museum you'll find this area that takes its name from the huge totem poles carved with the mythical thunderbird. There's also a workshop of Indian artists that you can visit during the week.

★ **Helmcken House** (map II, A3, **91**): Elliot Street Square. ☎ 361-0021 and 387-4697. Open May to September 11am–5pm. October to April noon–4pm. Also 10 days at Christmas. Dr Helmcken's house at the edge of

Thunderbird Park dates from Victoria's earliest days. Helmcken was one of the pioneers of the town and preferred hard work to political honours. The doctor's room, left intact by his daughter, includes contemporary furnishings and domestic objects, plus an extremely good collection of medicine. Note the three successive stages of construction of the house to accommodate his growing family. The rear section (from 1852) is the oldest. The surrounding garden is the old children's cemetery, with oaks that are many centuries old. The little school next door is believed to be the oldest dwelling in Victoria (1843), but it has been rebuilt here.

★ **Maritime Museum of British Columbia** (map II, A2, **92**): 28 Bastion Square, between Yates and View streets. ☎ 385-4222. Fax: 382-2869. Website: www.mmbc.bc.ca. Open daily 9.30am–4.30pm. This houses the very first Provincial Court House (from 1899). On the ground floor are models, navigational instruments, materials for repairing sails, a gruesome whale cannon, the local fishing skiff and a machine room.

First-floor rooms have displays about the life of Captain Cook and the great steamers, and more lovely models. You'll see sections of lighthouses, beacons and the navy at war, and, curiously, the oldest lift in North America, still in working order.

★ **Parliament Building** (map II, A3, **93**): ☎ 387-3046. Open Monday to Friday 8am–5pm. Guided tours every 20 minutes, lasting for 30 minutes. The building is classical in style, characteristic of the symmetrical and austere buildings from the end of the 19th century, with vestiges of Roman, Victorian and Italian Renaissance styles. Only the copper domes brighten up the various sections of the building. At the top of the dome, right in the middle, stands a statue of George Vancouver, the first person to circumnavigate the island. When the original copper statue of the famous mariner oxidized and turned green the inhabitants of Victoria were upset that he should be this colour: 'Who ever saw a sailor who was seasick?', people used to say, so the statue was covered with gold.

While you're here, note the window marking Queen Elizabeth II's Jubilee. It was made by a member of the clergy, but there wasn't enough time for it to be 'approved' by the royal family before the ceremonies. It was presented, but immediately rejected. The image of a sun setting underneath the British flag was considered unlucky, especially since 'the sun never sets on Her Majesty's Empire'. The symbol was consequently reversed.

★ **Empress Hotel** (map II, A3, **94**): 721 Government Street, right in the middle of the block. ☎ 348-8111. This was built in 1908 by the Canadian Pacific Railway at the time of the economic boom generated by the advent of the railway. The huge Victorian building was constructed over a marshy bog on hundreds of wooden pylons which go down as far as the rocky footing. Go to the Bengal Bar where the tiger skins and fans enchanted both the Queen of England and the writer and poet Rudyard Kipling (1865–1936). Director Michael Cimino filmed a scene here from the *Year of the Dragon* (1985) in the hall that's full of Chinoiserie and palm trees.

★ **Emily Carr House** (map I, B4, **95**): 207 Government Street; between Simcoe and Toronto streets. ☎ 387-4697. Fax: 387-5129. Open mid-May to mid-October, Thursday to Sunday 10am–5pm. This adorable house with its big garden is where the Canadian artist and writer Emily Carr was born in

1871. You can visit her bedroom and the dining room with family ornaments, and learn about what a Sunday dinner was like in this house. When the house was being restored, some original wallpaper (about 130 years old) was discovered.

★ **Butchart Gardens** (map I, off C1): 800 Benvenuto Avenue, West Saanich; about 21 kilometres (13 miles) from town. ☎ 652-5256 and 652-4422. Fax: 652-3883. Entrance charge around $16. By car, take Blanchard Street, which becomes Highway 17, then turn left into Keating Cross Road. No. 75 bus from Douglas Street. Open in summer 9am–10.30pm (sometimes closes earlier). Telephone for opening times during the rest of the year.

Imagine a huge park turned into a fabulous garden with thousands of species of brightly coloured plants, trees and flowering shrubs, plus fountains and stretches of water. The spaces are differentiated or grouped by style – Japanese or Italian gardens, etc. – in a combination of the natural and the cultivated. There are rose beds with species from all over the world. The whole place is pretty remarkable, and brilliantly done (although a tad expensive). From July to September there are fireworks on Saturday night and concerts in the evenings. It's very busy at the weekend.

★ **Art Gallery of Greater Victoria** (map I, C3, **96**): 1040 Moss Street. ☎ 384-4101. Fax: 361-3995. Open Monday to Saturday 10am–5pm (9pm on Thursday). Sunday 1–5pm. Entrance charge. The gallery has a permanent exhibition of works by Emily Carr that is changed periodically to show different themes (totems, trees, etc.). It also houses the only Shinto shrine in North America, purchased with funds from British Columbia's lottery. There's a small collection of European pictures and furniture. It also hosts temporary exhibitions that are sometimes very good.

★ If you have a car, go south down Douglas or Government streets to **Dallas Road** (the coastal road). You'll see rows of beautiful houses, both classical and modern with delightful flowerbeds outside. There are lovely viewing points along the bay, and this is a pleasant tour at the end of the day, when you'll see superb sunsets. A little farther east you'll come across the charming little historic cemetery of **Ross Bay** which is particularly romantic in the autumn.

★ **Market Square** (map II, A1, **97**): between Johnson Street and Pandora Avenue, not far from the youth hostel. An attractive group of brick buildings surround the square, with lots of passages and walkways where you'll find nice organic food shops, bookshops and gift shops. You'll also find the quirky Rubber Rainbow, a shop that specializes in selling condoms as gifts, with really colourful and original wrapping.

★ **Chinatown** (map II, A1): Starting from the beautiful Chinese gate on Fisgard Street (known as the 'door of harmonious interest'), this is the second oldest Chinatown in North America. For a long time it was known as the 'Forbidden City' because of the drug trafficking that went on, with opium dens, illegal gambling dens, throat-cutting alleys, false walls and secret passages that allowed the criminals and gangs to escape from the police. Take a look at Fan Tan Alley (between Pandora Avenue and Fisgard Street) and you'll be convinced that this was one of the most dangerous. It's now thought to be the narrowest alley in Canada.

WHAT TO DO

– **Tours of Vancouver Island**: If you're staying on the island for a few days, head to Tofino – the route alone is worth the trip. The mountainous landscapes are breathtaking and the Pacific Rim National Park is stunning (*see* 'Pacific Rim National Park' *in* 'Tofino'). The island is 500 kilometres (312 miles) long. Travel times can be quite critical in Canada, as services can be quite far apart, so you need to calculate realistic times:

Victoria → Nanaimo	110 kilometres (69 miles)	1 hour 30 minutes
Victoria → Port Alberni	195 kilometres (122 miles)	3 hours
Victoria → Campbell River	264 kilometres (165 miles)	5 hours
Victoria → Port Hardy	502 kilometres (314 miles)	8 hours
Port Alberni → Tofino	122 kilometres (76 miles)	2 hours
Campbell River → Gold River	91 kilometres (57 miles)	1 hour 30 minutes

– **Whale-watching**: Frustrating as it might be, you can't get any closer to the whales than 150 metres (490 feet). This is fine for them but it's annoying if you want to see them close up. Even so, this really is a pleasant outing, and it's best to take a boat from Tofino or go to the north of the island to see the whales.

SHOPPING

🔒 **Rogers'** (map II, A2, **81**): 913 Government Street. ☎ 384-7021. Fax: 384-5750. Open daily until 7pm. At the beginning of the 20th century, Charles W. 'Candy' Rogers had problems getting his sweets and goodies from San Francisco. So he decided to make them himself, including the famous Victoria Creams that are ordered by the White House and the British royal family. This is a charming little shop, with rich wood panelling and an elegant interior where you can stock up on plain creams, creams with hazelnuts, almond brittle, mint wafers, peppermint chews and much more.

🔒 **Christmas** (map II, A2, **100**): 1022 Government Street. Absolutely everything to decorate your Christmas tree. Business must be good because there are three specialist departments for baubles, garlands and all manner of small figurines.

🔒 **Victoria Eaton Center** (map II, A2, **101**): corner of Fort and Government streets. ☎ 389-2228. Open Monday to Saturday 9.30am–5.30pm (9pm Thursday and Friday). Sunday noon–5pm. Over 120 shops open onto this gigantic Victorian-style atrium with a huge clock that dates from the time of the Empire. The mall has some charm, with lots of green plants, a promenade, fountains, etc.

🔒 **A&B Sound** (map II, A2): 641 Yates Street, between Government and Douglas streets. Less attractive prices than in the Vancouver branch.

🔒 **Antique Row**: Fort Street. Several antiques shops will offer a more original souvenir of your trip than a replica totem pole.

🔒 **Munro's Book**: 1108 Douglas Street, opposite the Eaton Center. Open Saturday to Wednesday in summer 9am–7.30pm. Thursday and Friday 9am–9pm. The inhabitants of Victoria love this old building, with its colourful character, stained glass and wooden shelves. You'll find lovely books on Vancouver Island as well as lots on the local artists.

LEAVING VICTORIA

By Bus

🚌 **Pacific Coach Lines**: ☎ 385-4411 or 1-800-661-1725 (toll-free). Website: www.victoriatours.com/Home

– **For Vancouver**: Eight departures daily via the ferry from Swartz Bay to Tsawwassen. It's much cheaper to take local bus No. 70 from Victoria to Swartz Bay, and then buy your Pacific Coach Lines ticket on the boat to Vancouver.

– **Local buses**: from Tsawwassen take the No. 640 or No. 404 to Ladner Exchange, then No. 601 to Granville Street (or No. 17 then No. 99). At about 8am you can catch a bus direct to Vancouver International Airport.

By Boat

⚓ **Black Ball Transports** (map II, A3, **110**): 430 Belleville Street. ☎ 386-2202. Ferry service to **Port Angeles** in the United States. Two departures daily from March to May and October to November; one only from November to February.

⚓ **Victoria Express** (map II, A2, **111**): Leaves from the terminal at the Regent Hotel on Wharf Street. ☎ 361-9144. Website: www.ferrytravel.com/vexpress. Passenger boat only, also for Port Angeles. Tickets on sale at the tourist office. The journey takes 1 hour, with four daily departures in summer.

⚓ **Washington State Ferries**: ☎ 381-1551 or 656-1531. Website: www.wsdot.wa.gov/ferries. Services operate from Sidney (north of Victoria) to Anacortes in Washington State, USA.

⚓ **Victoria Clipper** (map II, A3, **112**): 1000A Wharf Street. ☎ 382-8100. In Seattle: ☎ (206) 448-5000 or 1-800-888-2535 (toll-free). Website: www.victoriaclipper.com. Express motorboat direct from Victoria to **Seattle**. Several daily departures from mid-June to end-September; three daily departures between 21 May and 17 June and one departure per day during the rest of the year.

By Plane

– **For Vancouver** and **Seattle**: Flights from Victoria International Airport take 25 and 45 minutes respectively.

CHEMAINUS
DIALLING CODE: 250

A little north of Duncan, 1 hour 30 minutes from Victoria, Chemainus is a multifaceted town – a blend of a well-preserved old village and a commercial street with a succession of gift shops and other tourist traps. This small logging village (population 4,000) chose to turn itself into a 'tourist attraction' with an eye to diversification. In 1980 a programme of revitalization was launched to address the decline in the logging industry, and a mural depicting the town's history was painted on the walls of the main building. This led to the Festival of Murals and today there are about 30 murals throughout the village, painted by many North American artists and mainly depicting scenes of local and industrial life of the past.

USEFUL ADDRESSES

🛈 **Chemainus Infocentre**: from Chemino Drive (the main road) turn right onto Willow Street. ☎ 246-3944. Open daily 9am–5pm. A catalogue of B&Bs with photographs is available to help you make your choice.

🛈 **The Arts and Business Council Office**: PO Box 1311. ☎ 246-4701. Fax: 246-3251. Website: www.chemainus.com.

🚌 **Island Coach Lines**: ☎ 246-3341. For buses to Victoria, Nanaimo, Parksville and Port Hardy.

WHERE TO STAY

🛏 **Chemainus Hostel**: 9694 Chemainus Road. ☎ 246-2809. This charming private house at the entrance to the village has six beds for men and six for women at $15 per night. It's well maintained and has a pleasant communal breakfast room and spotless washing facilities. There's also a sitting room and laundry.

🛏 **Olde Mill House B&B**: 9712 Chemainus Road. ☎ 416-0049 or 1-877-770-6060 (toll-free). Fax: 246-4457. Email: oldemill@gec.net. A small, white, wooden house with flowers and old-fashioned charm. Two rooms with bathroom for $75 and a suite with a terrace for $85. Not recommended if you don't like dogs.

NANAIMO   DIALLING CODE: 250

Despite a population of 72,000, Vancouver Island's second largest town (after Victoria) is not very touristy. It's more of an overnight stop when you come off the ferry. It's mainly dependent on the logging industry and has suffered severely from the economic crisis in the Far East.

USEFUL ADDRESSES

🛈 **Tourism Nanaimo**: 2290 Bowen Road, 4 kilometres (2.5 miles) from town, well signposted. ☎ 756-0106 or 1-800-663-7337 (toll-free). Fax: 756-0075. Website: www.tourism.nanaimo.bc.ca. Run by volunteers who can help with reservations.

■ **Budget car hire**: 17 Terminal Avenue South. ☎ 754-7368. Also **Avis** at the airport: 3350 Spitfire Rd, Cassidy. ☎ 245-4166.

🚌 **Island Coach Lines**: ☎ 753-4371. For buses to Victoria and Port Hardy.

■ **Tanis' Web Cafe**: 120 Commercial Street. ☎ 714-0302. Fax: 714-0312. Open daily 8am–10pm (8pm on Sunday). Internet access at $5.50 for an hour, fax services, printers, scanners, etc. Also drinks and sandwiches at modest prices. The decor can't have changed in 20 years, but there's a warm welcome.

WHERE TO STAY AND EAT

♠ **Nicol Street Hostel**: 65 Nicol Street (the main street). ☎ 753-1188. Fax: 753-1185. Open May to mid-September. Rooms for less than $20, with TV, showers and communal kitchens, but don't expect great comfort. Or you can set up your tent. Registration from 4 to 11pm.

♠ **Carey House B&B**: 750 Arbutus Avenue. ☎ 753-3601. One of the cheapest places in town, at about $50 for a double room. Nicely arranged basement rooms with kitchenette. TV room available.

♠ **B&B on the Green**: 2471 Cosgrove Crescent. ☎ 758-4565. You'll get a really friendly welcome in this superb place. Two pretty and com-

fortable rooms cost just over $55 for a double. There's a patio and garden, plus neighbouring golf course.

♠ **Beach Drive B&B**: 1011 Beach Drive. ☎ 753-9140. Well located, not far from the ferry terminal. Prices are $50 for a double and $35 for a single. You'll get a warm welcome.

✕ **Cactus Club Cafe**: No. 801 5800 Turner Road, at the junction with Island Highway. Another in the chain (see 'Where to Eat' in 'Vancouver'), with top-quality meat, speedy service and a cool and trendy ambience. A reliable spot for an overnight stay in Nanaimo, and one of the few places around that's open at night for a drink.

WHAT TO SEE

★ **Nanaimo District Museum**: 100 Cameron Road, next to the tourist office and train station. ☎ 753-1821. Fax: 753-1777. Email: ndmuseum@island.net. Open daily in season. Tuesday to Saturday the rest of the year. This interesting little museum has a reconstruction of a mine shaft, and a section on natural history with lots of fossils.

IN THE AREA

★ **Parksville**: Usually a really sweet, peaceful little town, but for a few days at the beginning of July – when the famous sandcastle competition takes place – the town is unrecognizable as tourists descend and the beer flows. One year attracted a record 30,000 visitors to the sandcastles.

★ **MacMillan Provincial Park**: The road linking Port Alberni, Qualicum Beach and Parksville runs through this park. There's an amazing and unmissable stretch called **Cathedral Grove**, between Cameron Lake and Port Alberni, where you can see the last vestiges of the almost equatorial forest that covered the island more than 1,000 years ago. You can choose from a range of prepared walking trails taking 15–30 minutes.

Coming from Nanaimo, there are two possible routes from the car-park. Start with the one on the left of the road (there's more light). The oldest tree on this trail is estimated to be around 800 years old. A vast expanse of this forest burned down three centuries ago and now the majority of the trees are Douglas fir. There are also some Western red cedars, the biggest trees in Canada. It's curious that these giant trees seem to rest only on airborne roots. The simple explanation is that a seed grows on a dead trunk (the nurse log), the roots progressively grow through the trunk down to the earth and then the nurse log rots away completely. The result is the extraordinary impression of a giant tree suspended in mid-air.

Several immense trees have been cut down, and one of them is used as a bridge. The area has an ingenious ecosystem involving several hundred different plants, fungi and animals. These include the Devil Club, a plant with very broad leaves that allow it to capture the maximum amount of light let through by the giant trees, and the *Oplomax horridum* (abominable weapon), so called because of its poisonous thorns. It's an impressive spectacle when the sun's rays play on the lichens and mosses that hang from the trees. Among the birds and animals here are woodpeckers, squirrels and deer.

PORT ALBERNI   DIALLING CODE: 250

You really should stop here en route from Victoria to Tofino, as this is the departure point for the Pacific Rim National Park. Don't waste too much time here, though, as the road down to the west coast is magnificent and it will take about another 2 hours to get to Ucluelet (*see below*).

USEFUL ADDRESSES

🛈 Tourist office: At the entrance to the town, as you approach from the east.

🚌 Island Coach Lines: ☎ 724-1266. Buses to Victoria via Nanaimo, and daily services to Ucluelet and Tofino.

🚌 Orient Stage Lines: ☎ 723-6924. Daily bus to Ucluelet and Tofino.

■ Alberni Valley Chamber of Commerce: Site 215–C10, Port Alberni. ☎ 724-6535.

WHERE TO STAY

🛏 Friendship Lodge: 3978 8th Avenue. ☎ 723-6511. Close to the centre of town, this small, budget hotel has 14 rooms costing around $15 (dorm bed) or $25–30 (private room) per night, with group rates available. It offers basic comfort and is fine if you're stuck for a place.

IN THE AREA

★ **Clayoquot Sound**: Continuing on the road to Tofino you'll cross this ancient temperate rainforest, which is under threat from felling and road-building. British Columbian ecologists, numerous Greens and nature lovers are all mobilized regularly to fight such projects. You can get an idea of the disaster at 'Black Hole', an area of bare hillsides razed in the 1980s. In the Clayoquot Peace Camps and the ecological shops in Victoria there is lots of information explaining the problem.

– For more information: **Friends of Clayoquot Sound**, Box 489, Tofino, BC V0R 2Z0. ☎ (250) 725-4218. In Victoria: ☎ 386-5255. Fax: 386-4453.

VANCOUVER ISLAND

UCLUELET

Once you get to Ucluelet (pronounced 'You-clou-let'), you're at the end of the road. The name means 'safe and welcoming port' in the local language. In winter there are about 1,800 inhabitants (mostly fishermen) and, in terms of tonnage of fish caught, Ucluelet is the third largest fishing port in British Columbia. It's the only place, besides Tofino, where you can stay near the Pacific Rim National Park, the most beautiful and most popular park on the island.

USEFUL ADDRESS

■ **Ucluelet Chamber of Commerce** (tourist information): ☎ 726-4641. Fax: 726-4611. Website: www.ucluelet.com/ucoc/. Open 10am–6pm. Information about fishing and visits to neighbouring islands, including Clayoquot.

WHERE TO STAY

In summer it's advisable to book.

Campsite

☎ **Ucluelet Campground**: ☎ 726-4355. Well situated at the ocean. At about $25 for two, it's not cheap and not very clean.

☆ – ☆☆ Budget to Moderate

☎ **Sheila's Country Cottages**: 2425 Pacific Rim Highway, 2 kilometres (just over 1 mile) before the village, on the left. ☎ and fax: 726-4655. Open all year. Attractive small cabins among the trees, well back from the road. Barbecue.

☎ **Suzie's Seaview B&B**: 249 Albion Crescent. ☎ 726-1281. The house doesn't look like much but it's really comfortable and the view of the ocean is superb. Rooms cost $65–70. Suzanne prepares gargantuan breakfasts.

☎ **Burley's B&B**: 1073 Helen Road. ☎ and fax: 726-4444. At the end of the village overlooking the ocean. A few nice rooms at reasonable prices ($55–60 for two in season and at the weekend), plus a big, bright sitting room with bay view, billiard table in the basement, large terrace and lovely garden. Non-smokers only. Visa and Mastercard accepted.

☎ **Pacific Rim Motel**: Peninsula Road (the main road). ☎ 726-7728. Well run and reasonable prices, with rooms at $75 in season.

☎ **Thornton Motel**: 1861 Peninsula Road, at the entrance to the village, on the right. ☎ 726-7725. Fax: 726-2099. Email: bjpeder@cedar.alberni.net. Pretty, flowery frontage, painted an eggshell colour. Some of the 18 rooms have kitchenettes and cost around $80.

☎ **Little Beach Resort**: 1187 Peninsula Road, as you leave the village. ☎ 726-4202. Fax: 726-7700. Small, Chinese-run houses with kitchenette and sitting room. Most important, the only hotel in Ucluelet where you can see the ocean from the terrace. Good value for money.

☎ **Canadian Princess**: On the quay, in the harbour. ☎ 726-7726 or 1-800-663-7090 (toll-free). Fax: 726-

7121. Open March to September. For $75 you can sleep in a real cabin on a boat, with a grand saloon and a bridge where you can promenade. Try for a cabin overlooking the water. But, since this is essentially a fishing boat, expect to be woken up very early. Alternatively, the motel next door is run by the same management, but expect to pay about $110.

⚓ **West Coast Motel**: on the harbour. ☎ 726-7732. Marc and Marcelle come from Québec and run this unpretentious hotel, with indoor swimming pool, gym, squash court and sauna. Rooms at various prices.

WHERE TO EAT

✕ **The Matterson House**: 1682 Peninsula Road. This family-run restaurant, popular with local fishermen, serves good soups and sandwiches, and specials of the day for less than $6. The dining room isn't that big but it doubles in size when the terrace is open in fine weather.

✕ **Wickaninnish**: halfway between Ucluelet and Tofino, on the beach of the same name. ☎ 726-2206 and 7706. Open 11am–11pm. It's great to walk along the immense beach before going to watch the sun set fire to the Pacific from the vast bay windows of the dining room here. You'll find the same prices as elsewhere. Free parking.

✕ **Eagle's Nest Pub**: Waterfront Drive; follow the signs for Island Fishing Resort. More a bar than a restaurant (most of the patrons come here for a game of billiards or to watch sport on the big screens), but the atmosphere is warm. Cajun-style cooking, fish and chips and seafood. Burgers for around $8, seafood chowder from $3–5, plus a choice of beers on draught.

FESTIVALS

– **Pacific Rim Summer Festival**: This is held during the last two weeks of July in Ucluelet and Tofino.

– **Pacific Rim Whale Festival**: This takes place in July.

TOFINO   DIALLING CODE: 250

A real corner of paradise, about 5 hours' drive from Victoria and 3 hours from Nanaimo, this fishing port has charming coves and the days seem too short. Tofino is more touristy than Ucluelet because of its excellent location on a peninsula, right on the edge of Tonquin Beach and MacKenzie Beach. Its temperate climate means it attracts visitors all year round, particularly young people for whom this is a special surfing spot.

USEFUL ADDRESSES

🏛 **Tourist office**: Campbell Street (main street). ☎ 725-3414. Open 10am–6pm. In season, if you haven't booked, they can help you find accommodation.

■ **Shuttle bus**: ☎ 726-7779.
🚌 **Island Coach Lines**: ☎ 724-1266.
■ **Tofino Car Rental**: ☎ 725-1221 or 1-800-593-9389 (toll-free).

WHERE TO STAY

Booking is advisable in summer because Tofino gets very full for the limited amount of accommodation, even though new hotels are being built all the time.

Campsites

⚑ Two campgrounds are located inside the Pacific Rim National Park itself. ☎ 726-7721. The one at **Point Green** is the more comfortable.

⚑ **Crystal Cove Resort**: 1165 Cedarwood, 2 kilometres (1 mile) before Tofino. ☎ 725-4213. Fax: 725-4219. About $50 for two, with good facilities, pleasant surroundings and accessible beach. Luxurious cottages also for rent. Sauna and swimming pool.

⚑ **Bella Pacifica Campground**: 400 Mackenzie Beach, about 4 kilometres (2.5 miles) from Tofino. ☎ 725-3400. Fax: 725-2400. From $24–33 in season, depending on the site (about $10 less out of season). Wild location on the edge of a superb beach. Wooden tables and fire pit at each site. Decent facilities and laundry.

⚑ **Hot Springs Cove Campground**: a few hundred metres from Hot Springs Cove Government Dock. Open all year. ☎ 725-3318. Rudimentary facilities, but for less than $10 per person.

☆ Budget

⚑ **The Windrider**: 231 Main Street. ☎ 725-3240. Fax: 725-3280. Email: whole@island.net. An above-average hostel, but for women only. Prices are $25 per night in dormitories and $65 for a private room. Very comfortable, open fire, jacuzzi. A real haven of peace on the seashore.

⚑ **The Wolf House** (Wilp Gybuu): 311 Leighton Way, 5 minutes' walk from town. At the end of the main street, turn left onto First Street then right onto Arnet Street. Leigton Way is the first on the right. ☎ 725-2330. Fax: 725-1205. Email: wilpgybu@island.net. Open all year round. $75–85 a night. Resident proprietors Wendy and Ralph have a modern, wooden house that doesn't look much from the outside. They rent out three really nicely decorated rooms, and a sitting room and living room is available for use. Spectacular ocean view in the winter. Ralph is Indian and makes silver jewellery. Booking advisable. Non-smoking.

⚑ **Whaler's Retreat B&B**: 450 Neill Street. ☎ 725-2669 or 1-800-613-9699 (toll-free). Email: whalers-retreat@island.net. Pretty, wooden house with two rooms at $75 and $85, plus a suite sleeping four at $90. Also a jacuzzi. You'll get a warm welcome, and a good, ample breakfast.

⚑ **B&B Edgar's**: 260 Campbell Street. ☎ 725-3923. Right at the end of the street; go any farther and you're in the ocean. Quiet is guaranteed in this very pleasant house with a superb front garden. It's run by a charming gentleman whose father was apparently the first inhabitant of Tofino. Cosy interior with pleasant rooms at $70 for two; the basement room has its own entrance and is very practical for families. Two bikes available for use. There's a barbecue in the garden. Good value for money.

⚑ **Tides Inn Bed & Breakfast**: 160 Arnet Road. ☎ 725-3765. Open all year. In the south of town; from the post office go down 1st Street, turn right onto Arnet and you'll find this charming oasis almost at the end.

It's one of the best places on the island, an adorable house in shades of brown, with a view over a dreamy little bay. Keep an eye out for the playful dolphin that seems to live there and does pirouettes to entertain the guests. You'll get a really nice welcome from owners Val and James Sloman. Comfortable rooms from $85 to $95 with open fire (one with jacuzzi), and a superb family room at garden level which sleeps five people. Seaside deck from where you can enjoy the landscape, and a hot tub to relax. You'll get a lovely breakfast. Book ahead.

Park Place: 341 Park Street. ☎ 725-3477. Open all year. At the end of the world, hidden in the woods. A green avenue leads to this ravishing house in wood and glass, with one of the best panoramic views in the area. A long flowery balcony, hanging over the rocks runs all around. It's ideal for watching whales, seals and dolphins, and incredible sunsets. Below, there's a deserted little beach. Hosts Joan and Jim Bristow welcome you most courteously and offer two rooms for around $85 for two, plus a generous breakfast. There's a supplement if you stay for only one night (but who could think of staying only one night?).

Schooner Motel: On the main road, very central. ☎ 725-3478. Attractively priced if there are a few of you. Facilities include fridge, cooker, bath and TV.

☆☆ – ☆☆☆ Moderate to Expensive

Weigh West: 634 Campbell Street. ☎ 725-3277 or 1-800-665-8922 (toll-free). Fax: 725-3922. E-mail: wwest@weighwest.com. This hotel looks onto the harbour next to the Blue Heron (see 'Where to Eat') and charges $100–130 for a double room with fireplace, hot tub and kitchen.

Ocean Village Beach Resort: 555 Hellsen Drive, on Mackenzie Beach 3 kilometres (2 miles) from Tofino. ☎ 725-3755. Expect to pay $105 from June to September, and very attractive rates out of season. The spacious cedar cottages in superb surroundings look like the hulls of overturned boats, and many have extensive ocean views. Equipped kitchens, swimming pool and laundry.

Crystal Cove Beach Resort: 1165 Cedarwood, 2 kilometres (just over a mile) before Tofino. ☎ 725-4213. Fax: 725-4219. Email: crystalc@cedar.alberni.net. Superb log bungalows located right on the water's edge can accommodate up to six people, at $170 a night. Better value for groups ($190 for two rooms). About $10 for each extra person. Very comfortable and nicely furnished, with equipped kitchen, sitting room with open fire, big bathroom.

Middle Beach Lodge: 400 Mackenzie Beach Road, 3 kilometres (2 miles) before Tofino. ☎ 725-2900. Fax: 725-2901. This is a small family hotel between the forest and the beach with a pleasant sitting room overlooking the ocean. Rooms are around $165 a night, and cabins $175. A second, equally elegant and restful, lodge opened recently. This is the most convivial of the hotels on the Pacific shore.

Best Western Tin Wis: just before Tofino. ☎ 725-4445 or 1-800-661-9995 (toll-free). Fax: 725-4447. Modern, wooden building looking onto lawns and pine forests at the edge of the beach. The location on the Pacific shore is superb and the bay windows overlooking the ocean distract you from the rather ordinary furniture. On the other hand, the prices are attractive, at around

$135 for rooms sleeping three or four.

🛏 **Pacific Sands Beach Resort**: 1421 Park Rim Highways, 7 kilometres (4 miles) before Tofino. ☎ 725-332 or 1-800-565-2322 (toll-free). Fax: 725-3155. Across from a superb bay, a very pleasant resort with a lawn overlooking the beach. Prices range from $150–195, and the rooms with corner kitchens are spacious. For a little more money you can even take a dip in a jacuzzi with an ocean view before warming up in front of the open fire in your room.

☆☆☆☆ Splash Out

🛏 **Wickaninnish Inn**: around 12 kilometres (8 miles) before Tofino. ☎ 725-3100 or 1-800-333-4604 (toll-free). Fax: 725-3110. Website: www.wickinn.com. A very romantic place; when there are ferocious storms in winter, the waves crashing onto the rocks are fabulous. Prices range from $300–380 in June and September, and around $100 less the rest of the year. All rooms have an open fire and a balcony with ocean view; some also have a jacuzzi. Saltwater and other beauty treatments extra. Non-smokers only.

WHERE TO EAT

🍴 **The Blue Heron Restaurant and Dockside Marine Pub**: Campbell Street. ☎ 725-3277. Seafood fans can really get stuck in at this bar-restaurant on the harbour serving salmon and French fries, Dungeness crab, cod and halibut. In the pub you can have snacks or choose from a selection of sandwiches (excellent homemade granary bread). There's a lovely view of the bay and the mountains beyond.

🍴 **The Common Loaf**: opposite the post office at the end of the village. A pleasant self-service restaurant for breakfast, to eat either inside or on the terrace, popular with backpackers and local surfers. Tasty muffins cost $1.25.

🍴 **Sea Shanty Restaurant**: 300 Main Street. ☎ 725-2902. Seafood platters cost from $8–15 at lunch-

time and $10–22 in the evening. Wood decor and a pleasant terrace from where you can watch the hydroplanes and enjoy the view over Clayoquot Sound.

🍴 **The Schooner**: 331 Campbell Street. ☎ 725-3444. Open daily in summer noon to evening. Around $25 per person. This lovely red house with a very nautical atmosphere has its bar in the prow of an overturned boat, and the kitchen in the hull. Marine charts and photos of boats cover the walls and complete the attractive decor. The speciality here is a seafood platter of shrimp, scallops, sole, salmon, halibut, snapper and grilled oysters. The seafood chowder is also most welcome after an expedition out on the ocean, followed by pecan pie with raspberries.

WHAT TO SEE AND DO

★ **Pacific Rim National Park**

– **Information Center**: at the park entrance going towards Tofino. ☎ 726-4212. Fax: 726-7721. Open daily 9.30am–6.30pm. You'll find all sorts of brochures and all the information you need, including details of the walks and trails. Buy your pass for the park, otherwise your car will be towed away if you park in the car-parks.

– **Wickanninish Interpretive Center**: Open 10.30am–6pm in season. Everything on the local fauna and submarine life, plus video shows and exhibitions (from mid-June to September).

Park Routes and Trails

There are lots of routes to follow, either along the ocean shore, out to sea or into the heart of the damp forest. This brief selection highlights the best of each kind. Contacts are given for tour operators and more information.

– **Ocean shore**: This walk on Frank Island (between Chesterman Beach and Cox Bay) is best done towards the end of the day, two hours before sunset. As you leave Tofino by car, and just after The Dolphin Motel (on the left), take the little road on the right (Lynn Road) that leads to a car-park. Then walk to the beach and turn left, following the coast. Before you get to Frank Island you'll see superb villas in all different styles that are widely spaced and completely lost in the wilderness. Note that Frank Island is only accessible at low tide, so be sure to go back before high tide. Here, amid superb wild surroundings, you'll find peace pure and simple.

– **The heart of the forest**: A trail lasting about 45 minutes is laid on logs and marked out by explanatory signboards. To get a really good view you have to climb Radar Hill, where you can see the radar that was built during the Cold War to track missiles. But it's quite difficult to see whales from here. If you have time, extend your journey and travel on to Spring Cove. It's not much more expensive, and it will take a good half day. You'll get the chance to see whales, walruses and sea lions, to walk through the damp forest and bathe in warm ponds. It's a really amazing experience to talk to the person next to you in these tiny pools while currents of iced water from the ocean chill your fingertips.

– **Boat trip out to sea**: You're almost certain to see whales when out on the ocean, because the various companies inform each other by radio about the best locations at any time. The grey whale only migrates from March to May, but some small schools sometimes delay until October.

■ **Chinook Charter**: 450 Campbell Street. ☎ 725-3431 or 1-800-665-3646 (toll-free). Fax: 725-2360. Email: chinook@cedar.alberni.net. Prices are the same as in Tofino: $50 to see the whales, $75 for a trip as far as the hot springs. Perhaps not the best company, but that doesn't detract from the shiver of anxiety you feel when you close in on a whale. They have flexible times and will even go out for only two people (in a zodiac). Trips also stop off at the bird reserves. All operators give you a second chance if you don't see any whales on the first trip.

■ **Seaside Adventures**: ☎ 725-2292 or 1-888-332-4252 (toll-free). Fax: 725-2390. Website: www.seaside-adventures.com. You can book up to an hour before departure, which means you don't have to take a risk with the weather. However, bear in mind that the boats can be full if you leave it to the last minute.

– **Salmon fishing** in Tofino will remain a memorable event for anglers. Guides set off with early risers on a long morning's fishing out on the ocean, in search of this noble fish that swims in these cold waters. Most of the guides have offices in the main street, with signs outside.

– You can also hire a **kayak** for a wonderful tour of the bay and its numerous islands.

– **Whale-spotting**: If you want to see them outside an aquarium, a motorboat trip can help you get close to them in their natural habitat. There are plenty of operators along the main road.

– A flight on a **hydroplane** is certainly pretty expensive, but absolutely unforgettable. Information and reservations available from the harbour at the end of the village. **Tofino Air-lines Ltd**: ☎ 725-4454.

CAMPBELL RIVER   DIALLING CODE: 250

A 5-hour drive from Victoria will only take you halfway up Vancouver Island, so to get this far, you have to be a determined angler or hiker. Campbell River is known as the capital of salmon fishing. If you're not a fisherman, Strathcona Provincial Park, 30 minutes away, is one of the wildest on the island and features some splendid walking trails.

■ **Campbell River and District Chamber of Commerce**: 1235 Shoppers Row. ☎ 287-4636. Fax: 286-6490. Website: www.vquest.com/crchamber. Tourist information office.

WHERE TO STAY

⌂ **Rivers Ridge B&B**: 2243 Steelhead Road. ☎ 286-9696. Two rooms with bathroom for $60. You'll get a warm welcome from hosts June and Frank, plus a generous breakfast of homemade bread, scones, muffins and jam. Kitchen and barbecue available on request.

⌂ **Sea Blue Salmon Charters**: 623 Holm Road, at Willow Point, 10 minutes from the beach. ☎ 923-6079. Fax: 923-7332. Doubles cost from $55–59 in this simple, pleasant house that also arranges salmon-fishing trips.

⌂ **Passage View Motel**: 517 Island Highway. ☎ 286-1156 or 1-877-286-1156 (toll-free). Fax: 286-1139. Classic motel in grey-and-blue wood on the edge of the ocean, 10 minutes' walk from the centre of Campbell River. Allow $50–70 for a room, plus $10 for a kitchenette. Peaceful, with a lovely view of Discovery Passage.

⌂ **The Anchor Inn**: 216 Island Highway. ☎ 286-1131 or 1-800-663-7227 (toll-free). Fax: 287-4055. Website: www.anchorinn.bc.ca. Overlooking the ocean, and appreciably more expensive, starting at $150 a night. They organize fishing trips (but they're expensive). Swimming pool and jacuzzi.

WHERE TO EAT

✗ **On Line Gourmet**: 970 Shoppers Row, just before the Chamber of Commerce on the left. ☎ 286-6521. Open Monday to Friday 8am–5.30pm. Saturday 8.30am–4pm. Simple and welcoming cyber-café, with a green painted wood decor. Particularly good for breakfast. Traditional set meals or muffins, bagels or sandwiches with different fillings from $6. Internet access at $5 an hour, $3.50 for 30 minutes (free on Thursday 3–5.30pm).

✕ **Moxie's**: 1360 Island Highway. ☎ 830-1500. In a new commercial complex, this is a family-run restaurant that's popular with the people of Campbell River. Substantial sandwiches and soups for less than $7. It's *the* place for Sunday lunch, when the kids get stuck into ice-creams that are bigger than they are. A real jostle for brunch.

✕ **Sushi bar**: in a wing of the Anchor Inn, overlooking the ocean (*see* 'Where to Stay'). Equally fascinating spectacle inside, because the sushi is made in front of you. An assortment of sashimi for $19, sushi $15 and tempura $4. If you still have doubts about eating raw fish, here it's so fresh it just melts in your mouth. Voted the best place for sushi.

✕ **Tex Mex**: located in the opposite wing of the Anchor Inn, in direct competition with the Sushi Bar. Noted mainly for its margaritas ($5) and relaxed atmosphere. Meals around $10 a head.

WHAT TO SEE AND DO

★ **Discovery Pier**: Access to this wooden pier going into the ocean is free if you're just interested in looking, but $2 if you want to fish for a couple of hours. You can hire rods and even take part in competitions to catch the biggest salmon.

★ **Quadra Island**: Ferries run roughly every hour, the journey takes about 15 minutes and costs just $0.50. There are lots of opportunities to hire zodiacs or fishing boats or go on organized tours – fishing, boat trips to see whales or bears or just to admire the scenery. The tourist office can advise you on the most suitable trip.

★ **Strathcona Provincial Park**: 50 kilometres (31 miles) from Campbell River. The biggest park on the island features lakes, glaciers, forests and the Delta Falls, which remains an untouched wilderness as it takes several days' walk to get there. They're the highest waterfalls in Canada at 440 metres (1,443 feet). There's a superb lodge (*see below*). When Jim Boulding inherited this land, he thought he'd make his fortune, as his father did, by chopping everything down. Then he changed his mind and decided to build a lodge so people could enjoy the wilds. In spite of his Québécois accent, David comes from Lille in France, and looks after the wilderness activities.

– Lots of trails start from Strathcona Park Lodge (*see below*), but don't be put off by the apparent length of the walks. For example, the walk to Lupin Falls, estimated to take 20 minutes, actually took just 10 minutes there and back, plus another 10 minutes for a rest and to take some photos. From the lodge you can also hire kayaks, scale the glaciers or set off to discover the wild animals.

⌂ **Strathcona Park Lodge**: 40 kilometres (25 miles) from Campbell River, at the park entrance. ☎ 286-3122. Fax: 286-6010. Website: www.strathcona. bc.ca. Small cabins scattered along the lake with simple, comfortable rooms at $40–70 with shared facilities and $70–90 with private bathroom (additional $20 for lakeside room). Cabin hire is $95 (with attractive deals for groups), and also beds in dormitories. They offer all-inclusive packages (meals, activities, etc.), including the 'Alpine chalet' on Mount Washington, which is ideal for doing ski trails in winter or climbing in summer.

IN THE AREA

★ **Sooke** (**East Sooke Park**): This isn't far by bus, and offers well-marked hiking trails, including an extensive one along the shore taking about 8 hours.

★ **Carmanah Pacific Park**: East of the West Coast Trail (*see below*) and accessible by car, here you'll find lush vegetation and a few more giant survivors of the rain forest, some as tall as 90 metres (295 feet).

★ **Goldstream Park**: On Highway 1 towards Duncan, this is easily reached by bus from Victoria; stop at Freeman King Visitor's Center. Many paths meander under the splendid Western red cedars or the Douglas firs, some of which are 500–600 years old. In the autumn there's a salmon run up the river. It's a lovely walk of about 1 hour to the top of Mount Finlayson for great views.

★ Any keen historians could go much farther north to **Gold River**, west of Campbell River, and then on to **Muchalar Inlet** from where you can take a boat to the place where Captain Cook first disembarked.

★ **Telegraph Cove**: Right in the north, just before Port Hardy, you'll find the prettiest village on Vancouver Island, built in the 1920s and '30s. Only a dozen houses were built, on piles, each bearing a plaque recounting the history of the inhabitants. This is also one of the best places to see orcas (killer whales).

THE WEST COAST TRAIL

This is a superb and sometimes challenging hiking trail, 77 kilometres (48 miles) long, that takes between six and eight days to complete. A shorter alternative is possible (from Pachana to Nitinat Narrows).

True to its name, it runs along the west coast from the village of Bamfield (in the north) to the village of Port Renfrew (in the south). The path was originally created to lead survivors of shipwrecks back to civilization.

The landscape varies immensely, the sunsets are unforgettable and you can spend evenings by the camp fire in places where few have trodden. But note that, once you've set out on the West Coast Trail, the only way to get off it is to turn around and go back. The northwest section is fairly easy going, but it becomes much more difficult in the southeast.

Note also that, because of the success of the trail and the resulting problems of pollution and erosion, you now have to book several months in advance. The park authorities want to keep the number of walkers down (to 52 a day) to avoid the path being damaged too rapidly.

If you plan to tackle the trail, staff at the information centres will help you plan your hike (*see* 'Useful Addresses'). Make sure you pick up a copy of the indispensable *Contour Map of the West Coast Trail* that shows all the campsites and springs, and details the dangers, etc. Let the rangers know your departure date. If you don't reappear, they will send out search parties. In any case, avoid leaving on your own.

GETTING THERE

By Car

– **From the north**: It takes about 2 hours to drive from Port Alberni to Bamfield (100 kilometres/63 miles) on an unsealed road. Alternatively, take the ferry from Port Alberni to Bamfield; it heads down the Alberni Inlet and takes 4 hours.

– **From the south**: It's also 100 kilometres (63 miles) from Victoria to Port Renfrew, of which 80 kilometres (50 miles) is sealed road, and the trip takes around 1 hour 30 minutes. You can also go via Cowichan Lake, 56 kilometres (35 miles) on an unsealed road, taking an hour.

By Bus

– The **West Coast Trail Connector** goes from Victoria to Port Renfrew daily. Departures are at 7am and 2pm, and the journey lasts 2 hours 30 minutes. The bus also goes via French Beach, Jordan River and China Beach.

– **For Bamfield**: **West Coast Trail**: 1299 Camrose Crescent. ☎ 380-0580. Information: ☎ 985-4301. Departures daily at 8am from opposite the Royal British Columbia Museum in Victoria. Journey time: 4 hours. Tickets are quite expensive. Alternatively, you could join the numerous hitchhikers on the two routes.

USEFUL ADDRESSES

❶ Two information centres (one at each end of the trail) are open daily 9am–5pm in summer:

– **Pachena Bay**: 5 kilometres (about 3 miles) north of Bamfield. ☎ 728-3234.

– **Port Renfrew**: next to the Recreation Centre. ☎ 647-5434.

– **Pacific Rim National Park**: ☎ 726-4212. Fax: 726-7721. *See also* 'What to See and Do' *in* 'Tofino'.

– **Provincial Park Office**: ☎ 387-4363.

WHERE TO STAY

Campsites are signposted all along the route and marked on the map. They're usually located near small rivers and, although the water is usually drinkable, it's wise to boil it first. Lighting fires is permitted on beaches only. Bring a long rope with you and use it to tie your food (in a sealed bag) up in a tree out of reach of the bears (along a branch, away from the trunk). When you leave, make sure to take *all* your rubbish with you and don't leave anything behind.

LEAVING VANCOUVER ISLAND

– **For Port Hardy**: From Victoria it's about 10 hours by bus.

– **For Prince Rupert**: Enjoy a stunning 15-hour ferry crossing from **Port Hardy**, spotting orcas and dolphins en route. The land- and seascapes are similar to the fjords of Norway. There's one departure every two days at around 7.30am, so you'll have to spend the night in Port Hardy. If you have a car, booking and payment in advance is essential in summer. Expect to pay about $420 for a car and two passengers. ☎ (604) 444-2890 or 1-800-724-5223 (toll-free). Fax 381-5452. Website: www.bcferries.bc.ca.

– For **Prince George**: You can get from by bus and then return to Vancouver by bus or, preferably, by train. It takes a bit longer, but the landscapes are wilder and the photo stops are much better.

Prince Rupert to Prince George

This is really just a way of getting to the Rockies, even though the route is sometimes very beautiful, especially at the beginning when it follows the Skeena River. Remember to fill up with fuel before the journey, as there's at least 100 kilometres (63 miles) between stations out here. Try to avoid spending the night in Prince George, which is a big industrial town (as you'll notice by the smell). A couple of more pleasant towns in which to overnight are Smithers, which has B&Bs, and Fort St James, which is on a lake. Rooms may be hard to find, so try to book ahead.

USEFUL ADDRESSES

Dialling Code: 250

🅱 Travel Info: 1st Avenue and McBride Street. ☎ 624-5637 or 1-800-667-1994 (toll-free).

🚌 Greyhound Lines: 822 3rd Avenue West. ☎ 624-5090 or 1-800-661-8747 (toll-free).

⚓ BC Ferries: The embarkation point is 3 kilometres (nearly 2 miles) from the centre. Ferries leave every two days for Port Hardy (north tip of Vancouver Island) and for the Queen Charlotte Islands. ☎ 624-9627 or 1-800-663-7600 (toll-free). If you have a car, don't forget to make a reservation and pay for your ticket to secure your booking. These ferries are often very full.

WHERE TO STAY

There are lots of hotels, but they're quite impersonal. Here's a selection of the best, located on the coast and charging fair prices.

In Prince Rupert

🛏 Inn on the Harbour: 720 1st Avenue. ☎ 624-9107 or 1-800-663-8155 (toll-free). Fax: 627-8232.

🛏 Ocean View: 950 1st Avenue. ☎ 624-6259. Clean, but otherwise only for emergency use.

🛏 Pioneer Rooms: 167 3rd Avenue. ☎ 624-2334. A blue house from another century with a weird atmosphere, but the rooms are very cheap and there's a communal kitchen and facilities outside.

🛏 Pacific Inn: 909 3rd Ave West. ☎ 627-1711. Fax: 627-4212. Comfortable hotel with average prices (doubles from $75–85). You'll get a friendly welcome.

BRITISH COLUMBIA

Elsewhere Along the Route

⌂ **Stuart Lodge**: 5 kilometres (3 miles) past Fort St James. ☎ 996-7917. Five rooms with facilities and balconies overlooking the lake. The charming host, Gerhard, will lend you a canoe or rent you a motorboat.

⌂ **Glacier B&B**: before Smithers, on the way to Glacier Gulch. ☎ 847-2020. Website: www.bbcanada.com/1503.html. Facing the glacier, this is one of the most pleasant B&Bs in British Columbia. The lovely wooden house is surrounded by a garden with a pond, and there's also a fountain. There's a sitting room with a billiard table. The host, Barbara, is charming and her three

rooms cost between $55 and $70. A canoe is also available.

⌂ **Lakeside B&B**: 1 kilometre from Smithers. ☎ and fax: 847-9174. A magnificent view of the glacier and the dock right on the lake. Four rooms at attractive prices.

⌂ **The Ptarmigan B&B**: take the road for Glacier Gulch just before Smithers and it's on the right. ☎ 847-9508. A little less attractive than the others because it doesn't have a view, but the three rooms in this cabin, deep in the woods, are incomparably nicer than the motel rooms in town. On top of that, hosts Margaret and Dave are delightful.

BRITISH COLUMBIA

WHAT TO SEE

★ **Prince Rupert**: You have no option but to stay here overnight, as the ferry arrives very late and leaves very early. Despite its beautiful location, it's not a town of great interest.

★ **North Pacific Cannery**: in the village of Port Edward, 20 kilometres (12.5 miles) from Prince Rupert. ☎ 628-3538. Open daily in summer 10am–7pm. Rest of the year Wednesday to Sunday 10am–4pm. Visiting a salmon cannery might seem like a ridiculous idea, but you also visit the village built on wooden piles. It was founded in 1889 and Japanese, Chinese, Indians and Europeans lived together here. It's one of the few well-preserved villages in British Columbia.

★ **Ksan Indian Village Museum**: 2–3 kilometres (1–2 miles) from the Highway and Hazelton. Open 10.30am–4.30pm. Closed Tuesday and Wednesday in winter. There are guided tours every hour around this reconstructed native Indian village, and they are the only way you can get into the houses. In the summer, there's a show every Friday.

★ **Fort St James**: A little village near the superb Lake Stuart. Open in summer 9.30am–5.30pm. Mid-June to September 10am–5pm. The fort has been restored to its original state of 1896 when the Hudson's Bay Company was in business here. In July and August, actors re-create scenes of life in the past.

MOUNT ROBSON PROVINCIAL PARK

DIALLING CODE: 250

At 3,954 metres (13,000 feet), Mount Robson is the highest peak in the Canadian Rockies. It's a superb, imposing mountain but its summit is often swathed in clouds.

USEFUL ADDRESS

🛈 **Travel Info**: at the foot of Mount Robson. Open May to September 8am–5pm. Mid-June to August 8am–9pm. You must register here if you want to camp near Lake Berg (*see below*).

WHERE TO STAY AND EAT

⌂ **Robson Meadows** and **Robson River**: Near the Travel Info office in the park. Two campsites, with 125 and around 20 spaces respectively. Showers, toilets and firewood available in both. Good departure points for hiking.

⌂ **Robson Shadows Campground**: a few kilometres past the Travel Info office, just after the eastern entrance to the park. ☎ 566-4821. Fax: 566-9190. Located on the banks of the Fraser River, with around 30 places for about $15 per night. There's a mini snack bar, and you can go rafting with the Mount Robson Whitewater Rafting Co. (☎ 566-4879) or do other activities. Pleasant atmosphere.

⌂ **Mount Robson Lodge**: same location, contact numbers and services as Robson Shadows Campground (*see above*). About 20 fully equipped cabins ranging from $70–100. Decent facilities.

⌂ **Terracana**: 30 kilometres (19 miles) from the Travel Info office going towards Prince George. ☎ 968-4304. Fax: 968-4445. The cabins are extremely comfortable and overlook the Fraser River. Very peaceful and isolated, and appreciably more expensive than Mount Robson Lodge. Horse riding, rafting, jet-boating available.

✕ **Café Mount Robson**: same location as the Travel Info office. A pleasant, well-run place for a snack (good burgers). Also self-service.

WHAT TO SEE

★ **Lake Kinney**: The loveliest walk in the area is up towards the lakes that surround Mount Robson, and a round trip to Lake Kinney takes about 2 hours 30 minutes.

★ **Lake Berg**: This is the more beautiful of the two lakes, but it's a hike of 22 kilometres (about 14 miles). Some parts of the trail up here may be tough going for soft urbanites used to getting around by car, but the wilderness is so superb that you'll soon forget the odd aches and pains and the weight of your backpack.

On offer are grand mountain vistas, very dense and rich undergrowth, torrents of water rushing under suspension bridges, impressive waterfalls that crash straight down, and continuous lines of rocks and gravel left by a glacier. Finally you get to Lake Berg where chunks of glacier sometimes break off into its turquoise waters.

There are several organized campsites near the lake or on the way, and campers must pay a fee and register at the Travel Info office. There are also two shelters (without beds) on the lake shore, and it's great to come across a few other bravehearts. It's a good idea to set up camp in one of the sites near the lake as a base for some of the other walks that go on from here, especially up to Snowbird Pass. This will easily fill two or three days. Alternatively, you could always get a helicopter to drop you at the lake on Monday or Friday – departures from Valemount cost just over $100 per person.

WELLS GRAY PROVINCIAL PARK

DIALLING CODE: 250

The entrance is about 40 kilometres (25 miles) from Clearwater. The park itself isn't particularly spectacular but you can tackle numerous trails, some on horseback, by mountain bike or canoe, and you can see the loveliest waterfalls in British Columbia. There are also dozens of inviting walking trails. Once inside the park you can drive on a certain number of the routes, even down to the lake. Some of the secondary routes are only accessible by four-wheel-drive vehicles. There are also several ranches out in the wilds – good enough reasons to stay for a day or two.

USEFUL ADDRESS

Information Centre: in Clearwater, 40 kilometres (25 miles) from the park entrance. ☎ 674-2646. Open 9am–5pm. As ever, you can get all the information you need about the park and the area.

WHERE TO STAY

The best option for accommodation in the area is to stay on a ranch, which generally offers you roof (usually a cabin), or a site to pitch your tent.

Wells Gray Ranch and Campsite: 27 kilometres (17 miles) from Clearwater. ☎ 674-2774. Fax: 674-2197. A Western feel to the 10 rooms, entirely fitted out in wood and overlooking fields of galloping horses. A tiny chapel and a few teepees complete the scene. In the saloon, an ancient Wurlitzer plays to accompany your meals, which are costly but of good quality; you'll get a good buffet and substantial breakfast. The campsite is reasonably priced, and there are lots of activities on offer if you can afford them.

Nakiska Ranch: about 30 kilometres (19 miles) from Clearwater. ☎ 674-3655. Fax: 674-3387. Three cabins and two rooms in a splendid landscape, but no campsite. Run by Swiss Germans. If you don't like dogs, you should consider staying elsewhere.

Trophy Moutain Buffalo Ranch and Campsite: 20 kilometres (12.5 miles) from Clearwater. ☎ 674-3095. Fax: 674-3131. The four rooms are rather charmless and the atmosphere is not very relaxing; it's good to see the bison.

Helmcken Falls Lodge: at the park entrance. ☎ 674-3657. Fax: 674-2971. Pleasant hotel rather like an Austrian chalet. More expensive than the previous places. You can get dinner here.

Wooly Acres: 5 kilometres (about 3 miles) from Clearwater, taking the road on the right. ☎ 674-3508. Fax: 674-2316. This B&B is the farthest into the park, but it's considerably less expensive than the others. Three big rooms in a chalet with lots of sheep close by. Warm welcome.

WHERE TO EAT

✕ **Flour Meadow Bakery and Café**: from Clearwater, take the road for Wells Gray Park; the bakery is 300 metres farther on, on the right. ☎ 674-3654. Perfect for breakfast, plus muffins, buns, biscuits and all sorts of bread. Also a few light salads at lunchtime.

Has a pleasant terrace for fine weather.

✕ **Clearwater Country Inn**: Clearwater. Not very luxurious, but the setting isn't bad and the food is decent, even though they don't serve anything surprising. You won't find much else around here.

WHAT TO SEE

Here are a few places you shouldn't miss:

★ **Helmcken Falls**: Enjoy spectacular views as the river thunders along and plummets 141 metres (463 feet) down the canyon.

★ **Bailey's Falls**: Around the end of August and the beginning of September you can witness the superb sight of salmon weighing at least 15 kilograms (33 pounds) desperately trying to jump the falls.

★ **Lake Clearwater**: Hire a canoe here and spend one or even several nights in the campsites on the lake shore. It's a sort of return to nature that's both calming and disorientating. If you're in more of a hurry you can take a boat trip to Rainbow Falls (about 4 hours) with Clearwater Lake Tours: ☎ 674-2121 or 674-3052.

MOUNT REVELSTOKE AND GLACIER NATIONAL PARKS   DIALLING CODE: 250

The town of Revelstoke can be a pleasant stopover on the way to the Rockies if you go through these national parks.

USEFUL ADDRESSES

🄳 **Revelstoke Tourist office**: Revelstoke, at the junction of Highway 1 and Highway 23 North. ☎ 837-7451. Open daily May to September 9am–7pm. Also at 204 Campbell Avenue in the town centre. ☎ 837-5345. Open all year Monday to Fri-

day 8.30am–5pm. Saturday in summer 10am–5pm.
– **Rogers Pass Information Centre**: in Glacier National Park. ☎ 837-7500 or 814-5253. Open 8am–8.30pm in summer. 9am–5pm midseason. 7am–5pm in winter.

WHERE TO STAY

🛏 There are two **campsites** in Glacier National Park at Illecillewaet, 3 kilometres (about 2 miles) west of Rogers Pass, and near the Loop River, 2 kilometres (just over a mile)

away. No need to book, they're on a first come, first served basis. Rudimentary facilities, no showers, but toilets and running water. Open June to the end of September.

⚓ **Canyon Hot Springs**: between the two parks on Highway 1. ☎ 837-2420. Fax: 837-3171. In a beautiful forest setting, really nice with two swimming pools with naturally hot water at 40°C (104°F) and 26°C (79°F). You can swim without camping, but there's a charge in both cases. Rickety washing facilities, and no showers.

Around Revelstoke

⚓ **The Regent**: 112 East 1st Street, Revelstoke. ☎ 837-2107. Fax: 837-9669. A somewhat old-fashioned hotel in the middle of town.

⚓ **Nelles Ranch**: 3 kilometres (2 miles) from Revelstoke, on Highway 23 South. ☎ 837-3800. A B&B in a real ranch on the edge of the forest, with a corral full of horses. If you can afford it, choose the largest of the nine rooms, which is three times the size of the smallest and hardly costs any more.

⚓ **The Peaks Lodge**: 5 kilometres (3 miles) west of Revelstoke, on Highway 1. ☎ 837-2176 or 1-800-668-0330 (toll-free). Fax: 837-2133. Pretty little hotel decorated with beautiful Provençal fabric. Lovely view but it's a bit close to the road.

⚓ **Three Valley Lake Château**: 19 kilometres (12 miles) west of Revelstoke, on Highway 1. ☎ 837-2109. Fax: 837-5220. Classic rooms with little balconies overlooking lovely gardens and the lake. It has a swimming pool, and is not very expensive for families or groups. The owner has built a ghost town next door, with relocated or rebuilt buildings. Guided visits take 45 minutes, from 8am to 5pm.

Around Glacier National Park

⚓ **Canyon Hot Springs**: between the two parks on Highway 1. You can rent cabins sleeping two to eight people. It's a really nice place, but expensive for what it is. *See also above.*

⚓ **Hillside Lodge**: 13 kilometres (8 miles) before Golden, coming from Glacier National Park. ☎ and fax: 344-7281. Four spacious rooms with balconies in a big chalet in the wilds, with a torrent below and mountains all around. Also five isolated cabins for rent. They serve breakfast and dinner in this very pleasant place, with warm decor and a friendly welcome.

⚓ **Blaeberry Mountain Lodge**: signposted about 12 kilometres (8 miles) before Golden, coming from Glacier National Park. ☎ and fax: 344-5296. Run by Renata, a German ex-pat, this lodge has a pond, some swings, and wild horses in the meadows, all surrounded by a magnificent amphitheatre of mountains. There are four rooms in a big cabin and two individual cabins at unbeatable prices. Renata and her husband also rent mountain bikes and organize rafting trips. It's the ideal place to chill out, and highly recommended.

☆☆☆ More expensive

⚓ **Glacier Park Lodge**: on the roadside at Rogers Pass in Glacier Park. ☎ 837-2126 or 1-800-528-1234 (toll-free). Fax: 837-2130. A hotel with no great charm but ideally located in the middle of Glacier National Park. About $150 for two in summer (half as much in low season). There's also a grocery store and a filling station that's open at night.

WHAT TO SEE

★ **Railway Museum**: Revelstoke, along the railway track (Victoria Road). Open in summer 9am–8pm. Out of season, check with the museum (☎ 837-6060) or the tourist office. Entrance charge. This includes excellent illustrated panels of old photographs recounting the building of the railway through the Rockies. There's a magnificent locomotive from 1948, and even one of the last mechanics to explain how it worked.

★ **Mount Revelstoke**: As you leave Revelstoke on the road to Golden, take the road on the left that snakes around for 25 kilometres (16 miles). From the car-park you can take a shuttle or walk up through the meadows. From the summit there's a magnificent (and very rare) 360-degree view of the Rocky Mountains.

★ **Glacier National Park**: This is just away from the highest ridge of the Rockies but it's really worth a detour if you have the time. There are not too many opportunities to walk, but the landscape is superb.

YOHO AND KOOTENAY NATIONAL PARKS

DIALLING CODE: 250

Continuing on the route to the Rockies from the last two parks, you'll get to Golden, a town of absolutely no interest except for its numerous motels and its strategic location for the various parks in the region. From Golden you can get to Yoho and Kootenay, two national parks which, although small, are of great interest. In Kootenay, Radium Hot Springs is a large village with well-built and attractive motels. The town owes it name to the hot-water pools which are certainly pleasant, but pretty small.

USEFUL ADDRESSES

🛈 Yoho information centre: Field, in Yoho Park. ☎ 343-6783. Open 8.30am–7pm in summer. 9am–5pm in spring and autumn. 9am–4pm in winter.

🛈 Kootenay information centre: In the swimming pool building at Radium Hot Springs. ☎ 347-9505. Open 9am–7pm in summer. 9.30am–4.30pm in spring and autumn. Closed in winter.

WHERE TO STAY

In Yoho National Park

🛏 The only campsite in the park with showers is at **Kicking Horse**, but it's quite expensive and you can't book ahead.
🛏 **Lake O'Hara**: There's a 30-site campground near the lake and it's essential to book far in advance.

☎ 343-6433. A few extra places, which are very sought-after, are made available at the Field information centre daily. It's impossible to book these.
🛏 **West Louise Lodge**: right in the middle of Yoho Park, not far from

Field and 11 kilometres (7 miles) west of Lake Louise, on Highway 1. ☎ 343-6311. Fax: 343-6786. Despite being near the highway, the lodge overlooks the lake and also has sumptuous views of the snow-capped mountains. Reasonable prices. Breakfast included.

☖ **Lake O'Hara Lodge**: 11 kilometres (7 miles) from the Trans-Canada Highway after Field. ☎ 343-6418 or (403) 678-4110 out of season. It's impossible to get accommodation at this magical place unless you book a long time in advance at Yoho Park (☎ 343-6783). It's on one of the loveliest and best-preserved lakes in the Rockies. In winter you can ski to the lodge; in summer you have to go by bus or on foot (but it's a 14-kilometre (9-mile) walk!). The lodge is strictly non-smoking.

In Kootenay National Park

☖ There are three campsites in Kootenay Park and, again, it's first come, first served. The only one with showers is **Redstreak**, but it's fairly expensive and very close to Radium Hot Springs.

☖ **Kootenay Park Lodge**: on Highway 93, right in the middle of the park. ☎ (403) 762-9196. The only hotel in the park has 10 cosy cabins with kitchenettes, and magnificent views. Inside you feel you're in a cocoon and you really want to settle down in front of the fire. Really decent prices, which makes it even better. Booking is essential.

In Radium Hot Springs

☖ **Motel Tyrol**: on Highway 93 before the park entrance. ☎ 347-9402. Fax: 347-6363. A well-equipped little motel that is pretty nice, especially when it comes to the prices.

☖ **Mount Farnham Bungalows**: on Highway 93, just before the park entrance. ☎ 347-9515. Fax: 347-9302. The cabins are sheltered under the trees very close to the swimming pools.

☖ **The Chalet**: 5063 Madsen Road. ☎ 347-9305. Fax: 347-9306. The big cabin dominates the whole valley and offers splendid views. Moderate to expensive prices.

WHAT TO SEE

★ **Takakkaw Falls**: This is the main attraction in Yoho Park – 380 metres (1,246 feet) of churning, spouting water. Wear a pullover and waterproofs if you want to get up close, as you'll get drenched. The other notable attraction is the **Burgess Shale**, a geological well.

★ **Emerald Lake**: Yoho Park, 11 kilometres (7 miles) from Field. This is a very beautiful lake in a superb setting and, on the whole, there aren't too many people. You can either walk around the lake (a circuit of about 5 kilometres/3 miles) or hire a canoe.

★ **The Paint Pots**: 20 kilometres (12.5 miles) from Castle Junction, heading towards Radium Hot Springs. Here you'll find mineral springs saturated with ferrous oxide, in enormous holes, surrounded by deposits of a red ochre clay. For many years these natural paint pots were used by the Prairie Indians for war paint and for decorating their teepees.

★ **Radium Thermal Springs**: Radium Hot Springs. ☎ 347-9485. Concessions for families and seniors. You can take a plunge in these pools of spring water. One is 40°C (104°F) and the other 27°C (81°F).

THE OKANAGAN VALLEY — DIALLING CODE: 250

This must be the only valley in British Columbia where the forests don't meet the horizon. The Okanagan, with its lakes, vineyards and orchards, is the second largest fruit-growing region in Canada. From June to October people come here to look for work picking fruit. Near Osoyoos there's a 'pocket desert' where the climate's hot and dry and you can swim in the lakes. Kelowna the is main town, and Osoyoos and Penticton are the most attractive towns to stay in.

USEFUL ADDRESSES

🏢 **Osoyoos tourist office**: junction of Routes 3 and 97. ☎ 495-7142.
🏢 **Penticton tourist office**: 888 Westminster Avenue West. ☎ 493-4055.

🏢 **Kelowna Travel Info**: 544 Harvey Avenue (the extension of the Highway). ☎ 861-1515.

WHERE TO STAY AND EAT

🛏 **Sandy Beach**: 6706 Ponderosa Drive, Osoyos (on the beach). ☎ 495-6931. One of the few motels where most of the bungalows have beach views.
🛏 **Hostelling International Penticton**: 464 Ellis Street, Penticton. ☎ 492-3992. The local youth hostel, with dormitories or private rooms. Laundry facilities and bike hire.

🛏 **Golden Sands**: 1028 Lakeshore Drive, Penticton. ☎ 492-4210. Fax: 492-0339. Practically the only motel around and most of the rooms overlook the lake and the boat *Sicamous* (not really worth visiting). The rooms on the first floor are nicer. Moderate prices.

In Kelowna

🛏 **Abbott Villa Inn**: 1627 Abbott Street. ☎ 763-7771 or 1-800-578-7878 (toll-free). Fax: 762-2402. For the same price as the dreadful motels along the road into town, this little establishment is ideally located near Waterfront Park, right in the centre. First-floor rooms have a balcony with table and parasol. Very good facilities.
🛏 **Willow Inn**: 235 Queensway Avenue. ☎ 762-2122. Fax: 762-2077. Half the rooms have views

of the lake and the port. Good value for money in the centre of town.
🛏 **Prestige Inn**: 1675 Abbott Street. ☎ 860-7900. Fax: 860-7997. In the centre next to the lake. Moderate to expensive prices.
🛏 ✕ **Eldorado**: 500 Cook Road, 10 minutes' drive from town. ☎ 763-7500. Fax: 861-4779. The hotel is really pleasant but expensive. However, you can have lunch (Monday to Saturday) on the dock, overlook-

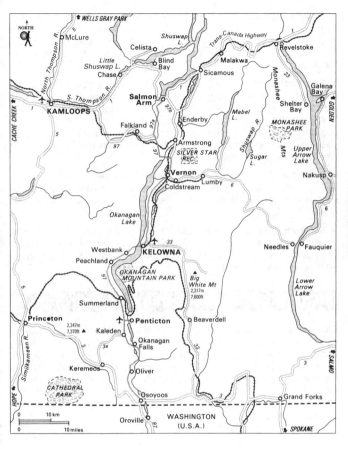

THE OKANAGAN VALLEY

ing the lake, for the same price as other places.

✕ **Marina Village Pub**: just after the floating bridge on the left coming from the north. ☎ 769-6666. Excel-lent place with a lovely terrace over-hanging the lake where you can enjoy amazing sandwiches such as hot turkey, crab and cheddar cheese melt.

WHAT TO SEE

★ **Osoyoos**: This small town, 3 kilometres (2 miles) from the border with the United States (open 24 hours) is touristy but full of charm. There are lots of motels near the lake but, for some inexplicable reason, most of the rooms overlook the car-parks. You can bathe in the lake and you won't find hotter water anywhere in British Columbia. Make the most of it.

★ **Osoyos Museum**: near Main Street on the lake shore. Open mid-June to September 10am–4pm. Without doubt this is one of the best little local museums in all of Canada. It's a real treasure trove, with a Falcon missile, a butterfly collection, dolls and even a patient being tortured by the dentist.

★ **The 'pocket desert'**: take Highway 3 East and turn left onto 45th Street, then carry on to the end. Entrance charge $2.50.This real mini-desert is, in fact, an outcrop of the Mexican desert but, in truth, there's not much to see. This is Inkameep Indian territory. You don't need a permit, but if you come across a native Indian, just be sure to ask if you are disturbing him. After all, you're on Indian land and as long as you respect that you'll help delay the time when access to others is not permitted.

★ **Penticton**: This small town is attractively situated between two lakes. It's best known for its zoo (8 kilometres/5 miles south of town), which house species from all over the world. You're allowed to feed the animals here, so kids will love it.

★ **Kelowna**: Coming from the north, your first impression is that it's awful, as endless rows of motels and shopping centres stretch before you. But, as soon as you leave the highway, you'll discover a charming town with private houses along the lake shore.

MANNING PROVINCIAL PARK   DIALLING CODE: 250

Rather like Wells Gray Park, this park doesn't boast the spectacular beauty of the Rockies, but it's perfect for all sorts of activities, including some wonderful walks. This is where the Pacific Crest Trail starts, a jaunt of just 3,860 kilometres (2,412 miles) from Manning to Mexico. Should the urge take you, allow yourself six months to follow the original trails of the Indians and trappers, later developed by the American Forests Service.

USEFUL ADDRESSES

🛈 **Park Information Center**: in the middle of the park, 100 metres from Highway 3 not far from the lodge. ☎ 840-8836. Open daily 8.30am–4.30pm. An illuminated map shows all the hiking trails.

■ **Horse riding**: Available near the lodge towards Lightning Lake. ☎ 840-8844.
■ **Mountain bike and canoe hire**: Information and equipment available at the lodge.

WHERE TO STAY

Accommodation is a big problem as there's only one lodge in the park. The alternative is to spend the night more than 50 kilometres (31 miles) away in Princetown or Hope.

🛏 **Manning Park Resort**: inside the park. ☎ 840-8822. Fax: 840-8848. The lodge is not remarkable (and neither is the view), but it's comfortable and ideally located. Moderate prices. Booking is essential.

♟ The most pleasant of the four **campsites** within the park is near Lightning Lake. You can reserve a site at the Information Center.

WHAT TO SEE

★ **Lightning Lake**: Even if you're only passing through Manning, you should visit this superb emerald-green lake where you can see the trout jump and climb up to Cascade Lookout for the view.

– The loveliest walks, through the mountain meadows high up, start from the summit at 1,960 metres (6,400 feet).

HOPE	DIALLING CODE: 604

BRITISH COLUMBIA

This big market town, while not exactly unattractive, isn't madly exciting either. But it's fine for a stopover because it's ideally located near the mouth of the Fraser River gorge, an important centre for rafting where hotels are rare. It's also not far from Manning Provincial Park where there's only one hotel.

USEFUL ADDRESS

🛈 **Tourist office**: 919 Water Avenue, near the Fraser River. ☎ 869-2021. Don't be surprised to find brochures about the actor Sylvester Stallone, as the original Rambo movie, *First Blood* (1982), was filmed here.

WHERE TO STAY

♟ **Swiss Chalets Motel**: on Highway 1, along Fraser River going north. ☎ 869-9020 or 1-800-663-4673 (toll-free). Fax: 869-7588. The chalets, 5 minutes' walk from the centre, overlook the Fraser River which is especially tumultuous at this particular spot.

♟ **Windsor Motel**: 778 3rd Avenue. ☎ 869-9944. Fax: 869-9975. A smaller motel looking out onto the park at the centre of town.

♟ **Skagit Motor Inn**: 655 3rd Avenue. ☎ 869-5220. Fax: 869-5856. A quiet motel, shaded by trees and two blocks from the centre.

Québec

Refer to the second colour plate section for a general map of the province of Québec, and maps of the Montréal Metro, Montréal and Québec City

MONTRÉAL Pop: 3.4 million   DIALLING CODE: 514

For maps of Montréal, see the second colour plate section.

Once the huge motorway network around the city finally deposits you into Montréal, your first sight of its centre may come as something of a let-down. After all, you might feel that you haven't come all this way just to see yet another North American metropolis, complete with skyscrapers, a geometric grid of streets and endless traffic. It's certainly true that an unfortunate mixture of poor urban planning and property developers' greed have done no favours to the city centre. But, scratch the surface a bit, and you'll find that although Montréal has certainly grown very fast, many of its old quarters continue to doze peacefully among the glass-and-concrete giants. You'll discover quiet roads flanked by small, brightly painted houses, each with its little bit of flower garden or vegetable patch. Life in these backwaters goes on at a gentle pace, and the locals are cheerful and friendly. There's certainly nothing here to remind you that you're in a metropolis: there's no litter, no dirt and no squalor. This is certainly a city of the New World, but it's built on a human scale. As you go from one district to another, you'll also find a wonderful and heart-warming diversity of lifestyles, cultures and ethnic origins. Add to this a buzzing nightlife, almost Mediterranean in its pace, and things really begin to look up!

Getting Your Bearings

Montréal is on an island, bounded by the St Lawrence river to the south and the Rivière des Prairies to the north. The **boulevard Saint-Laurent** cuts the city in two: the streets that cross it are defined by it, with Est (east) being added to their names on one side and Ouest (west) on the other. Their house numbers also start from this main artery. Make sure you take careful note of the Est and Ouest bit; getting it wrong may mean ending up several miles away from where you actually want to be. It's a bit easier as you go from south to north, since numbering starts from the river. House numbers on all these streets go up by about a 1000 (give or take a dozen) from one major intersection to the other, making the numbering very consistent from street to street. It's a very handy system, and you'll soon catch on.

The boulevard Saint-Laurent also forms a virtual boundary between social classes and cultures. To the west are the more 'desirable' areas, including the business quarter and **Westmount**, the smart residential district inhabited by the English-speaking middle classes. The francophone quarters and industrial districts, on the other hand, lie mainly to the east. The distinctive quarter of **Vieux Montréal**, separated from the rest of the city by the gash of the Ville-Marie motorway, is on the south side of town. Farther north, on the slopes of

Mont Royal, there's **Outremont**, the residential area of the French-speaking middle class. Other outlying districts house a variety of ethnic groups and recent immigrants. Nowadays, though, the boundaries between these districts are becoming blurred: the population moves around and new people keep moving in, resulting in a great deal of social and cultural shift, and a constant interchange of ideas. All this has resulted in a dynamic and complex city, with plenty going on to keep you busy, however long you stay.

GETTING THERE

International flights arrive at Dorval airport, 22 kilometres (14 miles) from Montréal, while charter flights and cargo planes land at Mirabel airport, 55 kilometres (34 miles) from the city centre.

✪ Mirabel International Airport: ☎ 394-7377. There is no tourist office at the airport, but the information desk (on the first floor in departures) has maps of Montréal and the region, as well as brochures listing things to do and see. Look out for Montréalscope, where you can change money and organize car hire. Note that none of the cash dispensers at this airport take MasterCard.

– Getting from Mirabel airport to Montréal: by Autocar Connaisseur coach (desk in arrivals lounge). ☎ 934-1222. The direct service (Express) takes an hour to get to Montréal's central bus station (Station Centrale d'Autobus Montréal, 505 boulevard de Maisonneuve Est; Métro: Berri-UQAM), and 50 minutes to get to the Centre-Ville terminal (777 rue de la Gauchetière Ouest; Métro: Bonaventure. Coaches leave at 5.15am, 8.15am, 11.15am, 2.15pm, 5.15pm, 8.15pm and 11.15pm. Prices are $8 single, $11 return. Getting to town by taxi costs about $60. A free shuttle-bus service runs between the Centre-Ville terminal and several hotels.

– Getting from Montréal to Mirabel: take the Express bus from the central bus station (leaving at 4am, 7am, 10am, 1pm, 4pm, 7pm and 10pm) or from the Centre-Ville terminal (10 minutes later). Going by taxi costs $60.

✪ Dorval International Airport: ☎ 394-7377 or 1-800-465-1213.

– Getting from Dorval airport to Montréal: take the La Québecquoise airbus (☎ 931-9002; every 20 minutes) to the Centre-Ville terminal (Métro: Bonaventure) or the central bus station (Métro: Berri-UQAM). The journey takes 30 minutes and costs $11 single and $20 return (more expensive than to Mirabel, though it's much nearer town). A taxi costs about $25.

– From Montréal to Dorval: departures every 30 minutes from the central bus station (5am–11pm; no 10.30pm departure) and 10 minutes later from the Centre-Ville terminal.

– **Shuttle bus between Mirabel and Dorval airports**: there is no direct service between the two airports. All services run via Montréal, where you have to change. Allow 75 minutes. Price $15 single and $20 return, reductions available.

– **Getting from Dorval to Québec**: by bus. Single $46.

USEFUL ADDRESSES

Tourist Information

🛈 Infotouriste (colour map II, B3): 1001 rue du Square-Dorchester, at the corner with Metcalfe. ☎ 873-2015; freephone number from Canada or the US ☎ 1-800-363-7777 (weekdays only, 9am–5pm). Email: info@tourisme. gouv.qc.ca. Métro: Peel. Open 8.30am–7.30pm from the beginning of June to mid-September, otherwise 9am–6pm. Free brochures and leaflets – but not maps – and a wealth of information about Montréal and the rest of Québec. Ask for the *Montréal Tourist Guide*, which covers all the main tourist attractions in the city. You can change money, make bookings with the travel agency, hire a car and buy phonecards. Maps of cycle routes are available, and you can book a hotel through the **Hospitalité Canada** service (☎ 393-1528; freephone within Canada ☎ 1-800-665-1528. Fax: 393-8942).

🛈 Old Montréal Tourist Office (colour map III, C1, **2**): place Jacques-Cartier, at the corner with Notre-Dame Est. Open 9am–7pm from the end of June to mid-September, otherwise Thursday–Sunday 9am–5pm.

■ Hospitalité Canada: 505 boulevard Maisonneuve Est, at the bus station. ☎ 284-2277. Fax: 523-7072. Métro: Berri-UQAM. Open 9am–9pm. A free, friendly tourist information centre where the Groupe qui Héberge accommodation service provides city maps and guidebooks. There's plenty of information about all levels of accommodation, from dirt-cheap to luxurious, and a free reservation service is available. On the ground floor, you'll find a café and three PCs offering Internet access ($6 per hour).

Embassies and Consulates

■ British Consulate General: Bureau 4200, 1000 rue de la Gauchetière Ouest, Montréal, Québec H3B 4W5. ☎ (514) 866-5863. fax: (514) 866-0202.

■ American Consulate: 1155 rue Saint-Alexandre. ☎ 398-0703 or 398-9695. Open 8.30am–2.30pm. Arrive early, as the queues can get very long.

■ South African Consulate: 1 Place Ville Marie, Montréal, Québec H3B 4S3. ☎ (514) 878-9217. Fax: (514) 878-4751.

■ Visa renewal: Canada Immigration, 1010 rue Saint-Antoine. ☎ 496-1010. Métro: Bonaventure. Open 8.30am–4.30pm. You can get application forms for visa renewal from this office.

Communications and Weather

✉ Post office (colour map III, B1): main office, 201 rue Saint-Antoine. ☎ 393-1177. Métro: Place-d'Armes. Open weekdays only, 8.30am–5.30pm. Note that there aren't any public phones here.

■ Public telephones: There are plenty of public phones on the streets and in shopping centres, restaurants and so on. You can usually phone abroad without too much hassle, or make reverse-charge calls. Some phone boxes take credit cards, but you'll pay heavily for the privilege: better to buy a La Puce (Bell) card. You can get these at some Métro stations, from the *tabagies* (newsagents), at the central rail station or at the Infotouriste centre. For more information, *see* 'Communications' *in* 'General Information'.

■ **Bell Canada** (colour map II, B3, **2**): 700 rue de la Gauchetière Ouest (at the corner of University).

■ **Telegrams**: Unitel, Or-Gold, 800 Victoria Square. Open weekdays only, 8am–4pm. Send telegrams by phone on ☎ 861-7311, 24 hours a day.

■ **Weather**: ☎ 283-3010.

■ **Snow and traffic information**: ☎ 1-873-4121.

Cybercafés

■ **Café McGill** (colour map II, B2-3, **12**): 3420 McTavish, where it meets Sherbrooke. ☎ 398-7444. Open 9am–4pm. Free Internet access in a café run by McGill University. It has eight computers and a bookshop, but no printing facilities. Coffee, juices, cakes and pastries are available.

■ **Cyberground Café** (colour map II, C2, **13**): 3672 boulevard Saint-Laurent. ☎ 842-1726. Website: www.cyberground.com. Open 10am–11pm. $8 per hour. The welcome is not particularly warm, but there are plenty of PCs.

■ **Café Électronique** (colour map II, B3, **14**): 1425 René-Lévesque Ouest, at the corner of Bishop. ☎ 871-0307. Open Monday to Friday, 9am–8pm. $4 for 30 minutes. Doubles up as a restaurant.

■ **Café Ludik** (map II, C3): 552 Sainte-Catherine Est. ☎ 844-1139. Website: www.geocities.com/cafeludik_2000. Open 11am–3am. This is a friendly place with a concert hall, a library and games tables (for backgammon, cards, etc.).

■ **Allô Copie** (colour map II, D1, **15**): 928 Mont-Royal Est. ☎ 523-2488. Email: allo@videotron.net. Open 8am–7pm; noon–6pm on Sunday. Ten cents per minute; Macs as well as PCs. Black-and-white or colour printing and photocopying services are also available.

■ **Club International Vidéo** (colour map I): 750 Beaubien Est. ☎ 273-6428. Website: www.videobeaubien.qc.ca. Métro: Beaubien. Open 9am–midnight. Ten cents per minute.

■ **Brasserie Internet** (colour map I): 855 boulevard Décarie, near the corner of rue Jean-Talon, northwest of the centre. ☎ 744-5345. Email: info@brasserie.ca. Open Monday to Saturday, 11am–1am. $3 for 30 minutes. As the name suggests, it's also a restaurant.

Emergencies

■ **Emergency number**: ☎ 911. For police, ambulance or fire service.

■ **Saint Mary's Hospital**: 3830 Lacombe (Côtes-des-Neiges area). ☎ 734-2690. Métro: Côtes-des-Neiges.

■ **24-hour pharmacy**: Pharmaprix, 5122 chemin de la Côtes-des-Neiges, on the corner of Queen-Mary. ☎ 738-8464. There's another late-night pharmacy (open until midnight) at 901 rue Sainte-Catherine Est, on the corner of Saint-André (☎ 842-4915).

Money

You can get money from most cash dispensers with a Visa card.

■ **American Express** (colour map II, B3, **6**): 1141 boulevard de Maisonneuve Ouest, at the corner with Peel). ☎ 284-3300. Métro: Peel. Open 8.15am–5.15pm. Also in the basement of the Eaton centre: 705 Sainte-Catherine Ouest (☎ 282-0445). Lost cards helpline: ☎ 1-800-268-9824.

■ **Visa**: Banque Royale (colour map II, A3, **7**), 1100 avenue Atwater. Information: ☎ 1-800-463-3135. Lost cards: ☎ 1-800-847-2911.

■ **Change**: to change money or traveller's cheques, go to a *kiosque de change*. There are several in the main tourist areas. Banks will often refuse to change money unless you have US dollars. At American Express (*see above*), there's no commission for changing traveller's cheques.

> **TIP** remember to keep $10 in cash for the 'departure tax', which you pay after you go through customs when leaving Québec.

Tourism and Travel

■ **Montréal Reservation Center**: 505 boulevard de Maisonneuve Est, office 205. ☎ 1-800-567-8687. Fax: (514) 284-7777. Sells packages for sporting and cultural events.

■ **Tourisme Jeunesse** (at Tout pour le Voyage, colour map II, C2): 4008 rue Saint-Denis, at the corner with Duluth. ☎ 844-0287. Freephone from outside Montréal: ☎ 1-800-461-8585. Métro: Sherbrooke. Open Monday to Wednesday 10am–6pm, Thursday and Friday 10am–9pm, Saturday 10am–5pm and Sunday noon–5pm. This is the commercial section of the Regroupement Tourisme Jeunesse (the equivalent of our Youth Hostels Association). You can buy an international YH card here, which will save you $3 a night if you stay in a youth hostel. Among the many services offered, they can make bookings at hostels throughout Québec. The shop sells travel accessories and guidebooks. There is also a branch in Québec (in the old town).

■ **Randonnées Plein Air**: 1260 Sainte-Catherine Est, office 200. ☎ 278-3577. Open Monday to Friday 9.30am–5pm (to 6pm on Thursday). A well-run, reliable and friendly place where you can sign up for a wide range of walks: day trips (every Saturday from December to March), walking tours lasting several days and trips that combine sightseeing, hiking and rambling. It's best to book several days in advance. The organization has branches across Québec, including offices in Charlevoix, Saint-Denis, Boston and Montagnes Blanches.

■ **Aux Quatre Points Cardinaux** (colour map II, D2, **10**): 551 Ontario Est. ☎ 843-8116. Website: www.aqpc.com. Métro: Berri-UQAM. Open 9am–6pm on weekdays (to 9pm Thursday and Friday), Saturday 10am–5pm. An essential stop for hikers and anyone planning to travel north of Montréal, this shop specializes in maps of Québec and the rest of Canada. It also stocks nautical charts of coastal North America, road maps of (almost) every country in the world and travel guides.

■ **Globe Trotter Adventure Canada**: 5140 Saint-Hubert, office 515, 2J-2Y3. ☎ 849-8768. Freephone: ☎ 1-888-598-7688. Fax: 286-3866. Website: www.aventurecanada.com. Open Monday to Friday 9am–6pm. The company was set up by two globetrotters to offer all-inclusive adventure holidays in Québec's most beautiful national parks. Activities available range from old standbys (canoeing, camping, quads, walking and riding) to the more unusual: snowmobiles, walking in snowshoes or training huskies. These packages give you an opportunity to really get to know the parks.

■ **Tourbec**: 3419 rue Saint-Denis. ☎ 288-4455. Open 9am–6pm on weekdays (to 8pm on Thursday and Friday) and Saturday 10am–4pm. Plane tickets only.

Entertainment and Media

– **Cineplex Odéon chain**: ☎ Cinecharge: 849-3456. Discounted tickets are available ($6 instead of $9.50) for Tuesday and Wednesday, and for screenings before 6pm on every other day. **Ex-Centris**: 3536 boulevard Saint-Laurent. ☎ 847-3536. Métro: Sherbrooke or Saint-Laurent. Built in 1999, this avant-garde, big-screen cinema complex cost $32 million to construct and screens the best independent, local and international films, as well as works that use state-of-the-art digital technology. Admission is $8 ($6 for students and senior citizens). The complex also houses a hip café-restaurant, **Méliès**, where the dish of the day costs $8–13. They also do soups, salads and even breakfast.

– **Radio**: excellent rock music is played on the English-speaking CHOM station (97.7 FM). Or try the French-speaking community radio station, CIBL (101.5 FM), where volunteer DJs play an eclectic mix of house, techno and *chanson*.

– **Concerts** and **nightclubs** are listed in the free weekly English publications *Mirror* (mostly rock) and *Hour*. The back pages of the free guide *Pom* (available at all tourist centres) include plenty of money-off vouchers for museums and attractions in Montréal and the surrounding area.

– **Ice rinks**: most are open-air. Try the ones by the lake in Lafontaine Park (3819 rue Calixa-Lavallée; bring your own skates) or at Vieux-Port (Bonsecours lake, open from the beginning of December to the beginning of March, 10am–10pm; skate hire available), where you can skate to music. There is an indoor rink under the illuminated glass roof of the Bell Amphitheatre (1000 rue de la Gauchetière Ouest, ☎ 395-0555; skate hire available).

– **Swimming pools:** Montréal has several indoor and outdoor swimming pools, including paddling pools for toddlers (the best being at Lafontaine Park). Entry to public swimming pools is free until 4pm during the week; entry to toddlers' paddling pools is free at all times. Information: ☎ 872-2237, ext. 651.

– **Beach**: the park beach on Notre-Dame island is an excellent place to hang out during the scorching summer months. Open 10am–7pm from mid-June until the third week in August; admission fee. ☎ 872-4537. Métro: Île-Sainte-Hélène.

Souvenirs and Shopping

Montréal's shopping is something of a revelation. Here are a few useful addresses:

🔒 **L'Échange**: 3694 rue Saint-Denis. Between Sherbrooke and carré Saint-Louis. ☎ 849-1913. Second-hand CDs in excellent condition, and a good selection of books.

🔒 **Sam the Record Man**: corner of Sainte-Catherine and Saint-Alexandre. ☎ 281-9877. For years, this has been Montréal's cheapest record shop, and the choice is better than at most. Music-lovers should also visit **HMV** (1020 rue Sainte-Catherine Ouest; ☎ 875-0765) or **Archambault Musique** (500 rue Sainte-Catherine Est; ☎ 849-6201; website: www.archambault.ca). Fans of world music should go to **Hibiscus** (288 rue Sainte-Catherine Ouest; ☎ 393-4090).

🔒 **Neon Clothing Co. of Canada**: 4251 rue Saint-Denis, 375 rue Sainte-Catherine Ouest and 1388 rue Sainte-Catherine Ouest. ☎ 393 4090. This clothing chain stocks keenly priced clobber by Levi's, Calvin Klein, Tommy Hilfiger, Dr Martens and the like. They charge $8 for alterations and will have your jeans ready by next morning. The huge Neon warehouse (6565 Saint-Hubert; ☎ 274-1221) has an incredible choice of end-of-season bargains and sale-price clothes.

🔒 **Le Baron**: 932 rue Notre-Dame Ouest. ☎ 866-8848. Closed Sunday. A supermarket that only sells camping gear (including camping gas, which is very rare in Canada), fishing gear, walking gear etc. The staff are friendly and helpful.

🔒 **La Capoterie**: 2061 rue Saint-Denis, at the top of Sherbrooke. ☎ 845-0027. Open until 9pm. As French-speakers may already have guessed, this shop sells nothing but condoms. They are available in any shape, flavour or colour you can think of (and several that you probably can't). There is another branch at 2015 rue Crescent.

🔒 **Pierre Gingras**: a friendly chap who sells natural honey, maple syrup, maple wax, organic fruit juices and cider vinegar at the Jean-Talon market. Open every day in season (7075 avenue Cassegrain, north of the town centre; Métro: Jean-Talon). ☎ 277-2140 for opening times or ☎ 469-4954 for information on where the produce is made.

🔒 **Markets** open to the public in Montréal are listed in the regional tourist guide available at Infotouriste. The Atwater market (138 avenue Atwater; Métro: Lionel-Groulx) is great for those who want to do their own cooking: it sells local vegetables, fruit and fish. Open every day (until 9pm on Thursday and Friday).

– Don't miss the *encans* (auctions) advertised in the papers. You might pick up some interesting bits and bobs.

– Traditionally, **26 December** is the day of the biggest department-store sales. Sales in most shops continue until 31 December.

– Don't buy any **Native American craft objects** here; they are much cheaper in the Native American reserves.

Laundrettes

■ **Duluth Laundromat and Dry Cleaning**: 106 Duluth Est, not far from boulevard Saint-Laurent. Métro: Sherbrooke or Mont-Royal. Open 9.30am–6pm (to 5pm on Sunday). This comfortable, inexpensive, but slightly bizarre laundrette is run by a scatty but charming Greek guy who will lend you a book to read while you are waiting, and might even offer you a coffee or an orange juice.

■ **Buanderie Net Net**: 310 Duluth Est. Open Monday to Friday 8.20am–10pm and Saturday to Sunday 9am–9pm. If you just want to wash and go, this is a more conventional laundrette, about 100 metres away from the first.

Car Hire

Car hire on the outskirts of the city tends to offer better value if you're willing to traipse out there. The addresses of the cheapest operators in Montréal are listed below.

■ **Discount**: 6740 boulevard Décarie. ☎ 340-1551. 607 boulevard de Maisonneuve Ouest, city centre. ☎ 286-1554. Freephone: ☎ 1-800-263-2355. Good prices.

■ **Hertz**: 1475 rue Aylmer. Métro: McGill. ☎ 842-8537. Freephone: ☎ 1-800-263-0678.

■ **Budget**: Mirabel airport. 895 rue de la Gauchetière Ouest. Métro: Bonaventure. ☎ 866-7675. Freephone: ☎ 1-800-268-8970.

■ **Via Route**: 1255 rue Mackay. Métro: Guy Concordia. ☎ 871-1166. 6250 boulevard Saint-Jacques Ouest. Métro: Vendôme. ☎ 482-1660. One of the least expensive; 10 other branches.

■ **Thrifty**: 1076 De La Montagne, at the corner of René-Lévesque and L'Allier, H3G-1Y7. ☎ 989-7100. Good rates.

Motorbike Hire

■ **Laval Moto**: at Laval (north shore of Montréal), 31 boulevard des Laurentides. ☎ 662-1919. Large bikes only.

Bicycle and Skate Hire

Cycling is the trendy way to get around in Montréal, so you might as well join in. The cycle paths are well managed, and are respected by drivers and pedestrians. Apart from the larger city-centre thoroughfares, the roads are usually not too busy. A series of bridges, a ferry service and the Métro (on which you can take bikes outside the rush hour) link the impressive cycling network on Montréal island with the suburban paths. The tourist office provides an excellent map of cycle routes for a small fee.

■ **Ça roule Montréal** (colour map III, C1-2, **1**): 27 rue de la Commune Est. ☎ 866-0633. Bicycle, tandem and rollerblade hire and sale. It costs $20 per day to hire out a bike or a pair of in-line skates, with reductions for children. Lessons $25 per hour.

■ **Bicycletterie J.R.** (colour map II, C1, **11**): 151 rue Rachel Est, at the corner of rue Bullion. ☎ 843-6989. Métro: Mont-Royal. Also at 907 Bélanger Est (☎ 278-4016). All kinds of bikes and equipment, at the best prices in Montréal.

■ **Vélo-Aventure**: at Vieux-Port de Montréal, quai des Convoyeurs, 100 metres to the right of the Imax cinema on the Vieux-Port promenade. ☎ 847-0666. Open 10am–8pm in summer. Mountain bikes, tandems and in-line skates available.

■ **La Cordée**: 2159 rue Sainte-Catherine Est. ☎ 524-1515. Métro: Papineau. Bicyle hire and equipment for outdoor pursuits.

■ **La Maison du Cycliste**: 1251 rue Rachel Est, at the corner of the Brébeuf and Rachel cycle lanes, opposite Lafontaine Park. ☎ 521-8356. The home of Association Vélo Québec (Québec Cyclists Association), which offers good advice and information about cycle routes. There's a travel agent specializing in cycle tours and a shop stocking maps and guides. No bike hire, though. La Maison du Cycliste is where cycling fans meet for *panini* and espresso at the Café Bicicletta (same address), where you can watch live coverage of the Tour de France.

TRANSPORTATION

Métro: modern, quick and easy. Runs from 5.30am–1am (1.30am weekends). STCUM (Montréal's transport company) sells good-value one-day ($5) and three-day ($12) travelcards, valid for Métro: and bus services, Buy them at the Berri-UQAM Métro station; from 15 April–30 October, you can also get them at the main Métro stations and at the Old Montréal tourist office on place Jacques-Cartier. A book of six tickets ($8.25) saves $2 on the normal ticket price.

Bus: the network is extensive and convenient. Dial AUTOBUS on any phone in Montréal for information on bus times and traffic updates. You must have the correct change to buy a bus ticket on board. If you don't have change, you could end up paying a lot more for the journey. Bus cards are available at the tourist office.

Métro and bus transfer tickets: free maps of the network are available at Métro stations. When you buy connecting tickets, the Métro ticket machines offer you the choice of finishing your journey by bus. Bus drivers can give you a connecting ticket that allows you to finish your journey by Métro, no matter how many changes you have to make. Transfer tickets are valid for up to 90 minutes.

Taxis: it's not hard to find a taxi in Montréal. Even better, if you book by phone, they don't charge you for the journey to your address. One of the best taxi companies is a small firm called **COOP**: ☎ 725-9885.

Trains to the suburbs: from Windsor station (☎ 395-7492; Métro: Bonaventure) or the central station (STCUM).

WHERE TO STAY

For maps of Montréal see the second colour plate section.

⭐ Budget

Campsites

There are 14 campsites around Montréal. Get a list from the tourist office when you arrive. Camping in the area is quite expensive, and the sites are a long way from the city. Without motorized transport, camping is pretty much impossible, so bear this in mind when booking.

🛖 **Oka Park campsite**: 2020 chemin Oka, in Oka Park, about 30 minutes' drive from Montréal. ☎ (450) 479-8337. From Montréal, take highway 15 (or 13), then turn off onto the 640, heading west. The campsite is tucked away in the greenery and has 800 pitches, of which about 300 are hooked up to water and electricity. This is one of the most beautiful campsites in the area.

🛖 **KOA Montréal-Sud**: 130 boulevard Monette, at Saint-Philippe-de-la-Prairie. ☎ 659-8626. Follow highway 15 going south. Take exit 38, turn left and it's another 3 kilometres (2 miles) down the road.

🛖 **Seigneurie de Soulanges**: 195 route 338, at Coteau-du-Lac.

☎ 763-5344. If you're coming in by highway 20 west, it's just before you cross to Perrot Island. Open from May to the end of September. It's near the main road, and it's noisy.

🛖 **Camping Camp Alouette**: at Belil, 3441 rue de l'Industrie. ☎ 464-1661. Take highway 20, exit 105. Open from 15 April until the beginning of November. It has an outdoor swimming pool.

– For **camping-gas refills**: Blacks Camping International, 3525 chemin Queen-Mary, near Saint-Joseph's chapel. ☎ 739-4451. Métro: Côtes-des-Neiges. Along with Le Baron (*see* 'Souvenirs and Shopping'), this is one of the few places in Montréal that sells camping gas.

Youth Hostels

🛖 **Auberge de Jeunesse de Montréal** (colour map II, A-B3, **20**): 1030 rue Mackay. ☎ 843-3317. Fax: 934-3251. Website: www.aj Montreal.qc.ca. Métro: Lucien-L'Allier. It's best to book by telephone, but you can only do so if you have a credit or debit card. From $19 per night in a dormitory if you have a Youth Hostel card; private rooms from $26 per night. Children under 12 stay free when accompanied by their parents. A non-smoking youth hostel with 264 beds in rooms for two, three, four, six or 10; all rooms have en-suite showers. If you forgot to bring sheets, you can hire them when you arrive ($2.30, no matter how long your

stay). The hostel has a left-luggage facility and parking for bicycles, and guests can use the washing machine/dryer. Self-catering is possible, but hide your food, as it tends to disappear. There's no curfew, and the hostel organizes bar crawls two or three times a week.

🛖 **Auberge alternative du Vieux Montréal**: 358 rue Saint-Pierre, in the town centre, about 15 minutes' walk from Métro Square-Victoria. ☎ 282-8069. Open 24 hours a day. From $18 per night in a dormitory (6–13 beds); a double with shared bathroom and toilet is $50. It costs $2 to hire a sleeping bag for the first night. This newish hostel near the old port is run by the very welcoming Angela, an Australian, and Bruno, who's from Québec. You can use the kitchen and laundrette for the same price as at the Auberge de Jeunesse de Montréal (*see above*), and you don't need a Youth Hostel card to do so. Rooms can be booked in advance, but debit and credit cards are not accepted.

â **Auberge de Paris**: 901 Sherbrooke Est, on the corner of Saint-André. ☎ 522-6861 or 1-800-567-7217 (toll-free). Fax: 522-1387. Open 24 hours a day. Dorm beds from $19 a night. Free minibus service from the railway station. The smart Hôtel de Paris (*see* 'Expensive') offers hostel-style accommodation in a converted old house. It's a clean, friendly place with proper bedding, a kitchen, a laundry room and a TV room with hi-fi, and a few private rooms are available, some with kitchen facilities. Prices are at their lowest between November and May.

Religious Organizations

â **Centre Maria Goretti**: 3333 chemin de la Côte-Sainte-Catherine. ☎ 731-1161. Métro: Côtes-des-Neiges. This friendly place with no curfew only takes women aged 18 or over. Single rooms with shared bathrooms and toilets $15 per night or $60 per week; discounts for long stays. The accommodation is good, clean and cheaper than at the Auberge de Jeunesse de Montréal. Rooms with basins are also available, as are smaller, cheaper rooms. It's a good place to meet people, with a library and two TV rooms, although the atmosphere isn't exactly wild. Credit and debit cards are not accepted.

â **YMCA** (colour map II, B3, **23**): 1450 rue Stanley. ☎ 849-8393. Fax: 849-7821. Métro: Peel. This pristine hostel with no curfew is right in the centre of town, and welcomes men and women. Single rooms are not cheap, at $46 per night (doubles $56), but rooms for three or four offer better value. It's a sociable place, with a cafeteria, swimming pool and a range of cultural and sporting activities. You get a $2 discount with a student card.

â **YWCA** (colour map II, B3, **24**): 1355 boulevard René-Lévesque Ouest. ☎ 866-9941. Fax: 861-1603. Métro: Peel, Lucien-L'Allier or Guy-Concordia. Open 24 hours a day. This central hostel for women only has single rooms from $49 a night (doubles from $66), all with basins, air-conditioning and TV. There is a bathroom on each floor. A bed in one of the single-sex dormitories is $22 a night, but they are very popular, so remember to book in advance. Credit cards are accepted. The place lacks charm, but it's extremely well maintained, with uniformed receptionists, a shop, a women-only swimming pool, a sauna, a library and cooking facilities. The cafeteria and laundrette are open to men and women.

Colleges and Universities

University accommodation is only available in summer. It's often overpriced, and it's not always that pleasant, but it's useful if you get stuck.

â **Collège Français** (colour map II, C1, **25**): 5155 avenue de Gaspé, next to the park of the same name. ☎ 270-4459. Fax: 278-7508. Métro: Laurier. From $15 per person per night in a dormitory. The college is a fair way from the city centre, but it's in an interesting neighbourhood (*see*

'Where to Eat' *and* 'What to See') and rooms are available year-round. You can opt for a seven-bed dormitory (less expensive than at the Auberge de Jeunesse) or a room for four, which comes with shower and toilet. It's not especially comfortable, but you can't really complain at these prices. The curfew varies depending on the time of year. In summer, they also serve breakfast (good value at $4).

🏠 **McGill** (colour map II, B2, **26**): 3935 rue de l'Université. ☎ 398-6367. Fax: 398-6770. Also 3425 rue de l'Université. ☎ 398-6378. Fax: 398-4445. Open 15 May to 15 August. Studio with kitchenette, bedding and towel $40 ($34 for students). Montréal's English-speaking university is quite a distance from the city centre, and the unspectacular accommodation is expensive compared with the youth hostels, but this is a useful

option if you're in need of a budget bed.

🏠 **Résidence des étudiants de l'Université de Montréal**: 2350 rue Édouard-Mont-Petit. ☎ 343-6531. Fax: 343-2353. Métro: Édouard-Mont-Petit. Open from the beginning of May until 20 August. Single rooms $23 per night (doubles $33). The hall of residence for the French-speaking University of Montréal is cheaper than McGill, but the Auberge de Jeunesse still offers better value. All the rooms have basins, and there are bathrooms on each floor.

🏠 **Collège Jean-de-Brébeuf** (just off colour map II, B1): 3200 Côte-Sainte-Catherine. ☎ 342-1320. Métro: Côte-des-Neiges. Open to tourists from the end of May to mid-August. Spotless single and double rooms with basins for $30 per person per night. Singles and doubles are available, and you can get a decent meal without busting your budget.

Bed and Breakfast Accommodation

B&Bs have two main advantages over hotels: breakfast (which is usually huge) is always included in the price, and you're likely to get a much warmer welcome. Unfortunately, in Montréal, both types of accommodation share one thing in common: you pay a $2 lodgings tax per room per night. It's best to book in advance in summer and you should always telephone before you arrive. If there are no vacancies, check out the Fédération of Agricotours guide (available at Infotouriste), or contact one of the groups listed below:

■ **Bed & Breakfast Downtown Network**: 3458 Laval Avenue, near Sherbrooke. ☎ 289-9749. Fax: 287-7386. Email: bbdtown@cam.org
■ **Chambres d'hôte Montréal Oasis**: 3000 chemin de Breslay.

☎ 935-2312. Fax: 935-3154. Email: bb@aei.ca
■ **Bed & Breakfast à Montréal**: 2033 St-Hubert, off Sherbrooke Est. ☎ 738-9410. Email: info@bb Montreal.com

If you're planning an extended stay, and don't want to spend all your time in a B&B, call Catherine, a French emigrée who lets private rooms and furnished apartments that belong to local residents who are out of town for anything from a couple of weeks to several months. Make sure you know any relevant house rules (on inviting friends round, use of domestic appliances, linen and so on). You must also accept visits from people interested in renting the property after you, so settle the terms at the start of your stay and you won't be surprised by an impromptu visit. Even if you don't decide to stay in one of these properties, Catherine can offer some helpful advice about Montréal, and organizes a wide range of activities. ☎ 524-8344. Fax: 524-6558.

Hopefully, you'll find something to suit you at one of the following addresses. These are more highly recommended than even the hotels in the 'Expensive' category.

⬦ **Auberge Chez Jean** (colour map II, C2, **36**): 4136 rue Henri-Julien, ☎ 843-8279. Métro: Mont-Royal. From $18 per person per night, including breakfast; sheets $2. The owner, Jean Bériou, is from France, and staying with him is more or less like living in one big family in one big house: if he is fully booked, he will offer you a place in one of his converted vans, under a canopy outside or even on the roof. Whatever the situation, he'll make sure there's room at the inn. The prices are unbeatable, and so is the atmosphere. It may be more intimate than what you're used to, but you'll have plenty of opportunities to meet fellow travellers. The best room is on the top floor, where you can sleep under the eaves and enjoy a wonderful view of Montréal in a room filled with light and backpackers. It really has to be seen to be believed. Jean edits a monthly newsletter about his hostel, complete with stories and photographs from past residents. Auberge Chez Jean is worth a visit even if you decide not to stay there; if you do, don't even think about going to bed early.

☆☆–☆☆☆ Moderate to Expensive

Studios to Rent

⬦ **Les Studios du Quartier Latin** (colour map II, D2, **49**): 2024 rue Saint-Hubert, office 5. ☎ 990-4091. Fax: 840-9144. Email: lestudio@ globetrotter.net. Website: www. microtec.net/lestudio. Métro: Berri-UQAM. Doubles $50–60 per night, depending on the season, with a 20 per cent reduction if you book for a week; monthly stays $20 per day for two. This collection of 60 studios in converted houses feels a bit like a small residential hotel. The staff are friendly, and you get plenty for your money. The kitchen is extremely well equipped and maintained, and some rooms have private bathrooms.

Guesthouses

In the City Centre
⬦ **B&B Le Zèbre** (colour map II, C2, **50**): 3767 avenue Laval, not far from carré Saint-Louis and Saint-Denis.

☎ 844-9868. Fax: 844-4665. Email: lezebre@mlink.net. Métro: Sherbrooke. Doubles $70 a night. This attractive, well-maintained house in the quiet Plateau neighbourhood is run by a charming Montréal-born duo called Éric and Jean-François, who spent several years in Brussels and Barcelona. The stylishly decorated rooms are beautiful, and the shared bathrooms are immaculate. It's no wonder that the place is popular with Montréal's arty crowd.

⬦ **La Maison Jaune** (colour map II, D2, **31**): 2017 rue Saint-Hubert, near the central bus station. ☎ 524-8851. Métro: Berri-UQAM. Doubles $68 per night, with discounts if you stay for five days or more. There's a touch of class about this chic, beautifully renovated Victorian residence with mahogany furniture and a rather British feel. Service always comes with a smile, and the breakfasts are excellent. You'll need to book, as there are only five rooms: a single on the ground floor (shared facilities); three doubles on the first floor (the yellow room is probably the best); and, also on the first floor, a splendid room sleeping four. It's not cheap, but you certainly get what you pay for.

♜ **Chez Marine Berthou** (colour map II, C2, **42**): 3490 rue Jeanne-Mance. ☎ 282-9861. Métro: Place-des-Arts. Doubles $75 a night. You'll get a warm welcome from the French owner, Marine, and her Québécois cat, Saskatchewan, at this peaceful house. From the outside, it looks pretty ordinary, but inside the whole place has been modernized and redecorated. The interior is calm and bright, with an attractive entrance hall and three cosy rooms, all sharing a bathroom. Free parking.

♜ **B&B À l'Adresse du Centre** (colour map II, D3, **51**): 1673 rue Saint-Christophe, on a quiet and colourful street near the Travellers' Terminus. ☎ 528-9516. Fax: 528-2746. Métro: Berri-UQAM. Doubles $68 a night. The long-time manageress, Huguette Boileau, has retired, but her daughter Natalie and her boyfriend continue Huguette's tradition of hospitality, and will happily give you tips on what to see and do in the city. The rooms in this little pink house are pretty and comfortable: the downstairs room at the back is the most spacious, but the '*café-crème*' room on the street side, with a fireplace, moulded ceilings and wood-trim panels, is the prettiest. The gourmet buffet breakfast, made using mom's old recipes, includes omelettes, homemade cakes, cornbread and banana bread. The delicious smell adds to the special atmosphere, which makes this the best little guesthouse in Québec.

♜ **B&B Le Chat Bleu** (colour map II, D2, **56**): 4098 Saint-Hubert, between Duluth and Rachel, two minutes from the main shopping area. ☎ 527-3421. Fax: 527-3006. Website: www.cybermtl.com/lechatbleu.

Métro: Mont-Royal. Doubles from $67. A lovely semidetached house on the Plateau, with four bedrooms (one three-bedded) on one extremely long corridor. The decor is cosy, and there's a pleasant breakfast room. You'll be greeted warmly, and offered tips about the town and local customs. It is not, however, suitable for those allergic to cats, as they are everywhere.

♜ **B&B Roger Bontemps** (colour map II, D3, **55**): 1441 Wolfe. ☎ 598-9587 or 1-888-634-9090 (toll-free). Métro: Beaudry. Doubles from $65, depending on season; also apartments for two to eight people. In a cluster of small brick houses, set around a courtyard and joined by a network of corridors and passages, are 10 lovely rooms with colourful individual decor; most have an en-suite bathrooms and large beds. Guests can enjoy the sunshine from the comfort of the terrace, and you can hire bicycles for $15 per day if you're feeling active.

♜ **Gîte touristique du Centre-Ville** (colour map II, C2, **33**): 3523 rue Jeanne-Mance. ☎ 845-0431. Fax: 845-0262. Website: www3.sympatico.ca/app. Métro: Place-des-Arts. Doubles with shared bathroom $75 a night; apartments $85. This stone house in a residential part of the city centre has three modern rooms (one single) with fans and TV. It's a pleasant place where everything runs smoothly, and breakfast is superb, although you can opt for a room with kitchen overlooking the back garden. The three small apartments (sleeping up to five) are in an anonymous modern tower block, but you do get a balcony and access to the swimming pool, sauna and laundrette – not to mention a breathtaking view of Montréal, its skyscrapers and Mont-Royal. So, a cosy house

MONTRÉAL

or a room with a view – the choice is yours.

â B&B chez Christian Alacoque (colour map II, C2-3, **34**): 2091 Saint-Urbain. ☎ 842-0938. Fax: 842-7585. Email: christian.alcoque @sympatico.ca. Métro: Saint-Laurent. Doubles with shared bathroom $70–90 a night; furnished accommodation on a monthly basis. In a quiet and central location, this is a classically Québécois guesthouse. The rooms are on the small side, but they're colourful and cosy, with old wooden floors. The staff are friendly and laid-back – even a touch bohemian – and breakfast is excellent. Facilities include a reading room full of French comic strips and books, a terrace, a kitchen and a laundrette. It's best to book.

â Le Gîte du Parc Lafontaine (colour map II, D2, **41**): 1250 Sherbrooke Est. ☎ 522-3910. Fax: 844-7356. Métro: Sherbrooke. Open from 1 June to 1 September, this is a cross between a gîte and a youth hostel, with dormitory accommodation ($20 per night) and double rooms ($45–65). The price includes breakfast, which is served on the

Out of Town

â Gîte du Passant Chez François (colour map II, D2, **53**): 4031 and 4037 rue Papineau. ☎ 239-4638. Fax: 596-2961. Doubles $85–100 a night. In a quiet area 10 minutes' walk from Saint-Denis via Lafontaine Park, this solid house with metal staircases on the facade offers luxurious, brand-new rooms overlooking the garden or the park. All are intimate and meticulously maintained, with blond-wood floorboards and reassuringly expensive materials used throughout. The more extravagant ones have a private bathroom with jacuzzi; otherwise, it's a shared but very pleasant bathroom. Breakfast, served in a quiet room at the back, helps you to start

terrace. It's clean and sparkling, although the rooms are a bit small. You can hire towels for $1 and use the kitchen between 5pm and 8pm.

â B&B Centre Ville-Downtown-Network (colour map II, C2, **47**): 3977 avenue Laval. ☎ 287-9635. Fax: 287-1007. Website: www. hostelMontreal.com. Métro: Sherbrooke. From $35 for a single room and $55 for a double. The painter and opera singer Martha Pearson and her daughter let rooms in this quiet street near the lively Saint-Laurent and Saint-Denis boulevards.

â La Maison du Jardin (colour map II, D2, **57**): 3744 rue Saint-Andre. ☎ 598-8862. Fax: 598-0667. Website: www.openface.ca/ ~durocher/jardin. Métro: Sherbrooke. Three comfortable double rooms and friendly, no-nonsense service are on offer in a house that's typical of the plush Plateau district. If it's free, take the big room ($105 per night), which has access to the garden and plenty of morning sun. The two smaller rooms upstairs are $65 and $80 per night.

the day the North American way. Free parking.

â La Dormance (colour map II, D1, **32**): 4425 rue Saint-Hubert. ☎ 529-0179. Fax: 529-1079. Email: dormance@microtec.net. Métro: Mont-Royal. Doubles $72, including breakfast. This comfortable, quiet house near a lively part of town is impeccably run by a charming young couple. The four double rooms are large, attractive and bright, with views of the street or the yard; there's also a relatively drab single on the ground floor. The first floor has three double rooms (one of which can easily hold a third bed; $15, free for a child under 10) and a fully fitted bathroom with a spacious separate toilet, both pristine. The last double and the single share another bathroom, this time with toilet, on the ground floor.

♠ **Gîte La Cinquième Saison** (colour map II, D1, **54**): 4396 rue Boyer. ☎ 522-6439. Fax: 522-6192. Email: cinquieme.saison@sympatico.ca. Website: www.bbcanada.com/1952.html. Métro: Mont-Royal. Doubles $65 a night. The friendly and attentive Jean-Yves Goupil runs this quiet, hospitable establishment in the smart, green Plateau area with great success, as a glance at the visitors' book soon reveals. The five comfortable, tastefully decorated rooms all have TVs, and there's a communal shower room as well as a shared bathroom. There's a good sweet and savoury breakfast with homemade pastries.

♠ **Gîte du Passant L'Urbain** (colour map II, C1, **48**): 5039 rue Saint-Urbain. ☎ 277-3808. Métro: Laurier. You'll pay a little over the odds for one of the three cosy rooms in this beautiful, turn-of-the-20th-century house, but it's worth splashing out: the hostess is charming, and it has a cosy terrace and a large TV room with video, newspapers and, unusually, a piano.

♠ **Au Bonheur d'Occasion**: 846 rue Agnès. ☎ and fax: 935-5898. Website: www.bbcanada.com/526. html. Métro: Place-Saint-Henri. Doubles with shared bathroom $75 a night (en suite $95). This is a magnificent early-20th-century house in a very quiet area. Everyone's very helpful – you can even borrow a bike if required. Be sure to ask for one of the first-floor rooms, which are stylish and new. If the weather's nice, have breakfast (which is huge) in the little garden. Free parking.

♠ **Monique et Christian**: 1508 rue Jeanne-d'Arc. ☎ 522-2869. Métro: Pie-IX. Bus No. 139. Single rooms from $40 a night (doubles $60), including breakfast. A great place for anyone visiting Québec for the first time, thanks to the family atmosphere and the warmth of your hosts, who can give you tons of information about Montréal or anywhere else in Canada. It's some way from the centre of town, so it's quiet, but you can reach the action within 20 minutes by public transport.

Hotels

Montréal's hotels tend to be rather costly, but there are a few bargains to be had. If you're staying for a while, it's better to rent a room: it's usually better value, and you should get a refrigerator, a shared bathroom and at least one telephone for the whole house. The best place to look is the rue Saint-Denis district (although the so-called 'Tourist Rooms' here are sometimes brothels). You could also try the Saint-Hubert neighbourhood, rue Berri, carré Saint-Louis, rue Duluth, rue Aylmer, rue Hutchinson or avenue du Parc. The Tours Richelieu Tower organization rents hotel rooms and apartments with fully equipped kitchens. ☎ 844-3381. Fax: 844-8361. Remember that, wherever you go, you'll pay a supplementary tax of $2 per night per room.

♠ **Hôtel Dynastie** (colour map II, D2, **27**): 1723 rue Saint-Hubert, 200 metres away from the bus station. ☎ 529-5210. Fax: 529-7170. Email: hoteldynastie@qc.aira.com. Métro: Berri-UQAM. Doubles $45–55 a night, depending on the time of year. This place is simple, clean and friendly, and the owners put a lot of effort into making your stay as pleasant as possible. The rooms, which are regularly renovated, are soundproof, and all have cable TV, air-conditioning and private bathrooms, as well as a small refrigerator and a kettle. Excellent value for money.

🛌 **Hôtel L'Abri du Voyageur** (colour map II, C3, **28**): 9 rue Sainte-Catherine Ouest. ☎ 849-2922. Fax: 499-0151. Email: info@abri-voyageur.ca. Website: www.abri-voyageur.ca. Métro: Saint-Laurent. Doubles with shared bathroom $45–60 a night. A stone's throw from the Chinese quarter, and right in the middle of the Sainte-Catherine red-light district, this small hotel has upgraded its image without raising its prices. The reception is at the top of a flight of steps, with rooms on several different floors. The decor is plain, but the place is bright, spacious and very well kept, with showers and toilets on the landing and fans to provide relief from the summer heat. It attracts a friendly young crowd who want to stay in the heart of Montréal without breaking the bank.

🛌 **Hôtel Manoir des Alpes** (colour map II, D3, **37**): 1245 rue Saint-Andre. ☎ 845-9803. Freephone: ☎ 1-800-465-2929. Fax: 845-9886. Email: admi@hotelmanoirdesalpes.qc.ca. Website: www.otelmanoirdesalpes.qc.ca. Métro: Berri-UQAM. Doubles $80 a night, including breakfast. Des Alpes is a small, family-run place on a quiet if dreary side street near Montréal's gay village. You're not guaranteed a warm welcome, but the service is generally of a high quality. Some rooms have en-suite bathrooms; all have air-conditioning and a TV. Coffee and croissants are served in a candy-pink lounge. Book well in advance, as it's often full. Free parking.

🛌 **Auberge des Glycines** (colour map II, D3, **44**): 819 boulevard Maisonneuve Est. ☎ 526-5511. Métro: Berri-UQAM. Doubles $75 a night, including breakfast. The attractive brick facade is perhaps the best thing about this hotel, which is typical of the area. There are rocking chairs in the entrance, the decor is a little old-fashioned and the staff are a little reserved. The clean rooms sleep two, three or four people, and they're all en suite, so it's a good choice if you can't bear to share. Otherwise, you'll get better value at a B&B. Free parking.

🛌 **Hôtel Pierre** (colour map II, C2, **29**): 169 rue Sherbrooke Est. ☎ 288-8519. Fax: 288-7181. Métro: Sherbrooke or Saint-Paul. Doubles $75–110 a night, depending on season; $5–10 per extra person. First the good news: this is a really friendly place. Unfortunately, it's on a noisy street, the rooms aren't much to write home about and 'breakfast' consists only of coffee. Not a great choice for couples, then, but the rooms for four or six with bathroom are good value at $120.

🛌 **Hôtel Le Breton** (colour map II, D3, **38**): 1609 rue saint-Hubert. ☎ 524-7273. Métro: Berri-UQAM. Doubles from $65 a night. A decent if old-fashioned hotel in an excellent location, offering refurbished rooms with TV, and, in the more expensive rooms, a private bathroom. Breakfast (very small) is included in summer. In winter, the prices are lower, but you only get coffee in the morning. Le Breton's saving grace is its friendly manager, Mme. Miron, who can offer advice on what to see and do, and even organize things should you so wish. Book in advance, as this place is popular. There also a few good-value four-bed rooms.

🛌 **Castel Saint-Denis** (colour map II, C-D2, **39**): 2099 rue Saint-Denis. ☎ 842-9719. Fax: 843-8492. Website: www.castelsaintdenis.qc.ca. Métro: Berri-UQAM. Doubles from $55 a night. If you want to be where the action is, this hotel is for you. It's very friendly, and everything is spotless. The rooms are quiet, and all have TV, air-conditioning or fans; some also have en-suite bathrooms. They don't do breakfast, but the owner, Anne-Marie, a friendly Breton woman, can recommend places to go and eat, and does everything she can to help her guests. This is one of the best budget hotels in Montréal, so book early.

☆☆☆ Expensive

In this section, you'll find hotels offering good rooms and very small suites at fairly reasonable prices. Rates vary depending on the size of the room.

⌂ Hôtel Manoir Sherbrooke (colour map II, C2, **29**): 157 Sherbrooke Est. ☎ 845-0915. Fax: 284-1126. Website: www.armormanoir.com. Métro: Sherbrooke. Doubles with shared bathroom $48–68 a night, en suite $58–109. Right on a noisy main road, the Manoir is a huge white building that looks vaguely like a medieval castle. The interior is rather more appealing. There are 20-odd rooms, each one different but all tastefully decorated, with mouldings and stylish furniture. Ask if you can see the rooms before choosing; if you can't, try to get one at the back. In the most expensive rooms, the decor is Victorian – and some have a jacuzzi to help you unwind after a day of sightseeing. Breakfast is available, but it's not included in the price.

⌂ Manoir Ambrose (colour map II, B2, **45**): 3422 rue Stanley. ☎ 288-6922. Fax: 288-5757. Website: www.manoirambrose.com. Métro: Peel. Doubles with shared bathroom from $50 a night (en suite from $65). The Manoir Ambrose is a classic Victorian-style Montréal house in a residential area. Inside, it has bags of charm, with pretty wood trims, fireplace and a library, while many of the flawless rooms have antique furnishings. The spacious suites are fantastic, and the service is as polished as the decor.

⌂ Hôtel de Paris (colour map II, D2, **46**): 901 Sherbrooke Est, on the corner of Saint-André. ☎ 522-6861. Fax: 522-1387. Métro: Sherbrooke. Doubles with en-suite bathroom $65–120 a night; there's also a youth hostel (see 'Where to Stay – Budget'). This charming old house has rooms with air-conditioning, TVs and telephones. The most luxurious ones have alcoves or four-poster beds. It's a genial place, though the service can be a little old-fashioned.

⌂ Le Taj Mahal-Thrift Lodge (colour map II, D3, **40**): 1600 rue Saint-Hubert. ☎ 849-3214 or 1-800-613-3383 (toll-free). Fax: 849-9812. E-mail: tajmahal@videotron.net. Métro: Berri-UQAM. Doubles from $75 a night. This is a chain-style business hotel, modern, comfortable, slightly pricey and short on charm. The staff are professional rather than friendly, and the well-maintained rooms all have air-conditioning, bathroom and TV. Local calls and parking are free.

⌂ L'Auberge de La Fontaine (colour map II, D1, **43**): 1301 rue Rachel Est. ☎ 597-0166. Fax: 597-0496. Website: www.aubergedelafontaine. com. Doubles $145–234 a night, depending on the season; $15 per extra person. If you want to spend a night in style, look no further. The individually designed rooms have views over the park, a lounge area or even a hot tub. The decor and the colour scheme are both extremely tasteful, with clever wallpaper effects to bring out hidden details. To make you feel more at home, you even get a kitchenette.

WHERE TO STAY IN THE AREA

⌂ Auberge de jeunesse Le Chalet Beaumont: 1451 rue Beaumont, Val-David. ☎ (819) 322-1972. About 80 kilometres (50 miles) away from Montréal, between Sainte-Adèle and Sainte-Agathe-des-Monts. You can get to and from the city by bus, but it's a real grind, so it's better to have a car. There are about 50 beds in rooms for two or four, and dormitories sleeping six to eight. Breakfast is available, and there are showers, toilets and basins, as well as a fully equipped kitchen. This lovely wooden chalet is perfect for sporty types: activities on offer in the area include swimming (in the nearby lake), walking, climbing, cycling and skiing. Or you could just relax on the veranda . . .

⌂ L'Anse du Patrimoine: 475 Émile-Nelligan, Boisbriand. ☎ (450) 437-6918. Fax: (450) 434-5130. Website: www.ansedupatrimoine. com. In the northern suburbs of Montréal, about 20 minutes from Mirabel airport, via highway 15 south. Doubles $60–75 a night. This charming, 200-year-old country-house hotel is perfect if you're flying in late and don't want to drive all the way to Montréal, or if you're looking for somewhere near the airport when you go home. There's a swimming pool, the service is excellent and you'll get a huge breakfast to send you on your way.

⌂ Gîte du Passant La Belle Vie: 1408 Jacques-Lemaistre. ☎ 381-5778. Fax: 381-3966. Email: alabelle vie@hotmail.com. Website: www. bbcanada.com/3399.html. From Dorval airport, take route 520 east (9 kilometres, or about 5 miles) towards highway 40 east, then exit 73 onto avenue Christophe-Colomb north; after 1 kilometre, turn right into rue Legendre, then left onto André-Grasset (200 metres on); Jacques-Lemaistre is the first on the right. Doubles $60 a night, including breakfast. La Belle Vie, in a quiet residential area near Montréal's two airports, is an appealing alternative to the anonymity of most airport hotels. It has bright, spotless rooms and a small swimming pool, and the excellent breakfast is served on the terrace, which opens out into a little garden.

⌂ Gîte du Passant La Villa des Fleurs: 45 rue Gaudreault, Repentigny, in a calm residential area. ☎ (450) 654-9209. Fax: (450) 654-1220. Doubles with basin and shared bathroom $50–60 a night. An ideal stopover if you're driving to Montréal from the north (Québec or Trois-Rivières) on highway 40. Mind you, it's well worth a detour wherever you're going, as the rooms are cosy and the welcome from Denise and Claude is lovely. Breakfast is delicious, as is dinner (available on request), with local specialities to the fore. There's a swimming pool, and it's a good base for winter sports. All in all, a very good gîte.

WHERE TO EAT

For maps of Montréal, see the second colour plate section.

Montréal is one of the gastronomic capitals of North America, and there's a staggering choice of restaurants offering cuisine from all over the world. The following is a selection of good-value restaurants, ethnic eateries and trendy establishments.

Don't hesitate to explore the northern area of the city. The livelier neighbourhoods, such as rue Prince-Arthur and rue Saint-Laurent, nearly always become touristy, and so lose some of their charm. Fads come and go: one day it's fashionable to eat near Fairmount, the next, Bernard and Van Horne are the places to hang out. If you're on a tight budget, you can sample modestly priced and speedily served world cuisine at the many food stalls in the sprawling underground shopping malls, or pick up breakfast in the cheap coffee houses in Métro stations.

Tax (15 per cent) and service (15 per cent) are not included in the prices listed on restaurant menus. Be warned, too, that wine is expensive in Canada, especially in restaurants, but you can take your own bottle to some restaurants in Montréal, and elsewhere in Québec, as many are not licensed to sell alcohol. If nothing else, this should save a bit of cash.

Saint-Laurent and Sainte-Catherine

This is a lively area at night and by day, and it's packed with snack bars and restaurants. Most of the strip clubs and porn cinemas lie at the intersection of Saint-Laurent and Sainte-Catherine, which also marks the start of Chinatown.

☆ Budget

✗ **Ben's Delicatessen** (colour map II, B3, **63**): 990 boulevard de Maisonneuve Ouest, on the corner with Metcalfe. ☎ 844-1000. Métro: Peel. Open 7am–4am; $8–15 per person. The decor is 1950s kitsch, with loads of chrome and plastic, the walls are plastered with posters of film stars, and you'll see some pretty frazzled customers in the wee hours. But it's not the look of the place that draws people here: it's the fabulous smoked meat on rye, and the fact that you can eat and drink here for a pittance. If you are starving, the Big Ben is a meal in itself. Alternatively, try something from the bilingual menu, which proclaims that 'Our customers are the most wonderful people in the universe.' The soups of the day and potato pancakes with '*crème sure*' or blueberries are a good bet. After you've eaten, you can even get your photo taken at the till. It's hard to imagine that this place will ever change, and let's hope it doesn't.

✗ **Da Giovanni** (colour map II, B3, **61**): 690 rue Sainte-Catherine Ouest, near the bus terminal.

☎ 393-3808. Métro: McGill. Open every day from 7am (7.30am Sunday) to 2am (3am Friday and Saturday, 1am on Sunday); set menus $8–12. This Italian restaurant is something of an institution: it's one of the least expensive, and most popular, restaurants in town. There's nothing particularly attractive about the huge, noisy room, the decor is haphazard and the food is not exactly gourmet, but people queue outside for the chance to down bucketfuls of cheap pasta and dessert. There's also a vast choice of pizzas, salads, sandwiches, omelettes and chicken dishes. A very generous breakfast is served until 11am, and there's a take-away service. There are two other Da Giovanni restaurants: at 5440 Sherbrooke Est and 572 Sainte-Catherine Est.

✗ **Le Commensal** (colour map II, B3, **73**): 1204 avenue McGill-College. ☎ 871-1480. Métro: McGill. Open 11.30am–11pm; $7–15 per person. Food is sold by weight at this popular, cafeteria-style self-service vegetarian buffet. You can sample a host of dishes and plump for as much as you like when you've found a favourite. This could take quite a while, with a huge array of starters, salads, pasta, pies and soups, a good choice of herbal and non-herbal teas and coffees and delicious desserts. Try raw vegetables, unusual dishes such as algae, quinoa and *seitan*, or a filling veggie pie. It's cheap, the staff are hip, and if you don't fancy a meal, you can drop in for coffee and cake. There are several other outlets in Montréal, including 2115 Saint-Denis and 3715 Queen-Mary.

✕ **Basha** (colour map II, B3, **64**): 930 rue Sainte-Catherine Ouest. ☎ 866-4272. Métro: Peel. Open from 11am (noon on Sunday) to midnight (1am Friday and Saturday); $10–16 per person. Ignore the drab, cafeteria-style decor: this popular, inexpensive Lebanese eatery serves good spit-roast meat and a dirt-cheap dish of the day on weekdays.

– Montréal's minuscule **Chinatown** is home to a host of good-value restaurants, most of them on rue Clarke and around rue de la Gauchetière (south of René-Lévesque). The following is a selection of the best places to eat for less than $20.

✕ **Le Jardin de Jade** (colour map II, C3, **97**): 67 rue de la Gauchetière Ouest. Métro: Place-d'Armes. A good find, with an all-you-can eat buffet for $7 and a mainly Oriental clientele.

✕ **Cristal Saigon** (colour map II, C3, **98**): 1068 Saint-Laurent. ☎ 875-4275. Métro: Place-d'Armes. This small, informal family restaurant serves generous portions of tasty home cooking. They occasionally serve fresh *durian* fruit, which is worth trying if you can cope with its off-putting smell.

✕ **Pho Minh** (colour map II, C3, **99**): 1021 Saint-Laurent. ☎ 866-8288. Métro: Place d'Armes. The delicious Vietnamese specialities on

offer at this slightly gloomy basement restaurant include pancakes, tripe soup and red beans, with coconut cream for dessert. The staff are young and trendy.

☆☆ Moderate

✕ **Biddle's** (colour map II, B3, **66**): 2060 rue Aylmer. ☎ 842-8656. Métro: McGill. Open 11.30am–11pm on Monday and Tuesday, until 11.30pm Wednesday and Thursday and until 1am at the weekend; at least $20 per person. The overblown rustic decor won't be to everyone's taste, but carnivores of all stylistic persuasions will be wowed by the gigantic, meaty Southern-style spare ribs. The half-portion is big enough for most, although gluttons can gorge themselves on the full whack, or on the equally gargantuan 'ribs and chicken'. If you've got any room left, the Caesar salad and desserts (cheesecake, carrot cake) are also good, while delicious sangria is available by the jug. At lunchtime, the place is teeming with workers, yuppies and English-speaking businesspeople, and it's noisy; it gets louder and more crowded in the evening, when there's decent live jazz (*see* 'Nightlife'). If you can't stand the crush, get a table on the terrace and gaze at the limousines sweeping past. It's not the most refined place in the world, but Biddle's offers a winning combination of good-quality food and ultra-professional service, no matter how packed the place gets. They also sell T-shirts, key-rings and nice aprons.

✕ **Quartier Saint-Louis** (colour map II, C1, **95**): 4723 rue Saint-Denis. ☎ 284-7723. Métro: Laurier. Evenings only; closed Sunday and Monday. This friendly place serves excellent French dishes and country food: calves' sweetbreads with noodles, rabbit fricassée, mussels and wild boar, all simply cooked but bursting with flavour. The decor is perhaps a little drab, with oilcloths on the tables, but one plus point is that you can bring your own wine.

✕ **Restaurant Place Milton** (colour map II, C2, **84**): 220 Milton Ouest. ☎ 285-0011. Métro: Place-des-Arts. Open 8am–8pm (until 4pm Saturday and Sunday); $6–10. This brunchtime gem is hidden behind a very ordinary shopfront, and is a great place to stoke up for a day's sightseeing if you're not getting free breakfast at your hotel. Head straight for the quiet, green terrace (heated in winter) and get stuck into delicious set menus of sweet and savoury breakfasts, including toast, eggs, sautéed potatoes, sausages, bacon, fruit and coffee. The staff are easy-going, and it's excellent value for money.

✕ **Cafétéria** (colour map II, C2, **93**): 3581 boulevard Saint-Laurent. ☎ 849-3855. Métro: Sherbrooke. At lunchtime, $5–14; in the evening, a *table d'hôte* is $13–17. One of Montréal's trendiest restaurants, this place attracts a hip young crowd in the evening. Needless to say, it doesn't look at all like your average caff: the interior is original and sophisticated, with soft lighting and a warm, modern feel, and the staff suit the place down to a tee. The pasta, omelettes, meat dishes, eggs Benedict and puddings are all good and surprisingly affordable, and the menu suggests that somebody has given a thought to those on a low-calorie diet. This is another good place for a hearty breakfast (8–11.30am).

✕ **Shed Café** (colour map II, C2): 3515 boulevard Saint-Laurent. ☎ 842-0220. Open 8am–11pm on the terrace; until 3am inside. A hip hangout with pumping music and postmodern decor, where the snack-type food is tasty and not very expensive. You can get sandwiches on wholegrain bread, toasties, good burgers and a range of salads, as well as scrummy desserts. People come here for the atmosphere as much as for the food, and it's worth popping in for a drink even if you're not hungry.

☆☆☆ Expensive

✕ **Primadonna** (colour map II, C2, **94**): 3479 boulevard Saint-Laurent. ☎ 282-6644. Métro: Sherbrooke. Lunch $25; double that for an evening meal. People come to this Italian restaurant to see and be seen, and to flash the cash while they're at it. You're waited on by a bevy of supermodels, supervised by the cool Roberto, and the cooking is original and inventive: grilled vegetables with olive oil and balsamic vinegar, a 'mosaic' of grilled fish and shellfish, octopus with herbs, black pasta with queen scallops and prawns, all with individual sauces. There's also an excellent sushi bar. The decor is attractive, in shades of yellow and blue, but the restaurant is on a busy main road, which makes it fairly noisy.

✕ **Chez Gautier** (colour map II, C2, **96**): 3487 avenue du Parc. ☎ 8445-2992. Métro: Place-des-Arts. Lunch $20; *table d'hôte* dinner $25–35. Slap-bang between two city-centre districts, this elegant restaurant looks like a 1900s-style Parisian bistro, and its terrace is one of the nicest in the area. The impeccable service is matched by the decor and the cooking. The à la carte menu is expensive, but the affordable set menus are well worth trying.

The West Quarter

This is the English-speaking part of the city, and it doesn't take long to realize that the vibes are different – it's a lot smarter, with prestigious real-estate businesses and lots of luxury shops. It's dead in the evening, apart from a few elegant streets with fashionable nightclubs, although the area around McGill University is lively during term time.

☆☆ Moderate

✕ **Bar B'Barn** (colour map II, A3, **65**): 1201 rue Guy, near Sainte-Catherine. ☎ 931-3811. Métro: Guy-Concordia. Open from 11am (weekends 11.30am) to 10.30pm (midnight on Friday and Saturday). Main courses $6–20. This vast, country-style restaurant is like a five-storey lumberjack's cabin, and the cooking is suitably robust. The specialities of the house are spare ribs with tomato rice and chicken and chips (both come in several different sizes), but whatever you choose, excellent food and generous portions are guaranteed.

Vieux Montréal

This is beautifully preserved area is full of charm, but there are coachloads of tourists everywhere, and finding good food at sensible prices is something of a challenge. Your best bet is to visit the old town for a morning walk or an evening drink (*see* 'Nightlife'), but eat elsewhere: nearby Chinatown is packed full of good-value restaurants (*see above*).

✕ **La Gargote** (colour map III, B2, **67**): 351 place d'Youville. ☎ 844-1428. Lunchtime menus $12–15; evening *table d'hôtes* $13–17. It's not far from the lively rue Saint-Paul and the busy boulevard René-Lévesque, but the only vehicles that drive past this restaurant are horse-drawn carriages full of tourists in search of romance. It's not especially friendly, but it's agreeably intimate and the French cooking is not bad at all.

✕ **Le Grill** (colour map III, C1, **68**): 183 rue Saint-Paul Est, near the corner of place Jacques-Cartier. ☎ 397-1044. Lunch $9–15; evening *table d'hôte* $20–25. Le Grill feels like a French restaurant, and the staff are all from France. There's a pretty patio where you can eat in summer, or you can sit inside in the subdued light, gazing at exposed beams and stone walls. The food is good, rather than great: at lunchtime, the '*spécial du jour*' is the thing to go for, while in the evening, the *table d'hôte* is ideal for a romantic tête-à-tête.

✕ **Menara** (colour map III, C-D1, **69**): 256 rue Saint-Paul Est. ☎ 861-1989. Open for lunch, but people only really come here in the evenings (until 10pm). *Table d'hôte* $28. If you fancy something a little more exotic than French cuisine, this is an authentic Moroccan restaurant in a mock Berber tent serving couscous, *mechoui*, tajines, pastillas and the like, all tasty and well prepared. In the evenings, dessert is accompanied by belly-dancers, complete with floaty veils, which can be a bit disorientating.

Rue Saint-Denis and Eastwards

On rue Saint-Denis (Nos. 1000–4000), there's a range of restaurants to suit all pockets. On '*bas Saint-Denis*', which is the main focus of this section, they're all crowded together in direct competition, although everyone seems to get on OK. The section between René-Lévesque and Sherbrooke is commercial and touristy in the worst sense of the word (i.e., all the eateries are packed out). That said, it's always lively, particularly during the Jazz Festival (first two weeks in July), and the Just for Laughs comedy festival at the end of that month.

☆ Budget

✗ **Spirite Lounge Restaurant** (colour map II, D2, **67**): 1201 rue Ontario Est, (Montcalm corner). ☎ 529-6204. Closed Sunday evenings and Monday. Set menu $13. Travelling is about seeing, doing and eating something different: the Spirite Lounge gives you the chance to do all three at the same time. Roz-Man and Patrice are the most unusual pair of restaurateurs in Montréal, and their charm, their food, their style and their flair for design make their restaurant one of the best places to eat in the city. The facade is graffitied, and the astonishing decor uses recycled materials such as aluminium foil, bits of mirrors, odd furniture and tablecloths. The result looks is somewhere between a rubbish tip and a cathedral: it's not to everyone's taste, but it makes a change from flashy places in other areas of the city. At the stove, Roz-Man, a self-taught chef, prepares succulent vegetarian cuisine using instinct alone. Patrice, meanwhile, lavishes attention on his customers, and can talk knowledgeably about the organic produce and anything else you might care to ask him. Even the food is eco-friendly: you ask for a portion that matches your appetite, and failure to clear your plate carries a fine of $1. Bring your own wine.

✗ **Restaurant Iza** (colour map II, D2, **68**): rue Ontario Est (Timothée end), in a fairly trashy area. Meals about $20. You'll spot this place straight away: a small, dilapidated building with traditional briquettes painted green and orangey-red. Inside, there are only a few tables, with music in the background, and you can see part of the kitchen behind the bar. You really are 'chez Iza' – or 'chez Iza's parents', to be more exact, as Iza is the little girl playing supermodel in the framed photos lining the walls. Her father, who's from the Dominican Republic, cooks up authentic family cuisine: delicious chicken fajitas, enchiladas and chilli con carne, followed by flambéed bananas for dessert, all made with fresh ingredients. You'll find the sangria and margaritas alarmingly easy to knock back. Unsurprisingly, this place has a sizeable regular following.

✗ **Chez Gatsé**: 317 rue Ontario Est. ☎ 985-2494. Meals $7–12. This is the only Tibetan restaurant in Québec. The decor is a bit drab, but it's a cheap and cheerful place where you sample *thupkas*, *shapalès*, *shaptas* and *momos*, delicious light steamed buns garnished with cheese, vegetables or meat. Gatsé offers a smiling welcome; she also owns a shop on the first floor above the restaurant, selling jewellery, books, incense and rugs imported from Tibet.

✗ **La Paryse** (colour map II, C2-3, **70**): 302 rue Ontario Est, on the corner with Sanguinet. ☎ 842-2040. Open 11am–11pm (2–10.30pm on Sunday); main courses $7. If you are put off by rue Saint-Denis, walk on a short distance and you'll get the best burgers in Montréal. The 1950s decor and crowded tables make for a friendly atmosphere, the lunch menu offers very good value and there's often a queue. One per cent of the restaurant's profit is used to sponsor contemporary artists.

✗ **Le Café Pellerin** (colour map II, C2-3, **82**): 330 rue Ontario Est. ☎ 845-0909. Open 11am–11pm; lunch $8–12, dinner $10–15. A Montréal fixture since the 1970s, Café Pellerin is basically a nice place to read a magazine and listen to good music. There's also a quiet terrace at the rear. The menu is not very original, but it's not very expensive either. They do brunch on Sundays.

✗ **Shezan** (colour map II, C-D2, **92**): 2051 rue saint-Denis. ☎ 845-8867. Dinner only on Saturday and Sunday; lunch $5–10, evening *table d'hôte* $10–16. One of the best Asian eateries in the area – and there are plenty of them – this simply decorated Indian restaurant offers good food at honest prices.

☆☆ Moderate

✗ **Le Petit Extra** (colour map II, D2, **71**): 1690 rue Ontario Est, near Papineau. ☎ 527-5552. Open for lunch and dinner (until 10pm), dinner only on Saturday and Sunday; lunch $9–12, dinner $13–20. This is a fashionable, lively bistro where you'll get flawless food and service with a smile. The lunchtime menu, which changes every day, offers a starter,

a main course and coffee, and is extremely good value. In the evening, the higher prices reflect the more elaborate cuisine. Make sure you book in advance.

✗ **Bato Thaï**: 1310 Sainte-Catherine Est, in the city's gay quarter. ☎ 524-6705. Soups and salads $3; main dishes $9. This modern and intriguing restaurant replaces conventional Thai decor with exposed ventilation shafts and swathes of fabric hanging in mid-air, all in vivid colours but with soft lighting. The waiters and waitresses bustle around the circular bar in traditional skirts, trousers or sarongs. The short menu includes a choice of salads, soups, and dishes flavoured with ginger, lemongrass or coconut. The starters are enormous, so stick to a main course with rice or noodles unless you're ravenous.

✗ **Mikado** (colour map II, C-D3, **72**): 1731 rue Saint-Denis. ☎ 844-5705. Open every evening and for lunch on Wednesday, Thursday and Friday; set menus $10–42. You will emerge from this Japanese restaurant with a warm glow of satisfaction after stuffing yourself with delectable sushi, sashimi and teriyaki in an elegant setting, complete with waitresses dressed in kimonos.

From Prince-Arthur to Mont-Royal

The parallel main roads of Saint-Laurent and Saint-Denis, and the adjacent streets, are happy hunting grounds for cash-conscious diners (Métro: Sherbrooke and Mont-Royal). They've yet to be overrun with tourists, and the original populations have not yet been forced out. This bit of Saint-Laurent also crosses part of Montréal's Portuguese district.

A few years ago, rue Prince-Arthur was home to the city's coolest restaurants, but it lost its soul when the tourists moved in. Rue Duluth was once full of nice little restaurants and Greek eateries, but has also lost much of its appeal, though there are still some pleasant streets in the area where you can go for a stroll (rue Drolet, rue Laval, carré Saint-Louis). In general, though, all you'll find in this part of town are dozens of Greek restaurants in cut-throat competition, in the middle of an area whose redevelopment has not lived up to its promise.

☆–☆☆ Budget to Moderate

✗ **Schwartz's** (colour map II, C2, **76**): 3895 boulevard Saint-Laurent. ☎ 842-4813. Open every day 9am–1am (2am on Friday, 3am on Saturday). This is the best Jewish restaurant in Montréal. You can't really miss it, as crowds of people gather outside to queue for a table – and most are prepared to wait for ages. The glass counters groan under the weight of smoked meats and jars of peppers, and if you don't fancy hanging around, you can pick up a huge smoked-meat sandwich with mustard and dash off. While you wait, you'll be entertained by the sight of old locals and middle-class types jostling for tables. On the walls, paintings and assorted paraphernalia testify to the fame of this establishment.

✗ **L'Anecdote** (colour map II, D1, **78**): 801 rue Rachel Est, at the edge of Saint-Hubert. Métro: Mont-Royal. Open 7.30am–10pm (weekends 9am–10pm); lunch menu (soup, main course and coffee) $6.75, full breakfast $8–10. A snack bar that smacks of yesteryear, with red leatherette seats and Formica everywhere. It attracts a local crowd, with lots of children at weekends, as well as a smattering of tourists who seem to dig the 1950s atmosphere. Either that, or they've heard about the generous and tasty breakfasts (fresh fruit juice, excellent omelettes, bagels, the burgers and the *poutine* (a local speciality: French fries topped with cheese and brown sauce). There are two rooms, one done up like an American diner, the second with amusing, slightly eccentric decor and retro kitchen furniture; the music is contemporary, though.

✗ **Porté Disparu** (colour map II, D1, **79**): 957 avenue du Mont-Royal. ☎ 524-0271. Métro: Mont-Royal. Open until 1am (2am on Saturday and Sunday); daily set menu $5.50. A magnet for the area's poets, philosophers and artists, this large, brick-walled place has an old wooden floor and a shelf full of books running all the way along one wall. Revolving displays and an out-of-tune piano add to the general ambience, and there's live jazz on weekends. The food isn't what you'd call up-market, but it's generous, nourishing and unfussy. The set menu is really good value, as you get soup, the dish of the day, a dessert and coffee: beef and vegetable broth, say, then chicken creole and date squares. There's a glass-roofed refuge at the back, so you can gaze up at the blue sky while you tuck in.

✗ **Le Bambou Bleu** (colour map II, C2): 3895 rue Saint-Denis. ☎ 845-1401. This little Vietnamese restaurant serves good-quality food at reasonable prices. The best set menu ($11.95) includes soup, spring rolls, kebabs, dessert and coffee and costs $11.95. You'll have trouble clearing your plate, as the portions are huge. There's a pleasant terrace for hot summer evenings. Le Bambou Bleu is not licensed to sell alcohol, so you can bring your own wine.

✗ **Santropol** (colour map II, C2, **80**): 3990 rue Saint-Urbain, on the edge of Duluth. ☎ 842-3110. Opens from 11.30am (noon at weekends) to midnight (1am on Friday and Saturday). Closed Monday in winter. This is a very popular place, especially with 'granolas' (a local term for vegetarians, though the food here is organic, not veggie). The bric-a-brac decor is colourful and fun, while outside you'll find a tiny Japanese garden and a rustic inner courtyard. They serve all kinds of teas, including their own herbal teas (apricot, raspberry, etc.), tasty homemade milkshakes and excellent sandwiches with weird names (smooth roots, midnight butter, pepper island), all made to order and absolutely huge. A quarter of Santropol's profit goes to charity.

✗ **Le Jardin de Panos** (colour map II, D2, **62**): 521 rue Duluth Est. ☎ 521-4206. Open noon to midnight; $12–20. It looks like a typical Greek taverna, and there's usually a queue outside the door. Inside, the atmosphere is like that of a university canteen, with a noise level several decibels higher than in most restaurants. It's a friendly place, the service is fairly swift and the Greek specialities are surprisingly good given the huge number of people who come to eat here; in fact, this is one of the best restaurants on rue Duluth. Start with an assortment of meze (taramasalata, aubergine caviar, stuffed vine leaves), enough for two to share, then move onto *souvlakia* or juicy marinated grilled meats. In summer, you can join the hordes on the huge terrace.

✗ **Le Nil Bleu** (colour map II, C2, **69**): 3890 rue Saint-Denis, between Roy and Duluth. ☎ 285-4628. Full meal $25. The Nile is the longest river in the world at 6,000 kilometres (about 3,750 miles), and runs through many countries on its journey to the Mediterranean. This restaurant follows a similar culinary course, offering specialities from Rwanda, Burundi, Kenya, Sudan and Egypt, all cooked by the charming Ethiopian restaurateurs. If you don't mind eating with your fingers, you'll have a great time here, particularly if you go in a group and have a buffet-style meal. The principle is simple: each of you chooses a different speciality (chicken, lamb or vegetables in spicy sauces), accompanied by small rolled pancakes. Instead of using plates, everything is served on a vast tray covered with a giant pancake that you eat at the end to mop up the sauces. To round

off your meal, you'll get beautiful cafetières full of the most sublime *moka*, which the Ethiopians have been drinking since the dawn of time.

✗ **Restaurant Mazurka** (colour map II, C2, **81**): 64 rue Prince-Arthur. ☎ 844-3539. Open until midnight; lunchtime menus $9–15, dinner $25. This Polish restaurant, frequented by Polish people, has a deservedly good reputation. The food is excellent, if a little overpriced, and portions are fairly generous.

☆☆ – ☆☆☆ Moderate to Expensive

✗ **L'Express** (colour map II, C-D2, **83**): 3927 rue Saint-Denis. ☎ 845-5333. Open until 2am (to 1am on Sunday); main courses $8–20. L'Express is a lively restaurant and bar, rather like a Parisian brasserie, that's frequented by 30-something beautiful people and an artsy crowd. Thankfully, its popularity hasn't gone to its head, and it has maintained its quality – and kept its clientele – over many years. It's not too expensive, the desserts are fantastic – try the raspberry and pear ice cream, or the astonishing 'Indulgent' gateau – and it has one of the best wine cellars in Montréal. Book in advance for dinner.

✗ **Jano** (colour map II, C2, **77**): 3883 boulevard Saint-Laurent. ☎ 849-0646. Open 5pm–midnight; $10–22. This popular Portuguese restaurant has a brazier in the window, bare brick walls and an impressive collection of bottles. You'll be treated to huge portions of Ribatejo specialities: grilled rabbit, skewered meat, spare ribs, sausage, chargrilled fish and more. There's a family atmosphere, with friendly service and simple cooking. It's not exactly a bargain, but a meal here won't break the bank.

☆☆☆☆ Splash Out

✕ **Laloux** (colour map II, C2, **85**): 252 avenue des Pins Est (two blocks away from rue Saint-Denis). ☎ 287-9127. Open noon–10.30pm (weekends 11.30pm); lunch (before 2pm) $10–17, evening *table d'hôte* $20–26. We're talking serious dining here: stylish waiters wearing long aprons pirouette around the sober, elegant space, laden with enormous ice creams and other goodies for a classy, yuppie clientele. The shortish menu offers imaginative and well-balanced nouvelle cuisine, with dishes such as rabbit and pepper *gateau*, shellfish gazpacho, fish with vanilla and calf's sweetbreads and marrow cooked in red wine, while there are some good wines available by the glass. The food is truly excellent, so come for lunch if you can't afford to have dinner here.

From Mont-Royal to Bernard

This is one of the city's most cosmopolitan districts – most of the locals are Greek, Portuguese or Italian, while some streets are frequented by Orthodox Jews, so it has a decidedly Mediterranean feel. In the rectangle bounded by Parc and Saint-Laurent, you'll discover a host of restaurants, most of which are well worth trying, while Parc is a kind of 'little Greece' for foodies. It's also the latest part of the city to undergo gentrification, especially on Saint-Laurent and between Saint-Joseph and Bernard. There have been no architectural upheavals, but restaurateurs, advertising agencies, trendy clothes shops and fashionable hairdressers have set up shop in premises that had been abandoned for some time. Outremont, to the north of this district, is the home of the middle-class French-speaking community, and you'll find chic restaurants aplenty there. All in all, this is a good place for a culinary adventure and a stroll through ethnic Montréal. To get there, take the Métro to Laurier station or the bus that goes up boulevard Saint-Laurent.

☆–☆☆ Budget to Moderate

✕ **Wilensky** (colour map II, C1, **86**): 34 rue Fairmount Ouest, at the corner of Clark. ☎ 271-0247. Métro: Laurier. Open Monday to Friday, 9am–4pm (closed from 15 to 30 July); $5–8. This kosher snack bar has been open since 1932, and it hasn't changed a bit in 70 years. It has an authentic prewar atmosphere, with ancient toasters and a decor that is pure cinema. Today, the narrow high stools are occupied by local kids and businessmen, who come in for breakfast or to stoke up with a Wilensky special, made with four kinds of salami. The sandwiches may not be the best in town, but the character of the place is unique: the drinks are made to order, with ladlefuls of concentrate topped up with soda – a moment of pure nostalgia.

✕ **L'Avenue**: 922 avenue du Mont-Royal Ouest, on the corner of Saint-Urbain. ☎ 523-8780. Open from 7am (8am on Saturday) to 11pm (10pm on Sunday); breakfast $8, hamburgers and pasta $5–10. This is the in place for weekend brunches, and hip young Montréalers come here in droves. During the week, it's a lot less frenetic, and you can linger over the giant sandwiches, hamburgers with delicious French fries, huge pasta dishes, invigorating breakfasts and eggs Benedict with all kinds of sauces. The cakes, meanwhile, are of the 'death by chocolate' variety. The decor is splendidly exuberant: benches in alcoves, a graffitied brick wall, a psychedelic toilet with a mirrorball and a water fountain. The music could do with being toned down a bit, though. Payment by cash only.

✕ **Maison de l'Original Fairmount Bagel** (colour map II, C1, **87**): 74 Fairmount, between Saint-Urbain and Clark. ☎ 272-0667. Open 24 hours a day. It's a case of love at first smell for this bakery in an old red-brick house. People come from far and wide for delicious, freshly baked bagels: the brown ones with raisins are rated the best in Montréal, and they certainly live up to expectation.

☆☆ Moderate

✕ **Beauty's** (colour map II, C1, **88**): 93 avenue du Mont-Royal Ouest, on the corner of Saint-Urbain. ☎ 849-8883. Métro: Mont-Royal. Open every day from 7am (8am Sunday) to 5pm; main courses from $8. Built in 1942, this place has a diner-type atmosphere, with typical blue and aluminium decor – but you don't get many diners this crowded, and there's something Tardis-like about the number of people they cram into the space. On Sunday mornings, fans wait patiently for ages to have their brunch, pouncing on tables as soon as anyone leaves. Beauty's has its share of celebrity fans as well, including the singer Leonard Cohen. The atmosphere is friendly and relaxed, but the main attraction is the good, fresh, appetizing Jewish food: sandwiches, omelettes, salads and burgers. Try the famous Beauty's Special (cream cheese, smoked salmon, tomatoes and onions on a crusty grilled bagel), delicious cheese *blintzes* or the 'mishmash' (omelette with sausage,

salami, green pepper and fried onions).

✕ **Pacific**: 837 avenue du Mont-Royal Est, near Saint-Hubert. ☎ 521-7035. From $20 for a starter, main course and rice. The setting is nothing if not exotic, with a giant Buddha on the wall, leopardskins on the wicker chairs and papyrus and bamboo lining the walls. The Far Eastern dishes are no less opulent: subtle, intense and with an endless variety of flavours. Peppered chicken soup with coconut milk, duck with five spices and sautéed vegetables in peanut sauce are all exquisite. Unfortunately, the wine list falls far short of the standard required: it's too short, the few bottles on offer are too expensive, and the house wine ($20 per litre) is not always available.

✕ **El Zaziummm** (colour map II, C1, **90**): 4525 avenue du Parc. ☎ 499-3675. Lunch $3–7; dinner menus $8–20. It is impossible to find two identical objects in this hectic, noisy Mexican restaurant, which is jam-packed with junk-shop odds and ends, from an Elvis bust and a plastic skeleton to bar seats made from bike saddles, bath tub tables and Aztec masks. The menu reflects the decor: it's crammed, cluttered and almost illegible. The Tex-Mex food is not up to much, but it's very cheap indeed. On Monday and Tuesday nights, a fortune-teller can reveal what your future holds, though you'll have to cross her palm with silver first . . .

✕ **La Petite Ardoise** (colour map II, C1, **89**): 222 rue Laurier Ouest. ☎ 495-4961. Open 8am–midnight; *table d'hôte* $9–17, weekend brunch $5–9. This trendy restaurant and bar, with a spruce turquoise facade, has a brick-and-wood decor and a quiet terrace. The service is charming and refined, and it's a tranquil place to have a snack (onion soup, salads, quiches) as you write postcards or watch the locals going about their daily business. In the evening, the *table d'hôte* offers tasty dishes like chicken stew in generous portions. Brunch is available on Saturday and Sunday.

✕ **Galaxie** (colour map II, C1, **91**): 4801 rue Saint-Denis, not far from the corner of Saint-Joseph. ☎ 499-9711. Métro: Laurier. Open until 11pm (1am at weekends); $12–15. Coming here is a bit like visiting another planet: a world of authentic American diners in huge aluminium caravans, with Formica seats and waitresses in bobby socks. This caravan dates from the 1950s, and was salvaged from a scrapyard. You can devour burgers, milkshakes, enormous banana splits and sundaes as you listen to your favourite rock 'n' roll hits on the jukebox. A nice place, although it sometimes lacks atmosphere.

✕ **Modigliani**: 1251 rue Gilford. ☎ 524-3812. *Table d'hôte* $9.95–18.95, excluding taxes and service charges. This friendly Tuscan 'gallery-restaurant' is in the heart of the Plateau-Mont-Royal area, but it's a fair distance from the lively rues Saint-Denis, Duluth or Prince Arthur, and your fellow diners are more likely to be local residents than tourists. You can sample divine pasta, gnocchi with peas and *sauce rosée* or lamb with rosemary in a truly eclectic environment: toy raccoons play in a dinghy above the entrance, and there's a huge bas-relief of a dozing drinker on the mirror at the back. Strange, but true.

✕ **La Moulerie**: 1249 avenue Bernard, on the corner of Champagneur. ☎ 273-8132. Métro: Rosemont or Outremont. Open 11.30am–midnight (weekends from 10am). Lunchtime *table d'hôte* $8–12, dinner $15–20. This chic, bistro-style establishment is one of the most popular restaurants in northern Montréal, especially at the weekend. As its name implies, the speciality is *moules* (mussels), with more than a dozen tasty preparations (the more unusual ones include Indian-style, Italian-style and in a salad).

In the North of Town

In this fast-evolving city, new restaurants develop all the time, then fade out again. In the north of the city, whole districts are being regenerated bit by bit; each time this happens, up spring the restaurants to cater for the latest 'invasion'. If you are an adventurous foodie, and you haven't seen anything that takes your fancy in the listings above, why not go farther afield? You could try Montréal's Italian quarter, for example, for sumptuous Mediterranean food. Métro: Beaubien or Jean-Talon.

☆☆ Moderate

✕ **Tre Marie (Les Trois Marie)**: 6934 rue Clark, on the corner of Mozart, to the west of Saint-Laurent. ☎ 277-9859. Métro: Jean-Talon. Open noon–9pm; $20–30. This is a neat and tidy restaurant with warm, tasteful modern decor, and the olive-skinned waiters and waitresses make you feel like you're in Italy. It attracts a fairly chic clientele, and fills up fast in the evening, while on Sundays, Italian families monopolize the tables. The food is delicious and typically Italian: lasagne, osso buco, cutlet *alla parmigiana*, Venetian calves' liver and oodles of pasta, all marvellously cooked by an authoritarian mamma and her gang. The desserts are good, but only the tiramisu is homemade, and it's so popular that you almost need to book it along with your table. You can round off your meal with a real espresso.

WHERE TO EAT IN THE AREA

Traditional Québécois Cuisine

✖ **Sucrerie de la Montagne**: 300 rang Saint-Georges, Rigaud, about 45 minutes away from Montréal, near mount Rigaud, on highway 40 towards Ottawa (exit 17). ☎ 451-5204/0831. This is a lumberjacks' camp, like those built in the early 20th century. It's impossible to get here by bus, so it's only for those who have their own transport, and you'll need to book in advance, as it's something of a tourist attraction. You can watch the harvest being gathered, or see how maple syrup is made, and the owner, who sports a splendid beard, is a real character. But the main reason for visiting is to taste pea soup, baked beans or pancakes with syrup, all prepared in the traditional way. It's far from cheap, but you'll find it impossible to clear your plate. You can stay for one or more nights in the two attractive log cabins (each sleeps six) at the entrance, and the whole enterprise is primarily geared towards groups. It's the perfect place to get back to nature, but skip it if you're looking for nightlife, as nothing happens in the evenings.

✖ **La Sucrerie À l'Orée du Bois**: 11381, La Fresnière, Mirabel, Saint-Benoît, 50 kilometres (about 30 miles) north of Montréal. ☎ 258-2976. Fax: 258-4757. To get there from Montréal, take Route 13 or 15 North, then autoroute 640 West. Leave this at exit 11, staying on the right-hand side on 148 West, then, at the third set of lights, take boulevard Industriel on the left. At the third stop sign, turn right onto Rivière Sud-Chemin La Fresnière; about 10 kilometres (6 miles) farther on, you'll find l'Orée du Bois on your left, shortly after you pass a junction with the Rochon hill on your right. The Pilon family run this large, rustic cabin in green and pleasantly undulating surroundings, You'll be served hearty portions of traditional pea soup, baked beans, *oreilles de crisse* (a kind of crunchy bacon consisting of boiled and fried salted lard), house marinades, and loads of puddings with maple syrup (peaches with maple syrup, maple tarts, maple mousse, maple meringues). The portions are gargantuan, and the prices are more-or-less reasonable. It's essential to book in advance: while you're on the phone, why not arrange a guided tour of the Sucrerie, led by Nicole, the housekeeper?

Other Cuisine

✖ **Le Bistrot à Champlain**: at Sainte-Marguerite du lac Masson, about 50 minutes from Montréal. Take Autoroute 15 North, exit 67, then the 117 North and finally the 370. This bistro is renowned for its good food, and its cellar is little short of legendary, with some 22,000 bottles of wine to draw on. This is the only restaurant in Canada to have received a Grand Award from the American magazine *The Wine Spectator*. People come here from all over America and even from Europe.

WHERE TO HAVE A DRINK, NIGHTLIFE

For maps of Montréal see the second colour plate section.

Montréal's nightlife could leave you feeling exhausted after a few nights. It's richly varied, intense and remarkably inexpensive, as you usually don't have to pay to get into clubs and you won't pay through the nose for drinks. The city's clubs don't make you feel that you're being fleeced, and there's a refreshing absence of cliquey, elitist venues that treat you like dirt. Montréal is a city that parties hard, but don't bother going anywhere before 11pm: the nightlife starts late here, even though the bars and clubs close relatively early (2–3am). It goes without saying that there is something for all tastes, but fashions change quickly here, and there's no guarantee that the places listed below will still be drawing the in-crowd by the time you get there.

For some time now, the division between francophone and anglophone Montréal (to the west of boulevard Saint-Laurent) has been growing more marked: you may even see queues outside certain English-speaking clubs, with an admission fee of up to $10. Dress to impress if you want to get in, or get there well before midnight. These clubs are becoming more and more popular, particularly with Americans from the state of Maine. On the French side, meanwhile, you'll find an explosion of life in the pavement cafés over the (all too short) summer months. These terraces are quieter in winter, but that doesn't mean that there's less going in the bars themselves.

For events, concerts and nightclubs, look in the free weekly *Voir*, which you can find practically everywhere (large hotels, restaurants, garages etc.). The places below are listed by area; for each address, there'll be some indication of whether the focus is on drinking, dancing, listening to music or all three. (In Canada, these different activities aren't necessarily distinct.)

Montréal is an important centre for jazz, as you can tell from the number of places dedicated to this kind of music, and many talented musicians hail from these parts. If you're a fan, then the best time to come is for the International Jazz Festival, in late June or early July (*see* 'Festivals and Events').

In the Centre: Sainte-Catherine and Saint-Denis

❦ **Jello Bar** (colour map II, C3, **103**): 151 rue Ontario Est. ☎ 285-2621. Entrance $6. Right in the centre of Montréal, but in a fairly quiet area, this is a great place to sip a martini and listen to excellent jazz, funk, soul and salsa, in a warmly coloured space with soft lighting. There's also a dancefloor should the mood take you.

❦ **Les Foufounes Électriques** (colour map II, C3, **101**): 87 Sainte-Catherine Ouest. ☎ 844-5539. This large, grungy bar-club is one of the best nightspots in Montréal, and it attracts a pretty colourful crowd,

from students in punk gear to skate fiends and even a few stray hippies. There's a huge terrace on the ground floor, while you can dance to pumping techno anthems in the upstairs room. Attitudes seem to be left at the door, which makes it a nice place to settle in for a serious drinking session (they do good-value beer by the jug). Occasional concerts.

❦ **Le Saint-Sulpice** (colour map II, C3, **117**): 1680 rue Saint-Denis. ☎ 844-9458. This is a café-bar in a pretty house with a garden and a wonderfully sprawling terrace, where a motley crew of students meets for drinks beneath the trees or by the fountain. There are six rooms on three levels, all with their own particular atmosphere: in the basement, there's a dancefloor, while upstairs you can pick up a book to read in one of the five bars, or play billiards. There's always a good atmosphere, despite the coachloads of tourists who appear on certain evenings, and the music covers most bases. A hidden door on the top floor leads to **Le Cabaret**: a little stage, about 15 tables, a bar, and shows every evening during the festivals. Look out for stand-up shows during the Just for Laughs festival in July. There's no cover charge, but they do a collection for the performers after each show.

♥ Café Chaos (colour map II, C3, **102**): 1637 rue Saint-Denis. Open until 2am if business is brisk enough. This laid-back, unpretentious, little bar with pretty, wood-panelled rooms is a great place to meet local students. The waiters and waitresses are charming, and all styles of music are on offer, from French chanson to alt-rock, while Monday is techno night. There's a small terrace on the street, and food is served during the day. Drinks-wise, it's well worth trying draught Boréale, a local beer that comes in blonde and dark flavours. If it's full, head across the road to Pégase for a game of chess.

♥ Biddle's (colour map II, B3, **66**): 2060 rue Aylmer. ☎ 842-8656. Métro: McGill. This is a great place to meet, as much for your stomach's sake as for your ears' (see 'Where to Eat'). There's good-quality jazz here every night from 6pm to midnight (until 2am on Friday and Saturday), in an elegant setting with art-deco lights. Entry is free since it's a bar-restaurant, but drinks are on the steep side. The owner, who really is called Biddle, plays the double bass, and the house band often get their friends in for a rowdy jam session.

♥ Le Di Salvio (colour map II, C2, **111**): 3519 boulevard Saint-Laurent. ☎ 845-4337. This place has a dancing room with a circular bar and a hall where you can hear rock and blues bands (Wednesday to Sunday, 10pm–3am). It's good fun, if a touch subdued, and attracts an upwardly mobile young crowd.

♥ Spectrum (colour map II, C3, **100**): 318 rue Sainte-Catherine Ouest. ☎ 861-5851. Website: www.admission.com. Métro: Place-des-Arts. Concert tickets $20–30. One of the best gig venues in the city: most of the concerts are rock, but it sometimes has dance acts or jazz. It's a big place, and there's never much of a crush, but get there early if you want to bag the best seats.

♥ Groove Society (colour map II, D3, **107**): 1288 rue Amherst, level with rue Sainte-Catherine. Open from Wednesday to Sunday until 3am. Entrance fee $6–8. You'll be frisked before you get past the door of this basement club, full of trendy young things who flit around among the very kitsch decor: fake fur on the ceiling, padded walls and so on. A succession of vaulted rooms take you on a journey from techno to hip-hop and from funk to house.

♥ Métropolis (colour map II, C3, **106**): 59 rue Sainte-Catherine Est. ☎ 288-2020. Métro: Saint-Laurent. This former theatre is the subject of much debate in Montréal. Its critics consider it to be a monument to pretension, from the doormen, the red carpet and the cordoned-off pavement to the exorbitant admission fee, the draconian door policy and the dress code. Once inside, you'll see an astonishing concentration of the beautiful people, joined on weekends by a bemused-looking bridge-and-tunnel crowd in their Sunday best. There's also a concert hall.

Rue Sainte-Catherine is the centre of Montréal's red-light district. Americans go there to slum it, and it's become rather seedy.

In the Old Town

Terrasse de l'Auberge du Vieux Port (colour map III, C1-2, **110**): 9 rue de la Commune Est. ☎ 876-0081. Website: www.aubergedu vieuxport.com. From the small but luxurious hall of the Auberge du Vieux Port, get the lift to the top floor. Take the first door on the right, then the stairs to the roof, and you'll be rewarded with a breathtaking view of the city: the port of Montréal, the dome of the Biosphere, the Saint Lawrence river, the boats. Service is fast and friendly, and snacks and drinks are available at all hours, at prices that look a lot more reasonable when you have the city spread out before you. You won't find a better place to take a break from sightseeing in Vieux Montréal.

Union (colour map III, B2, **111**): 600 rue d'Youville Ouest. ☎ 286-9851. A meal here costs $15. Union is the coolest café in the docks area. In fact, there's no competition: this part of the harbour is being renovated, but this place caters for the many Montréalers who aren't prepared to wait for the builders to finish the next hot area. It's a place to see and be seen, whether you want to pose over Sunday brunch (from 12.30pm) or just burn up the dancefloor.

Le Jardin Nelson (colour map III, C1, **108**): 407 place Jacques-Cartier. ☎ 861-5731. Website: www. jardinnelson.com. Open until 1am

from mid-April until the end of October. Main course $13. Right in the heart of Vieux Montréal, this bar-restaurant has a lovely shaded terrace that opens onto rue Saint-Paul. There are jazz and blues concerts in the afternoon and evening, and it's a great spot to sink a few sangrias as the sun goes down. It's a little expensive, but no more than you'd expect in a tourist area.

Les Deux Pierrots (colour map III, C2, **109**): 104 rue Saint-Paul Est. 861-1270. Email: pierrots@vidéo tron.ca. Métro: Champ-de-Mars. Open Thursday to Saturday, 8pm–3am. This club specializes in chanson, with concerts every evening in summer and a seemingly neverending show, throughout which there's a background hum of lively chat. It's rather touristy, but it's still a relaxed place with plenty of character.

L'Air du Temps: 191 rue Saint-Paul Ouest. ☎ 842-2003. Open 9pm–3am. Closed on Tuesday and Wednesday. Admission $5 from Sunday to Wednesday, $10 from Thursday to Saturday; students $5. This small but atmospheric joint is probably the best jazz club in the area, and it's the de rigueur rendezvous for the city's connoisseurs. They get excellent jazz bands in, as well as a few bluesmen. On Mondays out of season, there's a good 'big band'.

In the West Quarter

In the English-speaking area, you'll find plenty of fashionable clubs and cafés in the elegant rues Crescent, Bishop and Stanley.

♥ La Salsathèque (colour map II, B3, **119**): 1220 rue Peel. ☎ 875-0016. Métro: Peel. Open 10pm–3am. Admission $5 on Friday and Saturday (concerts). Amid an ultra-flash decor, a Cuban, Brazilian and Colombian crowd sway their hips to sensual Latin rhythms – salsa, baie-nato, meringue, mambo and lambada are all on the musical menu. This is definitely a student-free zone.

♥ Cock and Bull (colour map II, A3, **104**): 1944 rue Sainte-Catherine Ouest. ☎ 933-4556. Métro: Guy-Concordia. Open until 3am. A good-natured Irish pub with darts, billiards, slot machines and delicious beers. There are blues concerts from Thursday to Saturday, while on Sunday, the owner relives his youth by playing classic tracks by the Beatles and the Stones.

North of Prince Arthur

♥ Le Swimming (colour map II, C2, **113**): 3643 boulevard Saint-Laurent, between avenue des Pins and Prince-Arthur. Upstairs. ☎ 282-7005. Métro: Sherbrooke. Open noon–3am. Concerts from Thursday to Saturday ($4–5). This huge, very lively bar is a great place to sink a few beers, play billiards (free until 5pm; otherwise $10 an hour) or watch pop videos with a laid-back crowd. The gigs span funk, jazz, rock, pop and disco.

♥ Tokyo Bar (colour map II, C2, **120**): 3709 boulevard Saint-Laurent, near avenue des Pins. ☎ 842-6838. Métro: Sherbrooke. Open 10pm–3am. Admission varies; usually $6. Concerts from Thursday to Sunday. Once you've found the minuscule entrance, this is a super club on several floors. The vast, ultra-modern main room is packed full of young people getting down to funk, house, disco or hip-hop, while the 'jacuzzi' sofas might catch you by surprise. There is a DJ every night.

♥ Le Peel Pub (colour map II, B3, **118**): 1107 rue Sainte-Catherine Ouest, in the city centre. ☎ 844-6769. Métro: Peel. Open 6.30am–3am; happy hour Monday to Friday, 3–7pm. Sports-loving beer monsters will be in hog heaven in this immense, impersonal bar, where a very noisy crowd knock back vast quantities of booze at knock-down prices. Giant screens show non-stop ice hockey and American football, and it gets especially raucous when the local team is playing. You can line your stomach with a burger or a sandwich, though the food really isn't anything to write home about (and this place is sometimes less than spotless). If you don't like this kind of bar, you won't be converted, but at least it's cheap, especially if you're looking for breakfast.

♥ Le Sugar (colour map II, C2, **121**): 3616 boulevard Saint-Laurent. ☎ 287-6555. Métro: Sherbrooke. Open until 3am. It's impossible to miss this trendy place: look out for the two huge guys who block the doorway. If they let you in, you can mingle with Montréal's beautiful people in a wittily futuristic space and kick back to hip-hop, techno and alt-rock tunes. If you need a break from the action, the bright and pleasant terrace upstairs is a great place to chill out.

♥ Le Saphir (colour map II, C2, **122**): 3699 rue Saint-Laurent, upstairs, next door to the Tokyo Bar. Métro: Sherbrooke. Admission $6. Hip-hop fans should make a beeline for this Middle Eastern-themed club, with hangings on the ceiling and palm trees dotted about. The music is loud, the crowd is young and the DJ really knows his stuff. There are occasional theme nights.

♥ Café Central (colour map II, C1, **114**): 4479 rue Saint-Denis. ☎ 845-

9010. Métro: Mont-Royal. Open 3pm–3am. Admission $2. The music is varied at this studenty bar, but they don't play dance music of any kind, so it's perfect for those who can't bear repetitive beats. The decor is modern, and there's a mezzanine with little archways. It's buzzing in the evening, with drinks at reasonable prices.

❦ **Whisky Café** (just off colour map II, near C2): 5800 boulevard Saint-Laurent, on the corner at rue Bernard. ☎ 278-2646. Website: www. whiskycafe.ca. A classy bar with a calm, subdued atmosphere, ideal for a late-night liaison or a civilized nightcap. There's choice of spirits, and cigars are available (from $12).

❦ **Café Zazou** (Sports Bar Plus, colour map II, C1, **116**): 4597 avenue du Parc. ☎ 845-6060. Métro: Mont-Royal. This café looks fairly plain, but has about 15 TVs, and screens several sports events at the same time. Aficionados of American football, ice hockey and basketball meet here to relive the key moments of classic matches.

❦ **Le Belmont** (colour map II, C1, **124**): 4483 boulevard Saint-Laurent, on the corner with rue Mont-Royal. ☎ 845-8443. Métro: Mont-Royal. Open 8pm–3am. Admission $5. The

Belmont has a dance bar with all kinds of music (techno, funk, disco) and no dress code. It's also an English-style pub, with a snooker table, table football, video screens and a collection of pitchers and trays.

❦ **Le Diable Vert** (colour map II, C1, **123**): 4557 rue Saint-Denis. Métro: Mont-Royal. Open from 5pm–3am (from 3pm Thursday–Sunday). Shows $2–12. In this charming concert bar, built over an old theatre, you can tap your toes to jazz or techno, read your paper or admire the contemporary art on the walls. Bands booked for the Jazz Festival sometimes pop in to play a low-key set for an audience of laid-back, rather preppy 30-somethings. The soft lighting and immaculate decor (in shades of red) invite you to relax and chat, or sip a house cocktail while you prop up the bar.

❦ **Le Kokkino** (colour map II, C2, **125**): 3556 boulevard Saint-Laurent, on the corner of Prince-Arthur. ☎ 848-6398. Métro: Sherbrooke. Open 9pm–3am. Closed Tuesday and Sunday. Admission $7. Dress to sweat, as this lively place is a real disco inferno, with choice funk, house and hip-hop numbers burning up the dancefloor. Try the 'Staff Night' on Monday.

WHAT TO SEE AND DO

For maps of Montréal see the second colour plate section.

Although Montréal has the skyscraper skyline of so many modern cities, you'll also see a staggering number of church spires soaring into the heavens. So many, in fact, that the novelist Mark Twain once observed that it was impossible to throw a stone down a street without hitting a church. The reason is simple: the presence of both the English and French, and hence of Protestants and Catholics, resulted in a multiplication of places of Christian worship.

★ **L'Autre Montréal**: ☎ 521-7802. Uncover the many faces of Montréal with guided tours of various neighbourhoods. Subjects covered include the town's backstreets, its heritage, multiculturalism and the role of women in the city's history. Tours are conducted aboard an old yellow school bus.

★ **Vieux Montréal** (Old Montréal): This section of the city is bound by rues Notre-Dame, Berri, Saint-Paul and McGill, with place Jacques-Cartier (colour map III, C1–2) forming its historic centre. It's touristy, but still charming, thanks to the restaurants, cafés and general hubbub of the streets.

Don't expect the striking beauty and architectural coherence you might take for granted in the old towns of Europe: most of the buildings listed below are randomly scattered about between banks, office buildings and 19th-century warehouses. Try to get hold of a pamphlet called *Circuit de visite du Vieux Montréal*, which was published to commemorate the city's 350th anniversary. It includes a street map and a brief description of the most interesting buildings.

Most of the historic houses are on or near place Jacques-Cartier, although the **Château de Ramezay** (colour map III, D1, **1**) is a little farther out at 280 rue Notre-Dame Est. Built in 1705 and once the residence of the governor of Montréal, the château has a splendid interior, and it now houses a small museum (☎ 861-3708; open 10am–4.30pm, closed Monday; from 1 June to 28 September, open every day, 10am–6pm; entry $6, with reductions available). There's a small collection of period clothes, paintings, antique furniture and other interesting 18th- and 19th-century artefacts on display in the original wood-panelled rooms.

The **Maison Papineau** (440 rue Bonsecours; colour map III, D1, **2**) was built in 1785. Papineau, who once lived here, was the main instigator of the 1837 nationalist uprising.

There are several handsome 17th- and 18th-century town houses on **Rue Saint-Louis** (colour map III, D1, **3**). No. 442, a pretty, red-brick house that dates from 1890, has Victorian cornices, moulded skylights and attractive external stairways. The building opposite was constructed in two stages: the first part in 1755, the second in 1815. Continue to **Maison Brossard**, which dates from 1827. At No. 401 rue Bonsecours and No. 445 rue Saint-Paul Est, you'll find the **Maison du Calvet**, built in 1770 (colour map III, D1, **5**), and the **Maison Dumas**, constructed in 1800 (colour map III, D1, **4**). Look out for the elegant **Marché Bonsecours** (colour map III, D1, **6**), a domed 1845 building that's now home to stylish boutiques selling clothes by fashionable local designers. The **Maison Beaudoin** (colour map III, C1, **7**), built in 1780, is farther west at 457 rue Saint-Vincent. On **Place d'Armes** (colour map III, B1, **8**), another historic square, you'll find the **Vieux Séminaire** (colour map III, B1, **9**), an architectural gem erected in 1684 and boasting a handsome clock tower. The Gothic-style **Notre Dame** basilica (colour map III, B1, **10**) has an ornately decorated interior, with stained-glass windows portraying scenes from the city's early days as well as religious history. The other buildings on the square were once the offices and shops of 19th-century merchants and tradesmen.

Pause at **Place d'Youville** (colour map III, B2, **11**) to enjoy the carefully restored architecture. The square has a squat, solid look, thanks to the revived charm of buildings such as the **Hôpital Général des Surs Grises** (colour map III, B2, **12**), built between 1694 and 1765, and the **Ecuries d'Youville** (Youville Stables; colour map III, B2, **13**), which dates from 1827. The walled gardens inside the Ecuries are an oasis of peace and quiet.

Thanks to careful conservation and restoration work – and the end of the trend for modern redevelopment – Vieux Montréal's street life is flourishing, with the inevitable arrival of chic designer shops, antiques stores and other signs of gentrification. A hush descends on the area when the office and shops shut at 5pm, but by 8pm it comes back to life with a vengeance, especially around the nightspots. The restaurants are rather expensive, but the nightclubs are affordable and fun.

★ **Saint-Denis 'village'**: This is the section of rue Saint-Denis between rues Rachel and Sainte-Catherine, where the city's hippy fringe meets the newly moneyed upwardly mobile. Artists, students, commuters and tourists rub shoulders in the neighbourhood's many restaurants, terrace cafés and nightclubs. There's a rather Parisian feel to this area, especially around UQAM (Université du Québec à Montréal), south of Sherbrooke. It's overrun by tourists in summer, but even then, it's definitely worth a visit.

★ **Le Plateau**: Spread out along avenue du Mont-Royal, on both sides of rue Saint-Denis, this was *the* place to hang out in the 1990s. Today, it's famous for its brunches, but turn up early if you don't want to queue for a table. The bar- and club-lined streets are particularly lively at night, but stroll through the area during the day, heading east from Saint-Denis over Mont-Royal, and you'll find a grungy bohemian utopia: stalls selling colourful trinkets, hippy artists plying their trade and slices of pizza for $2.

★ **Catherine**: This neighbourhood between rues Bishop and Saint-Hubert is an odd mix of high style and seediness, with fancy department stores, stylish boutiques and cinemas a stone's throw away from the red-light district at the junction with rue Saint-Laurent. The driving here is pretty crazy, so you're best off exploring the area's contrasting sides on foot. The impressive **Place des Arts** complex, just before you get to Jeanne-Mance, houses several cinema screens and concert and theatre halls, as well as a superb contemporary art museum (*see* 'Museums' *below*).

South of Place des Arts is the maze-like **Complexe Desjardins**, with its skyway-linked buildings and hotels. It's less immediately striking than the rest of the Catherine district, but the restaurants, bars and shops between Saint-Hubert and Papineau are favoured by the city's gay community, and the area as a whole has a friendly and tolerant feel.

★ **West Quarter**: Predominantly English-speaking, this neighbourhood lies between rues Sherbrooke, Bishop and René-Lévesque, and stretches as far as Dorchester Square. The very British-looking rue Crescent is full of fashionable restaurants and classy nightclubs, while the glittering rue Stanley explodes into life every evening. It's not suited to travellers on a budget, but take a look anyway, as the area has a lot of charm, and there are a few reasonably priced spots.

★ **Chinatown**: Bordered by rues René-Lévesque, Saint-Laurent, Viger and Bleury, the area – or what's left of it – revolves around rue La Gauchetière. It has gone into decline since the construction of the east-west motorway and the regeneration of the town centre. Some red-brick terraces – a few covered with ivy – remain, however, and in recent years, an urban-renewal plan for the district has begun to bear fruit.

★ **La Ville Souterraine** and **Place Ville-Marie** (colour map II, B3): The 'underground city' is the world's second-largest shopping centre, and a triumph of modern urban development. Integrated into the road system and served by Métro stations as well as the city's bus service, the 'city' is a vast, multilevel spider's web whose halls and escalators extend for nearly 15 miles around more than 1,700 shops and 200 restaurants, bars, hotels, cinemas, theatres and art galleries. Shopaholics could spend days here without seeing any natural light. You can access the 'underground city' via several of the shops on place Ville-Marie, or from the Victoria or Bonaventure Métro stations.

Museums

As you would expect of a city this size, Montréal has its fair share of excellent art and history museums, but it also has a string of museums that will appeal to those with more specialized interests. If you're a real museum fiend, pick up an individual or family *carte musées Montréal*, which allows access to 21 museums on any two days within a three-day period. It is available at Infotouriste centres, or from any of the participating museums. The card (which costs $20) comes with a map of the city and a museum guide.

★ **Musée des Beaux-Arts** (Fine Art Museum) (colour map II, B3, **130**): 1379 rue Sherbrooke Ouest. ☎ 285-2000. Métro: Guy-Concordia and Peel, bus No. 24 (stop at Bishop). Open Tuesday to Sunday, 11am–6pm (to 9pm on Wednesday for special exhibitions). Permanent collection free; concessions available for temporary exhibitions. You can pick up a map at the entrance. The museum has a cafeteria, but you're better off going to the Californian-bistro-style Café des Beaux-Arts next door: 1384 rue Sherbrooke Ouest, ☎ 834-3233; lunch $20 à la carte, dinner $20–25.

This is reputedly the oldest museum in Canada. Housed in two buildings on opposite sides of the street, it is linked by an underground passageway. The first building was built in the 19th century, the second is brand-new. Between them, the two sections boast an impressive array of works from around the world, including Egyptian, African, Roman and Greek art, with Rembrandt, Picasso and Rodin among the star names on show. There's also a strong collection of Canadian and Native American (including Inuit) art, while several rooms are devoted to trends in 20th-century art and the decorative arts.

★ **Musée d'Art Contemporain** (Contemporary Art Museum) (colour map II, C3, **131**): Place des Arts, 185 rue Sainte-Catherine Ouest. ☎ 847-6226. Website: media.macm.qc.ca. Métro: Place des Arts. Open Tuesday to Sunday, 11am–6pm (9pm Wednesday). Admission $6; concessions available. Visitors can take a guided tour.

A brand-new, bright and airy building next to the Place des Arts complex, the museum is a superbly designed showcase for contemporary Canadian artists, in particular those from Québec. One wing contains the permanent collection, which comprises 5,000-odd works made between 1939 and the present; another is devoted entirely to temporary exhibitions, while sculpture is displayed in large, open-plan rooms. The museum also has a good information centre and a comprehensive bookshop. There are 'artists' workshops' for children on the ground floor, where the corridors are lined with works by budding young artists. Booking is essential: ☎ 847-6239.

★ **Musée d'Archéologie et d'Histoire-Pointe-à-Callière** (colour map III, B2, **138**): 350 place Royal, in Vieux Montréal. ☎ 872-9150. Website: www.musee-pointe-a-calliere.qc.ca. Métro: Place-d'Armes. In July and August, open 10am–6pm (weekends 11am–5pm); otherwise 10am–5pm (from 11am on weekends). Closed Monday. Admission $8.50; concessions available.

This is a great place to start your exploration of French-speaking Canada, as you can stand on the spot where the city was founded. An amalgam of two buildings – a former customs house and a purpose-built modern structure – the museum contains the spoils of several archaeological excavations. Begin your visit by watching an excellent multimedia presentation about local history, then turn your attention to the archaeologists' digs, which, though hardly earth-shattering in significance, are brought to life by an imaginative interactive setting. You can see Montréal's first Catholic graveyard, an old riverbed and the remains of a Native American settlement. The remaining floors use interactive technology to describe Québec's evolution, covering the French presence, architectural advances, the British conquest, the Industrial Revolution, Americanization, American-Indian history and the dominance of French language and culture. All in all, it's a thoroughly modern and very informative museum. The remains of the settlement were discovered only as the museum was being built, which meant the designers and architects had to adapt their plans to accommodate them.

★ **Musée Marc-Aurèle Fortin**: 118 rue Saint-Pierre, in Vieux Montréal. ☎ 845-6108. Fax: 845-6100. Métro: Square-Victoria (rue Saint-Jacques exit). Open Tuesday to Sunday, 11am–5pm. Admission $4; concessions available. Marc-Aurèle Fortin (1888–1970) painted landscapes across Québec, as well as old houses and historic buildings in Montréal. The museum, housed in a former warehouse, contains around 40 of the artist's works, in which he tried to create a style of landscape painting quite different from any in Europe. Judge for yourself whether he succeeded.

★ **Musée des Arts Decoratifs**: 220 rue Crescent. ☎ 284-1252. Métro: Guy-Concordia. Open Tuesday to Sunday, 11am–5.30pm (9pm Wednesday). Admission $4; concessions available. The Museum of Decorative Arts recently moved from Château Dufresne, its home since 1979, to its present city-centre location in the new wing of the Musée des Beaux-Arts (*see above*). The collection, which features jewellery, furniture, pottery and glassware, is devoted to 20th-century works, and offers a good overview of the different styles of the past hundred years.

★ **Centre Canadien d'Architecture** (colour map II, A3, **132**): 1920 rue Baile. ☎ 939-7026. Website: www.cca.qc.ca. Métro: Guy-Concordia. From June to September, open Tuesday to Sunday, 11am–6pm (9pm on Thursday); otherwise, open Wednesday to Sunday 11am–6pm (5pm on weekends, 8pm on Thursday). Admission $6; concessions available. Students can visit for free on Thursdays, while it's free for all from 6–8pm. A superb example of modern design constructed around an old Victorian town house, this museum is well worth a visit. The constantly changing exhibitions home in on styles of architecture through the ages, and are usually fascinating and well presented. While you're there, take a stroll through the manicured gardens. Guided tours are available, and there's also a good specialist bookshop.

MONTREAL

★ **Cinémathèque Québécoise, Musée du Cinéma** (colour map II, C3, **133**): 335 boulevard de Maisonneuve Est, not far from the junction with Saint-Denis. ☎ 842-9763. Métro: Berri-UQAM. Despite the various small exhibits and films on display (entry free), this is not really a museum, It's primarily a film archive, with one of the most important collections of animated films in the world. Films are shown twice a day (once on Sunday); screening times are available over the phone.

★ **Musée Juste pour Rire** (Just for Laughs Museum, colour map II, C2, **134**): 2111 boulevard Saint-Laurent. ☎ 845-4000. Métro: Saint-Laurent. In summer, open Tuesday to Sunday, 10am–5pm; phone for times during the rest of the year. Admission $5; guided tours are available every hour. Juste pour Rire is Montréal's world-famous comedy festival, and this museum is dedicated to the bizarre, the wacky and the hilarious. The exhibits change frequently, so phone in advance if you want to know exactly what's on offer. Public participation is usually part of the deal, so be prepared to get involved.

★ **Centre d'Histoire de Montréal** (colour map III, B2, **139**): 335 place d'Youville. ☎ 872-3207. Métro: Square-Victoria or Place-d'Armes. From May to August, open 10am–5pm; closed Mondays between September and April. Admission $4.50; concessions available. Somewhat overshadowed by the Musée d'Archéologie (*see above*), this former fire station is home to a modest interactive local-history exhibition. It's less spectacular than its neighbour, but it still has much to offer. The permanent collection traces the day-to-day history of Montréal from 1642, covering the creation of the city's railway system and public services, the development of the port and the restoration of old buildings. The museum staff are dedicated and dynamic, and they know just about everything there is to know about Vieux Montréal, so don't hesitate to ask for more information.

★ **Musée McCord d'Histoire Canadienne** (colour map II, B3, **135**): 690 rue Sherbrooke Ouest. ☎ 398-7100. Website: www.musee-mccord.qc.ca. Métro: McGill. From late June to early September, open 10am–6pm (5pm on Monday and weekends); closed Monday outside this period. Admission $7; concessions available. Guided tour on Saturday at 2pm. The permanent collection offers an overview of the development of Montréal, as well as snapshots of early colonial life and Canada's indigenous cultures, which are represented by some amazing Inuit ivory miniatures and traditional Native American clothing and artefacts ornamented with glass beads. The eclectic temporary exhibits focus on anything from Québec silverwork to ice hockey or photographs of Inuit women.

Other Attractions

★ **Parc des îles**: This is made up of two islands, Sainte-Hélène and Notre-Dame. ☎ 872-4537. Access by car is via the Jacques-Cartier and Concorde bridges (parking $10). Pedestrians and cyclists can take the Métro to Isle-Sainte-Hélène, or the No. 169 bus from Papineau Métro station. Between June and October, a water taxi runs from the Jacques-Cartier quay at Vieux-Port. Once you're there, you can take a ride through the park on bus No. 167, which you can board opposite the Isle-Sainte-Hélène Métro at the 'plage des îles' bus stop.

The largest of Montréal's parks is geared towards sports and leisure activities, and on weekends it's teeming with locals trying to unwind. It was used as a venue for Expo '67, and you can still see the gardens created for the event and a few converted exhibition halls. The Biosphere stands on the spot of the American exhibition, and the former French patch is now taken up by a casino which you can enter for free.

The park is a pleasant place for a stroll, especially on Sainte-Hélène, where you'll find most of the sights. If you're feeling sporty, however, head straight for Notre-Dame, where activities include cycling, rollerblading, pedalos, canoeing and windsurfing. The beach (for which there is an entry fee) is ideal for picnics, and you can swim in the St Lawrence River. The Parc des îles is also home to the Gilles-Villeneuve racing circuit, where the Canadian Grand Prix is held in mid-June.

Below is a summary of the attractions on Sainte-Hélène:

– **L'Homme**: A huge sculpture by Alexander Calder occupies an outcrop on the western part of the island, which offers splendid views of the city.

– **Musée David M. Stewart**: in the Vieux-Fort, 10 minutes' walk from Sainte-Hélène Métro station. ☎ 861-6701. Open 10am–6pm in summer; otherwise 10am–5pm; closed Tuesdays. Admission charged; discounts available for students. The museum's remit is the history of Canada up to independence, with displays devoted to national customs and traditions, exhibitions of old weapons and other unusual artefacts. Look out for the superb collection of globes or the model of the city as it looked in 1760.

In summer, you can see demonstrations of 18th-century military manoeuvres in uniforms of the time (Wednesday to Sunday, 1pm, 2.30pm and 5pm). There's more period fun across the way at Le Festin du Gouverneur (☎ 879-1141), a restaurant where diners attend banquets served by staff in period dress and are entertained by performances of heroic historical episodes. As you may have guessed, it's a bit of a tourist trap, and the prices reflect this.

– **La Ronde**: The îles' amusement park, which you can reach from the esplanade. ☎ 872-6222. Open from the end of May to Labor Day (the first Monday in September), 11am–11pm (until midnight on Friday and Saturday). There's a host of attractions, from fairground rides to variety shows for kids and adults, and all are of pretty good quality. It's crowded but well organized, so queues are tolerable, and there are plenty of places to grab a snack. In summer, the Ronde hosts an international fireworks competition, with displays twice weekly. You have to pay to get in, but you can get a good view from the Jacques-Cartier bridge, which you can drive onto, but not cross, during these events.

– Another international event staged at the Ronde is the **Fêtes gourmands international de Montréal**, a vast open-air food fair that takes place in August.

– **Biosphere**: ☎ 283-5000. Website: www.biosphere.ec.gc.ca. Open 10am–6pm from the end of June until the beginning of September; otherwise Tuesday to Sunday, 10am–5pm. Admission $6.50; concessions available. This former US Expo entry, an original work by the American architect Buckminster Fuller, is now Canada's leading centre for environmental observation and monitoring. Inside, an interactive museum focuses on water and tells you everything you need to know about the Great Lakes and the St Lawrence River.

★ **Le Vieux Port** (The Old Port): The riverside neighbourhood of Vieux Montréal, on the banks of the St Lawrence. ☎ 496-7678. Totally revamped, the riverbanks are now the site of extensive gardens and some of the city's tackier tourist attractions. These include children's playgrounds, an inter- active maze, miniature trains, pedalos, paddle-steamer cruises and rides in a jetboat. There's also an Imax cinema, a host of terrace cafés and, during winter, open-air ice-skating. The riverside information centre can provide details of the many free events that take place here.

★ **Dow Planetarium** (colour map II, B3, **137**): 1000 rue Saint-Jacques Ouest, near place Bonaventure. ☎ 872-4530. Métro: Bonaventure. Closed Monday off-season. Phone for details of show times. Admission $6; concessions available. There's a lot to take in during the one-hour sessions, but it's well worth it if you're keen on astronomy, and it's pretty exciting even if you're not. The planetarium's spherical screen, which looks a bit like a giant magic lantern and dominates the 400-seat circular auditorium, re- creates the night skies using sophisticated equipment: the slow movement of the planets of our solar system contrasts with the rapid trajectory of stars journeying through the heavens, while you'll be wowed by a series of epic events, including a solar eclipse.

★ **Mont Royal**: This spot offers superb views of Montréal, but you'll have to claw you way up to the 233-metre (764-foot) summit. The route on foot from the Youth Hostel is particularly picturesque; otherwise, you can shorten the trip by taking the Métro to Mont-Royal, then the No. 11 bus as far as the Lac des Castors. Next to the Mont, there's a 200-hectare (500-acre) park, laid out by F.L. Olmstead, the creator of New York's Central Park, and popular with picnickers. It's particularly animated on sunny Sunday afternoons, when the smell of organic snacks wafts through the grounds and musicians and a host of eccentrics gather to play drums, dance and watch or participate in other spontaneous artistic happenings. The Oratoire Saint-Joseph, a popular place of pilgrimage, stands at the foot of Mont Royal. You can reach it from the Côte-des-Neiges Métro station.

★ **Botanical Gardens**: access for cars at 4101 rue Sherbrooke Est. ☎ 872- 1400. Website: www.ville.montreal.qc.ca/jardin. Métro: Pie-IX. Open from 9am until dusk, but the greenhouses close at 7pm in summer and 5pm during the rest of the year. Admission $6.75–9.50, depending on season; concessions available. Second in size only to London's sprawling Kew Gardens, this site contains 26,000 species of plant, spread over 73 hectares (180 acres). There are 1,200 types of orchid alone. Visitors can explore the water garden, the Japanese and Chinese gardens, tropical greenhouses and an excellent insectarium (same opening hours as the greenhouses). It's best avoided around 3pm on Saturdays, when newly-weds and their guests flock to the place for photoshoots.

★ **Parc Olympique**: 4141 avenue Pierre-de-Coubertin. ☎ 252-8687. A free shuttle bus runs between the Parc (from the Viau Métro station or the information centre at the foot of the tower) and the Botanical Gardens (via the Insectarium). Guided tours in summer at 10am and 6pm. As you'll have guessed, this was the flagship venue for the Montréal Olympics in 1976, when its concrete architecture was considered pretty avant-garde, and it's something of a shrine for diehard sports fans. The structure itself is interesting, but the tours are predictably obsessed with the scale of the place, and there are only so many ways of saying 'big'. You'll learn, for example, that there are no fewer than 525,000 cubic yards (400,000 cubic metres) of concrete, 400,000 tonnes of steel, 225 kilometres of cable (about 140 miles) and so on. The leaning tower is the tallest of its kind in the world, and you can take the external elevator to the top for unbeatable views of the city (admission fee; closed from mid-January to mid-February). The tower also houses a small museum dedicated to the Olympics. The stadium is multipurpose and, if you're lucky, you'll be able to see its impressively speedy transformation from football pitch to athletics track or baseball field.

Montréal is home to some top-notch sports teams, such as baseball giants the Expos, and ice hockey champions the Canadiens. Every match is a major event, so a good atmosphere is guaranteed. For details of forthcoming baseball games: ☎ 253-3434.

★ **Biodôme**: 4777 avenue Pierre-de-Coubertin, next to the Parc Olympique. ☎ 868-3000. Website: www.ville.montreal.qc.ca/biodome. Métro: Viau. Open 9am–5pm (7pm in summer). Admission $9.50; concessions available. A combined ticket includes entry to the Botanical Gardens and Insectarium. This huge dome, used for indoor cycling events during the 1976 Olympics, covers 7,000 square metres (75,000 square feet) and now contains re-creations of four distinct ecosystems from across the Americas: tropical rainforest, the Laurentian forest, the St Lawrence marine habitat and the Arctic. The dome's animal inhabitants are a thoughtfully selected cross section of species. In one section, a family of beavers has adapted so well to the new habitat that they've built a dam in front of the filter that serves their artificial lake. In the basement, you'll find Naturalia, an interactive mini children's museum devoted to wildlife. It focuses on the animals' eating habits, they way they move, how they sense the world around them, and how they defend themselves.

★ **Cosmodôme**: 2150 rue des Laurentides, Laval, 30 minutes by car from central Montréal. ☎ 978-3600 or ☎ 1-800-565-2267 (toll-free). Fax: 978-3601. Website: www.cosmodome.org. Leave Autoroute des Laurentides (No. 15) at Exit 9 onto boulevard Saint-Martin, turn right into boulevard Daniel-Johnson and right again at rue Edouard-Montpetit. Take another right onto avenue Terry-Fox, and you can't miss the grandiose entrance, complete with a statue of Ariane (the French equivalent of Britannia). Open 10am–8pm (closed Monday from September to June). Discounts for children and student-card-holders.

The enormous Cosmodôme, which opened in 1995 and is dedicated to the observation and exploration of space, is a well-thought-out project that offers plenty of insights into space and the study of space. An introductory 20-minute multimedia presentation traces mankind's relationship with space from the Neolithic era through to modern times, and looks at the scientists who have contributed to our knowledge of the final frontier. After this, a series of displays explain space travel, how to survive in space, what we learn about Earth and the solar system from exploring space, and satellite communications. You can conduct your own space experiments using the interactive screens, and there's even a machine that enables you to experience weightlessness. One of the prize exhibits is a chunk of moon rock, brought back to Earth by astronauts. Should you crave a more in-depth experience, you could always join one of the workshops (up to five days). These are best done as a large group.

★ **Le Centre Molson** (colour map II, B3, **136**): 1260 rue de la Gauchetière Ouest. ☎ 932-2582. Métro: Bonaventure or Lucien-L'Allier. This 21,000-seater ice hockey stadium – home to the Canadiens – is frequently transformed into a venue for big-name American pop acts. The ice hockey season runs from April to September.

– **Lachine rapids descent**: Les Descentes sur le Saint-Laurent, 7770 boulevard La Salle, 15 minutes' drive from the city centre. ☎ 767 2230. Take Autoroute 20 Ouest and leave at exit 63 (La Salle); then take exit 2 and follow the signposts for '*rafting sur le Saint-Laurent*'. A free shuttle bus runs from the Infotouriste centre at 1001 square Dorchester; or take the Green Line Métro to Angrignon, then the No. 110 bus. White-water rafting can be an expensive business, so this is your chance to try your hand at an exciting sport in a safe, and affordable, environment. You can raft for $36, or skid through the rapids on the white-knuckle hydrojet for $42 (concessions available). Trips last two-and-a-quarter hours, including travel there and back, and depart between 9am and 6pm from the beginning of May to the end of October. It's a good idea to book places a day or two in advance, and to go in the afternoon, when the water is warmer. You're sure to get soaked through, so don't forget to take a change of clothes.

> **TIP** Don't leave your spare clothes on the minibus, because you'll get so wet that you'll freeze: wrap a spare T-shirt in three lots of plastic bags, tightly closed, and tie the whole lot to the raft so that you can change into it when passing through calmer sections of the descent.

Lachine is also home to the small but interesting **Musée du Commerce des Fourrures**, where you can find out all about the fur trade.

– Hire roller skates from **Patins à roulettes Montrean** (27 rue de la Commune Est; ☎ 866 0633). The shop is open all day, and there's a great path running down the banks of the St Lawrence and the Lachine Canal. Alternatively, hire a bike in Vieux Montréal and do the path on two wheels.

A WALK THROUGH 'LITTLE BURGUNDY'

Vast swathes of Montréal are currently undergoing a makeover, with old neighbourhoods being revamped, factories moving out and their remains being converted into condominiums. These changes are particularly apparent in **Petite Bourgogne** ('Little Burgundy'), which stretches along the Lachine canal and was once a workers' district. To get there, take the Métro to Lucien-L'Allier or Lionel-Groulx – or cycle there, as the roads are relatively quiet. The area is neatly enclosed by rue Saint-Antoine to the north, rue de la Montagne to the east, avenue Atwater on the western edge and the canal to the south.

Not much remains of the workers' houses and tenements that once stood here; they were demolished to make room for the red-brick housing projects that stand in their place. Of particular interest are the enormous O'Keefe brewery, which dominates the local skyline, and the **rue Notre-Dame**, one of the oldest streets in Montréal. It's mentioned in records as far back as 1660, and evidence of its importance can be seen at 1850 rue Notre-Dame Ouest: the site of the magnificent 19th-century Banque de Montréal, which sports Flemish-style sculpted gables; the red sandstone used in its construction was imported from Scotland.

Rue des Seigneurs leads you to the **Lachine canal**, where you'll find footpaths and cycle routes in the area around the canal's third lock. You can still see a few of the old factories, though they're doubtless destined to be transformed into bijou apartment blocks. The canal was built in 1825 as a bypass for the St Lawrence rapids and was used commercially for 130 years, propping up the country's economy. In the 1950s, it was superseded by the St Lawrence Seaway.

Turn back up rue des Seigneurs until you come to rue Saint-Jacques, where the **îlot Saint-Martin** is a fine example of how urban renewal can and should be carried out. The older buildings in this block have been renovated, but thought has been given to preserving their essential character so that the new constructions complement the old.

Rue Coursol is one of the last remaining old townscapes of Petite Bourgogne, with rows of tastefully renovated workers' housing and fine examples of 19th-century architecture. Past boulevard Georges-Vanier, you'll come across typical rows of coloured Montréal houses. The neighbourhood is partly inhabited by black families, descendants of the railroad gangs who came here in 1850, and by more recent immigrants from Haiti.

Finally, turn down avenue Atwater until you reach the market, the **Marché Atwater**, an art-deco style building that's vaguely reminiscent of fascist-era Italy (colour map II, A3). Have a drink or a snack at the Taverne Magnan (corner of Saint-Patrick and Charlevoix), where the beer is cheap and the large rooms and terrace gardens can accommodate more than 1,000 people. Alternatively, the Première Moisson bakery serves a dish of the day and mouthwatering desserts.

For a breathtaking view of the city, head for the 45th floor of the skyscraper at 1 place Ville-Marie and visit the **Resto-Lounge 737**. It's smart and rather expensive, and the dancefloor isn't exactly kicking, but having a drink 737 feet above Montréal (hence the name) is an experience worth risking your street cred for.

In fine weather, take a Sunday-evening stroll through **Parc Jeanne-Mance**, which resounds to the beat of African drums and has a youthful, festive feel. You'd never guess that this was once North America's first golf course.

FESTIVALS AND EVENTS

Montréal's cultural life is pretty extensive, and it's hard to do it justice in such a short space. Your best bet is to leaf through the *Mirror* and the *Hour*, the city's English-language weekly listings magazines. These, their French-language equivalents (*Voir* and *Ici*) and the bilingual monthly *Montrealscope* are available at the Infotouriste centre and at newsagents throughout the city.

– **Festival International de Jazz**: This 10-day event, one of the world's most prestigious music festivals, takes place between late June and early July. The festival headquarters are at 822 rue Sherbrooke Est. ☎ 871-1881. About 2,000 musicians from every continent take part in some 400 live concerts. Of these, 300-odd are open-air events, and completely free. The mood is good-natured, despite the crowds (1.5 million people come to enjoy the music), and the whole town gets into the swing of things, with the area around place des Arts transformed by fringe events. While jazz is the festival's core, a host of other musical styles is represented: recent headline acts include Dee Dee Bridgewater, George Benson, Lucky Peterson, Buddy Guy and Ben Harper.

– **Summer events at Vieux-Port**: Place Jacques-Cartier and quai de l'Horloge (rue Berri) host a range of activities from May to early September. These include exhibitions and performances of theatre, music and dance, as well as open-air jazz concerts in the evening. In July, you can browse through the offerings of the many booksellers who set up stalls here.

– Other notable events include: the **Festival de Théâtre des Amériques** (a theatre festival held every two years 2001, 2003 etc. in late May; ☎ 842 0704); the **Festival de Musique Francophone Francofolies** (concerts of francophone music on place des Arts and nearby venues in June, July and August); the **Festival des Films du Monde** (last week of August; ☎ 933 9699); the **Festival International de Nouvelle Danse** (a modern dance festival in late September; ☎ 287-1423); and the **Benson & Hedges International Fireworks Competition** (*see* 'Other Attractions').

– **Festival Juste pour rire** ('Just for Laughs'): second fortnight of July. ☎ 845-3155. Website: www.hahaha.com. Despite the carefree name, the locals take this 10-day street festival extremely seriously. From 6pm, rue Saint-Denis is closed to traffic and the revellers take over. Comedians from around the world mount free shows, transforming the area into a bedlam of street sketches, stand-up routines and practical jokes, and the mayhem lasts until midnight. A large car-park to the east of Saint-Denis is transformed into a giant stage with seating and a sand floor: an ideal venue for performances of comedy, poetry and circus tricks. It's good fun, and you should definitely go if you're in town when it's on.

– **Fête de Saint-Jean**: Québec's national saint's day, 24 June, is a public holiday for everyone, but for many it's also an opportunity to celebrate the province's Catholic character. Many of the roads are closed to traffic, filling instead with crowds attending the many shows staged to celebrate the day. The main event is the afternoon procession through Sherbrooke, which winds up at the Parc Olympique, where, mainly dressed in blue, crowds of separatists shout popular nationalist slogans like '*On veut un pays*' or '*Le Québec aux Québécois*' ('We want a country' and 'Québec for the Québécois').

– It's an altogether different story on **Canada day**, 1 July, when avenue Sherbrooke is decked out in red for the English-speakers' parade, which travels in the opposite direction to the Saint-Jean procession. Curiously, the festival coincides with Montréal's 'moving day', when property leases are renewed or come to an end, and you can see washing machines and fridge-freezers in transit all over the city.

– The **Ligue National d'Improvisation** mounts extraordinary theatrical sparring matches in which two rival teams seek to outdo each other in song and mime. Themes are chosen by drawing lots. Performances kick off in October, and take place on Sunday evenings. ☎ 849-9726.

– **Festival Coup de Cur francophone**: ☎ 253-3024. A 10-day celebration of the French language in song. It takes place in November, and it's the biggest music event of the season, with new and established singers of chanson and cabaret from across the French-speaking world.

– Finally, the **Formula One Grand Prix** takes place in early June.

IN THE AREA

★ **Mont Saint-Hilaire**, in the Vallée-du-Richelieu, is just 20 minutes from Montréal. You can reach it via McGill University. Locals will tell you it's a dormant volcano, though kill-joy gossips say this claim was cooked up to attract tourists. A path leads all the way up to the peak of the mountain, fondly known as Pain de Sucre ('Sugarloaf'), where you'll get spectacular views of Montréal and the Vallée-du-Richelieu on a clear day. Parts of the **Centre de la Nature de Mont-Saint-Hilaire**, a UNESCO Biosphere Reserve owned by Montréal's English-speaking McGill University, are open to the public, including a lake where you can see water birds in their natural habitat. At the foot of the mountain, pick-your-own apple orchards and cider factories attract hordes of townies.

While you're in the Vallée-du-Richelieu area, you should also visit **Fort Chambly**. Built in 1665 during the colonial conflicts between the French, British and Iroquois, the fort is now a museum that traces the valley's military and civilian history. Open from 20 June to 6 September, 10am–6pm. Outside these dates, telephone to check opening hours, ☎ (450) 658-1585.

★ Roughly 140 kilometres (85 miles) north of Montréal, off the Laurentides motorway, **Parc du Mont Tremblant** ('Trembling Mount') is a landscape of stunning wooded hillsides filled with lakes and waterfalls. Autumn visitors will see the park at its most colourful, as the trees burst out in amazing shades of yellows, reds and browns, while winter guests can ski at the Tremblant's alpine-like resort, a pretty if somewhat snooty place. The Laurentides region is also home to the **Parc Linéare du 'Petit train du Nord'**, a park that incorporates 200 kilometres (120 miles) of old railway line between Saint-Jérôme and Mont-Laurier. The line passes through Sainte-Agathe-des-Monts, Mont-Tremblant and Lac-Nominingue, and provides an excellent (and easy) route for cycling and cross-country skiing. Certain sections are also suitable for snowmobiles. Some of the old line's railway stations have been converted into restaurants, hostels, information centres and bike-hire and repair huts. Contact the Association touristique des Laurentides for more details: ☎ (450) 436-8532.

★ **Parc Omega**, lies 110 kilometres (68 miles) west of Montréal on route 323 North, Montebello, and is a good stop-off point between Montréal and

Hull (in Québec). ☎ 423-5487. Open year-round. From 1 June to 30 September, admission $12 for adults, $7 for children aged 6–15 and $2 for toddlers; out of season, it's $9 for adults and $6 for 6–15s. A safari park with a difference: instead of lions and tigers, you can see the wildlife of North America in its natural habitat. Spread along a 10-kilometre (6-mile) section of road, you can gawp at buffalo, moose, wapiti, Virginian deer, bears, wolves, beavers and raccoons. There is a panoramic restaurant on site, with a picnic-like atmosphere, and you can find out more about the park's animals at the visitor centre.

– The area's other attractions include what is reputedly the largest wooden building in the world: the **Château Montebello**, now a luxury hotel belonging to the Canadien Pacifique hotel chain. Nearby is the **Manoir Papineau** (open mid-May to early September), a stately home that once belonged to the liberal politician Louis-Joseph Papineau, who headed the 1837 Patriots' revolt.

If you've come this far, then head for **Hull**, on the Québec side of the river Outaouais; the federal capital, Ottawa, is on the other bank. There you'll find the **Musée Canadien des Civilisations** (100 rue Laurier; ☎ (819) 776-7000), an impressive structure housing an equally impressive museum of local anthropology. The main gallery contains an exhibition devoted to the culture and totem carvings of six indigenous nations. A thousand years of history are brought to life through a sensitive, original interactive presentation, and there's a superb section set aside for kids, who are even allowed to touch the exhibits. The museum is open 9am–6pm from 1 May to 30 June, and until 9pm throughout July. Entry is free on Sunday from 9am to midday.

★ **Les Cantons de l'Est** are worth a detour if you're travelling down to the US on Autoroute 10. Pitted with valleys and lakes, this beautiful region is home to many artists, whose villas surround the town of Magog; it's also a popular second-home location for Montréalers. There are plenty of activities on offer during the summer, sporty and otherwise, while in winter, there's skiing at Bromont and Mont-Orford. The Cantons are also renowned for their restaurants, many of which occupy attractive Victorian houses built by English loyalists who moved here after America gained its independence.

LEAVING MONTRÉAL

Hitchhiking

■ **Allô-Stop**: 4317 rue Saint-Denis, on the corner with Marie-Anne. ☎ 985-3032 or 985-3044. Open 9am–6pm (7pm on Thursday and Friday, 5pm at the weekend). Métro: Mont-Royal. This lift-share agency puts hitchers in touch with car drivers. The system generally works well, but you give as much notice as possible for long-distance trips. There is a fee for the service, and you're expected to contribute towards fuel costs.

– To hitch a lift to the **Laurentides** or the **north**, take the No. 100 bus from the Crémazie Métro stop to the Laurentides Autoroute.

– For the **Trois-Rivières**, along the north bank of the St Lawrence, take the No. 189 bus from the Honoré-Beaugrand Métro station and go as far as possible down rue Sherbrooke.

– For **Québec City**, take the Métro to Longueuil, not far from Autoroute 20.

– If you're going to **Sherbrooke**, take the No. 6 bus from the Longueuil Métro stop and get off at the Autoroute des Cantons de l'Est.

– For **Ottawa**, **Toronto** and the **west**, take the Métro to Crémazie station, then the No. 100 bus west to Autoroute 40.

> **TIP** The phrase to use when hitching is '*Je vais sur le pouce à . . .*' ('I'm thumbing a lift to . . .').

By Coach

Look out for special offers that apply to many destinations (including New York) and don't forget that reduced fares are available if you book tickets 24 hours in advance. You could save up to 40 per cent off the full price.

Station Centrale d'Autobus de Montréal (main coach station): 505 boulevard de Maisonneuve Est (colour map II, D3). ☎ 842-2281. Métro: Berri-UQAM. Several coach companies provide services to Sherbrooke, Hull, Ottawa, Trois-Rivières, Québec City (about three hours by express coach), the Gaspésie region (about 15 hours to Gaspé), Moncton, Charlevoix and the north coast, New York and many other destinations, including Mirabel and Dorval airports (*see* 'Getting There'). The Orléans Express and Intercar companies offer discounted fares for students and senior citizens. In summer, Orléans Express has a Tour Pass ticket valid for unlimited travel on certain routes in Ontario and Québec for periods of seven, 14 or 18 consecutive days. Always get there 45 minutes before your departure to ensure you have enough time to buy tickets.

– A **Montréal–Vancouver** service operates twice daily, taking about 72 hours coast-to-coast. Keep a camera handy, as opportunities for great pictures come up at the stops and in transit. You can't take bicycles on this service, so bikes must be wrapped up and sent via the Greyhound parcel service: prices vary according to weight, but expect your bike to arrive before you do. The trip is an epic journey to say the least; it's also quite expensive, but the road-movie feel provides ample compensation.

– **Taxi Philibert** (☎ 374-5252) runs 11-seater minibuses three times a week to Gaspé via Québec City and Rimouski. It's faster than the bus, and full-fare tickets are cheaper, but it's still a 12- to 14-hour trip, including food breaks and toilet stops. Book a seat at least a few days in advance.

By Train

Gare Centrale: 935 rue de la Gauchetiére Ouest (downtown, colour map II, B3). You can also access the station from rues University and Belmont. ☎ 989-2626 (9am–5pm); freephone ☎ 1-800-361-5390 (Via Rail). ☎ 1-800-872-7245 (Amtrak) for services to the US. Montréal's main railway station serves the rest of Québec and Canada, as well as the US.

– There are five trains a day to **Québec City** (four on Sunday and Monday, two on Saturday). Discounts are available if you book at least five days in advance.

– **For Gaspésie**: Three trains a week from Montréal, passing through Rimouski, Matapédia, Carleton and Percé. The trip takes 16 hours.

By Air

– **Mirabel and Dorval airports**: Take the Autocar Connaisseur service, which leaves from the Aérogare Centre-Ville (777 rue de la Gauchetiére Ouest; Métro: Bonaventure) and the central coach station (Métro: Berri-UQAM). The trip takes about an hour (for timetables, *see* 'Getting There'). ☎ 1-800-934-1212 or 934-1222.

> **TIP** An **airport tax** of $10 is payable by all passengers (except those in transit) flying from Mirabel and Dorval, so make sure you keep enough cash on you.

■ **Le Club D-7**: 3607 Saint-Denis. Recorded message service ☎ 843-6441; bookings ☎ 843-4413. A handy place if you're looking for cut-price tickets or last-minute deals on charter flights, mostly going south. Destinations include Cuba, Mexico and the Caribbean, but Vancouver is also covered.

Delivery Driving

■ **Westmount Drive-away**: Office 509, 345 avenue Victoria, Westmount. ☎ 489-3861. Drivers are required for vehicle deliveries to Toronto, western Canada and the Atlantic province, as well as California and New York. Between November and January, most deliveries are to Florida. The security deposit and your share of the petrol costs are negotiable.

BERTHIERVILLE Pop: 3,950   DIALLING CODE: 450

Berthierville, on the road between Montréal and Québec City, is a good place to spend the night if you prefer not stay in Trois-Riviéres (*see below*). It's genuinely rural, and there are two good places to stay in the area.

WHERE TO STAY AND EAT

⌂ **Chez Marie-Christine B&B**: 3120 Rang-du-Ruisseau, Sainte-Elisabeth, 15 minutes from Berthierville. ☎ 759-9336. Email: hivonmmp@citenet.net. Doubles $55 a night; open May to October. From Montréal, leave autoroute 40 at exit 122 and head for Joliette, on route 31 north. At Joliette, take route 131 north towards Notre-Dame-de-Lourdes. Chez Marie-Christine is on the right, two kilometres (one mile) after the traffic lights. From Berthierville, leave autoroute 40 and take route 158 west to Joliette. Turn right towards Sainte-Elisabeth on route 345 north, drive through the village, turn left towards Notre-Dame-de-Lourdes and continue for four kilometres (2.5 miles) after the village; you'll find the house on your right. This friendly, peaceful B&B, highly praised by Canada's agriculture minister, has three clean, comfortable bedrooms that share a bathroom. It's a cosy place, and an ideal base if you're going to the Joliette's classical-music festival (held every July).

â ✕ **Gîte Le Cheval Bleu**: 414 route 343, Saint-Alphonse-Rodriguez, one hour's drive from Montréal. ☎ 883-3443. Fax: 883-3443. Website: www.pages.citenet.net/users/ctmx2402. Doubles from $50

a night. From Berthierville, follow the directions to Chez Marie-Christine (*see above*), then continue past Sainte-Marcelline. The Cheval Bleu, which has a garden overlooking a small private lake, is ideally placed if you want to explore the 34 lakes around Saint-Alphonse-Rodriguez. Guests stay in the annexe, which has five clean bedrooms overlooking the surrounding forest. If you book in advance, you can get dinner for about $20. In the summer, they do barbecues, and there are plenty of activities on offer in the area.

WHAT TO SEE

★ **Musée Gilles-Villeneuve**: 960 avenue Gilles-Villeneuve; leave autoroute 40 at exit 144. ☎ 836-2714. Fax: 836-3067. Website: www.villeneuve.com. Opening times 9am-6pm everyday. Admission $6. The museum is dedicated to Berthierville's most famous son: the French-Canadian motor-racing legend, Gilles Villeneuve, whose brilliant career was cut short in 1982 when he died in a Formula One accident. There's a film about his life, while the exhibits include a collection of original race cars, among them a superb Ferrari, video games, trophies, photographs and a racing simulator. His son Jacques, who won the Formula One championship in 1997, also gets a mention.

★ **Église de Sainte-Geneviève**: rue Montcalm. This 200-year-old church has a fine interior.

★ **Chapelle des Cuthbert**: rue de Bienville. Open from late June to early September, 10am–6pm. ☎ 836-7336. Built in 1786, this chapel was Québec's first Protestant church. It's now home to the local tourist office, and hosts free exhibitions in summer.

SOREL Pop: 23,200   DIALLING CODE: 450

Sorel is on the opposite side of the St Lawrence River to Berthierville. Once favoured over Montréal and Québec City as a meeting place for Hell's Angels, the town was the site of several fights between rival gangs. Things have calmed down considerably since then, and ecological and historical tours in the area provide the excitement for visitors.

Saint-Anne-de-Sorel, on chemin Chenal-du-Moine, is the departure point for river cruises on the St Lawrence (☎ 743-7227. Fax: 743-7807), which visit the picturesque Îles de Sorel, home to a wide variety of bird life. You can also take a 10-minute ferry trip to the north bank of the St Lawrence, via Saint-Ignace-de-Loyola. The boat leaves every 30 minutes in summer and every hour during the rest of the year. You don't need to book, but if you want more information, call ☎ 743-3258 (in Sorel), or 836-4600 (in Saint-Ignace).

QUÉBEC

WHERE TO STAY

⚓ **Auberge du Lac Archambault**: 221 rue Aubin, Saint-Donat, opposite the lake. ☎ and fax 1-819-424-3542 or 1-888-745-0606 (both toll-free). Website: www.altern.org/aubarchambault. Doubles $55–92 a night, including breakfast. Parking available. Run by a friendly French couple, this spacious village guesthouse is 90 minutes from Montréal via autoroute 15, and just 15 minutes from the Mont-Tremblant national park. Most of the 12 clean and tastefully decorated rooms have their own bathroom, and the dining room has an open fire. Jazz bands play here during the summer, but the place is a welcome break from the road whatever the time of year.

TROIS-RIVIÈRES Pop: 48,400   DIALLING CODE: 819

This small industrial town, halfway between Montréal and Québec City, is unavoidable if you're travelling to the Mauricie National Park. Named after the three waterways that form the mouth of the St Maurice, it's a sleepy, provincial place, overhung by the smell of wood pulp from its paper mills. Not that Trois-Rivières is without charm: it was founded 350 years ago, and you can still see a handful of historic buildings in the pretty centre, while its strategic location between so many tourist attractions makes everyone here keen to help visitors have a good time. In early autumn, the town hosts an international poetry festival (*see below*).

USEFUL ADDRESSES

🛈 **Bureau du tourisme**: 1457 rue Notre-Dame. ☎ 375-1122. Email: tourismevtr@tr.cgocable.ca. Open 9am–6pm; closed weekends in winter. There's plenty of information, the staff are helpful and visitors can pick up a free street map. There's another tourist office at the entrance to the town (6560 Route 136 West; summer only).

🚌 **Terminus Orléans Express** (coach station): 275 rue Saint-Georges. ☎ 374-2944.

WHERE TO STAY

⚓ **Auberge de Jeunesse La Flottille**: 497 Radisson, 500 metres from the bus terminal. ☎ 378-8010. Email: flottille.cagm@cgocable.ca. Open 8am–midnight. Dormitory beds $20 ($16 for Youth Hostel members, free for children under six); breakfast $3.50. The staff at this clean, cosy hostel are friendly, and guests have access to laundry facilities, a safe, a communal kitchen and bike hire. There are two doubles, with rooms for four and ten as well as the dorms. You'll find plenty of tourist information on-site.

⚓ **Le Gîte du Huard**: 42 rue Saint-Louis. ☎ 375-8771. Doubles $50–60 a night. Mme Huard's attractive, century-old house, a stone's throw away from the St Lawrence River in the town's most historic neighbourhood, has seven comfortable rooms: one single and four doubles, including a self-contained, ground-floor studio flat with an extra sofa bed. All have en-suite bathrooms, kitchens, CD players, TVs and videos.

â **Maison Wickenden**: 467 rue Saint-François-Xavier. ☎ and fax: 375-6219. Doubles from $50 a night; credit and debit cards ac-

cepted. This small town house has three well-kept, moderately priced bedrooms, the smallest of which is a little cheaper than the others. Service comes with a smile, and the breakfasts are huge.

WHERE TO STAY IN THE AREA

The following establishments are a bit farther out, and are only really suitable if you have your own transport.

â **Gîte Saint-Laurent**: 4551 rue Notre-Dame Ouest. ☎ and fax: 378-3533. Doubles $55 a night; four-person apartment $100. Right on the edge of town (at the tourist office, take the small road that follows the river and you'll see a large building on the right-hand side), this roomy establishment has a large garden, with a swimming pool that stretches down to the river. The four spacious rooms with shared bathroom all have air-conditioning, and each takes its name from its colour scheme. Your host, Yolande, is a keen chef who makes a memorable three-course breakfast. You won't get better for the price, and it's deservedly popular, so be sure to book.

â **Gîte Baie-Jolie**: 711 rue Notre-Dame, Pointe-du-Lac, 10 kilometres (six miles) from Trois-Rivières. ☎ and fax: 377-3056. Doubles $55 a night; full-board $107. This quiet,

relaxing place next to the river has a garden with a swimming pool and three rooms with en-suite bathrooms. Breakfast is huge, and you'll find the Swiss-German couple who run the place especially helpful.

â **Grand Papa Beau**: 3305 rue Sainte-Marguerite, G8Z-1X1. ☎ 693-0385. Email: grandpapabeau@altavista.net. Doubles $50 a night; $10 for each extra person sharing. Credit and debit cards accepted. It's 10 minutes from the town centre by car, close to the Université du Québec: take exit 198 from autoroute 40, then follow boulevard des Récollets Nord as far as boulevard Jean-XXIII, and you'll see it on the right. This luxuriously decorated Québécois farmhouse has four (not very soundproof) rooms that sleep up to four people. The hospitable hosts rustle up a huge breakfast for their guests.

WHERE TO EAT

There are plenty of restaurants in town, most on rue des Forges, but many are pretty average.

✕ **Angéline**: 313 rue des Forges. ☎ 372-0468. Fax: 372-3881. Website: www.restoangeline.com. Main courses from $10. This pleasant Italian eatery with a large outside dining area serves enormous helpings of pizza, pasta with almost every kind of sauce imaginable, Italian-

style hamburgers and other specialities. It's all very Mediterranean, with a fountain, a balcony and Roman paving, and you can finish your meal with a proper cappuccino. There's also a shop selling Italian products.

✕ **Nord-Ouest**: 1441 rue Notre-Dame, on the corner of rue des

Forges. ☎ 693-1151. Open for lunch and dinner (until 3am). Main courses $10. This café, one of the best in the town centre, is built on the site of an old bank, and has a refrigerator instead of a safe, a safe instead of a refrigerator. Salads and Mexican dishes are served in a long, rustic-style dining room, or in the small garden. The café also serves as a venue for live music, exhibitions and other events, and there's a large upstairs room where you can play billiards during the day.

✕ **Souvlaki**: 338 rue des Forges. ☎ 371-2005. Main courses $10. The atmosphere of this large dining area of this popular Greek restaurant is rather dull, but the food is cheap, varied and well prepared – a great place if you're ravenous, but don't want to break the bank.

✕ **Cabane à Sucre Chez Dany**: 195 rue de Sablière, Pointe-du-Lac.

☎ 370-4769 or 1-800-407-4769 (toll-free). If you're coming from Montréal on autoroute 40, leave the motorway at exit 192 and head for Pointe-du-Lac (on chemin des Petites-Terres). Turn left onto chemin Sainte-Marguerite and Chez Dany is on the street to your left. From 24 June to 4 September, open 11am–2pm and 6–10pm; telephone to check the opening hours during the rest of the year. Full meal $14 per person. This large, red-roofed wooden restaurant is another good place to come if you've worked up a good appetite. The all-you-can-eat menus, with down-to-earth dishes like baked beans, ham with maple syrup and *oreilles de crisse* (crispy bacon chunks), are served in a relaxed, rustic setting, and you'll sometimes hear live music. Once you've finished gorging yourself, you can visit the on-site sugar refinery.

WHAT TO SEE AND DO

★ **Centre d'Exposition sur l'Industrie des Pâtes et Papiers** (Pulp and Paper Industry Exhibition Centre): 800 parc Portuaire, next to the river. ☎ 372-4633. From June to September, open 9am–6pm; otherwise weekends only, 11am–5pm. Entrance $3, including a one-hour guided tour. This intriguing museum is dedicated to the history of the paper industry. It explores the unusual applications of paper and the by-products of the manufacturing process with scale models of machines on show. This industry is very important in Canada and Trois-Rivières has two paper factories, a training centre for the industry's engineers and a research facility.

★ **The old town**, ravaged by fire in 1908, is still home to several historic buildings, including the neo-Gothic cathedral on rue Bonaventure and the Manoir de Niverville, which contains a permanent collection of antique furniture. You should visit the 18th-century Manoir de Tonnancour (864 rue des Ursulines; ☎ 374-2355), which houses an art gallery, and the Monastère des Ursulines (at No. 374), in which you'll find exhibitions devoted to local history. From May to October, open Tuesday to Friday, 9am–5pm, and 1.30–5pm on weekends; in March and April, open Wednesday to Sunday, 1.30–5pm; otherwise, by appointment only. ☎ 375-7922.

★ **Musée des Arts et Traditions Populaires du Québec**: 200 rue Laviolette, in the heart of the old town. ☎ 372-0406. From late June to early September, open Tuesday to Sunday, 11am–6pm; otherwise noon–4.30pm. Admission $6; guided tours available. Six rooms house permanent and temporary exhibitions on subjects as varied as the etymology of

Canadian French, domestic life, traditional crafts (toys, textiles, furniture, tools, etc.), archaeology and the arrival of the Native Americans, who travelled across the Bering Strait. A passageway takes you to the **old prison**, a maze of cells where you can see what life was like for inmates between 1920 and 1984.

★ **Les Forges du Saint-Maurice**: 10000 boulevard des Forges. ☎ 378-5116. From May to August, open 9am–5.30pm; otherwise 9am–4.30pm. Admission $4; guided tours available. This former foundry was one of the most important centres for the iron industry in Canada. The Grande Maison, once the site of a warehouse, a shop, a chapel, offices and living quarters, now houses a *son et lumière* display that re-creates the day-to-day tasks of the site's workers. The blast furnace, the main source of cast iron for 150 years, now houses an information centre and several displays. From the surrounding pathway, you can see the forge and the chimney once used in the refining process.

– If you want to find out more about the harbour and the St Maurice River, take a 90-minute **boat trip** aboard the *Draveur*. ☎ 375-3000 or 1-800-567-3737 (toll-free). Tickets $10; concessions available.

★ **Cité de l'Énergie**: in Shawinigan, a half-hour drive down autoroute 55, leaving at exit 211. ☎ 536-8516 or 1-800-383-2483 (toll-free). Fax: 536-2982. Admission $12. You'll need about three hours to do justice to this hydro-electric plant, some of which is still in use. Most of it, however, has been converted into a kind of science museum where you can learn the ins and outs of the production of hydro-electric power, aluminium, paper and electrochemistry. A multimedia exhibition charts the evolution of the industrial sector, and you can also to visit the Northern Aluminium Company's power station, where you can find out all about the production of electricity in an intelligent, accessible and interesting way. Wind up your visit with a drink or snack in the cafeteria.

QUÉBEC

FESTIVALS

– In late June and early July, the streets of the old town resound to the sound of religious, ethnic, traditional and popular song during the six-day **Festival International de l'Art Vocal**. This fast-growing event is extremely popular.

– The **Festival International de la Poésie** is a celebration of verse held in late September and early October, with concerts, films, public readings and exhibitions.

Le Parc National de La Mauricie

The La Mauricie National Park is 60 kilometres (about 38 miles) north of Trois-Rivières. Take autoroute 55 and leave at exit 217. For information, contact the park wardens in the La Mauricie district: 776 5th rue, Shawinigan (Québec). ☎ (819) 536-2638. Admission $3.50; free for campers. Free maps and information are available at the entrance. Visitors can stay in the well-equipped campsites or in gîtes (small guesthouses or B&Bs). You're advised to book ahead in summer: ☎ 537-4555.

This wild, beautiful park takes in nearly 550 square kilometres (220 square miles) of hills, lakes and waterfalls that can be reached via numerous footpaths. As you would expect, it's superb walking country, and you can also take a trip in a Native American canoe (*Rabaska*), accompanied by a guide, and go fishing, swimming or cross-country skiing. If you're lucky, you may also see some local wildlife, including beavers, the common loon or the Canadian elk. The village of Saint-Tite, on the edge of the park, was once the region's timber capital. Every year (10 to 20 September), Saint-Tite hosts one of Canada's most important rodeos, a kind of Western festival, complete with cowboys, wagons and feisty horses.

★ Don't miss the **Village du Bûcheron** (lumberjack village), in Grandes-Piles. It's superbly done, with 25 buildings evoking the harsh lives of the lumberjacks, timber drivers and other pioneers who made the region into one of the world's most important paper-milling centres. You can visit the buildings that make up a traditional camp, and dine in a big log cabin where typical lumberjack fare is served. The village is open 10am–6pm in summer; you'll get more out of your visit if you take a guided tour. ☎ 538-7895.

★ The **Musée d'Aviation de Brousse** (Museum of Aviation in the Bush), in Saint-Georges-de-Champlin, traces the history of civil aviation and its pioneers since June 1919, when the first commercial aeroplane landed on the Lac-à-la-Tortue. ☎ 538-6653. Open noon–9pm in summer (to 5pm on weekends). Guided tours take about 90 minutes, after which you can take a ride in a seaplane. Incidentally, 'Lac-à-la-Tortue' (Tortoise Lake) is named after the mines. One day, the miners struck ground water, which flooded the mines, and a lake was formed. It stretched from just 50 centimetres at its deepest point to a radius of several hundred metres.

WHERE TO STAY AND EAT

⌂ **La Maison Bellemare**: 2760 Principale, Saint-Jean-des-Piles. ☎ 538-2301. Fax: 538-7786. Leave route 55 at exit 226, then follow the signs for Parc de La Mauricie. Doubles $50 a night; cottages $55 for two and $10 per extra person. This large, family-run house in the middle of a beautiful park overlooks the River Saint-Maurice. There are four bedrooms (three double and one single) in the house, and five well-equipped cottages in the park. It's a tasteful, unpretentious place, and hosts classical-piano recitals in summer, which take place in the lounge, with its handsome fireplace.

⌂ **Maison Trudel**: 543 rue Goulet, Hérouxville. ☎ 365-7624. Fax: 365-7041. Email: maison-trudelquebec @concepta.com. From Trois-Rivières, take route 55 north, then follow the signs for Saint-Tite; cross the railway line and take the first left. Doubles $50 a night; triple room at $75. There are four bedrooms in this hospitable, friendly place, each with rustic decor. The owner will happily tell you about activities in the area, which include snowbiking. Breakfast is 'lumberjack style' (i.e., huge): French toast, waffles, syrup, home-made jams, bacon and eggs, cakes and baked beans. A real find.

⌂ ✕ **Village Innusit**: at Lac-Édouard. ☎ 653-2004. Fax: 653-2104. From Trois-Rivières, take route 155, and exit after 150 kilometres (93 miles). About $65 per person for dinner, bed (in one of six teepees) and breakfast. Your hosts, Vital and Lorraine, who cooks dinner, will also help you make the most of the area's natural beauty.

Route 138 between Trois-Rivières and Québec

Although autoroute 40 is faster, route 138 runs alongside the St Lawrence River and is much more enjoyable. You'll pass several attractive villages with elegant houses, including Deschambault (where there's a great place for an overnight stop), Cap-Santé and Neuville. The route, **chemin du Roy**, has linked Montréal to Québec since 1874, and was the first road in Canada that could take motor vehicles.

★ In **Grondines**, you'll find one of Québec's oldest windmills. Built in 1674, it used to serve as a river lighthouse. These days, it hosts exhibitions in summer. ☎ (419) 285-4616. The church, a listed building, was constructed between 1838 and 1840, and has an interesting presbytery.

★ If you are passing through **Batiscan**, pause to visit the village's old presbytery (340 rue Principale; ☎ (418) 362-2051; open 10am–5pm from June to October; admission $3). It's an impressive stone building built in 1816. There's an explanatory booklet if you want to look round on your own, or you can take a 40-minute guided tour.

★ Be sure to visit **Sainte-Anne-de-la-Pérade** if you are in the area during the '*poulamon*' ('little channel fish') season, between the end of December and mid-February, when the River Sainte-Anne is covered with hundreds of little huts with holes in their floors for fishing lines. The lure of the *poulamon* tempts 100,000 Québécois every year: the most dedicated fishermen have their own private huts, but the others are rented for 10-hour blocks, at all times of the night or day.

★ **Deschambault**'s presbytery dates from 1815 (☎ (418) 286-6891; open 9am–5pm in summer; weekends only, 10am–5pm, in May, September and October; admission $1.50). At the beginning of the 20th century, it was used for storing the parish tithe. Today, the building houses an exhibition about the Iroquois occupancy in the 15th century. The Moulin de la Chevrotière (Chevrotière mill), at the western edge of Deschambault, is also worth a look.

★ **Portneuf**, a charming town at the mouth of a river of the same name, is typical of the settlements along the St Lawrence. Fish, mainly eel, are caught in the deep-water harbour using a traditional method known as '*fascine*', which involves hanging nets from the jetty. There's a leisure park next to the quay for visiting yachts, with canoeing, windsurfing, bird-watching, hunting and fishing among the activities on offer.

★ **Cap-Santé**: Le Vieux-Chemin, which overlooks the St Lawrence, is one of the most beautiful streets in Canada. It's home to two of the last vestiges of French occupation: the house of Mademoiselle Bernard (built in 1890) and the church (built 1752–1768).

★ **Donnacona**: Following the old chemin du Roy, rue Notre-Dame leads to the Produits Forestiers Alliance paper mill, the mainstay of the town's economy. At the beginning of the 20th century, the company's English-speaking employees were relocated to the Quartier des Anglais ('English Quarter'), on boulevard Saint-Laurent.

QUÉBEC

– La Corporation de Restauration de la Jacques-Cartier manages a migration route for Atlantic salmon, where you can watch the fish coming in to spawn. There's an information centre where you can find out about the life cycle of the salmon. Fishing is allowed from 1 July to 30 September: you'll need a permit, which you can get on site. ☎ (418) 285-2210.

★ **Neuville**: rue des Érables is home to some fine, carefully preserved historic architecture. Look out for the Larue and Angers Houses, the Sainte-Anne chapel and the church of Saint-François-de-Sales. If you want to visit any of these places, call ☎ (418) 286-3002.

★ **Saint-Augustin-de-Desmaures**: the local church (built between 1809 and 1816) possesses several notable treasures, among them the two angels near the high altar and the pair of owls who stand guard in the walled graveyard outside. The calvary, erected in 1880, is adorned with bronze statues imported from France.

– **Érablière le Chemin du Roy**: 237 chemin du lac Nord, Saint-Augustin-de-Desmaures. ☎ 878-5085. Open mid-March to mid-October. This maple grove is named after the road that once ran through it. If you book in advance, you can eat in a typical Québécois *cabane à sucre* (maple shed), with traditional folk music to accompany your meal.

WHERE TO STAY AND EAT EN ROUTE

🛏 **Gîte du Passant Le Saint-Élias**: 951 rue Principale, Batiscan. ☎ 362-2712. Fax: 362-2081. Website: www.quebecweb.com. Take autoroute 40 and exit 229 south towards Batiscan. Doubles from $55 a night. This pretty late-19th-century house, in a quiet spot overlooking the river, has four lovely bedrooms with two shared bathrooms. It's a friendly, comfortable place, the owner is charming and breakfast is plentiful and well presented. In short, it's a wonderful hotel. Art-lovers should pop into the gallery of Québécois art next door.

🛏 ✕ **Auberge du Passant Manoir Dauth**: 21 boulevard de Lanaudière, Sainte-Anne-de-la-Pérade. Take exit 236 on autoroute 40, and it's just before the bridge. ☎ and fax: 325-3432. Email: manoir.dauth@tr.cgocable.ca. Doubles from $52 a night. Lise Garceau and Yvan Turgeon run a hospitable hotel with five pretty, romantic rooms, some with canopy beds, in a carefully restored mid-19th-century stone house that features on the village's heritage tour. Each room is named after an important figure in the history of Sainte-Anne. The newly refurbished bathrooms are spotless, and you can relax in the reading room, in the lounge or on the terrace. Depending on the season, you can go dog-sledging, fishing or canoeing (lessons are available). Breakfast and dinner are both excellent. Between May and October, the Turgeons also run a free museum devoted to old-fashioned gardens, bicycles and snow scooters.

🛏 ✕ **Maison de la Veuve Grolo**: 200 chemin du Roy, Deschambault, halfway between Trois-Rivières and Québec. ☎ 286-6831. Doubles from $60 a night. This attractive house, a listed building, dates back to 1715 and once belonged to a certain widow Grolo. Set in wooded grounds, it has four lovely rooms in 1930s, 1950s or Victorian style, with a pleasant shared bathroom. The interior is decorated in painted wood, and there's an elegant red lounge. Donald, the owner, is charming, and can provide meals if you book them in advance, although you'll have to supply your own wine.

QUÉBEC CITY Pop: 690,000   DIALLING CODE: 418

For maps of Québec City, see the second colour plate section.

If you come here after a stay in Montréal, you'll be in for a bit of a shock, as the two cities could hardly be more different. 'Nothing,' enthused Governor Frontenac in 1672, 'has ever seemed so beautiful and magnificent to me as the location of Québec.' His words ring true today, for Québec City is mercifully free of the skyscrapers and concrete monstrosities that have scarred so many American cities. Much of the city is pedestrianized, and it's so unspoiled that it's hard to believe noisy motorways run close by. Unsurprisingly, floods of American tourists come here every summer in search of Olde Worlde charm, but even in high season you'd be mad to miss out on this historic and hugely hospitable place.

The word 'Québec' comes from *kebec*, Algonquin for 'at the point where the river narrows'. The French explorer Samuel de Champlain gave this name to the site in 1608.

When to Go

The best times to visit are for the Fête de Saint-Jean (Québec's main public holiday), on 24 June, or during the Festival d'Été International de Québec (the international summer festival), a lively celebration of performing and street arts that takes place during the first two weeks of July. If at all possible, you should be in Montréal for Saint-Jean, then spend early July in Québec. The summer festival, a happy and spontaneous explosion of regional pride, is an infectious affair, and you will probably find yourself tempted to join the famous *farandole* dance (*see* 'Festivals').

The People

It is difficult to capture the essence of the Québécois in words. On the whole, they are warm-hearted, down-to-earth people with whom it's surprisingly easy to strike up a friendship, and there's nothing forced about their laid-back hospitality. That said, you'll also find a powerful sense of unity, particularly when it comes to defending the French language. Stubborn, generous, well versed in the art of heated discussion and extremely sensitive when it comes to politics, the Québécois are deeply rooted in their past, but resolutely forward-thinking at the same time.

QUÉBEC
CITY

USEFUL ADDRESSES

Tourist Information

🖪 Maison du tourisme de la province de Québec (colour map II, C2): 12 rue Sainte-Anne; near Château Frontenac. ☎ 1-800-363-7777 (toll-free). Website: www.bonjourquebec.com. Email: info@tourisme.gouv.qc.ca. From the end of June to the beginning of September, open 8.30am–7.30pm; otherwise, 9am–5pm. The provincial tourist office stocks road maps for the whole of Québec, and has a car-hire desk and a bureau de change.

🅑 **Office du tourisme de la communauté urbaine de Québec** (colour map III, B3): 835 avenue Wilfrid-Laurier. ☎ 692-2471. Fax: 692-1481. Website: www.quebecregion.com. Email: info@quebecregion.com. From the beginning of June until the first Monday in September, open 8.30am–7.45pm; in April, May, September and October, open Monday to Friday, 8.30am–5.30pm; from November to March, open Monday to Friday, 8.30am–5pm. This friendly tourist office deals with the city and its surrounding areas. It has a wealth of maps, brochures and information about what's on in town and a telephone you can use to call hotels free of charge.

– In summer, you'll find **mobile information points** scattered across the Old Town. These consist of young tourist-office employees on mopeds, marked with large question marks.

Communications

✉ **Post office** (colour map II, B1): 300 rue Saint-Paul. Open Monday to Friday, 8am–5.45pm. There is another one at 3 rue Buade.

Money

■ **American Express**: Galeries de la Capitale (in the La Baie shop). ☎ 627-2580.

■ If you want to take out money with a Visa card, most of the seven branches of **Banque Royale** have cashpoints. There are branches at 700 place d'Youville and 140 Grande-Allée Est.

Embassies and Consulates

■ **United States Consulate**: 2 place Terrasse-Dufferin. ☎ 692-2095. Open Monday–Friday 2–4pm, plus Tuesday and Thursday mornings 9–11am.

Health

■ **Brunet Pharmacy (24-hour)**: 4266 1ere Avenue, Galeries Charlesbourg. ☎ 623-1571.

■ **Emergencies**: ☎ 911.

Transportation

➊ **Québec Airport** is in Sainte-Foy (20 minutes from the town centre). The Dupont company runs a shuttle bus service between Québec and the airport, with a dozen or so round trips daily. In winter, there are only three a day. Timetables are available at the tourist office.

■ **Air Transat**: no office in Québec. For information on arrival and departure times ☎ 872-1011.

■ **Air Canada**: ☎ 692-0770. The airport office is open 5.30am–9.30pm in summer (variable hours in winter).

🚂 **Railway station** (Via Rail; colour map III, B1): gare du Palais, 450 rue de la Gare-du-Palais. ☎ 692-3940. There's a left-luggage service (24 hours maximum).

🚌 **Coach station** (colour map III, B1): gare du Palais, 320 Abraham-Martin. ☎ 525-3000. This is the arrival and departure point for all the private bus and coach operators. There's a service to Montréal every hour, on the hour, and the station has left-luggage facilities.

■ **STCUQ**: Québec's public transport organization. ☎ 627-2511. Make sure you have the correct change before you board buses. You'll save a little cash if you buy single-journey tickets in advance at grocers or newsagents. Alternatively, a $4 bus pass entitles you to a day of unlimited travel. Copies of the bus timetable are available at the STCUQ information counter.

Sightseeing Tours

■ **Grayline**: sightseeing tours in the town and region. ☎ 622-9722.

■ **Trolleybus**: city tours are run by Feuille d'Érable et Dupont. ☎ (418) 649-9226. The three 45-seater vehicles, done up to look like old trams, make regular trips between the hotels in the Haute Ville and the main tourist spots.

Car Hire

■ **Hertz** (colour map II, B2): 44 côte du Palais; in Vieux Québec. ☎ 694-1224. You can get a special weekend deal offering unlimited mileage. If you're planning a one-way trip from Québec to the US, ask whether the office has any vehicles that need to be taken back across the border. They often do, and this will save you having to pay a return fee.

■ **Pelletier**: offices at 5070 boulevard du Jardin, Charlesbourg (☎ 621-0678); 1600 boulevard Charest Ouest, Sainte-Foy (☎ 687-5454); and 6385 boulevard Hamel, Ancienne Lorette (☎ 872-6636). Bargains:

■ **Discount**: in the town centre. ☎ 692-1244.

■ **Tilden**: 295 rue Saint-Paul, ☎ 694-1727.

Bicycle and Skate Hire

■ **Cyclo Service**: in the Vieux-Port area. ☎ 692-4052. Friendly service.

■ **Vélo Passe-Sport**: 77A rue Saint-Anne. ☎ 692-3643. Rollerblades are also available for hire.

Hitchhiking

■ **Allô-Stop**: 467 rue Saint-Jean. ☎ 522-3430. Email: allostop@total.net

Entertainment and Media

The *Québec Chronicle Telegraph*, published on Wednesday, is your best bet for English-language information. For listings, try the free weekly paper *Voir* to find out what's going on. You'll find it in bookshops and restaurants, as well as on the street). Also see: *Aujourd'hui à Québec*, *Québec Scope* (free monthly) or the tourist guide *Région de Québec* (free).

■ **Maison de la Presse internationale** (colour map II, B2): 1050 rue Saint-Jean, opposite rue Sainte-Ursule. As well as carrying a wide range of newspapers from the US and Europe, this shop has a good choice of magazines and postcards.
■ **Bibliothèque Gabrielle-Roy**: 350 Saint-Joseph Est. ☎ 529-0924. This is the most beautiful library in the province. It heads a network of about 10 annexes, including the library in the Old Town at 37 rue Sainte-Angèle.

■ **CDs**: Archambault Musique, 1095 rue Saint-Jean and 2450 place boulevard Laurier, Sainte-Foy. Québec's largest music store is also its cheapest, and is particularly good for new releases.
■ **Public swimming pool**: boulevard Champlain, at the southern end of Vieux Québec, 20 minutes' walk from the ferry. ☎ 692-6211. There's another free pool on the Plaines d'Abraham, next to the Musée du Québec. Open only in summer. Swimming caps are obligatory.

Miscellaneous

■ **Laundrette** (colour map II, B2): 35 rue Saint-Flavien. Open 8am–9pm. This place also has drying facilities. There is another laundrette at 17 bis rue Sainte-Ursule: open 9am–9pm; closed on Sundays.

TIP There is only a handful of shops in Québec where you can buy **camping-gas refills**. One of these is Latulipe (637 Saint-Vallier Ouest, on the corner with rue Marie-de-l'Incarnation; ☎ 529-0024). Another is the Boutique de Chasse et Pêche (1221 boulevard Duplessis, near boulevard Hamel; ☎ 871-1216), which also sells hunting and fishing gear.

Cybercafés

These cafés come and go at an alarming rate, so phone before you go.

■ **Bar l'Étrange**: 275 rue Saint-Jean. ☎ 522-6504. Email: skippy @etrange.qc.ca. Website: www. etrange.qc.ca. Internet access $3 per hour; no printing facilities.
■ **Café Internet du Palais Montcalm**: 995 place d'Youville. ☎ 692-4909. Internet access $6 per hour; no printing facilities.

■ **Le Tribune Café**: 975 rue Saint-Jean. ☎ 694-0051. Internet access $6 per hour; no printing facilities, and only one computer.
■ **Dream City**: 2323 Galvani, Sainte-Foy. ☎ 686-0606. Email: games@games.qc.ca. Website: www.dreamcite.com. Internet access $5 per hour; printing facilities are available, and you can transfer information to disks.

QUÉBEC CITY

GETTING AROUND TOWN

Everybody walks in Québec City, so there's very little traffic. The Haute Ville is pedestrianized, and is connected to the Basse Ville by a funicular railway. The tourist office has a handy leaflet that shows the main car-parks: most of them are quite expensive, so try to get into the one between rues Saint-Paul and Saint-André (60 spaces) if you can.

A cycle path runs from the centre of Québec to Montmorency and Sainte-Anne-de-Beaupré via the old port and market. The cycle paths in and around Québec are marked on all the maps produced by the tourist office.

WHERE TO STAY

For maps of Québec City, see the second colour plate section.

It can be hard to find somewhere to stay during the summer and carnival time, so make sure you arrive early (before 10am) at youth hostels and hotels; better still, book in advance as much as possible. Most of the city's hotels are full along rues Sainte-Ursule and Sainte-Anne. Some people prefer to stay on the other side of the river at Lévis, where the guesthouses tend to be less expensive and less crowded. A ferry service connects the area to the centre of town.

☆ Budget

🛏 **Auberge de la Paix** (colour map II, B2, **11**): 31 rue Couillard. ☎ 694-0735. Bed and breakfast (as much as you want) $19 per person; sheet hire $2.50 (obligatory if you don't have a sleeping bag). Out of season, you'll get a free night if you stay for more than a week. Curfew at 2am; you must arrive before 6pm if you book by telephone.

You don't need a card to stay at this smallish, well-maintained youth hostel, which has 60 beds in rooms and dormitories with two to eight beds, and the price stays the same regardless of room size. Jean, the owner, is a mine of information about the town and the region, and if you park in the Richelieu car-park, opposite the hospital along rue McMahon, he'll usually refund half the parking fee. The Auberge has a free left-luggage facility, a courtyard and a kitchen, and you'll find a laundrette nearby. This is the best budget option in town, and it's also near rue Saint-Jean, which is always

bustling. For excellent salads and affordable snacks, join the young Québécois at Temporel, next door.

🛏 **Centre International de Séjour de Québec** (colour map II, B2, **12**): 19 rue Sainte-Ursule. ☎ 694-0755. Fax: 694-2278. Email: cisq@mail. org. Open 24 hours a day. Dormitories $17 per person; doubles $46 ($51 with breakfast). Add $4 a night if you don't have a YH card. You can book by telephone, and Visa cards are accepted. This is the city's official Youth Hostel, with 245 beds in rooms of three to six beds and three dormitories sleeping 10 to 12 people (one of these is mixed). Pillows and blankets are provided, but you have to hire sheets. It's a real rabbit warren, with a maze of stairs and corridors. There's a large common room with video games and a pool table, while the cafeteria dishes up large, cheap breakfasts. The staff are pretty laid-back and can offer sightseeing advice and guided tours of the town, sometimes free of charge. Other facilities include a phone booth, a washing

QUÉBEC
CITY

machine (coin-operated), a kitchen and Internet access.

♠ **YWCA** (off colour map III, A3, **13**): outside the town centre, at the intersection of 865 avenue Holland and chemin Sainte-Foy. ☎ 683-2155. Fax: 683-5526. Doubles $43 a night; singles $29. Men and women welcome. There's really not much to say about this place. There are lots of beds, so it's a good summer fall-back, but it has little else to offer. It's gloomy, character-less, expensive and a long way from the action. It has no cafeteria, but there is a small kitchen.

♠ **Laval University**: a 20-minute bus ride from the town centre. ☎ 656-5632 (extension 1618). Website: www.ulaval.ca/sres. Rooms available between mid-March and mid-August. Doubles $30 a night; singles $22. Another last-ditch option when there's no room at the Auberge. It's miles out of town, and it's not especially cheap, but it will do in an emergency.

– **Tourist rooms** (rooms to let) in private residences are a viable option if there are two of you. If possible, try to find somewhere in Vieux Québec (i.e., inside the city walls).

Hotels

Most of the hotels listed here are inside the city walls.

☆ – ☆☆ Budget to Moderate

♠ **La Maison du Général** (colour map II, B3, **15**): 72 rue Saint-Louis, by porte Saint-Louis. ☎ 694-1905. Doubles $45 a night; singles $33. Booking by telephone only; you must arrive after noon. This is the cheapest place to stay in town, and it shows: the rooms are dilapidated, the furnishings are not co-ordinated and there's no breakfast. Some rooms have en-suite showers, but these are more expensive. The earth won't move for you if you stay here, but you'll get a polite reception, and it's well worth hearing the anecdote about 'the General' (ask the staff to tell you).

♠ **Hôtel Manoir Charest** (colour map III, A2, **24**): 448 rue Dor-chester-sud, in Basse Ville, on the corner with boulevard Charest. ☎ 647-9320. Fax: 529-5120. E-mail: manoir@videotron.ca. Doubles $68–78 a night, including Continental breakfast and parking. This is a small, simple and rather charmless hotel, but it's not too expensive and you're just a short walk away from the town centre. The rooms on the

street side are a bit noisy, so try to get one at the back. The standard-issue hotel furniture has seen better days, but everything is tidy and the friendly manageress can tell you where to find the best restaurants in town.

♠ **Manoir des Remparts** (colour map II, C2, **14**): 3 rue des Remparts, a 5-minute walk from Château Fron-tenac. ☎ 692-2056. Fax: 692-1125. Doubles with shared bathroom $50 a night (en suite $70); rooms for four $70 (en suite $90). Breakfast is included. This is an ageing, slightly run-down guesthouse, but it's in a peaceful spot and it doesn't cost the earth. It's run by a friendly family, so there's a nice, homely atmosphere, and while the rooms are nothing to shout about, several overlook the port (not very pretty, but they do get a lot of light). No smoking.

☆☆ Moderate

♠ **Auberge de la Place d'Armes** (colour map II, C2, **22**): 24 rue Sainte-Anne, right in the centre of Vieux Québec. ☎ 694-9485 or ☎ 1-800-465-7847 (toll-free). Fax: 694-

9899. Doubles $65–105 a night, including parking. Rue Sainte-Anne is the most touristy street in the city, so the room rates at this three-floor hotel represent something of a bargain. To some extent, you get what you pay for: the rooms are small and sometimes a bit tatty, and while care has been taken over the decor, it's not especially tasteful. Avoid the rooms at the back, as there's a lot of noise from outside. Despite these reservations, it's good value for money, and the staff are friendly. There's a restaurant on the ground floor, and breakfast is served at the Swiss café next door.

≜ L'Hôtel particulier Belley (colour map II, B1, **23**): 249 rue Saint-Paul, place du Marché du vieux port, between the Gare du Palais and the Vieux Port. ☎ 692-1694. Fax: 692-1696. Website: www.oricom.ca/belley. Doubles $65–130 a night, and often far less out of season; breakfast $5. This is a nice part of town, and the hotel has a lot of character. There's a trendy café on the ground floor, and the comfortable rooms come with shower, TV, minibar, telephone and fan as standard. Some also have air-conditioning, while the biggest ones also have kitchens. The young staff are enthusiastic and friendly – but don't let them talk you into taking a room in the annexe, which is considerably less charming than the main building. Laundry facilities are available.

≜ Hayden's Wexford House (colour map III, off B3, **25**): 450 rue Champlain, between the cliff and the St Lawrence River. ☎ 524-0524. Fax: 648-8995. Website: www.bbcanada.com/hayden wexfordhouse. Doubles $85–125 a night, including breakfast. This old Irish guesthouse dates back to the 18th century, but has only recently been reopened, with four well-deco-

rated, inviting rooms (shared bathroom), a more expensive studio flat and a four-person apartment. You'll get a really friendly welcome from Louise, Françoise and Jean, who used to own a restaurant in Montréal. Breakfast is served in a beautiful brick-and-stone dining room, and you can get an evening meal in winter if you book it in advance.

≜ Auberge Saint-Louis (colour map II, B3, **20**): 48 rue Saint-Louis. ☎ 692-2424. Fax: 692-3797. Doubles $55 a night (en suite $85), including breakfast. This place is about as good as it gets in this price range: the staff are professional and courteous, and the tastefully decorated rooms are simple, comfortable and regularly refurbished. Rooms with en-suite showers offer particularly good value, while the suite has a fireplace and a private bathroom. Avoid the rooms overlooking the street, as the noise tends to seep in. Breakfast is served at the Crêperie du Château Frontenac, which is pretty good as well.

≜ Auberge de la Chouette (colour map II, B3, **29**): 71 rue d'Auteuil, opposite parc de l'Esplanade, near porte Saint-Louis. ☎ 694-0232. Fax: 694-9332. Doubles with en-suite bathroom $58–80 a night, depending on season; breakfast $2. This quiet, family-run hotel above the Aspara restaurant (see 'Where to Eat') has 10 spacious, air-conditioned rooms that have been individually furnished, some with antiques. They're not especially luxurious or original, but they're well maintained, and some have beautiful bathrooms. It's a friendly place, and very peaceful considering how close it is to town: the rooms overlooking the park have the best views, although the horse-drawn carriages make a fair bit of noise.

≜ Manoir La Salle (colour map II, B2, **16**): 18 rue Sainte-Ursule, opposite the Centre International de

Séjour. ☎ 692-9953. Doubles $55–75 a night; no breakfast. This cosy, old-fashioned hotel is owned by the charming Thérèse Lachance, who is a little absent-minded, slightly authoritarian and absolutely mad about cats (she keeps four at the hotel). A lovely varnished wood staircase takes you up to the bright, comfortable rooms, which are larger than you'd expect at this price but slightly sombre. Everything is kept spick and span, but you should give the place a miss if you're allergic to cats. You can also rent a studio flat by the week.

🛇 **Château de Léry** (colour map II, C3, **18**): 8 rue de Laporte, near Château Frontenac. ☎ 692-2692 or ☎ 1-800-363-0036 (toll-free). Fax: 692-5231. Website: www.quebec web.com/chateaudelery. Doubles $80–130 a night, including breakfast; parking $7. The only castle-like thing about this hotel is its name. The rooms aren't bad – they're regularly redecorated and spacious, and the more expensive rooms have en-suite bathrooms and air-conditioning – but the prices reflect the location, not the quality of the establishment. Breakfast is a pretty meagre affair, and the corridors and reception area have seen better days. On the plus side, the parking fee is much less than you'll pay at a public car park.

🛇 **La Maison Demers** (colour map II, B3, **17**): 68 rue Sainte-Ursule. ☎ 692-2487. Doubles $65–85, including breakfast (small and very basic) and parking. Book in advance for this 'bijou' residence, as it only has eight rooms: these are quaint, verging on kitsch, but they're all big (especially the four-bed rooms) and some have en-suite bathrooms and even terraces. The elderly owners are spontaneous and chatty, though the welcome during the high season is not always what it should be. The car-park, though free, is quite a way away.

🛇 **La Maison Sainte-Ursule** (colour map II, B3, **19**): 40 rue Sainte-Ursule, not far from porte Saint-Jean. ☎ 694-9794. Prices vary, so ask to see a room to find out what you're getting. Maurice Decker is not your average hotelier: he worked as a photographer, painter and translator in Britain before moving to Québec, his interests include collecting cacti and he has a cockatoo called Maurice who accompanies him wherever he goes. But then this is not your average hotel: the simple rooms in this 200-year-old building are as quiet as if you were in the countryside, whether they're on the street or the courtyard side, and there's a guesthouse atmosphere, laid-back and rather unconventional. Maurice gives everything the personal touch, and loves spending time with his guests, sometimes over a drink or late into the evening. It's not to everyone's taste, but some people will absolutely love it.

☆☆☆ Expensive

🛇 **Au Jardin du Gouverneur** (colour map II, C3, **27**): 16 Mont-Carmel, in the heart of Vieux Québec. ☎ 692-1704. Fax: 692-1713. Doubles $60–125 a night, including breakfast. This enormous building has rooms that match its wonderful views, with bathrooms, air-conditioning and TV as standard. The rooms on the third floor and at the back are the cheapest, but the $60 ones are tiny, so it's worth spending a bit more. If money is no object, Nos. 102 (for two people) and 202 (for four) are the best. The Continental breakfast, sadly, is run-of-the-mill.

🛇 **Hôtel Manoir d'Auteuil** (colour map II, B3, **28**): 49, rue d'Auteuil, not far from porte Saint-Louis.

☎ 694-1173. Fax: 694-0081. Doubles $90–150 a night, including breakfast. This beautiful hotel is full of character, with a subdued, well-heeled atmosphere and 1930s and 1950s furniture and woodwork. The rooms are really comfortable, with the whiff of luxury you'd expect at these prices. Édith Piaf once stayed in No. 8, which has a superb royal-blue bathroom and two queen-size beds, but you might prefer the room with a jacuzzi and power shower (which happens to be the most expensive). Your stay will be colourful and sometimes a bit over the top – but all in the best possible taste.

♠ **Auberge Saint-Pierre** (colour map II, C2, **38**): 79 rue Saint-Pierre, on a historic street near the Vieux-Port. ☎ 694-7981. Fax: 694-0406. Doubles from $90 a night. All the rooms are very comfortable, and the devoted staff provide flawless service. The suites are a bit expensive, but the decor is original and very tasteful.

♠ **La Maison Acadienne** (colour map II, B3, **26**): 43 rue Sainte-Ursule. ☎ 694-0258 or ☎ 1-800-463-0280 (toll-free). Doubles from $59 (en suites $79–225), excluding breakfast; discounts available out of season. This large, well-situated house attracts tourists in their droves. There are 40 single and double rooms, some of them rather lacking in charm, but well maintained, and the roof terrace offers welcome relief from the crowds below. The most expensive ones have exposed stone walls, a fireplace or a terrace. The staff at reception can be a little brusque, but otherwise you'll be made to feel right at home. There's a car-park, but you'll have to pay extra to use it.

Bed & Breakfast

For the most part, Québec's B&Bs are a little out of the way, but they're peaceful, comfortable and affordable, which makes them a better bet than many of the impersonal, overpriced hotels in the city centre.

☆☆ Moderate

Haute Ville, Inside the Walls

♠ **La Marquise de Bassano** (colour map II, C3, 21): 15 rue des Grisons, near Château Frontenac. ☎ 692-0316. Email: bassano@total.net. Doubles $65–95 a night, including breakfast and parking. This lovely Victorian house within the city walls has five cosy bedrooms on two floors, with a bathroom on each level. Two are reserved for long stays (more than 10 days); of the others, one has an impressively stocked library and another is an attic bedroom. Breakfast is served in a lovely dining room with a piano, and it's enormous. The warmth of the owners helps make this a great place to stay.

♠ **Maison James Thompson** (colour map II, B3, **25**): 47 rue Sainte-Ursule. ☎ 694-9042. Doubles $75 a night. The building is listed as a historic monument, but it's a house that lives and breathes. Several rooms are wood-panelled from floor to ceiling, and some are up in the attic. The decor shows a personal touch, and some of the furniture is custom-made, including the huge double beds, which have thick, snug-looking duvets. Breakfast is served in the large dining room.

♠ **Gîte du Quartier Latin – B&B Chez Hubert** (colour map II, B3, **30**): 66 rue Sainte-Ursule. ☎ 692-0958. Fax: 681-4678. Doubles $80 a night, including tax, breakfast and parking. As soon as you step through the beautiful glass-paned front door, you'll feel the peaceful atmosphere of this lavishly furnished family house. Climb the staircase to the second floor and you'll find four enormous, scrupulously clean bedrooms, sharing two bathrooms. All are decorated in delicate, well-chosen and co-ordinated colours, while the carpets and pictures give each of them a touch of class. Generous breakfasts are served in a superb dining room, and you'll be made to feel right at home by Guylaine and Hubert, and by Jean-Marc, their charming handyman.

Haute Ville, Outside the Walls

♠ L'Heure Douce (colour map III, A2, **29**): 704 Richelieu, in the Saint-Jean-Baptiste quarter. ☎ and fax: 649-1935. Email: hdouce@videotron.ca. Website: www.ifrance.com/hdouce. Doubles $65 a night, including breakfast; four-bed rooms $110. This recently renovated period house has two double rooms and one for four, a bathroom with a view (!), a kitchen and a little terrace. The rooms are very peaceful, even those that overlook the street, and they're not at all expensive. You'll be greeted by the charming owner, Diane, who also serves the lavish breakfasts. Bright and spacious studio flats are also available. A first-rate establishment.

♠ Chez Mimi (colour map III, A3, **31**):70 rue Fraser, not far from avenue Cartier. ☎ 524-9161. Fax: 843-7627. Doubles $70, including breakfast and parking. There are three double rooms, with one bathroom. Mimi, the owner, is lovely, and really makes you feel welcome.

Farther Afield

The following places are all accessible by bus, and if you're travelling by car, parking is free.

♠ Chez Stuart et Marie-Paule Fleet (colour map I, C2, **34**): 1080 avenue Holland, in the Sillery quarter, 10 minutes' drive from Vieux Québec. ☎ 688-0794. Doubles $75 a night, including breakfast and parking. This beautiful house on a large, quiet avenue is a great place to stay, if only for the warmth and kindness of the Fleets and their daughter, who

♠ A l'Étoile de Rosie (colour map III, A3, **40**): 66 rue Lockwell, near rue Cartier, René-Levesque and the chemin de Sainte-Foy. ☎ 648-1044. Fax: 648-0184. Email: etoilerosie@sympatico.ca. Doubles $75–80. There are three bedrooms with a shared bathroom in this bright maisonette, owned by Marie-Denise Saint-Gelais, or Rosie to her friends. The best room is the '*Africaine*', a mini suite with a living room and superb views of the Laurentides. The other rooms overlook the street, but are very quiet at night. Rosie's enthusiasm for helping her guests is boundless, and she goes out of her way to give you advice and tips on what to do in the city, which she knows like the back of her hand. She'll even book snowmobiles, sleigh rides or skiing trips for you. For breakfast, you go through the kitchen to the sitting room, where the stunning view of the Laurentides makes facing the morning seem a lot better.

are always on hand if you need anything. The air-conditioned rooms are rather small, but they're bright, comfortable and elegantly decorated, and the tranquil surroundings make a pleasant change after the throngs of tourists in the city centre. There's a wide choice of things for breakfast, and you can walk off any early-morning over-indulgence in the nearby Coulonges park. Book in advance during summer.

≜ Café-couette 4 Saisons (colour map III, A4, **38**): 287 rue René-Lévesque. ☎ 525-6426. Doubles $95 a night, including breakfast. There's nothing special about the en-suite rooms, which are comfortable and well looked after. Breakfast, on the other hand, is something of an occasion: Guy, your host, is a newly retired restaurant owner, and he cooks up a different breakfast every day, guaranteed to fill you up until nightfall. He's a typical Québécois, warm, spontaneous and happy to share his local knowledge. You can park your car behind the house.

≜ Fernlea (colour map I, B3, **33**): 2156 rue Dickson. ☎ 683-3847. Doubles $70 a night, including breakfast. The owner, Joyce Coutts, is a charming Englishwoman whose beautiful detached house has a magnificent garden. Upstairs, there are three large, comfortable and peaceful bedrooms (shared bathroom). The decor is Anglo-American – one room is painted in white and mauve – and there isn't a spot of dust. Breakfast is excellent, and so is the value for money.

≜ La Maison Bourlamaque (colour map III, A4, **39**): 1045 avenue Bourlamaque, on a quiet street between Grande-Allée and René-Levesque. ☎ and fax: 529-7171. Email: maugen@globetrotter.qc.ca. Doubles $65–75, including tax, breakfast and parking. This is a splendid wooden house built at the turn of the 20th century, with a veranda. Upstairs, there are three simple, bright bedrooms and two bathrooms. It's a no-nonsense – and no-smoking – family-run establishment, with everything you need for a great holiday and no complications. You'll get a gracious welcome from the owner, a retired university lecturer who used to teach ethics;

philosophy graduates may be surprised to learn that in spite of this, he's very good at working through any problems you might have. For breakfast, you'll get good, homemade produce in the large living room on the ground floor, or on the gallery if the weather's fine. You can also rent a house on the Île d'Orléans.

≜ La Maison Lesage (colour map I, C2, **35**): 760 chemin Saint-Louis. ☎ 682-9959 E-mail: bb maisonlesage@videotron.ca. Doubles $90 a night, including breakfast. A beautiful brick house, built in 1928, the Maison Lesage's looks suit summer greenery as much as winter snow. The reception rooms have bow windows, wood panelling, fireplaces and 1930s parquet floors. Upstairs, there are five huge bedrooms, tastefully furnished, peaceful and each with an en-suite bathroom and a little boudoir. Everything is spotless, and there is central air-conditioning. It's good value for money, especially when you consider the warm welcome and wonderful big breakfast. No smoking. Children not admitted.

≜ Les Corniches (colour map I, C2-3, **32**): 2052 chemin Saint-Louis, in the Sillery area. ☎ 681-9318. Fax: 692-1713. Website: www.bbcanada.com/3282.html. Sometimes closed out of season. Doubles $85 a night, including breakfast. This large, white house, built at the turn of the 20th century, is pleasantly set in greenery. Two of the upstairs bedrooms share a bathroom: the first is a little gloomy, but has a very large bed; the other is brighter, but with a 'normal' bed. The third bedroom is a bit more expensive, but it's definitely the best: it's vast, with an enormous bed and its own bathroom. Breakfast is different every morning, but the service is always charming, and after a hard day's sightseeing, you can unwind in the beautiful living room, which has a piano. This is a smart, peaceful and very pleasant establishment, but don't stay here unless you have a car, as it's a long way from the town centre.

â **B&B Le Manoir Rustique** (colour map I, C2, **36**): 850, avenue Marguerite-Bourgeoys, a stone's throw away from chemin Sainte-Foy. ☎ 686-1611. Doubles $70 a night, including breakfast and parking. Marieve and Daniel have worked hard to buy and restore this huge house, and it's more than just a business venture for them: as well as being a hotel, this place acts as a refuge for young Québécois who've strayed onto the wrong side of the tracks. And they do it without any help from the authorities. The house, a lovely manor painted pale yellow, is surrounded by a traditional veranda where you can have breakfast or just daydream. There are two beautiful bedrooms at the front, and a third, half a level below, looks out onto the garden. Even breakfast is a little bit different, with generous portions of food that fits the seasons, not the usual Continental conven-

tions. All that the owners ask of you is that you don't smoke or wear shoes in the house.

☆☆☆ Expensive

â **Manoir Mon Calme** (colour map III, B3, **41**): 549 Grande-Allée Est, G1R-2J5. ☎ 523-2714. Fax: 523-3078. Website: www.bbcanada.com/2379.html. Doubles $149 a night, including breakfast and parking. This striking town house is probably the best B&B in town. The first-floor rooms are enormous, with high ceilings, beautiful furniture and wooden floors, fireplaces and lovely en-suite bathrooms. It's not cheap – indeed, luxurious as the rooms are, they don't necessarily offer good value for money – but there's a four-bed room if you're travelling as a family or in a small group. The owners are professional and discreet, and will give you lots of advice on sightseeing and day trips. There's only one criticism: the breakfast corner is surprisingly dreary, which is a shame. Strictly non-smoking.

WHERE TO STAY IN THE AREA

☆ Budget

â **Le P'tit Bonheur Youth Hostel**: 183 côte Lafleur, Saint-Jean, on Île d'Orleans. ☎ (418) 829-2588. Thirty minutes by car from the centre of Québec. *See* 'Where to Stay and Eat' for Île d'Orleans.

Campsites

â **Camping Juneau**: 153 chemin du Lac, at Saint-Augustin-de-Desmaures, 12 kilometres (7.5 miles) west of Québec. ☎ 871-9090. Fax: 871-1642. Email: campingjuneau@videotron. Website: www.quebecweb.com/cjuneau. Follow autoroute 40 west, then take exit 300 south-

bound. Open between 15 April and 15 November; also open in winter, but with limited facilities (you can get electricity, but the toilet block is closed). A pitch for a tent sleeping two adults and two children costs $18 ($20 with electricity). This pleasant, user-friendly campsite, next to a lake in the middle of the forest, has 60 cheap pitches with tables and barbecues. Chalets are also available. The site is also extremely well equipped, with hot showers, a laundry room, a convenience store, open-air games, a snack bar and camping-gas refills available. The toilet block has facilities for the disabled, which is rare on Québécois campsites. Activities on offer include fishing and pedalos. Mr Juneau, the owner, will show you round his maple shed, where you can try – and buy – his maple toffee and other products. The menu at the on-site restaurant, meanwhile, includes the famous *poutine* (*frites* with cheese and brown sauce).

☎ **Camping Aéroport**: 2050 route de l'Aéroport, at Sainte-Foy, 10 kilometres (six miles) from Québec City. ☎ 871-1574. Fax: 877-0739. Email: campingaeroport@globetrotter.qc.ca. To get there, take Route 540 northbound; it's five kilometres (three miles) past the airport. Open from May to October. A pitch for a two-person tent costs $19; $3 for each additional adult. This is one of the closest campsites to the city, and it's well equipped, with a restaurant, a grocery and a swimming pool.

☎ **Camping municipal de Beauport**: 95 rue Sérénité, along boulevard Rochette at Beauport. ☎ 666-2228. From the city centre, take Métrobus No. 800 to the Beauport terminus, then take bus No. 50 or 55. The driver will drop you off about a kilometre from the campsite, which makes it easily accessible by bus. If you're driving, it's 10 kilometres (six miles) away from Québec along autoroute 40; take exit 321. Open from June to early September. Pitches $19–24. Situated in the woods, near a lake and the Montmorency river (and the waterfalls of the same name), this is a cheap, well-equipped campsite, with a snack bar, a laundry room, a convenience store, a swimming pool and sports facilities.

☎ **Camping de la base de plein air Sainte-Foy** (Sainte-Foy Outdoor Activity Centre Campsite): rue Laberge, Sainte-Foy. ☎ 654-4641. To get there, take Route 540, and turn off at rue Laberge. Open from May to early September. Good value for four people sharing, because pitching your tent costs the same as for one person. Now for the bad news: it's near a motorway, so it's noisy, and there are no showers. Campers have access to swimming, fishing and windsurfing facilities.

WHERE TO EAT

For maps of Québec City see the second colour plate section.

Québec, like Montréal, is a culinary paradise, with something to suit all tastes (and pockets). In July, you'll find 'lobster festivals' in many restaurants, but you can get your claws into it all year round.

There are three distinct restaurant areas in the city: 'Haute Ville inside the walls', 'Haute Ville outside the walls' (to the west) and 'Basse Ville'. Wherever you go, if you avoid the tourist traps, you'll be able to eat well at very reasonable prices – perhaps better than anywhere else in Canada.

> **TIP** In Québec, it's customary to dine out in the evenings, rather than at lunchtime. Restaurateurs have cottoned on to this, and try to encourage their countrymen to do lunch by offering special rates – up to four times cheaper than in the evening. Be sure to take advantage of their generosity. Also, in contrast to the unhealthy local habit of eating a colossal breakfast, skipping lunch and making up for it at dinner, why not make the midday meal your main one? Even in the best restaurants in town (*see* 'Expensive' in the sections *below*), lunchtime set menus will set you back only $15 or so. You'll get the same service and the same welcome, but for a lot less cash.

Haute Ville Inside the Walls

This area is usually full of tourists, so restaurants are often very expensive – except at lunchtimes, of course.

☆–☆☆ Budget to Moderate

✕ **Casse-Crêpe Breton** (colour map II, B2, **40**): 1136 rue Saint-Jean. ☎ 692-0438. Open 7.30am– midnight. Lunch menu $7; dinner $10–12. This place is really cheap, which helps to explain why so many young Québécois eat here. The crêpes have been adapted to the local taste buds: it's not gourmet food, but the decor's attractive and the staff are friendly. Credit and debit cards are not accepted.

✕ **Le Petit Coin Latin** (colour map II, A2, **42**): 8 rue Sainte-Ursule. ☎ 692-2022. Open from 8am (9am in winter) to 1am. Lunch menu (starter, main course, coffee) $7. This is a good place to try a few local specialities, although it's equally handy if you just want a snack, with quiches, toasted sandwiches and enormous baguettes all on the menu. If you're really famished, the sugar tart (*tarte au sucre*) with maple syrup will leave you feeling full for the next three days. It's especially busy at breakfast time, when you can feast on pancakes, maple syrup and eggs, washed down with huge bowls of *café au lait*. In summer, try to get a table in the indoor courtyard, which is surrounded by greenery. In the evenings the *table d'hôte*, which includes dessert, doesn't cost much more than lunch.

✕ **Le Figaro** (colour map II, B3, **54**): 32 chemin Saint-Louis, G1R-3Y9, opposite the Musée Brousseau. ☎ 692-4191. Lunch menus (two starters, main course, dessert and coffee) from $16; dinner menus $16–28. This is a good restaurant that takes its cue from the better Parisian brasseries. It strikes the

right balance between quality and price, with efficient service, above-average food and a menu that changes regularly. Starters include calf-liver terrine with carrots and sweet-and-sour onions, dumplings and a soup of the day, with generous helpings of rigatoni *au gratin*, steak with mustard sauce or Gaspé crab in hollandaise sauce to follow. Everything runs like clockwork, and the chefs take great pains with the presentation. It's no surprise to discover that Le Figaro shares a kitchen with the far swankier Continental, just next door. The brasserie connection ends at the wine list, which has distinctly Canadian prices.

✕ **Restaurant Apsara** (colour map II, B3, **29**): 71 rue d'Auteuil, opposite the parc de l'Esplanade. ☎ 694-0232. *Menu du jour* $9; evening set menu $25–30. This restaurant is run by the Khuong family, who also manage L'Auberge de la Chouette (*see* 'Where to Stay'). It's a lovely place, if a little spartan, without any of the usual dragons or red lanterns: the only ornaments are a few Thai statues and a solitary owl above the door, and the intimate dining area resembles the sitting room of an old bourgeois Québec house. The food, thankfully, is less minimalist: the Cambodian, Vietnamese and Thai dishes are always filling, with tasty soups and simpler mains at lunchtime, and more elaborate fare in the evenings. Service is fast and friendly, and you won't be pressurized into spending more than you want to.

✕ **Café-restaurant Le Rétro** (colour map II, B2, **41**): 1129 rue Saint-Jean. ☎ 694-9218. Open until 10.30pm. Lunch menus (soup, main course and dessert) $10–20; dinner menus $15–25. Another less-is-more eatery: wood, plants and not a lot else. It attracts its fair share of tourists, which makes it a little lifeless, but the service is charming and efficient, and the set menus are good whenever you eat. The à la carte menu features good old-fashioned home cooking – lasagne, good fish, coq au vin and so on – all at reasonable prices.

✕ **Les Frères de la Côte** (colour map II, B2, **43**): 1190 rue Saint-Jean. ☎ 692-5445. Lunch menus $10–13; dinner $18–22. This pleasant bar-restaurant has been done up in ochre tones, and attracts a young and sometimes noisy crowd, so look elsewhere if you're planning an intimate dinner à deux. Nor is it a temple of gastronomy: the mainstays of the menu are pizza (the usual suspects, with a few exotic options such as Greek-style with feta cheese and peppers, or even with camembert) and pasta. If you're after something a little more exciting, try one of the daily specials, which might include green pepper and goat's cheese salad, snail risotto with Dijon mustard, marinated salmon with dill, rabbit in ginger and various grilled meets. The food is quite expensive, but it's a fun place to hang out.

✕ **Chez Temporel** (colour map II, B2, **11**): 25 rue Couillard; next to l'Auberge de la Paix. ☎ 694-1813. Open 7.30am–1.30am. Full meal $20–25. Students and guests from the next-door youth hostel make up the clientele at this cheap and cheerful establishment. Actually, it's not quite as cheap as you'd expect, as it's basically an up-market snack bar, but it is a really nice place to eat or have a coffee. Head for the first-floor dining room, all in green with a window looking out over the road, for thick soups, rich cakes, quiches and salads.

✕ **La Caravelle**: 68 rue Saint-Louis. ☎ 694-9022. Lunch menus $9–17; dinner $20–40. A pleasant, stylish restaurant where the staff are friendly and Spanish folk music plays in the background. They do excellent lobster and pretty good paella, while the fish tank out front indicates how fresh their fish is: it's served grilled, meunière-style or with a choice of well-prepared, delicious sauces. You'll get more for your money if you go at lunchtime, and steer clear of the à la carte menu, as it's somewhat overpriced.

✕ **Le Saint-Amour** (colour map II, B3, **46**): 48 rue Sainte-Ursule. ☎ 694-0667. Open until 11.30pm; lunch Tuesday to Saturday only. Lunch menus $10–18; dinner menus $30–35. Book in advance, particularly for dinner. This is one of the best restaurants in Québec, and even the humble set lunch is a not-too-be-missed experience. There are two rooms, the larger of which is a magnificent winter garden, with pink tablecloths, candles and green plants. The food is imaginative and tasty, and portions are generous; the à la carte menu offers some pretty elaborate dishes. A chic crowd descends on the place in the evening, so put on your Sunday best if you don't want to feel out of place. The only criticism is that the service is a bit slow.

✕ **Aux Anciens Canadiens** (colour map II, B3, **45**): 34 rue Saint-Louis, on the corner with rue des Jardins. ☎ 692-1627. Open 11am–10pm. Lunch menu $14; dinner menu $25–45. This is one of the oldest houses in Québec (built in 1675), and as if that wasn't enough of a draw, the restaurant that now occupies it offers splendid regional specialities. Inevitably, it's always full of tourists, but then so are most of the places within the city walls. It's an intimate place, cluttered with antique plates, prints and beautiful objects, and there's even a gun room. The menu features a host of dishes you'll have trouble finding anywhere else in town: pork and bean hotpot, pig's trotter and meatball stew, duck in maple syrup or braised caribou. The lunch menu is really tempting, with soup, a main course (a choice of up to eight dishes), dessert, coffee and a glass of wine or beer. In the evenings, the menus are even more generous, with a starter, soup, main course (the part that dictates the price) and dessert. The speciality is the *assiette des habitants* (locals' platter) – a small feast of its own. Watch out, though: if you veer off the set menus, or have a couple of bottles of wine, you could get a nasty shock when the bill arrives.

☆☆☆ Expensive

✕ **L'Initiale** (colour map II, C2, **44**): 54 rue Saint-Pierre; at the corner with côte de la Montagne. ☎ 694-1818. Lunch menus $10–20, excluding drinks; evening menus $35–45. Here's an offer you can't refuse: come to this elegant establishment at lunchtime and you can enjoy some of the best cooking in Québec for the cost of a few slices of pizza. L'Initiale was awarded the Grand Prix 2000 de Gastronomie by the city's tourist office. It's discreetly luxurious, with very high ceilings and a airy, spacious feel. Rolande is the manager, and he'll offer you dishes concocted by Yvan (a Breton). These include homemade soups and ice-creams, and Yvan's own, French-inspired recipes, based on the finest local produce. You'd be mad to miss out.

✕ **La Crémaillère** (colour map II, B2, **63**): 21 rue Saint-Stanislas, on the corner with rue Saint-Jean. ☎ 692-2216. Menus $30–35. There's no lunch menu, but it's worth splashing out on medallions of calves' sweetbreads with chestnuts smoked in rosemary, noisette of venison in redcurrant and green pepper vinegar, or *feuilléte* of langoustines with chanterelles and spinach smothered in lemon saffron butter.

Haute Ville Outside the Walls

This includes the Saint-Jean-Baptiste area, a popular old district that's crawling with students during term time. It's fallen foul of the property developers in recent years, but its character remains largely intact, and restaurants there are generally cheaper and less touristy than inside the city walls. The area's main thoroughfare is the section of rue Saint-Jean that runs east from avenue Dufferin. Finally, the Grand-Allée Est (leading to porte Saint-Louis) houses a preposterous number of tourist restaurants, all crammed in next to each other.

☆ Budget

✕ **Café Sainte-Julie** (colour map III, B2, **47**): 865 rue des Zouaves, near the corner with Saint-Gabriel. ☎ 647-9368. Open 7am–9pm. Menus $6–8. This is one of the cheapest eating spots in town; it's basic, but it's good, and they'll even do 'off-menu' dishes if you can't see anything you fancy. It's smoky, noisy and full of students and eccentrics, with rock and blues music playing.

✕ **Croque M** (colour map III, A2, **49**): 585 rue Saint-Jean, at the crossroads with rue des Zouaves. ☎ 524-7832. Open 9am–5pm (9pm on Thursday and Friday). Daily menu $8. This is a small restaurant with an attractive, cosy interior. The menu of the day consists of soup or vegetable juice, a toasted sandwich or salad, and coffee. This is simple food, made with fresh produce and served with a big smile.

✕ **Les Crêpes Celtiques** (colour map III, A3, **60**): 151 chemin Sainte-Foy. ☎ 525-5101. Meals $5.50–12. This place is the brainchild of an expatriate Breton: a self-service *crêperie* where you pick your table, order your food at the counter, go back to get your meal when it's ready, then clear the table when you're done. You can start with a choice of soups and salads, and there's always one fish, one meat and one pasta dish on offer. But you're here for the crêpes, both savoury (Mexican chilli, ham, béchamel sauce) and sweet (the inevitable maple syrup). If you're crêped out after your main course, try *gâteau à la canneberge* (a local speciality made with cranberries) for dessert. It's a great place to eat if you're short of cash, as the price-quantity ratio is very much in your favour. On fine days, a small terrace is set out in the courtyard at the back, but it's just as cheerful inside.

✕ **La Piazzetta** (colour map III, B2, **48**): 707 rue Saint-Jean; on the corner with Sainte-Geneviève. ☎ 529-7489. Open 11.30am–11.30pm (weekends 4–11.30pm). Lunch menu $8–12; evening menu $13–18. This is a modern, slightly soulless place, but it does serve really good American and Neapolitan pizzas: square-edged and extra thin. The parmesan pizza is a good bet, but it's overshadowed by the three-cheese pizza, which is absolutely delicious. There's another Piazzetta at 1191 avenue Cartier.

✕ **Self et Pub de l'Université Laval** (Laval University refectory and pub): this is a fair way west of the Haute Ville. By car, go back up the chemin Saint-Louis, follow avenue Laurier for about five kilometres (three miles), then turn onto the av-

enue des Sciences. The refectory is in the Pollack and Desjardins pavilions, signposted at the entrance – ask someone if you get lost, as the campus is huge. It's an awkward journey unless you have a car, but this is a really good place to meet local students. From Monday to Friday, you can get a cheap lunch from one of the self-service counters, each of which has a different culinary theme. There's also an evening bar-restaurant, Le Pub, with good food and a vibrant atmosphere.

☆☆ Moderate

✕ **Chez Victor** (colour map III, A3, **51**): 145 rue Saint-Jean. ☎ 529-7702. Open for lunch and dinner (until 10.30pm; 9pm on Monday). Lunch menu $7; à la carte dinner $10. Victor's place is a little out of the way, but it's in a 'real' part of Québec and the only tourists who come here are lost. You'll get the best hamburgers and French fries in town in a cosy environment with exposed stone walls and folk music on the stereo. The lunch menu consists of a burger, fries or a salad, and a drink.

✕ **Hobbit** (colour map III, B2, **50**): 700 rue Saint-Jean. ☎ 647-2677. Open 8am–11pm. Lunch $9–11; dinner $11–16. Another studenty place, although this time they're the ones behind the counter, waiting on a clientele of cerebral-looking 30-somethings. The spacious, stone-walled dining area is crowded at lunchtime, but it gets quieter in the evening, which is the time to try a *table d'hôte* (soup, main course, dessert and coffee) that strikes the right balance between quality and price. Alternatively, pop in for breakfast (brunch at weekends) or a fortifying salad and sandwich between sights.

✕ **Le Cochon Dingue** (colour map III, A3, **58**): 46 boulevard René-Lévesque Ouest, near avenue Cartier. ☎ 523-2013. Lunch menus $8.50–16; dinner menus $18–24. This restaurant is at its best in summer, when you can sit out behind the main building on a huge covered terrace with a fountain in the middle. The name translates as 'the crazy pig', and you'll find plenty of porcine puns on the menu. The menus and the *table d'hôte* give you a choice of several daily specials. There's a branch in the Basse Ville, on boulevard Champlain, but it isn't as good.

☆☆☆ Expensive

✗ **L'Astral** (colour map III, B3, **52**): 1225 place Montcalm, on the Grande Allée Est, on the top floor of the Hôtel Concorde. ☎ 647-2222. Lunch menus $10–18; evening set menu $20–38; buffet menu $39. This is a revolving restaurant with spectacular panoramic views of Québec City, the St Lawrence and the surrounding area. It's expensive, but that's no surprise given the location, and you don't necessarily

have to eat here: you can go for a drink if you go in the afternoon or late in the evening. If you want a seat near the viewing window, you should book your table in advance. While there's no dress code or attitude, most of the people who come here are businessmen, and the international cuisine reflects their tastes. If you are starving, try the buffet lunch (although you'll have to really stuff yourself to get anything like value for money) on Saturday nights and some lunchtimes.

✗ **Momento Ristorante** (colour map III, A4, **64**): 1144 avenue Cartier. ☎ 647-1313. Lunch menus $13–18; dinner menus $15–25. This is an image-conscious, slightly flashy Italian joint, but it serves tasty and filling Italian dishes: beef carpaccio, oven-baked lasagne, *penne al arrabbiata* and tiramisu. The Italian wines, served in carafes, are a little expensive, but they are good. The waiters are charming, and there's also a small pavement terrace where you can see and be seen.

Basse Ville

This is one of the most picturesque parts of Québec, with its old port, quaint train station and venerable houses. Oddly enough, there are few tourists, even though there are plenty of great restaurants and lively cafés.

☆ Budget

✗ **Le Café du Clocher Penché** (just off colour map III, near A2): 203 rue Saint-Joseph. ☎ 640-0597. Lunch menus $8; dinner menus $14. This popular neighbourhood bar-restaurant takes its name from the leaning church steeple over the road, and you can study the steeple's wonkiness from one of the window tables in the lovely dining room if you're so inclined. It's smoky and full of chatter at mealtimes, as artists and students of all ages get stuck into simple no-frills bistro fare, cooked behind the bar.

The chef sometimes tries his hand at more exotic cuisines, and the results are usually pretty good. Service is efficient and friendly, even at the busiest periods.

✗ **Buffet de l'Antiquaire** (colour map II, C1, **53**): 95 rue Saint-Paul. ☎ 692-2661. Open summer only, 6am–11pm (7pm on Saturday and Sunday). Menus $6–13. This is one of the few down-to-earth restaurants left in this gentrified area. For the past 20 years, it has served simple dishes accompanied by the house mashed potato, in lime-green surroundings with small tables, a counter and a mezzanine. Plump for the set menu and you'll get soup, a main course and a drink, with up to 10 dishes to choose from. They also do lovely salads and large sandwiches. It's not at all expensive, and it has a lot of charm.

✘ **Pizza Mag** (colour map II, A1, **55**): 363 rue Saint-Paul; opposite the train station. ☎ 692-1910. Open 11am–midnight. Pizzas $8–13, depending on size. An excellent pizzeria whose owners had the courage to include taxes in the prices, and the good sense to set up shop near the train station. The pizzas are popular and original, with crusty bases and plenty of toppings.

✘ **Asia** (colour map II, C1, **56**): 89 rue du Sault-au-Matelot. ☎ 692-3799. Open 11am–2.30pm and 4.30–9.30pm. Lunch $10–15; evening *table d'hôte* $13–20. Good, cheap Vietnamese and Thai food and friendly service make this place a real winner, and you'll need to book if you want to have dinner. The lovely terrace is packed throughout the summer.

☆☆ Moderate

✘ **Le Saint-Malo** (colour map II, C1, **57**): 75 rue Saint-Paul. ☎ 692-2004. Open until 10.30pm. Lunch menus $8.50–15; dinner menus $19–24. This place attracts a sophisticated clientele, drawn by high-quality, French-inspired cuisine: black pudding with apples, *cassoulet* (bean casserole with meat), rabbit in mustard sauce, *bouillabaisse* and lamb's liver. There's a pleasant little terrace in summer, and the prices reflect the excellence of the food and the service.

✘ **Le Lapin Sauté** (colour map II, C3, **59**): 52 rue du Petit-Champlain. ☎ 692-5325. Lunch menus $8–14; evening *table d'hôte* $17–23. Although this street is crammed with

tourists, Le Lapin Sauté still attracts a fair number of Québécois. There's an agreeably Provençal feel to the decor, and the terrace is a gem. As the name suggests, the house speciality is rabbit, but it also does good salads and inventive main dishes. The tempting lunch menus usually offer a soup or green salad, followed by a main course (pasta or salmon). There is another branch at 120 boulevard René-Levesque Ouest. ☎ 523-8777.

☆☆☆ Expensive

✘ **L'Ardoise** (colour map II, C1, **61**): 71 rue Saint-Paul. ☎ 694-0213. Lunch menus $9–17; dinner menus $23–33. This is a good choice for anyone with a hearty appetite, as there's an 'all you can eat' deal if the other options don't look filling enough. Most people, however, will be more than satisfied by the set menus, which offer a starter, a main course, dessert and coffee, with plenty of choice and a high standard of cooking. This is the best place for mussels in Québec, and dishes such as omelette, black pudding, pasta and (huge) salads are also good. Bright colours and floral couches give this dining room a certain charm, which only adds to the appeal.

✘ **Le Péché Veniel** (colour map II, B1, **62**): 233 rue Saint-Paul. ☎ 692-5642. Open 7am–11pm (11am–11pm in winter). Lunch $9–13; dinner $20–25. This restaurant is famous for its interior decor: half bare brick, half orange-painted walls, with green plants and soft lighting. The food is French, not especially original but sophisticated and tasty: they also do hamburgers, though it would be a pity to have one in a place like this. The à la carte breakfasts are well worth trying, and there's a brunch option if you've got the mid-morning munchies.

In the Saint-Roch Quarter

✕ **L'Impasse des Deux Anges** (colour map III, A2, **63**): 275 rue Saint-Vallier Est. ☎ 647-6432. Menus $9–16. This small neighbourhood restaurant serves good, cheap, simple food in pleasant, rather fashionable, surroundings. The menus on display outside are often inaccurate: the lunchtime *table d'hôte*, for example, is generally served in the evening. They also do tasty breakfasts, but at the end of the week it only serves a brunch menu. A good place to line your stomach before a night at the nearby Mardi Gras bar (*see* 'Where to Have a Drink, Nightlife').

WHERE TO HAVE A PICNIC

If the sun is shining and you don't want to sit in a stuffy restaurant, why not do as the locals do? There are picnic tables aplenty in the Parc des Champs-de-Bataille, in the south of Vieux Québec (colour map I, C2). This spot is also called '*les plaines d'Abraham*'. Head for the west side of the park, as it's quieter than the rest and offers wonderful views of the river. You'll find everything you need at the nearest corner shop. Just remember not to leave any rubbish behind.

WHERE TO HAVE A DRINK, NIGHTLIFE

For maps of Québec City, see the second colour plate section.

Throughout Canada, there's no firm distinction between places where you go to drink, dance or listen to live music. Some places mix all three, others change their character from night to night. In this section, bars have been listed by area, and their speciality is indicated in the text. During the Festival d'Été (*see* 'Festivals'), music bursts out from all the bars, and the best approach then is to try as many places as possible.

Admission to most of Québec's bars is free, and live music is generally of a high standard. Even better, the town attracts thousands of young people, yet has no need for a huge police presence. If you want to sample a more authentic version of the Québécois nightlife, there are plenty of clubs full of die-hard folk fans.

Haute Ville, Inside the Walls

On rue Saint-Jean and the adjacent streets, you'll find plenty of pubs and trendy cafés. In fact, as in so many tourist towns, there are bars and restaurants everywhere you look. The list below offers a few good starting points, but you'll soon make your own discoveries.

♣ **La Fourmi Atomik** (colour map II, A2, **74**): 33 rue d'Auteuil, next to porte Saint-Jean. This rowdy rock bar with a large terrace that overlooks the rampart lawns is an ideal spot for a drink before or after a concert. There's a pool table (free on Sunday), and the music is good.

♣ **Chez Son Père** (colour map II, B2, **71**): 24 rue Saint-Stanislas, on the corner with Saint-Jean. ☎ 962-5308. Open 8pm–3am; concerts every night at 10pm. This is a friendly first-floor bar with canteen-style tables and a raised stage for musicians. This used to be a meeting point for local nationalists, who came to hear the cabaret singers. These days, the nationalists have moved on, but you'll still hear good cabaret tunes, as well as pop, folk and traditional Québécois music. It's also very cheap, which makes it ideal for an extended drinking session.

! Les Yeux Bleus (colour map II, B2, **72**): 1117 rue Saint-Jean, at the end of an alleyway. ☎ 694-9118. Open 8pm–3am (from 4pm in summer). Another rough-diamond establishment, although it's quieter than Chez Son Père. This place has a rather plain decor, but people from the area come here to strum a guitar or sing in jam sessions. Part of the Cap Diamant rock makes up one of the walls of the bar: in spring, the melting snow makes the stone weep as it would in a cave.

! Bar Saint-Laurent (colour map II, C3, **73**): in the luxurious Hôtel du Château Frontenac (*see below*), at the end of a corridor left of the reception. Open 11.30am–2am. This place is several cuts above the other bars in this area. In fact, it resembles a British pub more than anything else. It's a circular room in one of the towers of the castle, with a beautiful stone archway, comfortable armchairs and tables on the terrace above terrasse Dufferin. From the veranda, meanwhile, there's a romantic view of the St Lawrence River. The cocktails are pretty good value: try a Zombie (dark rum, grenadine, lemon juice) or a B-52 (Tia Maria, Baileys and Grand Marnier). It's classy but unpretentious: perfect for writing your postcards at the end of the afternoon.

Haute Ville, Outside the Walls

On Grand-Allée Est, you'll find several really lively clubs, where the mainly student crowd is swelled by tourists from all over the world. In general, the bars here are laid-back and informal, but you may see the odd designer outfit.

! Maurice (colour map III, B3, **74**): 575 Grand-Allée Est, on the first floor of an impressive-looking mini manor house. ☎ 640-0711. Free admission from Sunday to Tuesday; otherwise $3. Ignore the bizarre name: this is *the* place to go in Québec, and thankfully its popularity hasn't gone to its owners' heads. The music changes from night to night, and it's especially lively on Thursday, Friday and Saturday. At closing time, the young crowd gather at Ashton's, over the road, to wolf down *poutine* (French fries with cheese and brown sauce) or a burger. At the same address, you'll also find the Charlotte bar, where you can relax with a good cigar or sway to Latin rhythms on the steamy dancefloor.

! O'zone (colour map III, B3, **75**): Grand-Allée Est, opposite Maurice. ☎ 529-7932. Open 11am–3am (from 1pm on weekends). A huge, dimly lit but modern place with beer on tap, pool tables, rock and hip-hop tunes, and young bands. Great fun.

! Dagobert (colour map III, B3, **76**): 600 Grand-Allée Est; where the road meets the Chevrotière. ☎ 522-0393. Free entry; comedy nights $2. Free concerts every night except Wednesday. For more than 30 years, the 'Dag' has been the place to see and be seen in Québec. It's a huge, ultra-modern club in a distinctive red-brick building with a terrace and turrets, while on the mezzanine you'll find a large pub decked out in varnished wood with comfy benches, stained-glass windows and lamps dating back to 1900, as well as a stage and a giant screen for live bands. On the upper floor, there's a large balcony that overlooks the heaving dancefloor. The main space resounds to the sound of house and techno tunes, while live bands provide the atmosphere in the pub. Monday is disco night, and dressing the part is essential.

❣ **Le Drague** (colour map III, B2, **77**): 815 rue Saint-Augustin, between rues Saint-Jean and Saint-Joachim. ☎ 649-7212. Website: www.ledrague.com. Le Drague means 'The Chat-Up Line', and this popular gay bar lives up to its name. There are drag shows on Sunday, and sometimes during the week as well. There are two large, dim rooms, with pool tables, loud music and a giant electric guitar on the ceiling.

❣ **Le Cosmos** (colour map III, B3): 575 Grande-Allée Est, opposite Dagobert. ☎ 640-0606. World-music fans will love this friendly little bar with a terrace.

Basse Ville

You won't find much action on the streets, as everything happens in the cafés. Bars here are usually hipper and more design-conscious than in the Haute Ville.

❣ **Bistrot Le Pape Georges** (colour map II, C2, **78**): 8 rue Cul-de-Sac, a tiny pedestrian street on the corner of Champlain and Notre-Dame. ☎ 692-1320. Open 11am–10pm (until 3am from Friday to Sunday). This sociable wine bar, in a charming stone building with arched ceilings and rustic decor, is a good place to watch Québécois cabaret artists or listen to folk, jazz and blues. It also stocks a good range of local and French cheeses.

❣ **Belley** (colour map II, B1, **79**): 249 Saint-Paul, in a typical Vieux-Port house. ☎ 692-1694. Students and bohemian types frequent this buzzing café. Terrace in summer.

❣ **L'Inox** (colour map II, C1, **80**): 37 Quai Saint-André, in a converted warehouse. ☎ 692-2877. Fax: 694-6904. Website: www.inox.qc.ca/virtuel.asp. Open noon–3am. Inox is French for cask, and the three large, stainless-steel vats in the main room tell you that this is a microbrewery. A dozen beers are available (from $3). There are two pool tables, and a mixed crowd of students, locals and tourists keep things lively. You can visit the brewery room (by appointment only; an hour-long tour costs $5).

Avenue Cartier

This area is a fair distance from the city centre, but you'll see a slice of village-style life, and it's not as showy as the Old Town. It's becoming increasingly touristy, but it still has plenty of character, and there are masses of small lively cafés.

❣ **Jules et Jim** (colour map III, A3, **86**): 1060 avenue Cartier, at the junction of rue Fraser. ☎ 524-9570. Open 3pm–3am in summer (4pm–3am in winter). It's a brave move to name a bar after a French film classic, but Jules et Jim is as distinctive as François Truffaut's masterpiece, and is a great place for a quiet chat. In this little bar full of regulars, you can sip a glass of Scotch to a soundtrack of classic chanson (Édith Piaf, Jacques Brel and Serge Reggiani) or mellow Brazilian music. The little library at the back has plenty of books about film; ask the bar staff if you want to have a look at one. Don't miss it.

☙ Café Krieghoff (colour map III, A3, **87**): 1091 avenue Cartier. ☎ 522-3711. Open 7am–midnight (1am on Saturday and Sunday). The café takes its name from a Dutch painter who once lived in the area. The decor is run-of-the-mill, but it's pleasant enough, with a terrace, an indoor courtyard and cosy indoor spaces. You can get breakfast or a snack throughout the day, and B&B rooms are available, but most people just pop in for an evening drink.

☙ Le Quartier de Lune (colour map III, A3, **88**): 799 avenue Cartier, near the corner of chemin Saint-Foy. ☎ 523-4011. Open until 3am. This café-bar has a pool table, a large TV screen and an upstairs dancefloor (admission $4). There's a microbrewery on the premises, and they also serve Belgian beers. A set menu is available until 9pm, and you can get a snack at all hours.

☙ Le Merlin (colour map III, A4, **89**): 1179 avenue Cartier. ☎ 529-9567. Open 11–3am. This is a restaurant-cum-disco, and it's really more of a bar than a club. The decor isn't especially original, and it's not the liveliest place in town, but it's a good place for a boogie and there's a free buffet between 4 and 8pm.

☙ Pub Java (colour map III, A3-4, **90**): 1112 avenue Cartier. ☎ 522-JAVA. Open 7.30am–midnight (until 2am on weekends). This is a quiet, friendly bar-restaurant where you can wash down a snack or a cheap meal with one of more than 80 kinds of imported beer. Blues and Québécois music on the stereo. It gets fairly busy in the evening, especially on Fridays.

☙ Qué Sera (colour map III, A3, **91**): 7 boulevard René-Lévesque, by the corner of rue Salaberry. ☎ 523-6655. Open 11.30am–10pm (midnight on weekends). This is probably the only place in Québec where you can try your hand at ceramic painting. You choose a piece of earthenware (they cost about $9), then paint it as you please: you can even leave it for another visit if you can't finish your masterpiece in one go. The owners take care of the firing. It's an original way to introduce people to crafts, and even if you don't fancy yourself as an artist, the light, cosy mezzanine is a great place to while away a few hours. You can also get a cheap snack.

The Saint-Roch Quarter (in Basse Ville)

This is an old working-class district, unpretentious and tourist-free, where rents are among the lowest in town. It's populated by intellectuals, bohemians and the really hard up, and you'll find a few arty bars.

☙ Taverne Dion: 65 rue Saint-Joseph Ouest. Open until 11.30pm. In Québec, the taverns are the only places that make a real effort to keep down the price of beer. Until recently, Québec's licensing laws forbade women from entering such establishments: these regulations have now been abolished, although this was the last place in town to adopt the new rules. It's full of authentic local colour and a place for serious drinkers, and amateur ornithologists will be intrigued by the display cases full of stuffed birds.

☙ Dorchester Taverne (off colour map III at A2, **82**): 251 Dorchester, on the corner of rue Prince-

Édouard. Open 8am–midnight. Closed Sunday. This is another real tavern, where real Québécois drink vast quantities of real beer at realistic prices. You can watch baseball on the huge TV screen or play shuffleboard.

❢ Chez Léo: 449, rue Bagot, on the corner of Bayard, behind boulevard Charest Ouest. ☎ 525-5805. Open 10am–7pm. Serves the cheapest hot dogs in Québec. It's a tiny place, but the owner will be happy to find you a perch.

Laval University Campus

It's a long way from the town centre, but there is a really good bar here. Don't bother coming in summer, though, as it's pretty much dead. For directions, *see* 'Where to Eat'.

❢ Le Pub (colour map I, B2, **85**): in the Alphonse-Desjardins pavilion. Website: www.ulaval.ca/cadeul/pub. Open until 3am. Closed Sunday. This is a friendly student bar where you'll find a cheerful end-of-term atmosphere, good music and microbrewery beers. The huge terrace, nestled in the hollow of the square, is great when the weather's nice. The decor is futuristic and avant-garde, with a spherical aluminium sculpture at the entrance. There are always lots of people here, particularly at the start and end of the academic year, and students will feel right at home.

WHAT TO SEE

For maps of Québec City, see the second colour plate section.

Most of the sights in the old town are fairly central, so it's easy to explore on foot. In the evening, the illuminated squares, buildings and narrow streets take on a magical, theatrical look. The architecture in the historical streets of the Haute Ville, in particular the granite houses, with their tall chimneys and dormer windows, is reminiscent of the French town of Saint-Malo.

Haute Ville

This tour takes in all the major sites, museums and attractions, with a few small detours.

★ **Picturesque streets** (colour map II, B2): **rue Couillard**, which will already be familiar to you if you're staying at the youth hostel, is named after one of the first French inhabitants of Canada. Farther along, **rue Hébert** has an unmistakably French feel, while on **rue Sainte-Famille** (colour map II, C2), the **Maison Touchet**, at No. 15, is an unusual 18th-century structure, most of which is taken up by a large loft and chimney. Sadly, it's not open to the public. Next, take a look at the historic buildings on the pretty **rue Saint-Flavien**.

★ **Musée de l'Amérique Française** (Museum of French America) (colour map II, B2): 2 côte de la Fabrique. ☎ 692-2843. From the end of June to 1 September, open 10am–5.30pm; otherwise, open Tuesday to Sunday, 10am–5pm. The former seminary has been transformed into an impressive museum tracing three centuries of French presence in the region. Most of the objects on show once belonged to the priests of Laval University, who taught the first students in North America. Temporary exhibitions examine various aspects of Québec's cultural history and technical progress.

★ **Musée d'Art Inuit Brousseau** (Brousseau Museum of Inuit Art), (colour map II, B-C3): 39 rue Saint-Louis. ☎ 694-1828. Fax: 694-2086. Email: artinuit@globetrotter.net. Open 9.30am–5.30pm. Admission $6; concessions available. This superb museum, opened in 1999 by an Inuit art expert and his museologist wife, is devoted to the history, culture, country and sculpture of the Arctic-dwelling Inuit people. The Brousseaus' extraordinary private collection offers valuable insights into the development of Inuit sculpture from prehistoric times to the present. The thoughtfully designed exhibition spaces are filled with beautifully presented treasures from the far north: sculptures, engravings, drawings and everyday objects such as fishing and hunting equipment. One room hosts temporary shows of contemporary Inuit art.

★ **Musée des Augustines de l'Hôtel-Dieu** (colour map II, B2): 32 rue Charlevoix. ☎ 692-2493. Open 9.30am–noon and 1.30–5pm; afternoons only on Sunday. Admission free. This small museum contains the possessions of the Dieppe Augustinians, who built Canada's first hospital in 1639. The collection includes furniture, 17th-, 18th- and 19th-century paintings, silverware, household objects and a macabre collection of surgical instruments. If you're at all squeamish, avoid the 19th-century crank-driven machine for electric-shock treatment, and the cabinet displaying foreign objects swallowed by – and extracted from – patients.

★ Walk down the lively **rue Saint-Jean**, the main street in the old town, until you reach porte Saint-Jean. Then turn onto **rue d'Auteuil**, which climbs towards porte Saint-Louis and the street of the same name. In the 18th century, **rue Saint-Louis** was Québec's most elegant residential street, and you can still see several fine houses, in particular the **Maison Péon** (dated 1750), at No. 61.

★ **Parc de l'Artillerie** (Artillery Park): 2 rue d'Auteuil, between rues Saint-Jean and McMahon. ☎ 648-4205. From the beginning of May to the end of October, open 10am–5pm; otherwise, open Wednesday to Sunday or by appointment, and by appointment only in January. Admission fee. This strategic site has played a vital part in the history of Québec, and the fortifications were repeatedly strengthened by the French and the British. In the 20th century, it became a munitions factory, producing ammunition for the Canadian army in both world wars. Today, visitors can find out more about the city's defences at the interpretative centre, where attractions include a relief map of the town that dates from 1808 and audiovisual presentations. Guided tours are also available.

The white, buttressed Dauphine redoubt dominates the junction of rue d'Auteuil and rue McMahon. You can visit the officers' lodgings or stroll in the garden or on the ramparts, from which you'll get spectacular views, especially at sunset. Access is via the **Promenade des Fortifications** (100 rue Saint-Louis).

★ **Musée et Chapelle des Ursulines** (Museum and Chapel of the Ursuline Sisters): 12 rue Donnacona, on a tiny street linking rue Saint-Louis to rue Sainte-Anne. ☎ 694-0694. From May to August, open Tuesday to Saturday, 10am–noon and 1–5pm (Sunday 12.30–5pm); otherwise, open Tuesday to Sunday, 1– 4.30pm. Admission fee; concessions available. The former Ursuline convent is now home to a fascinating little museum that gives you a good idea of how the nuns once lived. The exhibits include paintings, prints, *objets d'art* and 17th- and 18th-century documents, as well as a beautiful mid-19th-century piano. One room is devoted to objects that once belonged to the sisters. On the second floor, you'll find an exhibition of Native American art and some remarkable embroideries created by the nuns, among them a splendid altar cloth made for Christmas 1739, an altar cloth for the feast of the Holy Spirit and third created for Pentecost, its centre piece is a lovely oil painting depicting the martyrdom of Saint Ursula.

You can visit also the chapel, which was built in 1902 but contains 18th-century ornamentation (same opening hours as the museum, but closed in winter; admission free). A printed notice at the entrance draws your attention to the chapel's main points of interest, which include a Nativity scene from the Le Brun school and a copy of a Philippe de Champaigne painting showing Jesus at the home of Simon the Pharisee (the original is in Nantes). Both paintings are above the high altar. Before you leave, take a look at the carved pulpit and altarpiece, one of the oldest in North America, and the tombstone of the Marquis of Montcalm.

★ Trace your steps back to rue Saint-Louis until you reach the **Duke of Kent's house** (dating back to 1700), at No. 25, and the **Maison Maillou**, built in 1736, at No. 17. Across place d'Armes, you'll find the crowded **ruelle du Trésor**, which is full of artists displaying their work. As is so often the case on touristy streets like this, the quality of the art is variable, but it's worth pausing to see the remarkable prints (mainly landscapes) by Jean Cencig. The **Musée Grevin** (22 rue Sainte-Anne), a franchise of the famous French waxworks museum, has models of important figures in Canadian history, while the **Musée du Fort** (open summer only, 10am–6pm), at No. 10, contains a diorama describing the city's many battles. It also houses a giant model of the town (from June to September, open 10am–8pm; otherwise 10am–5pm). The city's first skyscraper, the art-deco **Édifice Price**, stands next to the Hôtel Clarendon. Continue to the end of rue Saint-Anne until you come to **place de l'Hôtel-de-Ville**.

★ **Galerie Aux Multiples Collections**: 69 rue Sainte-Anne. ☎ 692-1230. Open every day. The gallery exhibits Inuit art, and is managed by a real enthusiast. Even if you're not planning to buy anything (and it isn't cheap), it's worth popping in to look at the works, which are carved in traditional materials such as whalebone, walrus ivory and soft soapstone. There's another branch at 43 rue Buade.

★ **Basilique Notre-Dame-du-Québec** (colour map II, C2): 16 rue Buade, on the corner of côte de la Fabrique. ☎ 692-2533. This is the oldest church in North America, although nothing remains of the original structure. It was established by Samuel de Champlain in 1633, but burned down soon afterwards. It was rebuilt by the Jesuits, only to be destroyed again during the siege of Québec in 1759. Reconstructed yet again in the 19th century, the church fell victim to another fire in 1922, but was rebuilt almost immediately after the fire, along the lines of the previous structure. Take a look at the Louis XIII-style canopy, the sanctuary lamp (a present from Louis XIV) and the bishops' crypt. In the evening, there's a *son et lumière* spectacular based on the history of the town; phone for details.

★ **Château Frontenac** (colour map II, C3): ☎ 691-2166. From 1 May to 15 October, open 10am–6pm; otherwise weekends only, 12.30–6pm. The Château Frontenac is to Québec what the Eiffel Tower is to Paris: a symbol of the city, but also of an era. Reminiscent of the wedding-cake castles built by mad King Ludwig of Bavaria in the 19th century, this much loved structure stands proud and elegant, in its mock French Renaissance style, above the St Lawrence. It also houses a self-sufficient hotel, complete with its own laundry, joiner's, electrician's workshop and bakery. Even the uniforms and curtains are made on the premises. A brand-new wing was built in 1993 to celebrate the castle's centenary.

Unless you can afford to stay here, the best way to see the grandiose interior is to take a 50-minute tour (admission fee). The guides are dressed in 19th-century costumes, and they do their best to act the part. It's all very Disney, and the Great Hall is usually packed with cruise passengers who stop off in Québec for a few hours, but you can always seek solace in the hotel's bar, which is genuinely classy and surprisingly inexpensive (see 'Where to Drink').

★ **Terrasse Dufferin**: at the foot of Château Frontenac. This long wooden terrace has superb views over the St Lawrence River, and it really comes alive in the evenings. It links up with the Promenade des Gouverneurs, a riverside walkway that runs parallel to the fortress, and eventually leads to the Plaines d'Abraham.

★ **Citadelle**: built after 1820, the citadel consists of a redoubt erected by the French in 1693 and an old gunpowder factory. It now houses a museum of weaponry, uniforms and other military artefacts (open summer only, 9am–6pm; admission fee). You can watch the changing of the guards every day at 10am between mid-June and Labor Day (the first Monday in September). In July and August, you can watch the Beating of the Retreat tattoo at 6pm, weather permitting.

★ You can follow the **fortified wall** that used to protect the city on foot. It's easy to find your way: start at the fortress, then follow the ramparts. These were built during the 18th century, and are still in excellent condition, although they have seen a few close calls. Around 1870, town planners decided to demolish the walls, which, they felt, were blocking Québec's development and hindering movement between the town centre and the new districts that had sprung up outside the walls. They started with the town gates, and would no doubt have knocked down the rest had it not been for Lord Dufferin, the new governor, who put a stop to the demolition, declaring that the walls had a certain charm. He even ordered the reconstruction of the four gates that were torn down, in the mock-Gothic style that was fashionable at the time. This explains why the gates of Vieux Québec are more ornate than the rest of the fortifications.

If you're following the rampart walk, **porte Saint-Louis** is the first of the reconstructed gates on the circuit. To the right of the gate, you'll see rue Saint-Louis and the Old Town, with its narrow streets and horsedrawn carriages; to the left is the modern Grand-Allée, clogged with traffic, and the vast building that houses Québec's parliament. A similar contrast is evident at porte Saint-Jean. You can leave the fortifications a bit farther on, near rue McMahon, by which time you will have completed three-quarters of the tour of Vieux Québec.

QUÉBEC CITY

★ **Parc des Champs-de-Bataille/Plaines d'Abraham** (Battlefield Park/ Plains of Abraham): leave Vieux Québec via rue Saint-Louis to reach this magnificent riverside park, site of the great battle of 1759, during which the Marquis de Montcalm lost his life. The French defeat saw the beginning of the British occupation of Québec. In their gallant last stand, the French won a victory at Sainte-Foy, but the long-awaited reinforcements turned out to be British soldiers. A bronze statue of Charles de Gaulle was erected on this spot, next to the statue of Joan of Arc, on 24 July 1997, 30 years after the General's famous 'Vive le Québec libre' ('Long live free Québec') speech.

★ **Musée du Québec** (colour map I, C2): 1 avenue Wolfe-Montcalm, Parc des Champs-de-Bataille. ☎ 643-2150. Take bus No. 11 from the stop opposite the Hôtel Concorde. Open summer only, 10am–5.45pm (9.45pm on Wednesday). Admission fee; free on Wednesday. The museum has strong collections of paintings, decorative arts, prints, and sculptures, and hosts interesting temporary exhibitions.

There are three interlinked buildings: a modern, airy central pavilion that houses the shop, auditorium and restaurant; the Pavillon Gérard-Morisset, a neo-classical structure that holds the main collection; and the Pavillon Baillairgé, a former prison that's now used for temporary exhibitions. It's an imposing yet, strangely uplifting place, and you can still see some of the red-brick vaulted cells.

The ground floor of the Pavillon Gérard-Morisset is home to an important collection of sacred and secular Québécois works of art. The first floor is devoted to 19th- and 20th-century works, and includes the *Apotheosis of Christopher Colombus*, an enormous (but unfinished) allegorical painting by Napoléon Bourassa. The rest of the museum is used for temporary exhibitions. On fine days, you can sit out on the terrace that overlooks the plains and the St Lawrence.

★ **Observatoire de la capitale** (City Observatory): 1037 rue de la Chevrotière, next to the Grand Théâtre. ☎ 644-9841. Open 10am–5pm (7pm from June to September). Admission fee; free for under-12s; concessions available. The 31st floor of the Marie Guyart building offers an exceptional panoramic view of Québec and its surroundings. There is an information centre with a permanent display.

★ For another superb **panoramic view** of Québec, visit the bar-restaurant L'Astral (*see* 'Where to Eat'), which you can reach via Grand-Allée Est.

★ **Assemblée Nationale du Québec** (Québec Parliament): Grand-Allée Est, in front of porte Saint-Louis. ☎ 643-7239. Open Monday to Friday, 9am–4.30pm, though it's best to phone in advance. Closed 1 to 23 June. Admission free. Join a guided tour of the building, built in 1877 in Second Empire style, and you can watch a debate if parliament is in session. While you're here, try out the assembly's restaurant, which is open every lunchtime from noon.

★ Beyond the ramparts, take a look at **St Matthew's Church** and its **cemetery** (755 rue Saint-Jean). The cemetery, which has been a park since 1987, contains the graves of many important Québécois figures, including Alexander Cameron (a soldier who died in 1759 – it's the oldest grave here) and Henry Hope, a former governor of the province.

At No. 669 on the same street, you'll see the picturesque **Épicerie Moisan**, which has a beautiful 19th-century wooden interior and wonderfully old-fashioned shop windows.

★ **Québec Expérience**: 8 rue du Trésor. ☎ 694-4000. A 3-D presentation about the origins of Québec. Shows take place every 90 minutes between 10am and 9pm. It's not expensive (and concessions are available), but the *mise-en-scène* and special effects are outdated, and it's basically a bit disappointing. Children seem to like it, though.

Basse Ville

The best way to get to the Basse Ville (Lower Town) is by taking the funicular railway from terrasse Dufferin. Alternatively, you can walk along côte de la Montagne and down the Casse-Cou (Breakneck) staircase.

★ **Maison Louis-Jolliet** (colour map II, C3): 16 rue du Petit-Champlain. The terminus for the funicular railway is a house built in 1683 for Louis Jolliet, who discovered the Mississippi river.

★ **Rue Petit-Champlain** is said to be the oldest road in North America. Québec's poorest inhabitants, mainly Irish immigrants, took refuge here in the 19th century. It has now been completely restored, and is a popular spot on the tourist trail.

★ **Place Royale**: this beautifully restored collection of historic buildings is one of the oldest architectural ensembles in North America. There's a tourist office at the Maison Thibaudeau, 215 Marché-Finlay. Open 10am–6pm from May to September. ☎ 643-6631. Samuel de Champlain built his first cabin in Canada here on 3 July 1608: the exact spot where it stood is marked by special paving stones. The square is edged by splendid 17th- and 18th-century buildings and residences, though the effect is rather spoiled by a curious white column covered in bathroom tiles, a 'work of art' donated to the city by the Jacques Chirac.

★ **Église Notre-Dame-des-Victoires**: constructed in 1688 on the foundations of the Champlain house, this is one of the oldest churches in Québec. On leaving the church you'll see, in the following order, the Maisons Marianne Barbel (the tallest, dating back to 1754), Veuve Rageot (1762), Pierre Bruneau (1791), Le Picart, and, at the corner of the square and rue Notre-Dame, the Maison Lambert-Dumont (1689). On rue Notre-Dame, look out for Maison Milot (also from 1689), and, opposite that, the foundations of the maisons Soullard and Gaillard. Some of the houses contain information centres and small shops (including the Maison des Vins, a wine merchant). Take a look at the painted wall at the end of rue Notre-Dame.

★ **Batterie Royale**: one of the principal elements of the city's defences since 1691, the battery stands at the end of the picturesque rue Sous-le-Fort. The 10 guns were gifts from France.

★ **Maison Chevalier**: this elegant bourgeois residence, constructed in 1752, contains interesting displays about the history, civilisation and ethnic culture of Québec. Open 10am–5pm; admission free.

★ **Musée de la Civilisation** (colour map II, C2): 85 rue Dalhousie. ☎ 643-2158. From 24 June to the beginning of September, open 10am–7pm;

otherwise Tuesday to Sunday, 10am–5pm (9pm on Wednesday). Closed 25 December. Admission fee; 40 per cent reduction for students; free on Tuesday out of season. Guided tours available. Allow plenty of time for you visit.

This highly original, cutting-edge museum uses interactive displays to explore 'civilisation' in its widest sense, taking in history, archaeology, sociology, ethnology and technology. At its core are three permanent exhibitions – 'Objets de civilisation', 'Mémoires' and 'Messages' – which are complemented by temporary displays on subjects as diverse as food, the Native American Indians and photography. It's the complete opposite of the traditional static museum, and most people should find something of interest within its walls.

Each of the permanent exhibitions is a museum in its own right, and the place is a maze of rooms where images, words, historical objects, avant-garde gadgets, explanatory signs, works of art and odds and ends all jostle for your attention. The idea is to make the visitor get involved in what's on show, rather than just staring numbly into display case after display case. In each section, the fixed and interactive signs and slogans provide a common thread, so you never lose track of the central theme.

It's been a huge success, attracting more than a million visitors in its opening year instead of the 300,000 its creators anticipated, and it's used as a model for museums around the world.

★ **Rue Sous-le-Cap**: this street, which is believed to be the narrowest in North America, was until recently one of the poorest streets in town. It's worth a visit to see the unusual exterior wooden steps and footbridges of the houses. They were once so close together that the footbridges linked the top floors. Most of the houses on the cliff side have disappeared, and only a few remnants of the original walls remain, but the footbridges are still intact. Take a look from rue des Remparts and you'll get a fine view of the street and its terraces, which have been done up by the houses' new owners, many of whom are antiques dealers.

The Vieux-Port District

This neighbourhood has undergone radical changes in recent years, as a series of old houses, warehouses and industrial buildings have been renovated to accommodate cafés, restaurants, antiques shops and apart-ments. The transformation has been fairly sensitive, and the result is a harmonious combination of past and present styles. The best way to get a feel for the area is to take a stroll through the lively rues Dalhousie, Saint-Paul and Saint-André. The Agora, a huge open-air arena that hosts pop concerts and recitals, is located at the Pointe de Carcy.

★ There are several buildings worth pausing to admire while you stroll through this area, including the beautifully restored **Société du port de Québec** and the Italianate **customs house**, with sculpted stone masks on the facade and a handsome colonnade that dates from 1856. A stairway once connected the building to the river. At **112 rue Dalhousie**, you'll see an elegant modern building in which glass and brick are strikingly combined. The former warehouses at **No. 94**, opposite the old fire station and tower, have been converted into luxury apartments.

★ Once a working-class neighbourhood, **rue Saint-Paul** is now a chic, up-market street lined with antiques shops and fashionable bistros. Despite its obvious charms, it has yet to be discovered by the tourist hordes.

★ Follow rue Saint-Paul to the river and you'll see two strikingly elaborate buildings: the **Santé et Bien-Être Social** (health and social security building), with its copper roof, turrets, pinnacles and gables with dormer windows; and, next door, the magnificent mock-Victorian **Gare du Palais** (railway station), with huge roofs and high skylights. It looks more like a manor house than a train station and its luxurious central hall is well worth a look.

★ The **Québec–Saint-Malo yacht race** takes place every four years at the end of July: the next one is scheduled for 2004. During the week leading up to the start, you can admire the giant single-, double- and triple-hulled boats lining up for their battle. There's always a great atmosphere around the port during the build-up to this event.

WHAT TO DO IN WINTER

– **Glissades de la Terrasse**: open 11am–11pm from mid-December to mid-March. This toboggan run for old-fashioned two-seater sleds occupies one of the loveliest spots in Québec, between Château Frontenac and the river, and at $1 a go, it's worth trying for the views alone.

– **Forfaits sports d'hiver-Canada** (winter-sports packages): 330, rue Saint-Jean, Saint-Marc des Carrières. ☎ 268-8846. A good place to book all-inclusive activity packages, including transfers, accommodation and so on. You can arrange snow-rafting, dog-sleighing, snowmobile trips and ice-fishing in a riverside hut, as well as tours of Québec City.

WHAT TO DO IN SUMMER

– **Vieux-Port Yachting**: Lake Louise, CP 1543, Québec Terminus. ☎ 692-0017 or 1-800-668-7428 (toll-free). Fax: 692-3728. You can buy or rent a boat at this sailing school, which is run by sailing enthusiasts Jocelyne and Michel, whose nautical achievements include a transatlantic crossing from Québec. From mid-May to September, you can arrange a three-hour introductory sailing trip, departing at 9am, 1pm or 5pm. They also offer boat hire with or without a skipper, aboard a choice of 10 vessels, ranging in length from nine metres (30 feet) to 15 metres (50 feet). The seven qualified instructors have all been approved by the Sailing Association.

– **Association Nautique de la Baie de Beauport** (Beauport Bay Nautical Association): you'll find this organization at the southern tip of boulevard Henri-Bourassa, on Beauport Beach. Take the Grande-Allée out of Québec, join autoroute 440 towards Montmorency Falls, take exit 23 and follow the signs for Port de Québec. ☎ 666-2364 in season, or 666-2155 out of season. Website: www.yachting.qc.ca/anbb. The association rents out sailboards, dinghies and catamarans, and can organize sailing lessons, weekly sailing courses and day trips aboard a cabin boat to L'Île d'Orleans (a boat for up to five adults, including skipper and picnic, costs $50 per person). Catamaran hire starts at $55 for 2 hours. Facilities at Beuaport

Beach include a children's swimming pool and a solarium. Snacks are available throughout the day.

WHAT TO SEE AND DO IN THE AREA

★ **IMAX**: 5401 boulevard des Galeries, next to the Galeries de la Capitale shopping centre, 15 minute' drive from Vieux Québec. ☎ 627-4688. Take autoroute 40 towards Sainte-Foy, then autoroute Vallon. Admission costs about the same as a cinema ticket in Britain; reservations essential. The Canadian IMAX company specializes in astonishingly realistic three-dimensional (3-D) films, which are shown in special theatres all over the world. Québec's IMAX cinema boasts the largest screen in Canada (in fact, at 20.50 metres (68 feet) high and 28.2 metres (93 feet) wide, it's not far off being the biggest in the world). The films tend to be factual in content – subjects include the life of fish, the migration of butterflies and the conquest of space – but most people come for a unique visual experience. The theatre is air-conditioned, so you may want to to take a jumper.

★ **Village de sports**: 1860 boulevard Valcartier, Saint-Gabriel-de-Valcartier. ☎ 844-3725. Take boulevard Laurentien (route 73) from the centre of Québec, and pass through Saint-Émile; in all, it's a half-hour journey. In summer, this looks like any other waterpark, with a wave machine, an 'adventure river', waterslides and fake waterfalls. In winter, however, it really comes into its own, with superb snowy slopes, ideal for hurtling down on inner tubes or huge inflatable boats, and superb ice slides. You can also try snow-karting, cross-country skiing and ice-skating, all at very reasonable prices.

QUÉBEC ON A SHOESTRING

– Take the **Québec ferry** from rue des Traversiers. Departures every 30 minutes. ☎ 644-3704. The 45-minute round trip is inexpensive, and you'll get splendid views of Vieux Québec. Keen photographers should board in the morning, when the light on the town is at its best.

– On the other side of the St Lawrence is **Lévis**, a pretty residential town with some interesting architecture. It's relatively tourist-free, the restaurants are less expensive and you'll have panoramic views of Vieux Québec. The following sights are worth a visit:

★ **Maison Desjardins**: 6 rue du Mont-Marie. ☎ 1-800-463-4810 (toll-free). Open 10am–noon and 1–4.30pm (weekends noon–5pm). Admission free. This Victorian house was the residence of Alphonse Desjardins, the founder of America's first public treasury.

★ **Économusée de l'Enseigne sur Bois** (Museum of Wooden Signs): 10965 boulevard de la Rive-Sud. ☎ 838-0871. From June to September, open Monday to Friday, 10am–4.30pm. If you look carefully around Lévis, you'll see several brightly coloured wooden signs, many of which were made at the workshop in this Victorian house. It's run by a highly skilled craftsman, who, in keeping with a tradition that dates back to the 18th century, sculpts hand-painted wooden signs gilded with gold leaf.

A TRIP BY SEAPLANE

It's not cheap, but you need to take to the air to fully appreciate the extensive landscape of lakes and forests around Québec. The plane flies at low altitude, so the views are fabulous, and it's an unforgettable experience. In case you were wondering, seaplanes are not allowed to fly over the city.

■ **Roger Forgues Aviation**: Lake Saint-Augustin. ☎ (418) 871-4455. Fax: (in summer) 871-8010. Take autoroute 40 towards Montréal and leave at exit 300 (Lake Saint-Augustin), 15 minutes from Québec. A 3-hour flight over the lakes and forests, with a picnic stop at a rural hut, costs $160 per person.

FESTIVALS AND PUBLIC HOLIDAYS

– **Carnival**: first two weeks of February. ☎ 626-3716. Despite the cold, Québec's carnival is a festive, if commercial, 10-day affair. In keeping with tradition, participants take snow baths wearing only underwear, gloves and shoes. Some revellers carry hollow canes through which they drink *caribou*, a warming mixture of spirits and wine.

– **Coupe du Monde de Vélo de Montagne** (Mountain-biking World Cup): on Mount Saint Anne in June. Not so much a festival, but an important local event, and great fun to watch.

– **Fête Nationale du Québec** (National Holiday): 24 June. Everything is closed.

– **Canada Day**: 1 July. The most important public holiday, celebrated throughout the country.

– **Festival d'Été de Québec** (Québec Summer Festival): during the first two weeks of July, the parks of Vieux Québec are overrun by thousands of locals and a host of theatre troupes, orchestras and folk and jazz bands. There's an eclectic line-up of concerts, variety shows and street theatre, with about 400 shows (most free) involving 800 artists from 20 countries, as well as plenty of activities for youngsters. For more information, contact the Festival d'Été International de Québec, 160 rue Saint-Paul. ☎ 692-4540. Fax: 692-4384.

– **Cirque du Soleil**: every two years in July, this acrobatic, animal-free circus mounts a breathtaking show in the car-park of the Galeries de la Capitale shopping centre. It isn't cheap, but you should really make the effort to see this spectacular and highly original 'circus' company, one of the world's most famous troupes. For reservations, call the Théâtre de la Ville: ☎ 1-800-361-4595.

– **Fêtes de la Nouvelle-France**: early August. ☎ 694-3311. First staged in 1997, this series of festivals tells the story of the American Indians and the newcomers from the Old World, with re-creations of historical battles, treasure hunts and much wearing of period costume.

– **Labor Day**: first Monday of September. Everything is closed, except some of the museums.

LEAVING QUÉBEC

Hitchhiking

■ **Allô-stop**: 467 Saint-Jean. ☎ 522-3430. Email: allostop@total.net. A ride-share agency.

– **To Montréal and la Beauce**: route 132, autoroute 20 west. Take bus No. 11 or No. 13 to the corner of rue Lavigerie and boulevard Laurier.

– **To Gaspésie**: route 132 east, autoroute 20. Take the ferry to Lévis, then bus No. 21 as far as route 132.

– **To le Saguenay and Lac Saint-Jean**: take bus No. 32 to Lac Clément, then walk to boulevard Talbot.

– **To Charlevoix, north side**: take bus No. 3 to Jacques-Cartier square, then bus No. 53 to Montmorency Falls. Start on route 138.

By Bus

🚌 **Central bus station** (colour map III, B1): Gare du Palais, 320 Abraham Martin. ☎ 525-3000.

– **To Montréal**: buses depart every hour on the hour, from early morning to late at night.

– **To Charlevoix, New Brunswick, Baie-Saint-Paul**, **Tadoussac** and **Baie-Comeau**: infrequent services. Phone to check times.

By Train

🚆 **Gare du Palais** (colour map III, B1): 450 rue de la Gare-du-Palais. ☎ 524-4161.

– **To Montréal**: four trains a day during the week; two or three at weekends.

🚆 **Gare de Lévis**: 5995 rue Saint-Laurent, Lévis. ☎ 833-8056. For departures heading east and south.

– **To Gaspésie**: three trains per week to Percé via Rimouski, Matapédia and the Baie des Chaleurs.

– **To Halifax**: three trains a week.

By Air

– The **airport bus** is run by Feuille d'Érable et Dupont. ☎ 649-9226. It leaves from Château Frontenac, and, in high season, from some of the bigger hotels.

Around Québec

Wendake – The Huron Village

This stretch of protected Native American territory lies about 15 kilometres (10 miles) from Québec. Take autoroute 73 north and leave at exit 154: you'll find Wendake on boulevard Bastien, towards Loretteville. If you're travelling by bus, take No. 801 from place de la Yonville to the Charlesbourg terminus, then bus No. 72 to the village. Admission $7. The journey by public transport is long and complicated, so it's worth getting a group together and hiring a car.

Don't expect this reserve to look anything like the villages you've seen in Westerns. Today's Hurons are Roman Catholics, and their reserve consists of houses with small gardens and American cars, just like those in the surrounding area. In fact, you could easily pass through without even realizing that you're in Native American territory; the wooden street signs are about the only give-away. From a cultural and social point of view, however, it is worth trekking out to this tiny patch, a kilometre long and 500 metres wide, inhabited by 1,000 Hurons. People pass freely in and out of the reserve, but the Hurons still have the right to maintain certain rights and duties within their community. The main tourist attractions are the re-created Huron-Wendat village and the shops selling Native American arts and crafts, including peace pipes, moccasins, statues, caribou-skin murals and dolls. Most of the shops are concentrated along boulevard Maurice-Bastien.

Life in the Reserve

The reserve, which is officially known as the Huron-Wendat Nation, has its own flag, which depicts a beaver, snowshoes and a rowing boat. The community is headed by the chief of chiefs, who is elected by vote, and has its own school and police force. Six sub-chiefs are responsible for the smooth running of the society, the preservation of its cultural heritage and defending the interests of the Hurons against encroachments by the ruling 'whites'. But all is not well at the heart of this community, where the influx of wealth from tourism seems to have benefited only a handful of leading families.

WHERE TO STAY AND EAT

🛏 **La Maison Aorhenché**: 90 François-Gros-Louis, in the Huron-Wendat village. ☎ 847-0646. Fax: 847-4527. Doubles from $65 a night, including an excellent breakfast. This friendly hotel with traditional Native American decor has three huge, warm and spotlessly clean rooms, each individually decorated, and two bathrooms.

✗ **Restaurant Nek8arre**: 575 rue Stanislas-Koska, in the Huron-Wendat village. ☎ 842-4308 or 847-9789. Website: www.huronwendat.qc.ca. From Québec, take boulevard Laurentien (route 73) northbound, leave at the De La Faune exit and take route 154 to Saint-Émile. Full meal $15; booking recommended. Dishes in this Native American restaurant, in a re-creation of a traditional log cabin, are made only from ingredients formerly used by the Hurons: maize, broad beans, potatoes, *banique* (unleavened bread), marrow, green beans, wild rice and a variety of woodland game, including bison, caribou, venison, stag, rabbit, partridge and duck and rainbow trout. You can also try a selection of smoked meats, pumpkin soup, soups with sunflower seeds or marrow and *sagamité*, the national dish of the Huron-Wendats, made with red beans, washed maize and a few pieces of meat. There's also a vege-tarian menu. Finish with a traditional dessert, followed by a herbal tea. The food is good, and this is a unique experience for which you don't have to pay through the nose. Further entertainment, in the shape of a dance troupe or storyteller, is optional. It is, of course, wholly tourist-oriented, but there's no better way to learn more about the Huron-Wendats, or for that matter the other Native American tribes in Québec.

WHAT TO SEE

★ **Huron-Wendat village of Onhoüa-Chetek8e**: 575 rue Stanislas-Koska. Open 9am–6pm (from 8.30am in summer; last visit 5pm). Admission $7. Guided tours with Native American guides leave every 30 minutes. The village stretches across about a hectare (about two acres) of land, and offers continual reminders of how the Huron-Wendats once lived. The tour takes in a traditional 'long house', made from bark and wood, a smokehouse and meat-drier, a 'sweating hut' and a series of exhibits about the shamanic Faux-Visages society (who make sculpted masks), the first contact with Europeans, the current status of the First Nations of Québec and contemporary life in Wendake. In the craft workshops, you can watch the manufacture of snowshoes and canoes. Throughout, panels are used to explain the history of the Huron-Wendat people.

Wind up your explorations with a traditional Indian meal (*see above*), and a visit to the Le Huron boutique, which stocks souvenirs, *objets d'art*, Iroquois sculpture, Navajo jewellery and much more. The bookshop, where you can buy CDs, books and cassettes about the Native American way of life, is a must for anyone keen to know more about the history, philosophy and current affairs of Canada's First Nations. Finally, Le Chamane sells a range of herbal remedies, herbal teas, fragrances and mysterious 'magic potions'.

Chute Montmorency

The Montmorency Waterfall is near Beauport, eight kilometres (five miles) northeast of Québec on the left bank of the St Lawrence River, opposite the Île d'Orléans. ☎ 649-2608. Beauport is well signposted, so it's easy to get there by car. It's a bit more complicated by bus: from Basse Ville and place Jacques-Cartier, take bus No. 53 (departures every 90 minutes) to get to the foot of the falls, or bus No. 800, followed by No. 50 (from the Beauport terminus), to get to the top. If you have a car, you could make a single trip to visit the Chute Montmorency and the re-created Huron village. Parking will cost you $7.

The waterfall itself is 30 metres (100 feet) higher than the Niagara Falls, though it's a bit less spectacular. Still, it deserves its status as a major tourist attraction. You can take a cable car ($5 one way; $7 round trip) to the top of the falls, or walk up one of several paths, one of which leads to a footbridge that runs alongside the waterfall and ends up at a former military camp where General Wolfe once stayed. Whatever route you take to the top, the views en route are superb. Hardy souls can return to the bottom via a 487-step path down opposite the waterfall.

The best time to visit is in winter, when the falls are partly frozen, forming an impressive 'sugar-loaf' effect, and experienced climbers and amateurs can scale the ice wall. You can book a one- to five-day course (☎ 663-2877); rates are reasonable and thrills are guaranteed.

Close by, a wildlife park runs along the St Lawrence, with a riverside path leading upstream into the woods. You could take a dip, but it's probably best not to: the water is cold, the currents can be dangerous and drownings are all too frequent. Still, that doesn't seem to bother the Québécois, who come here en masse to cool off in summer.

WHERE TO STAY AND EAT

🛏 **Gîte de la Chute**: 5143 avenue Royale, Boischatel, a few minutes' drive from Chute Montmorency. ☎ and fax: 822-3789. From route 138, take côte de l'Église and turn left into avenue Royale. Doubles from \$50 a night. This hospitable, if unspectacular Gîte de Passant has two upstairs rooms with views of the river; the three downstairs rooms are cheaper and a little cooler. Booking recommended in summer

🛏 ✗ **Le Petit Séjour**: 394 rue Pichette, Château-Richer, 15 minutes' drive from Québec. ☎ and fax 824-3654. By car, cross the Île d'Orléans bridge, heading towards Saint-Anne-de-Beaupré, then take route 138; take the Château-Richer exit, continue up the hill and it's the second

road on the right. Doubles \$60 a night; a four-bed en-suite room is \$115. Credit cards accepted. This is a friendly B&B in an attractive old house with a pleasant garden and panoramic views of the St Lawrence, the Île d'Orléans and Cape Tourment. It's a bit pricey, but the spectacular setting makes it popular, so do book ahead. All five rooms (three of which sleep four) have large beds and are tastefully decorated, with paintings on the walls. The upstairs rooms share two bathrooms and a shower room while the huge ground-floor room has a private bathroom and a small lounge. Breakfast is excellent, and a huge dinner costs about \$25 (bring your own wine).

Parc du Mont-Sainte-Anne

At Beaupré, 40 kilometres (25 miles) northeast of Québec. Open from 15 May to 1 November. Admission charge.

You can take a cable car to the top of the mountain, from which there are fine views of the St Lawrence, Cape Tourment (a bird reserve) and the Île d'Orleans. You should also see the spectacular waterfalls in the **Canyon Sainte-Anne** (Saint Anne Canyon), in Saint-Joachim, not far from the park: take route 138 east towards Baie-Saint-Paul, and it's about six kilometres (four miles) past the Basilica Sainte-Anne-De-Beaupré. ☎ 827-4057. Fax: 827-2492. Admission: \$6.50. A 55-metre-high (180-foot) suspension bridge spans the canyon, and it's a great place from which to observe the waterfalls, which are 75 metres (246 feet) high; you can also cross them at different levels via a succession of footbridges. According to an article once published in a Québec newspaper: 'The most powerful vocabulary is of limited use when trying to describe this splendid site. Only by paying a visit can you truly appreciate the richness of Québec's natural surroundings.'

There are seven more waterfalls (*les Sept Chutes*) at Saint-Ferréol, in the heart of the forest, but you'll have to splash out if you want to see them. A better bet is the **Chute Jean-Larose**, which plunges in three cascades from a height of 68 metres (223 feet). It's less spectacular than its neighbours, but it's less crowded, there's no admission fee and you can bathe at different levels in small, natural basins. Take the path from the golf course at the foot of Mont-Sainte-Anne.

Mont-Sainte-Anne Ski Resort

This excellently managed resort, well served by buses, has a skiing area of 170 hectares (420 acres), with 54 slopes on three faces. The highest are 800 metres (2,600 feet) above sea level. You can even ski after sunset (4pm), as the resort has 25 kilometres (9 miles) of illuminated slopes. A word of warning: the north face of the mountain, with its icy wind, is extremely cold.

WHERE TO STAY AND EAT

🏠 **Les Arolles**: 3489 avenue Royale, Saint-Ferréol-les-Neiges. ☎ and fax: 826-2136. Doubles $65 a night; $80 for a suite with bathroom. This cosy, hospitable establishment has four reasonably priced upstairs rooms, each bearing the name of a famous ski resort (Méribel, Zermatt, Chamonix and Kitzbühel). There's also a beautiful suite on the ground floor.

✗ **Le Café Colette**: 2190 avenue Royale, Saint-Ferréol-les-Neiges. ☎ 826-1963. Open Monday to Saturday, 5–11pm. This small, welcoming chalet serves French-inspired cuisine, with locally sourced meat and produce to the fore: *caribou au poivre*, bison *filet mignon* with Madeira and quails in wine. It's a high-quality restaurant, with prices to match.

Basilica Sainte-Anne-de-Beaupré

Built from local white granite, with an incredibly kitsch interior, this church attracts huge numbers of pilgrims and American tourists. It's hard to see what all the fuss is about, and it's more rewarding to head straight for avenue Royale, a picturesque road behind the church that's lined with beautiful traditional houses owned by Québec's elite. The avenue, which runs parallel to the motorway, follows the river and leads back to Québec City, but if you're not in a hurry, it's well worth making an overnight stop here.

WHERE TO STAY AND EAT

🏠 **Gîte du Passant La Maison d'Ulysse** ('House of Ulysses'): 9140 avenue Royale. ☎ 827-8224. Doubles $60 a night; triples $75.

This attractive house with a largely wooden interior stands on a quiet street set back from boulevard Sainte-Anne. The four charming rooms, some with en-suite bathrooms are done up in bright colours and bear names like Iliade, Odyssée and Pénélope. In the morning, country-style breakfast, complete with homemade bread, is served on the covered terrace, which overlooks the lawn.

✕ **Le Montagnais**: 9450 boulevard Sainte-Anne. ☎ 827-1071. Main course $5 during the week, $10 on weekends. It doesn't look like anything special, but this large restaurant on route 138 has a good selection of dishes and cheap, excellent breakfasts.

LE PARC DES LAURENTIDES

Not to be confused with the Laurentides region, Laurentides Park is about 50 minutes' drive from Québec City, and is a popular weekend escape for the city's inhabitants. If you're coming from Québec, take route 175 towards Chicoutimi.

Set in a hilly region with several summits more than 1,000 metres (3,300 feet) high, this is one of Québec's largest nature reserves, covering 10,000 square kilometres (4,000 square miles). It's divided into two parts, the Jacques-Cartier park and the Laurentides wildlife reserve, where if you're lucky, you'll see some of the many types of animal that live here, among them lynx, black bears, wolves, moose, beavers and 132 species of bird.

The Jacques-Cartier valley, which is dotted with fairly basic campsites, is a great place for mountain-biking and day-long hikes, or even just a short stroll. The Société de gestion des activités commerciales du parc de la Jacques-Cartier (☎ 843-1356) organizes a range of activities in the park, including kayaking, boating, camping and fishing. Faune Aventure offers similar activities (☎ 848-5099). Whatever you're doing, make sure you bring a good insect repellent; the area is swarming with bugs.

– **By bus from Québec**: Autobus Québec. ☎ 525-3000.

ÎLE D'ORLÉANS

Some 34 kilometres (21 miles) long, and encircled by the 67-kilometre chemin Royal, the Île d'Orleans is Québec's answer to Normandy. Discovered by Jacques Cartier more than three centuries ago, it was originally named 'Bacchus Island' because of the wild vines that once grew there, and 30 families descended from the first inhabitants still live here. For many years, the island was practically self-sufficient, and it needed to be: until the bridge was built in 1935, the only way to get here was by boat or, in winter, to walk across the St Lawrence. Today, there are about 7,000 residents, many disenchanted city-dwellers drawn by the quiet countryside.

The landscape is scattered with stone houses, some of which have stood since the days of the French settlers, as well as churches, tiny procession chapels and old farms. The island retains its agricultural heritage, and is renowned for its apples and strawberries. Jobs are available during the picking season in July, especially in Saint-François, and summer is also the time to try *tire d'érable* (maple twist), which you'll find in the island's many sweetshops.

ÎLE D'ORLÉANS

The best way to see the island is to cycle or walk around it. There isn't an awful lot to do, but this can be something of a blessing after the frenzied pace of **Montréal** or **Québec City**. In winter, you can go ice fishing, ski on the slopes or take a ride on a dog sled.

The island is dotted with B&Bs and guesthouses, but bargains are few and far between.

USEFUL ADDRESSES

🛈 **Tourist information kiosk**: 490 côte de Pont, one kilometre from the bridge. ☎ 828-9411. Open 9am–7pm (Friday to Sunday, 9am–5pm). The kiosk stocks brochures and a rough map of the island detailing the points of interest. For $10 (plus a $20 deposit) you can also hire audiocassette guides in English or in French.

■ **Bike hire**: at Le Vieux Presbytère Inn, Saint-Pierre, behind the old church.

Saint-Pierre

This is the first village you'll come to on the island, about three kilometres (two miles) from the crossroads after the bridge. It's the site of the oldest surviving church in Québec, a beautiful structure built in 1717. The stunning yellow floor and painted ceiling have remained unchanged ever since, although the PA system that broadcasts the church's story, set to music, is a more recent addition. Look out for the 'central heating', the long box pews with side doors and the 'church wardens' bench', a three-seater pew set well apart from the rest of the congregation and reserved for the prestigious church wardens, who helped the priest to run his parish. Next to the church, there's a shop selling local arts and crafts.

WHERE TO STAY AND EAT

🛏 ✖ **Au-Vieux Foyer**: 2687 chemin Royal. ☎ 828-9171. Website: www.auvieuxfoyer.qc.ca. Doubles $65 a night; cabins for two $65. Cross the threshold of this wonderfully rustic farmhouse cottage and you'll step 200 years back in time. It's a cosy, atmospheric place, with low ceilings, a piano, beautiful ornaments and wooden furniture in every room. There's a four-poster bed in the 'bridal' room, and a stone wall in the girls' room. The family suite has a foldaway bed, and there's a small bedroom tucked away in the attic. All bathrooms are en suite, and there are men's urinals in all the rooms. If you want to get closer to nature, try an outdoor cabin, one of which has two bedrooms and a fully equipped kitchen ($115 a night). A generous breakfast – yoghurt, croissant or pancake, grilled sausages, a choice of meats, cheeses and fruit – is served in the kitchen, and you can also order a traditional local dinner, featuring such delicacies as pea soup, pigs' trotter stew and *chômeur* pudding. You can hire bikes, snowshoes, cross-country skis, snowmobiles and a horse-drawn sled.

🛏 ✖ **Le Vieux Presbytère**: 1247 rue Royal. ☎ 828-9723. Fax: 828-2189. A courteous, professional establishment behind Saint Peter's Church. Doubles $60-105 a night; menus from $24; half-board for two $125. As its name suggests, this beautiful house with an exterior wooden gallery is set in a small garden next to the church. The cheaper rooms (shared bathroom) look out onto the village, while the more expensive en-suite rooms face the river. The largest room has stone walls and a beamed ceiling, and can sleep up to four. There's a charming sitting room with a harmonium and parquet flooring, and the dining room offers views of the St Lawrence. The food is excellent and inexpensive: the bison and ostrich dishes use meat from animals that have been reared in the fields behind the house. If that feels a little too close to home, try the scallop parcels or the game medley. You can hire mountain bikes by the day or hour.

🛏 ✖ **Auberge sur les Pendants**: 1463 chemin Royal. ☎ 828-1139. Double rooms from $65 a night; *table d'hôte* $24. This pleasant, unpretentious inn, decorated with wood panelling, dried flowers and flower tapestries, has several cosy attic rooms (with windows). The gourmet breakfast menu changes frequently, while the *table d'hôte* dishes include snails in pastry with pesto and beef with shallots. It's a friendly, relaxed place, if a bit pricey for a guesthouse.

🛏 **Le Crépuscule**: 863 route Prévost, in Saint-Pierre. ☎ 828-9425. Email: louise.hamel3@sympatico. ca. Doubles from $60 per night. This is a pretty guesthouse with two en-suite rooms on the ground floor and an upstairs room with en-suite shower and separate toilet. One of the ground-floor rooms even has its own entrance. Breakfast is a delicious spread of blueberry muffins, pancakes, homemade jam, baked beans and fruit, with coffee and fruit juice to wash everything down. Your hosts, Louise and Gilles, know the island inside out, and will offer you plenty of advice about what to see and do.

✕ **Buffet d'Orléans**: 1025 route Prévost, Saint-Pierre, not far from the tourist information kiosk. ☎ 828-0013. Open 6.30am–10pm. Full meal from $15. Florence Nolin has been in charge of this place for 40 years, and not much has changed under her stern and watchful eye: the tables are still topped with Formica, the waitresses still wear black skirts, and the menu remains strong on regional specialities. The reasonably priced, fortifying dishes include meat pie with mashed potatoes, kidney bean soup and Canadian *bouilli*. Make sure you leave room for dessert: exquisite maple syrup and homemade fruit tarts. Highly recommended.

Sainte-Famille

From Saint-Pierre, the chemin Royal heads north along the St Lawrence, with fine views across to the north bank. Sainte-Famille, the region's strawberry and raspberry capital, is home to several old farms, some dating back three centuries. It's worth taking a break from your walk to admire the architecture of the barns and the lovely chapel at the side of the road. Opposite the chapel stands one of the most delightful houses on the island, with a sculpted exterior gallery. The three-steepled church, built in 1749, has a lavishly decorated interior, its half-dome chancel flanked by two elegant balustraded galleries. In the lower part of Sainte-Famille, you'll find the superb Maison Canac-Marquis, with a bright-red roof and a huge field of flowers.

WHERE TO STAY AND EAT

🛏 **Le Gîte de la Picardie**: 3547 chemin Royal. ☎ 829-3832. Doubles from $55 a night. This clean, pleasantly decorated guesthouse, set in a large orchard, has a slightly dingy but cool 'old-fashioned suite' on the lower ground floor, which costs the same as an ordinary room. The upstairs rooms have lovely views over the countryside and the St Lawrence. Monique and Marcel will do their best to make you feel at home. In season, they serve fresh raspberries and garden fruits for breakfast, a reminder that the Île d'Orleans is Québec's vegetable garden.

✕ **Cabane à Sucre Le Relais des Pins**: 3029 chemin Royal, about eight kilometres (five miles) from Saint-Pierre bridge. ☎ 829-3455. Open noon–9pm in season. *Table d'hôte* $10–15. Regional dishes and delicious homemade desserts are served in a huge country-style kitchen. Try the farmhouse platter (pâté, potatoes and baked beans).

Saint-François

This parish is located at the end of the island, 15 kilometres (nine miles) from Sainte-Famille, where the St Lawrence opens up as it flows towards the sea. There are fine views of the Montmagny archipelago, Île Madame and Île aux Ruaux, while to your left you can see Cape Tourmente and Mont-Sainte-Anne.

The Breton-style church, originally built in 1734, is one of the most beautiful on the island. It was destroyed by fire in 1988, but has since been carefully restored. The Maison de nos Aieux, behind the church, is where the Québécois come to trace their ancestors.

WHERE TO STAY

⌂ **Camping Orléans**: 357 avenue Royale, on the way out of Saint-François. ☎ 829-2953. Open mid-May to mid-September; phone to check exact dates. A pitch for a four-person tent costs $27; $29 with water and electricity. Riverside pitches are more expensive. Set in a pleasant, wooded location, this is a hospitable, well-equipped but slightly overpriced campsite with showers and laundrette. Campers can use the swimming pool and hire bikes. Small chalets are available for let on a weekly, monthly or seasonal basis.

Saint-Jean

Some 12 kilometres (seven miles) from Saint-François, this village is a long chain of beautiful, smart houses with flower-decked balconies. Founded in 1679, it's regarded as the island's 'capital', and it was the traditional home for the pilots who towed the big ships out into the river. In 1834, there were 45 people living in Saint-Jean, all of them born there; the last of their descendants sold up and moved to Québec in 1975. Take a look at the seamen's cemetery opposite the river.

WHERE TO STAY AND EAT

⌂ ✕ **Auberge de Jeunesse Le P'tit Bonheur**: 183 côte Lafleur, near the little bridge over the River Lafleur. ☎ and fax: 829-2588. Follow the steeply climbing road to the top of the hill, then follow the directions for the equestrian centre. Dormitory accommodation $16 per night; sheet hire $3. Monique Simard opened this popular youth hostel, superbly located in a huge prairie with a magnificent view of the river, in 1995. You don't need a Youth Hostel card to stay here, and if you don't want to sleep in the house, you can opt for a teepee in front of the main building or in the middle of the forest, or stay even in the trappers' shelters. A generous breakfast costs $4, and you can order an evening meal for $9 or cook for yourself. The energetic, sociable Monique has plenty of ideas for keeping her guests busy: bike hire, sea-kayaking, motorboats or hang-gliding in summer; guided sleigh rides and snowshoe or snowmobile hire in winter. For just a few dollars, Monique will collect you by car from Québec or drive you around. If you're staying for a long time, she'll pick you up for free. This is the best place to stay on the island.

– If youth hostels are not your thing, Monique Simard offers more expensive accommodation in a nearby house that enjoys the same magnificent pastoral setting. Doubles $55 a night, including breakfast.

⌂ ✕ **La Maison de Pierres**: 3673 chemin Royal. ☎ 829-1166. Booking is advisable. Double rooms $55 a night, including breakfast; half-board for two $125. Set amid the meadows, this atmospheric 18th-century stone farmhouse has creaky parquet floors and rough old stone walls whose effect is amplified by the sparse furnishings. The four pretty rooms share two bathrooms: all brightly decorated, they have wonderful wide floorboards. The service is friendly, there's an impressive CD collection and the breakfasts alone make staying here worthwhile. If you book at least 24 hours in advance, you can order an excellent dinner of Canadian game, Asian cuisine or whatever else is on offer.

♠ **Gîte de la Lucarne Enchantée**: 225 chemin Royal. ☎ and fax: 829-3792. Doubles $60 a night, including breakfast. A small, steep road leads up to this guesthouse, a cavernous place with a high, timbered roof and splendid views of the St Lawrence. In winter, you park the car at the bottom of the hill, and the gîte's own husky takes your luggage up by sled. In the daytime, you're surrounded by nature in all its glory, while you can spend the evenings by the fireside in the cathedral-sized lounge. The enchanting Native American 'dream-catchers' guarantee a peaceful night. Three bedrooms (one much smaller than the rest) share a shower room and a

bathroom with jacuzzi. Breakfast is served at a huge wooden table.

♠ **Le Mas de l'Isle**: 1155 chemin Royal, at the top of a hill overlooking the river. ☎ and fax: 829-1213. Doulbes $60 a night, including breakfast. This pleasant wooden house with a lovely garden is run by a charming couple who will expect you to abide by two rules: smoking is strictly forbidden, and breakfast is at a set time (they'll wake you if you oversleep), with everyone eating together in the dining room. It's a pretty, peaceful place, with well-kept rooms and shared bathroom.

♠ **Le Giron de l'Isle**: 120 chemin de Lièges. ☎ 829-0985. Doubles from $70 a night. Lucie and Gérard Lambert run a large modern guesthouse just above the St Lawrence, set back from the main road. There are four large bedrooms, decorated in pastel colours and all with beautiful en-suite bathrooms. The two bedrooms at the front have a lovely terrace, great for enjoying the sunsets or sunrises. The most expensive room is a proper suite, which has its own living room. It's well worth paying a bit extra to stay here, especially in view of the generous homemade breakfast.

WHAT TO SEE

★ **Manoir Mauvide-Genest**: 1451 chemin Royal. ☎ 829-2630. This Norman-style manor was built in 1734 by Jean Mauvide, personal surgeon to Louis XV, and its facade still bears the scars of the cannonballs fired by the English fleet in 1759 during the siege of Québec.

Saint-Laurent

About 12 kilometres (eight miles) from Saint-Jean, this is the spot where Wolfe and his troops landed before the siege of Québec. Wolfe's officers included the famous navigator and explorer James Cook, who later discovered the great islands of the Pacific. Today, the old mill houses an excellent restaurant. From here, there are weekend departures to the Île aux Grues and Grosse Île. For information, contact Croisières d'Anty: ☎ 659-5489.

WHERE TO STAY

🛏 **Gîte de l'Eau Vive**: 909 chemin Royal, GOA-3ZO. ☎ 829-3270. Email: frack@mediom.qc.ca. Doubles $65 a night. Micheline Turgeon, a charming, hospitable host whose ancestors landed on the Île d'Orléans in 1664, has a bright, modern home with a beautiful living room, an open-plan kitchen and fine views of the St Lawrence from the terrace. The rooms are a good size and, like the rest of the house, they're immaculately kept. Add the perfect breakfast and modest prices, and you'll probably agree that this is a real find.

WHERE TO EAT

✕ **Auberge Le Canard Huppé**: 2198 chemin Royal. ☎ 828-2292. Fax: 828-0966. Lunch menus $10–18; evening *table d'hôte* $30–45. Discerning diners will appreciate the hushed atmosphere, the discreet background music and, above all, the gastronomic menu, which features scallops and asparagus with citrus fruits, smoked shark escalope and wild boar with ginger, mango and blueberries. Lighter and less expensive midday meals – salmon tartare, poultry liver mousseline on cedar jelly or salmon with orange and rose pepper – are served on the pleasant terrace. The Auberge also offers well-equipped, if rather soulless, rooms.

WHAT TO SEE

★ **Parc Maritime de Saint-Laurent**: 120 chemin de la Chalouperie. ☎ 828-2322. The park is on the site of an old shipyard, which closed down in 1967. A small *chalouperie* (boatshed) houses a mini exhibition about shipbuilding, with a collection of tools on display. Not far from here, next to a pond where you can fish for trout, you can visit a maple plantation.

Saint-Pétronille

In the 19th century, this was a well-heeled residential area populated by artists and rich Americans. Today, this incredibly peaceful village, with lovely villas, ancient trees and views of Québec City in fine weather, is perhaps the most beautiful on the island. Not the least of its charms is its vineyard, which produces a very respectable sweet white wine, made from a grape produced by crossing the hardy vines that grow on the island with the Chancellor and Prince of Wales varieties. You can sample and buy the wine from the Vignoble de Saint-Pétronille (1A chemin du Bout-de-l'Île; ☎ 828-9554; open mid-June to mid-October, 10am–6pm). In 1995, this small vineyard produced 5,000 bottles and planted 5,000 new vines, which produced their first crop in 1998.

The village is also home to a chocolate factory, which manufactures fabulous ice cream – the blueberry flavour is really something else – as well as chocs.

WHERE TO STAY AND EAT

✕ **Café d'Art Pingasuit Nukariit**: 148 chemin du Bout-de-l'Île. ☎ 828-0507. Open every day in season. Starters and salads $2.50–10; *table d'hôte* $15–20 for individual dishes, $30 for a full meal,

ÎLE D'ORLÉANS

including drinks. This small restaurant-cum-art gallery is right on a bend in the road, to your left as you come from Saint-Pierre. You can park in the courtyard behind the house. The menu features Inuit specialities: terrine or filet mignon of seal, *mattaaq* (whale), braised Greenland turbot, musk ox *bourguignon* and smoked arctic char. Less adventurous diners can tuck into pizza or sandwiches.

☆☆☆☆ Splash Out

⬢ ✕ Auberge La Goéliche: 22 avenue du Quai. ☎ 828-2248. Fax: 828-2745. Website: www.oricom. ca/aubergelagoeliche. Doubles $160–200; *table d'hôte* $25–35; half-board for two $210. The perfect place for a romantic stay, and ideal for tumbling straight into bed after an intimate dinner, this luxury inn has tastefully and individually furnished rooms, all of them immaculately kept, and all with beautiful bathrooms. Stylish furniture, comfortable armchairs and fine paintings add to the plush, refined atmosphere. The rooms and dining room overlook the river, and you can even see Québec City in the distance. The elegant but unpretentious five-star service is completely devoid of airs and graces, so you're bound to feel right at home. The food is good, and reasonably priced considering what you get: the *table d'hôte* includes a soup, starter, main dish and dessert, and the menu changes frequently. On Sunday morning, the refined brunch includes pancakes and maple syrup, baked beans and so on. It's popular with locals, so book ahead, especially on weekends.

Charlevoix

Whatever you do, don't leave Québec without visiting Charlevoix, a beautiful region shaped by a succession of glaciers that hollowed out and weathered the land. Much of the area was once covered by the Champlain Sea, which left clay deposits in its wake. The region is also home to the world's biggest crater: 56 kilometres (35 miles) in diameter, it was formed when a huge meteorite hit the land. Today, Charlevoix is a gentle landscape, its country lanes leading to backwoods places with strange, evocative names like Pis-Sec, Pousse-Pioche, Cache-toi-bien and Main-Sale ('dry udder', 'pickaxe-pusher', 'hide yourself well' and 'dirty hand'). In 1988, Charlevoix was the first inhabited region to be designated a UNESCO biosphere reserve.

BAIE-SAINT-PAUL Pop: 7,400　　DIALLING CODE: 418

Tucked away at the end of a valley is the peaceful, picturesque town of Baie-Saint-Paul, reached via a velvety, multicoloured landscape. There are no major tourist attractions here, just silvery bell towers and a host of historic streets (Saint-Joseph, Saint-Jean-Baptiste, Saint-Adolphe) and buildings, among them Maison Simard (87 rue Saint-Joseph), the 18th-century Moulin César (on route 362 east) and Moulin Remi. Baie-Saint-Paul is also famous for its handicrafts.

USEFUL ADDRESSES

🄸 **Association Touristique de Charlevoix** (B2 on the map): 4 rue Ambroise-Fafard, behind the church. ☎ 435-5795. Open summer only, 9am–5pm. The staff here are friendly and well informed, and the shop sells work by local artists. There's another tourist office at **Belvédère Saint-Paul** (444 boulevard Monseigneur-de-Laval, on route 138; ☎ 435-4160; open 9am–9pm), with information on the whole of Charlevoix.
✉ **Post office** (B2): 9 rue Saint-Jean-Baptiste. ☎ 435-2541.

🚌 **Bus terminal** (Intercar) (off the map at A1): at the Le Village shopping centre, on the left-hand side of route 138 if you're heading towards La Malbaie. ☎ 435-6569. Bus tickets are sold at the La Grignote restaurant.
– **Taxi**: for a taxi to Saint-Joseph-de-la-Rive (for Île aux Coudres), call Le Central (☎ 435-2596) or Real Fort (☎ 435-3860). The trip costs $25, and will save you the hassle of changing buses.

WHERE TO STAY

Campsites

⛺ **Camping du Gouffre**: 439 rang Saint-Laurent, six kilometres (four miles) from the centre. ☎ 435-2143. Website: www.quebecweb.com/campingdugouffre. Take rue Fafard, which becomes rue Leclerc, then turn left onto rue du Gouffre; the campsite, is five kilometres (three miles) farther on. Open 15 May to 10 October. Tent pitches $18–26 a night; caravans available. This riverside campsite isn't cheap, but it's a green and pleasant spot with plenty of shade. Facilities include a swimming pool, a playground, a tennis court and a shop, and you can fish on-site.
⛺ **Camping Le Genévrier**: 1175 boulevard Monseigneur-de-Laval, on route 138 heading towards La Malbaie. ☎ 1-877-435-6520 (toll-free). Fax: 435-6976. Email: labbe @cite.net. Tent pitches from $23 a night; two-bedroom chalets with kitchen and bathroom $50–100 a night in season. Again, this campsite is quite expensive, but it's very popular. Even if you're not staying here, you can use the on-site facilities; you'll pay $3 for a swim in the

man-made lake and $8 an hour for a tennis court.

☆ Budget

⛺ **Le Balcon Vert**: route 362. ☎ 435-5587. Fax: 435-6664. Website: www.balconvert.charlevoix.net. Reception open 8–11am and 5–9pm. Open mid-May to mid-October; bar, restaurant and facilities open mid-June to early September only. Tent pitches $16 a night; dorm beds $17; doubles $40. Turn left towards La Malbaie as you leave town; it's one kilometre from the road, up a very steep hill, and signposted. This superb campsite, which overlooks the valley and the bay, doubles as a youth hostel, and you also can rent a bungalow in the grounds. The accommodation is pretty basic, but the half-board option is good value for money, and if there's a vacancy, you can work part-time in the youth hostel in exchange for free board and lodging. Inside the main building, which has bathrooms on every floor, you'll find a large communal room with a cheap and cheerful café that serves brunch and dinner, a bar and a reading room, while you can play

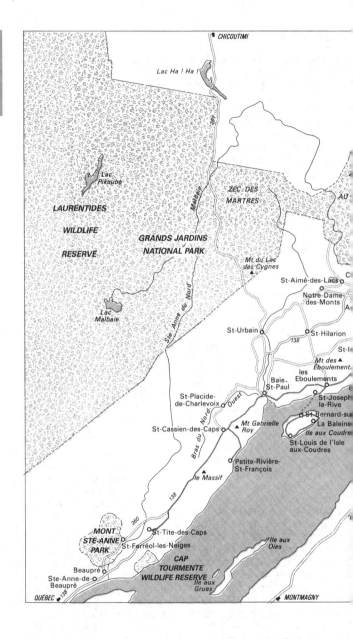

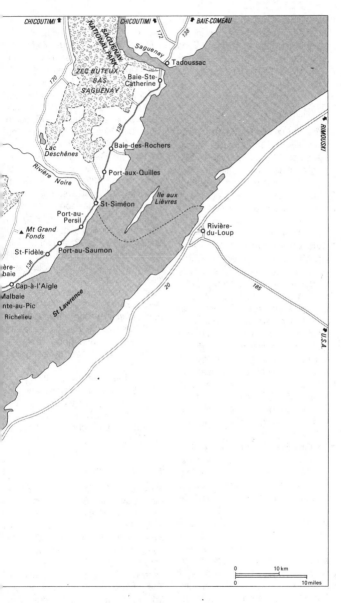

CHARLEVOIX

table tennis or volleyball in the garden. They also organize concerts, poetry evenings, campfire sessions and barbecues. If you're in search of a quiet break, this is not the place for you.

☆☆ Moderate

⌂ **Gîte Chez Marie-Marthe Bouchard** (B1, **10**): 43 rue Saint-Joseph. ☎ 435-2927. Doubles $50 a night, including breakfast. This simple, hospitable place is perfect for budget travellers, with four clean, basic rooms and a communal bathroom. The private garden has a pond with flamingos.

⌂ **Gîte du Passant La Chouette** (B2, **13**): 2 rue Leblanc. ☎ 435-3217. Website: www.quebecweb. com/gpc/alachouette. Doubles $80–95 a night. In a beautiful spot with views of Mont Cabaret, this house has a veranda, a sunny terrace and a reading room, with four en-suite rooms inspired by the four seasons. Breakfast is huge (try the pancakes with cheese and seasonal fruit) and guests can use the kitchen. Nearby, you'll find footpaths for summer walks, while in winter, you can go skiing. A delightful place to stay.

⌂ **La Grande Maison** (A1, **14**): 160 rue Saint-Jean-Baptiste. ☎ and fax: 435-5575 or 1-800-361-5575 (toll-free). Website: www.quebecweb. com/lagrandemaison. Doubles $70–225, including breakfast. Booking recommended. Built in 1920 and recently refurbished, this is the town's oldest hotel. A varnished parquet floor leads to the pleasant, sweet-smelling rooms: if you're feeling flush, try romantic room No. 1, which has a small terrace and an old-fashioned bath. The owners are charming, and the superb, if pricey, dinner menu includes lobster specialities and Qué-

bécois cuisine. There's also a health centre in the same building.

⌂ **Motel Royal** (A2, **15**): rue de la Lumière, near the centre of town, just past rue de l'Hôpital. ☎ 435-3540. Fax: 435-3542. Doubles $80 a night in high season; breakfast $5. This is an ordinary and rather expensive place to stay, but adequate if you can't find anything else. You can play mini-golf next door.

⌂ **Auberge Belle Plage**: 192 rue Saint-Anne, near the centre of town. ☎ 435-3321. Open in winter for skiing; otherwise summer only. This large, old-fashioned riverside house is easy to spot, thanks to the abandoned fishing boat right next to it. Doubles $65–97 a night. This hotel/motel has small attic bedrooms on the second floor, and larger en-suite rooms on the first floor; the most expensive have river views. Guests can use the outdoor pool or relax on the terrace, which overlooks the marina. It's a friendly place to stay, and good value for money. *Table d'hôte* meals are also on offer.

– If all these places are full, as is often the case in summer and on weekends, contact the Association Touristique de Charlevoix (*see* 'Useful Addresses') to check what else is available.

☆☆☆ Expensive

⌂ **Auberge La Muse** (B1, **12**): 39 rue Saint-Jean-Baptiste. ☎ 435-6839 or 1-800-841-6839 (toll-free). Fax: 435-6289. Website: www. lamuse.com. Email: lamuse@charlevoix.net. Doubles $70 in low season; half-board from $135 in high season. Booking recommended. This stunning 100-year-old house, fronted by four maple trees, has painted parquet floors and 10 pleasant en-suite rooms. It's a peaceful, relaxing place to stay, with a delightful garden, a terrace and, for more

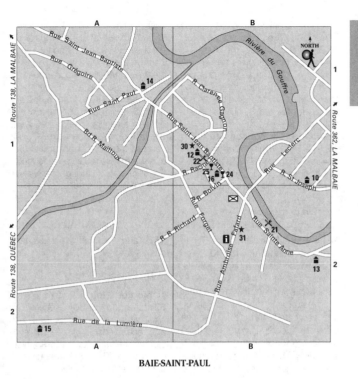

BAIE-SAINT-PAUL

■ **Useful Addresses**

🛈 Association Touristique de Charlevoix

🛈 Post office

🛏 **Where to Stay**

10 Gîte Chez Marie-Marthe Bouchard

12 Auberge La Muse

13 Gîte du Passant La Chouette

14 La Grande Maison

15 Motel Royal

16 Auberge La Maison Otis

✗ **Where to Eat**

21 Mouton Noir

22 Le Saint Pub

🍷 **Where to Have a Drink**

24 Le Scénario

25 Café des Artistes

★ **What to See and Do**

30 Randonnées Nature-Charlevoix

31 Centre d'Exposition

---

active visitors, a volleyball court. The evening *table d'hôte* offers you the chance to sample some regional cuisine, while breakfast comes with delicious homemade jam.

🛏 **B&B Le Cormoran**: 196 rue Sainte-Anne, next door to the Auberge Belle Plage. ☎ 435-6030. Website: www. cormoranbelleplage. com. Doubles $80–90 a night, including breakfast; motel rooms from $97. The luxurious, friendly B&B, which faces the bay, is owned by the people who run the Auberge Belle Plage. The en-suite rooms have all mod cons – some even have a jacuzzi – and breakfasts are generous and tasty. It's pricey, but worth every cent.

â **Auberge La Maison Otis** (B1, **16**): 23 rue Saint-Jean-Baptiste. ☎ 435-2255 or 1-800-267-2254 (toll-free). Fax: 435-2464. Website: www.quebecweb.com/gpc/maison

otis. Doubles from $173, half-board. This charming hotel is on the town's most attractive street, and the oldest part of the house has handsome fireplaces and fine wood panelling. The best room is a suite with a 2-metre bed, a TV, a video, a hi-fi and an enormous bath, but the low-end options are fairly basic, and some are in the modern annexe. Guests can use the indoor pool and sauna, and there's live music on weekends. For all its quality, though, La Maison Otis is a bit on the pricey side.

WHERE TO EAT

✕ **Le Saint Pub** (B1, **22**): 37 rue Saint-Jean-Baptiste. ☎ 240-2332. Open noon–3am. Lunch $8–13; evening *table d'hôte* from $16. Bar open evenings only. This pleasant restaurant has a delightful, shaded wooden terrace, and serves excellent beers from its on-site brewery (try the refreshing, spicy light ale). There's a good choice of tasty, good-value French-style

food, and the staff are polite and attentive.

☆☆☆ Expensive

✕ **Mouton Noir** (B2, **21**): 43 rue Sainte-Anne. ☎ 240-3030. This small, cosy wooden restaurant, with a terrace overlooking the Rivière de Gouffre, serves pricey but sophisticated food. The lunch menu offers considerably better value.

WHERE TO HAVE A DRINK

▼ **Le Scénario** (B1, **24**): 23 rue Saint-Jean-Baptiste, in the basement of the Auberge La Maison Otis (*see* 'Where to Stay'). ☎ 435-5002. Open Wednesday to Sunday until 3pm. This pub is one of the few places in town where you can hang out at night – there's even a dancefloor. You can play darts, pool or snooker, although you'll have to fight your way to the tables between Thursday and Saturday,

when locals flock here in search of cheap beer.

▼ **Café des Artistes** (B1, **25**): 25 rue Saint-Jean-Baptiste. ☎ 435-5585. Open 9am–midnight. You'll already have guessed that this is the place to find Baie-Saint-Paul's bohemian set. There are two terraces, one out front and one at the back, and it's a great place for a drink, with pizzas and paninis among the snacks on offer.

WHAT TO SEE

★ **Centre d'Art de Baie-Saint-Paul**, near the Association Touristique de Charlevoix: 4 rue Ambroise-Fafard. ☎ 435-3681. Open summer only, 9am–5pm. Baie-Saint-Paul's arts centre hosts exhibitions of work by local painters, and has a shop that sells locally produced silkscreen paintings, ceramics and so on. In August, there's a symposium for young Canadian artists at the Arena (behind the arts centre), where you can soak up the lively atmosphere and watch artists at work on a specially devised large-scale piece.

★ **Centre d'Histoire Naturelle de Charlevoix**: 444 boulevard Monseigneur-de-Laval, Route 138. ☎ 435-6275. From June to September, open 9am–5pm; otherwise 10am–4pm. This modern natural-history museum houses a permanent display on the origins of Charlevoix and the history of the crater, with the added bonus of fine panoramic views.

★ **Centre d'Exposition de Baie-Saint-Paul** (B2, **31**): 23 rue Ambroise-Fafard. ☎ 435-3681. From June to September, open 9am–7pm; otherwise 9am–5pm. Admission $3. Guided tours available on Wednesday, Saturday and Sunday. This place is devoted to the region's painters, and to anyone who has found inspiration for their art in Baie-Saint-Paul or Charlevoix. Most of the exhibitions are retrospectives of work generated by the annual symposium, but the top floor is given over to a permanent collection of sculptures and paintings on wood by Yvonne and Blanche Bolduc.

★ The unusual **church** has two asymmetrical towers.

★ There are several good **art galleries** in Baie-Saint-Paul, most near the town centre on rues Ambroise-Fafard, Saint-Jean and Sainte-Anne.

★ **La Laiterie Charlevoix**: 1167 boulevard Monseigneur-de-Laval, on route 138. ☎ 435-2184. Open 8am–7pm in high season; otherwise 8am–5.30pm (weekends noon–4pm). The town's dairy has an exhibition of old-fashioned equipment once used to make cheese. You can buy produce made in the traditional way, and if you arrive before 11am, you can watch the craftsmen at work.

WHAT TO DO

– **La Joyeuse Randonnée**: ☎ 435-6681. 'Happy Hiking' offers guided historical and architectural walks through the town. Most last about an hour.

– **Dog-sleigh and rafting lessons**: Descente Malbaie, 316 rue Principale. ☎ 439-2265.

– **Les Randonnées Nature-Charlevoix** (B1, **30**): 41 rue Saint-Jean-Baptiste. ☎ 435-6275. Open mid-June to mid-October, 9am–5pm. This company, which specializes in nature walks, is run by two young forestry engineers with a passion for the area. They organize a host of activities, all led by qualified instructors or nature guides. From late June to early September (and on weekends in autumn), you can sign up for a range of walks, most of which last about 2 hours: if you don't have a car, there's a shuttle bus to Parc des Grands-Jardins, which leaves early in the morning and brings you back at the end of the day. The group also offers bike hire, and runs a car pool. If you're feeling lazy, there are 2-hour bus tours around the countryside, taking in Charlevoix's famous crater.

WHAT TO SEE IN THE AREA

★ **Domaine Charlevoix**: route 362, five kilometres (three miles) northeast of Baie-Saint-Paul. ☎ 435-2626 or 1-877-435-2627 (toll-free). Open mid-June to mid-October. There's an admission charge. This vast private estate has been turned into a wonderful network of footpaths and cycle routes. The countryside throughout is beautiful and varied, with delightful river views, a beach, a cove and several waterfalls. The wildness is slightly spoilt by the tea-room, bar with games, terraces and exhibitions, but it's still well worth a visit.

★ **Parc des Grands-Jardins**: 35 kilometres (20 miles) north of Baie-Saint-Paul. By car, take route 138 for 10 kilometres (6 miles), then route 381, which goes through Saint-Urbain. If you don't have your own transport, you can get here with Randonnées Nature-Charlevoix (*see above*). At the entrance to the park, pick up a map at the Thomas-Fortin reception centre, then head towards Château-Beaumont. Which is the base for all the activities on offer.

The park is in the heart of the countryside, on a plateau that has its own microclimate. The vegetation resembles the Siberian taiga, with conifers and a thick carpet of lichen on the ground. You'll also see birch and black spruce trees. It's a bit like being in the far north, yet it's only 120 kilometres (75 miles) from Québec City. The wildlife, meanwhile, includes ducks, herons, squirrels and bears. Don't be surprised or put off if the ground you're walking along looks scorched: there were serious fires in the park in 1991 and 1999.

This is a fabulous place for hiking, but make sure you take some mosquito repellent, food and drink and a pair of binoculars.

At Château-Beaumont, you can watch a slide show about the park, hire a canoe and pick up leaflets about the footpaths. There are 10 routes through the park, which take between 1 and 6 hours to complete. The best of these is Le Mont du Lac des Cygnes, a 4-hour round trip that involves a 1,000-metre (3,300-foot) climb to get to an observation point with stunning views (it's chilly up there, so take a warm jumper). Some of the walks are unaccompanied, but for others you have to go with a guide: in summer, 3-hour guided walks leave Château-Beaumont at 10am and 1.30pm. If you want to stay overnight in the park, you can rent a chalet or use one of the two campsites.

SAINT-JOSEPH-DE-LA-RIVE Pop: 200

DIALLING CODE: 418

This is a lovely little village tucked between the sea and the mountains, 15 kilometres (nine miles) along the coastal road between Baie-Saint-Paul and La Malbaie. Whichever way you come into town, there are spectacular views as you descend into town, but be warned that there are steep gradients on either side. The oldest inhabitants in the village remember times in the 1920s when they had to drive in reverse in order to get up the hill: cars had no fuel pumps in those days, so this was the only way to get petrol into the carburettor. Even recently, the roads were no more than tracks. Saint-Joseph's was once one of Québec's most important docks, with ships going to Île aux Coudres.

WHERE TO STAY AND EAT

Tucked away among the trees are several stunning guesthouses with beautiful gardens. Unfortunately, they're usually very expensive.

☆ Budget

✕ **Le Loup Phoque**: 188 rue Felix-Antoine-Savard (the main street). ☎ 635-2848. Main courses less than $10. Overlooking the river, this charming wooden manor house has arbours and rather strange blue turrets. The speciality is seafood, and there's a pleasant terrace for those balmy summer nights.

☆☆ Moderate

⌂ ✕ **L'Été**: 589 chemin du Quai, near the ferry to Île aux Coudres. ☎ 635-2873. Open May to October. Doubles $55–75 a night; half-board compulsory. Credit cards accepted. This is a lovely little house near the beach with five comfortable, tastefully decorated bedrooms that share two bathrooms. There's a terrace tucked away in a pretty garden planted with cedars and lots of flowers.

⌂ ✕ **L'Auberge de la Rive**: 185 chemin de l'Église, on the riverbank.

☎ 635-2846. Fax: 888-935-2845. Doubles $85 a night, breakfast included. This large mauve-and-white building houses a hotel and a motel: the rooms in the former, though a little small, are nicer, cosier and less expensive than in the motel, and all have en-suite bathrooms. The facilities include a swimming pool, a restaurant, and a bar with a dancefloor. If you need a bike, ask the owner to lend you one.

⌂ ✕ **La Maison Sous les Pins**: 352 rue Félix-Antoine-Savard. ☎ 635-2583. Email: msp@clic.net. Doubles $120–150; half-board compulsory. No dinner Wednesday. Strictly non-smoking. There are six en-suite rooms in this wooden house; they're a little sombre, although a lot of effort has evidently gone into the travel-themed decor, and it's not without a certain quirky charm. A meal in the restaurant costs $15–25, and the food is excellent.

WHAT TO SEE AND DO

★ **Papeterie Saint-Gilles**: 304 rue Félix-Antoine-Savard. ☎ 635-2430. Open Monday to Friday, 8am–5pm; in summer, also open on weekends, 9am–6pm. Admission free; group tours $2 per person. This small paper mill, set up in 1965, is famous for its mottled handmade paper, decorated with local leaves and flowers. The processes used date back to the 17th century. You can try your hand at the various stages of paper-making – removing fibre impurities, sifting, pressing, drying and calendering (a special finishing process) – then watch a fascinating video that explains the whole process. You can also make personalized letter-writing paper, though it's not cheap.

★ **Exposition Maritime de Saint-Joseph-de-la-Rive**: 305 place de l'Église, opposite the paper mill. ☎ 635-1131. From mid-May to early October, open 9am–5pm; in May, June and September, open 11am–4pm. Admission $2; children under 15 free. Guided tours available in high season. From the end of the 18th century until the 1970s, one of this area's main industries was the construction of wooden schooners that carried supplies to villages (there were no reliable roads). This shipyard, which closed in 1952, has been transformed into an excellent open-air maritime museum, with two schooners in pristine condition to remind visitors of the old days. One of these craft is now used for cruises. You can visit the old sawmill and the workshop, and there's a small display of original tools and scale models of the boats once made here.

★ **L'Église Saint-Joseph-de-la-Rive**: chemin de l'Église, right by the river. Open every day in summer. The decor inside the parish church was inspired by the sea.

★ The **public beach** is just to the left of the quay.

L'ÎLE AUX COUDRES   DIALLING CODE: 418

The rugged, mountainous landscape of this little island lends it a rather Scottish feel. It was discovered in 1535 by Jacques Cartier, and takes its name from his surprise at seeing so many *coudres* (hazel trees). For almost two centuries, the island was used as a burial ground for sailors: the first settlers, who arrived in 1720, were a group of 1,600 missionaries, nicknamed *Marsouins* ('Porpoises') and famous for their hospitality. The island was also home to a ship-building industry, though the only trace of this is the odd piece of schooner scattered about the island. The road around the island is 23 kilometres long (14 miles), and you can easily cycle the whole way.

Foodwise, the local specialities include *soupe aux gourganes* (kidney bean soup), fried smelt (a fish), *tourtière grand-mère* (meat pie), *pâté croche* (a crescent-shaped pâté), and *tarte au sucre* (rhubarb tart). Don't expect much in the way of nightlife, though: the only option is a disco, appealingly named Le Donjon, and that's only open on Friday and Saturday nights. On the plus side, there's no shortage of peace and quiet . . .

GETTING THERE

If you're planning to come here by bus from Québec, bear in mind that the bus terminates at Baie-Saint-Paul. Hanging around for a bus to Saint-Joseph-de-la-Rive is a real pain, so you're better off hitchhiking, renting a car or taking a taxi from Baie-Saint-Paul (*see above*).

– **Ferry**: the 15-minute trip between Saint-Joseph-de-la-Rive and the island is free, and you'll even be given a map of the island while you queue. ☎ 438-2743. From mid-May to end-October, there are departures on the hour between 7am and 11pm; in July and August, there are extra trips every half-hour between 10am and 5pm, except on Wednesday and Thursday in July. Out of season, it's best to check the times in advance. Expect long queues on weekends.

USEFUL ADDRESSES

🅑 **Information kiosk**: on the seafront when you get to Saint-Bernard, near Pointe du Bout-d'en-Bas. ☎ 665-4454 or 1-800-667-2276 (toll-free). From 15 June to late August, open 9am–7pm; in September and early October, open weekends only, 10am–6pm. You

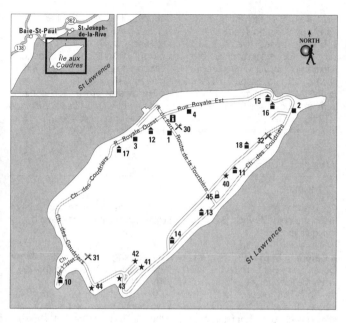

ÎLE AUX COUDRES

■ **Useful Addresses**

   🅸 Information kiosk
   1 Bike hire, Gérard Desgagnes
   2 Bike hire, Vél 'O'Coudres
   3 Michel Dufour
   4 Fer Plus

🛏 **Where to Stay**

   10 Motel L'Islet
   11 Motel La Baleine
   12 Motel Le Soleil Couchant
   13 La Marguerite
   14 La Riveraine
   15 Hôtel Écumé par la Houle
   16 Hôtel du Capitaine
   17 Camping Sylvie
   18 Camping Leclerc

✕ **Where to Eat**

   15 Hôtel-restaurant Écumé par la Houle
   30 Chez Ti-Coq
   31 La Mer Veille
   32 Hôtel Cap-aux-Pierres

★ **What to See and Do**

   40 Maison Leclerc
   41 Maison Bouchard
   42 Moulins de l'Île aux Coudres
   43 Musée de l'Île aux Coudres
   44 Musée des Voitures d'eau

🔒 **Shopping**

   45 Centre Artisanal

can pick up plenty of useful tourist literature and a detailed map of the island.

■ **Bike hire** (**1** on the map): Gérard Desgagnes, 34 rue du Port, Saint-Bernard-sur-Mer, a few minutes' walk from the jetty. ☎ 438-2332. You'll pay $3 an hour, or $15 a day. This is the closest hire shop to the jetty; they also offer mountain bikes. Alternatively, try Vél 'O' Coudres (743 chemin des Coudriers, La Baleine; ☎ 438-2118; **2**), 5 metres (3 miles) from the ferry, which has a good selection of bikes, mountain bikes, tricycles and four-wheelers; there's a courtesy bus from the harbour. At Harvey-vélos (27 rue Principale, La Baleine; ☎ 438-2343), bike hire costs $2.50 an hour or $16 per day. Group discounts and children's buggies are also available.

■ **Hardware store**: for camping gas and other useful equipment, go to Michel Dufour (☎ 438-2408; **3**) or Fer Plus (☎ 438-2334; **4**).

WHERE TO STAY

Campsites

The island is a perfect place to sleep under canvas, and every campsite on the island sells firewood ($3) for the obligatory campfire. Just watch out for mosquitoes.

♣ **Camping Sylvie (17)**: 191 Royale Ouest, Saint-Bernard. ☎ 438-2420. From the jetty, take the first road on the right and follow it for 1.5 kilometres (1 mile); you'll find the campsite on your right. Tent pitches $15. This is a friendly campsite with a lovely lawn at the front. As well as the campsite proper, there are several small, basic chalets in a beautiful area by a tree-lined lake. You can also hire pedalos here.

♣ **Camping Leclerc (18)**: 185 rue Principale, La Baleine. ☎ 438-2217. Tent pitches $18. There's room for 50 tents at this site, which has wonderful views of the river, and the facilities include hot showers, toilets, a wide range of games and a shop that sells fresh bread every day. You can also stay in one of the reasonably priced motel rooms although they're rather lacking in charm.

☆☆ Budget

The island is a popular holiday destination, and there's a good choice of hotels and motels. Unfortunately, many of them are always packed, so the list below focuses on places where you should be able to get a room.

♣ You can rent a **chalet** near the river, with a sitting room, a bathroom and two bedrooms, for $300 per week. Inquire at Harvey-vélos (*see* 'Useful Addresses').

♣ **Motel L'Islet (10)**: 10 chemin de l'Islet, at Pointe de l'Islet, at the very south of the island. ☎ 438-2423. From the jetty, follow the seafront and turn right at rue Royale; the motel is 8 kilometres (5 miles) farther on. Doubles $50 a night; bungalows with two bedrooms, sitting room, kitchen and bathroom $60 a night. This is a pleasant motel in an isolated little spot, with fantastic views of the St Lawrence (it goes silvery at sunset). It's cheap, clean and basic, and the staff are friendly.

♣ **Motel La Baleine (11)**: 138 rue Principale, La Baleine. ☎ 438-2453. Bungalows $50–60 a night. This place offers great value for money. The small white bungalows have lovely, spotless rooms and a fitted kitchen area, as well as superb views of the river.

⚓ **Motel Le Soleil Couchant** (**12**): 48 rue Royale Ouest. ☎ 438-2994 and 438-2393. Turn right at Saint-Bernard when you get off the ferry. Doubles $40 a night. The rooms here are cheap, simple and very clean, although most have views of the car-park. There's also a restaurant that serves cheap snacks and local specialities, including delicious *pâté croche* and smelt pâté. Bike hire is also available.

⚓ **La Marguerite** (**13**): 567 chemin des Coudriers, La Baleine. ☎ 438-2283. La Marguerite is an unusual stone house that looks out over the river, with large, clean rooms that share three bathrooms. Guests can also use the sitting room. If you want somewhere nice, quiet and friendly to stay at a reasonable price, look no further.

⚓ **La Riveraine** (**14**): 6 rue Principale, La Baleine. ☎ 438-2831. Doubles $55 a night, including breakfast. This friendly place offers excellent value for money. The five stylish rooms, all painted in fresh colours, share two bathrooms, and you can chat to other guests or read a book in the sitting room. Now and again, the owner treats visitors to a little tune on his accordion. The breakfasts are hearty and delicious.

⚓ **Hôtel Écume par la Houle** (**15**): 808 chemin des Coudriers, La Baleine. ☎ 438-2733. Doubles from $40 a night. This hotel was estab-

lished by Horace Pedneaud, a decidedly free spirit about whom you can read more in the 'What To See' section. Pedneaud set up this motel-style hotel opposite his restaurant (*see* 'Where to Eat'), in a garden just behind La Maison-Croche, and it's ideal for those with a taste for the bizarre. The rooms vary from very basic to extremely comfortable – some even have sitting rooms and kitchen areas – but all share a 1970s kitsch decor. You can also stay in the La Maison-Croche, which has four rooms with pre-war beds and a sitting room decorated in Pedneaud's inimitable style. The shared bathroom is absolutely stunning.

☆☆ Moderate

⚓ **Hôtel du Capitaine** (**16**): 781 chemin des Coudriers, La Baleine, near Pointe du Bout-d'en-Bas. ☎ 438-2242. This large, dark-wood chalet-style house is surrounded by a quiet garden next to the river, with several bungalows as well as the main hotel. Some of the comfortable rooms have en-suite bathrooms, and guests can use the salt-water swimming pool. In the evening, you can tuck into hearty helpings of good, traditional Québécois fare; the *table d'hôte* costs $22, and you can also stay on a half-board basis.

WHERE TO EAT

✗ **Hôtel-restaurant Écume par la Houle** (**15**): 808 chemin des Coudriers, La Baleine. ☎ 438-2733. Open for lunch and dinner; *table d'hôte* $16. Horace Pedneaud's bar-restaurant looks a little strange from the outside, but nothing can prepare you for the weirdness that lies within. There's a parquet floor and a breeze-block tower in the

centre, rather like a fortress, which is home to Le Donjon, the island's 'nightclub' (Friday and Saturday nights during high season only). The terrace, meanwhile, is like the bow of a ship moving along the river. The decor is basically Catholic kitsch, with strange religious relics and holy pictures all over the place, and added touches like an old stove, models of schooners sailing across a sea of feathers and hallucinatory paintings. Once you've adjusted your mind, you can tuck into cheap local dishes such as *pâté croche*, smelt pâté, *tarte au sucre* and *chômeur* pudding. If the interior puts you off your food, head for the tiny landscaped garden, which has superb views of the river and the mainland, as well as a water slide for children.

✕ **Chez Ti-Coq** (**30**): 29 rue du Port, on the left as you come up from the jetty. ☎ 438-2944. Open until midnight. This cheap little café offers a wide range of fast food and local dishes.

✕ **La Mer Veille** (**31**): 160 chemin des Coudriers, on the way to Pointe de l'Islet. ☎ 438-2149. This khaki-coloured house has a veranda overlooking the water, an excellent place to watch the sun go down. You can sample traditional snacks and dishes, including *soupe aux gourganes*, roast smelt and *pâté croche*, or try grilled lobster or lobster salad, followed by delicious homemade desserts. The set menus are not too expensive, but the á la carte probably offers better value.

✕ **Hôtel Cap-aux-Pierres** (**32**): 246 rue Principale, La Baleine. ☎ 438-2711. This classy hotel is always full of tourists, but it's worth coming here on a Sunday for the excellent brunch buffet (11am–1.30pm).

WHAT TO SEE

There's plenty to see on Île aux Coudres, with museums, ancient buildings and eye-catching details as well as the sumptuous landscapes. The main attractions are listed below; they're arranged as an anticlockwise trip around the island.

★ **La Maison-Croche**: opposite the Hotel-restaurant Écume par la Houle. Admission fee. This is another of Horace Pedneaud's creations. In 1963, Horace wanted to shock and annoy the strait-laced inhabitants of the island, so he built this odd little house with windows tilting at steep angles. One of his dictums was, 'You have to look beneath the surface' – and if you do, you'll see a few historical objects (a piano, a gramophone and a few bits of furniture), dozens of Horace's paintings and an awful lot of kitsch, from over-the-top light fittings and enormous ashtrays to a wacky baroque chair. It may have shocked the locals, but today it has a decidedly retro air.

★ **Maison Leclerc** (**40**): 124 rue Principale. ☎ 438-2240. Open 10am–6pm from 24 June to early September. Admission fee. This little stone house, built in 1750, has a small collection of local antiques and *objets d'art*.

★ **Maison Bouchard** (**41**): turn right as you get to Saint-Louis, then go to the end of chemin du Ruisseau. Built at the beginning of the 18th century, this is one of the island's oldest houses. The Bouchard family still live here, so it's not open to the public.

★ **Moulins de l'Île aux Coudres** (**42**): 247 chemin du Moulin, Saint-Louis. ☎ 438-2184. From mid-June to the beginning of September, open 9am–6pm; in late spring and early autumn, open 10am–5pm. Admission fee; discounts for students. In this beautiful spot, you'll find two 19th-century flour mills, the miller's house and a forge. In winter, the windmill took over from the water mill, and vice versa in summer, an arrangement unique in

Québec. The mills ceased working in 1948, and is now a museum, although you can buy flour made on-site at the shop. Start your tour by visiting the two mills, which have been expertly restored: the wooden gears are particularly impressive, while the steps slope towards the front to ensure that the miller doesn't lose his balance. There's also a lively talk about the life of the miller and his wife, who were called Desmeules ('Millstones'), while the artefacts on display include a petition, signed by the islanders in 1815, that begs for the mill to be built.

★ **Musée de l'Île aux Coudres** (**43**): 231 chemin des Coudriers. ☎ 438-2753. Open summer only, 8am–6.30pm. Admission fee. The history and layout of the island are explained by models made by a long-time inhabitant of the isles. It's of quite specialist appeal, though, and the staff are not particularly friendly.

★ **Musée des Voitures d'eau** (**44**): 203 chemin des Coudriers. ☎ 438-2208. Open June to September, 9am–6pm. This fascinating, well-presented museum, set up by a retired sea captain, explains the maritime history of the island. Part of the museum has been built using bits of wood from an old ship, and the place is full of extraordinary bits and pieces rescued from the sea: tools, instruments, scale models of ships, old photographs and so on. Outside, there's a display of buoys, and you can also visit the schooner *Mont-Saint-Louis*.

SHOPPING

🛈 **Centre Artisanal de l'Île aux Coudres** (**45**): 605 rue des Coudriers, La Baleine. ☎ 438-2231. Open 9am–9pm. For more than a century, the islanders used to make their own clothes and linen, and they continue this tradition even today. This crafts centre displays and sells handicrafts made by 150 craftsmen and women, including carpets, fabrics, fishermen's jerseys, pottery and ceramics. There are also regular weaving demonstrations. It's quite expensive, though, and the quality of the work is quite varied. There are plenty of similar shops dotted around the island.

LES ÉBOULEMENTS Pop: 1,020   DIALLING CODE: 418

This smart, pretty village, spread along the St Lawrence River, is best known as the site of the famous meteorite fall. It was also hit by an earthquake in 1663, when a huge landslide completely altered the shape of the landscape. From the terrace of the Auberge de Nos Aïeux, you can enjoy a truly spectacular view of the Île aux Coudres and the St Lawrence, while on the main street, rue Principale, you'll find the **Moulin Banal** (the communal mill, which dates back to 1790), the **Manoir de Sales-Laterriere** and the **Forge d'Arthur Tremblay**, a 100-year-old forge where you can still see all the old tools.

WHERE TO STAY AND EAT

⭐⭐ – ⭐⭐⭐ Moderate to Expensive

🛌 ✕ **Auberge Le Surouêt**: 195 rue Principale, on route 138. ☎ 635-1401. Fax: 635-1404. Doubles $95–105 a night; half-board available. The bedrooms here are all tastefully decorated, and if you're lucky, you'll get one that's been soundproofed; the more expensive rooms have views of the river. The restaurant is one of the region's finest: it's a formal affair, with veal, lamb and trout specialities cooked by a French chef. There's also a fantastic tea-room, where you can nibble tasty homemade pastries while you gaze out over the river.

🛌 ✕ **Auberge de Nos Aïeux**: 183 Route 362. ☎ 635-2405. Fax: 635-2389. Email: quebecweb.com/aieux. Doubles $70 a night in high season, including breakfast. You couldn't ask for a better view of the Île aux Coudres, but the rooms here are outdated and lacking in character, and the hotel is often full of coach parties. You can also stay in one of the two anonymous-looking modern motel buildings, where the rooms are bigger, but also much more expensive. On the plus side, guests can use the lovely garden and the swimming pool, there's a large car park, and the *table d'hôte* is a bargain.

WHAT TO SEE

★ **Cap-aux-Oies**: you'll find this hamlet at the point where the St Lawrence flows into the sea. There's a beach where you can swim in the sea, but watch out for the steep slope.

SAINT-IRÉNÉE Pop: 650   DIALLING CODE: 418

As you follow route 362, you suddenly plunge down towards Saint-Irénée, a chichi little spot with a long beach that's very popular with holidaymakers. The road climbs back up as you leave the village; look out for the pretty church with a shiny roof.

WHERE TO STAY AND EAT

⭐⭐ Moderate

🛌 **Auberge La Luciole**: 178 chemin Les Bains, on route 362. ☎ 452-8283. Email: lucie.tremblay2@simpatico.ca. From the main road, turn right just before the bridge. Doubles $55–75 a night. This large wooden house on the waterfront has pretty pastel rooms that share three bathrooms. It's a friendly place, and breakfast is delicious.

🛌 ✕ **Le Rustique**: 102 rue Principale, in the centre of the village.

☎ 452-8250. Open May to October. Doubles $55–65 a night, including breakfast. This is a beautiful 100-year-old house, surrounded by trees, offering a choice of eight charming rooms, some with views of the river. If the weather's fine, you can sit out on the veranda, while there are more views of the St Lawrence at breakfast, which is served on the terrace. The young, friendly owners also run the pub next door, and you can get a very good meal in the pastel-painted dining room (*table d'hôte* $19).

⌂ B&B La Cédrière des Thérien: 267 chemin Les Bains, on route 362. ☎ and fax: 452-3545. Doubles $70 a night; suites $120. This simply decorated guesthouse is perched above the St Lawrence as it flows down through Saint-Irénée. There are three mundane downstairs rooms; the first-floor rooms are much nicer, but, predictably, they're also more expensive. The best has a small terrace with a wonderful view of the river. The owner is very friendly, but has a tendency to rouse his guests in time to watch the sunrise.

☆☆☆☆ Splash Out

⌂ ✕ Auberge Les Sablons: 223 chemin Les Bains. ☎ 452-3594. Fax: 452-3240. Website: www.cite. net/sablons. Doubles $85–135 a night; various deals are available, including half-board from Monday to Friday. From the main road, turn left as you enter the village. This stunning blue-and-white building, overlooking the river, is the height of luxury. If you want to see the sun rise, ask for a room on the southeast side. The owner has converted an old hotel next door into four small flats with kitchenettes, all with river views. In the restaurant, the superb *table d'hôte* features traditional Québécois cuisine.

WHERE TO EAT AND HAVE A DRINK

✕ ⌑ Le Saint-Laurent Café-galerie: 128 rue Principale. ☎ 452-3408. Restaurant open Tuesday to Sunday, 11am–3pm. Main courses $8. The main dining area is a lovely wooden room in warm yellow-and-green colours, and the food is an original blend of various foreign influences, devised and cooked by the cheerful owner. It's good, cheap, and plentiful, and the service is excellent. There's a terrace in summer, and *table d'hôte* options are sometimes available.

⌑ Le Rustique: 102 rue Principale, in the hotel of the same name. This is a charming brick pub with a pool table and musical instruments hanging on the walls. Just as well, as it's the only decent bar in the village.

WHAT TO DO

– **Domaine Forget** is home to an academy of music and dance, which holds a fantastic **music festival** between 19 June and 21 August. ☎ 452-3535. Fax: 452-3503. You can book tickets by credit card. Throughout the year, it also hosts interesting art exhibitions. There are concerts on Wednesday, Friday and Saturday at 8.30pm and on Sunday at 3pm, although you should check before you go. There is an admission fee (students get a discount). Every Sunday (11am–2pm; about $20, including food), there's a musical brunch on the terrace, with live performances by an assortment of ensembles and soloists.

CHARLEVOIX

POINTE-AU-PIC

For rich Québécois, Canadians and Americans, the huge and ultra-pricey Manoir Richelieu is the main reason to come here. Nevertheless, this is a magnificent spot, its vast villas and luxury hotels surrounded by trees. The accommodation is usually excellent.

WHERE TO STAY AND EAT

Pointe-au-Pic is a little bit showy, so if you find that intimidating, you'll find plenty of less pretentious places to stay in nearby La Malbaie or the charming village of Cap-a-l'Aigle, a charming and totally unpretentious little village. If you want to observe the jet set at play, though, here's a list of Pointe-au-Pic's more reasonable options.

☆ Budget

≜ **Camping Les Érables**: 69 rang Terrebonne, on route 362, near the casino. ☎ 665-4212 (high season only). Tent pitches $15. This leafy campsite is right by the sea, and its attractions include hot showers and an on-site pond. There are also several bungalows available (☎ 665-2736).

☆☆ Moderate

≜ ✕ **Aux Douceurs Belges**: 121 boulevard des Falaises. ☎ 665-7480. Website: www.oricom.ca/DouceursBelges/. Open 15 June to 15 October only. Doubles $110 a night, including breakfast; half-board $140. Strictly non-smoking. This vast yellow-orange house has four bedrooms, all with parquet floors and wooden or thick stone walls. One has a balcony with a superb view, another has a corner lounge, and the last two are fitted out with whirlpool baths (bathrobes are provided). The owners are real Belgophiles: they've turned the dining room into an authentic-looking brasserie that offers Belgian food and a choice of 100-odd types of beer. Bike hire is also available.
≜ **Gîte du Passant Maison Frizzi**: 8 Coteau-sur-Mer. ☎ 665-4668. Doubles $60–70 a night. It's 2 kilometres (1 mile) past the Richelieu golf course; turn right onto a small road and the gîte is on the left. This clean and friendly place, surrounded by trees, looks a bit like a Tyrolean chalet. The three large, pleasant and comfortable rooms, all decorated in pastel colours, share two bathrooms; the most expensive one has a balcony and views of the river.

☆☆☆ Expensive

≜ **Auberge La Romance**: 129 chemin des Falaises. ☎ 665-4865. Fax: 665-4954. Website: www.quebecweb.com/laromance. Doubles from $110 a night. As guesthouses go, this place is very expensive, but then this huge old house with pale parquet floors is worlds away from your average guesthouse. The en-suite rooms are wonderfully intimate, and some have jacuzzis and sitting rooms, while the rustic decor is complemented by furniture painted by a local artist. There's a beautiful sitting room with fireplace, where you can sit and sip a cocktail (unusually for Québec, this place holds a licence to sell alcohol), and the buffet breakfast is served on the terrace in the garden.

COLOUR MAPS

SECTION 2

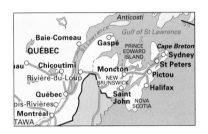

The colour maps in this section refer
to the second half of the guide and
primarily to the chapter on Québec

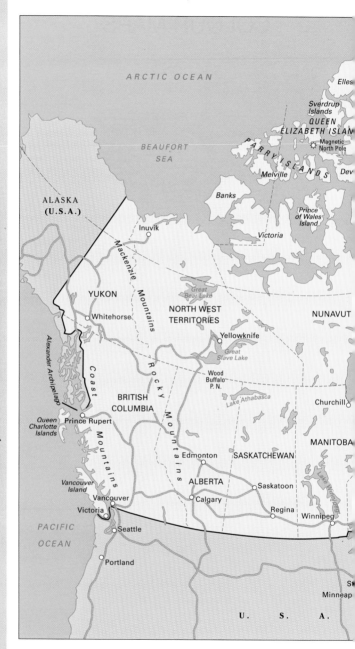

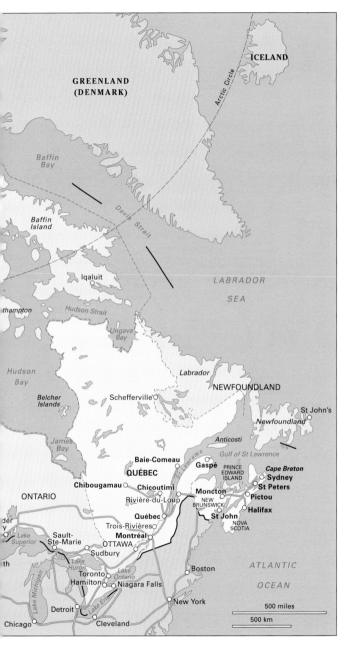

QUÉBEC, NEW BRUNSWICK AND NOVA SCOTIA

THE MARITIME PROVINCES

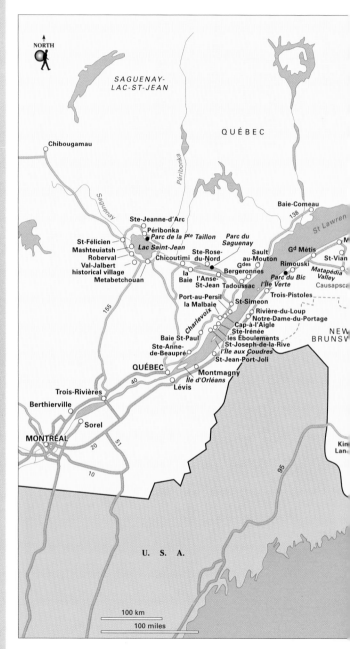

NORTH

SAGUENAY-
LAC-ST-JEAN

QUÉBEC

Chibougamau

Péribonka

St Lawren

Baie-Comeau

138

Ste-Jeanne-d'Arc
Péribonka
Parc de la P^{te} *Taillon*

*Parc du
Saguenay*

G^d Métis
St-Vian
M

St-Félicien
Mashteuiatsh
Roberval
Val-Jalbert
historical village
Metabetchouan

Lac Saint-Jean
Chicoutimi

Ste-Rose-
du-Nord

Sault
au-Mouton
G^{des}
Bergeronnes

Rimouski
*Matapédia
Valley*

la
Baie
l'Anse-
St-Jean Tadoussac

Parc du Bic
l'Île Verte

Causapsca

Port-au-Persil
la Malbaie

Charlevoix

St-Simeon

Trois-Pistoles

Rivière-du-Loup
Notre-Dame-du-Portage
Cap-à-l'Aigle
Ste-Irénée
les Éboulements
St-Joseph-de-la-Rive
l'Île aux Coudres
St-Jean-Port-Joli

NEW
BRUNSV

Baie St-Paul
Ste-Anne-
de-Beaupré

155

QUÉBEC
Montmagny
Île d'Orléans
Lévis

40

Trois-Rivières

Berthierville

Sorel

MONTRÉAL

20

51

10

Kin
Lan

U. S. A.

100 km

100 miles

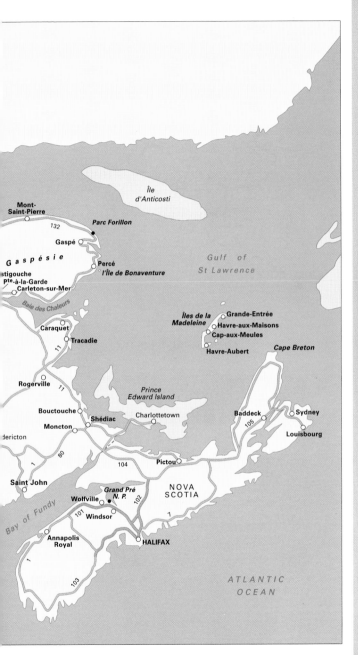

THE MARITIME PROVINCES

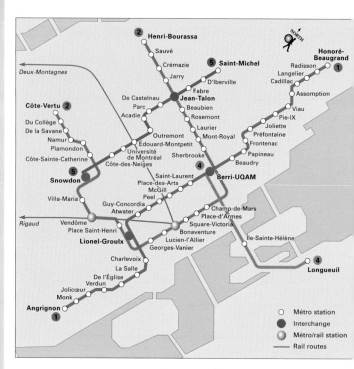

MONTRÉAL – MÉTRO

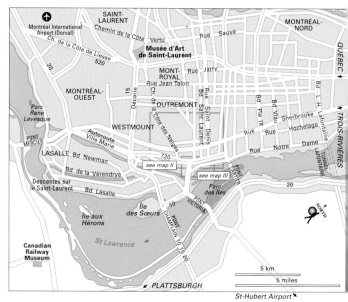

MONTRÉAL – (MAP I)

■ **Useful Addresses**

🏠 Infotouriste
🚌 Bus station
🚆 Railway station
2 Bell Canada
6 American Express
7 Banque Royale (Visa)
9 Air Canada
10 Aux Quatre Points Cardinaux
11 Bicycletterie J.R.
12 Café McGill
13 Cyberground Café
14 Café Électronique
15 Allô Copie

🛏 **Where to Stay**

20 Auberge de Jeunesse de Montréal
23 YMCA
24 YWCA
25 Collège Français
26 McGill
27 Hôtel Dynastie
28 Hôtel L'Abri du Voyageur
29 Hôtel Pierre and Hôtel Manoir
   Sherbrooke
31 La Maison Jaune
32 La Dormance
33 Gîte touristique du Centre-Ville
34 B&B chez Christian Alacoque
36 Auberge Chez Jean
38 Hôtel Le Breton
39 Castel Saint-Denis
40 Le Taj Mahal -Thrift Lodge
41 Le Gîte du Parc Lafontaine
42 Chez Marine Berthou
43 L'Auberge de La Fontaine
44 Auberge des Glycines
45 Manoir Ambrose
46 Hôtel de Paris
47 B&B Centre-Ville-Downtown-
   Network
48 Gîte du Passant L'Urbain
49 Les Studios du Quartier Latin
50 Le Zèbre
51 B&B À l'Adresse du Centre
53 Gîte du Passant Chez François
54 Gîte La Cinquième Saison
55 B&B Roger Bontemps
56 B&B Le Chat Bleu
57 La Maison du Jardin

✕ **Where to Eat**

61 Da Giovanni
62 Le Jardin de Panos
63 Ben's Delicatessen
64 Basha
65 Bar B'Barn
66 Biddle's
67 Spirite Lounge
68 Iza
69 Le Nil Bleu

70 La Paryse
71 Le Petit Extra
72 Mikado
73 Le Commensal
76 Schwartz's
77 Jano
78 L'Anecdote
79 Porté Disparu
80 Santropol
81 Restaurant Mazurka
82 Le Café Pellerin
83 L'Express
84 Place Milton
85 Laloux
86 Wilensky
87 Maison de l'Original Fairmount Bagel
88 Beauty's
89 La Petite Ardoise
90 El Zaziummm
91 Galaxie
92 Shezan
93 Cafétéria
94 Primadonna
95 Quartier Saint-Louis
96 Chez Gautier
97 Le Jardin de Jade
98 Cristal Saigon
99 Pho Minh

🍸 **Where to Have a Drink**

100 Spectrum
101 Les Foufounes Électriques
102 Café Chaos
103 Jello Bar
104 Cock and Bull
106 Métropolis
107 Groove Society
111 Le Di Salvio
113 Le Swimming
114 Café Central
115 Whisky Café
116 Café Zazou
117 Le Saint-Sulpice
118 Le Peel Pub
119 La Salsathèque
120 Tokyo Bar
121 Sugar
122 Le Saphir
123 Le Diable Vert
124 Le Belmont
125 Le Kokkino

★ **What to See**

130 Musée des Beaux-Arts
131 Musée d'Art Contemporain
132 Centre Canadien d'Architecture
133 Cinémathèque Québécoise, Musée
   du Cinéma
134 Musée Juste pour Rire
135 Musée McCord d'Histoire
   Canadienne
136 Centre Molson
137 Dow Planetarium

MONTRÉAL – MÉTRO AND MAP I

MONTRÉAL – KEY TO MAP II
(See over)

MONTRÉAL (MAP II)

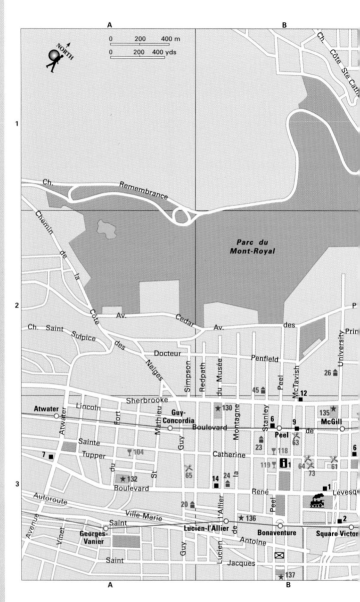

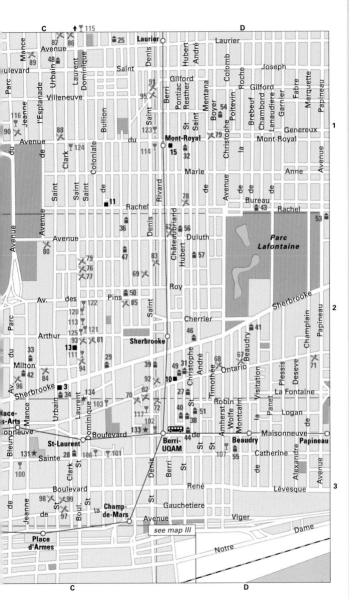

MONTRÉAL (MAP II)

MONTRÉAL – MAP II

MONTRÉAL (MAP III)

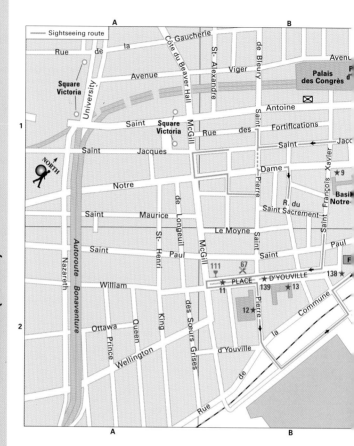

Sightseeing route

Rue de la Gaucherie
Côte du Beaver Hall
St-Alexandre
de Bleury
Avenu
Palais des Congrès
Square Victoria
University
Avenue
Viger
Antoine
⊠
Saint Square Victoria
McGill
Rue des
Fortifications
Saint
Jacc
Saint Jacques
NORTH
Dame
Saint François
Xavier
★9
Notre
de Longeuil
Pierre
Basi Notre-
Saint Maurice
R. du Saint Sacrement
Saint
Paul
Saint Le Moyne
Le Moyne
Saint
McGill
Saint
Paul
F
Autoroute Bonaventure
Nazareth
St-Henri
Paul
111
67
★ D'YOUVILLE
138★
William
★ PLACE
139 ★13
Commune
11
Pierre
12★
Ottawa
Prince
Queen
King
des Sœurs Grises
d'Youville
la
Wellington
de
Rue

■	**Useful Addresses**
🅗	Tourist information
📮	Post Office
1	Ça roule Montréal

✕	**Where to Eat**
67	La Gargote
68	Le Grill
69	Menara

🍷	**Where to Have a Drink**
108	Le Jardin Nelson
109	Les Deux Pierrots
110	Auberge du Vieux Port
111	Union

★	**What to See**
138	Musée d'Archéologie et d'Histoire Pointe-à-Callière
139	Centre d'Histoire de Montréal

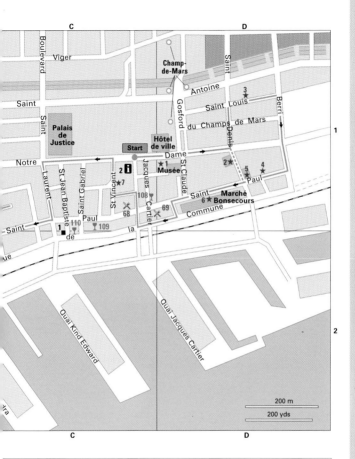

MONTRÉAL (MAP III)

★ What to See in Vieux Montréal

1 Château de Ramezay
2 Maison Papineau
3 Rue Saint-Louis
4 Maison Dumas
5 Maison du Calvet
6 Marché Bonsecours
7 Maison Beaudoin
8 Place d'Armes
9 Vieux Séminaire

10 Basilique Notre-Dame
11 Place d'Youville
12 Hôpital Général des Sœurs Grises
13 Les Écuries d'Youville

MONTRÉAL (MAP III)

QUÉBEC (MAP I)

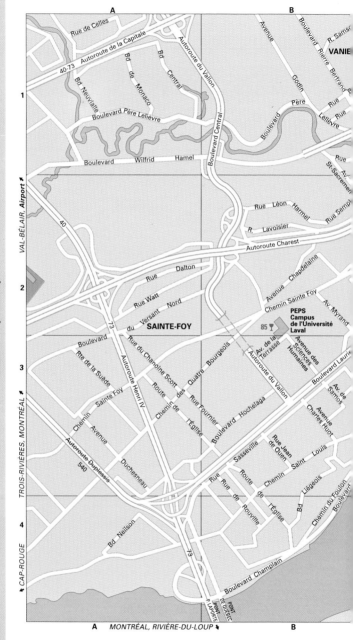

VAL-BÉLAIR, Airport

TROIS-RIVIÈRES, MONTRÉAL

CAP-ROUGE

A

B

Rue de Celles

Autoroute de la Capitale

Autoroute du Vallon

40-73

Bd Neuville

Bd de Monaco

Bd Central

Boulevard Père Lelièvre

Boulevard Central

VANIE

Boulevard Pierre Bertrand

R. Samso

Avenue

Godin

Père

Boulevard

Rue Lelièvre

Rue

1

Boulevard Wilfrid Hamel

Rue St-Sacrement

Rue Léon Harmel

Rue Sempl

R. Lavoisier

Autoroute Charest

40

Rue Dalton

Rue Watt

du Versant Nord

73

SAINTE-FOY

Avenue Chapdelaine

Chemin Sainte Foy

Av Myrand

PEPS
Campus
de l'Université
Laval

85

Av. de la Terrasse

Avenue des
Sciences
Humaines

2

Boulevard

Rte de la Suède

Autoroute Henri IV

Rue du Chanoine Scott

Rue des Quatre Bourgeois

Autoroute du Vallon

Boulevard Laurie

Av de Samos

Chemin Sainte Foy

Route des

Rue Fournier

Chemin de l'Église

Boulevard Hochelaga

Avenue Charles Huot

Rue Jean de Quen

Saint Louis

3

Avenue

Duchesneau

Autoroute Duplessis

540

Sasseville

Rue Rue de Rouville

Route de l'Église

Chemin

Bd Liégeois

Chemin du Foulon

Boulevard

Bd Neilson

73

4

Boulevard Champlain

PONT DE QUÉBEC

PONT P. LAPORTE

A

MONTRÉAL, RIVIÈRE-DU-LOUP

B

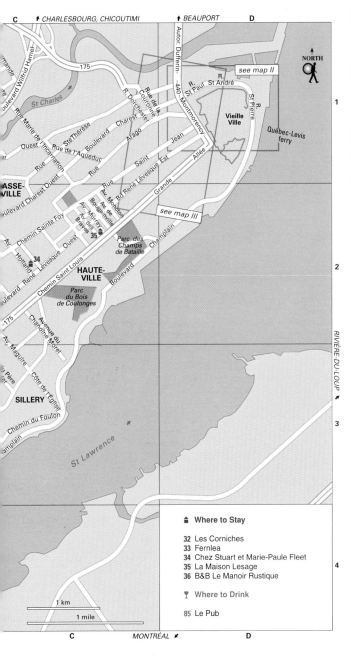

QUÉBEC (MAP I)

C ↑ *CHARLESBOURG, CHICOUTIMI* ↑ *BEAUPORT* **D**

see map II

NORTH

St Charles

Vieille Ville

Québec-Levis ferry

see map III

ASSE-VILLE

HAUTE-VILLE

Parc des Champs de Bataille

Parc du Bois de Coulonges

34

35

SILLERY

St Lawrence

RIVIÈRE-DU-LOUP

1

2

3

4

⌂ **Where to Stay**

32 Les Corniches
33 Fernlea
34 Chez Stuart et Marie-Paule Fleet
35 La Maison Lesage
36 B&B Le Manoir Rustique

🍷 **Where to Drink**

85 Le Pub

1 km

1 mile

C *MONTRÉAL* ↙ **D**

QUÉBEC (MAP I)

QUÉBEC (MAP II)

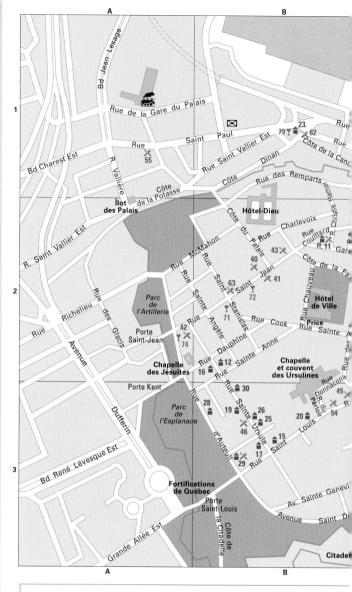

Bassin Louise

NORTH

Saint André
int Rioux Paul
R. 53 57 61
Sous le Cap
Rue des Remparts 56
14
Hébert
R. de l'Université
Séminaire
Archevéché
Chapelle
Basilique
O.-de-Québec) Parc
Je Buade Montmorency
du Trésor
1
h. du Fort
gl. Porte
PLACE Prescott
D'ARMES Escalier
Casse-Cou
Louis funicular
railway
Château
Frontenac 73
27
Mont-
Carmel
Parc des
Gouverneurs
21

BO

Prince de Galles

Rue Saint
Rue
Saint Jacques
Rue du Sault-au-Matelot

38
Musée
de la
Civilisation

Rue
St Antoine

Rue Saint Pierre

44
Montagne
R. du Porche

Dalhousie

Rue Notre Dame

PLACE
ROYALE
N.-D.-des-
Victoires
PL. DE
PARIS
78
R. du Marché
Champlain

Maison
Chevalier

59

R. du Petit Champlain

Champlain

Boulevard

Promenade
des
Gouverneurs

Dufferin

Terrasse

Haldimand

St Lawrence

Ferry

200 m
200 yds

C   D

QUÉBEC (MAP II)

	Where to Eat	46	Le Saint-Amour		Where to Have a Drink
1	Chez Temporel	53	Buffet de l'Antiquaire		
9	Apsara	54	Le Figaro	71	Chez Son Père
40	Casse-Crêpe Breton	55	Pizza Mag	72	Les Yeux Bleus
41	Café-restaurant Le	56	Asia	73	Bar Saint-Laurent
	Rétro	57	Le Saint-Malo	74	La Fourmi Atomique
42	Le Petit Coin Latin	59	Le Lapin Sauté	78	Bistrot Le Pape
43	Les Frères de la Côte	61	L'Ardoise		Georges
44	L'Initiale	62	Le Péché Véniel	79	Belley
45	Aux Anciens Canadiens	63	La Crémaillère	80	L'Inox

QUÉBEC (MAP II)

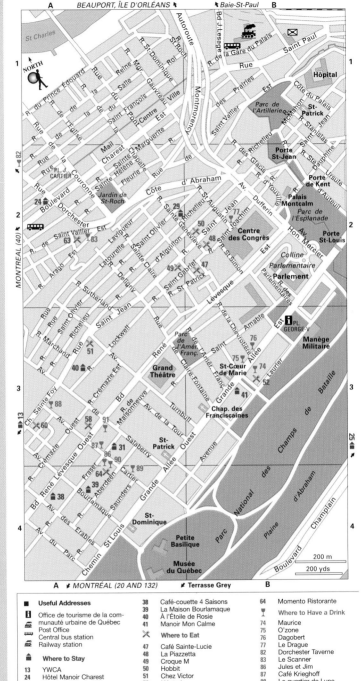

QUÉBEC (MAP III)

BEAUPORT, ÎLE D'ORLÉANS

Baie-St-Paul

MONTRÉAL (40)

MONTRÉAL (20 AND 132)

Terrasse Grey

QUÉBEC (MAP III)

	Useful Addresses
	Office de tourisme de la communauté urbaine de Québec
	Post Office
	Central bus station
	Railway station

Where to Stay

13 YWCA
24 Hôtel Manoir Charest
25 Hayden's Wexford House
29 L'Heure Douce
31 Chez Mimi

38 Café-couette 4 Saisons
39 La Maison Bourlamaque
40 À l'Étoile de Rosie
41 Manoir Mon Calme

Where to Eat

47 Café Sainte-Lucie
48 La Piazzetta
49 Croque M
50 Hobbit
51 Chez Victor
52 L'Astrale
58 Le Cochon Dingue
60 Les Crêpes Celtiques
63 L'impasse des Deux Anges

64 Momento Ristorante

Where to Have a Drink

74 Maurice
75 O'zone
76 Dagobert
77 Le Drague
82 Dorchester Taverne
83 Le Scanner
86 Jules et Jim
87 Café Krieghoff
88 Le quartier de Lune
89 Le Merlin
90 Pub Java
91 Qué Sera

▲ **Auberge Larochelle**: 68 rue Principale. ☎ 665-4622. Fax: 665-7833. Website: www.quebecweb.com/larochelle. Doubles from $115 a night. Tucked away at the bottom of a garden, this charming wood-and-brick house is kept in immaculate condition by the lovely couple that own it. There are 10 large, well-designed rooms with thick carpets, most of which have whirlpool baths; the most expensive one also has a fireplace. Hearty breakfasts are served in the large dining room.

▲ **Auberge Au Petit Berger**: 1 côte Bellevue, on Route 362, at the end of a long drive lined with trees. ☎ 665-4428 or 1-800-314-4428. Fax: 665-2343. Website: www.quebecweb.com/petitberger. Doubles from $95, including breakfast. Booking recommended. This is a traditional 1890s house in a huge garden, with elegant yet rustic decor. The five en-suite rooms in the main house are spotless, smart and spacious, though they're furnished in a slightly haphazard way. There are also several annexes with en-suite rooms, some with fireplaces, whirlpool baths and views of the river. Guests can use the swimming pool and the tennis court.

WHAT TO SEE

★ **Musée de Charlevoix**: 1 chemin du Havre. ☎ 665 4411. Open 10am–6pm in season; otherwise Tuesday–Friday, 10am–5pm (1–5pm on weekends). Admission $4. This museum houses a permanent exhibition of paintings, crafts, sculptures and *objets d'art* by local artists, as well as temporary shows about Charlevoix. The region's history is explained in a display in the building's rotunda, and there's a beautiful view from the terrace.

WHAT TO DO

– **Lighthouse and wildlife cruises**: Croisières aux Sentinelles du Saint-Laurent (☎ 665-3666) organizes cheap trips on large boats (May to October only). The trips last 3 hours, and leave at 8.30am, 11.45am and 3pm, but don't expect to see any of those elusive blue whales.

LA MALBAIE Pop: 5,000   DIALLING CODE: 418

The name means 'evil bay', but this is a pleasant little town near Pointe-au-Pic.

USEFUL ADDRESSES

🛈 **Association Touristique de Charlevoix**: 630 boulevard de Comporte. ☎ 665-4454. Open 8.30am–9pm in summer; otherwise 8.30am–4.30pm. The staff at this tourist office are very professional and knowledgeable.

🚌 **Bus station**: Dépanneur OTIS, 46 rue Sainte-Catherine. ☎ 665-2264. There are three buses a day to Québec (the journey takes 1 hour 45 minutes) and two buses a day to Tadoussac, one in the morning and one in the evening.

WHERE TO STAY

⚑ **Camping Chutes Fraser**: 500 chemin de la Vallée, 5 kilometres (3 miles) from La Malbaie. ☎ 665-2151. From Pointe-au-Pic, cross the river and turn left, then go straight on for about 3 kilometres (2 miles), until you reach the Jovi-P.E. Neron grocery store; the campsite entrance is on the right, and the reception is in the shop. If you're coming from the north, turn right before the bridge and it's signposted from there. Open 15 May to 15 October. Tent pitches $20 a night. This is a stunning setting for a campsite, although it's slightly spoiled by the electricity pylons that run across the hills. You can pitch your tent in the woods, or, if you prefer a little more luxury, stay in a chalet for two or four; these come with a small kitchen, but you have to bring your own sleeping bag. The campsite has a swimming pool, mini-golf, playgrounds, a grocery, a butcher and a launderette, and you can go trout-fishing in the area. If you're not staying here, you can visit the waterfalls or use the pool for a small charge.

⚑ **Camping Au Bord de la Rivière**: 60 boulevard Mailloux, on route 138. ☎ 665-4991. Open from June to early September. Tent pitches $19 a night. Sandwiched between two roads, this site can get rather noisy, but it has good facilities: a heated swimming pool, a small farm with animals that children can feed, mini-golf and shop. You can also rent a chalet.

⚑ **Gîte E.T. Harvey**: 19 rue Laure-Conan. ☎ 665-2779. Doubles $50 a night. Strictly non-smoking. There are three rooms and one communal bathroom in this small house, run by a friendly retired couple. It's within walking distance of the bus station, but the owners will pick you up if you prefer. Breakfast is generous, and guests can use the garden and the small swimming pool at the back.

⚑ **Auberge sur la Côte**: 205 chemin des Falaises, in a residential area overlooking the St Lawrence. ☎ 665-3972. Fax: 665-3231. Website: www.charlevoix.qc.ca/surlacote. Doubles from $95 a night; honeymoon suite $145. This charming building, erected in 1908, has nine tastefully decorated en-suite rooms, some with a Provençal touch, and a blue-carpeted sitting room with attractive white rattan furniture. The dining room has a central fireplace, and the food is delicious. This is an excellent place to stay, and if you want a bit more peace and quiet, you can rent one of the small villas, all of which are surrounded by greenery.

WHERE TO EAT

✕ **Restaurant Allegro**: 53 rue Nairn. ☎ 665-2595. Open 11am–2pm and 5pm–10pm; dinner only on weekends. Main courses from $8. Despite its smart appearance, this place serves cheap and delicious homemade pasta, lasagne and pizza. The food more than makes up for the rather sterile decor.

WHAT TO SEE

★ **Forge Riverin**: 218 rue Saint-Étienne, ☎ 665-2333. This old forge, managed by the same family for three generations, has been open to visitors since the 19th century. The grandfather, who still lives there, makes a variety of wrought-iron birds.

IN THE AREA

★ **Chutes Fraser** (Fraser waterfall): 5 kilometres (3 miles) from La Malbaie. Enter the Fraser campsite (there's an admission fee) and follow the road for 2 kilometres (1 mile). These huge waterfalls cascade spectacularly down rock steps. There are two car-parks, one above the waterfall and one below, and you'll find plenty of picnic tables in the area.

CAP-À-L'AIGLE Pop: 720   DIALLING CODE: 418

Despite its location below the highway, this is a pleasant, peaceful farming village that has hardly changed since the 19th century, except for the somewhat incongruous addition of a modern church. The pretty fields spread up into the surrounding hills, the locals are friendly and there are several great places to stay. Look out for the elegant **Ferme Cabot**, just off the road before you reach Cap-a-l'Aigle. In the village itself, it's worth visiting the **Grange Bhérer** at 215 rue Saint-Raphael, which was built in 1830. Take a look, too, at the delightful red church next door.

WHERE TO STAY AND EAT

☆–☆☆ Budget to Moderate

⚓ **Chez Claire Villeneuve**: 215 rue Saint-Raphaël, overlooking the river. ☎ 665-2288. Doubles from $50 a night. The five rooms in this long green-and-white house are pretty basic, but they're all clean and cheap.

⚓ **La Mansarde**: 187 rue Saint-Raphaël (the main street). ☎ 665-2750. Fax: 665-7216. Open June to mid-October. Doubles $55–75 a night. This beautiful old house, built in the first half of the 19th century and still surrounded by four hectares (10 acres) of land, once belonged to rich farmers. The seven bedrooms are decorated in floral, rustic style, and have basins or en-suite bathrooms. If you're looking for more basic accommodation, you can stay in an atmospheric rustic house at No. 451 on the same street; it's owned by the same people, and it's less expensive.

⚓ **La Maison Victoria**: 726 rue Saint-Raphaël. ☎ 665-1022. Doubles $60-70 a night, including breakfast. This pretty, flower-covered B&B has a superb view of the St Lawrence. There are five rooms, and guests can unwind in the quiet garden or admire the 100-year-old trees.

☆☆☆☆ Splash Out

⚓ ✕ **L'Auberge des Peupliers**: 381 rue Saint-Raphaël. ☎ 665-4423 or 1-888-282-3743 (toll-free). Fax: 665-3179. Website: www.que becweb.com/peupliers. Half-board $180 a night (obligatory in high season). One of the largest guesthouses in Québec, this elegant, cosy old place has been welcoming visitors for decades, and has a reputation for excellent hospitality and top-notch food. The rooms have all mod cons, and some have en-suite bathrooms with large baths, while the comfortable, air-conditioned dining room is full of old-fashioned Québécois furniture, including a beautiful piano. The *table d'hôte* features Charlevoix specialities: *pâté de foie maison*, cream of vegetable soup and fried caribou in a spicy caramel sauce. Finish your meal with a delicious selection of cheeses, dessert and tea. To work up an appetite (or make up for all that overindulgence), you can play tennis or volleyball in the garden. Or perhaps a leisurely game of croquet is more your style . . .

PORT-AU-PERSIL   DIALLING CODE: 418

Most people drive straight past Port-au-Persil, but it's one of the prettiest villages in Charlevoix, with a charming little port and a waterfall tumbling into the harbour. On the far side, you'll come across a chapel built in 1897. It's definitely worth a visit if you want to get away from it all.

WHERE TO STAY AND EAT

☆☆ Moderate

⌂ **Gîte L'Oasis du Port**: 535 route de Port-au-Persil. ☎ 638-5101. Doubles $50–60 a night. If your idea of paradise is sleeping in a small portside house, with water gently rippling onto the shore, a fantastic view and a nearby rocky island, then this is the place for you. The wooden gîte is simple, inexpensive and quietly elegant. There are five rooms, some with basins, and one large room on the ground floor with a huge bay window and an adjoining bathroom. It's a delightful, peaceful place to stay, and the owner is extremely helpful.

⌂ ✕ **Auberge de la Petite Madeleine**: 400 Route de Port-au-Persil, on the way to Saint-Simeon. ☎ and fax: 638-2460. Half-board $125 a night. Booking recommended. This cosy, peaceful guesthouse has a veranda and fine views of river and the surrounding area. The 15 small-ish rooms are pretty and inviting, with a separate bathroom for those on the ground floor. The evening *table d'hôte* offers a choice of delicious regional dishes, all served in large quantities (there are usually two dinner sittings, one at 6pm and the other at 8pm), while there's wonderful homemade bread for breakfast.

⌂ **Gîte Gens du Pays**: 490 Route de Port-au-Persil. ☎ 638-2717. Doubles from $40 a night. The rooms here are simple, elegant and clean, and you can sometimes see whales from your window. The motherly (or grandmotherly) owner, Bertrande, is very attentive, and cooks an excellent breakfast. Children's beds are also available.

WHAT TO SEE

★ **Pottery**: 1001 rue Saint-Laurent, on route 138. ☎ 638-2349. Open late June to September, 9am–6pm. Guided tours available. There's a display of beautiful earthenware crafts in a huge yellow shed.

IN THE AREA

★ **Centre Écologique de Port-au-Saumon**: between Saint-Fidèle and Port-au-Persil, next to the St Lawrence. ☎ 434-2209. Open 1 July to 31 August (except for 24 and 25 July and 7 August). Admission $5. Guided tours at 10am and 2pm. This open-air environmental centre offers a host of outdoor activities, including nature walks and marine observation.

SAINT-SIMÉON Pop: 1,020   DIALLING CODE: 418

At Saint-Siméon, the roads from Québec meet those from Saguenay and the north, and there's a ferry to Rivière-du-Loup, on the south bank of the St Lawrence. The town is the region's smelt capital, a fact celebrated by an annual festival in honour of the fish, which takes place in mid-July. For the rest of the year, there's very little to do here.

USEFUL ADDRESSES

🛈 Tourist Information: 135 rue Saint-Laurent (on the main road). Open from late June to early September, 9am–7pm.

🚌 Buses: you can buy tickets at Garage Irving, on the outskirts of the village as you head for Chicoutimi. The bus stop is at the L'Horizon restaurant (775 rue Saint-Laurent); there are three buses a day to Québec.

WHERE TO STAY AND EAT

You should only stay in one of the establishments on the main street as a last resort.

🛌 Camping Lévesque: 3 kilometres (2 miles) from Saint-Siméon, on the road to Tadoussac. ☎ 638-2290. Information and bookings: 400 rue Saint-Laurent in Saint-Siméon. Open early May to mid-October. Tent pitches $13 a night. At the end of a grassy track, this fairly wild site is right beside the sea, and there's a chance that you might spot whales from your tent. Facilities include showers, toilets and a laundrette, and you can buy basic supplies such as bread, milk, butter and eggs.

🛌 ✕ Auberge-sur-Mer: 109 rue du Quai. ☎ 638-2674 or 665-7251. Open 15 May to 15 October. Doubles from $75 a night. The rooms in this big blue-and-white motel are slightly sterile, but they're spacious and comfortable, and all have en-suite bathrooms, phones and views of the bay. The rooms for four offer particularly good value. There's a large, bright sitting room, and the hotel restaurant, in the building opposite, offers fairly basic fish dishes and snacks.

🛌 Rose-Aimée Tremblay: Couette et Café, 429 rue Saint-Laurent, near the landing point. ☎ 638-2416. Doubles from $45 a night. This friendly riverside B&B has four spotless, though slightly dated, rooms, a garden and a sitting room with views of the river. Breakfast is huge, and there's a car-park.

WHERE TO STAY IN THE AREA

🛌 Gîte de la Baie: 68 rue de la Chapelle, Baie-des-Rochers, 16 kilometres (10 miles) north of Saint-Siméon. ☎ 638-2821. Doubles from $45 a night. If you're driving, take route 138 through a spectacular stretch of countryside that's dotted with tiny lakes. Turn right at Baie-des-Rochers, and you'll see the green-and-white gîte a few hundred metres farther on. There are five modern, comfortable rooms, the most expensive of which have en-suite bathrooms. This house was restored by the owner, Maurice, who was born and raised here, along with his 10 siblings, and it's a wonderful place to enjoy the peace and quiet of the beautiful Baie des Rochers.

THE SAINT-SIMÉON–RIVIÈRE-DU-LOUP FERRY

– The crossing, on the *Trans Saint-Laurent*, takes just over an hour. For information, ☎ (418) 638-2856 (in Saint-Siméon), ☎ (418) 862-5094 (for a pre-recorded message), ☎ (418) 862-9545 (in Rivière-du-Loup) and ☎ (514) 849-4466 in Montréal. Visa cards accepted. There's no guaranteed booking, so arrive at least one hour before the departure time in summer. On the boat, you'll find a small tourist office, a restaurant and a children's play area. There usually five crossings a day in July and August, but check the times and frequency before you get there.

WHAT TO SEE AND DO IN THE AREA

★ **Baie des Rochers**: this pretty bay is 20 kilometres (about 12 miles) north of Saint-Siméon. From Baie-des-Rochers, turn right and follow the road, which becomes a track, until you reach the end. The views and surroundings are wonderful, and there are several footpaths.

– **Ranch La Licorne**: 1810 route 138, between Cap-à-L'Aigle and Saint-Siméon. ☎ 638-2359. You can hire a horse for an hour and go riding in the forest, accompanied by a guide. A paddock has been set aside for children. There's also a gîte here.

– **Centre d'Interprétation et d'Observation de Pointe-Noire**: on route 138, in Baie-Sainte-Catherine. ☎ 237-4383. From mid-June to early September, open 9am–6pm; from early September to mid-October, open Friday to Sunday, 9am–5pm. The Pointe-Noire promontory, in the heart of the Saguenay Marine Park, is one of the best places in the world to spot beluga and minke whales. There's an observation point near the centre, and in summer naturalists give regular talks about the area's wildlife. The centre itself contains displays about the confluence of the Saguenay and St Lawrence rivers.

– **Whale-watching**: two companies, both based in Tadoussac, organize whale-spotting boat trips from Baie-Sainte-Catherine in high season. Contact Famille Dufour (☎ 237-4421) or AML (☎ 237-4274).

WHERE TO STAY IN BAIE-SAINTE-CATHERINE

🏠 **Gîte du Passant Entre Mer et Monts**: 476 route 138, 4 kilometres (2.5 miles) before the landing point for the ferry to Tadoussac. ☎ and fax: 237-4391/4252. Doubles $45 a night. This good-value gîte has five clean, pretty rooms, three of them on the lower ground floor, and you can get an evening meal if you ask in advance. You'll get a warm welcome from your hosts, Anne-Marie and her husband, Réal, who makes excellent blueberry pancakes (the recipe is a closely guarded secret), and you can also buy tickets for whale-watching boat trips.

Inland Charlevoix

Charlevoix is famous for its coast, but it's well worth visiting the inland area as well. It's a land of gently rolling hills, dark woods surrounded by lush pastures, long plateaus and fertile valleys dotted with pretty farms. The area is a magnet for painters, photographers and other artists, who flock here from all over for inspiration, and you can spend hours wandering along the country lanes in Saint-Hilarion or soaking up the lovely, unspoiled atmosphere.

★ **Parc Régional des Hautes-Gorges-de-la-Rivière-Malbaie**: 44 kilometres (27 miles) north of Malbaie. ☎ 439-4402 or 665-4454. By car, take route 138 through Saint-Aimé-des-Lacs, then follow the signs along route de la ZEC des Martres. The river valley runs between steep rock faces, some of which are 700 metres (2,000 feet) high, so fantastic views are guaranteed. A network of old tracks once used by foresters has been converted into cycle paths, so you can pedal along peacefully while admiring the varied landscape and fascinating plant life. You can also rent dinghies in the park. You can easily spend a whole day here, and it's a great place for a picnic – though the ground gets very muddy when it rains. From mid-June to mid-October, Croisières Hautes Gorges runs cruises on the Malbaie River (☎ 665-7527).

★ **Monts-Grands-Fonds**: these remote mountains, 15 kilometres (9 miles) from La Malbaie, are home to a quiet, friendly ski resort. In winter, this spectacular area is perfect for cross-country skiing, while in summer, it's perfect walking terrain.

★ **Saint-Aimé-des-Lacs**: follow route 138 north from Baie-Saint-Paul to reach this peaceful lakeside holiday resort, where swimming and windsurfing are among the activities on offer.

WHERE TO STAY AND EAT

🛏 **Nadeau Provençale**: 193 rue Principale, Saint-Aimé-des-Lacs. ☎ 439-5402. Lakeside chalets sleeping up to 10 cost $1,100 a week.

🛏 ✕ **Auberge de la Miscoutine**: 62 rang 2, route Notre-Dame-des-Monts, Saint-Agnès. This friendly guesthouse and restaurant offers several activities. The rooms, however, are pretty basic, and a touch pricey.

WHAT TO SEE

★ **Notre-Dame-des-Monts**: from Saint-Aimé-des-Lacs, a spectacular minor road, lined with traditional wooden farmhouses and barns, zigzags through the highest peaks in the region, then drops down into the valleys. The village itself is tucked away in a dip in the mountains.

★ In **Saint-Urbain**, a small museum (open 9am–4pm; ☎ 639-2210) describes the 160-year history of Notre-Dame-des-Monts. Take route 381 towards Le Parc des Grands-Jardins, 6 kilometres (4 miles) north of the village.

– The 100-kilometre (62-mile) **cross-Charlevoix ski route** starts 15 kilometres (9 miles) from the village. For information, contact the Fédération Québécoise de la Montagne: ☎ (514) 252-3004 or (418) 639-2284.

Saguenay – Lac Saint-Jean

This area, one of Québec's 19 official tourist regions, extends along the Saguenay River and around Lac Saint-Jean, and reveals a completely different side to the province. Tourist attractions include the beautiful Fjord du Saguenay, part of which has been turned into a wildlife park, a Native American reserve, a haunted village and several pretty little hamlets. The lake itself is a bit disappointing, but the two roads that lead to it (from Saint-Siméon and Tadoussac) make the trip worthwhile on their own.

From Saint-Siméon to Lac Saint-Jean

If you're travelling via Charlevoix, take route 170 on the way up to the lake, a spectacular drive that's best enjoyed at a very leisurely pace. On the way back, head for Tadoussac along the north bank of the Saguenay on route 172, or cruise downriver on *La Marjolaine*.

PETIT-SAGUENAY Pop: 900   DIALLING CODE: 418

Petit-Saguenay nestles among the mountains, and its jetty offers one of the prettiest views of the fjord. The village takes its name from the river that runs through it before joining the real Saguenay. There are several footpaths by the river, and as you stroll, you'll see anglers skilfully reeling in salmon.

USEFUL ADDRESS

🖪 **Tourist information**: 126 rue Dumas. ☎ 272-3219. Open late June to late August, 9.30am–7.30pm.

WHERE TO STAY AND EAT

🛏 **Le Club des Messieurs**: by the river. ☎ 272-1169 or 1-877-272-1169 (toll-free). Rooms $40–100 a night. This place has five rooms, sleeping up to eight people, and a campsite with 30 pitches. It's the most authentic, rustic place to stay in the area.

🛏 ✕ **Auberge des Deux Pignons**: 117 rue Dumas, opposite the tourist information kiosk. ☎ 272-3091. Fax: 272-1125. Doubles from $100 a night, including breakfast. The rooms here are a bit too Laura Ashley, but all of them are different, and there's a pleasant garden at the back with views of the mountains. The excellent-value lunch menu ($10) offers the chance to taste several regional specialities.

🛏 **Village-vacances Petit-Saguenay**: 99 chemin Saint-Étienne. ☎ 272-3193. Fax: 272-3193. Email: village@royaume.com. Open late May to mid-October. Chalets from $72 a night. This 'holiday village' has a superb beach and a swimming pool, as well a campsite with 50 pitches. There's a programme of organized activities for children.

L'Auberge du Jardin: 71 boulevard Dumas. ☎ 272-3444 or 1-888-272-3444 (toll-free). Doubles from $72 a night; suites $135. The most expensive of this guesthouse's 12 double rooms have a fireplace, a whirlpool bath and a sitting room. Each additional person staying in the room pays $12, so the more you can pack in, the cheaper it gets.

WHAT TO DO

If you're a fan of the great outdoors, you certainly won't get bored here. The activities on offer range from walking and riding to salmon-fishing in summer, and from snowshoe walks to snowmobile hire in winter. For details, contact the tourist information centre in summer and the hotels in winter. You can buy one-day permits and hire equipment for freshwater salmon-fishing at one of the 30 official (and closely monitored) spots. It's worth taking a guide, as you have to put the fish straight back in the water; the guide can do this without harming the salmon.

– **Fishing**: in the Petit-Saguenay river. ☎ 272-1169 or 1-877-272-1169 (toll-free). A 3-hour starter session, including equipment and guide, costs $49.

– **Rambles**: there's a good choice of routes. The Sentier du Club des Messieur follows the Petit-Saguenay for 8 kilometres (5 miles); the Sentier Les Caps is a 9-kilometre (6-mile) hike from L'Anse Saint-Étienne to L'Anse Petites-Îles, where water taxis await those who can't face the long trudge back; and the longest path covers the 10 kilometres (6 miles) between the quays on the Petit-Saguenay and L'Anse-Saint-Jean.

– **Canot-Détente**: a laid-back dinghy trip along a 10-kilometre (six-mile) stretch of calm water on the Petit-Saguenay. You can also hire dinghies, plus transport and a guide. ☎ 272-1169 or 1-877-272-1169.

– **A walk along the quay**: there's a superb view of the Fjord du Saguenay from the end of the jetty. During the summer solstice, the sun sets exactly in line with the Saguenay river.

– **Guided tours with Sag-Tours**: a good way to discover the fjord's small villages and their heritage, with some stunning views thrown in. ☎ 272-3091/2592.

L'ANSE SAINT-JEAN Pop: 1,250 DIALLING CODE: 418

This delightfully verdant and floral village lies just beyond Petit-Saguenay. Founded in 1838, it was the first pioneer village built on the Saguenay, and it sprawls along the river for 10 kilometres (6 miles). The large covered bridge is a modern construction: the original one collapsed in 1986, and floated all the way down river to the marina quay. There are plenty of good B&Bs in the village, and walkers will enjoy the fabulous views on the Sentier de la Montagne Blanche.

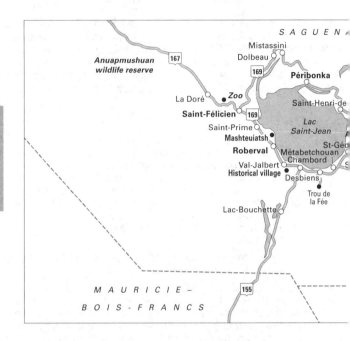

USEFUL ADDRESS

🛈 Tourist information: 17 rue Saint-Jean-Baptiste. ☎ 272-2199. Open late June to early September. In winter, there's a mobile tourist office (☎ 272-2633). The staff here can tell you everything you need to know about the Saguenay and Lac Saint-Jean.

WHERE TO STAY

⌂ Camping de l'Anse: 325 rue Saint-Jean-Baptiste, in the centre of the village. ☎ 272-2554 or 272-2633 (out of season). Open May to October. Tent pitches $17 a night. This riverside site is decidedly up-market, with swimming pools, tennis courts, a croquet lawn, sports equipment, shower blocks and whirlpool baths. It's very popular, and there are few vacant pitches in high season, so booking is a good idea.

⌂ Gîte Le Nid de l'Anse: 376 rue Saint-Jean-Baptiste. ☎ 272-2273.

Email: bilodeauronald@hotmail.com. Open from May to November. Doubles from $60 a night. This beautiful 100-year-old wooden house is a friendly place with attractive decor and superb views. The three rooms are small but pretty, and breakfast is huge.

⌂ La Maison des Lauriers: 7 chemin Saint-Thomas. ☎ 272-2695. From route 170, take rue Saint-Jean-Baptiste, then cross the first bridge on the left; it's on the right. Doubles from $60 a night. This

SAGUENAY – LAC SAINT-JEAN

spotless gîte, formerly a school, is straight out of *Little House on the Prairie*, with beautiful antique furniture and three lovely guest rooms.

⌂ **La Ferme des Trois Cours d'Eau**: 6 chemin de l'Anse. ☎ 272-2944. Turn left at the church, cross the covered bridge and continue until you see a wooden sign; turn right and it's 50 metres (50 yards) farther on, to your right. Doubles $55 a night, including breakfast. This delightful, quiet guesthouse, on a dairy farm not far from the Sentier des Caps et des Chutes (*see below*), has three simple, clean and comfortable first-floor rooms with wood panelling. The toilets are on the landing. Room No. 2 overlooks the Saguenay, the terrace has a lovely view over the fjord, and you can watch the boats go by from the dining room. The huge breakfasts are made with delicious farm produce, including ham, eggs and homemade bread and jam.

⌂ **Le Gîte Le Globe-Trotter**: 131 rue Saint-Jean-Baptiste. ☎ 272-2353. Email: andred@hotmail.com. Website: www.bbcanada.com/322.html. Doubles from $60 a night, including breakfast. This friendly guesthouse is near the road, so there's a bit of traffic noise, but it has lovely views of the river and wooded mountains at the rear. The three peaceful rooms are bright and airy, and you can sunbathe on the terrace or lawn.

⌂ **Le Gîte du Capitaine**: 274 rue Saint-Jean-Baptiste, near the church. ☎ and fax: 272-4444. E-mail: gdc.royaume@qc.aira.com. Doubles from $50 a night. If you're wondering about the name, this place was once owned by a retired sea captain, who built the house himself in 1920. Predictably, the four first-floor rooms are done up in nautical style, but there's a more interesting bit of heritage in one of the two bathrooms: the first bath to arrive in L'Anse-Saint-Jean. If the shipshape styling makes you uncomfortable, you can sit in the pleasant lounge or admire the fjord from the balcony. If you want to go whale-spotting, the owner will take you out on his 9-metre (30-foot) boat.

🛏 **Auberge des Cévennes**: 294 rue Saint-Jean-Baptiste. ☎ 272-3180 or 1-877-272-3180 (toll-free). Fax: 272-1131. Website: www.auberge-des-cevennes.qc.ca. Doubles $50–55 a night; rooms for four $70. This is a restful, reasonably priced guesthouse in an attractive, wood-panelled old house, with eight rooms arranged around a central gallery and excellent views of the fjord. You can hire bikes in summer, while winter guests can hire snowmobiles or go ice-fishing.

WHERE TO EAT

✗ **Le Restaurant de la Marina**: 335 rue Saint-Jean-Baptiste. ☎ 272-2144. Open 8am–11pm; brunch 8am–12.30pm. This friendly restaurant is spacious and beautifully decorated in pale wood, with exposed beams. The food is original and affordable: try *tourtière du Saguenay* (meat pie), prawn kebabs or delicious smoked salmon.

✗ **Auberge des Cévennes**: 294 rue Saint-Jean-Baptiste. ☎ 272-3180. Dinner only. *Table d'hôte* $17–25. The short menu offers tasty dishes such as langoustines in garlic butter, seafood, peppered caribou steak with wild fruit jelly, salmon and guinea fowl.

✗ **Le Maringoinfre**: 212 rue Saint-Jean-Baptiste, in the village centre. ☎ 272-2385 or 1-877-272-2385 (toll-free). Open from 5pm. This cosy, intimate restaurant serves local specialities – grilled meat, game, fish and seafood – and a few Native American dishes.

✗ **Pâtisserie Louise**: 328 rue Saint-Jean-Baptiste. ☎ 272-2611. This is the place to go if you feel like pigging out on delicious cakes and bread, all cooked in a traditional wood-burning oven. During high season, they also serve hot food, including *tourtières* (pies), pizzas, pasta, baked beans and homemade pâté. For dessert, try a fruit tart or blueberry pie. You're spoiled for choice, but you can taste before you buy.

WHAT TO DO

– **Site du 1,000 Dollars**: shelve any thoughts of getting rich quick. This is the place where the picture on Canada's $1,000 bills (which features the covered bridge) was taken. To get there, head towards the Saguenay and take the signposted path on your right, which leads to a visitor centre and an observation point.

– **Le Sentier des Chutes**: follow rue Saint-Thomas Nord until you reach the cemetery and a sign marks the start of this lovely footpath, which takes you through the woods to a waterfall and a superb panoramic viewpoint. If you keep walking, you'll reach the Montagne Blanche ('White Mountain').

– **Horse treks**: from the Centre Équestre des Plateaux, 31 rue des Plateaux. ☎ 272-3231. Open May to October. Three-hour ride $45. A two-day trek, including overnight accommodation and four meals, costs $245; a three-day trip, with two nights' accommodation, seven meals and use of a rowing boat, is $375. Riding lessons for beginners and advanced riders are also available. This is a clean, well-kept riding school with well-trained staff, and the treks take you through the conifers and along the twisting paths that follow the Saguenay. You'll pass old village houses and the famous $1,000-dollar bridge.

– **Kayak trips**: with Fjord en Kayak, Marina de l'Anse-Saint-Jean, 4 rue du Faubourg. ☎ 272-3024. Email: info@fjord-en-kayak.qc.ca. Website: www.fjord-en-kayak.qc.ca. Three-hour trip $39; five-day excursion to Tadoussac $655; discounts for children. You can take a trip to Île Saint-Jean or Île Saint-Louis, or simply mooch about the fjord. A boat will take you back after trips that last two days or more. Thermal underwear is provided, and the guides bring a VHF radio in case of emergencies.

– In the winter, you can go **cross-country** or **downhill skiing** at the Centre Touristique du Mont-Édouard (☎ 272-2927), named after the sixth-highest mountain in Québec. **Ice-fishing** is also available; call the Centre d'Hébergement des Gîtes du Fjord (☎ 272-3430 or 1-800-561-8060 (toll-free)).

– **Aventure Voile et Fjord**: 355 rue Saint-Jean-Baptiste in L'Anse-Saint-Jean. ☎ 272-2144 (387-3983 out of season). Email: joyo@globetrotter.qc.ca. Sailing packages $25–110. Staff take you on 2- to 7-hour trips where you'll learn how to handle the sails, take the helm and use navigational instruments. It's a fun, easy way to learn the basics of sailing.

PARC DU SAGUENAY

The entrance to this national nature conservation park is at **Rivière-Éternité**, on route 170, 65 kilometres (40 miles) before you get to Chicoutimi. ☎ 544-7388. Open late May to early September, 8am–7pm. Admission $7 per car. This huge park, which stretches from La Baie des Ha! Ha! ('*ha! ha!*' means 'cove' in Old French) to Tadoussac, is home to one of Québec's most beautiful natural sites: a fantastic fjord through which the Saguenay flows on its way to a merger with the salty waters of the St Lawrence. It's a stunning geological and marine phenomenon, and is unique in Québec. The fertile waters attract a variety of marine animals, including baleen whales (which do not venture into the fjord, but eat the rich supply of plankton from the estuary around Tadoussac) and beluga whales, which are present in considerable numbers in the Saguenay River. To cap it all, the fjord is also lined with lush forests.

The fjord is at its most spectacular in the Rivière-Éternité section of the park: around La Baie Éternité, the steep walls of Cap Éternité and Cap Trinité soar to a height of more than 300 metres (1,000 feet) above the water, which is about 300 metres deep at this point. The forest is crisscrossed by 30 kilometres (19 miles) of footpaths that lead to superb viewing points over the fjord.

WHERE TO STAY AND EAT

⬧ ✕ **Centre d'Hébergement Touristique de Rivière-Éternité**: the accommodation office for this area is at the entrance to the park. ☎ 272-3008 or 1-877-272-5229 (toll-free). Open 8am–4.30pm. Doubles in the motel $40 a night. Chalets (with fridge, stove, fireplace and bedding) for four to eight people $130 a night in high season; reductions in low season (May to mid-June and mid-October to mid-December). Staying here in winter is the best way to find out what life in Québec is really all about: activities on offer include ice-fishing and skiing, and you can work on a maple grove during the syrup-tapping season. The restaurant serves good-quality traditional food and snacks.

Campsites

⬧ **Camping Rivière-Éternité**: in the park itself, on the chemin de Baie-Éternité, 2 kilometres (1 mile) from the fjord. ☎ 1-888-272-3436. Tent pitches $20 a night. There are 16 pitches spread out among the trees and next to the river, and the facilities include a heated shelter, a laundrette, toilets and showers. The site offers guided evening trips to see beavers; book in the morning at the Centre d'Interprétation (*see below*). Film screenings and theatrical events are organized every evening in summer.

⬧ The park is home to several **wilderness camping sites** and **heated shelters**. Everything, including footpaths, is clearly marked on the map that's available at the park entrance.

WHAT TO SEE AND DO

★ **Le Centre d'Interprétation du Parc du Saguenay**: located in the park, 8 kilometres (5 miles) from Rivière-Éternité. The reception is at 71 rang Notre-Dame, in Rivière-Éternité. ☎ 272-2267 (reception) or 272-3027 (Centre d'Interprétation). Open from mid-May to mid-October, 9am–5pm (until 9pm in summer). This excellent visitors' centre has friendly, efficient staff, and slide shows about the park's fauna and flora. You can take a virtual helicopter ride over the fjord, and the nature guides organize a range of educational activities. The centre is also the departure point for the statue hike (*see below*) to Cap de la Trinité.

– You can go **hiking**, **rambling** or **riding** in the park: pick up a leaflet from the visitors' centre. The best hike is the 4-hour round trip to the giant statue of the Virgin Mary on top of Cap de la Trinité, which takes you past managed springs and offers stunning views of the Éternité River. If you're lucky, you'll see marmots, skunks, squirrels and various species of birds; even if you don't, the view from the top of the Cap is unforgettable. Wear sturdy shoes, and even if it's hot, a long-sleeved top to protect yourself from blackflies, which have vicious stings that leave nasty marks on your skin. There's a **shelter** with a huge fireplace but no electricity; make sure you bring a sleeping bag and mosquito repellent. The magnificent Vallée de la Rivière-Éternité, which is home to an astonishing variety of trees, is also worth exploring.

– **Fjord cruises**: a local company, Croisières du Cap-Trinité, runs several trips a day from La Baie-Éternité, near the Centre d'Interprétation. ☎ 272-

2591. The 90-minute cruise costs $18. Credit cards accepted. In May, June and September, there are two cruises a day, one at 11am and the other at 2.30pm; in July and August, there are three trips daily, leaving at 11am, 1.30pm and 3.30pm. The cruise takes you all around the bay, so you can admire the spectacular cliffs of Caps Eternité and Trinité, the Fjord du Saguenay and the statue of the Virgin Mary.

– **Site de la Nouvelle-France**: on Vieux-Chemin, in Saint-Félix-d'Otis, 16 kilometres (10 miles) from Rivière-Éternité. ☎ 544-8027. Fax: 544-9122. Website: www.royaume.com/robenoire. Head towards La Baie, then turn right 2 kilometres (1 mile) before Saint-Félix and take a minor road for 8 kilometres (5 miles) until you see the signposts. Open 11 June to 15 August, 9am–5pm; otherwise, open Friday to Sunday only. Guided tours $10 per person.

This picturesque riverside site at Anse-à-la-Croix was the location for the film *Robe Noire*, a big hit in Québec in 1991, and later for *Shehaweh*. To re-create the Québec of 1634, the film-makers built 24 authentic-looking buildings, including Samuel de Champlain's fort, the Jesuit mission, colonial farms and an Iroquois fort. After the shoot, the site was turned into a tourist attraction. The guided tour takes 1 hour 15 minutes, and is interesting, even if you haven't seen the films.

★ The people of Rivière-Éternité have kept up the tradition of placing life-size **Nativity cribs** in front of their houses. It's a striking sight, with mangers made out of a miscellany of local materials: snow and ice, old pieces of decorated wood, maple or cedar bark, bricks, moose or caribou antlers and cod bones. In late December, the church hall hosts an exhibition of miniature Nativity scenes from all over the world.

LA BAIE Pop: 21,000

In the 1960s, the pulp mills and aluminium works in this industrial town pumped vast amounts of pollution into the Saguenay and St Lawrence rivers. The situation has improved dramatically since then, with the waste now recycled or captured by biofilters, and the townsfolk are extremely friendly and hospitable. You may be surprised to see so many industrial complexes right by the river, but they were built long before the area starting attracting tourists. For an unobstructed view of the area, trek up to the hospital on the hill.

USEFUL ADDRESS

🛈 **Tourist office**: 1171 7e Avenue. ☎ 697-5050 or 1-800-263-2243 (toll-free) (out of season, try ☎ 697-5177). In summer, open 8am–8pm; out of season, open Monday to Friday, 8.30am–4.30pm.

WHERE TO STAY AND EAT

The tourist office has a long list of gîtes, but there's no reason to stay in La Baie unless you want to dine here.

Campsites

♠ ✕ **Camping municipal**: 400 chemin du Patro, in Saint-Félix-d'Otis. ☎ 697-5096. Take route 170 towards L'Anse-Saint-Jean. Open late May to mid-September. Tent pitches $18–25 a night. This delightfully rural lakeside campsite has a beach (with lifeguards), volleyball, games and a fast-food restaurant. Caravan and boat hire is also available.

☆–☆☆ Budget to Moderate

♠ ✕ **Gîte la Grange aux Hiboux**: 521 rue Mars. ☎ 697-6671. Website: www.sympatico.ca/grange. hiboux. Doubles from $50 a night. This fairly basic gîte has five rooms, a small studio that sleeps six and a fast-food terrace restaurant. The owners, who are keen sailors, have set up a small museum of the sea on the premises, and there's a craft shop selling local products.

♠ ✕ **Auberge des Battures**: 6295 boulevard de la Grande-Baie Sud, 20 kilometres (12 miles) from Chicoutimi, between La Baie and Le Parc du Saguenay. ☎ 544-8234 or 1-800-668-8234 (toll-free). Fax: 544-4351. Website: www. auberge-des-battures.qc.ca. Doubles from $100 a night. This barn-like wooden building overlooks the fjord and its own ice-fishing huts. The friendly owner, Georges, organizes several activities, including winter snowmobile and sleigh rides. The food, including breakfast (for which you pay extra), is good but pricey.

♠ ✕ **Gîte de la Basse-cour**: 271 rue Principale, in Saint-Félix-d'Otis, on route 170 between La Baie and L'Anse-Saint-Jean. ☎ 544-8766. Doubles from $45 a night; four-person room $75. *Table d'hôte* $15. Guests stay in the wooden chalet, which has three clean, simple rooms with air-conditioning. The owner, Huguette Morin, tends the garden, bakes her own delicious bread and looks after chickens, ducks and sheep. If you fancy fish for dinner, you can catch it yourself in the large nearby lake; if that sounds too much like hard work, just order dinner from Huguette in the morning.

☆☆☆ Expensive

♠ **Auberge des 21**: 621 rue Mars, La Baie. ☎ 697-2121. Fax: 544-3360. Doubles $78 a night ($110 from 1 July to 18 August); luxury suite $160. Lunch menu $12; evening *table d'hôte* $40–50. This is one of the largest and most expensive hotels in the area, and the suites have whirlpool baths and fireplaces. Its chief attraction, though, is the superb riverside restaurant, which serves regional specialities such as Native American smoked salmon with maple syrup or caribou fillets. It's run by Marcel Bouchard, one of Québec's best chefs and a former director of the Centre de Recherche de Cuisine évolutive de Montréal, a prestigious 'culinary research' organization. The superb Sunday brunch, which includes all the salmon you can eat, costs $16.

WHAT TO SEE

★ **Musée du Fjord**: 3346 boulevard de la Grande-Baie Sud. ☎ 697-5077. From 24 June to 5 September, open 8.30am–5pm (closed mornings on weekends); otherwise 8.30am–noon and 1–5pm (closed mornings on weekends). This museum is devoted to art and ethnography.

★ **Musée de la Défence Aérienne**: on route 170 between Chicoutimi and La Baie. ☎ 677-4000. Open June to August, 9am–5pm. Admission $4. Guided tours can be booked in advance. This is the only museum in Québec devoted to the history of military aviation. The exhibits include several vintage planes.

★ **Observatoire à Saumons**: 3232 chemin Saint-Louis, in the town centre. ☎ 697-5093. Open 15 June to 15 September. Admission $2. This salmon migration and observation point was built to boost the area's salmon population. You can see the fish from less than a metre away through the bay window of the observation post. There's a guided tour and you can have a go at salmon-fishing.

FESTIVALS AND EVENTS

– **La Fabuleuse Histoire d'un Royaume**: ☎ 1-888-873-3333 (toll-free). Fax: 697-5131. Website: www.grandspectacles.com. Shows take place in July and August, Wednesday to Saturday at 8pm. Admission $32; concessions available. Booking recommended. Every summer, 250 volunteer actors re-enact the history of Lac Saint-Jean and its people in 'The Amazing History of a Kingdom', a colourful, highly popular show that has been seen by more than 600,000 people in the past decade. The performances take place in a the huge 2,000-seater hall, and features real horses, cannon fire and a laser show. It's a family event, and it's also a fun way to find out more about the history of the region.

CHICOUTIMI Pop: 63,000   DIALLING CODE: 418

The region's capital is a modern, lively town with a university and a symphony orchestra. The party-loving locals are renowned for their hospitality throughout the year, but the town is at its best in July and August. Chicoutimi is also famous as a place where the female population significantly outnumbers the male.

■ **Useful Address**

🛈 **1** Office du Tourisme (tourist office)

⌂ **Where to Stay**

11 Gîtes La Maison sur la Butte
15 Hôtel Parasol
30 Gîte de la Bernache
31 Gîte du Passant Le Goût de l'Eau
32 Gîte Chez Monik Otis
33 Le Montagnais

34 La Maraîchère du Saguenay
35 Gîte et pension Aux Bons Jardins
36 Gîte du Passant Au Compte-moutons
37 La Maison du Passant, Chez Marie Gagné

★ **What to See**

50 La Pulperie/Maison du Peintre Arthur Villeneuve
52 Village de Sécurité Routière

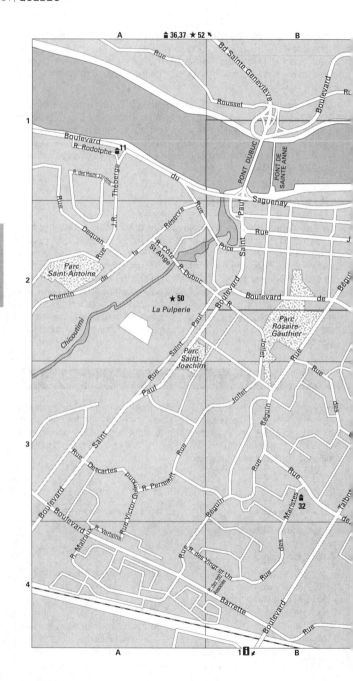

CHICOUTIMI

CHICOUTIMI

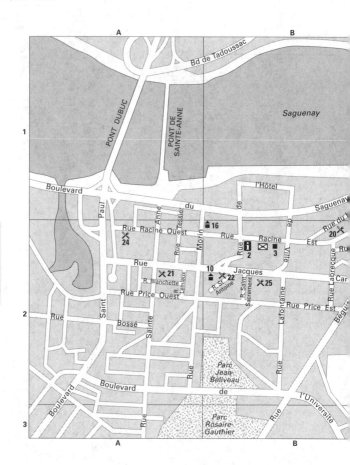

USEFUL ADDRESSES

🛈 **Tourist information**: boulevard Saguenay, near the port. ☎ 698-3254. Open late June to early September, 2.30–5.30pm. A good source of information about the town; there's also a list of 30 Gîtes du Passant.

🛈 **Office du Tourisme** (map I, off B4, **1**): 295 rue Racine Est. ☎ 698-3167. In summer, open 8am–8pm; otherwise 8.30am–noon and 1–4.30pm.

🛈 **Association Touristique du Saguenay–Lac Saint-Jean** (map II, B2, **2**): office 210, 198 rue Racine Est, opposite the town hall. ☎ 543-9778 or 1-800-463-9651 (toll-free). Open Monday to Friday, 8.30am–5pm. The staff here are professional,

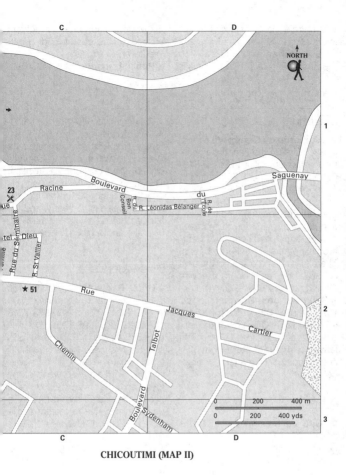

CHICOUTIMI

CHICOUTIMI (MAP II)

■ **Useful Addresses**

🏛 2 Association touristique du
Saguenay – Lac Saint-Jean

3 L'Aventurier

🛏 **Where to Stay**

10 L'Auberge du Centre-Ville
12 La Villa au Pignon Vert
14 Hôtel Chicoutimi
16 Hôtel du Fjord

✕ **Where to Eat**

20 La Cuisine Café-Resto
21 Café Mont Royal
22 La Sauvagine
23 La Tour Saint James Bar
24 Le De Vinci
25 Le Titanic

🍸 **Where to Have a Drink**

40 Guinness Pub

★ **What to See**

51 Musée du Saguenay

and there's plenty of useful tourist information.

■ **L'Aventurier** (map II, B2, **3**): 250 rue Racine Est. ☎ 545-2251. This is the place to find out about outdoor activities in the area, including rafting, kayaking and fishing.

■ **Public transport**: ☎ 545-CITS.

WHERE TO STAY

⊡ Budget

⌂ **L'Auberge du Centre-Ville** (map II, B2, **10**): 104 rue Jacques-Cartier Est, in the centre of town. ☎ 543-0253. Doubles from $60 a night. Although it's singularly lacking in charm, this popular hotel is one of the cheapest in town, and the location is excellent. Some rooms have newly refurbished en-suite bathrooms; others just have basins. There's a bar and disco downstairs, so ask for a quiet room if you're staying during the weekend.

⌂ **Services des Résidences du Collège de Chicoutimi**: ☎ 549-9520 ext. 257. Office open summer only, 8am–noon and 1–4pm. The university halls of residence offer accommodation during the summer holidays.

⊡–⊡⊡ Budget to Moderate

⌂ **Gîte La Maison sur la Butte** (map I, A1, **11**): 684 boulevard Saguenay Ouest. ☎ 549-7128. Take route 3720 towards Jonquière; the gîte is 2 kilometres (1 mile) from the centre of Chicoutimi, on the left-hand side of the road. Doubles from $50 a night, including breakfast. Built on a *butte* (mound), this clean, cosy white house has four rooms, three upstairs and one downstairs, two of which have twin beds. The owners go out of their way to make guests feel at home. Despite the nearby electric pylon and road, it's very quiet, but it's hard to get to unless you have your own transport.

⌂ **La Villa au Pignon Vert** (map II, C2, **12**): 491 rue Jacques-Cartier Est, in the centre. ☎ 545-0257 or 1-800-499-0257 (toll-free). Fax: 545-6184. Email: villapignon@multimania.com. Website: www.multimania.com/villapignon. Doubles from $60 a night. This large, central guesthouse has 10 snug rooms with basins. It's very friendly, breakfast is hearty, and the facilities include a washing machine, bike hire and a crèche. Good value for money.

⊡⊡ Moderate

⌂ **Hôtel Parasol** (map I, D1, **15**): 1287 boulevard Saguenay Est. ☎ 543-7771 or 1-800-363-7248 (toll-free). Fax: 693-1701. Doubles from $75 a night; $10 per extra person. Best reached by car, the hotel consists of three large, white, flower-covered buildings with views of the town and the river. Guests have access to a heated swimming pool, a solarium, a bar, a restaurant and a terrace. It's good value, especially for groups.

⌂ **Hôtel du Fjord** (map II, B2, **16**): 241 rue Morin, near the river. ☎ 543-1538 or 1-888-543-1538 (toll-free). Fax: 543-8253. Website: www.hoteldufjord.qc.ca. Doubles from $75, including breakfast. You can't miss this large, red-brick hotel, which is right in the centre of the town. The decor is stylish, and the rooms, some with terraces overlooking the fjord, are a good size. There's a bar and pool room.

⌂ **Hôtel Chicoutimi** (map II, C2, **14**): 460 rue Racine Est. ☎ 549-7111 or 1-800-463-7930 (toll-free). Fax: 549-0938. Website: www.hotel chicoutimi.qc.ca. Doubles from $80, including breakfast. Popular with businessmen and sales reps, this modern hotel has spotless en-suite rooms with TVs and tele-phones. It's very comfortable, but the decor is rather bland and impersonal.

WHERE TO EAT

☆ Budget

– There are several cheap bars and cafés on **Rue Racine**.

✕ **La Cuisine Café-Resto** (map II, B2, **20**): 387 rue Racine Est. ☎ 698-2822. Open 7am–midnight (from 9am on weekends). *Table d'hôte* $10. There's not much of an atmosphere at this café-bar and *pâtisserie*, but there's a good choice of breakfasts, and the cakes and pastries are delicious.

✕ **Café Mont Royal** (map II, A2, **21**): 6 rue Jacques-Cartier Est, at the corner with rue Sainte-Anne. ☎ 543-6427. Open 4am–7pm. Main courses $5. It doesn't look very appealing, but this restaurant offers cheap, hearty meals and snacks, many served with the ubiquitous baked beans.

☆☆ – ☆☆☆ Moderate to Expensive

✕ **Le De Vinci** (map II, A2, **24**): 42 rue Racine Ouest. ☎ 696-2002. Open Monday to Friday, 11am–4pm. All-you-can-eat buffet $7. This friendly eatery in an old wooden house specializes in delicately prepared vegetarian dishes: nut roast, ratatouille and filo pastry rolls. The desserts, which include papaya cake and pineapple muffins, are also delicious. In summer, soak up the sun on the delightful raised terrace.

✕ **Le Titanic** (map II, B2, **25**): 164 rue Racine Est. ☎ 543-5699. Meals for around $15. No prizes for guessing the theme of the decor here. Tourists and locals alike flock here for fish and seafood dishes. The food is good, if unoriginal, and there's a pleasant outside terrace.

✕ **La Tour (Saint James Bar)** (map II, C1, **23**): 517 rue Racine Est, opposite the cathedral. ☎ 543-1534. Full meal $15. This eatery attracts a mixed clientele: businessmen and office workers who come for the cheap lunchtime *table d'hôte*, and a smart young set who meet for drinks in the evening, when the bar gets quite lively. The terrace is lovely.

✕ **La Sauvagine** (map II, B2, **22**): 122 rue Jacques-Cartier Est. ☎ 690-2255. Open Monday 11am–3pm, Tuesday to Friday 11am–9pm, Saturday 3–10pm and Sunday 10am–1pm. Main courses $14. The decor's nothing special, and the food is neither cheap nor original, but there's a good, cheap *table d'hôte* that winds up with delicious cakes and pastries. Try the gourmet Sunday brunch, a real treat if you like homemade cakes, and try to get a table on the pretty terrace.

WHERE TO STAY AND EAT IN THE AREA

South of the Saguenay River

🛏 **Gîte de la Bernache** (map I, off D1, **30**): rang Saint-Martin, 10 kilometres (6 miles) from the town centre. ☎ 549-4960. Fax: 549-9814. Doubles from $55 a night; $20 for each extra adult. Strictly non-smoking. Take boulevard Talbot, then boulevard de l'Université Est; follow the Saguenay for 800 metres (800 yards), turn right onto rang Saint-Martin and follow the road for 7 kilometres (4 miles). Right on the Fjord du Saguenay, where the Canada geese stop during their biannual migration, this friendly gîte has four brightly coloured rooms and a shared bathroom. In winter, the owner will let you to do a spot of fishing from her riverside hut, and snowmobiles and snowshoes are also available. Breakfast is huge.

♠ **Gîte du Passant Le Goût de l'Eau** (map I, just off D1, **31**): 3483 rang Sainte-Famille, on route 170, 5 kilometres (3 miles) from the centre of town. ☎ 543-6306. You'll get a good welcome and a hearty breakfast at this riverside gîte, which has just two spotless and tastefully decorated rooms.

♠ **Gîte chez Monik Otis** (map I, B3, **32**): 1393 rue des Maristes, 3 kilometres (2 miles) from Chicoutimi

in a residential area. ☎ 549-4765. Doubles $45 a night, including breakfast. The charming elderly couple who run this gîte offer three rooms that share a bathroom on the lower ground floor of their house. The rooms are pretty basic, and have small windows, but they're also very cheap.

♠ **Le Montagnais** (map I, C3, **33**): 1080 boulevard Talbot, 2 kilometres (1 mile) from Chicoutimi on route 175. ☎ 543-1521 or 1-800-463-9160 (toll-free). Fax: 543-2149. Website: www.lemontagnais.qc.ca. Doubles from $70 a night. There are 300 large en-suite rooms at this huge motel; they're a bit dated, and lack charm, but there's nothing wrong with them, and guests can use the indoor and outdoor swimming pools, the sauna and the tennis court. The prices are about right for what you get.

North of the Saguenay River

♠ ✕ **La Maraîchère du Saguenay** (map I, just off C1, **34**): 97 boulevard Tadoussac, in Saint-Fulgence, 8 kilometres (5 miles) from Chicoutimi. ☎ 674-2247. Fax: 674-1055. Email: maraichere.saguenay@qc.aira. com. Website: www.maraichere. langevin.net. Doubles from $70 a night, including breakfast; four-person chalets $140. Credit cards accepted. This impressive old house covered with wooden slats has three rustic-style rooms and several chalets. It's right on route 132, so it's a bit noisy, but the place oozes charm: the decor in the gîte is delightful, with rural Québécois furniture, and the attic bedroom, decorated with an array of interesting objects, is just as charming.

♠ **Gîte et Pension Aux Bons Jardins** (map I, off C1, **35**): 172 Pointe-aux-Pins, Saint-Fulgence. ☎ 674-2896. Website: www.mariko. iquebec.com. Farm rooms $50 a

night; chalet rooms from $70. After Saint-Fulgence, turn left a kilometre (half a mile) after the Auberge de La Tourelle and head towards Parc Joseux, then follow the unpaved road for another kilometre. This is a remote spot that's ideal for nature-lovers and anyone who wants to get away from it all. You can stay in the rustic chalet overlooking the garden and the vegetable patch, or at the farm, which faces the fjord. It's a delightfully peaceful and verdant place, and you might even see a bear.

♠ **Gîte du Passant Au Compte-Moutons** (map I, off B1, **36**): 1141 Hôtel-de-Ville, Saint-Honoré, 12 kilometres (7 miles) from Chicoutimi. ☎ 673-7400. Doubles from $50 a night. Cross the Dubuc bridge in Chicoutimi, and follow route 172 ouest for about 3 kilometres (2 miles) until you reach the sign for Saint-Honoré, then turn left before the church. This unobtrusive green wooden house with three cosy rooms is run by a couple of elderly ladies, one of whom exhibits her own paintings on the first floor. It's a pleasant place, with plants, painted wooden walls and a wood-burning stove. Breakfast is huge, and includes *crêtons*, fresh eggs, yoghurt, muffins and homemade jam.

♠ **La Maison du Passant, chez Marie Gagné** (map I, off B1, **37**): 2605 boulevard Sainte-Genevière, Chicoutimi-Nord. ☎ 543-3923. Fax: 543-8469. Email: mathieu.barrette @sympatico.ca. Doubles from $50 a night. There are three comfortable rooms in this attractive house, with mountain-biking, dog sleighs and snowmobile rides among the activities on offer.

WHERE TO HAVE A DRINK

♟ **International Café Bar** (map II, C2): 460 rue Racine Est. ☎ 690-5129. This basement bar in the Hôtel Chicoutimi (*see* 'Where to Stay') comes to life on Thursday, Friday and Saturday evenings. There's a live orchestra on weekends. If you fancy a boogie, try the Loft Dancing club, next door.

♟ **Guinness Pub** (map II, C2, **40**): on the corner of rue de l'Hôtel-Dieu and rue Saint-François-Xavier. ☎ 693-5224. Open Monday to Tuesday 11am–3pm, Wednesday to Friday 11am–3am, and Saturday 7pm–3am. This place is a large, wood-panelled room with a good selection of beer, and attracts a young clientele, especially on Saturday nights. You can also get snacks here.

♟ **Le Cybernaute**: 391 rue Racine Est. ☎ 543 9555. Website: www. cybernaute.com. Internet access $3.50 per hour. This is a large, modern room with 28 computers and a selection of magazines and software for sale.

WHAT TO SEE

★ **La Pulperie** (map I, A2, **50**): 300 rue Dubuc. ☎ 698-3100. Website: www.reseau.qc.ca/pulperie. Admission $7. Guided tours available between mid-June and mid-September, 9am–6pm (8pm in July); they leave from the building 1921 every half-hour, and last for 2 to 3 hours. Chicoutimi's pulp mill, near a waterfall on the river, is a wild place, the huge old industrial buildings echoing to the sound of rushing water. The mill was built in 1896, and became the biggest producer of paper in Canada by 1910. With the onset of the Depression, however, the orders ran out, and the plant was shut down in 1930. It was saved from demolition in 1978, when the buildings were listed and an ambitious restoration programme began; disappointingly, though, not much of the original machinery remains. Nowadays, the site is used for a wide range of cultural events; ask for details at the tourist office.

★ **Maison du Peintre Naïf Arthur Villeneuve** (map I, A2, **50**): 300 rue Dubuc. ☎ 545-9400. Phone in advance to check the opening hours. This house belonged to the artist whose name it bears, and it's nothing if not distinctive: the walls are covered in frescoes depicting the history of the area and Villeneuve's musings on the world in general. When he wasn't painting his house, Villeneuve produced nearly 4,000 individual paintings, working on them right up to his death in 1990.

★ **Musée du Saguenay** (map II, C2, **51**): on the same site as the Pulperie. ☎ 545-9400. Open 8.30am–noon and 1–5pm (1–5pm only on weekends and public holidays). This fascinating museum has sections devoted to history, ethnography and the arts. The most compelling collection examines the culture of the Native Americans, with displays on their domestic life, hunting techniques and so on, all illustrated with superb photographs. There's a section devoted to the pioneers and their farming technology, while the ground floor is given over to an assortment of intriguing art works, including a calvary made out of bottles, a wax lyre and several wooden sculptures by Naïve artists. Other highlights include the reconstructed craftsmen's workshops and sections of an early-20th-century Canadian house.

★ **Village de Sécurité Routière** (map I, off B1, **52**): 200 rue Pinel. ☎ 545-6925. Email: villagesecurite@qc.aira.com. Open 19 June to 30 August, 10am–6pm. Admission $7. If you want to teach the kids about road safety, this child-sized town is the perfect place to do it. They can even drive special miniature cars.

WHAT TO DO

– **Vieux-Port**: 49 rue Lafontaine, off boulevard Saguenay. ☎ 698-3025. From June to September, there are shows every evening; from May to September, there's a daily market (9am–2pm); and from 21 June to 3 September, there's an art fair here (Wednesday to Sunday, 1–9pm). This spectacular park on the Saguenay River is at the heart of the city's social life. You can walk, cycle or rollerblade along the various paths, or make a day of it by bringing a picnic and letting the kids run riot in playgrounds. In the covered market, you'll find stalls selling vegetables, wild fruits, local produce and good-quality souvenirs.

– **Parc Rivière-du-Moulin**: 1625 rue des Roitelets, a minute away from the Place du Royaume shopping centre. ☎ 698-3235. Open 16 June to 4 September, 9am–9pm. This is a beautiful park in the heart of town, with plenty of picnic areas dotted around. There's no shortage of activities, from mountain-biking and hiking to fishing or sailing on the Moulin River. You can also hire dinghies, kayaks, pedalos and rowing boats. The park is also open in winter (mid-December to late March, 10am–5pm on weekdays, 9am–5pm at weekends; admission $3.50), when hiking and cross-country skiing are the main activities. There's a heated shelter if you get cold.

FESTIVALS AND EVENTS

– **Le Carnaval Souvenir**: in February. ☎ 543-4438. Fax: 543-4884. This riotous 10-day party has its roots in the pioneer days of 100 years ago: the locals dress up in period costumes, complete with crinolines, fur-trimmed bonnets and beaver-fur top hats and coats. If you're not too busy painting the town red, you can sample traditional recipes, watch all manner of plays and shows, and buy lots of vintage bric-a-brac.

– **Chicoutimi en Bouffe**: ☎ 698-3167. Website: www.chicoutimienbouffe. com. For 10 days in October, the town plays hosts to a feast of international flavours, as a dozen restaurants each pick a country and cook its food. A great chance to sample cuisines you may not get at home.

– **Regard sur la Relève du Cinéma Québécois au Saguenay**: Early spring. ☎ 698-5854. Website: www.regardsurlareleve.com. This film festival is dedicated to the early works of Québécois film directors. It's a friendly event where you can see short-, medium- and feature-length films, animated movies and documentaries, with readings and improvisation events among the other attractions.

– **Les Rendez-Vous du Film sur l'Art de Chicoutimi**: at the end of March. ☎ 543-2744. Website: www.sequence.qc.ca. Every year, La Galerie Séquence presents a varied assortment of films as part of the Festival International du Film sur l'Art.

– **Festival Jazz et Blues l'Héritage**: in spring. ☎ 549-7111. Website: www.jazzetblues.com. For one week only, Chicoutimi rocks to the rhythms of gospel, jazz and blues.

LEAVING CHICOUTIMI

By Boat

The crossing to Sainte-Rose-du-Nord (on *La Marjolaine*) leaves at 8.30am and takes 4 hours. You must book the day before at the ticket offices in the port; these are signposted everywhere. You go down the Saguenay River, which later joins the St Lawrence. This is a true fjord, 104 kilometres (65 miles) long, and the views are fantastic. If it's grey and cloudy in the morning, though, you might as well postpone your crossing, unless you want to spend 4 hours looking out at the fog from the boat's restaurant.

When it's clear, you'll see Caps Trinité and Eternité, and Le Tableau, an impressive rock face. The landing point, Sainte-Rose-du-Nord, is the prettiest village on the Saguenay.

– **Information and bookings**: Croisières Marjolaine, boulevard Saguenay Est, in the port. ☎ 543-7630. Cruises run between June and late September. The journey is quite expensive, and you should check the route, as some boats stop in the middle of nowhere, leaving you with no choice but to go back to Chicoutimi. Another trip leaves Sainte-Rose-du-Nord and goes towards the Caps.

By Bus

🚌 **Bus station**: 55 Racine Est. Autobus Laterrière. ☎ 543-1403. The Jasmin bus company runs local and regional services.

– **For Québec City**: Intercar Saguenay.

– **For La Malbaie**: Intercar Côte Nord.

– **For Tadoussac**: Tremblay et Tremblay.

– **For the Lac Saint-Jean area**: Jasmin runs services to Roberval, Dolbeau, Péribonka and Côte Nord (☎ 543-1403). Fournier runs services to Lac Saint-Jean, leaving from the bus station in Alma (☎ 662-5441).

JONQUIÈRE Pop: 7,000   DIALLING CODE: 418

Jonquière, 15 kilometres (9 miles) west of Chicoutimi, is a characterless modern town. The wide avenues testify to the town's former prosperity, derived from the presence in town of the world's biggest aluminium smelter. Sadly for Jonquière, the company that owned the smelter transferred its operations to an automated works in Laterrière, with devastating effect: for a while, Jonquière had the highest unemployment rate in the province. Despite the economic doom and gloom, the town's nightlife is much livelier than in Chicoutimi, and there are plenty of young people around. So you can help the local business just by having a good time.

USEFUL ADDRESSES

🛈 **Tourist Office**: Centre des Congrès, 2665 boulevard du Royaume. ☎ 548-4004 or 1-800-561-9196 (toll-free). Open 8am–8pm in summer; otherwise 8am–noon and 1.30–4.30pm. There's another tourist office at 3885 boulevard Harvey (☎ 542-7974; open mid-June to late August, 8am–8pm).

WHERE TO STAY

Campsites

♠ **Camping Jonquière**: 3355-122 chemin du Quai, on Lac Kénogami, 6 kilometres (4 miles) from the town centre. ☎ 542-0176. Open June to mid-September. Tent pitches $20 a night. There are 160 pitches for tents at this family-friendly campsite, where the facilities include children's playgrounds and a beach supervised by coastguards.

☆ Budget

♠ **Nouvelle Auberge de Jeunesse Jonquière**: 5 minutes from the town centre. ☎ 547-0845. Fax: 542-5617. Email: cricri.d@caramail. com. Open 15 May to 15 October. Beds $18 a night, including breakfast. Dinner $8; order in advance. You don't need the address of this youth hostel, as the manager, Christian Duschener, will collect you when you arrive in town; just phone when you get here. There are two rooms with four beds and two twin-bedded rooms. Christian loves his job, and treats his guests like friends, which helps make this a great place for budget travellers.

♠ **CÉGEP**: 300 metres from the 'nightlife' district, Saint-Dominique; look out for the two towers on the hill. ☎ 547-2191. Fax: 547-3359. Rooms from $25 a night. In summer, most of the rooms in this university hall of residence are rented by students from the language centre, but there are usually a few vacancies.

☆☆ Moderate

♠ **Gîte de la Rivière-aux-Sables**: 4076 rue des Saules, in a quiet residential area near the town centre. ☎ 547-5101. Fax: 547-6939. Website: www.pages.infinit.net/riosable. Doubles $50 a night. Take boulevard Harvey until you reach the tourist office, then cross the bridge, go straight ahead to the first set of traffic lights and turn left onto rue Saint-Jean-Baptiste. This is a friendly, non-smoking guesthouse with four appealing rooms, all soundproofed and with TVs. There's a lovely garden with a beach on the Rivière-aux-Sables, where you can go swimming. You can also hire a rowing boat or pedalo, go fishing or use the nearby cycle path.

≜ Le Mitan: 2840 boulevard Saguenay. ☎ 548-7388. Fax: 548-3415. Doubles $60 a night. This is a stylish, tastefully decorated guesthouse with three first-floor rooms that share a bathroom. Breakfast is served on a bright veranda.

≜ Gîte le Merleau: 2456 rue des Merles, not far from the town centre. ☎ 542-1093. Fax: 542-1031. Go south down rue Saint-Dominique and turn left opposite Station Irving onto rue des Hirondelles, then turn left again. Doubles $55 a night. The owners are extremely house-proud, and it shows: all the rooms have TVs, telephones, balconies and views of the park, and guests can use the swimming pool and solarium.

≜ CEPAL centre: 3350 rue Saint-Dominique. ☎ 547-5728. Fax: 547-4882. If you stay at the CEPAL Aventure hotel, you can take advantage of a variety of outdoor activity packages, including canoeing, sailing, tennis, skiing, rafting and snowmobiling. Qualified guides will help you discover the natural wonders of this area. The hotel has a bar, outdoor swimming pool, volleyball courts and a private beach, and you can hire bikes, canoes and windsurfers.

☆☆☆ Expensive

≜ Auberge Villa Pachon: 1904 Perron. ☎ 542-3568 or 1-800-922-3568 (toll-free). Website: www.aubergepachon.qc.ca. Doubles from $115 a night. Dinner $40–50. Head towards La Baie on route 170, go past the railway, then turn left straight afterwards. There are five rooms at this luxury guesthouse: it's a bit expensive, but it's very quiet and comfortable.

WHERE TO EAT

☆–☆☆ Budget to Moderate

✕ **Restaurant 400 Coups**: 2350 rue Saint-Dominique, at the corner with boulevard Harvey. ☎ 542-0400. Open until midnight. Main courses $16. As the Truffaut-inspired name suggests, this restaurant's decor is vaguely inspired by the cinema, but it's surprisingly cold and impersonal. The cheap lunch menus attract local workers, and yuppies make up the rest of the clientele. The food's good, though: regional specialities and fish, meat and pasta dishes.

✕ **Le Puzzle bar-resto**: 2497 rue Saint-Dominique. ☎ 542-6485. Fax: 547-8210. Open until 11pm; bar until 2am. A trendy young crowd come here for the inventive cooking, the stylish decor and the huge veranda.

✕ **Le Stade**: 2407 rue Saint-Dominique. ☎ 542-6119. Open until midnight. Simple but good-quality snacks are on offer at this friendly place, where a young crowd throngs the terrace day and night.

✕ **Resto-rétro Brillantine**: 2479 rue Saint-Dominique. ☎ 547-5060. Open until 4am. Main courses $7. Step into this café, and it's as if the 1950s and 1960s never went away. The decor and the mix of rock music and schmaltzy songs are perfect, and the hot dogs and burgers are absolutely in keeping with the time-warp feel. A great place for nostalgia freaks and night owls.

✕ **Le Barillet**: 2523 rue Saint-Dominique. ☎ 547-2668. Fax: 547-8210. Full meal $13. The dining room is utterly charmless, but you can stuff yourself with Chinese and Canadian food thanks to the all-you-can-eat buffet.

☆☆☆ Expensive

✕ **Le Bergerac**: 3919 rue Saint-Jean. ☎ 542-6263. Open 11am– 2pm and 6–11pm; dinner only on Saturday, closed Sunday. Full meal $37. This is a pleasant, if pricey restaurant where the specialities include carpaccio of caribou and medallions of ostrich in red wine. The lunch menu is cheaper, but still not cheap.

WHERE TO HAVE A DRINK

Jonquière's cafés, bars and discos are clustered along rue Saint-Dominique (known as 'Saint-Do'), especially at the junction with Saint-Thomas. Le Puzzle, L'Audace, Le Paradise, Le Zinc, Le Shooter, Le Stade, Le Singapour and L'Envol are the busiest bars, especially during Jonquière en Musique (late June to early August), when there are special events every weekend; the street becomes a pedestrian-only zone, and free concerts are organized on open-air stages.

WHAT TO SEE AND DO

★ **Centre d'Histoire Sir-William Price**: 1994 rue Price, between rue Ball and rue Bradet. ☎ 695-7278. From 15 June to 1 September, open 10am–8pm; otherwise, open Monday to Friday 8am–5pm. Admission $5. This museum, housed in an old Anglican chapel, explores the history of the Kénogami area and the life of one of its first and most important developers, Sir William Price.

★ **Centre National d'Exposition**: 4160 rue du Vieux-Pont. ☎ 546-2177. In July and August, open 10am–8pm; otherwise 10am–5pm. This free museum has collections devoted to art, science and the environment. If none of this appeals, it's perched on the side of the mountain, so the views are fantastic.

★ The art-deco **Centrale Hydroélectrique** was built during World War II. ☎ 699-1547. It's open to visitors every afternoon from Monday to Friday.

★ **Parc du Rivière-aux-Sables park**: 2230 rue de la Rivière-aux-Sables, in the heart of the town. ☎ 546-2177. A brand-new aluminium footbridge crosses the river, and the park's attractions include a covered market, water playgrounds, cycle paths, walks and the Parc de la Francite. Small boats and fishing equipment are also available for hire, and there are plenty of places to sit back and watch the world go by.

– **Québecissime** is a celebration of Québécois rhythm and song, from La Bolduc to Céline Dion. This musical extravaganza takes place during the summer at the Théâtre Palace Arvida, and involves 32 musicians, singers and dancers, 120 songs, hundreds of costumes and 15 changes of scenery.

WHAT TO DO IN THE AREA

■ **Auberge du Ranch des Érables**: 3737 and 3868 chemin des Érables, Lac-Kénogami, north of Jonquière. ☎ 542-1800 or 1-877-542-1800 (toll-free). Fax: 542-2170. This maple grove offers riding, canoe hire and an extensive network of footpaths. In winter, you can borrow snowshoes or go cross-country skiing. This place is also a guesthouse and a restaurant, and the food is delicious.

■ **Domaine de la Truite Mouchetée**: route Brassard, Shipshaw, facing Lac Kénogami, on the other side of the Saguenay River. ☎ 542-8600. This is a superb spot with ponds for year-round trout-fishing. You can hire all the gear – and eat your catch, provided you have somewhere to cook it.

METABETCHOUAN Pop: 4,900

This little village on the southeast corner of Lac Saint-Jean has a beautiful white-sand beach. The name Metabetchouan means 'meeting place' in the Montagnais language.

WHERE TO STAY

⌂ **Gîte Au Soleil Couchant**: 31 2ème rue Foyer-du-Lac. ☎ 349-2138. Fax: 349-2203. Doubles $50 a night; four-bed rooms $75. This quiet lakeside house, surrounded by flowers, has three spacious bedrooms full of hospitable little touches; ask for the room with the starry sky, and prepare to be amazed. Outside, there's a lovely garden with a pergola, while breakfast, lovingly prepared by the owner, Berthe, includes blueberry tarts and muffins. Self-catering accommodation is also available.

⌂ **Gîte Chez Christiane et Guy Voyer**: 34 2ème rue Foyer-du-Lac, next door to the Gîte Au Soleil Couchant. ☎ 349-2929. Fax: 349-3369. Doubles $50 a night. Outside, a lawn slopes gently down to the river, and you can watch the sun set over Lac Saint-Jean, a spectacular sight when the weather is good. Inside, here are three spotless, spacious and very pretty rooms, with two bathrooms between them. The owners, Christiane and Guy, are very chatty, and will offer plenty of tips about the area, as well as the chance to sample their superb blueberry wine. Breakfast is good – and huge.

WHERE TO EAT

✕ **Le Saint-Martin**: 118 rue Saint-André, at the junction with rue Saint-Antoine. *Plat du jour* $10. This friendly place offers a wide selection of cheap snacks: pizzas, sandwiches and submarines. The decor is humdrum, though, and the only reason to come here is that there's not much else in town.

LAC SAINT-JEAN

The Native American name for Lac Saint-Jean is Piekougami, meaning 'flat lake', but it's more like an inland sea, an ancient glacial trough fed by water from a dozen rivers. It's an uninspiring landscape, all dunes and sandy beaches, but the region is famous for being friendly, and it's home to several unusual tourist attractions, as well as cultural events and community festivals. The biggest of these is the **Traversée du Lac Saint-Jean à la Nage** ('Swim across Lac Saint-Jean'), which takes place in late July or early August. In Dolbeau-Mistassini, the **Fête du Bleuet**, in early August, celebrates the blueberry harvest: you can try the famous local blueberry wine, and buy a few bottles to take back to your friends, and sample local specialities such as *tourtière*, blueberry tart and salmon from the lake.

⛺ **Auberge de Jeunesse de Sainte-Monique-de-Honfleur**: on the Île du Repos ('Island of Rest'), at 105 route Île du Repos. ☎ 347-5649. Fax: 347-4810. Email: ilerepos@globetrotter.net. This youth hostel on the banks of the Péribonka river is ideal if you want a bit of peace and quiet.

– If you decide to **camp by Lac Saint-Jean** in summer, watch out for the mosquitoes.

WHERE TO STAY IN ALMA AND THE AREA

⛺ **Auberge des Îles**: 250 rang des Îles, in Saint-Gédéon, 11 kilometres (7 miles) from Alma. ☎ 345-2589 or 1-800-680-2589 (toll-free). Fax: 345-2683. Website: www.digicom.qc.ca/auberge. From Jonquière, follow route 170 and turn off at Saint-Gédéon; the Auberge is near the golf course. Doubles $68–98 a night. This is a quiet place, right on the beach. The rooms are good, and most have views of the lake. There's an English-style pub and a restaurant, and sporty types can rent catamarans, sailing boats and pedalos, or play volleyball.

⛺ **Gîte du Passant Belle-Rivière**: 872 rang Caron, Hérbertville. ☎ 344-4345. Fax: 344-1933. Email: bouchard@digicom.qc.ca. Doubles $50 a night. From Québec City, take route 169; when you get to the village, head towards Roberval for 6 kilometres (4 miles). Make sure you let the owners know exactly when you're planning to arrive. This guesthouse has four clean, simple rooms, and you'll get home-cooked regional dishes if you eat here. It's also a great place from which to explore the area by sleigh or snowmobile.

WHERE TO EAT

✕ **Restaurant-Traiteur Desbiens-Venue**: 1290 rue Hébert, in Desbiens. ☎ 346-1106. If you're hungry but short of cash, this is the place to go. The menu includes local specialities like *soupe de gourganes*, *ouananiche* salmon and blueberry tart. There are only 10 tables, so make sure you get there early.

WHAT TO DO AROUND LAC SAINT-JEAN

There are plenty of seasonal activities on offer: dog-sleigh rides, snowmobiling, ice-fishing and snowshoe hikes in winter, and sea-kayaking, white-water rafting and wildlife-watching in summer.

RAFTING IN DESBIENS AND SAINT-FÉLICIEN

■ **H2O Expéditions**: on route 169. Look out for the van marked 'H2O'. ☎ 346-7238 or 1-800-789-4765 (toll-free). Email: rafting.h2o@qc.aira.com. There are two 4-hour trips a day from Desbiens, leaving at 9am and 1pm. Excursions in Saint-Félicien, which cost $50, take place only on Saturday, and booking is a must: it's the roughest descent in Québec, but beginners are welcome. If you haven't had enough thrills on the raft itself, the staff will take you to a small ledge, 6 metres (20 feet) up, from which you can jump into the backwash. The trip takes you through spectacular countryside, with no roads and not another soul in sight, and is a once-in-a-lifetime experience. You can also go kayaking (prior experience essential). The highlights of the trip are recorded on video, and in the evening everyone watches the action replay together, drink in hand.

THE GHOST VILLAGE OF VAL-JALBERT

DIALLING CODE: 418

On route 169, 105 kilometres (66 miles) from Chicoutimi and 9 kilometres (6 miles) from Roberval. From 20 June to 5 September, open 9am–7pm; from 20 May to 15 June and 6 to 25 September, open 9am–5pm. ☎ 275-3132. Admission $12. A detailed map is available at the entrance. There's a programme of Disney-style shows (9am–5pm), with performers acting out the parts of labourers from the early 20th century. You can reach the village by bus from Chicoutimi. For information, contact the companies (*see* 'Leaving Chicoutimi').

Val-Jalbert sprang up around a large pulp mill, which was built at the turn of the last century and powered by a huge waterfall. A cable car takes you to the superb panoramic viewpoint at the top, or, if you're feeling energetic, you can walk up via the 750 steps. From the top, a footbridge leads to the Maligne waterfall.

The village become a municipality in 1915, and by 1926 it was inhabited by 950 workers and their families. Its growth came to an abrupt halt in 1927, when the pulp mill was forced to close because of a recession and mergers in the paper industry. Despite the coachloads of tourists who flock here and the rather melancholy look of the abandoned buildings, it offers an intriguing insight into everyday lives of this working community. There's a 2.5-kilometre (1.5-mile) walk around the site, and the visit takes about half a day.

WHERE TO STAY AND EAT

For information and reservations, contact the **Village Historique de Val-Jalbert**, CP 307, Chambord. ☎ (418) 275-3132.

⌂ **Campsite**: near the village. Tent pitches $19–23 a night. There are 70 pitches at this large site, some with water and electricity, and the facilities include a laundrette. If you stay here in May or June, watch out for the swarms of mosquitoes and blackflies.

⌂ **Hotel**: on the main street, at the entrance to the village. Doubles $70 a night. This beautiful old house has a Wild West feel. It's not cheap, but the rooms have showers and toilets, and it's a bargain compared with most of the other options in the area.

⌂ **Mini chalets**: most of these are moderately priced, and some have bathrooms and fridges; all guests have access to on-site washing facilities and bike hire. A trip to the historical village is included in the price.

– You can also rent one of the refurbished two-storey **houses** in the historical village. Each has a kitchen, a bathroom, a sitting room, a dining room and two bedrooms, with parquet floors throughout. They're ideal for small groups of friends, and they're not too expensive, either. In winter, when the place has an especially magical feel, you can go cross-country skiing in the area.

✕ For a snack, try **Magasin Principal** (11am–3.30pm). If you want something more substantial, head for the romantic **factory restaurant**, at the foot of the waterfall. Prices are reasonable, and there's a delightful terrace.

✕ **Restaurant de l'Ancien Moulin**: by the waterfall. There's a cheap set menu, and it serves snacks as well as full meals.

✕ **Restaurant Jalbert**: just before you reach the village, next to the junction with route 169. Booking essential. ☎ 275-6597. This restaurant serves typical Canadian cuisine, such as *tourtière* and blueberry tart, and also hosts cabaret shows.

WHERE TO STAY IN CHAMBORD

⌂ **Gîte du Passant chez Martine Fortin**: 824 route 169, 1 kilometre (half a mile) from the Val-Jalbert campsite. ☎ 342-8464. Doubles from $45 a night; chalets $60. This pretty, white house, surrounded by fir trees, has four cheap rooms that sleep up to four people. After a huge breakfast, you can wander off to see the animals on the neighbouring farm. There are also two small chalets with kitchens and air-conditioning, again sleeping up to four people.

WHAT TO SEE

★ **Avenues Labrecque and Tremblay** are particularly evocative.

★ If you're feeling up to it, climb the 750 steps to the **panoramic viewpoint** (or take the cable car). From the top, there's a superb view of Lac Saint-Jean, Roberval, Pointe-Bleue, Île aux Couleuvres, Pointe-Taillon and Chambord.

SAGUENAY–
LAC SAINT-JEAN

★ There's a small **cemetery** where the victims of the Spanish flu epidemic of 1918 are buried.

★ Visit the **disused factory** (the entrance is by the restaurant) for an insight into industrial life in the early 20th century. There are great views of the waterfall from the factory's windows.

ROBERVAL Pop: 12,000   DIALLING CODE: 418

Roberval, the biggest town on Lac Saint-Jean, is a quiet place where waves lap gently at pretty waterside gardens. The town is named after the first viceroy of Nouvelle-France, Jean-François La Rocque de Roberval, who unsuccessfully tried to gain a foothold in the Saguenay region in the 16th century. There aren't many must-see sights, but the town has some fine old houses, such as La Maison Donaldson (1873) and the old general store (464 boulevard Saint-Joseph). Keen anglers can fish for *ouananiche*, a freshwater salmon that lives in the lake.

Finding your way around Roberval can be confusing. If you're coming from Val-Jalbert, it helps to remember that route 169 becomes boulevard de l'Anse, then boulevard Marcotte and, finally, boulevard Saint-Dominique.

WHERE TO STAY

≜ Gîte du Voyageur: 2475 boulevard Saint-Dominique. ☎ 275-0078. Doubles $50 a night. Strictly non-smoking. Colette and Marcel offer a choice of three rooms that share a bathroom. The decor is slightly outdated, but there aren't many options in the area.

≜ Motel Roberval: 256 boulevard Marcotte. ☎ 275-3957 or 1-877-9903 (toll-free). Fax: 275-7333. Doubles from $67 a night. This is one of the cheapest places to stay in town, although rooms with whirlpool baths are more expensive. The facilities here include a restaurant and an outdoor swimming pool.

WHERE TO EAT AND HAVE A DRINK

✕ Brochetterie Chez Gréco: 979 boulevard Marcotte. ☎ 275-5705. Open until 10pm. Set menus from $14; *table d'hôte* $18. The restaurant specializes in Greek cuisine, but also serves large, if pricey, portions of fish, meat and seafood. It's half price from 4pm on Monday, but be prepared to queue.

✕ Restaurant de l'Hôtel Le Château de Roberval: 1225 boulevard Marcotte. ☎ 275-7511. Main courses from $20. The food here is relatively up-market and fairly pricey,

but it's about as good as it gets in these parts.

❢ Bistro 679: 679 boulevard Saint-Joseph. ☎ 275-6407. Open until 3am. This trendy bar is usually packed with youngsters from around the area. There's an eclectic range of music on the stereo.

❢ Bar Country: 887 boulevard Saint-Joseph. Open noon–3am. This huge wood-panelled bar has a pool table, and hosts line-dancing sessions from Thursday to Sunday.

WHAT TO SEE

★ **Centre Historique et Aquatique**: 700 boulevard de la Traversée. ☎ 275-5550. Email: vroberval@destination.ca. From 19 June to 28 August, open 10am–8pm; from 7 to 18 June and 29 August to 7 September, open noon–5pm. Admission $6; family tickets available. This is a museum and a cutting-edge ecology centre. There's an aquarium where you can see what lives in the depths of Lac Saint-Jean, while an unusual audiovisual presentation on the history of the region is shown in a submarine-shaped projection room.

MASHTEUIATSH (POINTE-BLEUE) Pop: 1,750

DIALLING CODE: 418

On the surface, Mashteuiatsh looks like any other Québécois village, but it's the people, not the sights, that make it interesting. This Native American reserve, home to the Montagnais, was created by the Canadian government in 1856, and there's no better place to find out about their nature-centred culture and philosophy. You can go on fishing or hunting trips with excellent Montagnais guides, and there are several shops in the reserve where you can buy beautiful handmade sculptures, snowshoes and moccasins. (For details, *see* 'What to See and Do').

Mashteuiatsh is not an easy place to get to, but you can hitchhike from the Terminus Voyageurs in Roberval, 6 kilometres (4 miles) away. Otherwise, you'll probably need to take a taxi; try Pointe-Bleue (☎ 275-0785).

USEFUL ADDRESS

🛈 **Tourist Information**: 1516 rue Ouiat-chouan (the main street). ☎ 275-7200. This tourist office is much like all the others in the area; you'll pass one every 5 kilometres (3 miles) or so.

WHERE TO STAY

🛏 **Auberge Kukum**: 1899 rue Ouiat-chouan, 4 kilometres (2.5 miles) from the centre. ☎ 275-0697. Doubles $50 a night, including breakfast. *Kukum* means 'grandmother' in Montagnais, and the name is a tribute to the grandmother of the French owner's Montagnais ex-husband. This unusual place is made entirely of logs: the well-kept rooms are small and simple, almost monastic, and there's not much in the way of heating. On the ground floor, there are youth hostel-style bunk beds, again with few frills, and breakfast is fairly rudimentary. But this not just a place to stay; it's a place to get a sense of the true Montagnais culture. It's also a convenient base if you're planning to visit the Musée Amérindien (*see below*), and the beach is a short walk away.

WHAT TO SEE AND DO

★ **Musée Amérindien**: 1787 rue Amishk. ☎ 275-4842. Email: museilnu@ destination.ca. From mid-May to October, open 10am–6pm; otherwise Monday to Friday, 9am–noon and 1–4pm; and by appointment only on weekends. Admission $6. This interesting, well-designed museum depicts the history, life and culture of the Montagnais Indians, with films and slide shows as well as more conventional displays. It also hosts temporary exhibitions about other Native American tribes.

★ **Magasin d'Artisanat**: 200 metres (200 yards) from the Auberge Kukum, and signposted. Gérard Siméon runs this craft shop/museum, and will happily share some of his many anecdotes about his ancestors. A little farther down the road, his son, Thomas, makes stone and wooden sculptures. The basement of his studio has been turned into an exhibition of his family's work, with crafts, sculptures, paintings and tools on display.

– There are two ways to find out more about the Montagnais themselves. You can spend some time chatting to the owner of the Auberge Kukum (*see* 'Where to Stay'), who can introduce you to local people and help you avoid any cross-cultural faux pas. Or you can get in touch with an organization that runs activities for visitors. These include **Mikuan II**, **Ilnu Tepiskau** (August to October only) and **Le Centre d'Interprétation de la Fourrure**. Details of all these companies are available at the tourist office. They run adventure trips into the bush, where you'll get a taste of the traditional way of life – setting traps, smoking meat, canoeing and portage, ice-fishing and more – and learn about the spiritual side of the Montagnais people. They're expensive and a bit contrived, but these excursions can be unforgettable.

SAGUENAY–LAC SAINT-JEAN

SAINT-FÉLICIEN Pop: **11,000**   DIALLING CODE: 418

This town is a crossroads on the Chamouchouane River, and is best known for its zoo.

USEFUL ADDRESS

🛈 **Tourist information**: 1209 boulevard Sacré-Coeur. ☎ 679-9888. Open 8am–4.30pm (8pm in summer).

WHERE TO STAY IN SAINT-FÉLICIEN AND THE AREA

Much of the accommodation in Saint-Félicien has a slightly battered look: the town is near a university, and the guesthouses are occupied by students out of season.

⌂ **Camping Saint-Félicien**: 2230 boulevard du Jardin, off route 167, near the zoo. ☎ 679-1719. Fax: 679-5410. Open mid-June to early September. Tent pitches $17–23 a night. This is a large campsite with good facilities, including an on-site shop, sports equipment and a swimming pool. Activities on offer in the area include go-karting and sea-plane trips.

🛏 **Auberge des Berges**: 610 boulevard Sacré-Coeur, 3.5 kilometres (2 miles) from Saint-Félicien, on the road to Roberval. ☎ 679-3346. Website: www.destination.ca/auberge. Doubles $60 a night, including breakfast; reduced rates for groups of six and for stays of more than three days. The decor here is a bit dull and old-fashioned, but the rooms are large, clean and air-conditioned, and each has a new bathroom, a TV and a fridge. Some even look out over the river. The owner is very friendly, and can tell you anything you want to know about the area.

Gîtes du Passant

🛏 **Gîte Au Jardin Fleuri**: 1179 rue Notre-Dame, near the bus stop and the tourist information centre. ☎ 679-0287. Doubles $40 a night. Of the seven gîtes in Saint-Félicien, this is the farthest away from the town centre. The five rooms are clean, if basic, but the decor is a little faded and there's only one shared bathroom. Still, you'll get a good night's sleep here, and you won't be disturbed by the traffic on the road or by the nearby railway – there's only one train a day. The delicious homemade breakfast features *crêtons* and bread with raspberry or blueberry jam.

🛏 **Gîte Ferme Dallaire**: 678 rang Double Sud, about 4 kilometres (2.5 miles) from the centre. ☎ 679-0728.

Doubles $45 a night. Go down rue Notre-Dame for 2.5 kilometres (1.5 miles), then turn left at rang Double Sud; it's a kilometre or so farther down, on your left. The rooms at this friendly farm-cum-guesthouse are spotless and quiet, and the owner makes lovely cakes.

🛏 **Au Domaine Tremblay**: 677 rang Double Sud, opposite the Gîte Ferme Dallaire. ☎ 679-0169. Doubles $45 a night. Booking recommended. This farm is run by a cheerful old couple who let out three country-style rooms (two doubles and one twin) that share a lovely big bathroom. It's not particularly special, but it's a pleasant, simple and unpretentious place to stay.

🛏 **Gîte des Peupliers**: 21 rang Saint-Isidore, Girardville, in the Dolbeau region, north of Lac Saint-Jean. ☎ 258-3889. Fax: 258-3529. Doubles $40 a night. From Saint-Félicien, head towards Sainte-Méthode on route 169; at Sainte-Méthode, take route 373 towards Normandin. The owners will collect you from Montréal airport, and take you back there when you leave. This friendly place has five very comfortable rooms with spotless bathrooms, and in the evening you can enjoy a traditional meal with Céline, Réal and their family. There are also several guided outdoor activities, including canoeing in summer or dog-sleigh rides in winter, both great ways to appreciate the vast open spaces of this region.

WHERE TO EAT

✕ **Le Café du Boulevard**: 1036 boulevard Sacré-Coeur, opposite the Provigo supermarket. ☎ 679-0324. Open until 11pm (until midnight from Thursday to Sunday). Full meal $10. This is a good place to stop for lunch, as the Québécois

menu offers a hearty soup (*potage*), *tourtière* (meat pie), blueberry tart and coffee at a very good price. You can also get breakfast, and there's a selection of sandwiches, salads and cakes. A small terrace looks out over the river.

✕ **Pâtisserie Grand-Maman**: 1883 boulevard du Jardin. ☎ 679-5551. Website: www.destination.ca/pgm. Delicious regional specialities like *tourtières* and blueberry tarts make this place very popular with the locals.

WHAT TO SEE

★ **Le Zoo 'Sauvage' de Saint-Félicien**: take route 169 towards Chibougamau, then, from boulevard Saint-Félicien, turn onto boulevard du Jardin (route 167). If you're going by bus, ask the driver to stop at the zoo entrance. ☎ 679-0543 or ☎ 1-800-667-LOUP (toll-free). Website: www.d4m.com/zoo sauvage. Open late May to mid-October, 9am–6pm; otherwise by appointment only. The last nature walk starts at 4.15pm. Admission $17. This is the best zoo in Québec. One area is designed along traditional lines, but otherwise the animals are free to roam, while the humans find themselves in cages on a little train that takes them through the site. The train journey lasts for an hour, and it'll take you at least half a day to see everything else. A wide variety of Canadian wildlife is represented here, including wolves, moose and buffalo. The polar-bear enclosure is divided into two sections by a big glass window, so you can watch them swimming underwater. The best time to do this is during feeding times, which are announced over the PA system. As well as the animals, you'll see reconstructions of a settlers' farm, a trapper camp, a trading post and a Native American village.

WHAT TO SEE AND DO IN THE AREA

★ **La Doré** hosts the Festival des Camionneurs (truckers' festival) at the end of June.

★ **Grands Jardins de Normandin**: 1515 avenue du Rocher-Normandin. ☎ 274-1993. Website: www.cigp.com/jardin.html. Open mid-June to late September, 9am–6pm (to 8pm in July and August). Admission $10. You'll need 1 hour 30 minutes to visit everything. This beautiful place charts the evolution of horticulture as an art, with examples of several styles of garden.

Winter Activities

■ **Aventure Maria-Chapedelaine**: 914 rang Saint-Louis, Mistassini. ☎ and fax: 276-5645. Website: www.glinx.con/users/aventure. Snowmobiles are the main attraction here, but there are other activities on offer, including dog-sleigh rides. It's pricey, but accommodation in a log camp is included in the cost, as are meals, and equipment hire, including thermal clothing and other gear to keep out the cold.

CHIBOUGAMAU Pop: 8,700

At the heart of the Chibougamau reserve is the Ashuapmuschan River, which was the return route for expeditions from the Hudson Bay. The name means 'meeting place' in the language of the local Native Americans. It's a vast area of low, gently sloping hills, with game and fish in abundance, and

SAGUENAY–LAC SAINT-JEAN

it's truly fantastic. It's also very remote – 232 kilometres (144 miles) northwest of Saint-Félicien.

SAINTE-JEANNE-D'ARC   DIALLING CODE: 418

It's worth stopping at this lovely village to see the picturesque **wooden mill** on rue de Moulin. ☎ 276-3166. Open 1 July to 1 September, 10am–5pm (to 7pm on Friday and Saturday). The free guided tour takes 30 minutes. The mill was built in 1907 and was in operation until 1974. All the machinery is still in place, and there's a small exhibition of antiques, though it's not exactly breathtaking.

WHERE TO STAY IN SAINTE-JEANNE D'ARC AND THE AREA

♠ Gîte La Chute aux Mûres-Mûres: 515 rue Principale, not far from Lac Saint-Jean. ☎ 276-1249. Doubles $45 a night. This guest-house is near a little river, and the owner will really make you feel at home. The rustic attic rooms are wonderful, and breakfast is delicious.

♠ Gîte Jardin des Quatre Saisons: 2562 boulevard Wallberg, on route 169, by the Mistassini Rver at Dolbeau Mistassini. ☎ 276-5561. Doubles from $65 a night. This lovely modern house with a garden has been beautifully designed and furnished by Marlayne and Robert. There's pale wood everywhere, and the four cosy bedrooms have each been decorated to represent one of the four seasons. There are two bathrooms, and guests can use the sauna. You'll find a beach and several footpaths nearby.

PÉRIBONKA Pop: 600   DIALLING CODE: 418

Péribonka is home to a museum dedicated to Louis Hémon, who put the village on the map with his novel *Maria Chapdelaine*. He was born in Brest, in France, in 1880, and spent much of his life in Canada before dying in a railway accident in Ontario on 8 July 1913. Sadly, he did not live to see his life's work published.

USEFUL ADDRESS

■ Les Excursions Ô Hameau: 119 chemin Plein-Air. ☎ 374-2031. This organization offers a range of soft-adventure packages, such as watching migratory birds on Île Boulianne (late April to late May). You can also go kayaking on Lac Saint-Jean and Lac Péribonka, do a spot of white-water rafting or go on a dog-sleigh ride in winter.

WHERE TO STAY

♠ Au Petit Bonheur: 374 rue Plante. ☎ 374-2328. Doubles $40 a night. This is a pleasant house with seven small rooms under the eaves. If a few of you share a room, it works out very cheap.

WHERE TO STAY AND EAT IN THE AREA

⌂ ✕ **AJ de l'Île du Repos**: in Sainte-Monique-de-Honfleur, at the mouth of the Péribonka River. ☎ 347-5649. Fax: 347-4810. Email: ilerepos@globetrotter.net. Dormitory beds $18 a night (a bit more if you are not a Youth Hostel member); private chalets with shower and toilet $60. There's also a campsite (tent pitches $20). Half-board available in the campsite and the chalets. Credit cards accepted. This youth hostel, run by a friendly young team, is on Lac Saint-Jean, on the aptly named Île du Repos ('Island of Rest'), and you have to cross a wooden bridge to get there. The chalets and tent pitches are scattered about in a forest edged by sandy beaches, and there are plenty of outdoor activities, including swimming, volleyball, croquet and cycling in summer, and snowshoe hikes, ice-skating, cross-country skiing and snowmobile rides in winter. Indoor facilities, meanwhile, include a laundrette, a bar where you can buy sandwiches and other snacks, and a good restaurant, Au P'tit Creux, open for breakfast and dinner in summer. The hostel hosts jazz and rock concerts and cabaret evenings throughout the summer (tickets $20). The opening of the restaurant, on June 20, is celebrated with a lamb roast, while the end of the tourist season is marked with a gourmet buffet and various shows. The youth hostel owns another island that's accessible only by boat; it's great if you want somewhere really peaceful to camp.

⌂ **Chalets du Centre Touristique Sainte-Monique**: 900 rang 6 Ouest, Sainte-Monique, at the north entrance to Parc de la Pointe-Taillon. ☎ (418) 3477/3592. These eight chalets have a bathroom and a kitchen, so they're good for families who want to stay in the area for a few days.

✕ **La Volière**: 200 4e Avenue, Péribonka, next door to Au Petit Bonheur. ☎ 374-2360. Full meals $16–40. The only restaurant in Péribonka is in an old house overlooking the river. The portions are generous, the cooking is good, and the fish come straight out of Lac Saint-Jean. The owner, Denyse Doré, has a couple of spare rooms, and can put up stray travellers who can't find anywhere else to stay.

WHAT TO SEE

★ **Musée Louis-Hémon**: 700 Maria-Chapelaine, between Péribonka and Sainte-Monique. ☎ 374-2177. From late June to early September, open 9am–5pm; otherwise 9am–4pm. Admission $6. This museum is dedicated to the writer Louis Hémon (*see above*). You can see La Maison Samuel-Bedard, where the writer worked as a farmhand for almost six months, while the modern reception building is home to a crafts shop and an excellent display that explains his life and work through photos, letters and personal memorabilia. The main building of the museum houses exhibitions of works by artists from Québec, Canada and elsewhere.

FESTIVALS AND EVENTS

– The **Traversée Internationale à la Nage du Lac Saint-Jean** (*see* 'Lac Saint-Jean'), which takes place at the end of July, starts from Péribonka.

PARC DE LA POINTE-TAILLON

This park has two entrances, one on the north side (admission $2 per person) and one on the south (admission $8 per car). You can also hire bikes at the entrances ($6 an hour; $12 for 3 hours). The park, a protected zone, is a long, low, tongue-shaped peninsula that sticks out into Lac Saint-Jean. It's wild, unspoiled and varied, with forests, rivers, lakes and freshwater beaches, dunes and peat bogs packed full of moose and other wildlife. On the south side, there's a 14-kilometre (9-mile) fine-sand beach, while the north side follows the Péribonka River up to its mouth.

In 1885, the pioneers who came here named the site Pointe-à-la-Savane ('Savannah Point'). However wild and bleak that may sound, it's actually a very pleasant blend of water and woodland, with firs, pines, silver birches and poplars. If you want to stay here, you can pitch a tent on one of the 'primitive campsites', and the activities on offer include walking, cycling, kayaking and swimming in the lake. Unfortunately, the mosquitoes are vicious, particularly during June, so make sure you take some insect repellent.

USEFUL ADDRESS

– **Parc de la Pointe-Taillon**: 825 Rang 3 Sud, Saint-Henri-de-Taillon. ☎ (418) 347-5371 (during high season).

GETTING THERE

– **From Sainte-Monique-de-Honfleur**: take Route 169, followed by rang 6. You'll reach a reception centre, after which there's a path for cyclists and pedestrians only. It crosses the peninsula from north to south across the Delta Digité, a vast peat bog.

– **From Saint-Henri-de-Taillon**: this is the best option for motorists, as cars are allowed through the south entrance to the park. Take Route 169, then rang 3; at the entrance, you'll find a reception centre and a beach, the Plage Taillon.

WHERE TO STAY

⌂ **Primitive campsites**: tent pitches $16, including the park admission fee. There are two campsites in the park. They're only accessible by cycle paths, and the facilities are so basic it's almost like camping rough. The Site du Castor is 2 kilometres (1.5 miles) from the chalet on the beach, facing the lake; if you're lucky, you might see beavers here. The Site du Prospecteur is 4.5 kilometres (3 miles) from the chalet on the beach, and also faces the lake.

WHAT TO SEE AND DO

★ **The beach**: the south bank of the peninsula is basically a long beach. Most people go to the 6-kilometre (4-mile) section by Saint-Henri-de-Taillon. The nearer you get to the mouth of the Péribonka River, the wilder and less busy it gets: the pedalos, dinghies and windsurfers gradually give way to a secret world of dense undergrowth, home to beavers, moose, Canada geese and other wildfowl.

– **Beaver observation**: in theory, the best places to spot these friendly beasts are near the waterways and little lakes behind the beach, including Lac à la Tortue ('Tortoise Lake'), the Bélanger canal and the Adélard canal. According to one local expert, however, you're better off looking for the elusive mammals at the end of the cycle track by the Péribonka River at dusk.

– **Bike rides**: the best way to get around the park is by mountain bike, as there are 30 kilometres (19 miles) of cycle tracks. If you want to hire a bike, go to one of the park's reception centres.

Between Parc de la Pointe-Taillon and Sainte-Rose-du-Nord

WHERE TO STAY

You can stay in Chicoutimi, Chicoutimi-Nord, Saint-Honoré or Saint-Fulgence. It's also worth having another look at the entries under 'Where to Stay and Eat in the Area' in the 'North of the Saguenay River' subsection.

WHAT TO DO

– **Les Chiens et Gîte du Grand-Nord**: at Lac Durand, lot 18, junction 2, in Saint-David-de-Falardeau. ☎ 673-7717. Website: www.chiens-gite.qc.ca. From Falardeau, turn right at the church, then take the third road on the right. Chalet rooms $20 per person per night; discounts available for stays of a week or more. Dog-sleigh rides $110. *Table d'hôte* available. This is one of the best places in Canada to experience the pleasure of riding on a dog sleigh. You can also try driving in snowmobiles (from $180), walking with snowshoes and ice-fishing, while summer activities include rafting (half-day $50).

– **Cascade Aventure**: Chute-aux-Galets, in Saint-David-de-Falardeau. ☎ 673-4949 or 1-800-420-2202 (toll-free). This company specializes in rafting excursions: a 3-hour rafting trip from Falardeau (late April to mid-October) costs $50, including equipment, a guide, a meal and the return journey in a shuttle bus. You'll get a 20 per cent discount if you have a student card. From mid-June to mid-September, free camping for participants is thrown in as well.

SAINTE-ROSE-DU-NORD Pop: 400

DIALLING CODE: 418

Just 3 kilometres (2 miles) off route 172, this is one of the most beautiful villages in Saguenay. Some 40 white houses are scattered around the main road in the middle of a velvety green valley, overshadowed by rocky, wooded peaks. It even has a tiny port. The landscape is beautiful and unspoiled, though the village is invaded by coachloads of tourists in summer, and has not escaped the inevitable souvenir shops and fast-food stands.

It's worth summoning up the energy to climb the highest peak, as the view is stupendous. This is also the departure point for a 4-hour trip on the Saguenay River, on the cruise boat *La Marjolaine*. For more information, visit the visitors' centres in the park.

WHERE TO STAY

⌂ **Camping La Descente des Femmes**: 154 rue de la Montagne, in the middle of the village. ☎ 675-2500/2581 or 1-800-463-9637 (toll-free). Tent pitches $12 a night; you pay extra for water and electricity. The facilities here include showers (again, you pay extra to use them), toilets and a laundrette with a tumble-dryer. Firewood is on sale, and there's a shop 200 metres (200 yards) away.

⌂ **Gîte le Manoir de l'Anse**: 489 Descente-des-Femmes. ☎ 675-1226. Doubles $45 a night. Credit cards are not accepted. This enchanting gîte is tucked away between two green valleys along the Saguenay, and is unquestionably the best place to stay in town. A whole floor if given over to guests to use, with three clean and adequate rooms, a kitchen, a big sitting room and a terrace with superb views.

⌂ **Gîte La Nichouette**: 125 rue des Artisans. ☎ 675-1171. Doubles $50 a night; three-bed rooms $60. Built in 1917, this is a large, white wooden house with balconies in a peaceful spot by the Saguenay. The three rooms are fairly basic, but they're light and pleasant, with handmade furniture. Facilities include a TV room and games.

⌂ **Chambres d'Hôte du Musée de la Nature**: 197-199 rue de la Montagne. ☎ 675-2348 or 1-800-463-9651 (toll-free). Doubles $50 a night, including breakfast. It's clearly signposted from the village. This place has a lovely view of the valley, but

the three rooms are austere and rather old-fashioned. At breakfast, you can try a selection of local cheeses and homemade jams. The owner is a taxidermy addict, and will take you to visit his little museum, which contains no less than 3,000 examples of his craft, including sharks caught in the Saguenay, bears, wolves and various birds of prey.

⌂ **Gîte Au Crépuscule**: 288 rue du Quai. ☎ 675-2307. Doubles $40 a night. Credit cards are not accepted. This green-and-white house is on your left as you enter the village. It's a very basic place, but the owners are friendly, and the five rooms have pleasantly old-fashioned decor.

☆☆☆ Expensive

⌂ **Auberge Le Presbytère**: 136 rue du Quai. ☎ 675-2503 or 1-800-463-9651 (toll-free). Fax: 675-1243. Doubles $65 a night; half-board $120. Claudette Laurier has been the boss here since 1984, and in 1998 she turned the establishment into a co-operative, making all the staff co-owners. This helps to explain the remarkably friendly and enthusiastic service. It's a pretty blue-and-white building with five lovely rooms, decorated in Laura Ashley style. The room rates are a little steep, though: the ground-floor rooms have no view, and those on the first floor share a shower room on the landing. Still, it's clean and quiet, and there's a large terrace overlooking the fjord where you eat between 11am and 6pm. Whatever time you choose to eat, the food here is excellent, though dinner is a touch expensive: the evening *table d'hôte* (booking essential) costs $20, while the lunchtime deal is just $10. The menu changes daily; the homemade soup and grilled salmon steak are particularly good, as is the melt-in-the-mouth *chateaubriand*.

â **La Pourvoierie du Cap au Leste**: in Sainte-Rose-du-Nord, on Route 172 heading towards Tadoussac, 88 kilometres (55 miles) along the Chemin de Cap à l'Est. Follow the road into the forest for 7 kilometres (around 4 miles). ☎ 675-2000. Fax: 675-1232. Doubles $120–150 a night, half-board. Booking recommended. Tucked away between three parks, this place looks out over the Fjord du Saguenay. The rooms are in wooden chalets among the trees, and all have lovely views. The staff are friendly, and the food is excellent, if rather expensive. The many activities on offer include forest hikes on snowshoes or snowmobile trips along the trails of nearby Mont Valin.

WHERE TO EAT

✕ **Café de la Poste**: 169 rue du Quai. ☎ 675-1053. Open 1 May to 15 October, 6am–11pm. Main courses $8; *table d'hôte* available from 24 June. This is a friendly café-cum-bakery in a pretty blue-and-yellow wooden house. It serves *tourtières*, quiches, *bruschettas* and homemade cakes at very appealing prices.

WHAT TO SEE AND DO

★ **Musée de la Nature**: 197–199 rue de la Montagne. ☎ 675-2348 or 1-800-463-9651 (toll-free). Open 8.30am–9pm. Admission fee. This curious little museum houses a comprehensive collection of local flora and fauna. The five little rooms contain a variety of things the owner has picked up on his long rambles, including mushrooms and strangely shaped roots and pieces of wood. There are also loads of stuffed birds and animals.

★ **La Chèvrerie 'la Petite Heidi'**: 504 boulevard Tadoussac, 10 minutes east of the village on route 172. ☎ 675-2537. 'Heidi's Goat House' is a cheesemaker's. A guided tour of the premises costs $2.50 (discounts for children), and includes a sampling session.

– **Cruises**: port de Sainte-Rose-du-Nord. ☎ 675-7630. *La Marjolaine* goes up the Saguenay and stops at Sainte-Rose-du-Nord. There are two 3-hour trips a day, each costing $30, and it's a unique opportunity to enjoy the views provided by the banks of this lovely river.

Between Sainte-Rose-du-Nord and Tadoussac

This is a wild and wonderful road that snakes through forests, and past rivers and rocky peaks.

★ **ZEC de la Rivière Sainte-Marguerite** (ZEC stands for 'zone d'exploitation contrôlée'): this magnificent valley stretches for 50 kilometres (31 miles) between Sainte-Rose-du-Nord and Sacré-Coeur. At the bottom is the

SAGUENAY-LAC SAINT-JEAN

Sainte-Marguerite River, a paradise for salmon- and trout-fishers. Two salmon pools (Nos. 23 and 46) have been turned into observation sites, while at the Bardsville site, at the 47-kilometre point, you can see the salmon floating around in the water and soaking up the sun. You can also rent a chalet here, and try some fresh salmon.

★ **Sacré-Coeur**: 14 kilometres (9 miles) from Tadoussac. This is the place to go if you want to see black bears. Contact Domaine de Nos Ancêtres, 1895 Route 172. ☎ 236-4836/9382. Booking essential. Bear-watching trips take place at dusk. A lovely old couple will take you out on 'safari' in an old school bus. It costs $20 per person, and a hair-raising time is guaranteed.

WHERE TO STAY

⌂ **Camping Sacré-Coeur**: 70 rue Jourdain, in the town centre. ☎ 236-9131. Open from mid-June to the beginning of September. The facilities here are pretty basic, but at least there's a laundrette with dryers.
⌂ **Gîte du Passant La Ferme de Camille et Ghislaine Gauthier**: 243 route 172 Nord. ☎ 236-4372. Doubles $45 a night, including breakfast. This modern house is right on the road, and the three bedrooms are in the basement. Still, it's a clean and friendly place, and it's not too expensive.
⌂ **Ferme Cinq Étoiles**: 465 route 172, Comté Saguenay. ☎ 236-

4551. This is a large farm surrounded by fields and woods. There are several types of accommodation, including fully equipped chalets ($80 a night for seven people), four gîte-type rooms, a campsite ($5 per person) and group accommodation. You can play tennis, use the swimming pool and go walking, while winter activities include cross-country skiing, walks on snowshoes or snowmobile rides. The farm is also home to a host of wild and domestic animals, including buffalos, deer, pheasants and hares. An ideal place for families.

WHAT TO DO

– **Tan Croisières**: 346 Anse-de-Roche, in Sacré-Coeur. ☎ 236-4562. Fax: 233-2272. This company offers 3-hour trips on Zodiac inflatables for $25. The guide, who is an experienced sailor, will take you around the fjord and in search of whales. Night trips are also available.

– **Sea-kayaking**: Ferme Cinq Étoiles. ☎ 236-4551. You can rent a kayak, or book a guided excursion.

TADOUSSAC Pop: 920   DIALLING CODE: 418

This beautiful little port sits at the mouth of the Saguenay. The word 'Tadoushac' means 'hillock' (or nipple) in mountain dialect, and presumably refers to the green and rocky hills to the west of the village. Tadoussac has many charming and picturesque houses, especially near the port itself, as a reminder that this was the original fur-trading post in the St Lawrence valley. The town's first tourists, Jacques Cartier and Samuel de Champlain, landed their ships here for rest and recreation, and many have followed in their footsteps. Despite this, Tadoussac remains unspoiled.

At low tide in the valley, the deep waters of the Saguenay disappear so fast that the tourist boats can no longer enter the mouth of the fjord, a strange phenomenon that accounts for the incredibly high levels of plankton in this stretch of water. As a consequence, marine mammals congregate offshore, making the area a mecca for whale-watchers.

Ecotourism

Only 20 years ago, the concept of whale-watching cruises simply didn't exist. Then, one day, a fisherman from Tadoussac offered to take a few backpackers out in his rowing boat. They were blown away by what they saw, to the great surprise of their guide, for whom the sight of the massive sea creatures was about as commonplace as pigeons in Trafalgar Square. Through word of mouth, demand grew, and the fisherman continued his new sideline, happy to let the awestruck Europeans tag along as long as this paid for the odd beer or wad of tobacco.

A few years later, a new company started to advertise whale-watching excursions, and brought with it sleek new 'rigid inflatable' boats. The pioneer of the trade, sadly, was forced to stop his 'cruises', as the authorities decided that his wooden craft was in breach of safety regulations. Since then, the whale-watching industry has brought in millions of dollars to the various businesses of Tadoussac, and now keeps the whole community going. As well as being extremely profitable, it also raises awareness about the plight of whales today. Once you've seen these magnificent creatures in their natural environment, you can't help but be converted to their cause.

Too Many Boats, Not Enough Whales

The expansion of the tourist industry in this region has created a paradoxical situation. In summer, the large number of observation boats on the water at any one time is posing a threat to the whales, which gather here to feed and build up fat reserves for the winter months. The local authorities have issued a guide on how to approach the whales, which all craft are supposed to observe, but navigation on the St Lawrence is unregulated, and it's hard to see how traffic-control laws could be put in place. A shipping code is a good idea in theory, but when you see the number of cruisers and speedboats on the water in the middle of summer, the scale of the problem soon becomes apparent. Indeed, the people of Tadoussac are beginning to ask themselves how they can safeguard the future of the whales and continue to provide an unforgettable experience for tourists. If you want to avoid the tourists, take a whale cruise from Grandes-Bergeronnes or Les Escoumins. They're less crowded, and the boats charge less.

To avoid disappointment, you should also be aware that the whales you'll see around Tadoussac are fin whales, which don't throw their tails out of the water when they dive. Only humpback whales do this, and they're predominantly found off the coast of Hawaii; only very rarely do they venture as far north as the St Lawrence. Even after 10 years in the job, there are guides who have yet to spot one. So, don't be fooled by the photos in the tourist office . . .

A Word About Whales

Although all whales belong to the order of Cetacea, there are several species, and it's easy to get them confused. Cetaceans are divided into two groups: those with plates of baleen, or whalebone, hanging from their upper jaw, through which they filter plankton (these are called Mysticeti, or baleen whales); and those with teeth (the Odontoceti). The most significant baleen whale species, listed in order of size, are the minke whale, about 7–10 metres (23–33 feet) long; the barnacle-encrusted grey whale; the hump-back whale, famous for its high leaps out of the water; the sei whale, about 20 metres (65 feet) in length; the fin whale; and the blue whale, probably the biggest creature ever to have existed on this planet. Blue whales can reach more than 30 metres (100 feet) in length, and over 150 tonnes in weight – the equivalent of 30 elephants. Its tongue alone weighs an average of four tonnes; its daily food intake comprises three tonnes of plankton and the tiny crustacea called krill; it shoots its famous water jet nine metres (nearly 30 feet) into the air; and it can dive down to a maximum depth of 200 fathoms (366 metres) for up to 50 minutes without resurfacing. According to some estimates, there are only 2,000 blue whales left in the world, which seriously reduces their chances of reproduction.

The second group, the toothed whales, includes a much greater variety of species. Among them, you'll find narwhals, porpoises and dolphins, beluga whales, pilot whales and orca, the killer whales (the only ones that eat other

TADOUSSAC

■ Useful Address		16 Hôtel-motel Le Béluga
🛈 Maison du Tourisme de Tadoussac et de la Côte Nord		17 La Maison Harvey-Lessard
		18 Domaine des Dunes
		27 Motel Chez Georges
🛏 **Where to Stay**		✕ **Where to Eat**
2 Camping Tadoussac		20 Le Bateau
3 Auberge de Jeunesse La Maison à Majorique		21 Le Gibard
4 Gîte Aux Sentiers du Fjord		22 Au Père Coquart Café
5 Gîte du Passant Maison Fortier		23 Roulotte à patates
6 Maison Clauphi		24 Café du Fjord
7 Gîte du Passant La Maison Hovington		25 Resto du Motel Chantmartin
8 Gîte du Moulin Baude		26 La Bolée
9 Auberge La Mer Veilleuse		27 Resto du Motel Chez Georges
10 Gîte La Galouïne		★ **What to See**
11 Hôtel Le Pionnier		30 Chapelle des Indiens
12 La Maison Simard		31 Grand Hôtel Tadoussac
13 Gîte du Goéland		32 Maison Chauvin
14 Auberge La Maison Gagné		33 Centre d'Interprétation des Mammifères Marins
15 Gîte de la Falaise		34 Centre de Pisciculture

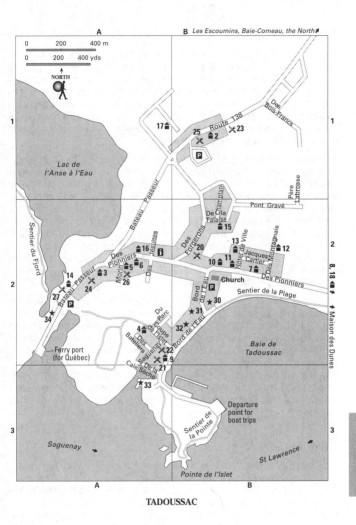

TADOUSSAC

whales). The biggest of them all is the sperm whale. It is half the size of the blue whale, growing to a 'mere' 15 metres (49 feet) on average, yet it has the biggest brain in the world, and can dive down as far as 1,000 metres (3,300 feet) and hold its breath for an hour. Although sperm whales have never been known to attack people (except, not surprisingly, when having harpoons thrown at them), they are the most feared of all the whales due to their colossal jaws. The most famous of them all is, of course, Moby Dick.

The Human Enemy

People have always hunted whales, but what was originally just a simple form of survival became an industry in the 12th century. The Basques were instrumental in this turnaround, as they used whale oil for cooking, and people soon discovered thousands of other uses for whales. Their fats became the basis for soap, lubricants and lamp oil; other whale products included ivory, leather, spermaceti oil and ambergris. Many European cities grew wealthy thanks to this industry, and nearly all the great voyages of discovery set out under the guise of whaling.

In the 19th century, the hunt for whales was transformed by the development of steamships and harpoon guns. Before this, the whaler had been a respected public figure because of the life-threatening struggle his job involved; after the Industrial Revolution, whales became a product like any other. The demand for their oils grew rapidly, and more and more countries tried to muscle in on the trade. The Americans built bigger and faster whaling vessels, providing jobs for more than 70,000 people. By the 20th century, the Scandinavians, Russians and Japanese were constructing giant industrial whaleboats, 100–160 metres (330–525 feet) long. These have been responsible for the massacre of 1.5 million whales, mainly for use in the cosmetics and pet-food industries.

The sheer scale of the killings led many nations, including the USA, where pressure due to public opinion was increasing, to conclude that some form of restriction was needed. In 1948, the International Whaling Commission was set up to regulate whaling and prevent the extinction of threatened species. The whaling nations were furious, and many openly rejected the Commission. Only the threat of widespread boycotts of whale-based products forced them to change their ways. Today, an end to whaling is in sight, but Japan and Norway, in particular, continue to defy international law; their whalers still capture thousands of tonnes of whale each year.

Rainbow Warriors

According to Native American legend, once the white man has all but destroyed Mother Earth through his greed, the 'warriors of the rainbow' will arise to save her. Sure enough, the past few decades have seen the rise of many outspoken environmental organizations, the most famous of which is Greenpeace, which was set up in Canada and has made the protection of whales one of its chief causes. Its supporters have risked their lives by placing themselves between threatened whales and the explosive harpoons of the whaling vessels. Their courage has paid off. After a near-fatal accident, when a Russian harpoon narrowly missed the head of the organization's founder, the Russians abandoned whaling for good. Despite such successes, though, Greenpeace would be the first to admit that widespread marine pollution poses as great a threat to sea mammals as any whaler – and attitudes will have to change a lot more before the seas are truly cleaned up.

USEFUL ADDRESSES

🄷 Maison du Tourisme de Tadoussac et de la Côte Nord (A2 on the map): 197 rue des Pionniers, near the Hôtel-motel Le Béluga. ☎ 235-4744. Fax: 235-4984. Open 9am–5pm (8am–9pm in June, July and August). An efficient centre where you'll find plenty of information about Tadoussac and the rest of the north coast as far as Blanc-Sablon, near the border with Labrador.
– You can also get plenty of info at the youth hostel (*see below*), which acts as a kind of second tourist office because of its location near the ferry disembarkation point. The managers will offer you the benefit of their local knowledge even if you aren't staying there.

■ Caisse Populaire: rue des Pionniers. You can withdraw cash and change money here.
🚌 Bus station: on route 138, about half a mile from the ferry, near the Petro-Canada station. ☎ 235-4653. Two departures a day in high season (none on Saturday) for Québec and Montréal. There are one or two buses per day in high season for Lac Saint-Jean, with two or three daily departures for Baie-Comeau. Most buses will pick you up outside the youth hostel.
■ Bike hire: at Maison Clauphi (*see* 'Where to Stay') and Boutique de Vélos Nature-Aventure (188 rue des Pionniers; ☎ 235-4303). About $12 for 2 hours; $5 per extra hour. You can hire mountain bikes, wetbikes and camping equipment, or book an archery session.

WHERE TO STAY

This area is nearly always packed in July and August, so book at least two days in advance.

Campsites

⛺ Camping Tadoussac (B1, **2**): 428 rue du Bateau-Passeur, about 800 metres from the ferry on route 138. ☎ 235-4501. Fax: 235-4902. Open mid-May to mid-October. A pitch costs $19. The stream of lorries heading for the ferry makes the site pretty noisy at all hours, but most of the 200 pitches have fantastic views of the river. Facilities include showers, toilets, washerdryers, firewood and a games area. Wheelchair access.
– If there's no room here, or if you want something less touristy, try **Camping Bon-Désir** at Grandes-Bergeronnes (*see below*).

☆ Budget

⛺ Auberge de Jeunesse La Maison à Majorique (A2, **3**): 158 rue du Bateau-Passeur, CP253, 200 metres away from the ferry port. ☎ 235-4372. Fax: 235-4608. Website: www.fjord-best.com/ajt. Dormitory bed $14 a night; private rooms $39–50; tent pitch $7. Prices are slightly higher for non-members. The local youth hostel is always full of people from all over the world, and the common room is a really good place to meet people. The dorms are pretty standard, most of them with 4, 6 or 10 beds, and some have bunk beds. For a bit more money, you can stay in the mobile home in the garden, which is family-friendly and offers wheelchair access. In winter, you can sleep over in an igloo. Make sure you have breakfast, as this place does the best one in Québec. The ingredients for pancakes (including ready-prepared mix) are provided, and you make your own. Often, people make their own speciality and share it with their neighbours, and there's always a great community atmosphere: even the washing-up is done together.

– If you're not staying here, you can pop in for breakfast ($3.50) or eat in the restaurant, which is open all day. Internet access is available ($2 per hour), and children can play on the grounded sailing dinghy in the garden, or in the teepee, which can be found in the camping area. The hostel organizes loads of activities, from hikes and beaver watches to minibus tours of the region, and can provide equipment for all the classic winter pursuits (snowmobiles, snow-shoes and more).

– If you want somewhere a little quieter, the youth hostel runs an annexe called **La Maison Alexis** on Rue des Pionniers. There are another 32 beds here, in dormitories, so you can usually find a place if the main hostel is full.

☆☆ Moderate

🛥 **Gîte du Passant La Maison Hovington** (B2, **7**): 285 rue des Pionniers. ☎ 235-4466. Fax. 235-4897. Doubles $60–100 a night, including breakfast. This pretty log cabin, built in 1800, is one of the oldest in the village. Its owners, Lise and Paulin Hovington, belong to an old seafaring family, and Paulin can tell you stories about his home town and about the St Lawrence during the age of the Canada Steamship Lines. The interior is cosy and tastefully decorated, and the five comfy rooms have en-suite showers and toilets. This is a classy establishment offering good value for money,

especially when you throw in the fantastic view of the bay.

🛥 **Auberge La Mer Veilleuse** (A2, **9**): 113 rue Coupe-de-l'Islet. ☎ 235-4396. Doubles $60 a night, including breakfast. This guesthouse dates back to 1887, and offers four spotless bedrooms, all with basins. Breakfast is served in the pleasant living room, which overlooks the port. The prices are reasonable given the location, and you'll get a warm welcome.

🛥 **Gîte aux Sentiers du Fjord** (A2, **4**): 148 rue Coupe-de-l'Islet, near the port and the departure point for whale cruises. ☎ 235-4934. Fax: 235-4252. Doubles $60, including breakfast. This blue house is hidden away at the end of a quiet little street, in a leafy spot where the forest path begins. The owners, Elizabeth and Xavier Mercier, are friendly, speak good English and are happy to answer any questions you might have about the region. They also whip up a delicious breakfast of homemade bread and yoghurt.

🛥 **Gîte du Passant Maison Fortier** (A2, **5**): 176 rue des Pionniers, opposite Dépanneur Murray. ☎ 235-4215. Fax: 235-1029. Doubles $60 a night, including breakfast. This central guesthouse has five spacious bedrooms, each with a basin. Madeleine Fortier, who runs the place, is charming, and she's also a great cook. Breakfast consists of fried eggs, orange juice, coffee, hot chocolate, cereals, jams, cheeses and *creton* (a kind of terrine) – and it's delicious.

🛥 **Maison Clauphi** (A2, **6**): 188 rue des Pionniers. ☎ 235-4303. Open May to October. Doubles $70 a night, including breakfast; motel room $44; chalet $95. The B&B rooms share a massive bathroom. This is a well-run place and breakfast is hearty. The owners can organize excursions and open-air weekend breaks, and you can hire a bike (with an itinerary).

Gîte du Goéland (B2, **13**): 261 rue de l'Hôtel-de-Ville, near Hôtel Le Pionnier. ☎ 235-4474. Doubles $50 a night. Half guesthouse, half hotel, the Gîte du Goéland is a quiet, central establishment offering five clean bedrooms with basins and a shared bathroom in the corridor. There's a separate entrance at the side of the house, so you don't have to come in through the hairdressers on the ground floor (run by the proprietor). It's good value, but you'll have to eat breakfast elsewhere.

Gîte du Moulin Baude (off B2, **8**): 381 rue des Pionniers, next to the golf course at the edge of the forest. ☎ 235-4765. Email: moulin baude@ihcn.qc.ca. Doubles $65 a night, including breakfast. This pretty log cabin is a little way out of Tadoussac, and it's a haven of tranquillity. There are four en-suite rooms, and the sitting room is really comfortable, so you can spend a long evening next to the fire listening to music or reading (there's a small library, but most of the books are in French). The owners will join you for breakfast.

Domaine des Dunes (off B2, **18**): 585 Moulin-Baude, 3 kilometres (2 miles) from the town centre, in a pleasant wooded area. ☎ 235-4843. Fax: 235-4695. Four-person chalets $120. Domaine des Dunes is a complex of well-designed new chalets with a ground-floor room and a mezzanine. The living area (with TV) is spacious, and there's a small kitchen in one corner. Ideal for families or those in search of peace and quiet.

Gîte La Galouïne (B2, **10**): 251 rue des Pionniers. ☎ 235-4380 or 1-888-465-4380 (toll-free). Doubles $45 a night. Credit cards accepted. Simple but satisfactory, this guesthouse has seven spotless bedrooms with cable TV; some also

have washbasins. You can make your own breakfast in the kitchenette, and the owners, Christian and Marie-Line, are very friendly.

Hôtel Le Pionnier (B2, **11**): 263 rue des Pionniers. ☎ 235-4666 (in summer) and 236-9271 (in winter). Fax: 235-4695. Open from May to October. Doubles $64–120 a night; discounts for three or four people sharing. The accommodation is arranged in three separate buildings, the most appealing of which is the old Town Hall. The other wings are newer and not as picturesque, but the rooms inside are perfectly adequate, with TVs and en-suite bathrooms. Prices drop outside high season.

Auberge La Maison Gagné (A2, **14**): 139 rue du Bateau-Passeur. ☎ 235-4526. Fax: 235-4832. Doubles $79 a night, including breakfast. The 10 colourful en-suite rooms here all have TVs; try to get one of the two with balconies. The owners are friendly, and breakfast is delicious, but it's a bit expensive.

Gîte de la Falaise (B2, **15**): 264 rue de la Falaise. ☎ 235-4344. Doubles $55 a night. Credit cards accepted. Five spacious and comfortable rooms with TVs at a very decent price, especially for four people sharing. The living room looks out over the St Lawrence and Saguenay rivers, while the focal point in the dining room is an impressive bearskin rug. You can use the kitchen to prepare your own food, and the breakfast provided is excellent.

Auberge de la Sainte Paix: 102 rue Saguenay. ☎ 235-4803. Email: saintepaix@mail.fjord-best.com. Website: www.fjord-best.com/sainte paix. Doubles from $75 a night. The young owners are warm and friendly, which makes up for the slightly glacial feel of the seven large bedrooms. The sitting room, done up in yellow and green, is enormous, and breakfast is on a similar scale. The pancakes are particularly delicious.

⌂ **La Maison Simard** (B2, **12**): 256 rue Montagnais. ☎ 235-4319. Doubles $55 a night. You can rent a studio flat on the ground floor of this little white house, with two large bedrooms, a shower and a TV room. The bedrooms can be rented separately, and there's also a double room on the first floor. Breakfast is traditional and well prepared. You'll feel right at home here, and it's good value for money.

☆☆☆ Expensive

⌂ **La Maison Harvey-Lessard** (A1, **17**): 16 rue Bellevue. ☎ 235-4802. Website: www.dreamsite.com/harveylessard. Doubles $90 a night; suite $145. This guesthouse is at one of the highest points in town, so you get a great view from every window. Choose from the three attractively decorated rooms with en-suite bathrooms and the luxurious suite, which has a jacuzzi. Each room has a balcony, which makes the views even more appealing. On the ground floor, you can relax on comfy tartan sofas in the handsome sitting room. It's expensive, but it's well worth treating yourself.

⌂ **Hôtel-motel Le Béluga** (A2, **16**): 191 rue Pionniers, opposite the church. ☎ 235-4784. Fax: 235-4295. Doubles $70–93 a night. The Béluga is a dark-blue modern building with comfortable en-suite rooms at sensible prices, especially in the motel. There's no air-conditioning, but you do get a rather noisy fan for those hot summer nights. For dinner, you could do far worse than the adjoining restaurant, **L'Auberge du Lac** (meals $18–24).

⌂ **Motel Chez Georges** (A2, **27**): 135 rue du Bateau-Passeur, near the ferry port. ☎ 435-3230. Doubles $90–100 a night. The en-suite rooms in the motel overlook the lake, and they're extremely good value for money here. Service is friendly and professional, and the location is perfect if you're planning to go whale-watching. If you're staying here, have breakfast at the youth hostel across the road.

WHERE TO EAT

☆ Budget

✕ **Le Bateau** (B2, **20**): 246 rue des Forgerons. ☎ 235-4427. Open 11am–2.30pm and 5–9.30pm. Lunch $11; dinner $17. The permanent buffet is laden with generous portions of traditional Québécois home cooking, and is popular with locals and tourists alike. The prices are very reasonable, especially at lunchtime, while the self-service buffet, available in the evenings, includes many elaborate dishes. You can try pea soup, cabbage salad, salmon paté, baked beans, apple tart, grape tart and even vinegar tart (not as bad as it sounds). If you've enjoyed the food, you can buy Le Bateau's recipe book.

✕ **Le Gibard** (A2-3, **21**): 137 rue du Bord-de-l'Eau. ☎ 235-4534. Open May to October, 10am–3am. Snacks $4–8. This cosy café-bar is in a lovely little red-and-black-painted house. Topped croissants, pizzas and cakes are on the menu, and there's a good selection of music.

✕ **Au Père Coquart Café** (A2, **22**): 115 rue Coupe-de-l'Islet. ☎ 235-4342. This café has an attractive wooden interior, and serves simple, good-value food, including submarines and other sandwiches, as well as game dishes, which are much more expensive. It's also a good place to come for a drink, as there's a good selection of local beers.

✗ **Roulotte à Patates** (B1, **23**): 452 rue du Bateau-Passeur, on the outskirts of Tadoussac. This place is a local institution, and should not be missed on any account. You can buy hot dogs, hamburgers and 'The Best Chips in Canada' (officially awarded in 1979), which you eat at the roadside picnic tables, but the star attraction is the owner, Claude Lapointe, or 'Le Blond', as everyone in the village knows him. An ex-sailor and an environmentalist ahead of his time, he's been telling stories to tourists and selling chips for more than 20 years.

☆☆ Moderate

✗ **Café du Fjord** (A2, **24**): 154 rue du Bateau-Passeur, next to the youth hostel. ☎ 235-4626. Open until 3am. Seafood platter $16. This lively café-restaurant is really popular with young people. In the evening, there's a self-service buffet with fresh vegetables, salads, soups, patés, filleted fish and several desserts. You can also choose from a range of fresh fish and seafood, which you pay for according to weight. Don't go overboard if you're on a tight budget, as the bill can rise very fast.

✗ **Resto du Motel Chantmartin** (B1, **25**): 412 rue du Bateau-Pas-seur, about half a mile out of Tadoussac towards Forestville (route 138). ☎ 235-4733. Fax: 235-4732. Open 7am–11pm (9pm out of season). This American-style eatery offers a wide choice of salads, chips, fresh fish, meats, pizzas and chicken, all simple, tasty, cheap and served in monster portions. As you'd expect in a waterfront town, the speciality is seafood.

✗ **La Bolée** (A2, **26**): 164 rue Morin, behind the youth hostel. ☎ 235-4750. Open June to October, 11am–2pm and 5.30–9.30pm. Main course $9–20. This huge, brightly painted house has a bakery on the ground floor and a restaurant upstairs. The staff are a mixture of French and Québécois, but the lunch menu is dominated by good-quality local dishes. The menu is strong on grilled meat dishes, which makes a nice change if you get bored with all that fish, and there's a good selection of beers.

☆☆☆ Expensive

✗ **Resto du Motel Chez Georges** (A2, **27**): 135 rue du Bateau-Pas-seur. Set menu $23. The specialities here are fresh lobster and crab, caught by local fishermen, but this excellent establishment also serves good meat and fish. The interior is stylish and the service is flawless.

WHERE TO HAVE A DRINK

❣ **Café du Fjord** (*see* 'Where to Eat'). Live rock, blues and jazz on Thursday, Friday and Saturday (admission $2). Tadoussac may be a small place, but it's not a total loss on the nightlife front, and this happening place with a dancefloor and a pool table is great for meeting new people. The music is good, and the bar staff can mix a mean cocktail.

❣ **Le Gibard** (*see* 'Where To Eat').
❣ **Au Père Coquart Café** (*see* 'Where To Eat').

WHAT TO SEE

Tadoussac is one of Canada's oldest fishing villages, and traces of its heritage can be found in and around the bay, most notably along rue Bord-de-l'Eau.

★ **Chapelle des Indiens** (B2, **30**): on the slope leading down to the harbour. ☎ 235-4324. Open June to September, 9am–9pm. Built by a Jesuit missionary in 1747, this is apparently the oldest chapel in North America. Whatever the truth of that, there's no doubt that it's absolutely charming. It's made entirely of wood and is painted red and white, in a similar style to the nearby Grand Hôtel Tadoussac (*see below*). The chapel bell, said to be the oldest in Canada, was brought over from France in the 17th century, in order to call the 'savages' to prayers. Even more curious is a tiny effigy of Jesus, thought to have been a present from Louis XIV. It wears a satin robe, supposedly made by Anne of Austria – although, according to one expert, it only dates back to the later half of the 19th century.

★ The **Grand Hôtel Tadoussac** (B2, **31**) has a pretty red roof with an ornamental steeple and a dreamy lawn scattered with parasols and deck-chairs. It was used for *The Hotel New Hampshire*, a screen adaptation of the John Irving novel. The hotel once belonged to the Canada Steamship Line, and was the first port of call for rich English tourists after travelling in the company's legendary white liners. It now belongs to the Dufour family, who also organize river cruises on board a magnificent schooner, painted to match the hotel. Rooms are available for those who are tempted by all this heritage (☎ 235-4421), although the Maison Harvey-Lessard (*see* 'Where to Stay') is a better bet if you're in the mood for extravagance.

★ **Maison Chauvin** (B2, **32**): 157 rue Bord-de-l'Eau. ☎ 235-4657. From the end of May to October, open 9am–8.30pm (to midnight from mid-June to mid-September); otherwise 3–6pm. Admission $3. This is a reconstruction of the first wooden house in Canada, built in 1600 by Pierre Chauvin, a Frenchman who was sent to Canada by King Henry IV. It was also the country's first trading post, where furs were exchanged between the Native Americans and the French. Inside, you'll find a trading counter with tools, a display of furs, an exhibition on mountain-dwelling tribes and documentaries about bears, the Native Americans, Québec's history and the village. Exhibits explain how beaver skins were used to make hats, how Jacques Cartier discovered that the Native Americans were using tobacco long before it arrived in Europe, and how oil from seal blubber was used for lighting in the first half of the 19th century.

★ **Centre d'Interpretation des Mammifères Marins** (Marine Mammal Education Centre; A3, **33**): rue de la Cale-Seche, opposite the marina. ☎ 235-4701. Open May to October, noon–6pm (9am–8pm from June to September). Admission $6; family ticket $14. As you'll guess from the half-size model of a rorqual in the entrance hall, this museum is dedicated to whales, especially the species (rorquals and belugas) that can be found in the St Lawrence. It's run by two organizations, the GREMM and the SIMM, which play an important role in marine science and ecology. They also run whale-watching excursions from time to time.

Inside the museum, a documentary on whales is shown throughout the day, and there are interactive games involving cetaceans, as well as educational displays about the life cycle of the whale (including a rorqual foetus) and the environment. One exhibit explains that the beluga whale faces extinction because of marine pollution: 15 to 20 a year are washed up on the banks of the St Lawrence alone, suffering from cancers or ulcers caused by toxic waste from nearby factories. If you feel moved to do something about it, the museum has a scheme for adopting whales.

★ There is a bizarre little green **Protestant chapel** on rue des Pionniers, opposite the Béluga hotel.

★ **Centre de Pisciculture** (Fish Farming Centre; A2, **34**): rue du Bateau-Passeur, between the ferry port and the Motel Chez Georges. ☎ 235-4434. Open 10am–6pm; guided tours every 45 minutes. There's a breeding station for Atlantic salmon here, and you can see the fish in their tanks.

★ Last but not least, there is a breathtaking view of Tadoussac from the **quayside**.

FESTIVALS AND EVENTS

– **Festival de la Chanson**: ☎ 235-4108. The 'Festival of Song' takes place at the end of the second week in June. It costs $8–26 to get into the various rock, jazz and blues concerts, which take place in the village's cafés. A season ticket is also available. It's great fun, and it attracts some pretty big names.

WHAT TO DO

Gentle Walks

There are several good walks within the village, the most popular being in the park along the banks of the Saguenay.

– **Sentier de la Coupe**: 40 minutes. There are two starting points: at the park information office or from rue Coupe-de-l'Islet, which joins rue Bord-de-l'Eau. The path circles the edge of the park, giving you panoramic views of the village and the river.

– **Sentier de la Pointe**: 30 minutes. Start from La Marée, a shop near the Centre d'Interprétation des Mammifères Marins, or at the far end of the quayside. The path follows the water's edge along the Pointe de l'Islet, skirting the peninsula, which is at the point where the Saguenay and St Lawrence rivers converge. There are information boards along the route, and you might see some whales swimming offshore.

– **Balade à Pointe-Rouge**: 15 minutes. Walk towards the dunes from rue des Pionniers, then stop at the golf course and take the path for Languedoc park. The tip of the peninsula is a good (and free) place for whale-watching.

Hikes

– **Sentier du Fjord**: mountain refuge bookings ☎ 272-3008 or 1-877-272-5229 (toll-free). Park your car at the Centre de Pisciculture, then take one of the regular shuttle buses (over land or water) to the start of the trail, or a bus to l'Anse de la Passe-Pierre, where the trail ends. This 45-kilometre (28-mile) path climbs up to l'Anse-à-l'Eau lake and follows the Saguenay fjord across the park, finally stopping at l'Anse de la Passe-Pierre. There are three brand-new mountain refuges along the route, with room for up to 12 people: one at l'Anse à la Boule, another at l'Anse à la Creuse and the third at l'Anse à la Barge. For serious back-to-nature types, there are also two sites for camping.

Unless you're planning an overnight stop, you're probably best off taking the shuttle all the way to l'Anse de la Passe-Pierre, then walking home, as the round trip is too much to do in one day. And don't try to do it on your own, as you're passing through some fairly remote terrain.

For the less adventurous, there's a shuttle to Cap de la Boule, from where you can enjoy a marvellous 10-kilometre (six-mile) walk back to Tadoussac. The tourist office can supply details.

Sightseeing by Plane

This is the only way to see this beautiful part of the world in its entirety. From the air, you can really appreciate the forests, the lakes, the beaches, the whales and the fresh, clean air. It's expensive, but if you don't do it, you'll regret it for the rest of your life. The companies listed below run tourist flights in the region.

■ **Aviation du Fjord**: 231 rue des Pionniers. ☎ 235-4640. Website: www.fjord-best.com. This is the ticket office in Tadoussac: it's a 10-minute bus journey to the lake, where the company's seaplanes are located. The agency organizes flights over Tadoussac for groups of up to seven people. A 20-minute flight costs $55, or you can hire a seven-seater plane privately at a rate of $500 per hour of flying time.

■ **Les Ailes du Nord**: 482 rue de la Mer. ☎ 232-6764. Fax: 232-6770. Flights leave from the Aéroport de la Mer. A 20-minute flight costs $40 per person; or $60 gets you 40 minutes in the air. Maximum three passengers. Special tours are avail-able: you pay per minute of flying time, and information is available on request from the office. This small agency was started by a French pilot, Éric Maillet, who moved to Québec after falling in love with a local lass. Everyone gets their own headphones and microphone, so you can communicate over the sound of the engine. The pilot gives an in-flight commentary, telling you the history of the villages below and about the region's flora and fauna, and is happy to answer any ques-tions. The plane, a Cessna, is so small that it feels as though you are flying it yourself. In fact, the pilot will even let you take over on the dual controls when it's calm enough, which is an adventure in itself.

Kayaking

■ **Tayaout Plein Air**: 158A rue du Bateau-Passeur. ☎ 235-1056 or 1-888-766-1056 (toll-free). Fax: 235-4608. Packages $25–80. The options include guided trips down the Saguenay River and the St Lawrence estuary. Prices include food, transport and protective clothing, but you'll need to take a sleeping bag for overnight excursions.

Whale-watching

Every summer, a dozen species of whale come to the St Lawrence estuary, including belugas, which are in danger of extinction in this region, and the blue whale, although you'd be very lucky to see one of these. Seals are a more common sight in the area, and they're fascinating, albeit not quite as impressive as their distant cousins.

The best time to go on a whale cruise is around midsummer. It's pretty unlikely that you'll see anything interesting earlier than June, although trips are available in spring.

Everyone in Tadoussac (even your hotel manager) will offer you a whale-watching trip, and all the companies, whether they operate Zodiac RIBs or bigger boats, charge roughly the same amount – $33 per adult for a 3-hour cruise. The price for children varies substantially, so shop around if you're planning a family trip. The bigger boats are more comfortable, but you'll be with a larger group. The best time to go is early in the morning, when there are fewer people around, but if you really want to avoid the hordes, skip Tadoussac and go whale-watching in one of the villages farther north. Two other things: book well in advance in high season (you can always postpone if the weather is bad), and check the timetables before you head for the boat.

■ **Croisière AML**: 175 rue des Pionniers. ☎ 235-4642 or 1-800-563-4643 (toll-free). Cruises every day from mid-May to late October, 9.45am–6.15pm from Tadoussac quay, and 15 minutes later from the quay at Baie-Sainte-Catherine; $30–35. As well as the traditional whale-watching routes, you can take a motor cruiser up the Saguenay and St Lawrence rivers, where you'll see beautiful landscapes but only be-luga and minke whales. There's also a trip to the picturesque Île Rouge, where you can visit a lighthouse made from Scottish granite, now populated by a colony of seagulls.

■ **Croisière 2001**: 1480 80e rue. ☎ 659-5489 or 1-800-694-5489 (toll-free). Hours and prices as above. You can buy tickets in the village shops. The *Katmar*, a large catamaran with room for 175, will take you to see the whales and the fjord in a single excursion.

■ **Les Croisières Express**: 161 rue des Pionniers. ☎ 235-4770 (summer only). Cruises from mid-May to late October, 8am–9pm; $32. A good choice if you want to travel in a small boat, as most of this company's vessels have space for just 12 people. However, it has recently added the 48-seater *Explorathor* to its fleet.

■ **Excursions Famille Dufour**: Grand Hôtel Tadoussac, 165 rue Bord-de-l'Eau. ☎ 235-4421 or 1-800-463-5250 (toll-free). A cruise costs $35. As well as owning the most beautiful hotel in Tadoussac, the Dufour family possesses four cruise boats, one of which is considered to be a historical monument. The schooner *Marie-Clarisse* was built in 1922, and has been restored several times. She has two masts, four sails and a crew of seven. Although she's not the fastest or most practical craft for whale-watching, the experience of being under sail is worth the price on its own. The Dufours organize three departures daily to the Saguenay and four to the St Lawrence. They are also members of GREMM, a marine-science group, so you'll get informed and informative commentary along the way.

■ **Croisières à la Baleine et au Saguenay**: 171 rue Bord-de-l'Eau. Three departures a day during summer, on 200-seater boats. Each cruise lasts 3 hours, and allows you to discover the Saguenay as well as see some whales.

– **Whale-watching from the shore**: you can see whales from the rocks that surround Tadoussac. The best time to do this is at dawn or dusk, when the whales come in as close as 15 metres (50 feet) from the shoreline. This is a magical experience, as you can also hear their distinctive call.

– Another good place for whale-watching is at **Cap de Bon Désir**, about 24 kilometres (15 miles) north of Tadoussac. There are fantastic cliffs from which you should be able to see whales. You have to pay to get to the main observation site, but it's much cheaper than a cruise. In the summer, there are guided tours, and you can also visit an open-air museum.

WHAT TO SEE IN THE AREA

★ **Maison des Dunes**: 6 kilometres (4 miles) east down rue des Pionniers. ☎ 235-4238. Open 9am–5pm (9pm in high season) from June to mid-October. This early-20th-century stone house is home to the Saguenay park interpretation centre, which contains information on Tadoussac's history and the formation of shelves on the sea floor. It is also an excellent site for observing the birds of prey that gather in the area during their migratory period. Outside, you'll find picnic tables and the start of a small trail that follows the beach back to the Grand Hôtel Tadoussac. The path passes Pointe Rouge, from where you can watch minke whales. It takes 2 hours to walk back this way, but it can be impassable at high tide.

★ **L'Île Rouge**: 20 minutes out to sea from Tadoussac. ☎ (418) 237-4274 or 1-800-563-4643 (toll-free). The island has an isolated lighthouse and a few houses on it. An inclusive package for whale-watching and the Île Rouge costs about $55. You can also stay the night at the lighthouse-keeper's home.

GRANDES-BERGERONNES Pop: 600

DIALLING CODE: 418

This small town, 20 kilometres (12 miles) north of Tadoussac, clings dramatically to the edge of the hillside; from a distance, it appears to be suspended over the valley. Grandes-Bergeronnes owes its name to the explorer Samuel de Champlain, who was reminded of wagtails (*bergeronnettes* in French) by the terns that populate the village's beach. It's less famous, cheaper and less touristy than Tadoussac, and it's just as good for whale-watching. In fact, it's easier to see whales around Grandes-Bergeronnes, as the village faces a particularly deep stretch of water: whale cruises from Tadoussac make for these waters for precisely that reason. Grandes-Bergeronnes has finally realized that it has missed the tourist boat, and is promoting itself with renewed vigour. It now offers many interesting excursions of its own.

WHERE TO STAY

Campsites

⬦ **Camping le Paradis Marin**: 4 chemin Émile-Boulianne, towards Les Escoumins. ☎ 232-6237. E-mail: coxy@saglac.qc.ca (September to April only). Open late May to late October (weekends only from September). Tent pitches $8 per person. This is the most beautiful and tranquil campsite in the area, with plenty of wide-open spaces, trees and even a small lake. It's right at the water's edge, which makes it an ideal base for whale-watching and diving. There's a cycle track, and the surrounding area is perfect walking country. An ideal spot for lovers of the great outdoors, miles away from any buildings or traffic.

⬦ **Camping Bon-Désir**: 160 route 138, on the way to Les Escoumins. ☎ 232-6297. Open June to mid-September. Tent pitches $22, but prices vary according to which of the facilities you use. This is a lovely site, tucked away among the trees and with seven lakes within easy walking distance. Milk, ice cream and firewood are on sale in reception, while other services include a convenience store, laundry facilities and showers. The site is surrounded by footpaths, and you can hire pedalos at the lakes.

☆ – ☆☆ Budget to Moderate

– If you're looking for B&B-style accommodation, ask for the list of '**Logements Chez l'Habitant**' from the information kiosk in the village (302 rue de la Rivière; ☎ 232-6326).

⬦ **Mer et Monde**: 53 rue Principale. ☎ 232-6779. Fax: 232-1007.

Website: www.mer-et-monde.qc.ca. Doubles $45 a night. There's a wonderfully peaceful feel to this friendly and welcoming guesthouse. There are three simple but comfortable bedrooms, and the living room has an open hearth. The owners, Alain and Andrée, also organize kayaking outings (in two-man canoes). A day trip along the Saguenay and St Lawrence rivers costs $100, and is a great way to see sea mammals and sites of interest. The price includes guide, meals and all taxes. It's worth asking about longer excursions, as they run fixed-rate packages that include accommodation (guesthouse or camping), meals and all equipment hire.

⬦ **Gîte la P'tite Baleine**: 50 rue Principale. ☎ 232-6756. Fax: 232-2000. Doubles $50 a night, including breakfast. This homely, tastefully decorated guesthouse, in the oldest building in the village, has five bedrooms (some with basins) and two shared bathrooms. The handmade bedspreads and antique furniture make the whole place rather special. Out of season, the owner puts up the local teachers, so you might find that the majority of the rooms will be taken.

⬦ **Gîte La Batture à Théophile**: 220 route 138. ☎ 232-6682. Doubles $50 a night, including breakfast. There are just two double rooms in this inventively furnished house, with a cosy log fire in the evenings. The owner has amassed an extensive range of tourist information, so you can read up about the local whale population over a leisurely breakfast.

⬦ **Gîte Bienvenue Chez les Petit**: 56 rue Principale. ☎ 232-6338. Fax: 232-1117. Email: gitepetit@ihcn.qc.

ca. Website: www.ihc.qc.calgite. Doubles $50 a night. This cosy house has five bedrooms, including a family room that sleeps five, and you can be sure of an excellent breakfast. The Petit family will offer plenty of advice about how to make the most of your stay, and have two bicycles for use by guests. They'll also let you use the Internet for free in the morning, and even lend you a Play Station. They can arrange 'safaris' that go in search of the bears and beavers that live in the nearby wilderness – and as if all this wasn't enough to make them the perfect hosts, they even give any tips they get to the Red Cross.

☆☆☆ Expensive

⚑ **Auberge La Rosepierre**: 66 rue Principale. ☎ 232-6543 or 1-888-264-6543 (toll-free). Fax: 232-6215. Email: rosepierre@fjord-best.com. Doubles $80 a night, including traditional Québécois breakfast. The decor is strangely kitsch, but the nine bedrooms are spick and span, and most have en-suite bathrooms.

FESTIVALS AND EVENTS

– **Festival de la Baleine Bleue** (Blue Whale festival): held in August. ☎ 232-6326.

WHAT TO SEE

★ **Centre d'Interprétation Archéologique**: 498 rue de la Mer, by the Essipit dock. ☎ 232-6286. Admission $5. This is a fascinating archaeology museum with interactive information screens, films, slide shows and a mini lab where you can learn how archaeology works. It also offers an overview of the prehistoric landscape of the north bank.

WHALE-WATCHING

■ **Croisière Essipit**: quai des Grandes-Bergeronnes ☎ 232-6778. Fax: 233-2888. Website: www.essipit.com. Cruises from mid-May to mid-October; $28, with child and group tickets available. Wheelchair access. There are two types of outing available, both of which last around 2 hours 30 minutes: a trip on the 100-seater catamaran *Kashkan*, with expert commentary from a naturalist, or an expedition in a Zodiac RIB, for which you'll be provided with protective clothing (but wear thick socks and a scarf, as it's freezing even in summer). The Zodiac excursions are more fun, as the boats tear along at speeds of up to 40kph (25mph), and there are only 12 passengers, but you might find yourself competing for the best vantage points with rival boats from Tadoussac. As on other trips, you should see seals, fin whales, belugas, minkes and, if you're really lucky, a blue whale.

■ **Les Croisières Neptune**: 507 rue du Boisé. Free parking at the centre; a free shuttle bus runs to quai des Bergeronnes, from where the boats leave. ☎ 232-6716. Fax: 232-6790. Cruises from mid-May to mid-October; $33, children $25. This company offers 2-hour excursions on Zodiac RIBs (again, protective clothing is provided). There are four departures a day between 6.30am and 6.30pm. If you don't see any whales on your first trip, they'll take you out again for free.

Farther North

LES ESCOUMINS Pop: 2,200   DIALLING CODE: 418

This area encompasses a fishing port and the Escoumins reserve, which is still populated by native mountain tribes. Its name is derived from two words in the mountain language, *esko* and *mins*, which apparently translate as 'there are still some seeds'. You can go out on the water with local fishermen to catch cod and halibut – and, of course, to see whales (for details, visit the information kiosk on route 138). Accommodation-wise, the Native American campsite is pretty expensive unless you camp in the designated wilderness area.

– A **ferry service** from Les Escoumins to Trois-Pistoles is available from mid-May to mid-October. There are two or three return crossings daily, depending on the tides and the time of year. The journey takes 1 hour 30 minutes, and costs $9 for a foot passenger and $22 for a car. For more information and reservations (a good idea in July or August), ☎ 851-4676 (in Trois-Pistoles) or ☎ 233-2202 (in Les Escoumins).

WHERE TO STAY

⌂ **Le Gîte Fleuri**: 21 rue de l'Église. ☎ 233-3155. Doubles $55 a night. A lovely guesthouse with four prettily decorated bedrooms, two of which have views over the St Lawrence, and two shared bathrooms. Breakfast and service are excellent.

⌂ **Motel Chez Gérard**: 520 route 138, at the water's edge, 3 kilometres (2 miles) east of the village. ☎ 233-2780. Open May to November. Doubles $43 a night. The rooms are nothing special, but they're about right for the price and you get the benefit of a wonderfully wild location. There's a good view over the estuary, where you might spot some whales.

⌂ **Manoir Bellevue**: 27 rue de l'Église. ☎ 233-3325 or 1-888-233-3325 (toll-free). Fax: 233-3277. Doubles $65 per person; $10 for a third person. This lovely guesthouse with views of the bay is tastefully decorated, and it's not at all expensive, especially for groups of three. You can also get an excellent meal for about $25.

WHERE TO EAT

✕ **Le Petit Régal**: 307 route 138. ☎ 233-2666. The decor is uninspiring, but there's a good view of the St Lawrence. The menu offers a wide choice of dishes – salads, sandwiches, pastas, pizzas, fish – at an equally wide range of prices.

WHALE-WATCHING

Two types of cruise are available in Les Escoumins:

– **Fishing-boat cruises**: Gérard Morneau, 539 route 138. ☎ 233-2771. From June to October.

– **Zodiac RIB cruises:** TAN Croisières. ☎ 233-3488, freephone 1-888-353-3488. Fax: 233-2272.

Good value for money, and children aged 5–12 go free. Reception is at port de l'Anse-aux-Basques, at the end of rue des Pilotes.

– Capitaine Ross. ☎ 233-3274. Another Zodiac option.

SAULT-AU-MOUTON

At Sault-au-Mouton, the river turns into an 18-metre (60-foot) waterfall, which rushes down into the torrents below.

WHERE TO STAY

⌂ **Base de Plein Air** (Outdoor Activity Centre): a big site offering overnight accommodation and breakfast, although it's quite expensive.

WHERE TO STAY BETWEEN SAULT-AU-MOUTON AND FORESTVILLE

⌂ **Gîte La Nichée, Chez Camille et Joachim Tremblay**: 46 rue Principale, route 138, Sainte-Anne-de-Portneuf , 84 kilometres (52 miles) north of Tadoussac. ☎ 238-2825. This particularly friendly guesthouse is a great place to stop before taking the ferry over to Baie-Comeau. Joachim is a mine of information on such diverse subjects as traditional hunting methods, ice-fishing, the local sugar festival and organic tomatoes. Camille, meanwhile, spoils everyone rotten with delicious pancakes, raspberry muffins and homemade jams.

WHAT TO SEE IN THE AREA

★ **Saint-Paul-du-Nord**: a little village about a mile from Sault-au-Mouton, with superb views over the bay. A panoramic viewpoint was built behind the church in 1997.

BAIE-COMEAU Pop: 26,000   DIALLING CODE: 418

Baie-Comeau is the departure point for visits to the giant Manic Dams, which are open from mid-June till the beginning of September. Manic 2 is a 20 minutes away from Baie-Comeau, but to see the mighty Manic 5, the world's biggest multiple-arched structure, you'll have to drive for nearly 3 hours. ☎ 294-3923.

– **Ferry for Matane, in Gaspésie**: ☎ 562-6560.

WHAT TO DO

★ **Domaine de l'Ours Noir**: 89 rue Maisonneuve. ☎ 296-5629. This is a wonderful place to see bears and wolves in their natural habitat, but in total safety. Between 15 June and 31 August, Réjean Chenel takes groups out into the wilderness, leaving at 4pm and returning late at night. You're almost certain to see animals, and the prices are very reasonable. You can also book trips out of season.

Chaudière-Appalaches

This vast region on the right bank of the St Lawrence, opposite Québec City, stretches south towards the US border. It's known as the Pays de l'Érable ('Maple Tree Country') because of the number of maple plantations in the area. Its many tourist attractions are not detailed here, as most visitors head for Charlevoix and then Gaspésie after leaving Montréal and Québec City. If you have time, however, it's well worth visiting **Montmagny**, one of the oldest towns on the river's south bank, especially during the snow goose festival (for details, visit www.montmagny.com/tourisme). It also has many interesting manor houses and, at the end of August, hosts an international accordion festival.

To get there, take the ferry from Québec to Lévis, then follow the scenic route 132 north along the St Lawrence.

From Montmagny, there's a free ferry service for the Isle-aux-Grues, the only inhabited island in a beautiful archipelago. There are two or three crossings a day, depending on the tides. ☎ 248-3549 or 248-2968.

You can also take a cruise from Montmagny or Berthier-sur-mer to Grosse-Île, which was a quarantine station for millions of immigrants on their way to America during the 1930s. ☎ 248-4832.

USEFUL ADDRESSES

⽇ Association Touristique Chau-dière-Appalaches: 800 autoroute Jean-Lesage, Bernières. ☎ (418) 831-4411. Fax: 831-8442. Plenty of useful information about the region.

⽇ Office du Tourisme de la Côte Sud (South Bank Tourist Office): 45 avenue du Quai, CP71, Mont-magny. ☎ 248-9196 or 1-800-463-5643 (toll-free). Fax: 248-1436.

WHERE TO STAY IN MONTMAGNY

⽄ La Belle Époque: 100 rue Saint-Jean-Baptiste Est. ☎ 248-3373. When you enter this luxury hotel, you'll feel as though you've stepped back in time. Everything is beautiful and/or antique. Sadly, the price reflects this.

⽄ La Cécilienne: 340 boulevard Taché Est. ☎ 248-0165. The own-ers, Doris and Cécile Boudreau, are charming, and the rooms are clean and well maintained.

WHAT TO SEE IN MONTMAGNY

★ **Le Manoir de l'Accordéon**: 301 boulevard Taché Est. ☎ 248-7927. Open 9am–5pm (weekends 10am–4pm); closed weekends out of season. This museum houses a collection of accordions of all ages and types, and has a workshop where you can see how an accordion is manufactured.

★ **Centre Éducatif des Migrations**: 53 rue du Bassin Nord. ☎ 248-4565. Open late April to mid-November. This is the place to find out about Grosse-Île's strange past – and its wildlife. The immigrants it shelters today are not human, but snow geese, which stop off here during migration.

SAINT-JEAN-PORT-JOLI Pop: 3,400

DIALLING CODE: 418

This pretty village at the edge of the St Lawrence owes its livelihood to woodcarving. There are several dozen working craftsmen in the village, who produce some real masterpieces as well as souvenirs for the tourists. If you're interested in learning the trade, you can sign up for one of many courses on offer.

USEFUL ADDRESSES

🄳 **Office du Tourisme**: 7 avenue de Gaspé Est. ☎ 598-9465. Fax: 598-3085.

🄳 **Kiosque Touristique**: 20 avenue de Gaspé Ouest. ☎ 598-3747.

WHERE TO STAY

🛏 **Au Boisé Joli**: 41 avenue de Gaspé Est, in the centre of town. ☎ 598-6774. This pretty wooden house with parquet flooring has five very comfy bedrooms. The service is friendly, and the breakfasts are huge.

🛏 **Hôtel Le Bonnet Rouge**: 76 avenue de Gaspé Est, on the waterfront. ☎ 598-3088. The rooms are nice and clean, and look out onto the quiet street or the backyard. There's a shared bathroom. Good value for money.

WHERE TO EAT

✕ **La Roche à Veillon**: 547 avenue de Gaspé Est. ☎ 598-3061. Open 8am–midnight. This is a real regional institution, and it's so busy in summer that they don't bother taking bookings. Even when it's heaving, though, the service is excellent, and the food is even better. The menu offers traditional Québécois cuisine 'like granny used to make', and there's a good-value *table d'hôte* at lunchtime. The dining room is large and rustic, and on summer evenings, a theatre troupe provides live entertainment.

✕ **La Coureuse des Grèves**: 300 rue de l'Église, off route 20. ☎ 598-9111. This charming bar-restaurant takes its name, 'The Siren of the Shores', from a poem about a mysterious and beautiful woman who swims naked near the shore, captivating every sailor who sees her. There's a good selection of salads, sandwiches and simple but tasty snacks, including mussels *en coquille* and smoked-salmon bagels, as well as a cheap lunchtime menu and a more expensive *table d'hôte* in the evenings. The restaurant stages exhibitions of Québécois art, and organizes various cultural activities. You can sit out on the terrace in summer.

✗ **Les Libellules**: 17 avenue de Gaspé Est. This US-style snack bar is on the church square, surrounded by souvenir shops. It's a good place to pick up a sandwich or a bagel at bargain prices.

WHAT TO SEE

★ **The Church**: this splendid red-brick building dates back to 1779. Its red roof is crowned with elegant silver bells. Inside, the pews and the altar are finely carved in wood.

★ **Lac des Trois-Saumons**: you can stroll around the lake and see more of the region from the panoramic viewpoint.

★ **Moulin à Farine** (Flour Mill): in Saint-Roch-des-Aulnaies, along the coastal road, next door to the Manoir des Aulnaies, which is also worth a visit.

★ **La Bigorne**: 711 avenue de Gaspé Ouest. ☎ 598-3887. This workshop belongs to Clermont Guay, who is a wrought-iron craftsman and a forest-keeper. He loves to tell tall tales to visitors, but even if you can't follow the French, his workshop will hold your attention.

★ **Théâtre d'Été** (summer theatre): at La Roche à Veillon (see 'Where To Eat').

★ **Les Bateaux Leclerc**: 307 route 132 west. ☎ 598-3273. From June to September, open 9am–9pm (workshops Monday to Friday, 9am–5pm); otherwise, Monday to Friday, 8am–noon and 1–5pm. Miniature boats are a Leclerc family tradition, and you can watch them being made here.

★ **Musée des Anciens Canadiens**: 332 avenue de Gaspé Ouest, on route 132 west, about 3 kilometres (2 miles) from the church. ☎ 598-3392. Open 8.30am–9pm in July and August; 9am–5pm from 15 May to 30 June; 9am–6pm in September and October. Woodcarving is very much the focus of this local-history museum.

★ **Maison Médard-Bourgault**: 322 avenue de Gaspé Ouest. 598-3880. Open late June to mid-August, 11am–5pm. Admission fee. This tiny stone house, hidden amongst giant cedars, once belonged to the woodcarver Médard Bourgault (1897–1967). He carved everything inside: the cupboards, doors, wardrobes, walls and furniture. From the outside, it looks unassuming, but once you cross the threshold, you'll see that Bourgault's creativity knew no bounds.

VISIT A MAPLE GROVE

Maple syrup is to Canada what vodka is to Russia: a national obsession – a maple leaf even adorns the flag – and you can't possibly go to Canada without visiting a maple grove (érablière).

The extraction of syrup takes place in winter and early spring (until March or April), but a summer visit is still enlightening. You'll learn about the maple tree itself, about how juice is extracted (they bore holes into the trunks and fit them with taps), and how the famous syrup is made.

★ **Érablière Bois Joli**: 896 rue de l'Église. ☎ 598-6686. From Saint-Jean-Port-Joli, take route 204 towards Saint-Aubert, cross the motorway, then go straight on along rue de l'Église. You'll find the entrance to the grove on the corner with 2e rang Ouest. Guided tours and syrup tasting take place in summer only. You can enjoy a tasty brunch in this beautiful location, then buy some maple syrup to take back with you.

★ **Érablière M.A. Deschêne**: 483 2e rang Ouest. ☎ 598-6606. Fax: 598-6517. From Saint-Jean-Port-Joli, take route 204 towards Saint-Aubert; cross the motorway, turn right (there's a signpost) and continue for 3 kilometres (2 miles). You can explore the maple grove in a 4x4, then taste the various products made on-site.

★ **Érablière de Rosaire Castonguay**: 40 route Bédard, Saint-Damase-des-Aulnaies. ☎ 598-6749. Plantation tours on Wednesday and Friday at 2pm; phone in advance to arrange a meeting point. This is probably the finest plantation in the Chaudière-Appalaches region, but it's difficult to find, as it's completely buried in the wilderness.

From Saint-Jean-Port-Joli, take route 204 west until you reach Saint-Damase (12 kilometres/7 miles). Go straight on at the church, and on leaving the village, turn left towards Sainte-Louise (route Elgin). Turn right as soon as the tarmac road becomes a dirt track, then carry on for 5 kilometres (3 miles) until you reach the Quatre Coins intersection. The Erablière is on the left, near the roadside. If you get lost, ask for 'Pinguet', which is the name of the area you need to find.

Although Rosaire Castonguay is unknown to most guidebooks and syrup connoisseurs, he almost certainly makes the best maple syrup on the planet, using traditional boiling methods to prepare the most luscious of syrups, which you can buy by the gallon, the half-gallon or in smaller bottles. To reach his cabin, which is hidden in the maple grove, you have to cross hillside meadows with stunning views of the St Lawrence Valley.

LOCAL CELEBRATIONS

– **Saint-Jean-Port-Joli festival**: every weekend in September. This is an international sculpture festival. The locals call it Maisons du Roy en Fête.

– **Festival du Poulet** (Chicken Festival): on the first weekend of September in Saint-Damase. Finger-lickin' good.

Bas-Saint-Laurent

The Bas-Saint-Laurent region stretches along the south bank of the St Lawrence River between Chaudière-Appalaches and Gaspésie. As you head north towards Gaspésie, following the coast, the views become ever more exciting as the river gradually turns into a sea. You'll pass many small villages surrounded by stark agricultural landscape. But suddenly, as you go round a hill, the landscape changes dramatically. The terraced landscape and plains are great walking country in a wilderness dominated by forests and lakes. Then there's the Parc du Bic, a big tourist attraction despite its small size, and tranquil yet lively villages such as Rimouski and Rivière-du-Loup. There are frequent ferry services between these villages (and Trois-Pistoles) and the towns on the opposite bank of the river.

Dégelis is a good destination for anyone who loves cycling, as a 130-kilometre (80-mile) cycle track has been built there on the old railway lines. It starts at Rivière-du-Loup and finishes at Cabano, passing the 'bottomless' Lake Témiscouata along the way.

🛈 Maison Touristique du Bas-Saint-Laurent: in La Pocatière. ☎ (418) 856-5040. From Saint-Jean-Port-Joli, take exit 439 on route 20.

RIVIÈRE-OUELLE Pop: 1,300

This small town on route 132 is a good place to break the journey north. The works of art in the church include the grand altar (18th-century French), paintings by Louis Dulongpré and 18th-century statues. The Casgrain manor house, built in 1834, was the home of the last remaining nobility of Rivière-Ouelle.

KAMOURASKA Pop: 700

Kamouraska means 'the place where the water rushes grow'. This was one of the first places to be colonized on the south bank, and it's now a beautiful village full of strange architecture: the rooftops are completely unique. There are Victorian-style homes with sculpted verandas and houses in the American Mansart style: very long with low shingle roofs (you'll find most of these on avenue Morel). There are also houses in the 'cubic style' and others in the 'American vernacular tradition', whatever that may be. Other than its architecture, the village's main point of interest is the Paradis flour mill, built in 1860 and still in use today. It's also a good place for eel-fishing and a prime meeting place for cormorants.

Though it's a tiny place, Kamouraska is the birthplace of several leading Québécois personalities, including the ultra-conservative René Chalout, who designed the province's fleur-de-lys flag; Eugène-Étienne Taché, who came up with the motto '*Je me souviens*' (I remember), which appears on all the local numberplates; and Adolphe Basile-Routhier, who wrote Canada's national anthem.

The tides are particularly dramatic here. The river (or rather the sea) subsides by 1–2 kilometres twice a day. Along the water's edge, notice boards give information on the tides and the local flora and fauna.

WHERE TO STAY

⌂ Gîte du Passant de Kamouraska: 81 avenue Morel, 100 metres from the church on the right hand-side (if you're coming from Québec). ☎ 492-2921. This pretty little guesthouse was once a school. The tastefully decorated bedrooms look out over the garden or the roads, and you can see the sea in the distance. The homemade jams are delicious.

WHERE TO STAY AND EAT IN THE AREA

⚓ ✕ **Auberge des Aboiteaux**: 280 route 132 west, in Saint-André-de-Kamouraska. ☎ 493-2495. Fax: 493-2779. This old blue-and-yellow-painted house, between the mountains and the river, has been tastefully renovated by the owners, René et Monique, who really make you feel at home. There are five cosy colourful bedrooms, four of which are named after the seasons; the fifth is an en-suite room up in the roof. The owners organize several activities, such as climbing and kayaking, and offer an excellent set menu.

⚓ ✕ **Auberge La Solaillerie**: 112 rue Principale, Saint-André-de-Kamouraska. ☎ 493-2914. This is a magnificent 19th-century home, both inside and out. The bedrooms are all different and all comfortable, and some have four-poster beds. The food is always delicious and plentiful, and the young owners, Isabelle and Yvon, are extremely friendly.

⚓ **La Maison au Toit Bleu**: 490 avenue Saint-Clovis, Saint-Alexandre, 26 kilometres (16 miles) from Kamouraska. ☎ 495-2701. An early-20th-century house with four immaculate bedrooms on the first floor (shared shower and toilet on the landing). All have views of the garden, which has a pretty swing seat. The wooden floors are painted pink, white and blue, and photos of daily life in times gone by are dotted about on the walls. Prices are very reasonable, and the owner is chatty and helpful.

WHAT TO SEE

★ **Musée de Kamouraska**: 69 avenue Morel. ☎ 492-9783. Open 9am–5pm from 20 June until Labor Day (early September). This small, well-designed museum brings Kamouraska's past vividly to life. All the items on show were donated by local people.

★ **Maison de la Prune**: 129 route 132 east, 3 kilometres (2 miles) east of Saint-André. ☎ 493-2616. Fax: 493-2141. Guided tours available. In the 19th century, this was one of the region's most important orchards, with more than 1,000 plum trees and dozens of apple and cherry trees. It fell into decline during the 1940s, but has since been revived. Products on sale include handmade wild berry jams, jellies, aromatic vinegars and, inevitably, maple syrup.

NOTRE-DAME-DU-PORTAGE Pop: 1,200

DIALLING CODE: 418

This peaceful little holiday village is the perfect hideaway if you want to get back to nature. It's full of lovely old buildings, while the rolling Charlevoix hills, on the edge of the village, help to create some of the most stunning sunsets in the area. A long time ago, Native American tribes pitched camp here in the summer for fishing, then carried their canoes inland to the lakes (hence the 'portage' in the village's name) for the winter hunting season.

WHERE TO STAY

La Sabline: 343 Fraser. ☎ 867-4890. On route 132, 5 kilometres (3 miles) north of Notre-Dame-du-Portage. This impressive early-20th-century house, with a pretty garden, used to belong to a furrier, then a famous brewer. The interior is modern and comfortable, and you're sure to sleep soundly in the three well-designed bedrooms (one en suite). There's a small solarium upstairs.

☆☆ Moderate

Maison Le Béluga: 553 route du Fleuve. ☎ 862-7165. This place used to be a restaurant, but the owners decided to convert it into a three-room guesthouse. Their culinary talent is evident when it comes to breakfast, which is huge and delicious. The house overlooks the St Lawrence, which only adds to its already considerable appeal.

Chute Couette et Café: 408a route du Fleuve. ☎ and fax: 862-5367. A modern house with four bedrooms (ask for the Belle Rose or the Pont d'Or) and two bathrooms. It's very peaceful, with good views of the St Lawrence and the magnificent local sunsets, but watch out for mosquitoes after 6pm. A coin-operated washer-dryer is available.

BAS-SAINT-LAURENT

RIVIÈRE-DU-LOUP Pop: 18,000   DIALLING CODE: 418

This pleasant little town is a good place to stay the night if you're heading from Québec to Matane or Gaspé. Nearby, the River Loup flows into the St Lawrence via eight successive cascades, from a total altitude of 1,090 metres (3,575 feet).

USEFUL ADDRESSES

Bureau d'Information Touristique du Bas-Saint-Laurent: 189 boulevard de l'Hôtel-de-Ville, opposite the Musée du Bas-Saint-Laurent. ☎ 862-1981. Fax: 868-1666. Open 8.30am–8.30pm in summer; otherwise weekdays only, 8.30am–5pm. The tourist office is in a slightly eccentric brown house that looks lost in the middle of a huge lawn.

Office du Tourisme de Rivière-du-Loup: 89 boulevard de l'Hôtel-de-Ville, at the ferry point. ☎ 862-1981. Fax: 868-1666. Open 8.30am–5pm.

Cashpoint: Caisse Populaire, 299 rue Lafontaine, in the shopping centre.

Terminal des Autobus Orléans SMT (bus station): 83 boulevard Cartier, a little to the north of town, opposite the Irving service station. ☎ 862-4884. There are two buses a day for Gaspésie and five a day for Québec.

WHERE TO STAY

Campsites

Camping Municipal de la Pointe: rue Hayward, at the junction with boulevard Cartier, not far from the jetty. ☎ 862-4281. Open from mid-May to mid-September. This well-equipped site is a good option if you're arriving on a late ferry.

BAS-SAINT-LAURENT

⬚ Budget

⌂ Auberge Internationale de Jeunesse: 46 rue de l'Hôtel-de-Ville, a 50-minute walk from the ferry. ☎ 862-7566. Fax: 868-1666. Credit-card bookings only. Curfew at 2am. If you call when you arrive, someone will pick you up in the hostel's minibus. This friendly youth hostel is in an old building, and some of the original layout and decoration has been preserved; otherwise, it's been carefully renovated, and the plumbing is brand-new. Double rooms are available, as well as family rooms and mixed or single-sex rooms sleeping three, four or more. There's a common room with a piano and a TV, and you can use the kitchen and the washing machine. Breakfast is included in the price, but linen is extra. The hostel can organize day trips on the St Lawrence and eight-day trips up-river on its magnificent old schooner, stopping at other youth hostels on the way. It also offers kayaking, mountaineering, cycling and storytelling evenings with a Native American chief.

⌂ Résidences du CEGEP de Riv-ière-du-Loup (University halls of residence): 325 rue Saint-Pierre. ☎ 862-6903. From late May to early August only. Single and double rooms available; it's much cheaper if you bring your own sheets or sleeping bag. Staying here can be an eerie experience, because the campus is deserted, but it's good for a one-night stopover.

– You can also stay on the **Bas-Saint-Laurent islands** (*see below*).

⬚⬚ Moderate

⌂ L'Auberge de l'Anse: 2 Anse-au-Persil, route 132 east, near the beach in Pointe de Rivière-du-Loup, two minutes' walk from the ferry for the north bank. ☎ 867-3463. Prices vary according to the season, but they're always reasonable. This welcoming motel/guesthouse will come in very handy if you arrive in town at the dead of night. The rooms are a little tired-looking, but they're clean and well lit, and each has a balcony with a superb view of the river. The largest room can sleep six. The meals are simple but tasty (*table d'hôte* until 9pm). The owners are building a stairwell that will lead straight down to the beach.

WHERE TO EAT

✕ **La Gourmande**: 120 rue Lafontaine. ☎ 862-4270. Open 7.30am–11pm (from 9am on weekends). This café-restaurant has an airy main room where you can tuck into a full breakfast or pop in at all hours for sweet and savoury pastries, cakes and various other snacks. The lunch menus offer soup, a main course, a dessert and coffee. Evening meals are more expensive.

WHERE TO HAVE A DRINK

Rue Lafontaine is jam-packed on a Saturday night, as all the young people in the area flock to its lively bars.

�️ Le Vol de Nuit: on the corner of rues Saint-Laurent and d'Amyot. This trendy bar is open every night until 3am.

�️ Le Jet: 409 rue Lafontaine, near the corner with rue Saint-Laurent. A wild cellar nightclub, complete with dancing girls.

♪ **Le Kojak**: next door to Le Jet, this is another storming place. The locals divide the night between the two, and when in Rivière-du-Loup . . .

WHAT TO SEE

★ **Loup River Waterfalls**: take rue Lafontaine, then rue Frontenac or rue de la Chute from the centre. A viewing platform offers spectacular views of the cascades.

★ **Musée du Bas-Saint-Laurent**: 300 rue Saint-Pierre, in a modern concrete building on the corner of rue de l'Hôtel-de-Ville. ☎ 862-7547. Open 10am–8pm from late June to early September; otherwise 1–5pm. Admission fee. This ethnographic museum has a permanent display about life in Rivière-du-Loup during the 1940s. Dotted all over the museum are works by contemporary artists.

★ If you're into **bells**, there's a private house with an impressive collection at 393 rue Témiscouata, 3 kilometres (2 miles) from the centre. ☎ 862-3346. The largest exhibit weighs 1 tonne.

★ **Musée de Bateaux Miniatures** (Miniature Boat Museum): 80 boulevard Cartier, in a souvenir shop next to the big Saint-Hubert restaurant. ☎ 868-0800. An interesting collection of replicas of boats that used to sail the St Lawrence. They're all made by local people, many of whom also work on the river.

WHAT TO DO

– **Circuit patrimonial**: the tourist office sells leaflets detailing this tourist walk round town, which takes in churches, parkland and some interesting Victorian buildings. From the Croix Lumineuse park, you'll get a good view of the town and the river.

– **Whale-watching**: Navimex organizes cruises from Rivière-du-Loup. It's the same trip you get in Tadoussac, but a bit longer. ☎ 867-3361. You'll get a discount if you have a Youth Hostel card.

– **Îles du Bas-Saint-Laurent**: Société Duvetnor (200 rue Hayward; ☎ 867-1660, fax: 867-3639) was founded by Jean-Hugues Bédard in 1979 to protect the wildlife on these islands. It raises funds by selling eiderdown to duvet manufacturers, and by organizing day trips to the Îles du Pot-à-l'Eau-de-Vie (a hike lasts 3 hours 30 minutes), the Île aux Lièvres (a 10-hour hike with wildlife-spotting) and the Îles Pèlerins (good for bird-watching). The prices are affordable, and groups get a special rate.

⚓ **Pot-à-l'Eau-de-Vie Lighthouse**: 'Nuitée au phare' ('Night at the Light-house') packages from around $120 per person; book at the harbourmas-ter's office. Available between June and October. The lighthouse was built in 1861 and abandoned in 1962 after use by generations of keepers. In 1989, Jean-Hugues Bédard renovated the place, and it's now open to visitors. The package includes a night's accommodation in the lighthouse, two meals featuring local specialities (dinner and brunch), a cruise with commentary and the ferry from Rivière-du-Loup. Gilles Rioux, the current keeper, is a brilliant cook, and will happily talk about the solitary lives of his predecessors. A once-in-a-lifetime experience.

🏠 You can hire a **log cabin** on the Île aux Lièvres: around $130 per day for a four-person hut. If you're really hardy, you can also camp on the island.

FERRY FROM RIVIÈRE-DU-LOUP TO SAINT-SIMÉON

There are frequent ferry services across the St Lawrence all year round (except in February and March), and it's a good way to get to Charlevoix. In summer, there are four or five return trips a day. You can't book, so make sure you get there in good time. Call ☎ 862-9545 (Rivière-du-Loup) or ☎ 638-2856 (Saint-Siméon) for up-to-date timetable information.

ÎLE VERTE Pop: 980   DIALLING CODE: 418

There's a ferry service to this island from the village of L'Isle-Verte, 27 kilometres (17 miles) north of Rivière-du-Loup on route 132. The service operates between May and late November (or until the first heavy frosts). Île Verte is the only island in Bas-Saint-Laurent that's inhabited all year round. Even in winter, about 40 islanders remain on this tiny islet. Until recently, it was isolated from the mainland, and had to be self-sufficient: as a result, it developed a rural way of life that has still survives today. It's also the only place in Québec where you can see (and eat) lamb raised on salt marshes similar to those in Normandy.

The best time to visit is the end of April, when 80 species of birds, including thousands of magnificent snow geese, pause on the island before heading for the eastern Arctic, where they spend the summer.

– **La Richardière Ferry**: ☎ 898-2843. There are three or four return crossings a day in July and August.

– You can also get to the Île Verte on the **Jacques Fraser bateau-taxi** (river taxi): ☎ 898-2199.

WHERE TO STAY AND EAT

– There are several B&Bs on the island, including **Au Chant du Coq** (☎ 898-2443); **Corporation des Maisons du Phare** (☎ 898-3451), in the old lighthouse-keeper's house; and **Le Bateau-Phare** (☎ 898-3444).
– There are also several guest-houses with restaurants: **La Bonne Bouffe** (☎ 898-3325), half-board and bikes available; **La Maison des Roses** (☎ 898-3268), a friendly place where you can hire bikes; **Entre Deux Marées** (☎ 898-2199), a motel, restaurant and bar where the room rates include bike hire; **La Maison d'Agathe** (☎ 898-2923), which offers picnics and light snacks; and **Mon Petit Lopin de Terre** (☎ 898-6166).
– The island also has a bistro, a tea-room and a convenience store that sells sandwiches.
🏠 **Aux Berges de la Rivière**: 24 rue Villeray, Isle-Verte, near the ferry for the island. ☎ 898-2501. Fax: 898-2501. This guesthouse on the mainland is a very pretty, old-fashioned house with lovely bedrooms and antique furniture. Highly recommended.

WHAT TO SEE AND DO

★ You can visit the oldest **lighthouse** on the St Lawrence, built in 1809. Take the chemin du Phare from the quai d'En-Bas, which is where the ferry drops you off.

– **Walking and cycling** in the protected landscape. Bikes can be hired from many of the island's guesthouses.

– With a bit of luck, you'll see **whales** surface off the northernmost tip of the island.

FESTIVALS AND EVENTS

– Many traditional festivities take place between June and September, including Soirée Folichonne ('Boring Night'), Journée des Écrivains (a celebration of local writing talent), a foghorn ceremony, Journée du Pêcheur (fisherman's day) and the Joyeux Bazar. A calendar of events is available at the tourist office in Rivière-du-Loup (*see above*).

TROIS-PISTOLES Pop: 3,800   DIALLING CODE: 418

The town got its name from a passing sailor who cried out *'Voilà trois pistoles perdues'* ('That's three gold pistols down the drain') when he dropped a valuable silver cup into the sea. It's opposite the Île aux Basques and the Razades, a bird sanctuary that attracts many species of sea birds. The town has a pretty church, and there's an island festival in July.

– **Ferry between Trois-Pistoles and Les Escoumins**: Two or three crossings a day between mid-May and mid-October depending on the weather and the tides. It takes 1 hour 30 minutes. ☎ 851-4676. If you take the last crossing of the day, you get a 50 per cent discount.

– **Day trips**: excursions are advertised along the quayside, in particular for Île aux Basques.

USEFUL ADDRESS

ⓘ Bureau d'Information Touristique: 55 route 132 west. ☎ 851-3698. Open 9am–7pm in summer. A friendly and efficient tourist office. Out of season, contact the Corporation Touristique des Basques (120 rue Notre-Dame Ouest, ☎ 851-4949) or visit www.icrdl.net/basques.

WHERE TO STAY

Campsites

⌂ Camping municipal des Trois-Pistoles: 100 rue Chanoine-Côté; signposted on route 132. ☎ 851-1377 or 851-4515; out of season, ☎ 851-1995. Open mid-June to be-ginning of September. Pitches $16–20. This is a large, well-organized campsite near the sea. If you don't fancy the beach, there's a heated pool (free for campers), and other on-site facilities include a shop, bike hire, mini-golf and botanical walks. You can try your hand at trout fishing nearby.

– There are two other campsites: **Camping Plage Trois-Pistoles**, to the north of town (130 route 132 east; ☎ 851-2403; fax: 851-4890; $15) and **Camping des Flots Bleus**, to the south of town (Rivière-Trois-Pistoles, on route 132; ☎ 851-3583).

☆☆ Moderate

☎ **Gîte La Rose des Vents**: 80 2e rang Ouest. ☎ and fax: 851-4926 or 1-888-593-4926 (toll-free). Doubles $65 a night. A pretty blue house on a hilltop that overlooks the St Lawrence. There are four bright, spacious and tastefully decorated rooms with en-suite bathrooms.

☎ **Gîte du Passant Le Terroir des Basques**: 65 2e rang Ouest.

☎ 851-2001. Doubles $50 a night. From route 132, take the 293 south for a kilometre (half a mile), then turn right. The guesthouse is about 1.5 kilometres (one mile) down on the left. A pleasant stone farmhouse with four simple bedrooms, one of which sleeps five. The friendly owners grow their own potatoes and keep cattle, and breakfasts consist of homegrown produce and homemade bread and jam.

☎ **Gîte aux Mille Souvenirs**: 96 rue Notre-Dame Ouest, above a souvenir shop. ☎ 851-4704. Doubles $45–55 per night. One of the few B&Bs in Trois-Pistoles itself, it has seven bedrooms, all with basins and some with showers. The interior is a bit old-fashioned, but this friendly place is the best option in town.

WHERE TO STAY AND EAT IN THE AREA

☎ ✕ **Auberge Saint-Simon**: 18 rue Principale, in Saint-Simon, 7 kilometres (4 miles) east of Trois-Pistoles on route 132. ☎ 738-2971. Open from mid-May to late September. Doubles $65 a night; 10 per cent discount for cyclists. An attractive wooden house with a cosy interior and nine bedrooms, all with footbaths. The nearby road is a bit noisy, so stay elsewhere if you're a light sleeper. Otherwise, it's a great place, and the cooking is excellent and varied: fish and shellfish, an excellent lamb stew with herbs, homemade yoghurt and so on. The food is sensibly priced, everything is fresh and it feels like you're eating it in a family dining room.

☎ **Gîte du Passant Chez Choinière**: 71 rue Principale, Saint-Siméon. ☎ 738-2245. Doubles $50–55 a night, including breakfast; $60 for the caravan on the beach, which sleeps four. Prices drop out of season. This roadside guesthouse is very appealing, and has been sensitively restored. It has five spacious bedrooms with beds and basins, all in period style, and a single shared bathroom upstairs. Alain, your relaxed host, bakes his own bread, and you can taste the results with the generous breakfasts. There's a BBQ corner in the garden. Prices are lower out of season.

WHERE TO EAT

✕ **L'Ensoleillé**: 138 rue Notre-Dame Ouest. ☎ 851-2889. Lunch menu $7–11; *table d'hôte* $10–18. This friendly restaurant is a haven for vegetarians, with delicious dishes such as chilli con carne. There are a few non-veggie dishes, such as chicken *à l'orange*, trout fillet and grilled prawns. The food is good, the service is excellent and the terrace is perfect for soaking up the sun.

WHAT TO SEE AND DO

★ **Musée Saint-Laurent**: 552 rue Notre-Dame Ouest. ☎ 851-2345. Open from late June to mid-September, 8.30am–6pm. Admission $3. In the 1960s, Adrien Coté, a motel-owner, bought a classic car in the hope that it would catch prospective customers' eyes. Over the years, vintage vehicles became an obsession, and, 15 years later, he ended up creating this museum to house them all. As well as a fine collection of classic cars dating from the 1930s to the 1970s, he's amassed several other automotive curiosities, including a bizarre snowmobile from 1919, mechanics' tools and car accessories, as well as other period pieces such as old bikes, harpoons and antique cigarette packets. Adrien is usually on hand to answer any questions you might have.

★ **Église Notre-Dame-des-Neiges**. This church is imposing both inside and out. Its architectural styles, its decoration and the many legends surrounding it have long been a local talking point.

★ **Parc de l'Aventure Basque en Amérique**: 66 rue du Parc. ☎ 851-1556. Open from 1 June to mid-October, 9am–8pm (from 10am between mid-July and mid-August). Admission $5. The park was built on the site where the first Basque community in Québec once lived, and the star attraction is the interactive exhibition about the arrival of the Basques in the region in the 16th century. After the tour, you can get a further taste of Basque culture at the bar or on the pelota court.

– **Boat trips to the Île aux Basques**: from the marina. ☎ 851-1202. From June to mid-September. There's a flat rate of $12 for guided trips, which take about three hours.

– **Sea kayaking**: Rivi-Air Aventure, 2175 route 132 east. ☎ 736-5232. Website: www.cam.org/£bsl/rivi-air.aventure. Half-day $33; full day $57. Three departures daily, between 7.30am and 8.30pm; one excursion at sunset. Booking recommended. The guided trips take you around the Bic islands.

LE PARC DU BIC   DIALLING CODE: 418

On Route 132, between Trois-Pistoles and Rimouski. There are two entrances: one is just after the village of Saint-Fabien, the other just before the village of Bic.

This National Park is in a beautiful location between the mountains and the sea. Legend has it that when God created the world, the angel in charge of mountains had too many; he dumped the extras into the sea, thus creating Bic and its islands. Whatever you make of the story, Bic is blessed with an abundance of rocky coastline, making it a great place to come for hiking, mountain-biking (on managed tracks) and wildlife-watching. The park attracts marine mammals, salmon, shellfish and sea birds, while the landscape is breathtaking.

> **TIP** If you go walking here, take plenty of insect repellent. The mosquitoes are fearsome.

USEFUL ADDRESSES

ℹ Park Information: by the second entrance next to the campsite. ☎ 736-5035. Open 8am–4pm in summer. You can pick up park maps and details of walks.

ℹ Tourist Information: 33 route 132, Saint-Fabien. ☎ 869-3333. Open from late June to early September 9am–7pm; closed weekends out of season.

WHERE TO STAY AND EAT IN THE AREA

⛺ There's a **campsite** in the park at the Pierre-Baudry entrance (the second if you're coming from Trois-Pistoles). ☎ 736-4711. A tent pitch costs $17. It's fairly basic, it's near the road, it's noisy and there's no shade, so avoid it unless you want to stay in the park.

⛺ ✕ **Auberge du Mange-Grenouille**: 148 rue Saint-Cécile, in Bic. ☎ 736-5656. Fax: 736-5657. Open 1 May to 15 October. Doubles $55–80 a night; booking essential. The Auberge is a former shop turned into a well-to-do home, and the place has a certain eccentric charm. Painted red, with a carved wooden gable, it has 15 comfy rooms, one of which is a magnificent bridal suite. Guests share two huge bathrooms, one of which has a jacuzzi. The rooms in the annexe have en-suite bathrooms. The restaurant and bar have a terrace with views of the park. Evening meals only.

⛺ **Gîte Aux Cormorans**: in Bic, near the pointe aux Anglais. ☎ 736-8113. Fax: 736-4216. From route 132, drive past the golf course; the guesthouse (with blue shutters and a white veranda) is a little farther down on the left. Doubles $50–75 a night. The location

is perfect – on the water's edge, facing rocky islets – and the five snug bedrooms with all-wooden fittings are not far off. Breakfast is served in the large dining room, with a fireplace and a lovely view, and behind the house is a pretty lawn planted with pine trees. This is a lovely, serene spot, and you'll be sad to leave.

⛺ **Gîte La Maison de l'Irlandais**: 182 1re rue Est, Saint-Fabien. ☎ 869-2913 or 1-888-869-2913 (toll-free). Website: www.bbcanada. com/2132.html. Doubles $55–65 a night. This former farm is on the roadside at the entrance to the park. It's painted green and yellow, and is full of character: the period interior design is simple yet stylish, with a rustic feel, and, as the name suggests, there's something of an Irish feel about the place, most obviously in the breakfasts and the music. There are four bedrooms, three with a basin and bath. The owner is also an artist and you can buy his works. Non-smoking.

⛺ ✕ **Gîte de la Maison du Cordonnier**: 26 7e Avenue, Saint-Fabien, in the town centre. ☎ 869-2002. Doubles $50 a night, including breakfast. This charming wooden house is painted pale yellow, with a silver-grey roof, and is surrounded by an elegant veranda. The three pretty bedrooms, which have an Olde Worlde atmosphere, share one bathroom. Bike hire is available.

WHAT TO DO

– **Seal- and bird-watching**: Aqua-tours. ☎ 750-1998. Website: www.cni pap/affaire/aquatour. Tours run from mid-April to mid-September, and cost $15–45. Discover grey seals, the coastline, and, thanks to a special underwater camera, shipwrecks and the seabed. You can also have an alfresco meal and camp at the water's edge.

– **Walking**: the park information centre suggests several gentle, scenic walks in the area.

– **L'Anse à Bouleaux Ouest** and **Cap-à-l'Orignal** are home to large colonies of grey seals, which come out to sunbathe on the rocks at low tide. Make sure you know when the tides are due before you go.

– No one is sure how the **Baie du Ha! Ha!** got its name. Some say it's because of the exclamations of awe people let out when they see the bay for the first time. Others believe it comes from an old French word for cove ('*ha-ha*').

RIMOUSKI Pop: 34,000　　　　　　DIALLING CODE: 418

Rimouski has seen more than its fair share of catastrophe. In 1950, more than a third of the town was destroyed by fire, and on 29 May 1914, the *Empress of Ireland* sank just offshore from Rimouski. There were more than 1,000 victims, making it the largest maritime disaster after the sinking of the *Titanic*. Despite this, the town is a lively place, and there's plenty to do if you decide to stay for a couple of days. The name, incidentally, comes from a Native American word meaning 'land of the moose'.

USEFUL ADDRESSES

🅱 Office du Tourisme (A1 on the map): 50 rue Saint-Germain Ouest, on the seafront. ☎ 723-2322 or 1-800-746-6875 (toll-free). From mid-June to mid-October, open 9am–8pm; otherwise weekdays only, 9am–4.30pm. There's loads of information about the region, and audioguides are available for visits to the town. You can hire a bike here, and there's a *poste restante* service.
Post office (B1): rue Saint-Germain Ouest.
■ **Banque Royale** (B1, **1**): 1 rue Saint-Germain Est, on the corner of rue Cathédrale. The cashpoint ac-

cepts Visa cards. There are several other banks in town.
■ **Allôstop** (B1, **2**) 106 rue Saint-Germain Est, in Le Perroquet bookshop. ☎ 723-5248. A good way to get lifts to Québec and Montréal.
🚌 **Terminus de Bus Orléans** (Orleans Bus Terminal) (off B1 on the map): 90 avenue Léonidas, on route 132 east. ☎ 723-4923. There are two buses a day for Gaspésie, and two buses a day for the Matapédia valley.
🚆 **Railway station** (B1 on the map): 57 rue de l'Évêché Est. ☎ 722-4737 or 1-800-361-5390 (toll-free). Three trains a week to Gaspésie.

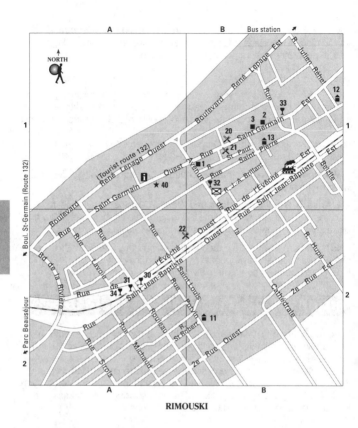

RIMOUSKI

■ **Useful Addresses**

🛈	Office du tourisme
✉	Post office
🚂	Railway Station
1	Banque Royale
2	Allôstop
3	Tabagie de la Cité

🛏 **Where to Stay**

11 CEGEP
12 Ô Toit Mansard
13 Gîte du Centre-Ville

✕ **Where to Eat**

20 Le Mix
21 La Maison du Spaghetti
22 Central Café

🍷 **Where to Have a Drink**

30 Café Le Campus
31 L'Étrier Pub
32 Le Sens Unique
33 Bar Country chez Dallas
34 Le Néo-taverne

★ **What To See**

40 Musée Régional

🚢 **Rimouski-Forestville Ferry**: ☎ (418) 725-2725. Up to four crossings a day in season. It takes 55 minutes to get to the other side of the St Lawrence. There's no service if the wind gets too high.

■ **Laundrettes**: 260 rue Saint-Germain Est and 167 rue Saint-Jean-Baptiste Ouest.
■ **Tabagie de la Cité** (B1, **3**): 102 rue Saint-Germain Est. Newsagent and tobacconist.

WHERE TO STAY

⚐ **CÉGEP** (B2, **11**): 320 rue Saint-Louis. ☎ 723-4636 or 1-800-463-0617 (toll-free). Fax: 722-9250. Website: www.cegep-rim ouski.qc.ca/residenc. Dorm rooms $20–28 a night. This student residence lets out 500 rooms between early June and mid-August. The buildings are a little soulless, but everything's clean.
⚐ **Ô Toit Mansart** (B1, **12**): 182 rue Ringuet. ☎ 724-2485. Doubles $50 a night. The three smallish but impeccable bedrooms are in the basement of an annexe. There's a fully equipped kitchen (with a microwave), and breakfast is served in a covered section of the garden.

⚐ **Gîte du Centre-Ville** (B1, **13**): 84 rue Saint-Pierre, on a quiet street near the centre. ☎ 723-5289. Doubles $50 a night. This smart, comfortable gîte is run by a kind and welcoming family. The four large, pastel-coloured rooms share a bathroom.
⚐ **Motel Lyse**: 543 boulevard Saint-Germain Ouest, on route 132, 3 kilometres (2 miles) from the centre towards Rivière-du-Loup. ☎ 723-1040. Fax: 723-1042. Doubles $50 a night. This roadside motel has clean but unspectacular en-suite rooms with cable TV. Ask for one that's away from the road. Breakfast is available, but only weekdays out of season.

WHERE TO STAY IN THE AREA

⚐ **Gîte 100-T**: 100 5e rang Est, Saint-Marcellin. ☎ 735-5224. From Rimouski, take route 232, exit 610, towards Sainte-Blandine. At Saint-Narcisse, take the track on the left, then follow the signs. Doubles from $50 a night. This good-value gîte-cum-health-club in the heart of the countryside is owned by the manager of a vegetarian restaurant, and offers excellent veggie and seafood dishes as well as a host of outdoor activities. Bring your own alcohol.
⚐ **Gîte Domaine du Bon Vieux Temps**: 89 chemin de l'Écluse, Saint-Narcisse-de-Rimouski. ☎ 735-5646. If you're coming from Rimouski, it's signposted after Mont-Lebes. From Québec City, take exit 610 off autoroute 20 east and follow signs for Sainte-Blandine until you

get to route 232 Ouest. Stay on the 232, past the Saint-Narcisse intersection and carry on for a kilometre (about half a mile), then take the first left and follow the directions from Rimouski. Doubles $55 a night. This wonderful stone-built 'refuge' in the middle of a forest, kept warm by the cast-iron stove in the fireplace, has three rooms and a shared bathroom. Guests can go swimming or canoeing in the nearby lake, and there's dog-sledding in winter. To cap it all, the breakfasts are excellent.
⚐ **Gîte Le Villageois**: 496 chemin Duchénier, Saint-Narcisse-de-Rimouski, 25 kilometres (16 miles) from Rimouski along route 232. ☎ 735-2335. This inexpensive, peaceful gîte is near the Canyon

RIMOUSKI

des Portes de l'Enfer ('Gates of Hell'). There are three bright, modern rooms, all equally comfortable and spotless. Breakfast is served in a glass conservatory with views of the surrounding countryside.

WHERE TO EAT

✕ **Central Café** (A-B2, **22**): 31 rue de l'Évêché Ouest, in an old, green-painted house among the trees. ☎ 722-4011. Open 11am–11pm (until midnight on weekends). Main courses $7–13. The menu includes good pasta and pizza dishes, 'luxury' hamburgers and fabulous *frites*. There's a good choice of eating areas, too: intimate ground-floor rooms, a conservatory, the terrace or the first-floor balcony, which is decorated with a bizarre assortment of birdcages.

✕ **Le Mix** (B1, **20**): 50 rue Saint-Germain Est, in the centre of town. ☎ 722-5025. Main courses $6–10. Open 2pm–3.30am (from 9am on weekends); food served until 8pm. This bright, spacious eatery with designerish decor attracts a young, trendy clientele.

✕ **La Maison du Spaghetti** (B1, **21**): 35 Saint-Germain Est. ☎ 723-6010. Fax: 723-8438. Open 11am–11pm. Full meal from $10. You can't miss this red-painted wooden house, which the locals still call 'Forge du Père Cimon' (it used to belong to a blacksmith, Henri Cimon). The interior is done up in pleasing shades of green and white, with checked tablecloths, and the menu majors in pasta dishes, though pizzas, grilled meat and seafood are available if you prefer. The portions are large, and the service is fast and friendly, so it's no surprise that this place gets very busy, especially on weekends. Booking recommended.

WHERE TO HAVE A DRINK

❢ **Le Mix** (*see* 'Where to Eat'). In the evenings, this venue lives up to its name, with an eclectic soundtrack of Irish, Mexican and Spanish folk, rock and blues, as well as a a good selection of beers from around the world. It hosts occasional theme nights. There's a terrace, and a chill-out room at the back.

❢ **Café Le Campus** (A2, **30**): 149 rue de l'Évêché Ouest. ☎ 722-0770. Open Wednesday to Sunday, until 3am. This is a lively student hangout with cheap drinks and Québécois singers providing the entertainment on Thursday, Friday and Saturday. There's also a pool table.

❢ **L'Étrier Pub** (A2, **31**): 155 rue de l'Évêché Ouest. ☎ 724-2266. Open until 3am; closed Sunday. This is your standard trendy bar-club. The atmosphere's good, but if you're looking for a night out, Le Campus is probably more fun.

❢ **Le Sens Unique** (B1, **32**): 160 avenue de la Cathédrale. ☎ 722-9400. Open until 3am. It sounds incongruous, but there's a disco every night in this mock-medieval bar. It attracts a mixed crowd, and the atmosphere's great. Get there early for happy hour.

❢ **Le Néo-taverne** (A2, **34**): 155 rue de l'Évêché Ouest. ☎ 724-2266. Open 2pm–3am; closed Sunday. This small, dingy club offers a good range of music and the occasional live band. The mini dancefloor is overhung by a giant spider, and there's a large terrace at the front.

❢ **Bar Country chez Dallas** (B1, **33**): 134 rue Saint-Germain Est.

☎ 723-4011. This is the place to go if you're in search of an authentic country-music bar, complete with line-dancing on Friday and Saturday nights. if you leave your preconceptions at the door, you'll have a ball.

WHAT TO SEE AND DO

★ **Musée Régional** (A1, **40**): 35 rue Saint-Germain Ouest. ☎ 724-2272. Open Wednesday to Sunday, 10am–6pm. This former church, built in 1824, houses good-quality art exhibitions.

★ **Maison Lamontagne**: 707 boulevard du Rivage, 6 kilometres (4 miles) from Rimouski, towards Pointe-au-Père. ☎ 722-4038. Open mid-May to mid-October, 9am–6pm. Admission $3; discounts for families, groups, students and senior citizens. The building dates back to the 18th century, and is one of only three half-timbered houses in North America. In the garden, there's a free exhibition about the development of Québécois building techniques over the past 300 years. Chamber-music concerts are held here in summer.

★ **Parc Beauséjour**: boulevard de la Rivière, on route 132. ☎ 724-3167. Attractions at this centrally located park include cycle tracks, walks, canoe and pedalo hire, picnic areas and open-air shows. New projects are in the pipeline, so phone if you want to find out more.

– **Sentiers d'interprétation du littoral et de la rivière Rimouski** (coastal paths with information en route): follow the river and pass through Parc Beauséjour. ☎ 723-0480. Walkers can explore 15 kilometres (9 miles) of footpaths dotted with information boards pointing out the area's bird and plant life. There are also 7 kilometres (4 miles) of laid out mountain-bike trails.

– **Excursions to Île Saint-Barnabé**: ☎ 723-2377. Tickets $12. Boats for guided island walks depart every half-hour between 10am and 3pm.

– **Expéditions Gallayann Aventure**: 199 rue Principale, Saint-Gabriel-de-Rimouski. ☎ and fax: 798-4642. Website: www.gallayann.com. Packages start at $85. This company offers expeditions into the heart of Rimouski's nature reserve, including guided nature walks that go in search of the region's animal life (parents of small children should bear in mind that this can mean spending an entire day in silence while you wait for the animals to appear), mountain-bike circuits, boat trips or trekking in traditional horse-drawn wagons. In winter, dog-sleigh trails take you into the woods and lakes of the Appalachians.

FESTIVALS AND EVENTS

– **Festi-jazz**: this jazz festival takes place every year around Labor Day (late August/early September) in venues all over town. For a programme, ☎ 724-7844.

– **Festival Musique en Fleurs**: from early July to 1 August, in Parc Lepage and on place Beaulieu. ☎ 723-2322 or 1-800-746-6875 (toll-free). Tickets, price $16, are on sale in the Rimouski Tourist Office. You'll hear music of all kinds during this summer concert season.

– **Carrousel International du Film**: every year during the last week of September, the Lido cinema shows films made by up-and-coming directors from all over the world. The movies are judged by a French-speaking panel. Tickets are available from the tourist office.

What to See in the Area

SAINTE-LUCE

This is a lovely stretch of seaside, 10 kilometres (6 miles) from Rimouski; in fact, it's probably the best beach along this coast. There's also a pretty church facing out to sea.

WHERE TO STAY, EAT AND HAVE A DRINK

☖ Campsite: route du Fleuve Ouest, Sainte-Luce. ☎ 739-5393. Fax: 739-5065. Tent pitch $20 a night; caravan space $23. This tiny site overlooks the sea, but it's more basic than you'd expect at these prices.

☖ Maison des Gallant: 40 route du Fleuve Ouest, right on the riverbank. ☎ 739-3512 or 1-888-739-3512 (toll-free). Website: www.gites-classifies.qc.ca/gallant.htm. Doubles $55 a night. A family-run gîte in an early-20th-century house and garden. There are three comfortable, well-kept bedrooms and two solariums. The breakfasts are amazing.

☖ ✗ L'Auberge de l'Eider: 90 route du Fleuve Est. ☎ 739-3535. Doubles from $60 a night. Open late June to late August. This is a lovely house in the middle of the cove, with direct access to the beach. The 18 en-suite bedrooms all have sea views, while the tastefully decorated dining room overlooks the St Lawrence River. The cooking is excellent, with regional specialities to the fore.

✗ La Boulangère de Sainte-Luce: 68 rue du Fleuve Ouest. ☎ 739-3244. You can get homemade pastries, bread, cooked meals, jams and sauces to eat in or take away. The staff are friendly, and the food is good and inexpensive: try the rhubarb and strawberry tarts.

✗ ❢ L'Anse aux Coques: 31 route du Fleuve Ouest, 100 metres east of the church. ☎ 739-4815. Email: sudanjou@cgocable.ca. Open late June until September, 7am–3am. Main courses $8–20. This is a decent café with a terrace and sea views; the house speciality is seafood. There's also a pool table.

SAINT-GABRIEL-DE-RIMOUSKI

Take route 298 from Sainte-Luce, then turn right onto route 234, then head to Sainte-Angèle. From Rimouski, take route 232 then turn left onto route 234.

WHERE TO STAY

☖ Le Bercail: 199 rue Principale. ☎ 798-4487. Fax: 798-4642. Website: www.gallayann.com/aubercail/index/html/. Doubles $45 a night. Josiane Vouillon runs this clean, simple establishment, and makes the excellent breakfasts. Her husband, Gilles, organizes horse-and-cart excursions in summer, and sleigh rides in the winter (about $85).

WHAT TO SEE IN THE AREA

★ **Musée de la Mer**: 1034 rue du Phare, Pointe-au-Père, 10 kilometres (6 miles) from Rimouski on route 132 est. ☎ 724-6214. Email: museemer@ globetrotter.qc.ca. Open June to mid-October, 9am–5pm (until 6pm from June to August). This maritime museum is located in the village lighthouse. There's an exhibition on the sinking of the *Empress of Ireland* on 29 May 1914, which claimed the lives of 1,192 people. The shipwreck has been re-created using video screens, and an exhibition of diving equipment explains how the wreck was discovered and investigated. You can also take a guided tour (1 hour 30 minutes).

★ **Canyon des Portes de l'Enfer**: 30 kilometres (18 miles) south of Rimouski on route 232. ☎ 750-1586. Open mid-May to late October, 9.30am–5.30pm. Admission $5. The 'Canyon of the Gates of Hell' was discovered by the French pioneers on their trip down the Rimouski River. It's 5 kilometres (3 miles) long, with several guided paths for hikers and 20 kilometres (12 miles) of mountain-bike trails.

Gaspésie

This peninsula encompasses a range of landscapes millions of years old, and much of it remains entirely unspoiled. Your time here will be one of the high points of your trip to Québec.

Forming the northern tip of the Appalachian Mountains, Gaspésie resembles Brittany in its climate and rocky coastline. At other times, the wild loneliness of the landscape seems more like Norway. In some places, its north side falls dramatically into the sea. Gaspé comes from the Micmac word *gespeg*, which means 'the place at the end of the Earth'. The Orléans bus company runs services throughout the region, and although there's only one bus a day from many places, this is often a better option than hitchhiking.

The people are almost exclusively French-speaking, and still have a very traditional lifestyle. This is because, until quite recently, the peninsula was economically isolated from the rest of Québec. A former prime minister, René Lévesque, was born in New Carlisle, on the south coast.

USEFUL ADDRESS

🄱 **Association Touristique Régionale de Gaspésie**: 357 route de la Mer (route 132), in Sainte-Flavie, the first village in Gaspésie if you're coming from Bas-Saint-Laurent. The tourist office is on the right-hand side of the road, in a white house with a red roof. ☎ 775-2223. Fax: 775-2234. Open June to mid-October, 8am–8pm. A good place to pick up a regional guide, maps, and leaflets on accommodation and sites of interest.

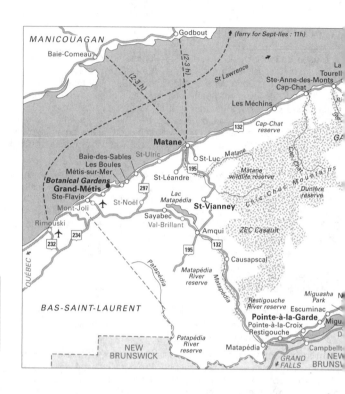

GRAND-MÉTIS Pop: 300   DIALLING CODE: 418

This pretty village is on the banks of the St Lawrence, midway between Rimouski and Matane, and just past Sainte-Flavie.

WHERE TO STAY AND EAT IN SAINTE-FLAVIE

⚓ ✕ **Centre d'Art Marcel-Gagnon**: 564 route de la Mer, on the left past the Sainte-Flavie exit, towards Matane. ☎ 775-2829. Fax: 775-9548. Doubles $60–80 a night. A hostel, café, restaurant and art gallery in a large wood-and-stone house by the sea. The most expensive of the 10 rooms have sea views, and all are very clean and tidy. The owner is a painter and sculptor, and made the series of Madonna-type figures who follow one another down to the water's edge.

✕ **Capitaine Homard**: 180 route de la Mer, on the outskirts of Sainte-Flavie, on the Rimouski side. ☎ 775-8046. Fax: 775-9308. Open May to September, until midnight. Daily specials $15. 'Captain Lobster' serves up good-value fish and seafood, especially cod and lobster, all caught locally around the Îles de la Madeleine and the Baie des

GASPÉSIE

Chaleurs. The restaurant is in a large, white-painted building with a red roof. The ambience is calm and laid-back, as is the service.

✕ **Le Gaspesiana**: 460 route de la Mer. ☎ 775-7233 or 1-800-404-8233 (toll-free). Fax: 775-9227. Lunch $15; dinner $23. This is a classy venue with excellent views of the river. The food is a bit unadventurous, but it's good value for money at lunchtime.

WHERE TO STAY AND EAT IN THE AREA

🛏 **La Villa du Vieux Clocher**: 179 rue Beaulieu, Saint-Antoine-de-Padoue. Take the road that crosses route 132 at right angles, opposite the Métis gardens, towards Saint-Octave-de-Métis. When you get to Saint-Antoine, take rue Gagnon, which leads to rue Beaulieu. Follow this road until you get to a church; the hotel is next door, in the old presbytery. ☎ and fax: 775-9654. Email: aggite@gites-classifies.qc.ca. Doubles $55 a night. The seven rooms are rather kitsch, but they're entirely in keeping with the rest of the house, which is full of eccentric religious ornaments, trinkets and pieces of furniture. The outside annexe can sleep 10, so it's a good choice for families or large groups of four or more. The landlady is a real character, and she's wildly enthusiastic about everything. In the winter, she organizes murder-mystery evenings. Meals are available, but you'll have to ask in advance.

🛏 ✕ **Auberge du Grand Fleuve, chez Raynald et Marie Pey**: 47 rue Principale, Les Boules, not far from Grand-Métis on the way to Matane. ☎ 936-3332. Doubles $60–80 a night; half- and full-board packages available. Opposite a church and not far from the riverbank, this pretty green-and-yellow wooden house has a dozen inviting rooms. The owners are a very pleasant French-Canadian couple. The evening meals are expensive, but the food is truly fabulous.

✕ **La Meunerie**: 202 route 132, Baie-des-Sables. ☎ 772-6808. This restaurant is inside an old flour mill, and the pretty waterwheel makes an interesting backdrop. The dining room has been cleverly designed to preserve the building's rustic charm, while the pleasant upstairs room has a fireplace. They serve bargain lunches and more expensive evening meals, with seafood and grilled meat among the specialities.

WHAT TO SEE

★ **Jardins de Métis** (Botanical Gardens): 200 route 132. ☎ 775-2222. Open early June to mid-October, 8.30am–6.30pm. Admission $8; family ticket $20. 'Métis' *(mitis)* is a Native American term meaning 'little poplar'. It is also the name of the river that runs through the gardens. The river is famous for its salmon population, which is what attracted a wealthy aristocrat to the area. His heir designed the English-style gardens, introducing several hundred species of plant. Today, there are more than 100,000 specimens, including day lilies, blue poppies, nasturtium, peonies and rhododendrons. You don't have to be green-fingered to appreciate the enchanting beauty of the place, complete with tumbling brooks and miniature bridges. Classical-music concerts are held here in summer.

At the centre of the gardens is a magnificent 19th-century **villa**, which has had 15 of its rooms transformed into a museum of crafts and domestic history. Guided tours are available (about 1 hour 30 minutes).

– There's a stunning **restaurant** in the villa's three luxurious dining rooms. ☎ 775-3165. Open 9.30am–6.30pm. The food is surprisingly affordable.

– Also inside the house is a **souvenir shop** selling fine examples of local craftsmanship. The prices may seem high at first, but the quality is far superior to that found in most of the similar shops in town.

★ **Centre d'Interprétation du Saumon Atlantique** (Atlantic Salmon Centre): 900 route de la Mer, on route 132, past Sainte-Flavie. ☎ 775-2969. Open mid-June to late October, 9am–5pm; times may vary in September. Admission $7. Exhibitions, films and aquariums tell you everything you ever wanted to know about these fascinating creatures.

★ **Le Grand Rassemblement**: Saint-Flavie. This sculpture by Marcel Gagnon (of the local Centre d'Art, *see above*) comprises 80 cement figures rising out of the waters of the St Lawrence.

MATANE Pop: 13,000   DIALLING CODE: 418

The name 'Matane' also has Native American origins, and means 'beaver breeding ground'. Today, however, Matane is essentially an industrial town, and is a key destination for ferries bringing passengers to the Gaspé Peninsula from Baie-Comeau or Godbout. Nonetheless, it's a pleasant town, thanks to its large squares and the beautiful sunsets over the water. There's no bus service from the port to the centre, which is a 30-minute walk away, so you may want to call a taxi.

USEFUL ADDRESSES

Bureau d'Information Touristique: in an old lighthouse at 968 avenue du Phare Ouest, by the sea. ☎ 562-1065. From June to August, open 9am–8.30pm; in September and October, open 9am–5pm. As well as the usual tourist services, there's a small museum.

■ Banque Nationale: 390 Saint-Jérôme.

WHERE TO STAY IN THE MATANE AREA

⌂ Camping Rivière-Matane: boulevard L.-F.-Dionne, Saint-Jérôme de Matane, about 3 kilometres (2 miles) from the ferry. ☎ 562-3414. Open from mid-June to the beginning of September. Tent pitches $12; caravan site $18. To get there, follow the river past the industrial park; the campsite is signposted a little farther down on the right. This is a spacious, pleasant site in the middle of the countryside. Facilities include a shop and a laundrette.

⌐☆–☆☆⌐ Budget to Moderate

⌂ Gîte du Passant Le Panorama: 23 chemin Lebel, Saint-Luc-de-Matane. ☎ and fax: 562-1100 or 1-800-473-9319 (toll-free in Canada only). Website: www.chez.com/gite panorama. Email: gitepanorama@ chez.com. From Matane, follow avenue Saint-Rédempteur for 8 kilometres (5 miles), turning left before you get to Lac Saint-Luc; it's 700 metres (half a mile) farther down on the left. Doubles $50 a night. This modern guesthouse, run by a really friendly couple, is surrounded by rolling hills, green fields and forest. The three bedrooms share two communal bathrooms, one with a jacuzzi, and there are great views of the town and the river from the living room; you can even use a telescope if you want to take a closer look. European-style coffee is available at breakfast. Nearby, there's a beaver pond and some good walking; the owners will show you around if you ask.

⌂ Le Lové du Pionnier: 1 rue Noël, Saint-Luc-de-Matane, in the heart of the village. ☎ 562-1935 or 1-866-211-7202 (toll-free). Email: lelovedupionnier@hotmail.com. Doubles $45 a night. This 100-year-old house has four well-kept bedrooms. Michel, the landlord, is passionate about the local wildlife, and can take you to see the beavers in a nearby reserve. He'll also advise on the best places to find moose in the wild. A snowmobile is available for use in the winter.

⌂ Le Jardin de Givre: 3263 route du Peintre, Saint-Léandre. ☎ and fax: 737-4411. Email: jardin-de-givre @globetrotter.net. When you get

GASPÉSIE

to Saint-Ulric, on route 132 between Rimouski and Matane, take the road that leads south to Saint-Léandre. Once you're there, turn right, go straight on for 2 kilometres (1.5 miles), then turn left onto route du Peintre; it's signposted from there. Doubles $65 a night. Le Jardin de Givre stands in the middle of 100 acres of woodland with managed forest paths, well away from the noise of the coastal road. The decor in each of the five bedrooms is inspired by the poem that hangs on its door, and your hosts will do their utmost to ensure that you have everything you need. Ginette makes generous, excellent breakfasts, complete with flowers on the table, and will help you put together a picnic; Gérald, a forester and writer, will take you horse-riding. Even the dog does his bit: you can follow him to the nearby waterfalls, where you can enjoy a refreshing dip in summer. In winter, you can use the snowmobile.

☆☆☆ Expensive

⌂ **Hôtel-motel Belle Plage**: 1310 avenue Matane-sur-Mer, at the edge of town on route 132. ☎ 562-2323 or 1-888-244-2323 (toll-free). Fax: 562-2562. Doubles from $64 a night. This hotel-cum-motel, decorated in 1950s style, is extremely

handy if you have a car, as it's just 500 metres (500 yards) away from the ferry, and you can just leave your car in the queue (see below). It isn't cheap, but most of the spacious rooms can sleep four, and all have a lounge area with pleasant views. Avoid the motel rooms, which are more expensive than those in the hotel, and don't have views. The restaurant is also pretty good.

⌂ **Auberge La Seigneurie**: 148 rue Druillette/621 rue Saint-Jérôme, in an imposing Victorian building near route 132. ☎ 562-0021 or 1-877-783-4466 (toll-free). Fax: 562-4455. Website:www.pages.infinit.net/mer canti/seigneurie. Doubles $70 a night. Credit cards accepted. The decor here is fairly tasteful, if a little quaint, and the communal ground-floor rooms are huge. The bedrooms, the largest of which can sleep four, are upstairs, and some have basins. It's a friendly place, and the landlord has plenty of good advice on what to see and do in the area.

⌂ **Motel Marina**: 1032 rue du Phare Ouest. ☎ 562-3234 or 562-3235. Doubles from $52 a night; breakfast $6. A welcoming place with a heated swimming pool and spacious, clean, comfortable bedrooms with views of the beach.

WHERE TO EAT

✕ **Café Aux Délices**: 109 rue Saint-Jean, near the bridge. ☎ 562-0578. Open until midnight from Sunday to Wednesday, and all night from Thursday to Saturday. There's a huge choice of food here, from sandwiches, pizza and pasta to grilled meats, with a Chinese buffet between Thursday and Sunday (5–8pm). The surroundings are nothing special, but it's cheap, the food's not bad and the staff are very friendly.

✕ **Café Bistro l'Estuaire**: 50 rue d'Amours, in the centre of town. ☎ 562-2939. Open until 10pm; 4pm–10pm on weekends. Main courses $12. Choose from excellent fish and seafood dishes, or pizzas cooked in a proper wood-fired oven. There's a very respectable table d'hôte.

– **Les Fumoirs Raoul Roux**: 1259 rue Matane-sur-Mer, near the sea, between the ferry point and the tourist office. ☎ 562-9372. It's a long way from the town centre, so you'll need a car to get here. If you're planning a picnic, you can pick up excellent smoked fish and seafood, including prawns, trout and halibut.

WHAT TO SEE AND DO

★ Between June and September, you can watch the **salmon migrating** upstream. A special aquarium has been built into the river, and the fish have to pass through it, so you can watch this amazing animal as it returns to its birthplace in time for the breeding season.

– **Promenade du Capitaine**: a walk by the Matane River, on rue Saint-Jérôme. All along the wooden walkway, there are information boards explaining the town's maritime history.

FESTIVALS AND EVENTS

– **Festival de la Crevette** (Prawn Festival): 23 June to 3 July. You'll find a panoply of prawns here, prepared in every imaginable way.

WHAT TO DO IN THE AREA

– **Seigneurie du Chevreuil**: 5 kilometres (3 miles) from the town centre, next to the main road and the river. ☎ 562-1528. Open May to October. Admission $3. There's a herd of 80 roe deer in this park, and you're bound to see them from the many footpaths.

– Matane is also the gateway for hikes in the **Chic-Choc mountains**, home to caribou, roe deer, bears and moose. The biggest population of moose in Québec can be found around the Étang-à-la-Truite.

FERRIES: MATANE–BAIE-COMEAU OR MATANE–GODBOUT

Tickets are $11 per person and $27 per car. Crossings take 2 hours 30 minutes. You'll have to queue for hours in the summer, as there are only two or three crossings a day for Godbout and one or two for Baie-Comeau. It's a good idea to book several days in advance; even then, you'll have to get there at least an hour before departure, or your place will go to someone else. If you get there the night before, you can leave your car in tomorrow's queue, stay at a nearby hotel, then rejoin your car 45 minutes before the first departure the next day.

– **Timetable information**:

– Online: www.traversiers.gouv.qc.ca

– Baie-Comeau: ☎ 294-8593.

– Godbout: ☎ 568-7575.

– Matane: ☎ 562-2500.

– **Car and group booking line**: ☎ 562-2500 or 1-877-562-6560 (toll-free). Fax: 560-8013.

GASPÉSIE

On the road from Matane to Mont-Saint-Pierre

LES MÉCHINS

This is a fishing town in a pretty cove. The Micmacs in the area attributed any misfortunes they suffered to the presence of underwater reefs, and, above all, to the great Outikou, who uprooted trees to hunt them down. Hence the name 'Méchins', probably a corruption of '*méchant*' ('evil').

WHERE TO STAY

⚓ **Gîte du Ruisseau à Sem**: 808 Bellevue Ouest, 6.5 kilometres (4 miles) from Les Méchins on route 132. ☎ and fax: 729-3484. Email: ruisasem@gîtes-classifiés.qc.ca. Doubles $50 a night. This is a lovely gîte in a fine house on the banks of the St Lawrence, midway between Grosses-Roches and Les Méchins. You'll be welcomed by humans Nicole and Richard, Vladimir the African grey parrot and Bébé Coco the budgie. There are three recently redecorated bedrooms with sea views, and breakfast is always excellent. You can head down to the sea via a 93-step staircase.

⚓ **Gîte La Vieille Maison**: 170 rue Principale, off route 132, near the church. ☎ 729-3318. Doubles $45 a night. This is an early-20th-century house, set back from the road, with four spick-and-span bedrooms. It's run by Marius, whose ancestors settled here in 1820.

CAP-CHAT

The village is named after a rock that resembles a crouching cat ('*chat*' is the French for 'cat'); you can see the feline effect from the river. Cap-Chat also has the tallest vertical-axis windmill in the world, 110 metres (360 feet) high. It is no longer operational, because it is so tall that it would be destroyed in high winds. There are guided tours (45 minutes) from late June to October (☎ 786-5719).

Next door, near the lighthouse and the Cap-Chat rock, is **Tryton**, an education centre that explains the relationship between the wind and the sea (open June to October, 8.30am–sunset; ☎ 786-5543). Multimedia displays show how the elements affect nature, human lives and Cap-Chat, while other exhibits explain the legend of the rock, the workings of the enormous windmill and the more recent collection of windmills built on the hillside around it.

WHERE TO STAY AND EAT

⚓ ✗ **Auberge Au Crépuscule**: 239 rue Notre-Dame Ouest, on route 132. ☎ and fax: 786-5751. Doubles from $55 a night; *table d'hôte* $20. This friendly, professionally run establishment in a large stone house by the sea has five pristine modern bedrooms. The room at the back of the house is brighter and more peaceful than the others. The owner, Jean, is an excellent cook, you can sample his creations in the homely dining room.

⚓ **Gîte Rêve et Réalité**: 216 rue Notre-Dame Est, on route 132. ☎ and fax: 786-2465. Doubles

$50 a night. There are five extremely comfortable bedrooms in this old house with views of the St Lawrence. The owners are very hospitable, and cook up truly magnificent breakfasts: blueberry *crêpes*, eggs, bacon, cheeses, orange juice and more. It's a lovely place, and offers excellent value for money.

SAINTE-ANNE-DES-MONTS

This stretch of jagged, rocky coast is the departure point for excursions in the **Parc de la Gaspésie**, 16 kilometres (10 miles) away.

USEFUL ADDRESSES

🅱 Kiosque d'Information Touristique: 96 boulevard Saint-Anne Ouest. ☎ 763-5832. From 1 to 15 June, open 4–8pm; from 15 June to mid-August, open 8am–8pm; from mid-August to mid-September, open 8.30am–8pm.

■ **Épicerie Sobeys**: at the intersection of routes 132 and 299. This is a good place to stock up on food before entering the park.
■ **Quincaillerie Keable**: 170 1ère Avenue. ☎ 763-2345. Camping-gas refills.

WHERE TO STAY AND EAT

♠ Auberge de Jeunesse: 295 1ère Avenue Est, G0E 2G0. ☎ 763-1555 or 1-800-461-8585. Fax: 763-9229. Beds from $15 for Hostelling International members; a private room costs $40; fixed-price packages are also available. This recently built hostel can sleep up to 80 people in four-bed rooms or singles with en-suite bathrooms. It's a good base for exploring the park, as it runs a shuttle to the park entrance, and organizes various outdoor activities.

♠ Gîte au Lever du Jour: 313 1ère Avenue Est. ☎ 563-9177. Doubles $50 a night. This place is an old house with fairly basic facilities but a good atmosphere. In summer, there's a youth-hostel feel: the four bedrooms are full to bursting point, and everyone talks late into the night. Serge, the owner, is very laid-back and friendly: he's also crazy about the sea, and sometimes offers to take guests out on his 26 foot yacht. If you prefer to stay on dry land, there's a lovely view of the St Lawrence from the gîte itself.

♠ Gîte l'Écume de Mer: 21 rue des Écoliers, La Martre. ☎ and fax: 288-5274. Website: www.bbcanada.com/3202.html. Open 15 May to 15 October. Doubles $70 a night. Credit cards not accepted. This lovely yellow house and its fenced-off garden are perched on a hill above the St Lawrence. The interior has been beautifully decorated in rustic style, and the four bedrooms are cosy and peaceful. There's a private forest walk nearby, and you can enjoy splendid views from the terrace. For breakfast, try *crêpes fourrées* (filled pancakes). If you're short of cash, it's worth knowing that the owner, Andrea, occasionally needs some extra help around the place, and is happy to negotiate a reasonable deal.

♠ Motel Beaurivage: 245 1ère Avenue Ouest, on the riverbank, at the junction with 5e rue Ouest. ☎ 763-2291. Doubles $65 a night. This is a clean and tranquil place, with rooms overlooking fields and the river.

⌂ **Sous la Bonne Étoile**: 30 5e rue Est, accessible via route 132 or 1ère Avenue. ☎ 763-3402. Doubles $50 a night. The four bedrooms are clean and attractive, and breakfast is generous, making this place extremely good value for money.

⌂ **Gîte des Deux Colombes**: 996 boulevard Sainte-Anne Ouest, near Cap-Chat. ☎ 763-3756. Doubles $50 a night. This is a small, old whitewashed house with a red roof. It used to be run by two sisters – the two *colombes*, or doves, in the gîte's name – but one of the doves has flown the nest. The remaining sister, Julie, runs the place alone, and does so very well, especially when it comes to breakfast, which is plentiful and mostly homemade.

✕ **Poissonnerie du Quai**: 3 1ère Avenue Ouest, opposite the church. ☎ 763-7407. Open June to mid-October, 11.30am–2pm and 5.30–10pm. Full meals $10–30. Credit and debit cards are not accepted. This is a fishmonger's with a restaurant in an attractive blue-painted room next to the shop. Unsurprisingly, it specializes in fish and seafood, but it also does decent meat dishes and good desserts, all at very reasonable prices. It gets very busy, so the service can be slow.

WHERE TO STAY AND EAT ON THE WAY TO MONT-SAINT-PIERRE

✕ **Chez Pierre**: 96 boulevard Perron Ouest, Tourelle. ☎ 763-7446. on Route 132, 1 kilometre (half a mile) from Sainte-Anne. Open from early June to mid-October. The place is run by a talented Belgian chef who learned his trade on the Côte d'Azur. He sources the best products from local fishermen to produce excellent seafood dishes, including lobster, crab, baby scallops and smoked fish, all at bargain prices.

✕ **La Couquerie**: in a white house with red shutters in Marsoui, next to route 132. Open until 9pm. This is a canteen-style restaurant, and plates laden with cakes and pastries are spread out on large tables inside. The daily specials, which offer soup, a fish or meat dish and a dessert, are very good value, while the layout is original yet somehow very Canadian.

GASPÉ NATIONAL PARK

This is one of the most spectacular natural wonders in Québec. To make the most of it, you'll need to hire a car (or a 4x4, if you can afford it) and spend a few days here, as the park covers a huge area (800 square kilometres, 320 square miles), and most of the roads are more like rough trails. You'll also need to stock up on food and petrol in Sainte-Anne, as the park's shop has a limited range, and is only open from June to September.

There are two mountain ranges within the park's boundaries: the Chic-Chocs (meaning 'craggy mountains' in the Micmác language) and the MacGerrigle Mountains. The landscape is alpine, with dense forests that shelter the last remaining population of wood caribou. In summer, the education centre organizes guided 3-hour excursions to visit the caribou ($15); there's also a free, 1-hour guided caribou-watching trip to Mont

Jacques-Cartier. When you plan your trip, bear in mind that Mont Jacques-Cartier is closed until 24 June because of the caribou calving season; find out about Mont Albert in advance as well, because it is often covered in snow.

The park's plant population is almost as impressive as the fauna. Species to look out for include Lapland rhododendrons and dwarf azaleas. The woodland changes gradually from stretches of mixed pine and birch to boreal forest.

The ideal time to come to the Gaspésie National Park is probably autumn, as the flies are less of a nuisance and your food will last longer. A pair of binoculars will come in handy, and whatever time of year you come – but especially in summer – don't forget your mosquito repellent.

– **Information**: in the Centre d'Interprétation (☎ 763-7811; open June to mid-October); or from the Bureau du Parc (124 1ère Avenue Ouest, Sainte-Anne-des-Monts; ☎ 763-3301).

WHERE TO STAY AND EAT

⬧ **Camping Mont Albert**: on route 299. ☎ 763-2288. Tent pitches $16. Credit cards accepted. This is the best of the park's four campsites, with well-equipped bathrooms and plenty of facilities, including telephones, ice machines, a laundrette and a swimming pool ($2 a dip). Try to get a pitch in the shady area by the riverbank.

⬧ **Camping de la Rivière**: just past the Auberge-gîte du Mont Albert, by the river. ☎ 763-2288. This place is a bit more isolated than the Camping Mont Albert, but it's well equipped and right next to the park shop.

⬧ ✕ **Auberge-gîte du Mont Albert**: inside the park. ☎ 763-2288 or 1-888-270-4483 (toll-free). Fax: 763-7803. Website: www.sepaq. com. Doubles $115 a night. This luxury gîte is ideally placed for the mountain trails, and is a kind of mecca for outdoor types, so booking is essential. The owners also let out chalets across the park; it's best to phone for details. The restaurant is exclusive and expensive, but the food is of high quality, and they also do decent snacks.

⬧ There are several **mountain shelters** for hikers: you can get more information at the Centre d'Interprétation.

WHAT TO DO

– Activities on offer in the park include mountain-biking, fishing, boating, skiing (winter only) and caribou-watching with a guide (*see above*).

– **Hiking in the Chic-Choc mountains**: this is a paradise for experienced walkers. Accommodation en route is in managed shelters. There are several itineraries, which take between two and seven days. You'll need proper hiking boots, warm clothes (even in summer) and plenty of insect repellent.

– **Mont Jacques-Cartier**: open 10am–4pm. Closed until 24 June because of the caribou calving season. Guided excursion $24. This is one of the park's most popular day hikes, although Mont Albert (*see below*) makes for more exciting walking. The main path up Mont Jacques-Cartier is an old military trail that goes up to an altitude of 1,270 metres (4,166 feet). It's a good place to see caribou, but it gets pretty crowded in summer. If you're not up to a long hike, you can take a bus for the first leg (every 30 minutes; the last one leaves at noon; return buses run until 4pm), then walk the last 4 kilometres (2.5 miles) to the summit. The path to the top passes through deciduous forests and pines before reaching the stark, wind-eroded stone of the summit. The views from the peak are stunning.

– **Mont Albert**: the scenery here is completely different to that in the rest of the park. This is a Québécois version of an Arctic plateau, with echoes of tundra. If you want to reach the summit, you'll need a decent map, and you'll have to start very early in the morning; it will take you a good day's hiking to get up and down the mountain. You can stock up with water from a number of springs en route. The walk begins at the Auberge-gîte du Mont Albert. The marked route is circular, taking the Sentier de la Montée on the way up and coming back along the Sentier du Lac du Diable. You should be able to do this superb 17-kilometre (10-mile) walk from the end of June onwards – but check that the mountain is open the day before you're planning to walk it, as snow can make the trail impassable, even in the middle of summer.

– **Lac Paul**: a good place to see moose, especially at sunrise or sunset. To get there, take route 11 Ouest (for Lac Cascapédia). There is a signposted observation point.

– **Lac aux Américains**: to get there, take route 299, then Route 16 for 15 minutes. Guided visit $15. The lake forms part of Québec's only cirque, a glacier formation that looks like an amphitheatre. It used to be the only place where Americans had exclusive rights to go fishing. This is a short walk, but the scenery is magnificent.

MONT-SAINT-PIERRE · DIALLING CODE: 418

A winding river runs through the stunning village of Mont-Saint-Pierre, which nestles between sea and tall, steep hills in a wide cove just past Ruisseau-à-Rebours. A precarious path leads to the top of the mountain, but you can also reach it by bus. The tourist office runs guided visits.

🄗 **Bureau du Tourisme**: the tourist office has plenty of brochures and leaflets about the area, and the Chasseurs pêcheurs (Hunting and Fishing) association should be able to answer most of your questions (☎ 797-5101).

– **Hang-gliding and Paragliding Championships**: late July to early August. ☎ 797-2222. You can watch the contestants hurl themselves from the top of Mont-Saint-Pierre or, if you're feeling brave, make your own tandem flight, accompanied by an experienced flier, for about $100.

WHERE TO STAY AND EAT

⌂ **Camping Mont-Saint-Pierre**: off the main road, 3.5 kilometres (2 miles) from the village on the way to Parc de la Gaspésie. ☎ 797-2250. Tent pitch $13. This spacious, wooded campsite is a good place to go if you've got your own transport. The facilities on offer include a small heated pool and a laundrette.

⌂ **Camping du Pont**: on the outskirts of the village as you head towards Gaspé. ☎ 797-2951. Open

1 June to 30 September. Tent pitch $17; group rates available. Credit cards accepted. This is a pleasant site, and they'll let you build a campfire, but it's a bit too near the road.

☎ ✗ **Auberge de Jeunesse Les Vagues**: 84 rue Prudent-Cloutier, in a former motel near the beach. ☎ 797-2851. Half-board available. Credit cards accepted. Currently closed while awaiting new manager. Do phone to check it's reopened before you arrive. Don't expect to get much sleep in summer, when this youth hostel fills up with young people from Québec, Chicoutimi and Montréal, who come for a laugh and for the live music in July and August. There are plenty of decent single rooms, and the four-bed rooms have access to the kitchen. You can hire mountain bikes here, and the restaurant's decent and cheap (you can ask for half-board).

☎ **Chalets Bernatchez**: on the outskirts to the village, on the right-hand side of the road if you're coming from Sainte-Anne-des-Monts. ☎ 797-2733. Doubles $25; self-catering chalets $50. There are six simple but peaceful rooms in the main house, and the well-equipped are the cheapest in the village.

☎ ✗ **Motel Mont-Saint-Pierre**: on the main road, opposite the sea. ☎ 797-2202. Doubles $60 a night. The rooms are passable, and a meal in the restaurant costs $10–15.

✗ **Les Joyeux Naufragés**: 7 rue Pierre-Mercier, on the outskirts of the village. ☎ 797-2017. Fax: 797-2027. Open for lunch and dinner (until 11pm). Lunch $10–15; *table d'hôte* $17–26. The food here is good, with specialities including lobster, crab, cod, snails, prawns, pizzas and steak, but the service is a little sluggish. In summer, sit out on the pleasant terrace.

On the road from Mont-Saint-Pierre to Parc Forillon

On the way to Parc Forillon, the countryside becomes increasingly gentle, dotted with small fishing villages and secluded coastal coves. This is the place to go for the best, and cheapest, *catalognes* (multicoloured rag rugs). You can visit several fish canneries, particularly in **Rivière-au-Renard**.

WHERE TO STAY AND EAT

☎ ✗ **Auberge du Passant La Maison Lebreux**: 2 Longue Pointe, Petite-Vallée, in the next village after Grande-Vallée. ☎ 393-2662. Fax: 393-3105. Email: bscetjoe@globe trotter.qc.ca. Doubles $50 a night; six-person chalets $80. Booking essential in high season (10 to 30 July). Evening *table d'hôte* $15. This tranquil gîte is in a breathtaking spot – at the foot of a hill on a promontory, surrounded by water – and the eight first-floor rooms all have superb views of the sea and endless green fields. If you're lucky, you'll even see seals sunbathing outside the house. For breakfast, you'll get delicious pancakes with wild-berry jams and maple syrup, *cretons* and home-made bread. The hospitable owner will happily tell you all you need to know about the region. He also owns a café-theatre, the Café de la Vieille Forge (open summer only; ☎ 393-2222; fax 393-3060; email fcpv@globetrotter.qc.ca).

GASPÉSIE

⬧ ✕ **Restaurant l'Étoile du Nord**: Pointe-à-la-Frégate, the village after Petite-Vallée. Full meal $10–23. This place serves excellent seafood. There are eight small rooms with sea views if you want to stay the night.

PARC FORILLON

Parc Forillon is another of the Gaspé peninsula's natural wonders, its sheer cliff faces and a chiselled coastline bringing the Appalachian Mountains to an abrupt end. The climate is much milder than in the rest of the region. Unfortunately, as with so much of this region, it's hard to get around without a car.

The sea has worn down this huge, rocky peninsula into a series of rock faces, coves and underground caves. The highest crags are made of hard rock, some soaring to 600 metres (1,970 feet) above sea level, but the lower geological strata are much less durable, hence the stunning, jagged landscape. The vegetation, meanwhile consists mainly of boreal forest and alpine tundra.

Forillon has some exceptional flora and fauna, with more than 200 species of bird alone, so a pair of binoculars will come in very handy. Serious wildlife-lovers should look out for black bears, moose, red foxes or lynx, but you'll need a lot of patience – and luck – to see any of these animals. Seals, on the other hand, are easy to find, and you may well see a few humpback whales.

The park authorities place great emphasis on the interdependence of man, earth and sea, and on the evidence of this park, it's hard to argue with that. There is an admission fee; for more information: ☎ 368-5505.

USEFUL ADDRESSES

🛈 **Poste d'accueil** (information centre): on route 132, between Rivière-au-Renard and L'Anse-au-Griffon, on the north side of the park. ☎ 892-5040. Email: parc canadaque@pch.gc.ca. Admission $4. This information centre offers an excellent assortment of leaflets and maps showing park footpaths.

🛈 There's another **information centre** in Penouille, on the south side of the park: ☎ 892-5661. Again, it has plenty of useful brochures.

– There are no **shops** inside the park, so you'll need to stock up on provisions in the surrounding area. You should be able to hitch a lift into the park from any of the neighbouring villages.

WHERE TO STAY

⬧ **Camping**: there are four popular campsites in the park, all well managed and very crowded in summer. ☎ 368-6050. Book at least five days in advance. The Anse-au-Griffon site is open all year round; the others are open in summer only. In the southern sector of the park, you'll find a laundrette, a café, a swimming pool and tennis courts, while the Cap Bon-Ami site, to the east, has fine views over the cliffs. There's a small site just outside the park, which usually has a few spaces (☎ 892-5100), and you can sometimes see whales from your tent. If all else fails, try the moderately priced Baie de Gaspé campsite, in Cap-aux-Os, on a pleasant spot near the park gates.

⌂ Auberge de Jeunesse de Cap-aux-Os: 2095 boulevard Grande-Grève, Cap-aux-Os, near the park entrance. The Orléans Express bus stops here between July and September. ☎ 892-5153. Fax: 892-5292. Open May to October; otherwise, group bookings of five or more only. Dorm bed $18 ($16 with a Youth Hostel card); private room $19. Sheet hire available. Lights out at midnight. This youth hostel used to be a go-go bar, but there's no trace of its former function, and it's now one of the area's best places to stay. The dorms sleep between four and eight, with a 27-bed room in the basement, and there are five family rooms, one with an en-suite bathroom. The cafeteria, open from mid-June to mid-September, serves cheap and delicious lobster dishes, and there's a kitchen for those who prefer to self-cater. Breakfast is not included in the price, but if you decide to pay extra, you've a choice of three types: Canadian, English or Continental. The staff are friendly, and there's plenty to do in the area, with bikes, snowshoes and cross-country skis all available for hire. Slide shows on Forillon's flora and fauna are held three evenings a week, and every evening there are guided car trips to see beavers. Other excursions include guided bear-spotting, walking or cycling tours, and whale- and seal-watching walks (at low tide) on Cap

Gaspé, where you can also go swimming. Out of season, you get two tours for the price of one. There's a swimming pool 3 kilometres (2 miles) away.

⌂ Gîte Haut-phare: 1321 boulevard Cap-des-Rosiers. ☎ 892-5958. Doubles from $45 a night. This seaside guesthouse with five rooms is next to Canada's tallest lighthouse. It's not the most comfortable place to stay, but the large veranda has stunning views.

⌂ Gîte aux Pétales de Rose: 1184 route 132, Cap-des-Rosiers. ☎ 892-5031. Doubles from $40 a night. This friendly, modern establishment has three clean, ever-so-slightly twee rooms.

⌂ Gîte des Trois Ruisseaux: 896 boulevard Griffon, Anse-au-Griffon. ☎ 892-5528. Doubles $50 a night. The decor here is a touch eccentric, but there are three spotless rooms, and you'll get homemade bread and jam for breakfast. The friendly owner, Micheline Deschênes, is a mine of information about local customs and places of interest.

⌂ Les Petites Maisons du Parc: 910 boulevard Forillon, opposite the Penouille information centre. ☎ 892-5873. Chalets $550 per week. Book at least three weeks in advance. This is a good base for families planning to spend a fair amount of time in the Gaspé region. The well-equipped chalets, perched on a pretty, wooded hillside, have simple but spacious interiors, and you can hire a TV if you feel the need.

GASPÉSIE

WHERE TO EAT

✗ **Restaurant Mona**: 1275 route 132 Est, Cap-des-Rosiers, 1 kilometre (half a mile) from the lighthouse. ☎ 892-5057. Daily specials from $8; *table d'hôte* $11–23. The *bouillabaisse* (fish soup) here is excellent, and not at all expensive.

WHAT TO SEE AND DO

★ **Cap-des-Rosiers Lighthouse**: open July and August only, 10am–5pm. The Cap-des-Rosiers Chamber of Commerce runs guided tours. Built in 1858, this lighthouse is believed to be the tallest in Canada, at 37 metres (121 feet) high, and became a listed building in 1977. There are 122 steps to the top, but you'll get a fine view of Cap-des-Rosiers and Cap Bon-Ami when you arrive.

★ **Clocher Capien**: open July and August only, 10am–5pm. The Capien bell tower is part of a uniquely designed modern parish church, with an interior that resembles an upturned boat. The previous church was demolished in 1964, but its treasures are on display inside its replacement.

★ **Centre d'Interprétation de la Nature du Secteur Nord du Parc** (Wildlife Interpretation Centre): in the north of the park. Open 9am–6pm. This environmentally friendly building offers a host of supervized activities.

– **Boat trips**: take a guided trip aboard the *Félix-Leclerc*, off the northern coast of the Forillon headland, and you'll see fantastic colonies of seals and birds. You must book the night before in July or August. For details, contact Croisières Baie de Gaspé (☎ 892-5000, fax: 368-7277) or Croisières 3 D (2172 Grande-Grève, Cap-aux-Os, ☎ 892-6088 or 368-6374). Cruises last 2 hours 30 minutes.

– **Walk along Cap Gaspé**: en route, you can visit the charming fisherman's cottage of Anse-Blanchette, which has been reconstructed to show how local fishermen lived.

– The pretty **Pointe-Penouille beach** stretches along the Pointe-Penouille promontory.

– **Walking**: there are several trails in the park. The Sentier de la Chute (waterfall walk) is a 30-minute circular route; the Sentier Les Graves is a 13-kilometre (8-mile) round trip that takes about 3 hours 30 minutes to complete; and Mont Saint-Alban is a spectacular 9-kilometre (5-mile) round trip marked in green. For more details, inquire at the park's information centres.

– **Cap Bon-Ami cliffs**: there's a beach littered with starfish on this beautiful stretch of coastline. A steep walk takes you up to Mont Saint-Alban, where you'll be rewarded with stunning panoramic views from the summit. On a clear day, you can see the Rocher Percé, 80 kilometres (48 miles) away.

GASPÉ Pop: 17,000   DIALLING CODE: 418

The name Gaspé comes from the Micmac word *gespeg*, meaning 'the ends of the Earth'. The town played an important part in Québec's history, and a mountain-top granite cross (similar to the one erected here by Jacques Cartier when he won Canada for the King of France) was placed here to commemorate the 400th anniversary of the discovery of Canada. The bay is picturesque, but the town is an industrial and commercial centre, and has little to offer in the way of sightseeing.

Between June and October, Via Rail runs a night train from Montréal to Gaspé, with one stop at Rivière-du-Loup. It arrives at about 11am.

USEFUL ADDRESSES

🛈 Bureau d'information touristique: 27 boulevard York, near the bridge. ☎ 368-6335. Open June to mid-August, 8am–8pm. A well-stocked tourist office.

🚆 Railway station: 3 rue de la Marina. ☎ 368-4313 or 1-800-361-5390 (toll-free).

🚌 Buses: 2 rue Adams. ☎ 368-1888.

WHERE TO STAY

⌂ Camping Municipal de Gaspé: 1029 Haldimand, on route 132, 10 kilometres (6 miles) from Gaspé on the way to Percé. ☎ 368-3820. This is a small roadside camp. There's very little shade, but it's close to the sea, so sun-worshippers will probably love it.

⌂ CÉGEP de la Gaspésie: 94 rue Jacques-Cartier. ☎ 368-2749. Email: residence@cgaspesie.qc.ca. Open mid-June to mid-August. From $35 per night per person. Linen and towel hire available. This student hall of residence offers well-equipped self-catering apartments that sleep six or eight people, and 50 rooms with communal bathrooms. The decor leaves a lot to be desired, but the rooms offer good value for money.

⌂ Motel Plante: 137 rue Jacques-Cartier, in the town centre. ☎ 368-2254. Fax: 368-5885. Website: www.motelplante.com. Doubles $60 a night. This blue-and-white motel has a large car-park right outside, and that pretty much sums up its character. That said, it's a good base for exploring the town, and the rooms are pretty well equipped, with kitchenettes, TVs and bathrooms. The cheapest rooms, in the annexe share a kitchen. Some of the accommodation is used by university students during term time.

⌂ Gîte La Normande de Gaspé: 19 rue Davis. ☎ 368-5468. Fax: 368-7336. Email: gitenord@glob trotter.qc.ca. Doubles $55 a night, including breakfast. Booking recommended. This red-brick house in a leafy residential area has five first-floor rooms, arranged around a large landing with a handsome carved chaise longue as its centrepiece. It's a bit like an old-fashioned manor house. The staff are not especially friendly, but the garden and the swimming pool more than make up for it.

⌂ Gîte de Gaspé La Maison Blanche au Toit Vert: 201 rue Guignion. ☎ 368-5273. Fax: 368-0119. Doubles $60 a night. Non-smoking. This spotless guesthouse has three pleasant en-suite rooms and a guests' lounge with views of the St Lawrence. The hosts own a maple grove, and will happily organize a visit, but you could content yourself with sampling their products at breakfast.

⌂ Le Gîte Terre et Mer: 562 montée Sandy-Beach. ☎ 368-1335. Website: www.page.infinit.net/terre mer. Doubles $55 a night. Overlooking the bay, and not far from the beach, this white-painted, green-shuttered gîte has a rustic feel, as do the three recently renovated rooms. From the veranda, you can see the St Lawrence and the Appalachian Mountains.

⌂ Gîte-auberge Le Fournil Rustique: 776 montée Sandy-Beach, on route 132, 8 kilometres (5 miles) from the town centre. ☎ 368-1394. Doubles from $30 a night. From Gaspé, take the coastal road towards Percé and you'll see it on the right-hand side, set back from the

GASPÉSIE

road. This peaceful place on the edge of a wood has a youth-hostel feel and suitably rustic decor. The landlord, Denis Brodeur, built this traditional Canadian log cabin himself, so there's no doubting his commitment to the enterprise; he even gives informal cello recitals for guests. The ground-floor rooms have toilets and basins. This is a great place, but it's pretty much impossible to reach using public transport.

🏠 **Gîte du Passant Baie Jolie**: 270 montée Wakeham, on route 198. ☎ 368-2149. Doubles from $45 a night; apartment $100. This welcoming establishment, in a modern house overlooking the bay, has three spotlessly clean bedrooms (shared bathroom) and a basement apartment that sleeps six.

WHERE TO EAT

✕ **Café des Artistes**: 101 rue de la Reine, on route 132 as you head towards Parc Forillon. ☎ 368-3666. Open June to September. *Table d'hôte* $25. This friendly, Olde Worlde establishment oozes charm, and the cooking is tasty and original. Try stuffed croissants, goat's cheese tart and banana and cream cheesecake, then wind up your meal with excellent freshly ground coffee. Upstairs, you'll find an artist's studio and a pretty veranda where you can see works by local artists. Breakfast is also available.

✕ **Jardin Oriental**: 110 rue de la Reine. ☎ 368-8888. Snacks from $5; set menu $40. The main reason to come here is the self-service Oriental buffet, ideal if you have a huge appetite and not much cash.

✕ **L'Ancêtre**: 55 boulevard York, near the tourist office. ☎ 368-4358. Dinner only. *Table d'hôte* $15–25. Situated in a handsome 19th-century house with views of the river, this restaurant offers excellent dishes made with ultra-fresh ingredients. Fish and seafood are the chef's specialities.

WHERE TO HAVE A DRINK

🍷 **Brise-Bise**: 2 côte Carter, a staircase off rue de la Reine, level. ☎ 368-1456. Snacks $7. This bistro-restaurant hosts exhibitions and concerts (rock, blues, jazz) from 9pm onwards in summer. If you're eating, you can sit on the terrace, which overlooks the river.

WHAT TO SEE

★ **Musée de la Gaspésie**: 80 boulevard Gaspé, on the way into town if you're coming from Parc Forillon. ☎ 368-1534. Open 9am–5pm in summer; otherwise, weekdays only, 8.30am–5pm (also weekends 1–5pm from September to mid-October). Admission $4. The museum houses permanent displays about the Micmacs, Jacques Cartier and the colonization of the Gaspé peninsula, as well as pieces of religious art and exhibits illustrating the daily lives of fishermen, lumberjacks and craftsmen. The collection is somewhat overshadowed by the view over the bay.

★ Behind the museum, a **monument** erected in honour of Jacques Cartier illustrates the first meetings between Europeans and American Indians. The six wrought-iron columns represent menhirs from Brittany, the explorer's homeland.

★ Gaspé is home to the only wooden **cathedral** in North America (open 8am–8pm). Don't expect anything quaint and rustic, though: it's a thoroughly modern structure.

★ **Le Site d'Interprétation des Micmacs**: 783 boulevard Pointe-Navarre, Gespeg, immediately after the bridge that crosses the river's mouth if you're coming from Parc Forillon. ☎ 368-6005. Email: micmac@quebectel.com. Open June to September, 9am–5pm. Admission $4. Visits last 2 hours 30 minutes. You can wander through a reconstruction of a Micmac village, where Micmac guides will explain the lives and traditions of their ancestors, then visit the museum and the shop at the entrance.

On the road from Gaspé to Percé

The scenery changes dramatically along this stretch of coast, where the incursions of the sea have left the landscape pitted with lakes. The picture-postcard landscape, dotted with small, whitewashed houses and mini cliffs, takes on a softer look. In some places, it looks almost Finnish, with pine trees and bright-green prairies spread with yellow flowers.

– Good places to stop off en route are Barachois, a little fishing centre (the name derives from '*barre à choir*', meaning a stretch of white sand where boats can be pulled up), and Coin-du-Banc, a tiny hamlet at the foot of a hill that leads to Percé. The surrounding countryside is stunning.

PERCÉ Pop: 4,000   DIALLING CODE: 418

This has been an established tourist magnet since the 1930s, when the remarkable Rocher Percé began to attract large numbers of artists. Today, visitors come to cut souvenir chunks out of the rock, and to enjoy the natural highs of the surrounding area: the village is set inside a semicircle consisting of Cap Blanc, Mont Sainte-Anne, Mont Blanc, Les Trois-Sœurs and Cap Barré.

The rock has inspired many a legend: according to one, it was once the home of a lioness with the head of a sorceress, who captured sailors foolhardy enough to disembark here at night and hurled them over the edge of the cliff.

USEFUL ADDRESSES

🚩 **Kiosque d'Information Touristique** (B1, **1** on the map): 142 route 132, in the centre of the village. ☎ 782-5448. Fax: 782-5565. Open late May to mid-October, 8.30am–5pm (until 8pm in July and August). The staff here are efficient and friendly, and they have loads of useful information to hand.

🚃 **Railway station**: 44 rue de l'Anse. ☎ 782-2747 or 1-800-361-5390 (toll-free). Open only when trains are due to arrive or depart (9–10am and 3–5pm on Monday, Thursday and Saturday).

👕 **La Boîte à T-shirts** (B1, **2**): on the main street. Open until 8pm. T-shirts from $12. The owner can print

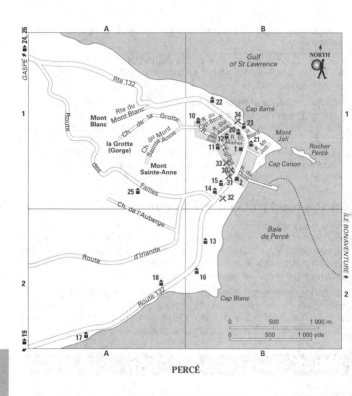

PERCÉ

■ **Useful Addresses**

1 Tourist Information
2 La Boîte à T-shirts

⌂ **Where to Stay**

10 Gîte du Mont Sainte-Anne
11 Maison Avenue House
12 Gîte du Passant La Rêvasse
13 Hôtel Motel Pavillon Côte Surprise
14 Motel Le Macareux
15 Gîte L'Extravagante
16 Gîte du Capitaine
17 Chalets Rainbow
18 Gîte chez Despard
19 Gîte Les Jardins Levêque
20 Maison Le Havre (The Haven)
21 Gîte La Maison Rouge
22 Gîte Marie-Josée Tommi
23 Hôtel et Motel Rocher Percé
24 Auberge Le Coin du Banc
25 Camping du Gargantua
26 Camping Tête d'Indien

✕ **Where to Eat**

30 Percé-Brasse
31 Les Fous de Bassan
32 La Morutière
33 Le Matelot
34 Restaurant Biard

T-shirts and baseball caps with a range of slogans and patterns while you wait. It's pretty cheap, but the motifs are quite entertaining.

WHERE TO STAY

Percé is not short of motels, B&Bs, gîtes and campsites, and strong competition means prices are lower here than in the much of Canada, especially in low season. It gets pretty busy in summer, so it's a good idea to book in advance. That said, you'll often find people queueing up to offer you rooms as soon as you get off the bus.

Campsites

⚑ Camping du Gargantua (A1, **25**): route des Failles, a few kilometres outside Percé. ☎ 782-2852. Tent pitches from $18 a night; caravan sites $22. This is the best campsite in the area, high above the bay with breathtaking views of Île Bonaventure. It's small, quiet and pleasantly wild, but there aren't many toilets or washing facilities, and not all the pitches are shaded. You'll need your own transport to get here.

⚑ Camping Tête d'Indien (off A1, **26**): in Saint-Georges-de-Malbaie, on the road to Percé. ☎ 645-3845. Fax: 645-2713. Email: danrose@bellsouth.net. Tent pitches $17 a night; caravan sites $25. This place, which has an English-speaking manager, owes its name ('Indian's head') to a rock that bears an uncanny resemblance to the profile of a Native American. You can see it from the campsite – unfortunately, though, it's about the only interesting thing to see in the area. If you're sensitive to the sun, give this place a miss, as most of the pitches are not shaded.

– There are several campsites in Percé itself, and two at Cap Blanc, both of which have beautiful views. The prices and services are all roughly the same.

☆ Budget

⚑ Maison Avenue House (B1, **11**): 38 rue de l'Église, in a quiet, green area near the centre. ☎ 782-2954. Situated. Doubles from $35 a night. This pretty wooden house with a veranda, full of potted plants, keepsakes and paintings, offers some of the cheapest rooms in Percé. It's run by an elderly English-speaking woman, and there's a faded, old-fashioned feel, although it's perfectly clean and tidy.

⚑ Chez Georges et Rita: 16 rue Sainte-Anne. ☎ 782-2990. This establishment has three reasonably priced double rooms and a kitchen for guests. Breakfast is not usually available, but you can pick something up from the bakery across the road.

⚑ Maison Le Havre (B1, **20**): 114 route 132, opposite the Hôtel Rocher Percé. ☎ 782-2374. Doubles from $40 a night; summer cottage $45. Ask for a quiet room at the back of this wooden, green-roofed house, which has five slightly faded but inexpensive single rooms, all with basins. There's no breakfast.

☆☆ Moderate

⚑ Gîte du Passant La Rêvasse (B1, **12**): 16 rue Saint-Michel, a stone's throw from Maison Avenue House. ☎ and fax: 782-2102. Doubles from $55 a night. An oasis of calm after the bustle of the town centre, this renovated wooden house is surrounded by lovingly tended gardens and meadows. The charming couple who run the place can provide you with plenty of information about the town and the surrounding area. There are four upstairs double or twin-bedded rooms, some with basins and all offering views of the garden and the countryside beyond. Breakfast is served in the kitchen.

âš Gîte Marie-Josée Tommi (B1, 22): 31 route 132 ouest, just past the Pétro-Canada station on the way to Gaspé. ☎ 782-5104. Doubles from $45 a night. This isn't a guesthouse in the conventional sense, but a large household of artists who share one big gallery-cum-studio, and rent three rooms to guests. The original decor is by Marie-Josée Tommi, a ceramicist and painter. It's a great place to get in touch with your inner bohemian, but the bathroom facilities are limited and the standards of cleanliness wouldn't pass muster in a proper hotel.

âš Gîte du Mont Sainte-Anne (B1, 10): 44 rue du Cap-Barré, above the Église de Percé, near the start of the footpath that climbs to Mont Sainte-Anne. ☎ 782-2739. Doubles $55 a night. This friendly gîte in a new residential area is modern and comfortable. There are three bedrooms upstairs and three on the lower ground floor, with shared toilets in the corridor and a view of the quiet garden. Ideal if you're just passing through.

âš Gîte L'Extravagante (B1, 15): 222 route 132 ouest. ☎ 782-5347. Doubles from $50 a night. No smoking inside. This hospitable gîte can't offer the sweeping vistas you get in many Gaspésie hostelries, but it's set back from the road and surprisingly quiet. It's run by Danielle, Denis and Léon and there are two bedrooms, both imaginatively decorated by Danielle.

âš Gîte La Maison Rouge (B1, 21): 125 route 132 ouest, in a meadow opposite the Rocher Percé. ☎ 782-2227. Doubles $63–67 per night;

four-bed rooms $93. You're guaranteed an extremely friendly reception at this pretty, maroon-painted, Jersey-style residence. There are rooms in the main house, but try to get one in the barn, as they're spacious and full of rustic charm: in one, an old manger has been converted into a bunk bed, while the chairs have been cobbled together from tractor parts. There's also an indoor swing, and in summer, the owners host barbecues on the terrace. If you're travelling with a large group, you can rent the entire barn.

âš Gîte du Capitaine (B2, 16): 10 rue du Belvédère, Côte Surprise. ☎ 782-5559. Fax: 782-5171. Website: www.gites-classifies.qc.ca/cap.htm. Doubles from $60 a night, including breakfast. A stone's throw from Cap Blanc, this house has staggering views of the Rocher Percé. The three delightful rooms share one bathroom: not all of them have views, but it doesn't really matter, as you can gaze at the famous rock through the window in the living room. Your hosts are Réjeanne and the dashing, larger-than-life Captain Flynn, known in the village as 'the Legend'. Join one of his exceedingly popular cruises around the rock to Île Bonaventure and you'll learn everything there is to know about the island; make sure you book in advance, though.

Hotels and Motels

âš Hôtel et Motel Rocher Percé (B1, 23): 111 route 132 ouest. ☎ 782-2330 or 1-888-467-3723 (toll-free). Doubles from $50 a night, including breakfast; motel rooms $70. All the rooms have toilets and basins, with shared showers on the landing. As you'd expect from the prices, the motel is more comfortable.

âš Motel Le Macareux (B1, 14): 262 route 132 ouest, on the southern fringes of the village. ☎ 782-

2414. Doubles from $55 a night; discounts available for stays of three or more nights. This cheap but run-of-the-mill motel has clean, spacious rooms, all with TV. The cheapest rooms have shared bathrooms, but they're still pretty good value. The more expensive ones, meanwhile, are en suite and have fully equipped kitchens. It's well worth haggling over the room rates, especially in low season. There's also a cheap and cheerful craft shop on site.

WHERE TO EAT

✕ **Les Fous de Bassan** (B1, **31**): 162 route 132 ouest, in the village's arts centre. ☎ 782-2266. Open summer only, 7am–10pm. Main courses $9; *table d'hôte* $12. This bistro-style restaurant has a great atmosphere with live music in the evening and full-blown concerts on weekends. The house specials include seafood and crêpes.

✕ **Percé-Brasse** (B1, **30**): same address as Les Fous de Bassan. ☎ 782-5350. Restaurant open until 10pm; bar open until 3am. The Latin rhythms playing in the background give this modern, colourful restaurant a non-stop party atmosphere. If you like moules-frites (mussels with chips), you can eat as much as you can handle for the fixed price of $12. If not, try chicken, pizza, salad or cod fillet, all with a pleasingly home-cooked feel.

✕ **Restaurant Biard** (B1, **34**): 99 route 132 ouest. ☎ 782-2873. Open May to October. Lunch menu $11; *table d'hôte* $18–27 (out of season only). This large restaurant has a good-value all-you-can-eat buffet for lunch (except in summer) or

dinner; the lunchtime version is much more limited. Otherwise, fish and seafood dishes take up most of the menu, though you should give the bouillabaisse (fish soup) a miss. You can get a free lift to the restaurant from wherever you're staying (☎ 782-2102).

✕ **Le Matelot** (B1, **33**): 7 rue de l'Église. ☎ 782-2569. *Table d'hôte* $16–30. A good time is guaranteed at this pleasant, spacious restaurant, which hosts concerts and even theatrical events in summer. There's a good choice of fish and seafood dishes, including crab, scallops, cod and excellent lobster. Highly recommended.

✕ **La Morutière** (B1, **32**): 249 route 132. ☎ 782-2802. Open for lunch and dinner (until 10.30pm in season). Full meal $13–29. This seaside café-restaurant has a pleasant dining room and superb views, especially from the terrace. It's popular with the locals, and the food is good: try the stuffed rainbow trout, seafood spaghetti, pizza and fish pâté. There are inexpensive menus at lunchtime.

WHERE TO STAY AND EAT IN THE AREA

☆ Budget

⌂ **Chalets Rainbow** (A2, **17**): 511 route 132, two minutes west of the village. ☎ 782-2254 or 782-2318. Two-person chalets $35; five-person chalets $65. If you're prepared to rough it a little, these chalets offer excellent value for money. They're in a pleasant, peaceful spot, with splendid views of the Île de Bonaventure, and each of the fairly spartan cabins has a bathroom and kitchenette, albeit with limited facilities. The owner, an elderly Briton, has a passion for local history, so don't hesitate to quiz him about the region.

☆☆ Moderate

🛏 Gîte Chez Despard (A2, **18**): 468 route 132 west. ☎ 782-5446. Set back a little from the main road, a couple of kilometres (1.5 miles) from the town centre. Doubles from $50 a night. The owner of this large violet-coloured house, built by her father in 1920, goes out of her way to make her guests feel at home. It's a bright, cheerful and slightly bohemian family residence, with four decent rooms and a large flower garden.

☆☆☆ Expensive

🛏 Gîte Les Jardins Levêque (off the map near A2, **19**): 931 rang 2, Anse-à-Beaufils, Cap-d'Espoir. ☎ 782-2441. Fax: 782-5147. Website: www.gites-classifies.qc.ca/jarl.htm. From Percé, take route 132 west and turn right onto the road that leads to Anse-à-Beaufils. At the end, turn right onto the minor road and continue for 300 metres (300 yards). Doubles from $65 a night; reductions for four people sharing. Situated on a hill and surrounded by greenery, this charming gîte with tastefully decorated rooms has a terrace overlooking the bay. The owner keeps poultry, rabbits and various creepy-crawlies, which should keep the kids amused. Guests can use the kitchen, and there's a barbecue in the large garden.

🛏 ✕ Auberge Le Coin du Banc (off the map near A1, **24**): 315 route 132 east, in Coin-du-Banc, 7 kilometres (4 miles) from Percé on the road to Gaspé. ☎ 645-2907. Doubles and chalets $42–90 a night; open by reservation only in winter. Pleasantly located on a crescent of beach in the Baie des Morues, this inn is especially suited to groups. There are 11 rooms, each individually decorated, some with en-suite bathrooms, and all with an appealing, slightly shambolic rustic feel. The seven chalets, all on the edge of the beach or the slopes of the mountain, have well-equipped kitchens. Even if you don't stay, it's well worth coming for a meal in the superb dining room, arranged around an old Gaspésian stove. The food is excellent, and though it's not cheap, you'll get good value for money. All in all, this place is highly recommended.

🛏 Hôtel Motel Pavillon Côte Surprise (B2, **13**): 367 route 132. ☎ 782-2131. Fax: 782-5323. Website: www.quebectel.com/rest. Open from June to late September. Doubles $116 a night, including breakfast; rooms for six $125. This clean, comfortable motel with fantastic view of the Rocher Percé and Île Bonaventure is great if you're travelling with a few friends.

WHAT TO SEE

★ The **Rocher Percé** is an immense wall of limestone, 433 metres (1,420 feet) in length, excluding the gap at the far end. It's thought to weigh more than 5 million tonnes. You can reach it on foot at low tide, though you'll find yourself knee-deep in water at times. It's worth getting wet for, especially if you're interested in birds, but make sure you're well informed about the movement of the tides before setting off.

★ **Centre d'Interprétation du Parc de l'Île Bonaventure et du Rocher Percé**: 343 rang de l'Irlande, on the southern fringes of the village. ☎ 782-2240. Open late May to mid-October, 9am–5pm. This visitors' centre offers a useful introduction to the Île Bonaventure's rich natural heritage, with well-

PERCÉ

presented displays devoted to the region's flora and fauna, and an audiovisual presentation on the gannets and their habits.

★ **Le Chafaud-Musée**: 145 rue Principale. ☎ 782-5100. Open June to September, 10am–10pm. Admission $5. Once used for fish processing, this historic building houses temporary exhibitions of paintings, poetry, sculpture and precious stones, all with a link to the Rocher Percé.

WHAT TO DO

– **Whale-watching**: Observation Littoral (249 Route 132, near the restaurant La Morutière; ☎ 782-5359) runs 3-hour boat trips between mid-May and late October. They cost $30, including equipment: the same price as in Tadoussac, and there are fewer boats around. If you're a student, ask for a discount on the price; the company offers them, but doesn't advertise the fact. There are three or four departures a day in high season, and you should book 24 hours in advance. You should see Atlantic white-sided dolphins (from the end of July), humpback whales, minke whales, fin whales and even a few belugas. If you're very lucky, you might even glimpse a blue whale. Whatever marine life you find, the helpful guides will happily tell you all about it.

> **TIP** If you want to take photos, expect the whales to stay on the surface for eight breaths before they dive again.

– You can also spend a day **cod-fishing** at sea. It's great fun, and it's not too expensive. If you want to keep the fish that you catch, make sure you say so before you board the boat.

– There are beautiful **walks** in the surrounding hills, which offer wonderful views of Percé. On the flat summit of Mont Sainte-Anne, the Micmacs used to worship the sun, presenting their newborn babies to it. One of the best routes starts from behind the Gargantua restaurant and leads to the Crevasse, a series of large natural faults. It takes about 40 minutes.

– There are several **beaches** around Percé where you can hunt for agates.

– You can hire **sea canoes** or go **scuba-diving**: inquire at the swimming pool in Percé (open mid-June to mid-September, 8am–5pm, ☎ 782-5403; out of season, ☎ 534-3800). Make sure you hire a canoe with a cover, otherwise you'll find yourself sitting in freezing water.

ÎLE BONAVENTURE

Bonaventure means 'good adventure'. Some say the name dates back to the early 16th century, when grateful Breton and Basque fishermen made their way to this part of the world and found it to be teeming with fish. Others maintain that it was on Saint Bonaventure's Day, 15 July 1534, that Jacques Cartier (originally from Rothéneuf, in Britanny) dropped anchor off the island.

After the British conquest, Bonaventure was settled by adventurers from Ireland and the Channel Islands. In 1831, 35 hardy families lived there, despite the high winds and tides. The last inhabitants left in 1973,

GASPÉSIE

abandoning their summer chalets and cabins: you can still see them, overgrown with weeds, on the Sentier du Roy footpath.

Nowadays, the island is ruled by gannets, which make up a quarter of the island's 200,000-strong sea-bird population; indeed, the Île Bonaventure is now a bird sanctuary. The gannets' colony on the cliffs is a spectacular sight, and all the more fascinating because you can only get there by boat, then on foot via a long and scenic route through woods and along the coast. Take a picnic, as you can easily spend a whole day on the island.

– You can't get drinking water anywhere on the island's footpaths, so make sure you bring some with you.

GETTING THERE

– **By boat**: there are four private companies at the port. Most offer 1-hour tours around the island before dropping you off. The leisurely trip gives you a chance to observe the cliffs, which are inhabited by seven species of bird – on the island itself, you'll probably see only gannets. Two companies, including Les Bateliers de Percé, also run a ferry service between Percé and the island; inquire at Les Fous de Bassan (*see* 'Where to Eat'). The crossing takes just 15 minutes, but there are only two departures: at 8am and 9am. From then on, you'll have to take the island tour.

Boats leave from the port's main quay. In summer, the companies pool their services and boats leave more or less every 15 minutes; after 15 August, crossings from the mainland to the island become less frequent, so check the times at the tourist office the day before your trip. The last boat back from the island to Percé leaves at 5pm.

> **TIP** Go as early in the morning as possible to avoid the crowds.

WHERE TO EAT AND HAVE A DRINK

✕ ❢ **Casse-croûte 3 'C'**: 4 rue du Quai, just above the landing stage. Open from early June to early October, 8am–5pm. This friendly place serves hamburgers and hot dogs and other simple snacks.

WHAT TO SEE AND DO

The island was designated a park in 1985 and is open to the public between June and mid-October, 8.15am–5pm. At the landing stage of l'Anse à Butler, where all boats arrive and depart, you'll be met by guides, who'll give a brief introductory talk about the island.

– **Footpaths**: four paths lead from the landing stage to the other side of the island. The shortest is the Sentier des Colonies, which is 3 kilometres (2 miles) long, and takes you through pretty undergrowth. If you have a little more time, try the Sentier des Mousses, an equally picturesque trail that curls around the northeast coast of the island (a protected zone) before bringing you to sea-bird territory; the whole walk takes 1 hour 15 minutes.

The most spectacular path, though, is the 5-kilometre (3-mile) Sentier du Chemin du Roy, which runs along the south coast of the island between the bird sanctuary and the quay, with fantastic views of the cliffs and sea. It's a wonderful way to head back to the port after visiting the bird colony, with a brief pause at the hauntingly beautiful Baie des Marigots, home to several abandoned houses and a cemetery. It takes about 3 hours to walk round the whole island.

★ The **sea-bird colony** is on the cliffs of island's eastern coast. The signposted footpath allows you to see thousands of birds close up, especially gannets. It's fascinating to see so many birds packed into so small a space, especially when they take off en masse to hunt for fish on the open sea.

★ **The gannets**: 80 centimetres (2.5 feet long), with a wingspan of up to 2 metres (7 feet), the northern gannet is bigger than any other gull. Its plumage is white, with a yellow neck and black-tipped wings, and it has blue eyes with distinctive black borders and a long, straight beak, which together form the gannet's characteristic 'smile'.

Gannets always live close to the sea, so you rarely see one inland. They feed on young fish or elvers, seizing them in their beaks after diving spectacularly into the icy water: they swoop down, building up momentum, before disappearing into the water in search of prey, which they gulp down before flying off again. The gannet spends the summer in Canada, and winters on the coasts of Florida and Gulf of Mexico.

This is the one of the world's most important bird colonies, and one of the most accessible. Amazing numbers of birds, young and old, mingle here: from a distance, they seem to have scant regard for personal space, but look more closely and you'll see just how aggressively they protect their tiny patches of territory, with beak-to-beak clashes breaking out when anyone steps out of line. You can spend as much time as you like watching the gannets and taking photographs from the footpath or the observation tower (you'll need a telephoto lens). Be warned, though: the smell can be somewhat overpowering.

★ **Baie des Marigots**: this pretty inlet with a shingle beach lies to the south of the island on the Sentier du Chemin du Roy. In the days when cod stocks were plentiful, Breton and Basque fishermen used to shelter here for an unofficial day off, eating, drinking and temporarily forgetting the hardships of work.

★ The **cemetery**, the most unassuming and touching in Québec, is on the Sentier du Chemin du Roy, about 500 metres (500 yards) from the jetty. It's a mown meadow facing the sea, surrounded by wild vegetation and with six small gravestones, a large, black wooden cross and a few information points. The pioneer families of Bonaventure lie buried here, most of them originally from the island of Jersey.

★ Dotted about the wild meadows on the west coast of the island are several **ghost houses** that once belonged to emigrant families from Jersey and Ireland. Today, they are abandoned and in an advanced state of dilapidation, although all are still covered with cedarwood tiles, and some of the houses are now being restored. The humblest of the dwellings, little more than shacks, housed families with as many as 12 children in exceedingly cramped conditions. The more elaborate houses are more like summer chalets, with bathrooms and panoramic views; in fact, the **Maison Paget**, built in 1858 by Michel Pagé, was used as a guesthouse until the 1950s. No matter how tempting it might seem, don't squat here for the night, as it's strictly forbidden.

BAIE DES CHALEURS
DIALLING CODE: 418

This bay reveals a completely different side of Gaspésie. The mountain retreats progressively as the strip of green between it and the sea grows wider, and the landscape, though pleasant, is considerably less spectacular. The fishing industry is still active here, hence the cod-drying sheds that line the coast.

The Road to Matapédia

There are two places worth visiting before you reach Port-Daniel.

★ **Centre d'Interprétation du Bourg de Pabos**: 75 chemin de la Plage, Pabos Mills. ☎ 689-6043. Open mid-June to mid-September, 9am–5pm. Admission $5. Guided tours available. This historical and archaeological centre examines the arrival of the first settlers in the 18th century, the lifestyle of the fishermen and the history of a local *seigneurie* (manor) that existed until the arrival of the British. You'll also find out how various excavated objects were dated, which should help you to get a sense of the area's history.

★ **Site Mary-Travers**: 124 route 132, in Newport. ☎ 777-2401. Open June to October, 9am–5pm. Admission $4. Guided tours available. This museum tells the story of a famous Québécois singer, born in Newport in 1894. When she was 13, she moved to Montréal, and eventually married Édouard Bolduc: hence her nickname, 'La Bolduc'. The display includes photographs and copies of her lyrics: she was inspired by everyday subjects and current events, as you can see from titles like *La Grocerie du coin* ('The Corner Shop') or *Le Nouveau Gouvernement* ('The New Government'). More curious is *Si j'pouvais tenir Hitler* ('If I Could Get My Hands on Hitler'), in which she threatens to stuff Hitler with cod, replacing his moustache with a cow's tail and smoking him like a herring. The visit ends with live renditions of some of the songs by a local singer, Angèle Poirier.

PORT-DANIEL

The village of Port-Daniel, built on a deep bay with a sandy beach, appears abruptly as you crest a hill. Unusually for Gaspésie, tuna is the main catch here. The village's main attraction is a wildlife reserve, dotted with small lakes and plenty of footpaths. From Percé, take a right as you enter the village; the reserve is 8 kilometres (5 miles) farther on.

USEFUL ADDRESS

ℹ There's a small **tourist office** on the outskirts of the village, just before the bridge if you're coming from Percé. ☎ 396-3215. Open in high season only, 8am–8pm.

WHERE TO STAY IN THE PORT-DANIEL AREA

⌂ There's plenty of budget accommodation in **chalets** or at the **campsite** at the wildlife reserve. ☎ 396-2789 (in high season) or 1-800-665-6527 (toll-free; reservations only). The campsite is top-notch in terms of location, cleanliness, bathroom and service. Campers can also go fishing.

⌂ Gîte Les Âcres Tranquilles: 252 route 132 west (Route Lévesque). ☎ 396-3491. Fax: 396-2014. Email: mynor@globetrotter.net. Doubles from $45 a night, including breakfast. This is a peaceful house with a lumberjack-style interior, surrounded by a large, carefully maintained garden. The four pleasant rooms share a bathroom (which has a basin built into a barrel), while the kitchen is done up in natural wood. In the morning, you'll be woken by the delicious smell of freshly baked bread.

⌂ Gîte à la Ferme MacDale: 365 route 132, Hope West, Paspébiac, 20 miles west of Port-Daniel. ☎ 752-5270. Website: www.bbcanada.com/399.html. Doubles from $45 a night. This fantastic, hospitable guesthouse is set back from the main road in the midst of a sweeping lawn. There are three fairly small but light and clean rooms, of which the best (and largest) is No. 4, with an all-wood decor and sea views from the en-suite bathroom. The homemade breakfast is excellent, and you can order dinner if you book in advance. To cap it all, the owners will happily ferry you to and from the train station.

PASPÉBIAC

The name of this natural harbour comes from the Micmac word *tcha kibiac,* meaning 'breached sandbank'.

Apart from the Banc de Paspébiac, the only reason to come here is the Don Lynn bar, on the main street, a lively place that attracts a young local crowd. You'll have to pay to get in at the weekend.

★ Site historique du Banc de Paspébiac: Route du Banc. ☎ 752-6229. Open June to mid-October, 9am–6pm (until 4pm out of season). Guided tours available. This astonishing complex was once a centre for the region's cod industry. Long since abandoned, it has been converted into an open-air ecological museum with an array of beautifully preserved buildings, including a carpenter's workshop and a forge. You'll need at least an hour to see everything.

Charles Robin, a merchant adventurer who emigrated from Jersey, established the site in the 18th century. Two influential fishing companies, CRC and Le Boutillier Brothers, were founded here: they used to import produce for the local population, but their main trade was fishing for cod, drying it, storing it, then exporting it all over the world. At the height of their success, hundreds of people worked in Paspébiac, which was the hub of the fishing industry on the Gulf of St Lawrence, attracting labourers from Germany, Britain, Portugal, France and even the Basque country; several families in the village still have Basque surnames.

NEW CARLISLE

This English-speaking village on the Route de Bonaventure, 7 kilometres (4 miles) from Paspébiac, is populated by descendants of the Loyalists, who left the United States after the American War of Independence because they wanted to remain under British rule.

WHERE TO STAY

â **Maison de Juge Thompson**: 105 rue Principale, near the law courts. ☎ 752-6308/5744; in summer, ☎ 752-6308. Doubles $60 a night, including breakfast. Built in 1844 by Judge John G. Thompson, and surrounded by a garden and lush green lawns, the house is pretty but unremarkable, with a pleasant veranda overlooking the sea. Inside, however, there's a wonderfully authentic 19th-century feel, with paintings, engravings, trinkets, Victorian-style furniture and French windows on the ground floor. The three spacious, cosy rooms overlook the garden. It's an up-market establishment, and the charming owners cook up an excellent English breakfast.

â **La Clé des Champs**: 254 route 132 east, Hope Town, between Port-Daniel and Paspébiac. ☎ 752-3113 or 1-800-693-3113 (toll-free). Doubles from $50 a night. Ideal for an overnight stop, this award-winning establishment has spotless rooms with views of the bay, and the breakfasts are excellent. Bernard, a skilled horseman, offers tours of the surrounding countryside in his cart.

BONAVENTURE

This is one of the last Acadian strongholds in Gaspésie.

USEFUL ADDRESS

🛈 **Bureau d'information touristique**: next to the museum. ☎ 534-4014. Open mid-May to late August, 8am–8pm.

WHERE TO STAY, EAT AND HAVE A DRINK

â **Gîte au Foin Fou**: 204 chemin de la Rivière. ☎ 534-4413. Website: www.gites-classifies.qc.ca. Open 15 June to 15 September. Doubles $50 a night. This charming house in a remote spot is extremely popular with artists, who come to this peaceful retreat to work; you can see, and even buy, some of the results. There are five beautiful and individually decorated rooms, and the house is full of unusual touches: in the lounge, there's a bizarre telephone fixed in an old sewing machine, while in the upstairs bathroom, the water runs through a tangle of cast-iron pipes, then pours into a ceramic bowl. Breakfast, meanwhile, is made with organic produce, including fresh eggs, and the pancakes are delicious. Guests can use the ground-floor massage room and the terrace, or go swimming or canoeing in the river at the bottom of the garden. In summer, everyone gathers round the campfire. This is the best place to stay in Bonaventure.

🛏 ✖ **Auberge du Café Acadien**: 168 rue Beaubassin, opposite the marina. ☎ 534-4276. Doubles $50 a night. This hospitable, family-run guesthouse has five pretty rooms, all with basins; the shower and toilet are on the landing. Two of the rooms have views over the meadows, the campsite and the sea; the others, rather less romantically, overlook the car-park, which is thankfully quiet at night. There's a large, pleasant bar

on the ground floor, while the restaurant serves substantial portions of herring, smoked salmon, cod and seafood pâté at reasonable prices.

✖ **Le Rendez-vous**: 108 rue de Grand-Pré, near the church. ☎ 534-3499. Open until midnight. This modern restaurant is short on charm, but it's worth trying the good, inexpensive fish and seafood dishes, as well as the usual burgers, pasta and pizzas.

✖ ❦ **Bistro-Bar Le Fou du Village**: 119 rue de Grand-Pré, near Le Rendez-Vous. ☎ 534-4567. Open 2pm–3am. This quiet bar has a pool table, a large terrace and a mezzanine. There's live music several times a week.

WHAT TO SEE

★ **Musée Acadien du Québec**: 95 avenue Port-Royal. ☎ 534-4000. From 24 June to September, open 9am–8pm; otherwise, open weekdays only, 9am–noon and 1–5pm. Admission $5. This interesting little museum looks at the origins and culture of the Acadians, a group of French settlers whose turbulent history is described in more detail in the New Brunswick chapter.

★ **Grotte de Saint-Elzéar**: 198 Route de l'Église, 20 kilometres (13 miles) north of Bonaventure. ☎ 534-4335. Fax: 534-2611. Admission $37. This is the oldest cave in Québec – almost 500,000 years old – with two chambers packed with stalagmites and stalactites. The only way to see the cave is on a tour, which lasts 4 hours, must be booked in advance. Make sure you wear warm clothing and sports shoes; a hard hat and torch are provided.

SHOPPING

🔒 **Les Cuirs Fins de la Mer**: 76 avenue Port-Royal; near the Musée Acadien du Québec (it's well signposted). ☎ 534-3821. Open 8am–8pm in high season; phone in advance during the rest of the year. This is a unique business selling items made from cod and salmon skin: purses, spectacle cases, make-up bags, ties, jackets, mobiles, pictures, bracelets and so on. They're as strong as leather, and surprisingly attractive, but the prices are unbelievable. Still, that hasn't stopped it becoming an extremely successful business venture.

NEW RICHMOND

New Richmond is a small, typically English town, with several luxurious houses in the town centre.

– **Tourist information kiosk**: on route 132. ☎ 392-7075.

GASPÉSIE

WHERE TO STAY

🛏 **Gîte du Passant Les Bouleaux**: 142 Route de la Plage, a kilometre (half a mile) from the centre. ☎ 392-4111. Fax: 392-6048. From Percé, turn left off route 132 at the New Richmond exit, at the intersection with route 299. Doubles $50–60 a night. This is a pleasant wooden house surrounded by greenery and silver birches. The lounge has a terrace overlooking the bay, and there are four little rooms with basins, and two bathrooms; the ground-floor room is the best, and has the most beautiful view. It's run by a pleasant and welcoming couple, and the breakfasts are great.

🛏 **Gîte de la Maison Lévesque**: 180 avenue Leblanc. ☎ 392-5267. Fax: 392-6948. Doubles $50 a night. This place offers excellent value for money. Mme. Lévesque is kind-hearted and considerate, and cooks wonderful food, including an enormous breakfast.

🛏 **Auberge La Maison Stanley**: 371 boulevard Perron Ouest, in the woods at the mouth of the Grande Cascapédia River. ☎ 392-5560. Fax: 392-5592. Doubles $90 a night. This classy, colonial-style residence, full of character and completely unpretentious, was once the home of the governor-general of Canada. The interior is rustic but stylish, and the huge lounge is full of antique furniture. The pretty veranda looks out onto a meticulously kept lawn, and guests can use the private beach on the Baie des Chaleurs.

WHAT TO SEE

★ **Centre de l'Héritage Britannique de la Gaspésie** (Gaspesian British Heritage Centre): 351 boulevard Perron Ouest. ☎ 392-4487. Open June to September, 9am–6pm. Admission $6. This is a wonderful reconstruction of a Loyalist pioneer village. The Loyalists, faithful to the British throne, sought refuge in Canada after the Americans gained their independence. Many settled on the Gaspé peninsula and in the Maritime Provinces (New Brunswick and Nova Scotia).

From New Richmond to the St Lawrence River

From New Richmond, you can travel across Gaspésie via the Vallée de Cascapédia to Sainte-Anne-des-Monts (on the south bank of the St Lawrence). Or you can head farther south to the Vallée de Matapédia, which brings you to Mont-Joli or Matane. In terms of time, there's not much in it.

It's a difficult choice: on your right is the imposing route 299; on your left is route 132, colourful and varied. The former passes through beautiful mountains covered with fir trees, a solitary landscape that's reminiscent of the Alps; the scenery along the Matapédia route is more diverse and inviting.

– In **Maria**, 18 kilometres (11 miles) before you get to Carleton, there's an amazing church on the Micmac reservation. From route 132, turn left before the Micmac craft co-operative, which has a giant wigwam. The interior of the church is warm and pleasant, but its most notable feature is a little altar dedicated to Catherine Tekakwitha, the Iroquois Virgin. She was a young Mohawk who left her tribe to convert to Christianity and follow the missionaries. She was martyred in 1680, at the age of 24, having already suffered more than most during her short life.

CARLETON-SUR-MER POP: 3,000

DIALLING CODE: 418

Carleton is a lovely seaside resort, stretching over a strip of low ground at the foot of a range of wooded hills. It's a pleasant place to stop for a night or two, to get a taste of its marvellous mild microclimate and spot several species of birds as they migrate south. Founded by the Acadians after the 1755 expulsions, Carleton is set out on a grid system, with all the streets at right angles to each other. It doesn't take long to get out of the town, and a green belt of forest soon replaces the cultivated fields. It's rather nice to be able to go straight from the sea to the mountains.

USEFUL ADDRESSES

🛈 **Tourist Office**: 629 boulevard Perron (this is the main street). ☎ 364-3544.
Post Office: 716 boulevard Perron.
🚌 **Bus stop**: at Le Héron restaurant, 561 boulevard Perron. ☎ 364-3881. You can get a timetable and tickets at the restaurant.

🚋 **Railway station**: on rue de la Gare, near the Belle Plage motel. ☎ 364-7734, or 0-361-5390 (toll-free). Only open when trains are due to arrive or depart. There are three evening departures to Montréal a week.

WHERE TO STAY

Campsite

⌂ **Camping Carleton**: on the Tracadigash peninsula, on the left if you're coming from Percé. ☎ 364-3992. Tent pitches $20; discounts available for long stays. This is a large campsite, a stone's throw from the beach, but there's not much shade and it lacks a shop or a restaurant.

☆–☆☆ Budget to Moderate

⌂ **Chambres du Café de la Baie**: 608 boulevard Perron. ☎ 364-6186. Doubles $40 a night. This is the cheapest place in town, with rooms above the restaurant and a bathroom on the landing. It's a bit gloomy, and gets noisy when the

restaurant's busy, but guests can use the kitchen.
⌂ **Gîte Chez Lulu**: 21 rue de la Montagne, in a quiet residential area. ☎ 364-6080. Fax: 364-6086. Doubles $55 a night. This friendly, good-value establishment is the best place to stay in the area. It's a new house with spotless rooms that share a bathroom, and guests can use the small swimming pool and the lawn behind the house. The owner, Gerry, is passionate about the great outdoors, and goes hunting with a bow and arrow in the forests of Québec. His wife, Lulu, is very friendly.
⌂ **Gîte de la Mer-La Montagne**: 711 boulevard Perron. ☎ and fax: 364-6474. Doubles from $50 a night. It has four small bedrooms,

two luxurious bathrooms and one suite with a balcony that overlooks the sea. It's clean and friendly, and the room rates are very reasonable.

⌂ **Auberge La Visite Surprise**: 527 boulevard Perron, at the fork in the road down to the port. ☎ 364-6553 or 1-800-463-7740 (toll-free). Email: liselebl@globtrotter.net. Doubles $48–60 a night. The seven rooms, some with basins, are airy and spacious, but lack charm. There are three bathrooms, and the service is friendly and considerate.

⌂ **Gîte La Rêverie**: 9 rue Gauthier, on a peaceful residential street. ☎ 364-7525. Email: bady@globe trotter.qc.ca. Doubles from $45 a night. This modern house, run by a really lovely couple, has one large three-bedded room, one double and one single, all moderately priced and very clean.

☆☆☆ Expensive

⌂ **Hôtel-motel de la Baie Bleue**: 482 boulevard Perron. ☎ 364-3355 or 1-800-463-9099 (toll-free). Fax: 364-6165. Doubles $100 a night. Evening *table d'hôte* $15–25. This place is slightly expensive, but the rooms are comfortable and the staff are extremely professional. Guests can use the heated swimming pool, the tennis court (you can borrow racquets and balls), the golf course and the play area. The manager, Richard Gingras, loves snowbiking, and will enthusiastically tell you all about it.

WHERE TO STAY IN THE AREA

⌂ **Motel Leblanc**: 1778 Boulevard Perron, on route 132. ☎ 364 7370. Take the exit for the village of Maria, 7 kilometres (4 miles) from Carleton. This is a friendly place with well-equipped, moderately priced rooms. Some even have kitchens.

⌂ **Gîte du Passant Wanta-Qo-Ti**: 77 chemin Pointe-Fleurant, in Escuminac, 20 minutes' drive from Carleton. ☎ and fax: 788-5686. E-mail: bwafer@globetrotter.net. Doubles from $58 a night. '*Wanta-qo-ti*' is a Micmac word meaning tranquillity or serenity, and though it's not far from Carleton, this beachside guesthouse near Miguasha Park truly lives up to its name. It's a large wooden building, homely and tastefully decorated, with eight comfortable rooms; the best is No. 5, with Scottish furniture and a rocking chair. Breakfast is a feast of muffins, crêpes, bread and jam, all home-made. The owner, Bruce, was born here, and knows the area like the back of his hand. Although he's a native of these parks, he's proud of his Scottish and Irish roots, as the giant shamrock fixed to the garage suggests.

WHERE TO EAT

✕ **Restaurant Le Héron**: 561 boulevard Perron, in the heart of town. ☎ 364-3881. Full meal $10–16. If you're after a snack, but don't fancy yet another burger, this is the place for you. There's a good choice of fish dishes, including cod and trout, and you can also get a take-away. There's a pleasant terrace, and in the bar, you can watch live rock, blues and folk bands (Tuesday to Saturday).

✕ **Le Marin d'Eau Douce**: 215 route du Quai, on the way to the harbour. ☎ 364-7602. Open 7am–10pm. Lunch $14–17; set menu

21. This is a friendly place with a veranda overlooking the sea. The waitress, Mimi, is extremely jolly, if a little slow, and food is simple and tasty: salads, *sous-marins* (the Québécois submarine sandwich) and plenty of fish and seafood, including sole, cod, salmon or halibut. There's a lunchtime special on weekdays, and you can get breakfast or a snack throughout the week.

WHERE TO EAT IN THE AREA

✗ **Café du Vieux Quai**: 192 boulevard Perron Est, in Saint-Omer, west of Carleton on route 132. ☎ 364-6204. This is a pleasant little restaurant with a small terrace. There are good à la carte dishes and several set menus, all at reasonable prices.

WHERE TO HAVE A DRINK

! Bar Saint-Barnabé: next door to Café l'Indépendant'e. ☎ 364-7304. Open mid-May to mid-August. Not so much a bar as a rusty old boat washed up on the beach: this red-and-white American minesweeper has been transformed into a trendy bar with a great atmosphere. A great example of how recycling can improve our lives.

WHAT TO SEE AND DO

★ **The beach in Carleton**: on the south side of the Tracadigash peninsula, near the campsite. The lighthouse has an information point explaining the history of the local lighthouses.

– **Bird-watching**: Carleton's lagoon attracts several species of sea bird, including great blue herons, seagulls, cormorants, black ducks, gulls and terns, long-distance migrants who think nothing of flying from pole to pole. They arrive here in mid-May to lay their eggs, then battle to protect them from the predatory seagulls. There's a splendid walk along route du Quai to the tip of the peninsula, where you'll find a bird sanctuary and an observation tower that offers great views and information about the birds and the creation of the lagoon.

– **Sea trips**: Mer Nature (☎ 364-7643) organizes fishing and diving trips in the Baie des Chaleurs between mid-June and mid-September. Excursions last 2 hours 30 minutes, and tickets can be bought from the marina in Carleton.

★ **Mont Saint-Joseph**: this wooded mountain, 555 metres (1,820 feet) high, dominates the resort. From Carleton, take rue de la Montagne and follow the signs for Oratoire Saint-Joseph. It's a 10-minute drive to the summit, or take the footpaths from the village of Maria to Mont Saint-Joseph and Mont Carleton. Admission $3. There's a 1930s chapel here, but the main reason to come is the fantastic view of Carleton, the Baie des Chaleurs and the wooded hinterland, especially at twilight. The 15-kilometre (9-mile) network of paths is dotted with waterfalls and superb panoramic viewpoints.

GASPÉSIE

FESTIVALS AND EVENTS

– **Maximum Blues**: ☎ 364-6008. For five days in early August, Carleton rocks to the rhythm of the blues, with musicians coming from Europe and the US as well as Québec. There are 70 performances, in the main marquee and in bars and restaurants all over town.

IN THE AREA

★ **Parc de Miguasha**: ☎ 794-2475. Open early June to late September, 9am–6pm. A host of remarkable fossils are displayed in evolutionary order, with staff on hand to provide clear and simple explanations of the site.

– A **ferry** links Miguasha to Dalhousie, in New Brunswick, with several departures daily in summer.

POINTE-À-LA-GARDE   DIALLING CODE: 418

This village is home to a fantastic youth hostel, housed in a Renaissance-style castle in the middle of a wood. It also hosts several unusual festivals (*see below*).

WHERE TO STAY AND EAT

🛏 ✕ **Auberge de Jeunesse**: 152 boulevard Perron, on route 132, 100 metres (100 yards) from the bus stop. ☎ 788-2048. Rooms $40–58, including breakfast; it's more expensive if you don't have a Youth Hostel card. The main building has private rooms and dormitories, but the star turn is the '*château*' Bahia, 500 metres (500 yards) behind the hostel on a small hill in the woods. This curious, Disneyesque building, built in 1983, is like a cartoon version of a chateau on the Loire. The double rooms, some with en-suite bathrooms, are all pretty, and there's a laundry and a telephone. It's best to book ahead if you want to stay in the château, which is closed out of season: it's more expensive than the youth hostel, but it's still pretty cheap, and you get a delicious breakfast of blueberry pancakes into the bargain. Try to have dinner somewhere else, though.

Guests can bathe in the 'warm' waters of the bay, try a variety of sports, go hiking or attend one of the hostel's many festivities, in honour of anything from the full moon to the strawberry season, a type of fish or St John's day. Between May and October, there are parties in the castle, including a lavish fancy-dress ball on the last Saturday in September, when revellers wear period garb from the chosen era.

WHAT TO SEE

★ **Musée de la Bataille de La Restigouche**: in Pointe-à-la-Croix. ☎ 788-5676. Open June to mid-October, 9am–5pm. This well-organized museum is home to the superbly preserved remnants of the *Machault*, which was sunk during a 1760 naval battle between the French and the British, then brought to the surface in 1939. You can also see its cargo (weapons, bullets, cannonballs, shoes, china, plates, earthenware jugs and so on), and an animated film describing the ship's fatal final engagement.

FESTIVALS AND EVENTS

– **Salmon festival**: in Campbellton, New Brunswick, in mid-June.

– **'Le Pistoli' Acadian festival**: in Campbellton, New Brunswick, on 15 August.

WHAT TO SEE IN THE AREA

★ **Restigouche:** The Micmac name for this village, which is home to the biggest Native American reservation in Gaspésie, means 'river divided like a hand'.

– The **church** in Restigouche is something of an enigma. It burned down 11 times before someone gave the church a relic: a fragment of bone from the right arm of St Anne. There has not been a single fire since.

MATAPÉDIA VALLEY

The road follows an old Indian track for about 50 kilometres (30 miles) before it enters the valley of the Matapédia River, known as the 'river of 132 rapids'. The steeply sloped banks form a clear boundary between the Chic-Choc Mountains and the highlands of the west. The landscape is sublime: along both sides of the river, the wooded hills look as if they're on fire, the leaves an eruption of reds, golds, pinks and oranges. At Routhierville, a covered bridge towers 80 metres (260 feet) above the river. Salmon-fishing is allowed down the length of the Matapédia.

Starting from **Causapscal**, the valley opens out, with beautiful views as the Causapscal and Matapédia rivers merge. At **Amqui**, turn right onto route 195 to get back to Matane. Amqui, which used to be written 'Humqui', means 'Where the water plays': the road crosses a wide valley with another impressive view.

GASPÉSIE

WHERE TO STAY AND EAT

⚑ **Amqui Campsite**: 686 route 132 west, in Amqui, on the riverbank. ☎ 629-3433. Tent pitches $16; caravan sites $19. There are plenty of activities on offer, and the site has clean toilets and showers.

⚑ ✕ **Auberge de Jeunesse**: 13 rue des Saumons, in Amqui. ☎ 865-2444/2422. Dorm beds $13 a night; doubles $30. Just beyond the railway, on a deserted street in a god-

forsaken spot, this youth hostel occupies a shack that looks like a Wild West saloon bar. It has two eight-bed dormitories and a few private rooms. The facilities are just about adequate, and there's a restaurant and bar on the ground floor.

⚑ **Gîte du Passant Aux Bois d'Avignon**: 171 Rustico, in Saint-Alexis-de-Matapédia, 9 kilometres (6 miles) from Matapédia. ☎ 299-

2537. Fax: 299-2111. Email: bois davi@globtrotter.qc.ca. Doubles up to $60 a night. This back-country guesthouse, run by the outgoing Laura Chouinard, is a good place to stop before you rejoin the Matapédia Valley. It's a superbly designed, bright and modern house, and there's a family annexe with its own bathroom. Other facilities include a large swimming pool and bike hire.

🛏 **Gîte J.-A Dufour**: 170 rue Principale, Saint-Alexis-de-Matapédia. ☎ 299-3040 or 299-2500. Fax: 299-2502. Doubles $50 a night. This place has five superb bedrooms and two fully equipped bathrooms, one of which is decorated like a ship's cabin. You get an excellent choice at breakfast, and Luce and Daniel, the friendly owners, can organize evening trips in search of bears and moose.

🛏 ✕ **Auberge La Coulée Douce**: 21 rue Boudreau, in Causapscal. ☎ 756-5270. Fax: 756-5271. This excellent, if expensive, guesthouse offers a wide range of outdoor activities, including snowmobile rides, hiking in snowshoes, horse-drawn calashes, skiing and fishing.

🛏 **Domaine du Lac Matapédia**: 780 route 132 west, in Amqui, 5 kilometres (3 miles) from the lake. ☎ 629-5004. Doubles $55 a night. This sprawling establishment has five very clean rooms, prettily decorated in pastel shades, and two bathrooms. There's also an enormous kitchen, where you'll get a hearty breakfast. A pleasant stay is guaranteed.

🛏 ✕ **Pourvoirie du Domaine du Lac Malcolm**: 123 route du Lac-Malcolm, in Sayabec, between Amqui and Mont-Joli. ☎ 536-3322. Doubles $55 a night. Built well away from route 132, this house looks out over a lake, and is a good place to spend your last night in Gaspésie. You can sleep, eat and even camp here, all at reasonable prices. Breakfast is served on a floating terrace, and there's cabaret at weekends; canoe and pedalo hire is also available. Think twice before coming here in July, however, as the constant whirr of agricultural machinery can play havoc with your peace of mind.

SAINT-VIANNEY

From Saint-Vianney, the road soon joins the course of the River Matane, then lazily follows its banks up to the port. This is a charming little valley with farming villages clustered around white churches.

GETTING BACK TO THE NORTH BANK

There's a choice of ferries at Matane: one goes to Godbout, the other to Comeau Bay. If you're heading south, it's quicker to go to Comeau Bay, but you'll miss out on Franquelin Bay.

THE ÎLES DE LA MADELEINE

A visit to the Îles de la Madeleine (Magdalen Islands) is a must for anyone with a touch of romance in their souls. Its charms include, in no particular order, deserted, wind-lashed beaches, red sandstone cliffs, wild berries and

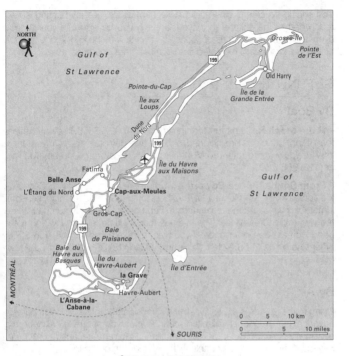

ÎLES DE LA MADELEINE

chanterelle mushrooms, brightly coloured wooden houses and cheap lobster dinners. Of the seven inhabited islands, five are populated by French-speakers; on the other two, English is the mother tongue. **Île aux Loups Marins** (meaning 'seal island') is overrun with cormorants; farther afield, Île Brion has been the site of a staggering 450 shipwrecks. Brion is also home to a wildlife reserve, while the **Rocher aux Oiseaux** ('Bird Rock') is home to several colonies of sea birds.

Although they were used by Micmac and then European fishermen for centuries, it was not until 1762 that this group of islands was inhabited on a permanent basis. In 1798, the seven islands had 500 inhabitants; today, about 14,500 people live there. Most are descended from the itinerant Acadians; as for the 750 English-speakers, most have their roots in Scotland.

The islands' tourist industry was kick-started in the 1970s by an influx of hippies, who were no doubt attracted by the laid-back pace of life. These days, the holidaymakers who come to the islands are more conventional, but the hotel infrastructure is still relatively developed, so you'll need to book accommodation in advance if you're coming between mid-July and mid-August. If you can, though, try to come in June or September (when the sea is warmer), as the islands will be much less crowded. If you're coming from Québec, remember to put your watch forward one hour.

THE ÎLES DE LA MADELEINE

You should be careful when discussing baby seals, as seal-hunting is very much part of the culture on these islands. If you have to bite your tongue every time the issue comes up, console yourself with the knowledge that the culling is more strictly regulated than in most other countries.

GETTING THERE

By Boat

– **From Montréal**: trips run fortnightly. ☎ (514) 937-7656. It's no cheaper than flying, but meals are included, and the two-day cruise is an adventure in itself. If you want to return to Montréal from by boat from Cap-aux-Meules, ☎ (418) 986-6600.

– **From Souris (Prince Edward Island)**: there's a daily ferry to Cap-aux-Meules (except for Monday at the beginning and end of high season). Timetables vary, and there's no ferry in February or March. In summer, there are two departures a day. The average journey time is 5 hours, and it's a good idea to book in advance. If you want to take a car, ☎ (418) 986-3278; otherwise, ☎ (902) 687-2181 (in Souris) or ☎ (418) 986-6600 (in Cap-aux-Meules).

By Air

Flying to the islands is expensive, but it's considerably cheaper if you book in advance; inquire about available discounts when you phone. Air Alliance is a subsidiary of Air Canada; for more details, ask for an Air Canada brochure. Several flights a day are available with the following companies:

– **Air Alliance**: ☎ (418) 969-2888, freephone (from Québec) 1-800-361-8620.

– **Régionnair**: ☎ 986-6565. The 12-seater planes make several stops between Montréal and the islands.

GETTING AROUND

If you're walking or cycling, the best way to approach the Îles de la Madeleine is to travel up or down the archipelago, which is 60 kilometres (37 miles) from end to end. If you've hired a car, you'll find it easy to get around using route 199, which spans the length of the islands. The seven islands are treated as a single entity here; in each section, they're listed from north to south.

Grosse-Île and Île de la Grande Entrée

These two islands, one English-speaking, one francophone, make up the northeast corner of the archipelago. They are linked by Pointe de l'Est, home to the national wildlife reserve. After crossing the Dune du Nord, a near-desert whose wilderness feel is slightly tainted by ugly electricity pylons, the rolling green hills of Grosse-Île offer quite a contrast. When you arrive on the island, you'll see the Seleine mines on the right; here, enormous quantities of salt are extracted for use in de-icing the roads in winter.

Île du Havre-aux-Maisons

To get from Grosse-Île to Île du Havre-aux-Maisons, follow the magnificent route 199, which is bordered on both sides by the sea. A thin band of sand is all that separates you from the waves; if you ever wondered what an atoll was, this is your chance to find out. With its red sandstone cliffs and rolling green hills, dotted with houses in bright and pastel shades, the island offers superb vantage points and magnificent vistas, especially at sunset.

◉ The **airport** is on this island, just before Dune du Sud.

Île du Cap aux Meules

An iron bridge links Île du Havre-aux-Maisons to Île du Cap aux Meules. This is the most densely populated island in the archipelago, as well as the commercial and administrative centre, and is made up of three municipalities:

CAP-AUX-MEULES

This is the most important community on the islands; the ferry docks here, and it's near the airport. It's also home to an excellent tourist office, which will provide you with comprehensive information about every aspect of the archipelago. It's the liveliest place on the islands (*see* 'Where to Have a Drink'), so it's a useful base if you like your creature comforts, but look elsewhere if you want to feel at one with nature.

FATIMA

Don't stay in Fatima unless you have a car, because there's really nowhere nice to eat. You'll have to go to Cap-aux-Meules for dinner.

L'ÉTANG-DU-NORD

This little village is an important fishing port. Near the harbour, a sculpture pays tribute to the hard work of the local fishermen.

Île du Havre Aubert and Île d'Entrée

Île du Havre Aubert is linked to Île du Cap aux Meules by two long sand spits, Dune de l'Ouest and Dune du Havre aux Basques, which encircle a lagoon. It's a windsurfers' paradise: the wind blows constantly, but there's no danger of ending up on the open sea. Île d'Entrée, meanwhile, is the second English-speaking island, and is the only island in the archipelago that can only be reached by boat.

HAVRE-AUBERT

This is the oldest village in the archipelago and, although it's rather touristy, there's no disputing its charm. At its heart is **La Grave**, a pebbly beach once lined with salting tubs, shops and fishing warehouses, and now awash with guesthouses, cafés, restaurants and souvenir shops.

BASSIN

You enter Bassin on a panoramic road that goes as far as Dune de l'Ouest. The village is of little interest in itself – **L'Anse-à-la-Cabane** is a better base – but the forest that surrounds it is the biggest on the islands, and is good walking territory.

ÎLE D'ENTRÉE

The inhabitants of Île d'Entrée, an English-speaking stronghold, wouldn't leave their island at any price. It's too expensive to provide the island with electricity and telephone lines, and the government has tried hard to get these people to go elsewhere, but nobody wants to move. When you've seen the island's vast, craggy cliffs and bare, windswept hills, you'll understand why.

Options for getting to the island from Cap-aux-Meules include:

– **Bonaventure Ferry**: leaves at 8am and 3pm, and returns at 9am and 4pm. ☎ 986-5705. Tickets $16.

– **Boat trips**: summer only. These leave at 10.30am and return at 2.30pm. ☎ 986-4745. The crossing takes an hour, which leaves 3 hours to explore the island unless you want to spend the night there. At $20, it's a touch more expensive than the ferry.

USEFUL ADDRESSES

🏠 Tourist office: 128 chemin du Débarcadère, at the intersection with route 199, Cap-aux-Meules. ☎ 986-2245. In summer, open 7am–9pm; otherwise Monday to Friday, 9am–5pm. The staff are efficient and helpful, and really know their stuff.

🚌 Tourist bus around the island: leaves from the Cap-aux-Meules tourist office at 9.30am, and returns at 4.30pm. Tickets $32, including lunch; discounts available for children. The bus stops at the main places of interest in the archipelago, and is a good way to get an overview of the islands.

■ Car hire: booking is essential if you want to hire a car in high season.

– **Thrifty**: ☎ 969-9006. Ask to speak to Nadine. If she doesn't have a car available for you, she'll find someone who does.
– **Tilden**: ☎ 969-2590.
– **Location HCR**: ☎ 969-4209.
– **Location du Berceau**: 701 chemin Principal. ☎ 937-5614. This company hires out used cars, so it's a good budget option. Scooter hire is also available.

■ Taxis: Taxi Archipel (☎ 986-2101); Taxi 2000 (☎ 986-2000); Taxi Madelin (☎ 986-2555).

■ Bike hire: Le Pédalier, 365 chemin Principal, at the traffic lights on the corner of chemin Petipas. ☎ 986-2965. A day's hire costs $18.

■ Activities: for information about exhibitions, concerts, shows and festivals on the islands, and for tickets, go to Dépanneur du Village, the local convenience store (325 chemin Principal; ☎ 986-4177).

WHERE TO STAY

🛏 **Agence Toit et moi**, an agency based in Bassin, offers good-quality chalets, rooms and caravans to hire all over the island. ☎ 937-2838.

Grosse-Île and Île de la Grande Entrée

🛏 **Domaine de la Grenouille sur Mer**: ☎ 985-2365. Doubles $65–110 a night. A nice little hotel.

🛏 **Club Vacances Les Îles**: 377 route 199. ☎ 985-2833. Fax: 985-2226. There are 24 rooms, let for a minimum of three nights: expect to pay $240 per adult, full-board, for a double room, with discounts available for children. You can also camp here (there's no shade, but there is a convenience store nearby). Club Vacances offers packages including meals and activities (*see* 'What to See and Do'), as well as Club Med-style evening entertainment. It's good fun, especially for families, but it's basically a holiday camp. Even if you're not staying here, you can come for a meal (lunch $10; dinner $15). There are three computers with Internet access (free for guests; otherwise $2 an hour).

Havre-aux-Maisons

🛏 **Camping des Sillons**: just off route 199, at the edge of Dune du Sud, right next to the beach. ☎ 969-2134 or 969-2126. Tent pitches $15 a night; chalets from $70 a night. This is a well-equipped site with a laundry room, a small shop, a restaurant and a playground, and prices are pretty reasonable. On the down side, there's no shade or shelter from the wind. The chalets have fully equipped kitchens.

🛏 **Domaine des Vacanciers**: 290 chemin Dune du Sud. ☎ 969-4312. Chalets $550 a week. These pretty, modern two-bedroom chalets have all mod cons and exceptional views of the sea. At these prices, they're a bargain.

🛏 **Gîte Chez Antoinette Leblanc**: 507 route 199, next to the Coop supermarket. ☎ 969-4454. Run by a nice retired couple, this guesthouse offers three ultra-clean and reasonably priced bedrooms. Breakfast is extra.

🛏 **Au Vieux Couvent**: 292 route 199. ☎ 969-2233. Fax: 969-4693. This carved-stone building was originally a convent, but now offers excellent accommodation at modest prices. Upstairs, the classrooms have been converted into simple, bright bedrooms (with en-suite showers or bathrooms), all in white and with views of the sea or the hills. In what used to be the chapel and the Mother Superior's residence, there's a bar-restaurant with terrace. At weekday lunchtimes, there's an all-you-can-eat mussel deal for $10; dinner costs $20–30. The food isn't haute cuisine (mussels and chips, squid, fish soup and the like), but it's not too expensive and portions are generous.

🛏 **Maison d'Eva-Anne**: ☎ 969-4053. Doubles $70 a night, including breakfast. This is a lovely place with absolutely no pretensions.

☆☆☆ Expensive

🛏 **Auberge la P'tite Baie**: 187 route 199, near the bridge that links Île du Havre-aux-Maisons to Île du Cap aux Meules. ☎ 969-4073. Doubles $65–95, including breakfast. This friendly place has five en-suite rooms, not huge but comfortable and tastefully decorated. The owners will pick you up at the airport or from the harbour. Breakfast is served in the cosy dining room, where you can also get good, traditional food in the evening; the *table d'hôte* offers the best value for money.

Cap-aux-Meules

≜ **Auberge des Pas Perdus**: 169 chemin Principal, opposite rue de l'Embarcadère. ☎ 986-5151. Fax: 986-6745. Doubles $40 a night, excluding breakfast. Once a bistro, this hotel was set up by three young locals who wanted to recapture the 'backpacker' atmosphere that they encountered during their travels round the world. It has four spotless bedrooms, an inviting bar on the ground floor and a restaurant (main courses $12) where armchairs and coffee tables are dotted about among the conventional dining tables. Internet access is available in the living room, and there's a lively disco most evenings. On Monday nights, they hold a jam session, with people bringing their own instruments, while the ground floor has been turned into a 'creative laboratory', where musicians play all kinds of different music on all kinds of material. It's well worth a visit, even if it's only for a coffee.

≜ **Auberge du Village**: 205 rue Principale, near the ferry. ☎ 986-3312. Fax: 986-3928. The rooms here are bland, but they're clean and very comfortable, with en-suite bathrooms and TVs as standard. It's a good location, too.

At Fatima

≜ **Camping Le Barachois**: 87 chemin du Rivage, near Anse des Baleiniers. ☎ 986-6065 or 986-4525. Tent pitches $15–20 a night. The owners of this large campsite have planted several small conifer trees, so it's well shaded and sheltered from the wind. There are plenty of outdoor activities on offer, and the facilities include a laundry room, a small convenience store and a restaurant, but there's only one toilet block.

≜ **Oasis Laliberté**: 462 chemin de l'Église, near chemin du Grand-Ruisseau. ☎ 986-2330. Doubles $45–60 a night, including breakfast. This place is pleasant, peaceful and reasonably priced. Spa addicts should opt for a special package that includes a 2-hour beauty treatment with an algae bath and an expertly delivered massage.

≜ **La Maison du Cap-Vert**: 202 chemin L.-Aucoin, a continuation of chemin Noël. ☎ 986-5331. Doubles $55 a night, including breakfast. This pretty sea-green house is near Cap Vert, a magnificent vantage point on the Dune du Nord. The rooms are very clean, but they're smaller and more basic than you'd expect at this price.

L'Étang-du-Nord

≜ **Camping-motel Pluvier des Îles**: 37 chemin du Radar, near the north end of the Dune du Havre aux Basques. ☎ 986-9858. Tent pitches $14–19. This is a good-size, good-value campsite, with conifers providing plenty of shelter. There's also a small swimming pool.

≜ **Bourque Jeannine**: 429 chemin Boisville ouest, near chemin Delaney and Cap à Savage. ☎ 986-2626. This tiny green-and-white house offers three small, very clean rooms for the lowest prices on the island.

♿ Auberge Chez Sam: 1767 chemin de l'Étang-du-Nord. ☎ 986-5780. Sam's place is a su-perb 19th-century wooden house, painted red and grey. The five pleasant and impeccably clean rooms, all with basins, share two bathrooms. Prices are very reasonable, but breakfast is not included.

Havre-Aubert

♿ Camping Belle Plage: 445 chemin du Bassin, next to Dune du Bassin beach. ☎ 937-5408. Tent pitches $12–16 a night. The site is on a grassy slope with no trees. It's not expensive, but it's not great, either.

♿ Club Nautique de l'Istorlet: 100 chemin de l'Istorlet, off route 199, near the fork with chemin du Bassin. ☎ 937-5266. Tent pitches $10 a night; doubles $40 a night. The campsite is well sheltered and shaded, and there are several nice rooms with basins in the main house, all leading onto a balcony that overlooks the sea. Whatever type of accommodation you choose, you'll have to use the shared toilet blocks. The holiday centre offers lots of activities (*see* 'What to See and Do'), and there's always a lively atmosphere.

♿ Armand Leblanc: 69 chemin Bouchard. ☎ 937-5793. Doubles from $35 a night, including breakfast. At the Dune aux Basques exit, take the first street on the right, then the next right; the house is on the left, hidden behind a cluster of pine trees. There are four spacious, clean, bright and pleasant rooms in this peaceful, inexpensive place, but breakfast is a bit token.

♿ Gîte Le Berceau des Iles: 701 chemin Principal. ☎ 937-5614. Doubles $40–110 a night. This large, violet-painted wooden house is on a patch of high ground set back from the road. The owner, André, built it himself, and it's turned out rather well. There's a bright and pleasant en-suite room on the ground floor, while the three cheaper upstairs rooms share a bathroom. If you're feeling flush, go for the huge 'suite', with its high ceiling and wonderful picture windows. André and his wife, Gisèle, are both charming, and will pick you up from the airport or the harbour. They can also arrange a hire car, and organize all sorts of activities; in winter, you can go kayaking to caves and ice cliffs, or take a helicopter trip to see baby seals on the ice floes (less expensive than you might think). This is an excellent place to stay.

♿ Chez Charles Painchaud: 930 chemin Principal, in the middle of the village. ☎ 937-2227. Doubles $55–65 a night. This friendly place has six comfortable rooms with basins, all sharing two bathrooms and a kitchenette. The buffet-style breakfast is served on the sunny upstairs terrace.

Bassin

♿ Havre-sur-Mer: 1197 chemin du Bassin, L'Anse-à-la-Cabane, on a cliff overlooking the beach. ☎ 937-5675. Fax: 937-2540. This luxury guesthouse is in a wonderful spot, best appreciated from the sweeping expanses of the lawn. There are eight comfortable en-suite rooms, but the prices are rather steep.

🏠 **La Coulée Douce**: 137 chemin de la Pointe. ☎ 937-5109. Doubles $65 a night, including breakfast. This pleasant place offers excellent value for money, and the breakfasts are fantastic.

Île d'Entrée

You can't get much farther away from it all than this, but there's not much choice when it comes to accommodation.

🏠 **Chez McLean**: ☎ 986-4541. Doubles $45 a night, including breakfast.

WHERE TO EAT

Grosse-Île and Île de la Grande Entrée

✗ **Le Délice de la Mer**: 907 route 199, on Grande Entrée, near the fishing port. ☎ 985-2364. Open 9am–9pm. Main courses $10–20. Fresh fish and seafood are the specialities here, and the seafood casserole is particularly good. There's also a lobster tank, full of crustaceans caught by the local fishermen. It can get pretty crowded, though.

Cap-aux-Meules

✗ **La Table des Roy**: 1188 route 199, at La Vernière, southwest of Cap-aux-Meules. ☎ 986-3004. Open Monday to Saturday from 6pm. Booking recommended. This is a trendy restaurant where the cooking is inventive and refined. The seafood dishes are particularly good, and the service is flawless. As you may have guessed, though, it's not cheap.

✗ **Boulangerie régionale**: 1397B chemin Principal, Cap-aux-Meules. ☎ 986-3614. This traditional bakery also serves snacks and light meals, including pizzas.

L'Étang-du-Nord

✗ **La Factrie**: 521 chemin Gros-Cap, on the southeast tip of Île de Cap aux Meules. ☎ 986-2710. Open 11am–10pm (from 4pm on Sunday). It looks like a glorified canteen, but this is a great place to eat freshly caught lobster, fish and seafood at bargain prices. You can walk off your meal by taking chemin Gros-Cap along the cliffs, pausing to admire the spectacular views.

✗ **La Côte**: in the port. ☎ 986-5085. Lunch menu $10; dinner $15–25. This is a nice little place with a beautiful view.

Havre-Aubert

✗ **Auberge Chez Denis et François**: 44 chemin d'En-Haut. ☎ 937-2371. Open 7am–9pm. Lunch menu $11; dinner $20–30. The pastel-green dining room is extremely pleasant, and the seafood-heavy cooking is pretty good. At lunchtime, you can have as many helpings of mussels and chips as you can handle for a very reasonable set price. In the evening, there's a *table d'hôte*, but more adventurous diners should go à la carte and try *loup marin* (seal): it's a stringy meat, prepared rather like *boeuf bourguignon*, but with an unexpectedly subtle flavour. For dessert, try 'Sauterelle', a delicious mint ice cream on a chocolate waffle. The Auberge is also a guesthouse, with several nice bedrooms upstairs, but at $85 a night, they're a bit pricey.

✖ **La Saline**: 1009 route 199, in La Grave. ☎ 937-2230. Dinner only. Set menus $20–27. This large wooden building with red shutters, a former warehouse, has been converted into a very pleasant restaurant. The *table d'hôte* offers you a chance to sample a local delicacy, *pot-en-pot* (hot seafood and potato pie), and you'll get a little glass of brandy to aid the digestion between the main course and dessert. It's well worth booking in advance.

☆☆☆ Expensive

✖ **La Marée Haute**: 25 chemin des Fumoirs, south of La Grave. ☎ 937-2492. Dinner only. *Table d'hôte* $30. Set back from the main road and not far from the sea, this cosy restaurant has a wood-panelled dining room. The *table d'hôte* offers a wide choice of starters, main courses and desserts, while the à la carte menu offers scallops, snow crab, breast of duck and even seal tournedos. If you want to stay the night, there are two pretty attic rooms with splendid views (good value at $60–75 a night; full-board available); downstairs, meanwhile, there's a larger and more expensive room with a big stove and an en-suite bathroom, but it's a little gloomy.

Bassin

✖ **Au Quai de l'Anse**: 20 chemin du Quai, at L'Anse-à-la-Cabane. ☎ 937-5346. Open 11am–11pm. This tiny restaurant on an old fishing boat offers sole, scallops, *pot-en-pot* and other seafood dishes at very reasonable prices.

WHERE TO HAVE A DRINK, NIGHTLIFE

Havre-aux-Maisons

♼ **Chez Gaspard**: in summer, the refectory of Au Vieux Couvent (*see* 'Where to Stay') has live music or theatre every night. It's a cheerful, noisy place that offers a welcome pick-me-up after the sleepy pace of the islands, and it's open until the wee small hours.

Cap-aux-Meules

♼ **Bar Le Central**: not far from the Auberge des Pas Perdus (*see* 'Where to Stay'). ☎ 986-3212. This lively little bar attracts folk and country groups from the island and beyond. The concerts are free, the music's good and the beer is cheap, all of which makes for a great atmosphere.

♼ **Chez Wendel**: opposite Le Central. An ace bar-restaurant with an art-house cinema attached.
♼ **Bar Laitier Au Cornet**: along route 199, to the southwest of the village. This place serves excellent ice-creams in generous portions, with an amazing range of flavours on offer.

L'Étang-du-Nord

❣ **Bar des Îles**: ☎ 986-6398. This large, friendly bar has country and blues bands every Wednesday night in summer.

❣ **La Côte**: in the port. ☎ 986-5085. This café hosts concerts on summer evenings (there's an admission fee).

Havre-Aubert

❣ **Le Petit Mondrain**: along the main street, opposite the aquarium. This lovely little bistro with a local clientele dishes up the cheapest seafood on the island. There's live music on some nights.

❣ **Le Café de la Grave**: 969 route 199. ☎ 937-5765. This cosy café in the old general store hosts exhibitions of photography and paintings. It's a great place for breakfast, afternoon tea, an aperitif or an after-dinner liqueur, and musical patrons are encouraged to play the piano.

❣ **Bar-terrasse La Saline**: next to the restaurant of the same name (see 'Where to Eat'). This is a good place to come for live folk and rock music.

❣ **Au Vieux Treuil**: 971 chemin de la Grave. ☎ 937-5138. In July and August, it hosts a wide range of shows; booking recommended.

WHAT TO SEE AND DO

Grosse-Île and Île de la Grande Entrée

★ **Centre d'Interprétation du Phoque**: at Club Vacances Les Îles. ☎ 985-2833. Open 10am–6.30pm in high season. Admission fee. Guided tours available. A good place to learn about the lives and habits of these curious marine mammals. Commendably, it doesn't shirk the issue of seal-hunting.

★ Club Vacances Les Îles can also organize a **tour of the caves and cliffs of Île Boudreau**: ☎ 985-2833. There are two or three 90-minute tours a day. You put on a wetsuit, get into the water and let yourself be jolted around by the current in the eight caverns. It's an unmissable experience. Club Vacances can also organize kayaking trips, cycling, windsurfing and many more activities.

★ **Pointe de l'Est National Wildlife Reserve**: ☎ 986-6644. Bird-watching tours available (through Club Vacances Les Îles). Dunes, moors, salt meadows, marshes, beaches and ponds are among the attractions of this reserve, an important bird migration stopover that provides sanctuary for the endangered piping plover during the nesting season. You can explore the area on your own, but don't stray off the footpaths, as the fragile vegetation is easily damaged. The panoramic road that encircles the reserve will take you to the **Grande Échouerie beach**, which is a staggering 20 kilometres (13 miles) long.

– There are several other good **walks** along the cliffs at the end of chemin des Pealey, or as far as Île Boudreau, where you can wallow in mud before rinsing off in the sea; make sure you do the rinsing on the Bassin aux Huîtres side, as the water there is a lot warmer than in the Gulf of St Lawrence.

– For a more organized **mud bath**, contact the indispensable Club Vacances Les Îles.

★ At **Old Harry**, on route 199, you'll find a pretty little whitewashed Anglican church, with two beautiful doors that are carved on the interior side; the chancel is decorated with scenes from the Bible, set against a backdrop of landscapes from the Îles de la Madeleine. A little farther on, the old school, all in red wood, houses a museum dedicated to the history of the Scottish community on the islands (open 9am–4pm). Old Harry was once the archipelago's economic centre; walruses were killed there when they came out onto the rocks to bask in the sun. Today, it's just another peaceful little village. There are no safe points for ships to drop anchor here; instead, a wooden ramp is used to haul boats in and out of the water every day.

Havre-aux-Maisons

★ **La Méduse Verrerie d'Art**: 35 chemin de la Carrière, signposted from route 199. ☎ 969-4245. Open 10am–5pm Monday to Saturday. At this interesting shop-cum-studio, you can see a small team of glass-blowers at work. Despite the intense heat, you could spend hours watching the craftsmen take blob after blob of molten glass from a large pot, blow and twist them skilfully into shape, then transform them into paperweights, vases, fruit, bottles, lamp shades and the like. If you're inspired to buy anything, the price-quality ratio is very favourable.

★ The last working **smokehouse** on the islands is on chemin du Quai, near the fishing port of Pointe-Basse, to the south of the island. How long it will stay open, it's hard to say; the family business produces only 350 crates of smoked herring a year, compared with 20,000 crates a few years ago. After a tour of the premises, you can try some of the produce. When you leave, follow chemin des Échoueries and enjoy the beautiful views.

– **Lagoon trips**: the departure point is at the kiosk that looks like a lighthouse in the Marina de la Pointe, near the bridge that links the island to Cap-aux-Meules. ☎ 969-4550 or 969-2088. Discover the flora and fauna of the lagoon on a glass-bottomed boat, with onboard demonstrations of lobster-, clam- and cockle-fishing. There are three 2-hour trips a day in high season.

– The countryside is full of little **hills** (known as '*buttes*') that offer views of the islands' varied landscape. You can climb them on foot, by bike or on horseback (for details, contact the Au Sabot d'Or equestrian centre, *see below*).

– **Centre Équestre Au Sabot d'Or** (equestrian centre): 28 chemin Philias. ☎ 969-4948. Open 9am–9pm. A 2-and-a-half-hour ride costs $35. In July and August, wear a long-sleeved shirt to deter the mosquitoes.

– **Le Fumoir d'Antan**: 27 chemin du Quai, Point-Basse. ☎ 969-4907. This recently resurrected old smokehouse is a good place to sample smoked herring. An exhibition of old photographs shows how the business worked in days gone by.

Cap-aux-Meules

– **Boat trips**: from the Cap-aux-Meules marina. ☎ 986-4745. All sorts of packages are available: a guided nature cruise costs $15, an excursion to Île de la Grande Entrée is $20, and a trip to the cliffs in an inflatable boat is $20. There are discounts for children and seniors.

Fatima

★ **The church** has a roof shaped like a clam shell, and the inside is decorated with odds and ends that symbolize the daily lives of the fishermen. The confessionals have ship's doors with portholes, and fishing nets and trawlermen's lanterns are dotted about all over the place. A leaflet explains the objects' significance.

– **Kite hire**: from Au Gré du Vent, L'Anse des Baleiniers. ☎ 986-3177. Fax: 986-5624. The stiff breezes that blow here really make kites go. You can also have a go at flying a traction kite ($40 a lesson); you sit in a low-set car, pulled by an enormous flying sail and driven by a pro. In July, the Festival Sable Eau Vent (sand, water and wind) features demonstrations and competitive stunt-kite flying, night flying and sand-yachting.

– There's a superb **clifftop walk** between L'Anse des Baleiniers and L'Anse de l'Étang-du-Nord. The magnificent red sandstone formations have been sculpted into caves and arches by the wind and waves. At sunrise, they look as if they're on fire. The sunsets at Belle Anse ('beautiful cove') are equally appealing, but you'll have to share them with every other tourist on the archipelago. The cliffs are very crumbly, so stay away from the edge.

– With rolling, flower-speckled hills and grazing cows, the countryside around the **Butte du Vent** brings Switzerland to mind. You'll find wild strawberries here in season, and in clear weather there's a beautiful view of the whole archipelago.

L'Étang-du-Nord

– **Aventure Plein Air**: 1252 route 199, at La Vernière, opposite the Coop supermarket. ☎ 986-6161. You can hire a sea kayak here, and the company offers guided tours to the caves and cliffs and kayak-camping packages that take several days.

– **Parc du Gros-Cap**: ☎ 986-4505. Sea-kayak hire.

– **Au Gré du Vent**: on place du Marché, in La Côte. ☎ 986-5069. You can hire a sea kayak here, but, as mentioned above, the company specializes in kites and traction kites.

– **Walking**: you can climb the Butte du Vent, or head along the cliffs as far as Cap du Phare and Belle Anse. You can also go swimming in the sea at la Dune de l'Ouest.

Havre-Aubert

★ **Musée de la Mer** (Maritime Museum): 1023 route 199, at Pointe Shea. ☎ 937-5711. From late June to late August, open 9am–6pm (from 10am at weekends); otherwise, open 9am–noon (Monday to Friday) and 1–5pm (weekends). Admission $4. As well as the usual maritime memorabilia – photos, scale models of boats and lighthouses, navigational and fishing equipment, objects from shipwrecks, birds and stuffed seals – the museum offers a recent film about the islands through the seasons, and a film about fishing, made in 1956, when the stocks were considerably less depleted.

★ **Aquarium**: chemin de la Grave. ☎ 937-2277. Open mid-June to mid-September, 10am–7pm (to 9pm from mid-July to mid-August). Admission $4. The fish here are caught each spring, then released into the wild in the autumn.

– **Les Artisans du Sable**: 907 route 199. ☎ 937-2917. Sand as you've never seen it before. The craftsman here work on the grains with wood or a milling machine, creating castles, seals, plates, vases, lamps and lots more. They make wonderfully original souvenirs, although they're quite heavy.

– **Club Nautique de l'Istorlet**: 100 chemin de l'Istorlet. ☎ 937-5266 or 1-888-937-8166 (toll-free). Fax: 937-9028. Email: istorlet@sympatico.ca. Website: www.sympatico.ca/istorlet. There's a wide range of activities on offer, including sea kayaking, surf kayaking, windsurfing, cycling and bird-watching. Club Nautique also has a registered daycare centre for children, making it a godsend for parents who need a break. If you want to learn how to windsurf, there's a range of courses, with or without accommodation. Dinghy hire starts at $30; windsurfers cost about the same. The Club also offers accommodation and food (see 'Where To Stay').

– **Cruises** to Île d'Entrée or elsewhere depart from the Havre-Aubert marina. ☎ 937-4266.

– **Shopping**: there are several art galleries and shops at La Grave.

– The best **walks** are on the sand along Dune du Bout du Banc, where the sandcastle contest is held every year in mid-August.

Bassin

– **La Chevauchée des Îles**: chemin des Arpenteurs, near chemin de l'Étang des Caps. ☎ 937-2368 or 937-3453. This equestrian centre is well placed for long gallops along the Dune de l'Ouest beach or in the woods. Sleigh rides are available in winter.

– **Archery club**: 150 chemin Massé, near L'Anse-à-la-Cabane. ☎ 937-2582. The club has set up archery targets shaped like animals among the woods and mountains.

– **Walking**: along chemin de la Dune de l'Ouest at sunset.

SHOPPING

Grosse-Île and Île de la Grande Entrée

🔒 **Au Tour de la Terre**: at the end of la Grande Entrée. ☎ 985-2805. The owner of this arts and crafts shop, Bernard Langford, works china in an unusual but beautiful way, giving it a matt finish, then painting it. The finished products include eggs, nests, birds (some have real feathers) and seals lazing on real rocks. The make beautiful souvenirs, but they're quite expensive.

Between Grosse-Île and Havre-aux-Maisons, there are dunes and beaches almost as far as the eye can see. In this bleak landscape, the little green dot that is Pointe-aux-Loups looks like a real oasis. You can buy mussels there, or look for them yourself at low tide in the sandy lagoons. Look out for a vertical-axis windmill near the bridge that links the Dune du Nord and the Dune du Sud.

New Brunswick

Along with Nova Scotia, Prince Edward Island and Newfoundland, New Brunswick is one of Canada's four Maritime Provinces. With a French-speaking population of nearly 35 per cent, it's also the only officially bilingual province in Canada. The early settlers were a mixture of French-speaking Acadians and English loyalists who sought refuge here after the American War of Independence; more recently, their numbers have been swelled by Irish and Scottish immigrants. Some of the province's 730,000 inhabitants still speak the local dialect: 'chiac', an unusual blend of French and English.

From Campbellton, in the north, to Saint John, in the south, most of New Brunswick's attractions can be found by following the coast, with a few trips inland here and there: to the provincial capital, Fredericton, for instance, or to Moncton, home of New Brunswick's French-speaking university. Wherever you go, don't forget to set your watch one hour ahead.

ACADIA

When some 40 French families landed in Poitou in 1632, who would have believed that this was the birth of one of North America's most remarkable civilizations? The Acadians first settled in the Bay of Fundy (now part of Nova Scotia). Thanks to the rich local soil, they were soon producing better crops than the people of France and Québec. This enabled the settlers to become self-sufficient at a time when France was obsessed with its own internal affairs, and with Québec's booming fur trade.

In 1713, the Treaty of Utrecht gave Acadia to the British, who renamed the province Nova Scotia. The Acadians brokered a deal whereby they could retain their land and practise their own religion provided they remained neutral in the event of conflict between France and Britain. This arrangement worked well for a while, but in 1744, the British tried to pressurize the Acadians into swearing allegiance to the Crown. They refused, but managed to dodge the issue for another decade.

In 1755, however, the governor of Nova Scotia expelled the Acadians from their land. More than 6,000 of them were evicted from their villages and either exiled to England or deported to Maine and Massachusetts, where the locals proved equally hostile. Some returned to France, while others wandered for years before setting up home in the unwelcoming swamps of Louisiana. There they founded the famous Cajun community, whose descendants are members of modern-day Louisiana's 800,000-strong French-speaking population. Another group of Acadians sought refuge among the Indian tribes on the coasts of New Brunswick and Gaspésie. When the whole of Canada, with the exception of Saint-Pierre-et-Miquelon, was ceded to the British in 1763, the surviving Acadians, who had ended up on a narrow strip of coastline from the Baie des Chaleurs to Moncton, were allowed to stay. In 1847, Henry Wadsworth Longfellow popularized the story of the Acadians in his poem *Evangeline*.

The Acadians became deeply attached to their new land, and preserved their customs, language and identity, taking '*L'union fait la force*' ('Strength through unity') as their motto. In 1884, they adopted a blue, white and red tricolour flag, with a yellow star on the blue representing the Stella Maris (star of the sea). Today, the flag flies proudly in many Acadian villages and gardens to signal that New Brunswick is the only Canadian province where the French-speaking population is not in decline. In fact, many English-speakers apparently feel threatened by Acadian patriotism: a new political party, the COR (Confederation of Regions), which has as its aim the abolition of bilingualism in New Brunswick, is now the main opposition party in the provincial government.

Agriculture still plays an important role in Acadian life, but other industries have also developed, such as lobster-fishing (in the 19th century, this delicacy was still a poor man's dish), peat-digging and mining for coal and other minerals. The province's zinc deposits are among the world's largest.

– **Fête Nationale des Acadiens**: 15 August.

– **New Brunswick Day**: 2 August.

USEFUL ADDRESS

🛈 **Tourist information**: ☎ 1-800-561-0123 (toll-free). Campbellton number ☎ 789-2367. Open 8am–9pm. The main tourist office for New Brunswick is in Campbellton, near a big shop called The Met.

From Gaspésie to Caraquet

The coastal route is picturesque rather than spectacular, with clusters of traditional wooden farmhouses, English hamlets in the middle of French-speaking areas, and old churches and lighthouses. One roadside sight is unmissable: a farmer has rounded up his 'vintage agricultural machinery' and painted the whole lot red.

CAMPBELLTON

The town's main attraction is the Sugarloaf park, which is set on high ground and has fine views of Gaspésie. The nearby River Restigouche was the site of a crucial naval defeat for the French in 1760.

– **Salmon Festival**: held in late June and early July. ☎ 789-2897.

WHERE TO STAY

🛏 **Campbellton Lighthouse**: 1 Ritchie Street, near the river. ☎ (506) 759-7044. Take route 134 towards Dalhousie, pass the intersection with Andrew Street and turn left shortly afterwards. Open from June to the end of August; reception open 4pm–midnight. Dorm beds $15 ($12 for YHA members); a tent pitch costs $5. The lighthouse-keeper's house has been transformed into a clean, pleasant hostel with 20 beds in single-sex dormitories. Guest can use the kitchen and the laundry.

DALHOUSIE

Founded by the Scots in the 19th century, this village is now home to a mainly Acadian population. It's also the landing point for the ferry from Miguasha, in Gaspésie, which cuts 80 kilometres (50 miles) off the journey south.

– **Festival du Bon Ami**: last week in July. ☎ 684-5395.

GRANDE-ANSE

★ **Musée des Papes** (the popes' museum): 184 rue Acadie, in Grande-Anse, 18 kilometres (11 miles) from Caraquet on route 340. ☎ 732-3003. Open mid-June to mid-August, 10am–6pm. Admission $5. Guided tours available. This is the only museum in North America devoted to the papacy and the principles of the Roman Catholic Church, and it shows how deeply attached to their spiritual heritage Acadians are. The exhibits include a huge scale model of St Peter's Basilica in the Vatican; a dizzying portrait gallery of all the popes, going as far back as Saint Peter; a life-size rubber replica of John Paul II; a weird collection of mannequins wearing a host of religious habits; and a host of chasubles, chalices and other ecclesiastical treasures. It's a well-presented museum where you'll learn plenty of surprising facts about the papacy – in the 10th century, apparently, the pope had the right to get married – but there's no mention of the Vatican's often malign influence on society down the years.

VILLAGE HISTORIQUE ACADIEN

Situated a few kilometres west of Caraquet. ☎ (506) 726-2600. Fax: 726-2601. Website: www.gov.nb.ca/vha. Open from the first Sunday in June until 4 September, 10am–6pm (to 5pm in low season). Admission $10. Parking available. There are several motels and hotels in the area.

The village, created in 1977 in a region that symbolizes the determination and resourcefulness of the Acadians, is one of the most beautiful sites in New Brunswick. Having been forced to settle on this marshy soil after the deportations of 1755, the Acadians survived by creating a complex system of dykes and ditches to reclaim the wetlands and grow crops.

Surrounded by parkland, the village consists of 40 authentic houses and other scrupulously restored buildings that have been brought here from all over the province. Wander along the rustic paths and you'll find a host of farms and workshops, some 150 years old: an ironmongery, a flour mill, a joiner's, a grocery, a cobbler's workshop, a printing press, a tavern, a school, a church and several barns and warehouses.

The staff, who wear period dress, carry out traditional agricultural activities or crafts, and all will happily explain the techniques they're demonstrating. A visit here will tell you more about the Acadians than any book or museum, which is why it's so popular with school groups.

–The **Information Centre** has a cafeteria and restaurant, a craft shop and a well-stocked bookshop.

CARAQUET

DIALLING CODE: 506

The fishing port of Caraquet, founded in 1757 by a handful of families who escaped deportation, is one of the oldest Acadian villages in New Brunswick, and it's a good place to stay after a visit to the Village Historique Acadien.

USEFUL ADDRESS

🅱 **Tourist Office**: 51 boulevard Saint-Pierre Est, in the Carrefour de la Mer complex, near the ferry quay. ☎ 726-2676. Follow the signs marked with a question mark.

WHERE TO STAY AND EAT

Campsites

⛺ **Camping Colibri**: in Bertrand, west of Caraquet. ☎ 727-2222. Website: www.sn2000.nb.ca/comp/colibri. Tent pitches from $14. The region's biggest campsite is at its liveliest in July and August, when it gets pretty packed. The washing facilities and toilets are basic, but there are two fantastic water-slides (open 10am–7pm), which helps to make it a fun place for children.

⛺ **Camping de l'Île Caraquet**: if you want to get away from it all, the uninhabited, car-free île de Caraquet should do the trick. The ferry leaves from the quay at Carrefour de la Mer. There are three crossings per day, at 11am, 2pm and 4pm, but phone the tourist office to check the timetable. The waterside campsite, near a beach, has clean washing facilities, and you can stock up with fresh supplies on site.

☆–☆☆ Budget to Moderate

⛺ **Auberge de Jeunesse**: 577 boulevard Saint-Pierre, on the western edge of Caraquet. ☎ 727-2345. Open 23 June to 2 September. This friendly youth hostel on the coast has a large garden.

⛺ **Maison Touristique Dugas**: 683 boulevard Saint-Pierre Ouest, on the Bertrand and Bathurst road, 6 kilometres (4 miles) from the village centre. ☎ 727-3195. Fax: 727-3193. Doubles from $34 a night; suite $45; four-person chalet $40. Tent pitches $5; camper van pitches $15. Credit cards accepted. A 10-minute walk from a private beach, this beautifully furnished residential house is a cheap, friendly and extremely pleasant place to stay.

⛺ **Gîte Paillasse et Croûte**: 211 boulevard Saint-Pierre Est. ☎ 727-5086. Doubles $50 a night. This blue, beachside house has four first-floor rooms, two with sea views. The interior is simple and clean, and the prices are fair. The owner, Anne-Marie, goes out of her way to make guests feel at home.

⛺ **Gîte L'Auberge au Pignon Rouge**: 338 boulevard Saint-Pierre Est, 3 kilometres (2 miles) from the centre on the Bas-Caraquet road. ☎ 727-5983. Doubles $45–50 a night. This striking Acadian house, built in red wood, has been beautifully converted by Raymond Albert, a musician and piano-tuner, and offers excellent value for money. Once inside, you head through the vast kitchen, then up to the stylish first-floor rooms; a little spiral staircase takes you to yet another floor, where two more rooms (with twin beds, but no view) nestle beneath the roof timbers. The pretty communal bathroom is on the landing. Guests can sit on the veranda and enjoy Raymond's playing while looking out to sea. All this, and air-conditioning as well . . .

â **Gîte Chez Rhéa**: 236 boulevard Saint-Pierre Ouest. ☎ 727-4275. Doubles $43–55 a night. Rhéa, the cheerful landlady offers blue, floral rooms, some with en-suite bathrooms, in this small, attractive house near the church.

☆☆☆ Expensive

â **Gîte du Passant Le Poirier**: 98 boulevard Saint-Pierre Ouest. ☎ 727-4359. Fax: 726-6084. Doubles $65–70 a night, including breakfast. This beautiful little house was built in 1928 by Maître Poirier,

a schoolmaster, magistrate and judge. There are five comfortable, attractively designed en-suite rooms, some with queen-size beds. It's a friendly place, and breakfast is huge.

â **Auberge de la Baie (Savoie Motel)**: 139 boulevard Saint-Pierre, in the centre of town. ☎ 727-3485. Doubles $60–80 a night. The rooms at this motel are comfortable, but not cheap.

â ✕ **Hôtel Paulin**: 143 boulevard Saint-Pierre Ouest, in the town centre. ☎ 727-3165 and 727-9981. Fax: 727-3300. Doubles from $65 a night. This small, picturesque hotel is set back from the road, so you're guaranteed a quiet night. It's not especially friendly, but the decor's nice and its restaurant has a reputation for good food.

WHERE TO HAVE A DRINK

❢ **Bar Studio Au Vieux-Sage**: 28 boulevard Pierre Ouest, in a red building near the Bellevue cinema. ☎ 727-7243. This unpretentious place has live music to suit all tastes (rock, alternative), and club nights on Friday and Saturday. It's a large, modern space with a dancefloor and pool tables, and there's a sports bar upstairs. Breakfast and snacks are served in summer, when you can sit out on the terrace.

WHAT TO SEE AND DO

★ **Musée Acadien**: between the quay and the fishing school, just past the Enfant-Jésus hospital. Open June to mid-September, 10am–8pm (from 1pm on Sundays). Admission $6. Housed in a small wooden building on stilts, the museum has several collections depicting the life and history of the Acadians. There's also a small crafts centre.

★ **Sanctuaire de Sainte-Anne-du-Bocage**: built in 1880 on a beautiful site to the west of the town, this white church was modelled on the chapel that was founded here a century earlier. In the cemetery, you'll find the grave of Alexis Landry, one of the town's founders.

★ **Écomusée de l'Huître** (Oyster Museum): 675 boulevard Saint-Pierre Ouest. ☎ 727-3226. Open 1 May to 22 November, 10am–5.30pm. Closed Sunday, 26 July and 15 to 31 August. Admission free. A series of interesting displays explore the history of the Caraquet oyster, the fishing methods of yesteryear, and modern breeding and harvesting methods.

– **Tour Kayaket**: 51 boulevard Saint-Pierre Est, at the Centre Extra-vacance. ☎ 727-6909 or 1-800-704-3966 (toll-free). A guided tour, including food, costs $45; without a guide, it's $12. This company runs 3-hour walks to the Dune de Maisonnette, towards the île de Caraquet or to the oyster sandbars. Don't forget to bring a hat, suncream and a windcheater.

– **Fishing tours**: $20 for about four hours. ☎ 727-0813. Boats leave Carrefour de la Mer at 5.45am. The catch will be mackerel or cod.

– The picturesque **Théâtre Populaire d'Acadie** (Acadian People's Theatre) is home to the region's best francophone theatre company. You'll find it behind the Musée d'Acadie at 217 boulevard Saint-Pierre Ouest (☎ 727-0920). It also hosts a summer festival.

FESTIVALS AND EVENTS

– During **the Acadian Festival** (first fortnight of August), Caraquet bursts into life, with music, comedy, street theatre, dancing, parties, folk groups and boat-blessings. Events culminate on 15 August with the Tintamarre, an exceptionally noisy procession.

In the Area

SHIPPAGAN

This important fishing port is home to several beautiful beaches.

– **Festival Provincial des Pêches** (Fishing Festival): is held in July.

WHERE TO EAT

✕ **Au Marinier**: in the centre, inside the Ultramar service station. ☎ 336-8775. Main courses $7–16. This popular place has a huge choice of cheap, simple dishes, including seafood, and is open round the clock.

WHAT TO SEE

★ **Centre Marin** (Marine Centre): ☎ 336-4771. Open 10am–6pm in season. A series of displays describes the life of local fishermen and the region's marine life. There's also a superb aquarium with marine species from the Gulf of St Lawrence, including small sharks. The seals are fed at 11am and 4pm.

ÎLE DE LAMÈQUE

This island is not what you'd call spectacular, but it has lots of charm and several typical Acadian market towns (most of its inhabitants are French-speakers). It's also home to a beautiful fishing port, where there's a baroque music festival during the first two weeks of July. At Petite-Rivière-de-l'Île, you'll find spruce, white houses and a colourful church, and there's a tiny zoo at Pointe-Alexandre.

A road bridge takes you to the **île de Miscou**. On your way back from Miscou, take the coastal road, route 113, which passes through a series of pretty villages: Pigeon Hill, Saint-Raphaël and Sainte-Marie-sur-Mer.

WHERE TO STAY AND EAT

– There are two **campsites** on the île de Lamèque.

★ ✕ **Auberge des Compagnons**: 11 rue Principale, just past the bridge. ☎ 344-7766 or 344-7762. Fax: 344-0813. Website: www. sn2000.nb.ca/comp/auberge-d-compagnons. Doubles $95 a night. This up-market, pricey establishment has been completely renovated, and has a comfortable, luxurious feel. The 16 rooms overlook a stretch of sea where you might see herons flying by.

✕ **Au P'tit Mousse**: 5182 route 113, Haut-Lamèque, just before the bridge on the right if you're coming from Caraquet. ☎ 344-8005. Main course $7. A popular place with haphazard decor and a mainly family clientele, this restaurant serves good, cheap food, including cockles, scallops, prawn sandwiches, lobster with bread, chicken and pizza.

ÎLE DE MISCOU

The explorer Jacques Cartier was the first to visit this island at the point where the Baie des Chaleurs meets the Gulf of St Lawrence. Today, it's a quiet, peaceful place with just 1,000 inhabitants, 25 per cent of them English-speaking. Rest and relaxation are guaranteed, but it can be a little dull. The main attractions are three beautiful beaches, a coast lined with lagoons and peat bogs, and the only wooden lighthouse in the region, built in 1856. You can also try your hand at sea-fishing.

– The island has two campsites, one gîte (English-speaking) and a restaurant.

– The most lively time to visit is during the **Tuna Festival**, held in late July or early August.

INLAND ACADIA

A few of the peninsula's agricultural villages are worth a visit.

★ **Paquetville** was the birthplace of the singer Édith Butler. It has a huge church, and a 'temple of fame' in the tourist office pays tribute to local celebrities, among them a kick-boxing world champion.

★ **Rang-Saint-Georges**, with its gently hilly countryside and the Poke-mouche River, is an ideal spot for an idyllic interlude.

★ **Saint-Isidore** is home to a small museum dedicated to the history of the region (open June to September).

TRACADIE-SHEILA   DIALLING CODE: 506

NEW BRUNSWICK

The two language communities in these towns, which were amalgamated in 1992, get along extremely well: in fact, many English-speakers consider themselves to be Acadian, and some are actively involved with the Acadian movement. Founded in 1784, the village of Tracadie owes its name to the Micmac Indian for 'great place to camp'.

USEFUL ADDRESS

🄱 Tourist Office: 3416 rue Principale. ☎ 394-4029. Fax: 394-4025. Out of season, ☎ 394-4020. Website: www.rpa.ca/ts/. If you're coming from Caraquet, it's on the left before the bridge. Open mid-June to early September, 10am–8pm (from 8am on Saturday).

WHERE TO STAY AND HAVE A COFFEE

🛏 There's a **campsite** at Val-Co-meau, south of town.

❢ Roger Godin, a sculptor, runs the **Art Café** (rue Sam-Robichaud, Val-Comeau. ☎ 395-3042), a pleasant place that's decorated with his works (in stone and wood). He offers 30 varieties of coffee, a rare treat in a region devoted to tea-drinking.

WHAT TO SEE

★ **Musée Historique de Tracadie**: ☎ 394-4020. Open summer only, 9am–6pm (noon–6pm on weekends). This local-history museum is housed in a former convent where the nuns used to tend to lepers: a little farther down the road, you'll find the convent's cemetery. The museum, on the second floor of this 19th-century building, comprises exhibits describing the treatment of leprosy and a series of objects and tools used by the Micmacs, local farmers and craftsmen.

WHAT TO SEE IN THE AREA

★ **Tabusintac**: on route 11, opposite No. 483, in a pretty white house surrounded by a garden. ☎ 779-9261. This small museum is devoted to the life of the pioneers, woodcutters, fishermen and farmers who colonized the region.

★ **Néguac**: the main attraction in this pretty village is the stained glass windows in the Saint-Bernard Church. There's also a beautiful beach at Île aux Foins. The Festival du Rendez-vous takes place at the end of July

– Nearby, there's a Micmac reserve at **Burnt Church**.

★ **Miramichi**: this place owes its name to the merging, in 1995, of Chatham and Newcastle, two industrial, predominantly English-speaking towns that both have large Irish communities. Its main claim to fame is as the birthplace of Samuel Cunard, founder of the famous Cunard shipping company, whose ships include the *Lusitania* (torpedoed in 1915 by a German submarine), the *Queen Mary* and the *Queen Elizabeth*.

WHERE TO STAY IN THE AREA

⌂ **Auberge de Jeunesse Beaubear Manor**: in Nelson, 10 kilometres (6 miles) from Newcastle, near the Miramichi River. ☎ 622-3036. It's about 5 kilometres (3 miles) from the coach and railway stations; youth-hostel staff can collect you. Dormitory rooms $25 a night, $18 for YHA members; doubles $75 a night, including lunch. This charming old manor house is home to one of the best youth hostels in the province, run by Father Mercereau, a retired priest. Its facilities include a kitchen, a sitting room, a library and even a private beach. You can also hire canoes.

★ North of Chatham, in **Bartibog** (on route 11), you can visit the MacDonald Farm Historic Park, a restored 19th-century farm with displays describing the life of the Scottish colonists.

KOUCHIBOUGUAC NATIONAL PARK

The best, though not the quickest, way to get here is to take the coastal road that passes through Bay-du-Vin and Pointe-Sapin, with several quiet beaches en route. The main entrance is on route 134, south of Kouchibouguac village if you're coming from Chatham. If you're coming from Pointe-Sapin, route 117 leads directly to it. It's open year-round, and there's plenty of parking.

The largest park in New Brunswick, Kouchibouguac covers more than 26 kilometres (16 miles) of superb coast, dotted with dunes, forests and beaches. There's an extensive network of footpaths and cycle routes, so you can lose yourself among the peat bogs, dried-up marshes, woods, lagoons, ponds, rivers and estuaries. In winter, you can try cross-country skiing.

– The **Visitors' Centre** stocks excellent material on the park. ☎ 876-2443. Fax: 876-4802. Website: parkscanada.pch.gc.ca. From 13 June to 2 September open 8am–8pm; from 19 May to 13 June and 2 September to 12 October, 10am–6pm; otherwise 9am–5pm. Admission $4 a day.

WHERE TO STAY AND EAT

You can camp in the area (May to October) for about $20 a night. Facilities include toilets, showers and shelters for cooking. Visit the Visitors' Centre for bookings or information.

⌂ The main campsites are the well-managed and comfortable **Kouchibouguac Sud**; **Camping de l'Étoile de Mer**, at Pointe-Sapin, near the beach; **Camping Park d'Aigle**, at Saint-Louis-de-Kent, at the southern end of the park; and **Camping du Parc Municipal Jardine**, by the Richibucto beach.

⌂ **Camping rough** costs $13. You can pitch your tent in one of the following three locations: Sipu, on the Kouchibouguac River; Petit-Large, reached by cycle path; or Pointe-à-Maxime, in the Saint-Louis lagoon, at the mouth of the Kouchibouguac River, which is by far the wildest option. You watch seals from a canoe, or see the terns on the neighbouring Île des Sternes ('Tern Island').

✘ A handful of pleasant, reasonably priced restaurants are dotted along the coast, and there's a small eatery at Ryans, inside the park.

– **Fresh supplies**: unfortunately, little or nothing is available inside the park; the nearest place for supplies is 1.2 kilometres (half a mile) from the entrance. You can buy bread and milk at Kellys, near Kellys Beach.

WHAT TO SEE AND DO

Activities on offer include rowing ($7), kayaking in the park at Ryans ($7), swimming in the warm waters of the lagoons, fishing, bird-watching (piping plover and osprey) and golf (outside the park). There are also playgrounds for children. Hire a bicycle (price $5) and you can explore the 25 kilometres (15 miles) of cycle paths, including 6 kilometres (4 miles) of mountain-bike terrain. Callenders beach (unsupervised) boasts fine sand, while Kellys, with a tranquil lagoon and picnic tables, is ideal for children.

– **Beaver-watching**: on the Kouchibouguac River.

– **Seal-watching**: the best way to see these gentle, playful creatures up close is to board a canoe on the Saint-Louis lagoon. Leave from Pointe de Maxime and cross the sea inlet to the islets opposite, near Île des Sternes. You can take a boat cruise from Claire-Fontaine ($25; children $12.50).

– **Tern-watching**: take a canoe to Île des Sternes, home to 19,000 birds.

ROGERSVILLE

This village to the west of the park, on route 126 from Chatham to Moncton, is in the parish of Bishop Richard, the Acadian patriot who inaugurated the tricolour flag. Founded in 1869 by workers who came to build the railway between Halifax, Québec and Montréal, the village is home to the **Monument National Acadien Notre-Dame-de-l'Assomption**, built in 1955 to commemorate the 200th anniversary of the deportations. It also honours the Virgin Mary for her protection of Acadia, a reminder of how much Catholicism helped to preserve Acadian (and Québécois) identity. The monument itself is strikingly kitsch in appearance, but it's surrounded by an attractive group of buildings, including the village church, and the museum at the entrance to the monument (admission free) explains the complex links between religion and national sentiment in Acadia.

– The **Fête des Choux de Brussels** (Brussels sprout festival) takes place during the last week of July.

USEFUL ADDRESS

🛈 **Tourist office**. ☎ 775-9183. Fax: 775-2090.

BOUCTOUCHE

This is the home of New Brunswick's most distinguished French-speaking author, Antonine Maillet, whose heroine, la Sagouine, has become an icon of Acadian culture. Some of her words, in Acadian dialect, welcome you to the town's main tourist attraction, the Musée Le Pays de la Sagouine, where you're transported back to early-20th-century Acadia.

USEFUL ADDRESS

🏛 **Tourist Office**: ☎ 743-8811. This friendly, efficient office is near the bridge that crosses the sea inlet.

WHERE TO STAY AND EAT

🛏 ✕ **Gîte du Passant Domaine-sur-Mer**: 3821 route 535, Saint-Thomas. ☎ 743-6582. Fax: 743-8397. Website: sn2000.nb.ca/comp/domaine-sur-mer. Follow the signs for Shédiac, taking route 11 north to Miramichi, then take exit 15 (Cocagne/Notre-Dame) and follow route 535 north until you see a large blue-green house facing the ocean. Doubles from $55 a night; suite $115. Spick and span throughout, this pleasantly decorated guesthouse has attractive rooms with views and en-suite bathrooms; if you can afford to splash out, the suite is quite wonderful. The owner, Éveline, is a cookery teacher, and runs 3-hour courses that will teach you the best way to prepare lobster. There's also a restaurant, but it's expensive.

🛏 **Gîte du Passant Aux P'tits Oiseaux**: 124 rue du Couvent. ☎ 743-8196. Email: oiseau@nbnet.nb.ca. Doubles $50–55 a night. The two rooms in this lovely gîte are named after birds (in fact, the name trans-lates as 'guesthouse of the little birds'). The owner is a bird-watching fanatic, and should be able to offer plenty of top twitching tips. Judging by breakfast, she's a pretty good cook as well.

🛏 ✕ **Bouctouche Bay Inn**: about 5 kilometres (3 miles) south of Bouctouche on route 134, in a pleasant spot facing a bay. ☎ 743-2726. Fax: 743-2387. Doubles $50–85. This large inn, built in 1850 by one Colonel Serredon, has 27 reasonably priced rooms with single or double beds. The least expensive have twin beds and share a toilet on the landing; you'll pay more for the privilege of en-suite facilities. You can choose to stay in the old part of the building, where the rooms could do with a bit of a make-over, or in the annexe, which is rather motel-like. The owners are of German origin, and the restaurant serves German, Canadian and European dishes (for about $15), though the service isn't always the friendliest.

WHAT TO SEE

★ **Musée Le Pays de la Sagouine**: on route 134, south of town; turn right past the tourist office and Bouctouche bridge. ☎ 743-1400. Open from mid-June to early September, 10am–6pm. Admission $10. This museum faithfully reconstructs the romantic universe of *La Sagouine*, by the Acadian author Antonine Maillet. It's a fishing village, complete with colourful houses and a small red-and-white lighthouse, on a small island (the Île aux Puces) that's linked to the mainland by a long wooden footbridge. The information centre is devoted, unsurprisingly, to Acadia, the Acadians and the works of Antonine Maillet. Each of the meticulously rebuilt dwellings houses one of the characters from the book, played by actors in period costumes, so you can literally stroll through the story. Even if you haven't read the book, you'll get a feel for what life in these parts was like 100 years ago.

★ **Musée de Kent**: on route 475. ☎ 743-5005. Open June to September, 9am–5pm (from noon on Sunday). Guided visits until 5.30pm in July and August. Admission $3. The main reason to visit this museum is the building itself: the former Convent of the Immaculate Conception dates back to 1880, and has a fine wooden exterior and an equally interesting interior, with wooden panels, large staircases and a neo-Gothic chapel. As for the museum, it explores the history of the region through an array of artefacts and *objets d'art*.

SHÉDIAC
DIALLING CODE: 506

Shédiac is the lobster capital of the world: the world's largest lobster is proudly displayed at the entrance to the village. It's also extremely popular, especially in July and August, when tourists flock to the beautiful beaches that stretch towards Cap-Pelé, and to summer events like the sand-sculpture competition and the Lobster Festival, a shellfish orgy held in early July. So, book ahead if you're looking for accommodation in summer, and be prepared for weekend traffic jams.

USEFUL ADDRESS

🖺 **Tourist office**: 229 Main Street. ☎ 532-7788. Fax: 532-6156. Open 21 May to 8 October, 8am–10pm. Closed on 4 September.

WHERE TO STAY AND EAT

Shédiac has no youth hostels and very few gîtes, but there are plenty of campsites between Shédiac and Cap-Pelé. They're usually packed in summer, especially in July, so if you want a bit of peace and quiet, head for the Cap-Pelé area.

Campsites

🏕 **Parlee Beach Provincial Park**: ☎ 532-1500. Tent pitches from $19. This is one of the biggest campsites in the area, with car-parks to match, and it's not the place to go if you're looking for tranquillity or privacy. There's a beach (open 9am–7pm), but you have to pay to use it.

🏕 **Jason Riverside Trailer Park**: another packed-out site.

🏕 **Gagnon Trailer Park**: at Cap-Pelé, 12 kilometres (about 7 miles) west of Shédiac on route 950, past the bridge at the entrance to the village. ☎ 577-2519. Another gargantuan site, but not as crowded as the two above. You could also try the nearby **Sandy Beach** campsite.

Silver Sands Trailer Park: Petit-Cap. ☎ 577-6771. This site is more remote than the rest, and consequently much more peaceful. It's primarily for trailers and caravans, but you're welcome to pitch your tent here, and there's a beautiful beach close by.

☆☆ Moderate

Auberge Chez Françoise: 293 Main Street, in the town centre. ☎ 532-4233. Doubles $50–80 a night. Credit cards accepted. This magnificent colonial-style residence, which once belonged to an old Scottish family, has 15 spacious rooms, some with en-suite bathrooms. It's charming and very hospitable, so book ahead in high season. If you order in advance, you can enjoy an excellent meal in old-fashioned but elegant surroundings for about $25. Try veal crêpes Oscar, fillet of halibut with almonds and mandarins, giant prawns stuffed with crab or *délices de la mer* (a luscious assortment of seafood, including half a lobster, scallops with bacon, fillet of sole and giant prawns). The restaurant is a little expensive, but this place is highly recommended.

Hôtel Shédiac: in Parc Pascal-Poirier. ☎ 532-4405. Doubles from $55 a night. The Shédiac is less charming and authentic than Chez Françoise, but it offers extremely good value for money, especially as guests can use the rear garden and swimming pool. The building dates from 1853, and has quite a history. John Alexander MacDonald, Canada's first prime minister, spent a few nights here when he missed his train after a huge party in 1864, after the first meeting of the Confederation of

Canada. Several famous film stars have also graced its beds, among them Clark Gable, Walter Pidgeon and Bob Hope, while Queen Wilhelmina of the Netherlands stayed here after fleeing from the Nazi occupation. There's a whiff of past prestige about the place: all the rooms have period decor, and you can see the old stagecoach counter at reception. The restaurant serves Acadian specialities such as Miramichi salmon, lobster in cream served on toast and platters of seafood (lunch $20; dinner is a bit more expensive).

Au P'tit Sommeil: 21 Hamilton Street, near the sea. ☎ 532-3546. Doubles $94 a night. The plain exterior of this low-roofed house hardly prepares you for the stunning decor inside. The five air-conditioned rooms, some with mezzanines, are tastefully decorated in warm colours, and everything is smart, comfortable and beautifully kept. Breakfast is served on a pretty veranda at the back of the house. Nice, but expensive, too.

Gîte Maison Vienneau: 426 Main Street. ☎ 532-5412. Email: mvienau@nbnet.nb.ca. Doubles $80; four-bed room $85. This attractive but rather old-fashioned house has four bedrooms, three with en-suite bathrooms. There's a kitchen for use by guests.

– There are several **motels** between Shédiac and Cap-Pelé. The clean and modern **L'Edco**, on route 15, is about a kilometre from the junction for Cap-Pelé (☎ 577-4111; doubles $36–40 a night). The **Neptune Motel** is the closest to Shédiac, but it's in a busy area. Still in Shédiac, the **Four Seas**, on the fringes of Main Street, is a bit more expensive.

Restaurant Four Seas: 762 Main Street. ☎ 532-2585. Main courses up to $15. The decor in this large restaurant is rather slapdash, but the food is good, and it's less crowded than the neighbouring Paturel and Fisherman's Paradise. Look out for the 'summer lobster special', a 500-gram lobster with clam soup, corn and roast potatoes. The all-you-can-eat lobster buffet (early July to late October, 4–10pm) is also a good deal.

✗ **Maison du Homard**: in the Bombardier building, exit 37 to Parlee Beach. Open 4–8pm. ☎ 532-6816. The 'Lobster House' offers fresh lobster, salad, brioche, dessert and coffee at a very reasonable price.

☆☆☆ Expensive

✗ **Paturel (Maison du Rivage)**: in Barachois, 7 kilometres (4 miles) from Shédiac. ☎ 532-4774. Dinner $8–20. Open from 4pm. This restaurant is next to a fish-processing factory, but don't let that put you off.

The locals certainly aren't deterred: they come here in droves, so booking ahead is a good idea. There's a panoramic view that's perfect for watching the magnificent sunsets, the atmosphere is relaxed and the food is excellent: try oysters in their shells, seafood or cockle chowder, stuffed lobster, seafood casserole au gratin, a seafood platter or the fried-fish combo. If you don't fancy fish, the menu offers tried-and-tested favourites like chicken and chips and spaghetti at tasty prices.

✗ **Fisherman's Paradise**: Main Street, on the outskirts of Shédiac. ☎ 532-6811. Full meal $20–35. This is one of the smartest restaurants in town, and it's suitably formal and subdued. Fish and seafood specialities are served in an opulent decor. Booking essential.

WHAT TO SEE AND DO

The original town of Shédiac, with its timber houses, was destroyed by fire, so don't expect much Olde Worlde charm.

★ **Saint-Martin-in-the-Wood**: this church was built in 1821.

– **Shédiac Beach**: 3 kilometres (almost 2 miles) from the town centre, on the left off Route 133. Admission $5 for the day, including parking; there's a carpark at the foot of the sand dunes. Much used by the urbanites of Moncton, this pleasant if slightly mannered beach has fine, brownish sand.

FESTIVALS AND EVENTS

– **Festival du Homard**: first fortnight in July. As you'd expect, there's much cooking and consumption of lobster, with a theatre and crafts festival to occupy the pauses between meals.

WHAT TO SEE IN THE AREA

The region isn't bristling with important monuments, but it's charming in its simplicity, with the odd picturesque detail to look out for as you pass through.

★ **Barachois**: 7 kilometres (4 miles) from Shédiac on the Cap-Pelé road. This village's main draw is the beautiful beach at Pointe-à-Bouleaux, 300 metres from the small historical wooden church. Open 11am–5pm.

★ **Cap-Pelé and Petit-Cap**: take the scenic coastal route, lined with pretty houses and well-kept gardens. Founded in 1800, Cap-Pelé has an almost entirely French-speaking population, and proudly flies the Acadian flag. You'll see few signs of the herring smokehouses for which the village is famed: instead, there's a clean and harmonious feel, with simple, discreet architecture that blends in well with the countryside and the impeccably tended fields and gardens. In the evenings, families sit out on their porches to enjoy the last of the sun. There's a quiet and relaxing beach at Petit-Cap.

MONCTON

DIALLING CODE: 506

Moncton, a university town with a young population, is not especially charming, but it's interesting enough to merit a short stay. Main Street gets pretty lively on summer evenings, and there are one or two monuments, a few old houses and some interesting museums to see. The French-speaking university, founded in 1963, has helped to support the cause of the town's sizeable francophone minority.

USEFUL ADDRESS

🛈 **Tourist Office**: 774 Main Street, on the ground floor of the town hall. ☎ 853-3333. Fax: 856-4352. Open Monday to Friday, 8am–6pm.

WHERE TO STAY

☆☆ Moderate

⛫ **B&B Downtown**: 101 Alma Street, on a quiet street in the centre of town. ☎ 855-7108. Doubles $60 a night. This stone house, built in 1920, has four comfortable rooms, including one with twin beds. The owners, Jocelyne and John Harrisson, are charming, and it's probably the best place to stay in this category.

⛫ **Park View B&B**: 254 Cameron Street, in a residential neighbourhood 10 minutes' walk from the centre. ☎ 382-4504. Doubles from $55 a night. All the rooms in this large, comfortable brick house have TV and telephone, which is rare for a B&B, and some even have air-conditioning; the bathroom is on the landing. The English-speaking owner is friendly and helpful, and there's a park across the road.

⛫ **Jones Lake Motel**: 1650 West Main Street. ☎ 389-1718 or 1-800-399-8510. Fax: 854-9034. Email: adsnb@istar.ca. Doubles and rooms for four $80 a night. If you don't want a room overlooking the car-park, ask for No. 6 or No. 12. This place is perfect if you drive into town late at night. The price includes 10 minutes' worth of calls within Canada or to the US.

☆☆☆ Expensive

⛫ **Auberge Canadiana**: 46 Archibald Street, near Main Street, in an attractive neighbourhood of 19th-century houses. ☎ 382-1054. Doubles $80 a night, including breakfast. This delightful inn in a former maternity clinic has pleasant rooms with TV and bathroom. The interior is prettily decorated with original wooden panels and antique furniture, and Roland, the French-speaking owner, is charming. Strictly non-smoking.

⌂ **Colonial Inns**: 42 Highfield Street. ☎ 382-3395. Fax: 858-8991. Website: www.colonial-inns.com. Doubles from $65 a night.

This modern establishment, near the most vibrant part of 'Main', has pleasant, spotless rooms.

WHERE TO EAT

✕ **La Planche à Fromage**: 581 Main Street. ☎ 859-7487. Open 10am–7pm from Monday to Wednesday, 9am–9pm on Thursdays and Fridays and 11am–5pm on Saturdays. Main courses less than $10. This friendly, inexpensive place offers jazzed-up fast food: chicken *à la dijonnaise*, seafood pasta and so on. Desserts include an excellent cheesecake and a good choice of cheeses from around the world.

✕ **Graffiti**: 897 Main Street. ☎ 382-4299. Open until midnight. Full meal less than $10. The chef at this colourful, unpretentious restaurant specializes in Mediterranean food, from traditional dishes – couscous and Greek salad – to more inventive recipes, such as chicken breasts grilled with parmesan. The homemade cheesecake is wonderful.

✕ **Pastalli**: 611 Main Street. ☎ 383-1050. Main courses $10–15. This is an excellent Italian restaurant.

WHERE TO HAVE A DRINK, NIGHTLIFE

🍷 **Spanky's**: on the corner of Main and Botsford Streets, just past Burger King. ☎ 382-2582. Open Wednesday to Saturday, 8pm–2am. This student haunt is a large, dingy room with a small dancefloor where you can get down to rock and house tunes.

🍷 **Cosmopolitan**: 700 Main Street. Open Wednesday to Sunday, 8pm–2am; Ladies' Night until 11pm

on Thursday; Men's Night on Friday, with live jazz from 5–10pm. Admission $4. This is the town's 'in' club, and it gets pretty crowded. You have to fight your way across the terrace to reach the club area, with its sophisticated decor and lasers, but once you get there, the atmosphere is electric. The music is a mixture of house, techno and indie.

WHAT TO SEE

★ **Musée de Moncton**: 20 chemin Mountain, on the corner of avenue Belleview. ☎ 856-4383. Open mid-June to early September, 9am–4.30pm (Sunday 1–5pm). This modern building incorporates part of the old town hall's facade. It houses a small, well-presented ethnographic museum, with reconstructed period shops and workshops displaying domestic items and the tools of various trades. There's even a provincial railway-station office. The temporary exhibitions are usually very interesting.

★ **Musée Acadien**: in the Clément-Cormier building of the Université de Moncton. ☎ 858-4088. In June, July and August, open Monday to Friday, 10am–5pm (1–5pm on weekends); otherwise, Tuesday to Friday, 12.30–4.30pm (and 7–9pm on Wednesday), and 2–4pm on weekends. Admission $2. The permanent collection consists of mementos and objects relating to the history of Acadia since the 17th century. The university is also home to the Centre d'Études Acadiennes (Centre of Acadian Studies; ☎ 858-4085).

★ **Free Meeting House**: at the intersection of Mountain Road and Steadman. Moncton's oldest building, erected in 1821, was a meeting place for people belonging to religious denominations that did not have their own place of worship. Next door is New Brunswick's oldest cemetery, which contains the headstone of John Charters, dated 1816.

★ **Thomas Williams' residence**: 103 Park Street. ☎ 857-0590. Open June to September, 9am–5pm (1–5pm on Sunday). Thomas Williams, an accountant for the Intercolonial Railroad company, commissioned this magnificent Victorian-style residence for his wife, Analena, and their many children in 1883. It was originally built some way out of town, and gives you a good sense of what a middle-class house of the time would have looked like. You can take a break at the tea-room (open 11am–4pm, 1–3pm on Sunday).

★ **Magnetic Hill**: take exit 488B off the Trans-Canada Highway, at the northwest corner of Moncton. Admission fee. This strange place is supposedly the centre of a magnetic field that can make cars reverse uphill without their engines on. Even pedestrians walking down the hill say they feel as if they are being pulled back from behind. It could be something to do with the uranium deposits beneath the surface, or it could be a bizarre optical illusion: nobody knows for sure, though it's claimed that about 250,000 cars go through the experience every year.

There's a large **theme park** (☎ 384-0303) for children next to the hill, which features a wave machine and a 'kamikaze' water slide, where you'll plunge into the water at more than 50kph (30mph), as well as gentle slides for toddlers. Other attractions include paddle boats, restaurants, shops and a zoo.

– In summer, concerts and open-air events are held in the natural amphitheatre inside the park. Information is available from the park office.

★ **The tidal bore**: you can watch the highest tides in the world here, and see what happens when the sea rushes up the Petitcodiac River. The best vantage point is Bore Park, in the centre of town. In a little more than an hour, the water level can rise by more than 10 centimetres (4 inches). For timetables: ☎ 856-4399.

FESTIVALS AND EVENTS

– **Frolic Acadien**: a series of festivities featuring dance, theatre and song, beginning on the evening of 14 August and ending two days later. The Tintamarre procession usually passes through the town on 15 August, towards the end of the afternoon.

What to See in the Area

If you're in a car, take the picturesque countryside route southeast towards Nova Scotia. You'll see Acadian and 'Loyalist' villages dotted about, as well as some interesting historic sites.

NEW BRUNSWICK

SAINT-JOSEPH

The 'capital' of the Memramcook Valley, an important place in Acadian history, is on a hillock off route 925, about 30 kilometres (19 miles) from Moncton. The valley is unusual for two reasons: it was one of the only sites in New Brunswick to be colonized before 1755, and it was one of the few to escape the deportations. Today, Saint-Joseph is a spruce little village that proudly displays the tricolour flag – you'll even see it painted on walls.

★ **Lieu Historique National de l'Odyssée Acadienne**: this historic site is on the campus of the Institut de Memramcook (Collège Saint-Joseph). Open 1 June to 15 October, 9am–5pm. There's a fascinating exhibition about the history, traditions, customs and culture of the Acadians.

DORCHESTER

This leafy, British-looking village with superb mansions and churches tucked away among the trees, is on route 6, between Moncton and Sackville. Its elegance and austerity contrast with the more colourful, lively feel of the Acadian villages.

WHERE TO EAT

✗ **Bell Inn Restaurant**: on the main crossroads. ☎ 379-2580. Open Tuesday to Sunday, 11am–7pm. Built in 1811, this is believed to be the oldest stone house in New Brunswick. It serves healthy, moderately priced food – soup, salads, sandwiches, chicken and lasagne – though you can wind up with something a little more wicked, such as an excellent home-made cake, sundae or slice of cheesecake.

WHAT TO SEE

★ **Keillor House**: 9 Main Street. ☎ 379-6633. Open 1 June to mid-September, 10am–5pm (10am–1pm on Sunday). This building, which dates back to 1813, is worth a visit for its fabulous furniture. Next door, there's a Presbyterian church.

While you're in the area, take a look at Chandler House, built in 1831, which stands opposite the fire station, and the beautiful Eglise de Sainte-Trinité, on chemin de Sackville.

SACKVILLE

This attractive anglophone university town is known mainly for its cultural life. It was also the first place in the whole of the British Empire to grant a woman a university diploma (in 1875). The English-style campus is dotted with ancient trees, while there are several fine old residences in town, as well as the Owen Gallery, which hosts interesting exhibitions (☎ 364-2574).

USEFUL ADDRESSES

🛈 Tourist information: 6 King Street, next door to McDonald's. ☎ 364-4967.

WHERE TO STAY

♠ The Different Drummer: 7 West Main Street, near Sackville Memorial Hospital. ☎ 536-1291. Fax: 536-8116. Email: hanrahan@nbnet.nb.ca. Doubles $65 a night; four-bed room $90. This splendid house, surrounded by greenery, has four elegant rooms with neat floral decor and en-suite bathrooms. There are four more rooms in the annexe, an old converted stable, some of which sleep four.

♠ Marshlands Inn: 55 Bridge Street. ☎ 536-0721 or 1-800-561-1266 (toll-free). Fax: 536-0721. Website: www.marshlands.nb.ca. Suites $80–125 a night. Meals $15–25. This magnificent residence, set among sweeping lawns, oozes period atmosphere: the entrance, with its Ionian pillars, resembles a grand rotunda. Most of the rooms have en-suite bathrooms. In 1984, Queen Elizabeth II visited the establishment, and the owner very properly prepared tea – but she opted instead for a G&T.

THE FORT DE BEAUSÉJOUR NATIONAL HISTORICAL PARK

In **Aulac**, not far from Sackville and 40 kilometres (25 miles) from Moncton. ☎ 364-5080. Fax: 536-4399. Email: fort-beausejour@pch.gc.ca. Open 1 June to 15 October, 9am–5pm. Admission $2.50. Built by the French in 1751, the fort was captured by Colonel Monckton for the British in 1755. The nearby town was named after the conquering hero, but when they held the naming ceremony, the government official made a spelling mistake, and Moncton was born. The fort was later renamed Fort Cumberland. Several buildings have been restored, and there's a welcome centre with an exhibition explaining the history of the fort and the region.

CAPE TORMENTINE

There isn't really much of great interest here, unless you're planning to visit Prince Edward Island, home of Anne of Green Gables. The Confederation Bridge, which is 12 kilometres (7 miles) long, opened in June 1997, replacing the old ferry service to the island (crossing it costs $36 for a car). You pay the toll on the return journey, although you can avoid it by taking the ferry from Wood Bland to Caribou.

HOPEWELL ROCKS

At Hopewell Cape, 35 kilometres (22 miles) from Moncton on route 114. The main features of this small park are the 'flowerpots': rocks that have been completely worn away at the base by the huge waves of the Bay of Fundy. These waves are the highest in the world, reaching heights of up to 14 metres (46 feet). At low tide, you can walk between the 'flowerpots', under the arches, and visit the grottoes.

NEW BRUNSWICK

FUNDY NATIONAL PARK

Though it's relatively small for a national park, Fundy has a beautiful, rugged coastline and a host of footpaths, small creeks, forests, lakes, brooks, streams and covered bridges. There are also several campsites here.

KING'S LANDING HISTORICAL SETTLEMENT

At **Prince Williams**, on the banks of the St John River on route 2, 37 kilometres (23 miles) west of Fredericton (exit 259 off the Trans-Canada Highway). ☎ 363-4999. Fax: 363-4989. Website: www.gov.nb.ca/kings landing. Open from the first weekend in June to mid-October, 10am–5pm. Admission $10; family ticket $25.

This pioneer village is the British equivalent of the Village Historique Acadien, near Caraquet. You can visit old houses, shops and workshops that are scattered about in a large park, with 'villagers' wandering about in period dress. Don't miss the sawmill, the impressive flour mill and the forge.

WHERE TO EAT

✕ Try the **Kings Head** restaurant, which offers 19th-century dishes.

SAINT JOHN Pop: 75,000

From here, you can take the ferry to Digby, in Nova Scotia. The old-fashioned town, located at the mouth of a river, has a series of well-preserved Victorian buildings, and is easy to explore. Take a walk down Prince William Street and Germain Street to soak up its retro atmosphere.

Some History

Saint John was one of the first French settler camps in Nouvelle-France, along with Annapolis Port Royal, on the southern coast of the Bay of Fundy in what is now Nova Scotia. When the explorer Samuel de Champlain discovered the site on 24 June 1604, he named it Saint-Jean, after the saint who is celebrated on that day. As winter approached, the little colony withdrew farther south onto Sainte-Croix Island (now called Deer Island). It was a terrible winter, and 35 of the 79 members of Champlain's group never saw spring. Despite this setback, France now had a foothold in the New World, and Acadia was born. Thirty years later, when Saint-Jean had become a prosperous trading post, Franco-British rivalry degenerated into war. In 1713, as a result of the Treaty of Utrecht, France ceded Acadia to Britain, and Saint-Jean became Saint John. The Acadians were deported in 1755, and the region was later settled by Loyalists fleeing the newly independent American colonies. The town's most famous son is Donald Sutherland, of *Don't Look Now* and *M*A*S*H* fame.

USEFUL ADDRESS

🛈 **Saint John Visitor and Convention Bureau**: 16 Market Square. ☎ (506) 658-2990. Open Monday to Friday. The *Prince William's Walk* brochure details a pleasant walk through the Victorian streets of the town centre.

WHERE TO STAY

☆ Budget

⚑ **YMCA**: 19–25 Hazen Avenue. ☎ 634-7720. Fax: 637-0783. Dorm rooms $17. Ugly but practical and right in the centre of town, the hostel has clean rooms, a swimming pool and a weights room. Meals are also available.

☆☆ Moderate

⚑ **Mahogany Manor**: 220 Germain Street, near the town centre. ☎ 636-8000 or 1-800-796-7755 (toll-free). Website: www.sjnow.com/mm. Doubles from $65 a night, including breakfast. Credit cards accepted. This inexpensive, friendly establishment offers great value for money. The 100-year-old building, complete with pretty turrets, has an elegant interior, with thick carpets and mahogany panels. There are five bright and comfortable rooms, all with queen- or king-size beds and en-suite bathrooms. Guests share the lounge upstairs with the owners, Wayne and Ross, and there's a pretty flower garden.

⚑ **Garden House B&B**: 28 Garden Street. ☎ 646-9093. Email: dianem @nbnet.nb.ca. Doubles $65–75 a night. Despite the tranquil-sounding address, this fine Victorian residence is near a busy road, and it's rather noisy compared to Mahogany Manor. The interior is beautifully laid out, though, with soft carpets, floral walls and five large, sweet-smelling rooms with en-suite bathrooms and queen-size beds. Guests can also use the small garden.

B&B Earle of Leinster: 96 Leinster Street. ☎ 652-3275. Fax: 652-7666. Email: leinster@nbnet.nb.ca. Doubles $65 a night. Visa cards accepted. Somewhere between a guesthouse and a small hotel, this is one of the most central B&Bs in town. The well-equipped rooms all have TVs, videos and telephones, while the quieter ones have twin beds, en-suite showers and toilets. There's a basement living room with a pool table, a video and plenty of information about the town, and children can play in the garden. It isn't cheap, but it has plenty of charm.

WHERE TO HAVE A DRINK

🍷 **The Well**: a stone building on Princess Street, at the intersection with Water Street. Open until 2am. This is a large, convivial place with a pool table and rock music on the stereo. The landlord is particularly friendly.

🍷 **Darcy Farrow's Pub**: 43 Princess Street. ☎ 657-8939. Open until midnight (2am on weekends).

This fine old house is now home to a friendly, unpretentious bar that hosts regular gigs, usually featuring local musicians, with Celtic music on weekends. The decor is humdrum, but there's a good atmosphere. Highly recommended.

– You'll find several **terrace cafés** on the ground floor of an industrial brick building opposite Loyalist

Plaza (at the intersection of Saint Patrick and Water Streets). Outside terraces are not usually allowed in the English-speaking provinces, so they're worth a visit for that reason alone. Prince William Street and Princess Street also have a few good options.

LEAVING SAINT JOHN

– **For Québec**: take route 7, then Trans-Canada 2, which you join at Fredericton. It's a 709-kilometre (443-mile) trip.

– **For Digby, Nova Scotia**: on the other side of the Bay of Fundy. There are two or three ferry crossings a day from 24 June to 10 October: one in the morning, one in the afternoon and one late crossing around midnight. It takes 2 hours 45 minutes in summer and 3 hours during the rest of the year, and cuts 582 kilometres (360 miles), or around 7 hours, off your car journey. The schedule changes frequently, so phone to check fares and times. You must book in advance: ☎ 649-7777 or 1-888-249-7245 (toll-free). Website: www.nfl-bay.com

Nova Scotia

If you don't want to see anyone you know while on holiday, this is the place to go. Lapped on all sides by the sea, the Maritime Province of Nova Scotia truly feels like the edge of the world. On the map, it looks like a whale or a shark, its head pointing south, opposite the mainland, and its tail (Cape Breton island) pointing north, though some ungenerously say it looks more like a prawn.

Regardless, remote Nova Scotia, sparsely populated except in its towns, is a beautiful province, with luxurious wooded countryside around Cape Breton and more cultivated areas, such as the coastal plain along the Bay of Fundy. The bay, which stretches from Windsor to Annapolis Royal, is home to some fine orchards and also, less predictably, a couple of vineyards. The wine isn't bad, so one can only assume that Samuel de Champlain and his crew knew what they were about when they landed here, more than 100 years before the arrival of English and Scottish settlers in the 18th century.

There's a strong French connection to this fertile, faraway place; after all, it was they who settled here and worked hard to tame the land. When the Treaty of Utrecht handed the province to Britain in 1713, the new occupants renamed it Nova Scotia because the scenery reminded them of the Scottish Highlands. The Acadian population was deported in 1755, and far fewer traces remain than in neighbouring New Brunswick. That said, there are still a few francophone pockets: Cheticamp, on the west coast of Cape Breton, the breathtaking fortress of Louisbourg (the 'Gibraltar of the New World') and Saint Peters, to the south of Cape Breton. Grand Pré, meanwhile, was the site of a key moment in Acadian history.

Wherever you go, you'll meet the descendants of the Scottish settlers who came here from the Highlands in the 18th century. Their spirit permeates everything – the people, the houses and the culture. The Scottish inventor Sir Alexander Graham Bell liked Nova Scotia so much that he spent many of his summers here; in fact, this is where he died. You can visit his home in Cape Breton by following the magnificent Cabot Trail along the clifftops, and Baddeck, Bell's retreat from the stresses and strains of the outside world. The clear air and stunning natural beauty of the Cape's highlands are as refreshing as a week in a health spa, and the food is probably better – don't leave without trying the local cod and lobster.

– The best way to tour Nova Scotia is to take route 104 to Amherst and Pictou, and to leave via Annapolis Royal, taking the Digby–Saint John ferry across the Bay of Fundy. It will take about a week to do everything suggested in this section, including two days in Cape Breton – and you'll need more time if you want to do justice to the natural parkland, the hills, the highlands, the wildlife and, of course, the sea.

🛈 Tourist Information: arm yourself with a copy of *The Doer's and Dreamer's*, an excellent free guide available at tourist offices throughout the province. If you can't find it, ☎ 1-800-565-0000 (toll-free).

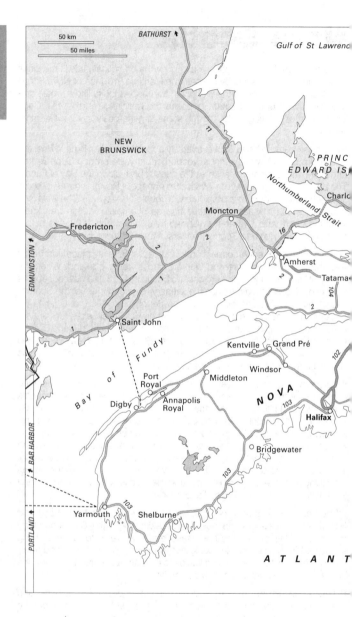

50 km

50 miles

BATHURST

Gulf of St Lawrenc

NEW
BRUNSWICK

71

PRINC
EDWARD IS

Northumberland Strait

Charlo

Moncton

2

2

16

EDMUNDSTON

Fredericton

1

2

Amherst

2

Tatama

104

2

Saint John

1

Bay   of   Fundy

Kentville   Grand Pré

Windsor

Port
Royal

Middleton

NOVA

103

102

Digby   Annapolis
Royal

Halifax

BAR HARBOR

Bridgewater

103

PORTLAND

Yarmouth   Shelburne

103

ATLANT

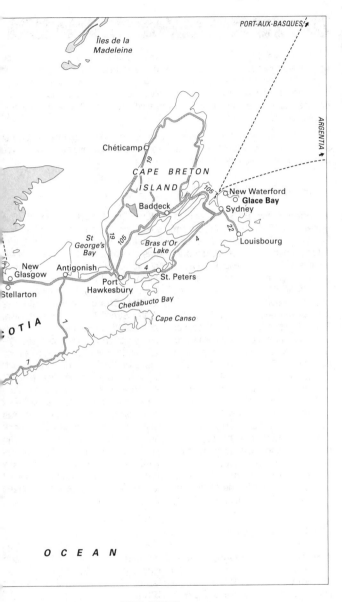

Îles de la Madeleine

PORT-AUX-BASQUES

ARGENTIA

Chéticamp

*C A P E   B R E T O N
I S L A N D*

19

105

New Waterford
Glace Bay
Sydney

Baddeck

22

*St
George's
Bay*

*Bras d'Or
Lake*

Louisbourg

19

105

4

New
Glasgow

Antigonish

4

Port
Hawkesbury

St. Peters

Stellarton

Chedabucto Bay

OTIA

7

Cape Canso

7

O C E A N

NOVA SCOTIA

PICTOU Pop: 4,500

Pictou is a small harbour town on the north coast of Nova Scotia, sheltered by the Northumberland Strait. The scenery is beautiful, with picturesque wooden houses coating the slopes of the gentle hills as they run down to the sea, and it's a good place to stop on the way to Cape Breton. The only stone houses you'll see are in the centre, where you could easily imagine that you were in Scotland or Brittany.

Pictou is where the first Scottish settlers landed on 15 September 1773, after a perilous journey aboard the *Hector*. An impressive quayside replica of the boat commemorates the landing.

WHERE TO STAY AND EAT

⌂ Linden Arms B&B: 62 Martha Street. ☎ 485-6565. Doubles from $40 a night. This traditional wooden establishment in a quiet neighbourhood is well situated and hospitable, and the pleasant, clean, non-smoking rooms all have TVs. Guests can use the garden.

⌂ ✗ Consulate Inn: 157 Water Street. ☎ 485-4554 Website: www.pictou.nsis.com/consulateinn. Suites $55–75 a night. Credit cards accepted. The former American Consulate is now a comfortable inn with antique furniture and an old-fashioned atmosphere. In all, there are five rooms, all en suite and with harbour views, but try to get one in the original part of the house, rather than the modern extension. Guests can use the pleasant garden.

⌂ Willow House Inn: 3 Willow Street, next door to the Consulate Inn. ☎ 485-5740. Doubles $60 a night. Credit cards accepted. This large green building, just a few minutes' walk from the town centre, has a comfy, old-fashioned feel. All eight rooms overlook the street or the garden. It's smarter and a touch more expensive than its rivals.

✗ The Stone House Café: 12 Water Street, in the centre of town. ☎ 485-6885. Open Monday to Saturday from noon. Main courses $7–20. Made entirely of stone, a rarity in these parts, this is the oldest building in the area, dating back to 1815. It was a shop and an office before becoming a café, and the third floor has hardly changed since it was built. There's a terrace at the back (for those rare occasions when the sun actually shines) and the unpretentious menu includes tasty local dishes such as haddock, halibut and pork *schnitzel*, as well as pizzas and sandwiches.

WHAT TO SEE

★ **Hector Heritage Quay**: on the port's main quay. ☎ 485-4371. Open mid-June to mid-September, 9am–9pm (from 10am on Sunday). Admission $4; family ticket $12. This is a wooden replica of the *Hector*, which brought the first Scottish pioneers to Pictou in 1773.

★ **Hector National Exhibition Centre**: Old Haliburton Road. From 1 June to 15 October, open Wednesday to Saturday, 9.30am–5.30pm, and 1.30–5.30pm on Sunday.

Cape Breton Island

There's nothing remarkable about the town of **Port Hawkesbury**, which is on the way to Cape Breton, but it's worth stopping at the tourist information centre, which you'll find just after the bridge on the hill.

🄗 **Nova Scotia Visitor Information Centre**: 96 Highway 4, Port Hastings, Nova Scotia ☎ (902) 625-4201 fax: (902) 625-4085. Email: wapgac@gov. ns.ca. Website: www.gov.ca/dtc. The friendly staff here can book you a hotel room for free (highly recommended in July and August). The office also stocks free road maps that highlight the main points of interest.

This village of small, scattered houses is not especially stunning, but its countryside and fresh air will whet your appetite for the rest of the island. You can explore the canal, which was dug into the wooded flanks of the mountains to link the Atlantic Ocean with the Bras d'Or Lake. From St Peters, sometimes referred to as the 'Gateway to the Bras d'Or Lake', you enter a totally different world.

This little village, home to a population of 730, has had a chequered history. Portuguese fishermen discovered the place in 1521, while looking for cod, and called it So Pedro. When Nicolas Denys, a relative of Cardinal Richelieu, landed here in 1650, he changed the name to Saint-Pierre, and turned it into the first fur-trading post on Île Royale (the old name for Cape Breton). It then became Port Toulouse, a trading post for the Compagnie de la Nouvelle-France, which Denys used as a base for controlling his newly conquered territories, stretching from Canso to Gaspé. Following the Treaty of Utrecht and the onset of British rule, Port Toulouse became St Peters.

GETTING THERE

St Peters is best reached on route 104, 53 kilometres (33 miles) east of Port Hastings. The 220-kilometre (140-mile) road from Canso to Louisbourg, known as the Fleur de Lys Trail, passes through wild and beautiful landscape.

WHERE TO STAY AND EAT

⛺ **Camping Saint Peters R.V.**: at the intersection of routes 14 and 247. ☎ 535-3333 Fax: 535-2202. Open June to September. Tent pitches $20 per night; extra for showers. The biggest campsite on the Bras d'Or Lake, with a heated pool and plenty of space.

⛺ **Youth Hostel**: ☎ 535-2404. This tiny hostel is actually a bungalow attached to Joyce's Motel and Cottages (*see below*), with two bedrooms, one with a double bed and bunk beds, the other with a double bed. There are washing facilities and toilets on the landing, and guests can use the laundrette at the motel. As space is limited, it's worth booking in advance. The prices are comparable to those at other youth hostels.

⌂ Joyce's Motel and Cottages: on route 4, heading towards Louisbourg, 1.5 kilometres (1 mile) from St Peters, facing the Bras d'Or Lake. ☎ 535-2404. Fax: 535-3727. Email: joyces motel@sympatico.ca. Open May to October. Cottages $45–105 a night. The 'cottages', or wooden bungalows, are dotted about on a hillside that slopes gently down to the lake. Some have kitchens, and all have bathrooms. You can get more expensive bungalows with better facilities at the motel. Guests can use the outdoor pool and laundrette, and you can hire bicycles here.

⌂ Carter's Lakeside Cottages: Main Street, Sampsonville, 5 kilometres (3 miles) from St Peters. ☎ 535-3744. This is a good place for families, with two log cabins (authentic trappers' cabins), one with one bedroom ($59) and one with two bedrooms ($79). Weekly rates are also available. Guests can swim in the nearby sea.

✗ There's a good, inexpensive restaurant in the centre of town, while more elaborate dishes are available at the restaurant in the MacDonald Hotel and at the Inn on the Canal.

WHAT TO SEE

★ **The St Peters Canal**: at the foot of the hill that's home to the Nicolas Denys museum. The canal was built in the 19th century so that merchant ships could travel between the Atlantic and the Bras d'Or Lake. These days, the canal is used only by pleasure boats.

★ **Nicolas Denys Museum**: east of route 4, at the end of rue Toulouse. ☎ 535-2379. Open June to September, 9am–5pm. This modest building houses a host of objects illustrating the life of Nicholas Denys, a neglected pioneer who took an interest in the indigenous people and respected their way of life. He also wrote the first history of America, published in 1672 with the snappy title *Description géographique et historique des costes de l'Amerique septentrionale avec l'histoire du pais* ('A Geographical and Historical Study of the Northern Coasts of America and a History of the Country').

LOUISBOURG

This French stronghold, nicknamed the 'Gibraltar of the New World' in the 18th century, sits at the edge of the Atlantic, on the south coast of Cape Breton. The imposing fortress, a symbol of French power in the New World until it was razed to the ground by the British in the 18th century, has been faithfully reconstructed at huge expense. It took about 20 years to complete. Whatever you do, don't miss this site during your visit to Nova Scotia.

A Brief History

Though small, Louisbourg was an important centre for the fishing industry – cod exports from Cape Breton were once worth three times as much as the fur trade in the whole of Canada. Hence the French decision to build a large fort here. In 1718, when the French provinces of Terre-Neuve and Acadia passed to the British following the Treaty of Utrecht, France hung on to her ports for a while, notably those on Île Royale (Cape Breton) and Île Saint-

Jean (Prince Edward Island). A colony began to emerge in Louisbourg, consisting of soldiers and officers, sailors, craftsmen and merchants. Eventually, the workforce was supplemented with slaves from the French West Indies and Native American labourers.

Built in 1713, the fortress provided shelter for a population of 2,000 by 1744. It was a costly project: it was said at the time that Louis XV's recurring nightmare was to see the roofs of Louisbourg from his bed at Versailles. After three decades of prosperity and relative peace, the Anglo-French war broke out anew. This time, the British targeted the lucrative cod business in Louisbourg. When the settlement fell to them in 1745, after a 40-day siege, it marked the end of French power in the New World. The fortress was destroyed in 1760, and Louisbourg fell into decline, effectively wiping the town off the map for 200 years. It could have been left that way, but somebody decided to help revive the area by rebuilding the fortress from scratch. Given that the reconstruction cost millions of dollars, it sounds like a crack-brained idea, but it has made a real difference to the local economy, reversing the 30-year decline that followed the collapse of the coal industry.

USEFUL ADDRESSES

🛈 Tourist Office: on the right as you enter Louisbourg on route 22, next door to the Railway Museum. You can pick up good maps of the town here.
■ **Lieu Historique National de la Forteresse de Louisbourg** (National Historical Fortresses of Louisbourg): CP 160, Louisbourg. ☎ 733-3100 (answerphone) or 733-2280 (information). The visitor centre for the fortress: this is the place to buy tickets and catch the bus to the site.

WHERE TO STAY AND EAT

In summer, particularly July and August, there are hardly any rooms to be had in Louisbbourg, so booking is essential. If you can't find anything in town, try Sydney, 32 kilometres (20 miles) away.

🛏 **The Manse, Brooks B&B**: 10 Strathcona Street. ☎ 733-3155. When you get to the centre of town, follow the main street towards the fortress, then take the first left after the petrol station. Open 1 April to 31 October. Doubles $35–50 a night. Outside, it's an attractive Victorian house in pastel green; inside, there are three prettily furnished double rooms with views of the sea and the harbour, and two shared bathrooms. This is a quiet, friendly place with a central location, but it fills up fast on weekends and in summer.

🛏 **Wilson's B&B**: 75 Wolfe Street, on the left of the road leading to the Royal Battery, just after the intersection with the road to the fortress's visitor centre. ☎ 733-2659. Open 15 May to late September. There are just two rooms in this quiet guesthouse, one with a double bed, the other with a single: both have views over the bay, with the fortress in the distance, and they share a shower and toilets, as well as a nice sitting room. It's run by a charming retired couple, and you're guaranteed good value for money.

🛏 **Levy's B&B**: 7 Marvin Street, near the port. ☎ 733-2793. Open 1 May to 31 October. Doubles $35–50 a night. Coming into Louisbourg on route 22, it's the second turning on the left after the tourist office. The location is perfect – right in the middle of town, but on a quiet side street – and, like most of the B&Bs in the area, this place has a cosy family atmosphere, The three double rooms have views over the port and the bay, and share two bathrooms.

🛏 **Cape Breton B&B**: 81 Pepperell Street. ☎ 733-2833. Coming into Louisbourg on route 22, it's the second street on your right after the tourist office. This is a quiet little place on a nice grassy slope. Two of the three bedrooms on offer are small, but they both have lovely views over the bay. Shared showers and toilets.

🛏 **Fortress Inn Louisbourg**: 7464 Main Street, 1.5 kilometres (1 mile) from the fortress. ☎ 733-2844 or 1-888-367-5353 (toll-free). Doubles $50–70 a night. With 45 motel-style rooms, the Fortress is lacks the intimacy of Louisbourg's guest-houses, but it's a useful standby if everywhere else is booked up.

✕ **Fortress View Restaurant**: Main Street, past the Banque Royal du Canada. Open 7am–10pm. There's a dining room facing the street, but try to get a table in the Ocean View Dining Room (you'll see why). The food is moderately priced and modest, but it is tasty, and they do a huge breakfast, the King Louis Special.

☆☆☆ Expensive

🛏 ✕ **Cranberry Cove Inn**: 12 Wolfe Street. ☎ 733-2171 or 1-800-929-0222 (toll-free). Doubles from $110 a night; full meal $20. This is an efficiently run, luxurious place with a lovely veranda, but the Laura Ashley-style decor may not be to everyone's taste.

In the Fortress

You can't stay here, but there's no shortage of on-site eateries.

✕ **Maison Destouches**: on the quay, facing the bay. Good for a quick, cheap snack.

✕ **Hôtel de la Marine**: a recon-structed 18th-century inn, where the waitresses, like everyone else around here, wear period dress. There's a tavern-style ambience, and the air is thick with tobacco smoke. English- and French-speak-ers sit shoulder to shoulder on wooden benches, and there are some unusual pictures on the wall, including one of Bacchus holding court on his barrel. The food is in keeping with the 18th-century theme – soups, sausages and cab-bage, beans, fish and chicken stew. You eat and drink from pewter plates and goblets, and there are no forks, only spoons: not very practical, but the American tourists love it. The prices are reasonable, and the gim-micks don't spoil the fun.

✕ **L'Épée Royale**: next to the Hôtel de la Marine. ☎ 733-3230. Open June to October. *Table d'hôte* $15. This is a classier establishment than its neighbour, and should come as a great relief for anyone who can't bear bad table manners. The food is traditional, and the set-ting has been faithfully re-created, right down to the last detail.

WHERE TO STAY IN THE AREA

⌂ **Sunlit Valley B&B**: 821 Brickyard Road, Albert Bridge, about 15 minutes from Louisbourg. ☎ 562-7663 or 1-877-808-8883 (toll-free). On the way to Louisbourg, cross the Mira River, then take a left just before the petrol station. Doubles $40–60 a night. The staff at reception are grumpy, and there's nothing special about this place, but you're more or less certain to get a room here, even in high season, so it's handy in an emergency.

WHAT TO SEE

★ **The Fortress of Louisbourg** is built on an imposing stretch of Louisbourg Bay, about 4 kilometres (2.5 miles) south of town. Although it looks authentic, with French-style houses and thick Breton walls, it was completely rebuilt between 1960 and 1980 (*see above*). It's the biggest reconstruction of its kind in Canada, and employs 100 or so actors in period attire, living life as it was in 1744. You'll feel as though you've stepped onto a film set, or travelled back in time. If you ask one of the 'residents' a question, the reply you get will be from an 18th-century viewpoint. Soldiers in tricorne hats stand guard, sentries stride across the street, beating their drums and making public announcements, stopping to question a prisoner or filling their muskets in the guardhouse. In the distance, an elegant lady plays her harpsichord, and an important-looking man in a wig writes his accounts with a quill pen. The bakery makes bread to 18th-century recipes, and even the children run around in costume. The only thing missing is the sea of masts that used to fill the bay.

As you look around, bear in mind that only 20 per cent of the original fortress has been reconstructed. It's not hard to see why the place was such a symbol of French power in those days.

– **Opening times**: from June to September, open 9.30am–5pm. It's open at the same times in May and October, but there are no performers. During the rest of the year, you can go around on a pre-arranged guided tour.

– You should set aside a whole day to look around the fortress properly.

– Admission is $11, with discounts for children. The price includes transport by bus from the Visitors' Reception Center, just outside the fortress. You have to leave your car there. If you buy a ticket after 3pm, you can use it the next day as well.

– **Visitors' Reception Center**: pick up a map of the fortress here, or a guidebook ($4).

Inside the Fortress

There isn't enough room here to list all the different things you can see in the Fortress, but here are a few of the best.

– **La Résidence du Commissaire-Ordonnateur Bigot**: the colony was ruled from this residence, and its treasury was here as well. François Bigot, who ran Île Royale between 1739 and 1745, had an excellent reputation. He was the province's last paymaster before the English took over. All the rooms have been furnished in 18th-century style, and there are actors here, too, writing with quill pens and going about their daily business.

– **Maison de la Plagne**: you can watch a film about Louisbourg here, and it's also the departure point for guided tours. In the garden, the staff cultivate the vegetable beds.

– **Maison Carrerot**: displays describe the building techniques of the period.

– **Hôtel de la Marine**: a reconstructed 18th-century inn (*see* 'Where to Stay and Eat').

– **Maison des Gannes**: come here if you want to learn the secrets of cooking on an open hearth, and of lace-making.

– **Maison d'Étienne Vernier**: the King's engineer, Étienne Vernier, lived here. His 'son' will tell you how the fortress was designed and why it was necessary.

– **Bastion du Roi**: this is the King's Bastion, the jewel in the crown of Louisbourg. It's inside the fortress itself, like a kind of mini citadel. Make sure you visit the chapel, the barracks and the exhibition that tells the story of the reconstruction.

– **Boulangerie du Roi**: open summer only. The King's bakery offers delicious fresh bread in soldier's rations.

– **Footpath around the ruins**: once you've been round the reconstructed fortress, why not take a stroll along the sand dunes, through the ruins of the parts that haven't been rebuilt? The path starts behind the Maison de la Plagne.

SYDNEY

Sydney is an industrial and administrative town on the banks of a large river, and it's not got much to offer in the way of tourist attractions. That said, there are plenty of hotels, restaurants and bars, so it's a good urban base for exploring the open spaces of Cape Breton, or for visiting Louisbourg if you can't get a room there. Sydney was founded in 1785 by American Loyalists, and it's not unusual to see pictures of the Queen hanging proudly in the shops even now.

WHERE TO STAY

⚓ **Park Place B&B**: 169 Park Street, near the centre. ☎ 562-3518. Fax: 567-6618. Website: www.bbcanada.com/&.html. Open 1 May to 31 October; out of season, by reservation only. Doubles $40–60 a night. This is a attractive Victorian house at the end of a long, shady avenue in a residential area. Run by a jolly old lady, it's cosy and full of attractive old furniture, with three very nice rooms and a circular living room. A lovely, quiet place to stay.

⚓ **The Gathering House B&B**: 148 Crescent Street, in a residential area about five minutes from the town centre. ☎ 539-7172. Fax: 539-6665. Booking essential out of season. Doubles $45–55 a night. Crescent Street is between Kings Road and Argyle Street, near three little lakes and the Court House. The Gathering House is a big, lively place with a Louisiana-style veranda, and it's full of backpackers and cyclists in summer. Despite that, it's a bit expensive for what you get. The lady of the house, Jean Philips, likes nothing better than a good natter.

â **Royal Hotel**: 345 Esplanade, in the centre. ☎ 539-2148. Doubles $29–50. The hotel dates from 1898, and the main features of the entrance hall are a moose's head and a picture of the *Titanic*, but the warm reception you'll get should put an end to any sinking feelings. The 18 clean, quaint rooms, all with washbasin and TV, have views the street or the yard at the back (these are quieter at night), and some have wooden floorboards

â **Paul's Hotel**: 10 Pitt Street, on the corner with Esplanade. Doubles $50–65 a night, including parking. This hotel has a certain *fin-de-siècle* charm, and the 17 rooms, some with en-suite shower and toilet, offer good value for money.

â **Paradise Found B&B**: 62 Milton Street, off route 125 (exit 8). ☎ 539-9377. Email: paradisefound@ns. sympatico.ca. Doubles from $60. This hotel is not very central, but it's on a quiet street lined with trees, so you can be sure of a good night's sleep. It's a big old house that retains much of the original woodwork and plaster mouldings. There are two big rooms, and guests can also use the library.

WHERE TO EAT AND HAVE A DRINK

✕ **Daniel's Bar and Restaurant**: 456 Charlotte Street, parallel to Esplanade and the river. Open 11am–10pm. Daniel's is a bar-restaurant with a friendly atmosphere: pool tables, music, TV screens and a little corner with video games. The food includes soups, salads, nachos, steaks, sandwiches and lobster, while the house speciality is 'Awesome Blossom', an enormous onion fried in vegetable oil.

❢ **Smooth Hermans**: 424 Charlotte Street, underneath Joe's Warehouse. This huge bar has a small stage where rock bands sometimes play. The local youth throng to this place on weekends.

IN THE AREA

★ **Marconi National Historic Site**: Timmerman Street, Table Head, in Glace Bay, a small town 23 kilometres (14 miles) northeast of Sydney. Open 1 June to 15 September, 10am–6pm. Admission free. This well-designed little museum is dedicated to Marconi, the wizard of the wireless. Born in Bologna, in northern Italy, on 23 April 1874, Guiglielmo Marconi first dreamed of sending messages across long distances, without wires, when he was a teenager. He was hopeless at school, but started his experiments at his home in Italy, then moved to London to pursue his ideas when he was 22 years old. After some early successes (his inventions impressed the Post Office), he moved to Cornwall, because he needed to be on the coast to test his ideas.

A couple of years later, Marconi moved to Saint John, in Newfoundland, and set himself up at Signal Hill. It might seem strange that he chose such a remote place, but Saint John is the closest place to Europe on the American landmass. He kept in contact with Cornwall all the while, and it was from there that he received his first message in Morse code – the letter S – on 12 December, 1901. This was the first time Europe and America had communicated across the Atlantic Ocean without the use of wires.

Marconi left Newfoundland and moved to Table Head, where he succeeded in sending a complete message to England in October 1902. In a sense, global telecommunication began in this remote part of the world.

BADDECK

This is one of the nicest villages on Cape Breton Island. Alexander Graham Bell, the inventor of the telephone, lived here in a manor house. The waters of Bras d'Or Lake and Saint Patrick's Channel wash the harbour, and the countryside is gorgeous, especially the forest. Even better, this stretch of sea has not been spoiled by the tourist trade, which makes it a great place to spend a couple of nights. As there are few hotels and B&Bs, make sure you book ahead in July and the first two weeks of August.

WHERE TO STAY, EAT AND HAVE A DRINK

Campsites

⌂ **Camping Baddeck Cabot Trail KOA**: 8 kilometres (5 miles) west of Baddeck, on route 105. ☎ 295-2288 or 794-7952. Open 15 May to 15 October. Tent pitches $22. This is the best campsite in the area, on a lovely, shady part of the riverbank. The toilets, showers and sinks are impeccably clean, and firewood is on sale. Other facilities include a swimming pool and a children's games area.

⌂ **Camping Bras d'Or Lakes**: 5 kilometres (3 miles) west of Baddeck, also on route 105. ☎ 295-2329. Open 15 May to 30 September. Tent pitches $19. Another good spot for camping, this time at the edge of the lake.

☆☆ Moderate

⌂ **Restawyle B&B and Cottage**: 231 Shore Road, on the road that joins route 105 as you leave Baddeck. ☎ 295-3253. Doubles $50 a night; cottage $110. The tall, wooden main building, prettily painted in blue and white, has a south-facing veranda that's perfect for basking in the sun (and for having a cigarette, as smoking is forbidden in the rest of the house). There are four rooms, all of which overlook the lake, with shared bathrooms, while families should go for the two-bedroom cottage, which has its own kitchen, as well as great views and lots of space. At breakfast, try the delicious blueberry muffins.

⌂ **Heidi's B&B**: 64 Old Margaree Road, in the middle of town. ☎ 295-1301. Open June to October; booking essential (deposit required). Doubles $45 a night. This lovely, late-Victorian building is a gem, with a lovely view over the lake from the veranda, but there are only two rooms.

☆☆☆ Expensive

⌂ **Duffus House Inn**: 108 Water Street. ☎ 295-2172. Website: www.capebretonet.com/baddeck/ Duffus House. Doubles $95–135. Kept lovingly by Judy Langley, this is the most charming place to stay in Baddeck, There are seven rooms, including three with balcony. The nicest bit of the inn is the old part, which is full of ornaments, antiques and books, but there's only one bedroom in it. The other rooms are in a modern annexe, tastefully arranged but less 'authentic' than the main house. The atmosphere is as romantic as you could hope for, and there are great views of a tree-covered island in the lake.

⚓ **Cabot Trail Motel**: off route 105, 1.5 kilometres (1 mile) west of Baddeck. ☎ 295-2580. Open 15 May to 31 October. Doubles $85 a night. This motel is rather lacking in character, but it's very comfortable, and the surroundings are stunning. All the rooms have lake views, TVs, radios and telephones, there's an outdoor (heated) pool, and guests can use the private lake for all manner of aquatic activities, so this is a good choice for families.

⚓ **Ceilidh Country Lodge**: on the road that leads to the port. ☎ 295-3527 or 1-800-565-5660 (toll-free). A room sleeping four costs $100; $10 extra per child sharing. Another family-friendly option, with water-sports galore – canoeing, kayaking, pedalos, boat trips – as well as bike hire and tennis courts. The hotel in front of the lake is more elegant, but also more expensive.

✕ **Lakeside Café**: just below Ceilidh Country Lodge. ☎ 295-3523. Main courses $10. The food is fine, if not fantastic, and the lakeside views are really romantic.

🍷 **Bras d'Or Yacht Club**: Water Street. ☎ 295-2107. The Yacht Club dominates the marina, and the first-floor bar is the only decent place to get a drink after 10pm. It's a friendly place with an American feel: you can play pool and shuffleboard, and everyone talks to everyone else, so it's great for solo travellers.

WHAT TO SEE

★ **Alexander Graham Bell National Historic Site**: on the east side of Baddeck, off route 205. ☎ 295-2069. Form July to September, open 9am–9pm; otherwise 9am–5pm. This excellent museum is crammed full of objects relating to the life of the inventor of the telephone. Alexander Graham Bell (1847–1922) was born in Edinburgh, and began his career teaching deaf-mutes before emigrating to Canada with his parents. His mother was partially deaf, and his father was a leading authority on speech therapy. Bell married a deaf woman called Mabel, initially one of his students. It was through his persistent attempts to break through the barrier of his students' deafness that he came up with the idea of transmitting voices along a wire.

As the museum reveals, Bell was a true Renaissance man: he understood genetics, studied medicine and agricultural science, learned the language of the Mohawks and loved aeroplanes.

He was a also fierce defender of his inventions – and his tenacity helped him get extremely rich. In 1892, he moved to Baddeck, to his manor house 'Beinn Bhreag' (Gaelic for 'beautiful mountains'), where he spent the last 30 years of his life.

There are some wonderful photos of the great man testing various inventions, and a purpose-built room houses the hull from the fastest hydrofoil in the world, a kite designed by Bell and documents about the history of the Silver Dart – the first British plane to get off the ground. Bell kept on inventing until his death in 1922, and always stayed true to his humanist ideals. Incidentally, you might like to know that the first words ever spoken over the phone (by Bell himself) were, rather disappointingly, 'Watson, come here; I want you!'

CAPE BRETON NATIONAL PARK AND CHÉTICAMP

The countryside here is reminiscent of Finland, with deep forests dotted with lakes, but the wildlife is a bit different – you'll see moose as well as bears and deer. There is a strong hint of Celtic scenery, too, in the rocky outcrops and especially in the ways of the inhabitants – there's even a Gaelic college in Baddeck. And some of the French-speaking pockets, like Chéticamp, are still home to the descendants of the Acadians. All in all, this is probably the most beautiful place in Nova Scotia.

To get to this 'world apart', follow the Cabot Trail, a beautiful coastal road that snakes between the sea and the forests. It's named after John Cabot (1450–1499), who first landed here in 1497: he was a Venetian, looking for the fabled passage to China, so perhaps he took a wrong turn.

USEFUL ADDRESSES

★ **Cape Breton Highlands National Park**: at Ingonish Beach. ☎ 285-2535 or 224-2306 (summer and autumn), and 285-2691 (winter and spring).

🄗 **Information and Visitors' Centers**: there are two of these. One is on the trail itself, a few kilometres north of Chéticamp; the other is at Ingonish. Open 8am–8pm from 24 June to 4 September; 8am–5pm between 20 May and 23 June, and between 5 September and 10 October. During the rest of the year, information can be obtained by telephone only. At the Center in Chéticamp, you can get a camping permit, walking maps and suggested itineraries, and use an extensive library devoted to the region's natural history.

■ **Mountain bikes** can be hired from the information centre at Chéticamp.

■ **Internet**: there are various places where you can surf the web, including Chéticamp's **Bureau Touristique des Trois-Pignons**, a big building with a red roof, two kilometres (about a mile) north of town ($2 an hour); at **Celtic Vision** in Pleasant Bay; and at the **Public Library** or the **Fire Hall** (fire station) in Ingonish.

GETTING THERE

– **From Baddeck**: this pretty port is the start or end point of the 296-kilometre (184-mile) Cabot Trail. The trail takes a day to drive if you are speedy, but it's best enjoyed at a more leisurely pace: the park literature claims that you need three or four days to explore the area properly. It's best to follow the trail clockwise, from west to east. From Baddeck, head for Chéticamp via the Upper Middle River and Margaree Forks.

– **From Québec and New Brunswick**: follow the Trans-Canada Highway route 104 (Sunrise Trail) until you reach the Canso Causeway, where there's a bridge to Cape Breton Island. Once you reach Port Hastings, you have two options: follow Route 105 to Baddeck, then take the trail from there, or go straight to Chéticamp along the Ceilidh Trail, which is 120 kilometres (75 miles) long, between the Canso Causeway and Margaree Harbour, and from there onto the Cabot Trail.

WHEN TO GO

– **Summer**: July and August are the warmest months, but they're also the busiest. The weather is at its best at this time of year, and you can swim in the lakes and even the sea (if you're feeling brave). The temperature is 20–25°C during the day, and 10–20°C at night. Pack a jumper and a waterproof, as the weather can be unpredictable (British readers should think Lake District).

– **Late September/early October**: this is also a good time to visit, especially if you like to escape the crowds. The trees in the forests turn a wonderful colour.

WHERE TO CAMP

Camping is free between mid-May and mid-October, but you need a permit to stay in the 'wilderness' sites (these are available from the information centres; *see above*). You'll get a reduction if you stay for more than four nights.

⛺ **Chéticamp**: at the west entrance to the park, just past the Visitors' Center. Along with Broad Cove, this is the biggest campsite in the area, with drinking water, clean toilets, showers and kitchens with wood stoves among the amenities. There are 14 pitches with electricity.

⛺ **Corney Brook**: also on the west side of the park, in a stony cove before the ascent to Lake French. Running water, shelters and stoves.

⛺ **Fishing Cove**: this 'wilderness' site in an exposed spot at the edge of the sea feels like the end of the world. It's accessible only via an 8-kilometre (5-mile) footpath between Lake French and Pleasant Bay, and it's for hardened campers and the foolhardy only. You need a camping permit to stay here.

⛺ **Broad Cove**: near the east entrance to the park. A nice big site, well maintained and near the titular cove and Ingonish.

WHERE TO STAY AND EAT

Between Chéticamp and Belle Côte

✕ **Hungry Skipper**: General Delivery, just past the bridge as you go towards Chéticamp. ☎ 235-2660. Main courses from $5. It looks like a fast-food joint, and the prices and the clientele do nothing to change this image, but the food is something else entirely: a vast array of fresh fish and seafood. You could easily miss this place, but you won't regret making the effort.

✕ **Margaree Lobster Pound**: from the bridge, follow the road to Chéticamp for about a kilometre (half a mile), then take the coastal road in the opposite direction until you reach the pier. ☎ 235-2608. There are no prizes for guessing what's on the menu here. You can pick a live lobster from the tank, which is then taken away and cooked, or, if you're squeamish, you can have one that's already been prepared. There's no dining room as such, but you can be sure that everything is absolutely fresh.

Chéticamp

⚓ **Germaine's B&B**: Point Cross, on route 19, 8 kilometres (5 miles) south of Chéticamp; it's on the left-hand side of the road. ☎ 224-3459. Doubles $50 a night. This well-kept establishment, owned by a friendly Acadian couple, has three clean, comfy rooms with exceptional views of the ocean. Next to the house, a sign reads: 'Wild Herbs, Unusual Art'. It belongs to a shack facing the sea, which houses all sorts of unusual *objets d'art*. Nearby, a footpath leads to the shore.

⚓ **Chéticamp Outfitters Inn**: Box 448, at Point Cross; 2 kilometres (just over a mile) south of Chéticamp. ☎ 224-2776. Fax: 224-2382. Coming from Margaree Harbour, past Point Cross, it's on your right: take an earth track for 400 metres (400 yards), and you'll reach the Inn, a brown wooden building perched on a hill. Open 1 May to 15 December; by reservation only out of season. Doubles $45–65 a night, including breakfast. Credit cards accepted. This is a quiet place with recently refurbished rooms in the basement and two new studio flats with kitchens. Shared toilets and showers are in the corridor. The owners are really friendly, and can tell you all about the National Park. You can join in their memorable barbecues, hire a bike and even indulge in a day's salmon-fishing, although the trips are quite expensive.

⚓ **Chéticamp Motel**: 14762 piste Cabot, at the southernmost end of the village. ☎ 224-2711. Doubles $45–65 a night; chalets $75. The motel has a lovely garden near the water, with views of the mountains and swings for the little ones. It's good walking territory, and the owners can also organize whale-spotting trips. A great place to stay.

✕ **Restaurant Acadien**: in the centre of town. ☎ 224-3207. Open 9am–9pm. Run by a local artist's co-operative in Chéticamp, this is a gastronomic godsend if you're fed up with the predominantly British-style restaurants in the area. The waitresses wear red-and-white check uniforms, the chairs are wooden and you'll sometimes see customers in Acadian costume. The à la carte menu features local specialities such as chicken stew, fish chowder, baked beans, meat and vegetable *chiard* and lobster, to mention just a few. Try to leave room for pudding: blueberry cake or *tarte aux raisins*. This is also a good place for breakfasts – they're huge – or a daytime snack.

✕ **Harbour**: 15299 Cabot Trail, a kilometre (half a mile) north of the church. ☎ 224-2042. This bar-restaurant serves hamburgers for less than $10 and proper seafood meals for less than $15. You eat in a lovely room overlooking the sea and the island off Chéticamp, which is especially pretty at sunset. The grilled scallops are delicious.

Dingwall

🛏 **The Inlet B&B**: just off the Cabot Trail, on your left if you're heading for the tiny port of Dingwall. ☎ 383-2112. Open 1 May to 31 October. Doubles $40 a night. The house is unpretentious – spartan would be more like it – but the three rooms are cheap, and have views over the charming little cove.

White Point

🛏 **Two Tittle B&B**: south of Aspy Bay, past South Harbour and Smelt Brook. ☎ 383-2817. Doubles $40–55. Booking essential. This place is right in the middle of nowhere, and much the better for it. The little wooden building, painted light green, overhangs a cute little port where a few coloured shacks huddle against the slope of White Point. There are just three rooms: the best is 'Rose's Room', which has twin beds and overlooks the port and pebbly beach. There's a double room in the basement, but there's no view. Overall, this is a simple but comfortable place to stay.

WHERE TO HAVE A DRINK, NIGHTLIFE

You probably didn't come here for the nightlife, but if the urge suddenly takes you, you'll have to take your chances in Chéticamp.

– **Bowling-Dancing du Centre Acadien**: not far from the church. This is Chéticamp's sole nightclub – but it's open only to 13- to 17-year-olds, who are supervised, and there's no alcohol. At least you can go bowling . . .

– **Le Gabriel**: on the main road, a kilometre (half a mile) north of the church. ☎ 224-3685. This place at-tracts a more mature crowd (35 and over). At the beginning of August, it hosts a decent 'festival', with local bands and traditional music.

❢ **Harbour**: just before Le Gabriel. ☎ 224-2042. Open until 1am. This place attracts a 20- and 30-something crowd. Don't get your hopes up, as Studio 54 it is not, but it's good for a quiet drink.

From Chéticamp to Ingonish

This section of the Cabot Trail is 106 kilometres (66 miles) long, and the countryside is breathtaking. In fact, it's one of the most beautiful coastal roads in Canada. The best bit is between Chéticamp and Neils Harbour.

★ Before you get to Chéticamp, at **Cap-le-Moine**, look out for the strange collection of scarecrows in a meadow to the right of the road. You'll see clowns, a golfer, a miner, George Bush and Princess Diana dancing, Ronald Reagan, François Mitterrand, Margaret Thatcher and a crowd of assorted unknowns. They all wear plastic or rubber masks, and are labelled just in case you can't recognize them.

★ **Chéticamp** is the main village in the area, and it's French-speaking. It was founded in 1755 by Acadians who were fleeing from Grand-Pré (*see below*). Fishing is the main source of income here. You can also visit the minuscule Musée Acadien or the artist's co-operative.

– **Skyline walk**: level with Lake French, this walk is a round trip of 7 kilometres (4 miles), and takes about 2 hours. You go past a vertiginous cliff that plunges away to the sea. If you're lucky, you'll spot a whale or a bald eagle along the way.

★ **Lake Benjies**: between Lake French and Pleasant Bay. A 3-kilometre (2-mile) path passes through coniferous forests and boggy ground before arriving at the lake. It's a good place to see moose and various northern birds.

– **Lone Sheiling**: this 800-metre footpath plunges you into the wilderness for 20 minutes or so, leading you to a Scottish shepherd's hut that's surrounded by 300-year-old maple trees.

★ **Dingwall**: to the northeast of Cape Breton island. There's nothing particular to see here, apart from the sea, but there is a decent B&B here (see 'Where to Stay and Eat').

– **Scenic Loop** is a panoramic road that runs past South Harbour to New Haven, passing through some forgotten but beautiful corners of the coast, including **White Point** (see above). It's also known as the 'Alternative Scenic Road'.

★ **New Haven** has a sandy beach, but swimming here can be a rather bracing experience.

★ **Ingonish**: one of the gateways to the national park, Ingonish is tamer and more urban than other parts of the west coast. The road from New Haven is nothing special, but hikers will love the 8.5-kilometre (5.5-mile) footpath around Lake Warren. It will take 3 hours to walk if you pause to admire the views, or sight any moose or deer.

Southern Nova Scotia

HALIFAX Pop: 122,000   DIALLING CODE: 902

Halifax is the capital of Nova Scotia. It sits on the banks of a river that speeds away to the Atlantic. It's a busy port town and a university town, the embodiment of 'old and new Canada'. You'll need a good day to do it justice.

One of its claims to fame is that it is home to the bodies of those who died aboard the *Titanic*. It was founded in 1749, as an English stronghold designed to counteract the French fortress at Louisbourg (see above). Halifax also has the oldest Protestant church in Canada and the remains of the only slave quarter in the province, Africville, where the boxer George Dixon (1870–1909) was born.

GETTING THERE

– **By bus**: there is a direct bus from Québec to Halifax, but the journey takes 16 hours (it leaves at 1am and arrives at 6pm). There are also buses from Edmundston, Baddeck and Sydney. The bus terminal in Halifax is at 6040 Almon Street, on the corner with Robie Street.

– **By road**: if you take the ferry from Saint John, it's 235 kilometres (146 miles) from Digby to Halifax. It should take 3 hours 30 minutes at most. If you're coming from Sydney, you'll have 423 kilometres (262 miles) to go, or about 6 hours 30 minutes. From Moncton, New Brunswick, it's 290 kilometres (181 miles), about 4 hours on a clear road.

– **By plane**: there are direct flights from London and Amsterdam, and domestic flights from Montréal. The airport is 40 kilometres (25 miles) from Halifax on route 102.

USEFUL ADDRESSES

◻ Nova Scotia Visitor Information Center: at the port, in the Historic Properties quarter. ☎ 424-4247.

✉ Central Post Office: 1680 Bedford Row. ☎ 494-4734.

■ Banque Royale du Canada: 5161 George Street. ☎ 421-8330.

■ Car hire: Rent-a-Wreck, ☎ 454-2121.

■ Alternative Passage: 1266 Hollis Street. ☎ 425-5781. A car-sharing agency where you can get lifts to Sydney, Digby, Moncton, Saint John and Montréal. It costs $7 to register. Travelling by car is actually cheaper than taking the bus in these parts.

■ The Bike People: ☎ 420-0777. Bike hire.

WHERE TO STAY

✩ Budget

♠ University of King's College: 6350 Coburg Road, within walking distance of the town centre. ☎ 422-1271. Fax: 423-3357. Website: admin.ukings.ns.ca. Open to the public 1 May to 15 August. Singles $16–32 a night. There are 80 hall-of-residence-style rooms with shared bathrooms in one of the oldest universities in North America. Though the students are largely absent at this time of year, there are always posters up advertising summer activities.

♠ Halifax Heritage House Hostel: 1253 Barrington Street, five minutes' walk from the town centre. ☎ 422-3863 or 1-800-663-5777 (toll-free). Fax: 422-0616. Website: www.goldeye.com/hostel. From the bus station, take the No. 7 bus from Robie Street or Almon Street to the corner of Barrington and South Street. Open 7am–10pm. Dorm beds $20 a night; private room

$30. Credit cards accepted. This is an appealing youth hostel in a building that's full of character, with the beds arranged into small dormitories. It has a kitchen, a laundrette and plenty of tourist information, and you can even surf the Internet ($6 an hour).

♠ YMCA: 1565 South Park Street. ☎ 423-9622. Fax: 425-3180. Dorm rooms $28 a night. It's more expensive than the youth hostel, and the rooms are smaller and a bit dreary, with no washbasins. The people who run it are very friendly, but you'd be better off finding a B&B for the same price.

✩✩ Moderate

♠ Rebecca's B&B: 2719 Windsor Street, in a quiet area near a park. ☎ 455-5802. Doubles $45 a night. There are three old-fashioned rooms, and the living room has a huge fireplace. The owner is charming, and it feels like a real home from home. Guests can also use the garden and patio.

â Fountain View Guesthouse: 2138 Robie Street, opposite a park. ☎ 422-4169. Doubles from $30 a night. This turquoise guesthouse has eight bedrooms, with bathrooms on the landing. Try to get a room on the garden side, as it's on a very busy street. You won't get breakfast here, but there are plenty of places to pick something up in town.

☆☆☆ Expensive

â Cambridge Suites Hotel Halifax: 1583 Brunswick Street. ☎ 420-0555 or 1-888-417-8483 (toll-free). Email: reservation@hfx.cambridge suites.ns.ca. Mini suites from $95 a night; breakfast is included if you go for a suite at $125 or more. All the rooms are air-conditioned, and all have cable TV, a hairdryer, a microwave and a fridge. Washing machines are also available. It's very comfortable, and good value for money.

WHERE TO EAT

✕ **The Diamond**: 1663 Argyle Street, in the liveliest area of Halifax. ☎ 423-7463. Full meal $10. This vast, bustling restaurant offers an unusual twist on fusion cuisine: Mexican-Provençal. The decor is immaculate, with softly lit, intimate alcoves if you're dining *à deux*, and a terrace if you prefer to eat alfresco. You can even combine the two by eating under an indoor tree. Worth a visit for the surroundings alone, but it is busy.

✕ **Mediterraneo Café**: 1571 Barrington Street, right in the centre of town. Main courses $3–8. Good for a quick snack – sandwiches, hamburgers, felafel, and Lebanese and Italian dishes.

✕ **Atrium Restaurant**: 1742 Argyle Street. ☎ 422-5453. Opening times are fairly ad hoc, but it's open 4–9pm on Sunday. On Saturday, brunch is served between 11am

and 3pm. The food here is good and simple, with soups, salads and house specialities such as lemon pepper chicken, deep-fried scallops and baked haddock. From 9pm, it turns into a nightclub, with a dancefloor where you can strut your stuff to chart tunes.

☆☆–☆☆☆ Moderate to Expensive

✕ **Nemo's**: 1865 Hollis Street. ☎ 425-6738. Main courses $10–23. The chefs here blend Breton, Canadian, Italian, Indian and Mediterranean influences to excellent effect, all at extremely reasonable prices. Try the strudel with spinach, chicken *aglio e olio* (garlic and oil), veal in white wine or shrimps *puttanesca*. Red and white wines are available by the glass or by the bottle.

WHERE TO HAVE A DRINK

For up-to-date information about the local nightlife, pick up *Light Up The Town,* the tourist office's guide to the bars and clubs in Halifax.

♪ **The Diamond**: *see* 'Where to Eat'. Open until 2am.

♪ **Granite Brewery**: 1222 Barrington Street. ☎ 423-5660. Website:

www.interlog.com/Ègranite. Open until 12.30am. This lively bar is in a huge stone building that dates from 1834. It's somewhere between an

English and an Irish pub, and they brew several beers on tap: Best Bitter, Peculiar (a warm treacly modelled on the Theakston's classic) and Keefe's Irish Stout. They do brunch from 11.30am to 4pm on Saturday, and from noon on Sunday.

❢ **Café Mokka ultra Bar**: 1588 Granville Street. ☎ 492-4036. By day, you can get the best coffee in Halifax; at night, the barmen mix a mean martini. There's live jazz, hip-hop or rock at weekends (admission $4), and the bar displays work by students from the city's art school. The cool, eclectic decor blends 1960s and 1970s styles.

❢ **Breakers**: 1661 Argyle Street. ☎ 425-4297. Website: www.breakersbilliardclubs.com. Open until 2am. Pool is the big thing here – there are two rooms full of tables

that you can hire for $9 an hour – but you can come for a drink and bury yourself in one of the comfy armchairs, or try your luck at chess, table football, pinball or video games. Pizza is available at the bar.

❢ **Bearly's Bar and Grill**: 1249 Burlington Street. ☎ 423-2526. Open until 2am. It's dark inside, and the music is loud, but this is a laid-back place that's popular with 30-somethings. There are live rock and blues bands most evenings, with a bluegrass evening on Saturday and music from 5.30pm on Sunday.

❢ **Midtown Tavern**: 1684 Grafton Street, on the corner with Prince Street. ☎ 422-5213. This is a pretty humdrum bar, but it's popular with students and sports fans. Fast-food snacks are available at the bar.

WHAT TO SEE AND DO

★ The **historic quarter** is on the seafront, at the foot of a hill spiked with modern tower blocks. It's a pretty little neighbourhood, though ultra-touristy, and the tourist information centre has loads of information on things to do in the area. Of particular interest are three blocks of 19th-century houses in a kind of Italo-Victorian style: this is the heart of old Halifax, where the pioneers first landed. The town has radiated outwards from this point, and the only trade left in the Old Town is tourism. Whatever you do, make time to visit *Bluenose II*, a racing boat built in 1921. It's a Canadian icon that's almost as important as the maple leaf. It's anchored near the information centre and the Privateers' Warehouse.

★ **Maritime Museum of the Atlantic**: 1675 Lower Water Street, in the port. ☎ 424-7490. Fax: 724-0612. From June to October, open 9.30am–5.30pm (from 1pm on Sunday); otherwise, 9.30am–5pm (from 1pm on Sunday). This museum houses documents concerning the sinking of the *Titanic*, which went down off the coast of Nova Scotia. The bodies recovered from the most famous shipwreck in history were buried in two of the town's cemeteries: at Mount Olivet, in Fairview, and at Baron de Hirsch. Another display describes a less famous, but no less cataclysmic, maritime disaster: the explosion of the French ship *Mont Blanc*, which went up in 1917 while carrying a cargo of TNT. The middle of the town was destroyed, and windows were shattered 80 kilometres (50 miles) away. The blast killed 2,000 people and injured 9,000, and it is said that reverberations were felt as far away as Sydney, on Cape Breton Island.

★ **Halifax Citadel**: on the hill that dominates the port. The Citadel was constructed between 1828 and 1856, and is star-shaped, to guard against invasion from all sides. In summer, actors in period costume are on hand to answer your questions about the place. If you're here at noon, you'll hear the cannons being fired, a ritual that takes place every day. If you walk to the top of the hill, you'll be rewarded with views of the whole town. Look out for the **Old Town Clock**, presented to Halifax by George III's son, Prince Edward (who also gave his name to the island).

★ **Atlantic Canada Aviation Museum**: exit 6 on route 102, on the far side of Halifax International Airport. ☎ 873-3773. Email: acam@ednet.ns.ca. Admission free, but donations are welcome. A magnificent assortment of flying machines, from early contraptions to modern-day jets, as well as photographs of various planes, pilot's uniforms and even some missiles. You can also test your aviation skills in a flight simulator. There's even a surprise as you leave: the exit is made from two aeroplanes.

■ **Hatfield Farm Cowboy Adventures**: 18212 Hammonds Plains Road, at Hammond Plains, 15 minutes' drive from the town centre. ☎ 825-2271. Fax: 835-0019. If you want to camp here, you'll only be allowed in on horseback. The farm offers all sorts of treks and lessons, at all levels, and there are ponies for children. It's worth ringing before you arrive to see exactly what is on offer.

LEAVING HALIFAX

By Bus

Three different bus companies run **shuttle buses** to various towns in Nova Scotia.

– **Eastern Comfort**: ☎ 1-800-528-1222. As the name suggests, it serves the towns to the east of Halifax, towards Yarmouth.

– For Sydney, try **Starline Shuttle** (☎ 1-800-239-9811) or **Caps Shuttle** (☎ 1-800-349-1698).

– For other destinations, you can get information at the tourist office, the station or the youth hostel.

WINDSOR

From Halifax, take Route 101 for 80 kilometres (50 miles). This very British village is suitably green and pleasant. You can still feel the presence of the American Loyalists, who fled here after the War of Independence. Windsor's most distinguished resident was Thomas Chandler Haliburton, a fervent supporter of the British Crown and the author of the 19th-century comic novel *Sam Slick the Clockmaker*. You can visit the writer's house, which is pretty, if a little reserved (open 1 June to 15 October, Monday to Saturday, 9.30am–5.30pm). All in all, Windsor is a lovely place to stay on the way to Annapolis Royal, especially if you don't take to Halifax.

WHERE TO STAY

B&B Clockmaker's Inn: 1399 King Street, at the crossroads with route 14. ☎ 798-5265 or 1-800-565-0000 (toll-free). Doubles $65 a night. Credit cards accepted. Non-smoking. A phenomenon that's all too rare in Nova Scotia: a place with character that also offers excellent value for money. The Inn, run by a retired couple, is a traditional Victorian wooden house surrounded by 100-year-old trees. Inside, the decor is like something out of a Hitchcock movie. A grand staircase leads to the first floor and its corner lounge, complete with divan, TV, video and books you can borrow. Your affable host, Denis Connelly, will offer you a cup of tea, which you can sip to the strains of classical music. The rooms are wonderfully quaint, and all have names: try to get Frederick Fraser or Joseph Howe, which have wooden beds and original fireplaces. The two others aren't quite as good, but they're quieter. Overall, there's an authentic Victorian ambience: a real taste of Old Canada.

GRAND-PRÉ Pop: 325

This is a small place with a big reputation. Everyone of Acadian descent, however tenuous, have been here or plans to come one day, as this is where the flight of their ancestors from Nouvelle-France began. The Acadians settled here in 1672, but in 1713, the area was ceded to the British under the terms of the Treaty of Utrecht. In 1755, the British demanded that the Acadians pledge allegiance to the Crown and convert to Anglicanism. They refused, and on 5 September 1755, Lieutenant-Colonel John Winslow ordered that they be assembled in the Church of Saint Charles, then deported. Their homes and lands were taken from them. This went on until 1762, by which time nearly 8,000 Acadians had fled to other French-owned lands, including Belle-Île-en-Mer, in Louisiana, and the Antilles. The heroine of Longfellow's poem *Evangeline* became, and remains, the 'emblem' of their cause.

WHERE TO STAY AND EAT

Evangeline by the Sea Cottage & Motel: 127 Evangeline Beach Road, North Grand-Pré. ☎ 542-2039. Doubles $48–52 a night. This little hotel is right on the water, in a very quiet area, and has a lovely swimming pool. The rooms are not lavish, but they are comfortable. Try to book No. 6 if you can – it's the cosiest, and overlooks the beach. Even if you're not staying, it's worth coming here to splash around in their mud pools, where you can pick your own winkles.

Evangeline Snack-Bar et Motel: on route 1, on the cross-roads with the road that leads to the National Historic Site of Grand-Pré. ☎ 542-2703. Open May to October. Doubles $44 a night. Convenience is the watchword here: it's the sort of place you can tumble into after a hard day's driving. It's not very charming, but the rooms are off the road, so it's not too noisy, and a warm welcome is guaranteed. The snack bar serves sandwiches and other simple dishes.

Inn The Vineyard B&B: 264 Old Post Road. ☎ 542-9554 or 1-800-565-0000 (toll-free). Website: www.bestinns.net/canada/ns/vine

yard.html. Take the road to the National Historic Site, then turn right; it's a little farther up on the right-hand side. Open 1 June to 30 September. Doubles $55–75 a night, including breakfast. This is a charming 18th-century building, carefully looked after and tastefully decorated by a couple of French Canadians who live in Montréal, but spend their summers here. It's set amid orchards and apple trees in the heart of the countryside; in summer, you can even hear crickets chirping. The rooms are a more expensive than elsewhere because of the surroundings, but you get a huge breakfast and friendly service for your money.

WHAT TO SEE

★ **Grand-Pré National Historic Site**: on a road leading to the sea, and clearly signposted. ☎ 542-3631. This is one of the sacred sites of Acadian history. It's now occupied by a kind of open-air memorial, consisting of a replica of the Église de Saint-Charles (the original was burned down by the British), a plaque with the names of 300 deported families and a bronze statue of Evangeline, the symbol of their plight. At the end of a footpath, a cross marks the spot from which the Acadians were led to the ships that took them into exile.

WOLFVILLE Pop: 3 500

Five kilometres (three miles) away from Grand-Pré, Wolfville is a small university town where the streets are lined with huge elm trees and grand Victorian houses. It's a little strange to find such opulence in a small place like this, and there doesn't seem to be any convincing explanation. There's not much to do here, but it's a nice place to stop off for a cup of tea or a bite to eat after visiting Grand-Pré.

WHERE TO STAY AND EAT

⌂ **In Wolfville**: 40 Main Street. ☎ 542-0400. Email: in.wolfville@ns. sympatico.ca. Doubles $85–125 a night. This is a brand-new B&B with four en-suite bedrooms, two of which are huge and stylishly decorated. It's bright and tastefully furnished, with an elegant living room (the floor is made from local wood), and there's also a pleasant veranda. You'll be warmly received by the owners, Ken and Sally, but you may find the prices a little steep.

✗ **Restaurant Acton's**: 268 Main Street. ☎ 542-7525. Main courses $15–18. This is a smart place, and it makes a change from the usual burger joints. At lunchtime, there's a hot and cold buffet, while à la carte dishes include Honfleur mussels, salads and *petatou* (potato gratin). The cooking is elaborate, and the wine list is good as well. In summer, head straight for the terrace.

WHAT TO SEE

★ **Thomson's Barber Shop**, in a little street at right angles to the main road, at the foot of a huge tree, is full of rock'n'roll memorabilia.

ANNAPOLIS ROYAL

The name may be terribly grand, but Annapolis Royal is little more than a rural village on the banks of the Annapolis River, which heads out to the Bay of Fundy. It hasn't always been so sleepy: this was the capital of Nova Scotia before Halifax, from 1713 to 1749. In the morning, sometimes until 11am, the whole town is bathed in fog, but this burns off to leave a sunny day. The bay has some of the fastest tidal currents in the world, producing breakers that hit the beach at tremendous speeds. The Canadians have exploited this natural phenomenon by installing a tidal power station here, the only one of its kind in North America.

Annapolis Royal is lovely, with maples, oaks, elms and poplars bathing the superb 19th-century houses in a sea of green, and it's a good place to stay the night before taking the ferry from Digby to Saint John. While you're here, it's well worth visiting Port Royal, on the opposite bank of the river, the first settlement founded by the French pioneers.

USEFUL ADDRESS

Ⅱ Tourist office: 236 Prince Albert Road. ☎ 532-5454. Open mid-May to mid-October.

WHERE TO STAY AND EAT

▲ Hébert House: 124 Victoria Street. ☎ and fax: 532-7936. E-mail: areid@ns.sympatico.ca. Website: www3.ns.sympatico.ca/areid/. Doubles $60–70 a night. Credit cards accepted. Huge trees fill the garden of this old, French-looking farmhouse, and the rustic charm continues inside. There are renovated en-suite rooms in the main house – these are more expensive, but breakfast is included in the price – or rooms in the motel opposite.

▲ The Turret B&B: 372 Saint George Street. ☎ 532-5770. Doubles $60–70 a night. The Turret is opposite an old cemetery, with huge black crows circling the trees. Don't

be put off, though, as the rooms in this 100-year-old building are really well kept, and some have queen-size beds. It's very comfortable, and the owners, a youngish retired couple, are very friendly. They also do a proper English breakfast – bacon and eggs, toast, porridge and all the works.

✕ The Fat Pheasant: 200 Saint George Street. ☎ 526-0042. Main courses $4–19. Despite its rather imposing exterior, this Scottish-style restaurant is warm and quiet inside. The food is nothing special, but it has a relaxed atmosphere, the owner is laid-back and the prices are reasonable.

WHERE TO HAVE A DRINK

♟ The Olde Towne Pub: 9–11 Church Street, a waddle away from the Fat Pheasant. This is one of the only watering holes in Annapolis Royal. The terrace is the place to sit in summer, but the inside is warm and welcoming enough to shut out the cold, dark nights. It's along the lines of an Irish pub, with a traditional 'maritime' theme, but the music is good and the staff are friendly. Books are strewn about the place for the use of patrons, and the pub also serves good, cheap brunches.

WHAT TO SEE

★ **Historic Gardens**: 441 Saint George Street. ☎ 532-7018. Open mid-May to early October, 8am to dusk. These Victorian gardens are great for an early-evening stroll. As well as a host of beautiful trees and flowers, you'll see a 17th-century kitchen garden and a reconstructed Acadian cabin. Below the gardens, a footpath leads to a sort of marsh, where you might see some herons.

★ **Fort Anne**: Saint George Street. ☎ 532-2321. Open 15 May to 15 October, 8am–6pm. The fort was held by the French between 1635 and 1713, when the British took over and renamed it in honour of Queen Anne. It's very genteel for a strategic stronghold: the barracks look more like a well-kept house. Strangely, the building is hidden from view by a series of grassy mounds arranged in star formation. Look out for the monument to Pierre du Gua, who sports a musketeer's moustache and hat. He was among the pioneers who arrived here in 1604, along with Samuel de Champlain and 80 other men, and he helped to construct the Port Royal Habitation (*see below*), a fortified wooden camp.

WHAT TO SEE IN THE AREA

★ **Port Royal National Historic Site**: 10 kilometres (7 miles) west of Annapolis Royal, on the north bank of the Annapolis River. ☎ 532-2898. This is an astonishing reconstruction of the first fortified French camp ('*habitation*') in North America. It's full of the ghosts of the past, and well worth a visit.

The French colonial story began here in 1605, and not in Québec or Gaspé, as is often thought: there was a sister encampment in Saint John, across the Bay of Fundy in New Brunswick, but no trace of the original site remains. As at other historic sites in the area, there are actors in period costume who can answer your questions.

If you've been to Louisbourg, don't expect a fortress on the same scale: this place is tiny by comparison. The log cabins are arranged around an interior courtyard, complete with well, entered through a plain-looking door. You can see the forge, the kitchen, the bakery, the chapel (sparse and monastic) and the dormitories under the eaves, with straw mattresses for the soldiers to sleep on. You can also visit the austere gentlemen's residence, and see the plans Samuel de Champlain drew up for Port Royal.

Index

Note: Page numbers in *italics* refer to maps/plans

INDEX

INDEX